THE PINK AND THE BLACK

The Pink and the Black

HOMOSEXUALS IN FRANCE

SINCE 1968

Frédéric Martel

Translated by Jane Marie Todd

STANFORD UNIVERSITY PRESS

STANFORD, CALIFORNIA

The mention of a name in this book does not imply that the individual in question possesses some dubious "homosexual identity." Similarly, books, films, and songs are cited not because they are "homosexual works"—an expression with little meaning—but rather because they play a role in the collective memory of "homosexuals," regardless of their creators' intentions.

Stanford University Press
Stanford, California
©1999 by the Board of Trustees of the
Leland Stanford Junior University
Printed in the United States of America

Library of Congress Cataloging-in-Publication Data

Martel, Frédéric
  [Rose et le noir. English]
  The pink and the black : homosexuals in France since 1968 / Frédéric Martel ;
translated by Jane Marie Todd.
       p.   cm.
  Includes bibliographical references.
  ISBN 0-8047-3273-6 (cloth : alk. paper) — ISBN 0-8047-3274-4 (paper : alk. paper)
  1. Gays—France—Social conditions.   2. Homosexuality—France—History—
20th century.
HQ75.6.F8M3713   2000
306.76/62/0944 21   99-049932

This book is printed on acid-free, archival-quality paper.

Original printing 1999

Designed and typeset in 10/12.5 Minion by John Feneron

To My Parents
To RSM, to RLG

Acknowledgments

Since this book's subject lies at the intersection of individual life histories and collective history, I needed to question a large number of participants before I could write it. I would therefore especially like to thank all those named in the Interview Sources, who were kind enough to meet with me over a period of three years. Beyond the views that may unite or separate us, I hope this book will contribute to a social debate in which both they and I are involved.

The French title of this book is taken from a book on Walter Pater and Oscar Wilde, written by the art critic Georges Duthuit (*Le rose et le noir*, Renaissance du Livre, 1930). It is more than a nod in that book's direction. I also wish to express my gratitude to Edgar Morin, who let me borrow the title of one of his essays, which is marked by a "critical sympathy" toward the Socialist Party (*Le rose et le noir*, Galilée, 1984). Another nod. Finally, the title of this book alludes to the name of one of the main feminist reviews in Quebec (*La vie en rose*), proof that it also has to do with women, and to the name of an ACT UP–Paris broadcast on Radio Libertaire in 1991, proof that it applies to homosexual life in the age of AIDS.

⌐

To complete this project, I received countless bits of advice. Many people read over the book as a whole, and others offered help on specific matters. I wish to acknowledge the contributions of the following friends.

For archival material, Alain Brillon (of *Libération*) and Yves Builly were of great help to me. I also consulted the archives of *Le Monde* and *L'Express*. I am grateful to those in charge of these archives as well, especially to Jean-François Laforgerie for his patience, availability, and kindness. Jean-Pierre Meyer-Genton and Stéphane Costa of the bookstore Les Mots à la Bouche, Alexander Wilson of Editions Passage in the Marais, Patrick Cardon of Cahiers Gai-Kitsch-Camp, and Chantal Bigot of the bookstore Les Amazones provided valuable advice regarding the bibliography. For the history of the fight against AIDS in France, I met with Jean-Bernard Senon, Frédéric Kurt, and Robert Wintgen every Tuesday evening in 1993, and they conducted research with me. The editors of the *Journal du Sida*, who allowed us into their offices and let us examine their archives, greatly facilitated the task.

Many individuals entrusted personal documents to me. Since their archives are usually inaccessible and unpublished, I wish to thank by name André Baudry (Arcadie archives), Marie-Jo Bonnet (Gouines Rouges documents), Jean-Baptiste Brunet (archives for the Groupe Français de Travail sur le Sida), Jean-Marc Choub (medical archives of the Comité d'Urgence Anti-Répression Homosexuelle, or CUARH), Eric Conan (AIDS archives at *Libération*), Daniel Defert (for showing me his notebooks regarding the first meetings of the organization Aides), Catherine Deudon (documents on the Mouvement de la Libération des Femmes, or MLF), Marc Epstein (documents on the radio project Fréquence Gaie), Olivier Fillieule (who provided the still unpublished results of a survey he conducted on ACT UP–Paris), Philippe Fretté (archives of the CUARH), Alain Huet (newspaper collections of the Front Homosexuel d'Action Révolutionnaire, or FHAR, and the Groupes de Libération Homosexuelle, or GLH), Guillaume Lallier (who conducted research for me on Quebec), Annie Le Brun (documents on the Situationists), Pierre Lascoumes (documents on Aides), Claudie Lesselier (many documents on lesbian groups), Philippe Mangeot (many documents and details on ACT UP–Paris), Jean-Yves Nau (AIDS archives at *Le Monde*), Alain Neddam (archives on GLH–Lyons), Albert Rosse (brochures on the Parti Socialiste Unifié, or PSU, and the CUARH), Carole Roussopoulos (who let me view tapes of the FHAR at the Entrepot), Willy Rozenbaum (archives of the Groupe Français de Travail sur le Sida), Alain Sanzio (documents of the GLH), and René Schérer (documents of the FHAR).

Thérèse Clerc and Claude Rejon lent me many of their own books. Jean-Loup Champion helped me obtain priceless books. Dominique Fernandez generously opened his library to me, making a great number of books available for several years.

In the provinces, several friends welcomed me, housed me, or organized my visits. I wish to thank them in particular: Michel Bourrelly in Marseilles, Christophe Clergeau in Nantes, Stéphane Cola in Nice, Jean-Michel Dorlet in Dijon, Alain Molla in Marseilles, Samuel Planet in Mâcon, Myriam Poitau in Lyons, and Xavier Rosan in Bordeaux. In addition, for three summers I enjoyed the hospitality of Dominique Fernandez, Ferrante Ferranti, Robert Lion, Gilles Ringuet, and Albert Rosse, who welcomed me into their homes to work on this book.

A few individuals were kind enough to look over particular passages or chapters of this book: André Baudry, Cathy Bernheim, Marie-Jo Bonnet, Christine Delphy, Renée Dufourt, Thierry Gamby, Mirko Grmek, Frédéric Gros, Gérard B. Ignasse, Jean-Noël Jeanneney, Hervé Liffran, Antoine Lion, Maurice McGrath, Bernard Minoret, Jean-Paul Montanari, Aquilino Morelle, Denis Olivennes, Denis Peschanski, Françoise Picq, Arnold Pire, Mathieu Potte-Bonneville, Henry Rousso, Willy Rozenbaum, and Michel Setbon.

Jérome Le Cardeur kindly looked over passages of the book having to do with dance, as did Jacques Siclier those having to do with film. Didier Eribon, Claude Rejon, and Jean Stern were kind enough to reread the first draft of this manuscript in its entirety, and in meticulous detail. I thank them all the more warmly inasmuch as they did not always share my views.

Although I assume sole responsibility for this book, several people helped me and contributed remarks or criticisms or simply shared their own reflections over these last few years. This book owes a great deal to them: Michel Braudeau, Eric Conan, Daniel Defert, Claire Dufour, Frédéric Edelmann, Pierre Encrevé, Dominique Fernandez, Alain Finkielkraut, the late François Furet, the late Jean Gattégno, Jacques Julliard, the late Pierre Kneip, Emeric Languérand, Alain Molla, Evelyne Pisier, the late Michael Pollak, Laurent de Villepin, and Michel Wieviorka.

At Editions du Seuil, I received an immediate and warm welcome. Hervé Hamon believed in this project from the beginning; he is an attentive editor who respects his authors. Anne Sastourné, Elisabeth Franck, Isabelle Bardet, and François des Accords were kind and patient in the help they provided, going far beyond what professional conscientiousness requires. Monique Cahen in particular reread and followed the manuscript step by step, giving me constant friendly help and motherly support. I am very grateful to all those who have shown such confidence in me and am very aware of the "Seuil spirit."

The memory of my friend Pierre Marc is closely associated with this book.

Finally, my closest friends bore with me on this project for three years. They reread all the drafts of this book, provided much criticism and encouragement, and constantly responded to my requests: Julien Bousac, Gwénaële Calvès, Cyril Chain, Jean-Loup Champion, Christophe Clergeau, Jean-Luc Eyguesier, Ferrante Ferranti, Stéphane Foin, Renaud Le Gunehec, Maxime Lefebvre, Emmanuel Pierrat, Réda Soufi-Merzoug, and Robert Wintgen. This is also their book.

F.M.

Contents

Acronyms Used in This Book

[The following list, although not comprehensive, includes important acronyms that appear frequently in the chapters that follow. Unfortunately, it was not always possible to discover the precise meanings of acronyms referring to long-defunct political groups and other organizations.—Ed.]

AFLS	Agence Française de Lutte contre le Sida
AMG	Association des Médecins Gais
ARCL	Archives Lesbiennes
BEH	*Bulletin Epidémologique Hebdomadaire*
CADAC	Coordination Nationale des Associations pour le Droit à l'Avortement et à la Contraception
CAPR	Comité d'Action Pédérastique Révolutionnaire
CERM	Centre d'Etudes et de Recherches Marxistes
CFES	Comité Français d'Education pour la Santé
CGL	Centre Gai et Lesbien
CGT	Confédération Générale du Travail
CNIL	Commission National Informatique et Libertés
CNTS	Centre National de Transfusion Sanguine
CUARH	Comité d'Urgence Anti-Répression Homosexuelle
CUC	Contrat d'Union Civile
CUS	Contrat d'Union Sociale
CVS	Contrat de Vie Sociale
DGS	Direction Générale de la Santé
EHESS	Ecole des Hautes Etudes en Sciences Sociales
FHAR	Front Homosexuel d'Action Révolutionnaire
FLJ	Front de Libération des Jeunes
FLN	Front de Libération Nationale
FMA	Féminin, Masculin, Avenir
GLH	Groupes de Libération Homosexuelle
GP	Gauche Prolétarienne
JCR	Jeunesse Communiste Révolutionnaire
LCR	Ligue Communiste Révolutionnaire
LO	Lutte Ouvrière

LSD   Lesbiennes Se Déchaînent
MDC   Mouvement des Citoyens
MIEL   Mouvement d'Information et d'Expression des Lesbiennes
MLAC   Mouvement de la Libération de l'Avortement et de la Contraception
MLF   Mouvement de la Libération des Femmes
OCT   Organisation Communiste des Travailleurs
PCF   Parti Communiste Français
PSU   Parti Socialiste Unifié
SID   Service d'Information et de Diffusion
SIS   Sida Infos Service
SNEG   Syndicat National des Entreprises Gaies
UEC   Union d'Etudiants Communistes
UNADIF   Union Nationale des Associations de Déportés
UNEF   Union Nationale des Etudiants Français
VLR   Vive la Révolution

Preface to the English-Language Edition

With its Stendhalian title, this book on homosexuals in France since 1968, now being published in English, may give its anglophone readers the impression of being a little too French. English-speaking readers will probably be surprised that the United States, the standard-bearer of the global homosexual cause, is so rarely mentioned. When it is mentioned, in the margins of the book, they will certainly judge that the little information given is too fragmentary. And this is true. Finally, the references that are cited, the debates that are mentioned, and the positions that are supported in this book will appear a bit baroque, perhaps even byzantine, outside their French context. It is thus with some uneasiness that I see this book appear in English.

There is a second reason for this apprehension: I wrote, between the ages of twenty-three and twenty-seven, what is a book of collective but also individual emancipation, and I published it when I was twenty-eight years old, at the end of a militant and political period in my life.[1] It was therefore a book of my youth, an apprenticeship, and—dare I say it?—a "coming out" book. Overall, if I had it to write today, I would do it somewhat differently, with more distance and nuance, and with less passion. I would probably modify the epilogue in the light of concrete political confrontations and my recent experience in a situation of political responsibility with respect to the debates on the Pacte Civil de Solidarité [Civil Pact of Joint Responsibility], or PACS.[2]

In spite of these worries, I insisted, out of concern for authenticity, that the published English version of my book be identical[3] to the French edition, even at the risk of causing some misunderstandings about me or of giving—wrongly, I think—the impression that France is a truly backward country in terms of its social mores.

⟺

The book, then, is French in more ways than one. Should it be seen as part of our penchant, so often criticized, for Franco-French navel-gazing? Do the antagonistic positions mentioned in this book have meaning only in the national context of France? Is there a French specificity that in itself would justify this treatment of the "French exception"?

I do not think so. It is up to readers to evaluate whether this history differs no-

ticeably from their own history in the country where they live. For myself, I will
speak only of a French singularity. Above all, I believe it is necessary to remind
readers that I neither intend to give an internationally valid interpretation of the
history of homosexual men and women nor claim to draw a universal lesson about
the best possible approach to facilitating the integration of homosexuals world-
wide. Most important, I do not claim to make any judgments about the overall attitude that homosexual militants ought to have taken during the early years of the
AIDS epidemic.

A FRENCH SINGULARITY

This book's only ambition is to offer a reading of the history of homosexuals
in France since 1968. To be sure, it is the first such book (in France there has been
no book of this kind before), but it will not be the only one (since this history will
also be written, I hope, by other historians and will be elaborated, completed, and
reevaluated in books that have yet to appear).

Readers are invited, then, to immerse themselves in the history of another
country—it is up to them to decide whether this history is slightly or vastly different from their own—and, by considering the elements specific to their own country, to assess the political power structure that exists in that other country. I hope
they will then find this book to be both of documentary interest and a basis for
comparison—a small thing, and also a great deal.

Since *The Pink and the Black* appeared in France (in April 1996), two issues—
public recognition of homosexuality, and the fight against AIDS—have undergone
an evolution.[4] To put it rather cavalierly, and just as succinctly, I feel that the major
hypotheses offered in this book have been confirmed in the last three years.

In this preface, then, I propose to return to these various evolutions and to go
into more detail about the most recent context of the subject in France, but also to
bring some perspective to two major debates provoked by my book: first, the debate about the attitude of "denial" on the part of gay activists in France, between
1982 and 1985, in the face of the AIDS epidemic; and, second, the more general debate about the advisability of building a political community of homosexuals.

The book discusses many other issues—for example, the persistent homophobia in France (on the religious and political far right); the discovery, by Luc Montagnier's team in 1984–85, of the retrovirus named HIV; "homosexual culture" in
the country of Marcel Proust and Jean Genet; the role played by François Mitterrand in suppressing homosexual discrimination in 1981–83; and the major role
played by female homosexuality within the history of the women's movement.[5]
Nevertheless, the debates about AIDS and about communitarianism have been the
most important ones, partly because my book marked a departure from the usual
language of "homosexual spokespersons." It is to these debates, then, that I wish to

return, even though I cannot devote to them all the space that is necessary. Still, I feel that the book sets these two debates out clearly enough for a non-French reader to understand their ins and outs. Therefore, with some regret, I will limit myself to retracing their main outlines.

    ↩

With respect to the first debate, in chapters 10 and 11 I examine the reaction in homosexual circles between 1981 and 1985 to the appearance of AIDS. All my questions are directed toward a single inquiry: Why, during those years, but especially between 1983 and 1985, were homosexual militants and the owners of commercial establishments slow to react to the disease? Of course, I take into account the context of the time (the lack of medical knowledge, the lack of visibility of the "epidemic") and the reactions that surfaced in those years (the renewed stigma attached to homosexuals by means of a "gay cancer"; the birth, 1984, of Aides, an AIDS organization; the political errors made in 1984–85, under the government of Laurent Fabius).

The issue of "denial" of AIDS in French gay circles between 1982 and 1985 is not unimportant. On the contrary, I found it to be essential, "the darkest chapter of that dark history" (to quote Hannah Arendt). The issue had to be raised, discussed, and commented on, even if this "wait and see" attitude (a term I would now choose over "denial") remains a fundamentally embarrassing problem. This book will make clear how things developed in France.

One further note: at no point in my book do I situate myself inside a logic of culpability; rather, I seek an explanation. Was an explanation possible, given that these were events and an epoch that I did not personally live through? Yes, of course: otherwise, "neither the administration of justice nor the writing of history would ever be possible."[6] I therefore attempt to understand the past—and to judge it—in order to illuminate the present and, perhaps, attempt to get a better grasp of the future.

From this perspective, the decision handed down by the Cour de Justice de la République on March 9, 1999, exonerating former prime minister Laurent Fabius in the contaminated-blood scandal, tends to complement my own analysis and confirm its relevance: the context did make the dangers of the epidemic "indiscernible." On the whole (and the book details all these elements), political leaders, physicians, and even hemophilia organizations and drug treatment centers did no better than homosexual militants at assessing the scope of the epidemic in France between 1983 and 1985. That's the way it is.

    ↩

I now come to the second debate: the one about communitarianism. This debate, considered primarily in the book's epilogue, has been a recurring one in France since the early 1990s (and in the United States as well, it seems to me, but earlier). France—through the so-called Islamic head-scarf affair,[7] the re-Islamization of certain outlying districts, and the move toward political parity for women—has become tuned in on a daily basis to issues surrounding the notions of "republic," "nation," "identity," and so on, and to the often passionate confrontations that these issues entail.

Let me say, briefly, that I take a line both very moderate and, to tell the truth, rather unoriginal (for France). Of course, I am probably the first in my country to have applied the terms of this debate to homosexuals and the fight against AIDS, but my position is completely classic in a country that never tires of commemorating the Revolution of 1789, the Republic of 1875, and the Constitution of 1958. In fact, I feel as far removed from a nervous (and stereotypically French) republicanism as from an extremist communitarianism. I have attempted to show, with equal vigor, why it was necessary to reject the arguments of those advocating the "right to difference" as well as the arguments of those who, in the name of an idealized and largely make-believe French republic, reject diversity and are altogether too satisfied with a "right to nonexistence"; why it was necessary to reject a blind communitarianism as well as an incantatory, nervous republicanism that denies social realities and different lifestyles; and why it was necessary to reject the dictatorship of the majority as well as the dictatorship of minorities.

In reality, there is something rather polarized and certainly artificial about this debate, since no one in France has ever feared or even claimed that French gays were going to leave the republic, transform the Marais district into the State of Sodom, opt for separatism, or mint money. And is it necessary to point out how much I like a number of the gay bars in the Marais, and that I frequent them regularly?

This is why I gave my epilogue the title "A Dubious Communitarianism." Nevertheless, it seemed to me that certain attitudes and kinds of behavior, especially during the early years of the AIDS epidemic, had to be analyzed and, as necessary, criticized.

Are my positions close to those of the conservative camp? A few radical gay militants and communitarians have claimed that they are.[8] It seems to me that a response to this criticism can be found simply in the reading of this book.

I agree with my critics on one point, however: the persistence of "official" homophobia. Over the last few months, in fact, during the debate on the PACS legislation—even though this legislation is cautious and moderate—we have seen a few rightist members of the National Assembly refuse, in profoundly discriminatory ways, any legal recognition to homosexual couples. A few (especially one, Christine Boutin, a fundamentalist Catholic, antiabortion militant, and religious fanatic) have even distinguished themselves by truly hateful and violent homophobia. Hence, for them, homosexuals, by supporting the PACS legislation, are threatening the family, marriage, filiation, the country's finances, public order, and who knows what else—and all in the name of "the republic"!

It will be clear that I do not identify in any way with such arguments, which distort the idea of the republic and, under cover of unconditional support for the French republican model of integration, thinly veil not just a desire to prohibit manifestations of collective identity and eradicate diversity but also what must, after all, be called by its name: homophobia. These "republican" arguments also overlook the specificity of the French model of integration, which guarantees every individual the right to choose an affiliation without being confined to it.

This is why, in the epilogue of my book, I insisted on the necessity of recognizing homosexuals, why I have fought for equal rights for unmarried couples (whether heterosexual or homosexual), and why I do not confuse the "right to indifference" with the "right to ignorance" that is so often used against homosexuals as a way of not recognizing their rights.

Thus it seems to me that the PACS legislation is directly in line with my book's epilogue. The PACS legislation is universalist because it is applicable to all unmarried couples (heterosexual or not) and rejects the conferring of a specific status on homosexuals. It is modern because it is not encumbered by the constraints or symbols specific to the unions of another era. It is generous because it proposes a number of concrete rights (economic and social rights, inheritance rights, rights for couples who are government workers). Finally, it is cautious because it does not raise questions involving next of kin or adoption, and it avoids taking on or provoking heterosexuals by tampering with marriage.[9]

On the whole, the aim of the PACS legislation, and my goal in the epilogue of the book, is integration, normality, and indifference. These words are not very appealing by comparison with the flamboyant terms "marginality," "specificity," and "community," but they nevertheless correspond to an essential pursuit for French homosexuals: to find a place in society—a comfortable place—and hence finally to become adults.

To be "like other people," to live as mature and free people, requires seeking a harmonious way of living together with our differences. It is a difficult quest, of course, but also a necessary one, and it inevitably entails rejecting the temptations of uniformization and of a fixed identity. It is at this price that we will be able to invent a new model: a modern state, hospitable to "the other" and protective of individuals, of their similarities as well as their differences.

In the last part of this preface, I would like to deal briefly and directly with a serious question raised by my book's publication, a question that seems intrinsically linked to the objective of maturity that I wish gays to be able to achieve: How should a homosexual situate himself in relation to "his" community, and what type of solidarity should he demonstrate with "his" "people"?

Contrary to what certain militants sometimes believe, the true defender of homosexuals is not, it seems to me, the one who, for demagogic, political, or commercial reasons, flatters "his" community, but the one who is sadder than anyone else when he is reminded of the errors of the past and of the many who have died. This is why it is up to him to "speak," to "tell," since even at this stage, it seems to me, no one should be displaying unconditional solidarity with his people.

Moreover, in the course of the debates over my book, the issue of "solidarity" has become conflated with an opposition between two political notions (not right versus left, but reformist left versus radical left), and especially with a certain aspect of the generation gap. It has been more than thirty years since 1968. Those who participated in the movements for "sexual liberation" have preserved a certain indulgence for their bold acts of yesteryear, and they continue to commemorate the utopia that most certainly was inherent in these acts. The late 1960s survive in the form of nostalgia for a paradise lost, even though no one has risked predicting what this utopia might have looked like. In France, this nostalgia feeds our daily fantasies by perpetuating the myths of "May": the right to plural desires, sexual indetermination, "desiring machines" (along with their contradictions), an overinvestment in the political realm, the rejection of half-measures, erasure of the separation between public and private.

Then along comes a book that casts doubt on the radicalism and love of provocation that spiced up a whole generation's youth (the AIDS epidemic having become, in the meantime, that generation's swan song): it is easy to understand why people would find the self-criticism difficult to carry out. And then the French left supports the proposal for the Pacte Civil de Solidarité, modest in its way and yet reformist, supportive of a certain "banalization" of the stable homosexual couple, respectful of the rights and demands of heterosexuals: it is easy to see the uneasiness that such an event might inspire in the far left, which even today is too often content to believe that having multiple partners is the only fulfilling form of sexuality, that revolutionary acts are the basis of political action, and that provocation and subversion are the only public discourse possible for the militant homosexual.

But the contemporary world has changed a great deal. Condemned to live in this world, deprived of the horizon of a bright new tomorrow, reminded of our finitude—reminded, that is, of the future's unpredictability—we need to rethink our possibilities for happiness.

In a period when sexual life is still marked by AIDS, when the search for homosexual autonomy is expressed only sporadically in the critical activism of student movements and antiestablishment "fronts," it is time to reestablish ties with a less impossible happiness. To achieve it (since the dynamic of generational conflict is a chronic illness), must we oppose our predecessors absolutely, support the gay couple, and criticize the gay community? No. But we must demand a new right to a "historical" reading (we need to write history, not "our" history) and a right to take stock of homosexual liberation and the fight against AIDS. On the whole, to apprehend the past and judge it, a "minority" must reach adulthood (must reach, in some sense, its "majority").

This is why a gay man, with a favorable bias and a show of courtesy, but with an equal measure of lucidity and, at times, even a certain intransigence, when necessary, must criticize the gay community, just as he must pay tribute to its many battles and demonstrations of courage.

Paris, March 1999

THE PINK AND THE BLACK

Prologue

Certain topics are in the air of a particular age; they are also in the fabric of a life.
—Marguerite Yourcenar

Sex will not be captured in any typology—for example, there will be only homo-sexualities, and that plurality will thwart any constituted, centered discourse, so that he will find it almost pointless to speak of them.
—Roland Barthes

"Ravaillac is still hiding in the well." In the early 1980s, that flash of wit could catch you off guard. Legend has it that in 1610, after assassinating Henry IV, the ribald king of France, Ravaillac hid at the bottom of a well in the cellar of the inn Au Coeur Couronné, on rue de la Ferronnerie in Paris.

Many years later, the inn became a banana storehouse and, in the early 1980s, its cellar was converted into a homosexual club, Le Broad Side. "To go looking for Ravaillac" became a humorous excuse to go down to the cellar, or right next to it, into the back room of Le Broad disco. There, in that dark room with a "high sexual yield," as sociologists demurely put it, was a sexual smorgasbord, a coded and highly ritualized universe, where bodies in ecstasy achieved the "systematic disordering of all the senses" advised by Arthur Rimbaud.

It was there, between Les Halles and the Marais, that the "homosexual district" of Paris began, a temple of pleasure for some, a kitsch ghetto for others. Between 1978 and 1985, this new neighborhood replaced rue Sainte-Anne, which had been deserted because of its prohibitive prices, vice squad roundups, and omnipresent gigolos. As the 1980s began, the Marais was the apotheosis of homosexual liberation—of coming out of the closet. Invited to take their pleasure, homosexuals were becoming gays.

Let us begin our visit to the homosexual district of Paris via rue de la Ferronnerie. The street is a promise: it announces the Marais and leads us into it. Leaving Les Halles and taking rue de la Reynie, then rue Saint-Merri, we arrive at Beaubourg. Within a triangle whose points are formed by the Centre Georges-Pompidou, the Saint-Paul metro, and the Picasso Museum—the three men for whom these structures are named would have been astonished to see their names map the geography of male pleasure—Parisian homosexual life begins anew every evening.

Its main artery is rue Saint-Croix-de-la-Bretonnerie. In the early 1980s, every new bar opening between the two rues du Temple (the old one and the new) is joyously celebrated as a new milestone in the triumphal march of desire. In the neighborhood, male barkeepers, waiters, lawyers, pharmacists, and even taxi drivers in their off hours now fancy men. A florist says, ironically, "Even the number 29 bus, when it comes through the Marais with its open-air rear platform, seems to be swishing." The Marais has become the neighborhood where gays converge.

But the uninitiated do not suspect the bond uniting the passersby. It takes a certain experience to detect the furtive glances, or to catch men turning their heads as in *Rencontre fortuite* [Chance encounter], a series of photographs by Duane Michals. The regulars, however, are not fooled: they are well acquainted with that curious atmosphere described in Patrice Chéreau's *L'homme blessé* [The wounded man] or depicted in Copi's play *Les escaliers du Sacré-Coeur* [The stairways of Sacré-Coeur].

In late 1978, Joël Leroux unveils Le Village, the first gay bar in the Marais. In late 1980, Maurice McGrath opens Le Central. There are subtle differences between them: at Le Village, the homosexuals are butch, with checked lumberjack shirts and leather bomber jackets; at Le Central, "clones" sport mustaches and make fun of "fairies." In both cases, the social mix is typical: trainees at the hotel workers' school rub shoulders with proprietors of fashion houses; readers of Roger Peyrefitte's *Amitiés particulières* [Special friendships] hold discussions with readers of André Gide's *Caves du Vatican* [*The Vatican Cellars*]. A member of the Council of State toys with a dancer. The customers are on a first-name basis. They listen to the Village People's "YMCA" (1978), Dalida's "Depuis qu'il vient chez nous" [Since he's been coming to our house] (1979), and Diane Tell's "Si j'étais un homme" [If I were a man] (1980). They do not dance. They are looking for a partner for the night, rarely for a life partner. It's the era of "I like you, you like me, let's get it on," as in Renaud Camus's *Tricks*. Taxi Girl sings "Cherchez le garçon" (1980). Gays are obsessed with the quest for the erotic grail.

A short walk from the strategic intersection of rue Saint-Croix and rue Vieille-du-Temple is the bookstore Les Mots à la Bouche. There, between original editions of Proust and Montherlant, you can buy Yves Navarre's *Le jardin d'acclimatation* [The zoological gardens] (winner of the 1980 Prix Goncourt) or Dominique Fernandez's *Dans la main de l'ange* [In the hand of the angel] (winner of the 1982 Prix Goncourt). As of 1983, you can leaf through *Gai Pied*[1], a weekly newspaper. Downstairs, the bookstore gallery has erotic books and photo exhibits of men, since the search for pleasure is the common denominator of all these spots in the Marais.

At Les Mots à la Bouche, you can also find the review *Lesbia*, established in 1982, and everything about love between women, from Sappho to Marguerite Yourcenar. Nevertheless, few homosexual women frequent the Marais. They prefer more discreet neighborhoods to the ghetto, places where they have their own bars and bookstore tearooms. The era of bisexual dowagers glittering in brocade

and baubles, of viragos in three-piece suits who with gloved hands, and with cigarette holders between their lips, would read Colette and imitate the sapphic love
affairs of Natalie Clifford Barney—that era is long gone. Instead of stereotypes,
female homosexuals are discovering the joys of ordinary life and gradual integration. Places for women have appeared throughout Paris, but without forming a
specific neighborhood. There is La Champmeslé, a "gay bar" opened in 1979 on rue
Chabanais by Josy—who does not like the word "lesbian." There is Le Katmandou,
on rue du Cherche-Midi, a disco where Elula Perrin brings in a mixed crowd at
night, offering *danses du tapis,*[2] a VIP area, and a more working-class basement.
Feminists who were once "card carrying" Gouines Rouges [Red dykes] meet up
again here in 1981, only to observe that it has become hard to talk to the new generation of lesbians, who call themselves "lesbos" [*goudous*] and flaunt their sexuality. Nevertheless, as mothers (which some of them are), the protagonists of a wom-
en's movement that is losing steam remain optimistic. The mood is always bright.
The sexual liberation movements have just swept François Mitterrand into power.

꩜

For male and female homosexuals alike, the Socialist victory is a turning
point. Announced during the gay tea dance at Le Palace on Sunday, May 10, 1981,
Mitterrand's election to the presidency of the republic is greeted with thunderous
applause. Fabrice Emaer, owner of the disco, sings "La vie en rose." The same
night, at Le Village in the Marais, one customer asks, "What's going to change?"
Another, dressed in leather, replies, "We're gonna fuck all over the place, with no
cops around." A few days later, *Gai Pied* runs the headline SEPT ANS DE BONHEUR?[3]

On rue des Blancs-Manteaux, in June 1981, Jürgen Pletsch opens a new bar
called Le Piano Zinc. Everyone comes with a song: customers perform "Lili Marlene," the repertoire of Zarah Leander, or the *Threepenny Opera.* Everyone parties.
Everyone laughs. It's a carefree time.

In 1982–83, after Mitterrand lowers the legal age of consent for homosexual activity, there are fewer militants around. Gays prefer to dance to Frankie Goes to
Hollywood's "Relax" and Queen's "I Want to Break Free" (1984). They dress like
Brad Davis, hero of *Querelle,* the 1982 Fassbinder film based on Jean Genet's novel.
But even though a party atmosphere is the rule, some loneliness remains. Every
night the language of love has to be reinvented; when sexual conquest is no longer
a possibility, the sounding of the two o'clock bell announces it's time to go home
and to bed—alone.

꩜

Was it March 10, 1985? Witnesses to the event are hard to find now, but that
seems to be the right date. On that night, stunned customers at Le Piano Zinc saw
three activists of a new sort appear for the first time at a gay spot in France. The
first man was named Daniel and said he had been the lover of Michel Foucault,
who had died the previous year. The second, Frédéric, claimed to be a journalist

for *Le Monde*. The third, Jean-Florian, was a geriatrician. Incongruous and doggedly persistent, they had come to Le Piano Zinc to distribute condoms.

At Le Central, Le Village, and Le Piano Zinc, AIDS had struck. Its presence in the heart of the Marais revealed the epidemic's existence within gay life as a whole. These three men, founders of the organization called Aides, appeared at Le Piano Zinc that evening in 1985 and settled in for many long years, soon to be joined in all the gay meeting places of France by "buddies," volunteers for the organization.

Homosexual activists and owners of gay establishments took a long time to react. The hecatomb was not really noticeable until the late 1980s, when bad news had supplanted doubt. At that time, in the Marais, taciturn boys whose "blood had declared bankruptcy" (Hervé Guibert) began to track their prospects in the *Journal du Sida* [AIDS journal], published a few streets away. Thirty-year-old homosexuals acquired the habit of reading the obituaries and went as often as three times a week to Père-Lachaise Cemetery. Soon, gay bars began to display a "patchwork quilt of names": with each death, friends of the victim added a square yard of colored material, somber or gay, simple or ornate, alluding to poets or priests, a patch that further expanded the interminable work of art. On the walls, the stenciled slogans of the activists in ACT UP began to appear, tragically reminding customers of the drama being played out beneath the windows of these seventeenth-century townhouses. Wearing pink triangles on black T-shirts, militants "zapped" a personality whose position on the disease was judged unacceptable, or they organized "die-ins," lying on the ground to evoke the implacable succession of deaths. Beginning in 1989, the slogan SILENCE = DEATH set the tone for the fight against AIDS.

AIDS tended to demobilize rather than promote unity in the gay "community." Divisions between groups became more pronounced, individual identities more rigid. Finally, total war broke out. The protest movements of the halcyon days—the Front Homosexuel d'Action Révolutionnaire [Homosexual front for revolutionary action], or FHAR, of 1971; the Groupes de Libération Homosexuelle [Groups for homosexual liberation], or GLH, of 1974; the Comité d'Urgence Anti-Répression Homosexuelle [Emergency committee against homosexual repression], or CUARH—died a second death after the demise of Guy Hocquenghem, who had been the emblematic figure of the French homosexual movement as a whole, the guiding light for gay liberation.

How distant it all seems now: Jean-Louis Bory's sketches in *L'Observateur*, the "Chéri(e)" personal ads in *Libération*. Nightwalkers settled down, and homosexuals changed. The heyday of public toilets and street urinals, of back rooms, seemed to be over for a while in the Marais of the early 1990s. *Gai Pied Hebdo* had recently folded. And the Marais remained the key observation post for a new generation of gays.

↜

Arriving at rue Michel-le-Comte via rue du Temple, you come to one of the new bars, the kind the Marais invented: Le Duplex, one of the first to promote the prevention of AIDS. Students, young bohemians, and aspiring artists mingle in this café of "homosexuality lite." It costs you nothing to read *Illico*, a monthly that follows and analyzes the gay lifestyle in the age of AIDS. In this minuscule smoke-filled spot, people talk about the civil union contract, a legislative bill awaiting a sponsor, whose aim is to recognize "homosexual unions" and to address the problems of gay couples. It seems that "cocooning," along with safer sex, may be the most significant revolution in homosexual lifestyles.

At Le Duplex as well, the new homosexual militants, a gay community trans-figured by the virus, gather to rebuild after the storm, around individuals who have "suffered together." Militancy has taken on new life, and identity struggles seem to have gained strength since the early 1990s. A gay and lesbian center has been created. Completing this movement, the Lesbian and Gay Pride Parade of June 24, 1995, attracts nearly 60,000 marchers to the streets of Paris. Fifteen years after AIDS first appeared, here is something that has never been seen before: between the pom-pom girls, the drag queens, and the Sisters of Perpetual Indulgence, homosexuals parade with heavy hearts and rediscover their "gay pride." It is a time of red ribbons and the Rainbow Flag, a new gay emblem. Within twenty-five years, from 1971 to 1995, the first phase of the French homosexual movement has run its course.

There are two ways to leave the homosexual streets of the Marais: by heading east toward the Place des Vosges via rue des Rosiers, or by heading west. To the east, the homosexual community in gestation gives way to the communitarian model put in place by the Jews. Gay kitsch, fashion victims, flyers, and go-go danc-ers make way for the Pletzl, the Jewish quarter, with its *kippah*, its *glatt kosher* butcher shops, and its Lubavitcher Hassidim in beards and hats. The Marais is a neighborhood of minorities, where the heterosexual goy sometimes feels out of place.

To the west, taking rue Saint-Denis, which is packed with prostitutes and sex shops, including an old Philippe Starck shop, you can leave the Marais and enter Les Halles. Homosexuals are more dispersed there; the neighborhood seems more working class and conforms to the characterization of Jacques Chirac, mayor of Paris at the time, for whom Les Halles "smells of french fries."

The walking tour ends where it began, on rue de la Ferronnerie. This short ar-tery has changed a great deal since the early 1980s. As is only fitting, the banana storehouse has become Le Banana Café, where "boys like boys who like girls who like girls." Bisexuality is in fashion. Young lesbians say they have adopted the den-tal dam as a means of preventing AIDS, and "straight" men sometimes indulge in an affair with a male pal. After all, as the old saying goes, it's not cheating on your girl to sleep with a guy.

Across from Le Banana Café is the surprise of a marble slab with three fleurs-de-lys. "Henry IV was assassinated over there, coming out of Le Banana Café," whispers the bouncer, friendly for once. Homosexuals have loved these flashes of witty anachronism ever since 1981, when they were promised seven years of happiness.

The continuities are even more striking than the breaks, however. The back room of Le Broad, closed for a time, has reopened under a new name, and the fourth volume of the *History of Sexuality*, which AIDS prevented Foucault from completing, is being written there today. House music has replaced disco as drag queens have replaced the old transvestites. Gay militants are back, and the language of love has to be reinvented every night. Fifteen years after AIDS first appeared, the Marais has remained faithful to itself. Ravaillac has still not come out of the well.

⌐

This book is a history of male and female homosexuals in France, from 1968 to the present. It is not *the* history, or even *a* history, of a minority or a community—dubious terms—but rather the history of a dual revolution: the homosexual revolution and the AIDS revolution. My objective is to assemble the scattered elements of a collective memory in search of itself. Therefore, this book comprises several books; it is a history with several points of entry. It is a book on organized political movements (the women's movement and the homosexual liberation movement), a book on lifestyles, a book on cultural figures and intellectual debates, and, finally, a book on gays confronting AIDS. Homosexuality exists as a thread running through larger stories of which it is a key part: stories of sexual liberation, of women's liberation, of changes in mores, of AIDS in France.

This book is the result of four major choices.

The first choice was to avoid following a "minority" by way of its most visible fringe element—in this case, a certain way of life in the Marais district of Paris, with which this intentionally anecdotal prologue opened. There are probably between 500,000 and two million male and female "homosexuals" in France.[4] Very few actually live in the gay district of Paris. This "chosen ghetto," though highly symbolic, is nevertheless artificial for most homosexuals, and it is inaccessible to anyone who does not acknowledge his or her sexuality or leads a double life, to anyone who cruises the bucolic little stretches of Les Gravières in Strasbourg or "goes out for a bit of fresh air" in Mi-Forêt on the road between Fougères and Rennes. How do those unacquainted with this ghetto live, love, bear the great consequences of their little difference?

These questions raise others, which form part of a recurring debate: Is homosexuality more like a road with various stops along the way, a multitiered sexuality in which bisexuality plays a bigger role than has been claimed? Might homosexuality be more like a personal itinerary and less like an identity, as generally believed? To these questions I offer no definitive answer. But to reduce an individual to his sexual particularity, to assign her an identity, is certainly a pernicious operation, and Foucault has shown how it plays into the hands of the power it is supposed to be combating. My first choice, therefore, was not to limit myself to those for whom homosexuality is an identity.

The second choice stemmed from the first and took the form of a question: How to write the history of a "minority" that is so difficult to grasp? My aim is not to produce yet another discourse on homosexuality but rather to take note of those that already exist, to shed light on lines of descent, to situate them or even set them against one other in the context of an era, to "pin them down," as Barthes would say. To write the collective history of a population that is not—yet—organized, I could find no better solution than to give an overview of individual life stories, to shed light on the sociohistorical dimensions of homosexuality. This choice explains the importance of the portraits scattered throughout these pages: of key personalities (Guy Hocquenghem, Simone de Beauvoir, Monique Wittig, Jean-Louis Bory, Michel Foucault, Daniel Defert, Hervé Guibert), but also of lesser-known individuals who reveal unique destinies, scenes from private life. Through these intersecting life stories, it seems to me, we can better understand the major internal conflicts pervading the homosexual question: the double life, mechanisms of self-loathing or of pride in oneself, the complex dialogue with family and with the social environment. Around these shared elements, group operations take shape—collective behaviors as well—and it becomes possible for isolated individuals to come together and form a critical mass, to organize as a power base. To assess this phenomenon, to explain how homosexuality has "taken shape," I had to take note of the signs (cruising codes, cultural elements, commercial sites) that accompanied the slow birth of a cause, of a social group, from its collective awareness of exclusion to its specific vulnerability to AIDS. This choice of individual life stories as a means of re-creating a collective history is, I believe, the least inadequate solution to the problem of grasping what cannot be grasped.

The third choice had to do with how to define the subject matter. Since my intention was to follow the interaction between homosexuality and society, I believed it was indispensable to treat both male and female homosexuality. Various authors have taken men as their subjects; others, less frequently, have studied women. Rarely has the dynamic relation between the two been the object of attention. My approach is therefore resolutely relational. In addition, given the changes in women's condition, I find that today homosexuality has a stronger symbolic role for many female homosexuals than does their place within a hypothetical "féminitude."[5] As we shall see, this postulate may not have been true in the early 1970s. It seems to me, however, that the 1990s have revealed connections between homosexuals of both sexes, suggesting essential links and secondary differences, even as the distance between lesbians and feminists has become more pronounced. These questions are being debated within the women's movement, and tensions remain for every female homosexual. Is "being a lesbian" primarily a way of "being a woman" or a way of "being sexually different"? Without providing a definitive answer to this question, we need to avoid two pitfalls: first, that of giving a strictly lesbian interpretation of the women's movement, forgetting the characteristics of women's specific condition; and, second and conversely, that of denying the importance of the homosexual question within that movement. Some believe, moreover, that the histories of male and female homosexuals cannot be told side by side. After all, the women's movement has its own specificity, and lesbians stand largely outside the AIDS problematic. According to this view, the history of homosexual women in France remains to be written.

The fourth choice had to do with the question of AIDS. This book is necessarily a book about AIDS. How could I have neglected to show the primordial place that the disease now occupies in the collective memory of homosexuals? Therefore, I made the choice to treat the issue of homosexuals and AIDS head on. This was the only way to shed light, from a new historical perspective, on the history of AIDS in France. This choice also allowed me to follow the path of a "minority" as it reconstituted itself, on the basis of an identity, after confronting the epidemic. I want this to be an optimistic history, however, even though tragedy bursts forth in the middle of my study, and even though the narrative, as in Shakespeare's historical plays, suddenly takes the form of a series of deaths. This fact should not be interpreted as a tragic conception of homosexuality, even less as a dialectical argument (thesis: liberation; antithesis: socialization; synthesis: AIDS). The 1970s were years of celebration, and the 1990s seem to be becoming so once again, even though, for homosexuals, pleasure and happiness may have to take new forms.

ᔕ

A final word: I have a personal relationship to the subject I am discussing. This is probably an advantage in terms of access to information, familiarity with the debates, and experience of the problematics. For someone who aspires to rigor, however, it is also a handicap in many respects. Contrary to what is often believed, we do not give the best analyses of those objects that are closest to us. To protect myself from straying off course, and to construct tools for establishing distance, I made two additional choices. First, I adopted a critical position with respect to "my" minority. The writer Bernard Dort gives a good summation of this problematic in an interview in *Gai Pied* (March 1983): "Homosexuality is a life situation. It certainly involves more constraints than heterosexuality does. It requires you to invent and assess your own behavior. In that respect, it is also a choice, in the end. It leads us to disobey the authorities that society proposes to us, including the homosexual authorities." In this book, I have opted to assert total independence, to cast a critical gaze and maintain distance even with respect to "homosexual discourse." This attitude will be particularly clear when I discuss the reactions of homosexual militants when AIDS first appeared in France.

On the basis of this critical stance, I decided to take a clear position. This was my second way of protecting myself from becoming too close to the subject under discussion. "Let us be serious. And let us be cautious," Jean-Louis Bory writes about any and all reflections on the homosexual question.[6] The following principles underlie this book: I cast my lot with the individual who is capable of consciously mastering his relation to the world, and of doing so in opposition to his fantasies and fears. I shed light on the mechanisms surrounding AIDS and make observations instead of seeking out guilty parties. I choose "factual truths" (the "modest truths" of which the philosopher Hannah Arendt speaks) instead of privileging broad generalizations, homophobia as a general law, and the antigay conspiracy as the rule. Finally, I show a preference—and clearly articulate it in the epilogue to this book—for universalism over multiculturalism, for *French-style* integration over communitarianism, for the "right to indifference," the right to be left alone, over the "right to difference."

Beyond these choices, in this book I propose "spaces for dialogue," a new state of mind that marks a departure from traditional militant discourse, "since the issue of homosexuality has changed so much that we need new terms coming from your generation."[7] These spaces for dialogue are designed especially for those who have discovered their homosexuality in the era of AIDS. I hope that this book will provide them with a link to a certain history—from which they will then feel free to disassociate themselves—or that it will serve as a calm message for "explaining what they are" to friends or family. These dialogues are very urgent today, if only for reasons of prevention. In a sense, they are also a way of bearing witness—the duty of memory—of attempting to understand what has happened now that several tens of thousands of homosexuals in France have been infected by AIDS.

   ↩

A provisional assessment, a space for dialogue, a working tool, a locus of memory. With these choices made, and with these positions formulated, the history of the homosexual population in France—a population that could be called, for lack of a better term, a "destiny group"—from the initial unspeakableness of homosexuality to the final unspeakableness of AIDS, from radicalism to socialization, from acceptance of responsibility to retreat into a fixed identity, is, in short, the subject of this book.

PART I

The Revolution of Desire (1968-79)

1

"My Name Is Guy Hocquenghem"

May '68 taught us to read the walls, and since then, we have begun to decipher the graffiti on prisons, asylums, and, today, on street urinals. An entirely "new scientific mind" has to be configured!
—Félix Guattari, "Trois milliards de pervers"

Against those who think "I am this, I am that," we must think in vague, improbable terms. . . . No queer will ever be able to say with certainty, "I am a queer."
—Gilles Deleuze, "Lettre à un critique sévère"

"My name is Guy Hocquenghem. I am twenty-five years old." Thus began the historic article in *Le Nouvel Observateur* (January 10, 1972), an article that would set the tone for the homosexual movement in France. The article caused a stir. This homosexual version of General de Gaulle's "appeal of June 18," so to speak, bore a title as grave as its consequences would be significant: "The Revolution of Homosexuals."

Who was this young man with the curly brown hair, his thin neck swimming in a loose sweater, this man of angelic beauty, who revealed himself in the great Paris intellectual weekly, claiming to transfer the idea of revolution to sex, this man whose personal self-portrait appeared under the collective title "The Revolution of Homosexuals"? Who was Guy Hocquenghem, who publicly "confessed" his homosexuality in the France of Georges Pompidou, where even the most timid would soon be humming along with Charles Aznavour, "I am a homo, as they say," and where others would smile at the scandal triggered by Michel Polnareff's baring of his bottom on posters for his show at the Olympia and singing, "I am a man; what is more natural, after all"?

In this article in *Le Nouvel Observateur*, Hocquenghem simply said "I" and recounted his life, an unstable mixture of guilt and revolt, the classic route to revolutionary utopianism. He told how his "meticulous" father addressed his mother with the formal *vous* and required his children to prepare the family's breakfast. How the young man left his father's office in tears. How, by contrast, he loved to be sick so that his mother would put him in her own room and take care of him. He moved on to what he claimed were anti-Oedipal confessions, but he avoided none of the clichés. His mother wrote a reply for the next issue of the newspaper, using an incestuous turn of phrase that would have made Freud smile: "I won't hide from you the fact that I would have preferred you to be a little bit 'straight,' for the very simple reason that . . . I was curious to know what a child of yours would be like." Madeleine Hocquenghem proved understanding, however, and wondered: "Could your exhibitionism be an opportunity for your liberation?"[1]

An opportunity for liberation? Hocquenghem had a knack for staging events. He made his personal history part of a larger movement that conferred a collective meaning on it. In *Le Nouvel Observateur*, he continued his account: he described his life, after a difficult time of loneliness and internal exile in his family, as an adolescent, a pariah at school: "Our shame begins with parents and continues with friends and comrades," he explained. In high school he was called a "faggot": "I was a bit of an eccentric. Hostility crystallized around me immediately." Bored to death, Hocquenghem did not have the same self-assurance as his peers at surprise parties and could not even put on a suit and go to parties. During recess, shyly withdrawn, he kept to himself. "I wrote my Memoirs, and, failing to understand the world in which I was living, I developed my sensibility: I was a pathetic little Rimbaud, a minor looking for someone to contribute to my delinquency."

It was then that Guy Hocquenghem, like the hero of Stefan Zweig's *Verwirrung der Gefühle* [Confusion of feelings], had an affair with his philosophy teacher, René Schérer: "I was becoming homosexual," Hocquenghem wrote. Because of this "pivotal passion" (in the sense given to that expression by Fourier), at the age of fifteen he was subjected to the ordeal of a double life: "High school and sex came at the same time."[2] Schérer recalls today the sort of high school student Guy was: "I found him striking because of his bushy head of curly hair, which gave him the look of an angel with, at the same time, a great authority in his manner of speaking. He had an unimpeachable presence. I established a Socratic dialogue with him: intellectual and increasingly amorous. This term implies reciprocity. It was he who, little by little, confided his homosexuality to me, which he had never dared admit."[3]

As a parallel to this homosexual initiation, Guy Hocquenghem, who was originally rather attracted to Gaullism, discovered political militancy in high school: "I emerged a leftist and a homosexual," he concluded. "On the one hand, the militant life, revolution. On the other, the life of feelings, homosexuality." Like many other students before 1968, Hocquenghem rapidly adopted the Marxist-Leninist catechism. He joined the Union d'Etudiants Communistes [Union of Communist students], or UEC, and sold *Clarté*. He also read Charles Fourier, Wilhelm Reich, Herbert Marcuse, Jean-Paul Sartre, Roland Barthes, and, soon, Gilles Deleuze and Michel Foucault. Hocquenghem was an exemplary product of what was called, in a strikingly compressed phrase, "the '68 philosophy." A member of the Communist Party, which he left in 1966 to join the Trotskyists—that is, Jeunesse Communiste Révolutionnaire [Revolutionary communist youth], or JCR, led by Alain Krivine and Henri Weber—he was also one of the leaders of the Union Nationale des Etu-

diants Français [National union of French students], or UNEF. Hocquenghem
seemed like an ordinary apparatchik: first a Marxist, he became a Trotskyist, and,
soon, a Maoist. One of his "comrades" remembers the first appearance Hocquenghem made at the Ecole Normale Supérieure, where he matriculated in 1965: "He
was running because he had just swiped a rudimentary copier, a kind of mimeo-
graph machine that at the time was called a 'Vietnamese' model. In fact, he was
moving from one Maoist group to another and didn't want to arrive empty-
handed." An appealing if not authentic image of the committed militant, already
involved in the fratricidal battles of the splinter groups within far-left movements.
"I was a minor leftist chief," Hocquenghem explained. At the time, to assert his
authority, he even went so far as to publicly deny his homosexuality.[4]

In short, Hocquenghem's political itinerary was typical for the late 1960s: Jeunesse Communiste, French Communist Party, UNEF, JCR. Naturally, in May 1968
the young student at the Ecole Normale Supérieure found himself on the barricades of rue Gay-Lussac.

↬

In 1968, a small group of fanatics lowered the Sorbonne's grand piano into
the courtyard and proposed to paint a revolutionary motif on the Puvis de Cha-
vannes fresco in the large amphitheater. Mom's washing machine, it seems, had
not kept up with the times—throw it out the window! Dad's jalopy represented
alienation—set it on fire! Although not openly a "sexual revolution," the student
movement erupted in Nanterre when students occupied the women students'
residences and demanded coed facilities. The posters and slogans of the time were
not unrelated to the question of desire: "The more I make love, the more I make
revolution; the more I make revolution, the more I make love." "Power is at the tip
of the phallus." "Let's invent new sexual perversions." "I get my rocks off" [Je jouis
dans les pavés]. Nevertheless, there was no real mobilization related to sexual mores during the events of May '68.

Unnoticed in the turmoil of May, the minuscule and mysterious Comité
d'Action Pédérastique Revolutionnaire [Revolutionary pederast action commit-
tee], or CAPR, which rapidly achieved the status of myth after the fact, had attempted to put up eight handwritten notices in the occupied Sorbonne, to denounce the repression of homosexuals, their isolation, their shattered careers, and
their rough treatment by the police. These notices also condemned the submissive
attitude of homosexuals themselves, the "stereotypical cowering homosexual"
with "the eyes of a beaten dog": "For every glorious Jean Genet, there are 100,000
apologetic pederasts condemned to unhappiness," one of the notices concluded.
The authors of these notices, whose message reached no one, were two students
from the Latin Quarter: Philippe Guy, future cofounder of the Front Homosexuel
d'Action Révolutionnaire [FHAR], and Stan, a young live-in prefect at the Lycée
Saint-Louis. The notices were immediately torn down, however, by the "official"

occupiers of the Sorbonne, who did not want to see their revolution "soiled."[5] This time, supposedly bourgeois homosexuality was on the side of revolt, and the supposedly orthodox revolutionaries were on the side of order. The relations between the leftists and the militants of sexual liberation did not begin under the best auspices. What was to follow only served as confirmation of this fact.

↩

In spite of the short-lived Comité d'Action Pédérastique Révolutionnaire, and apart from a few individual incidents at the Odéon Theater, it has often been said that May '68 forgot homosexuality in its smoke-filled meetings. However, the May movement contained, in embryo, all the ingredients of sexual liberation, for which it was a "dress rehearsal."[6] The shift from one revolution to another, from the "class struggle" to the "sex struggle," was now possible. The annexation of lovemaking by the serious business of revolution was under way.

In the early 1970s, the idea of sexual revolution was in the air. Before it took the form of a revolutionary movement, it was fostered ideologically by authors rediscovered for the occasion, and it was already playing an illustrious role in the arts.

In March 1971, a young dance star, Rudolf Nureyev, performed a pas de deux largely inspired by Mahler's lieder: Maurice Béjart's *Le chant du compagnon errant* [The song of the wandering companion]. In this duet of initiation between men, Nureyev was a romantic student furious with himself until Destiny (Paolo Bortoluzzi) took him by the hand and finally calmed him. In the ambiguity of bodies, the sexual give-and-take, the confusion of different partners, and the polysexuality, Béjart decreed the "emancipation" of sexuality before his time.[7]

In *Cabaret*, Bob Fosse depicted an androgynous master of ceremonies; in *Sunday, Bloody Sunday*, John Schlesinger showed the first kiss between homosexual men, not as a militant act but as a gesture of desire; and in *The Damned*, Luchino Visconti retold the homosexual orgy of the Night of the Long Knives. But it was surely Pier Paolo Pasolini who contributed the most, combining the history of cinema with that of homosexuality. Thus *Teorema* occupies a particular place in the memory of homosexuals and especially of militants. When an eruption of homosexuality is set off in an immaculately turned-out Italian bourgeois family by a guest (Terence Stamp) passing through, it brings revolution along with it. The archangel turns the libido of the capitalist, Catholic tribe on its head by sleeping with the whole family. Soon the mother (Silvana Mangano) is turning tricks along the highway; the son, passionate about painting, is urinating on his own canvases; and the father, Paolo, having acquired a taste for homosexuality, offers his factory to his workers and strips naked in the middle of the Milan train station. Liberated from social and economic conventions, the rich industrialist family finds a new life.

Pop music also illustrated this revolution, for which David Bowie was the international symbol. The performer of *Ziggy Stardust*, who publicly alluded to his bisexuality, could now dress as a woman, wear fishnet stockings, or simulate fellatio with his guitarist, Mick Ronson. Similarly, in France, Patrick Juvet took the stage of the Olympia encased in satin, wearing high heels and with silver stars on his face. The era no longer forbade itself scandal.

In the realm of ideas, the German author Wilhelm Reich, though dead for more than ten years, became all the rage. This Freudian-Marxist psychoanalyst, while nevertheless an enemy of Marxists and psychoanalysts alike, attributed political significance to orgasm.[8] His work went beyond Freud's analyses of homosexuality, which had championed the mastery of individual drives in the interest of social well-being: for Freud, "psychoanalysis and familialism were thick as thieves."[9] By contrast, Reich and the Sexpol movement he spawned demonstrated that repression of sexuality served to maintain the social fabric, and hence the social order. If sexual energy were freed, the shattering of the patriarchal family, the basic cell of capitalist society, would be close at hand.

In France, the most important book on desire appeared in 1972: Deleuze and Guattari's L'anti-Oedipe [Anti-Oedipus]. Representing an unexpected marriage between the thinking of a Nietzschean philosopher and that of a Lacanian psychoanalyst, the book was to be of key importance in the sexual liberation movement. "Being yourself," "being an anti-Oedipus" became a lifestyle choice. Libido and revolt were the new combination after May '68. This mixture soon had its own intellectual formulation: "Our assholes are revolutionary." As a complement to these theoretical works, however, the concrete model that inspired homosexuals came from the United States. In those years, the wind was not blowing from the East, as Marxists and Maoists still believed, but from the West.

↜

The act that gave birth to the homosexual movement is given the same date all over the world: June 27, 1969. On that night in New York, six plainclothes police officers went into a homosexual bar, the Stonewall Inn, at 53 Christopher Street, in Greenwich Village. It was the usual raid: in the end, the police closed down the bar while customers, most of them African-American and Puerto Rican transvestites, were roughed up. Just routine. That night, however, the homosexuals reacted, perhaps mobilized by the recent loss of their idol, the singer and actress Judy Garland: police reinforcements were answered with bricks—and high heels. Militants and historians generally agree that the first person to hurl a bottle at a police officer was Sylvia Rivera, a flamboyant transvestite.

Three nights of rioting followed. For the first time, homosexuals adopted an attitude of offense. It was the birth of what was called "coming out of the closet." This romantic event, which the American writer Edmund White, in Skinned Alive, calls "the taking of the Bastille," still plays an important role in the collective memory of "gay activists," though its scope may have been exaggerated. Symbolic dates are priceless.[10]

Philippe Guy, who had posted homosexual notices in the occupied Sorbonne, was teaching in the United States that year and witnessed the events at the Stonewall. When he returned to France, he found himself teaching at a high school in Gonesse, where he appeared in a star-studded white jumpsuit at a time when far-leftist instructors were reinventing education with "uncourses" by having their students read Rimbaud in the dark. "I learned everything in the United States," Guy recalls today. In France, the emancipation of homosexuals was beginning, an integral part of the larger history of sexual liberation. It was one small story within a greater history.

THE FRONT HOMOSEXUEL D'ACTION
RÉVOLUTIONNAIRE

"Something altogether extraordinary is happening. . . . The crowd . . . homosexuals . . . have stormed the stage." Ménie Grégoire could not get over it. On March 10, 1971, the star moderator of the radio network RTL was presenting her famous live broadcast, which little by little had replaced the confessional, deserted in the 1960s, before her listeners hurried off instead to psychoanalysts.[11] On this day, the theme of the broadcast was "That Painful Problem, Homosexuality," and various personalities representing the positions of the law, medicine, and the church were on the set. Ménie Grégoire had her guests give their "confessions" in the most perfect tradition later denounced by Foucault. Incongruously, even the Frères Jacques took part in the broadcast. Grégoire, although a liberal on principle, had trouble disguising her uneasiness with the subject: "Imagine what would happen if homosexuality became a social model. We would very soon be unable to reproduce ourselves. . . . For all that, there's a negation of life in homosexuality; I think one can say this without hurting anyone. . . . Even so, it's not a good thing to be homosexual." In response to a question from a female homosexual in the audience, who challenged her on the question of male domination, Grégoire added, "You know very well that the happy women are those who have met men who have satisfied them; that's obvious." She then declared, in a conciliatory tone, "In any case, if those people [homosexuals] are suffering, one cannot let them suffer without doing something for them." At approximately 3:35 P.M. (this detail comes from *France Soir*, where Grégoire worked), the moderator handed the microphone over to Abbot Guinchat. The priest declared, "For my part, I welcome many homosexuals—they are also my brothers—who come to speak of their suffering. One cannot be insensitive to this suffering." At that precise moment, militant homosexual women interrupted the debate, yelling from the back of Salle Pleyel, "Don't talk to us any more about *your* suffering!" Armed with Reich's formulations and with texts from the Situationist Internationale, and inspired by the American example of Stonewall, the women then shouted, in an indescribable brouhaha, "It's not true, we're not suffering! Transvestites on our side! We are a social scourge!"

and they came up with an expression destined for a long future: "Down with the heterocops!" As they went on to storm the stage, the militants forced the station directors to cut the live program off. RTL abruptly switched to the program's theme music: Barbara's *La petite cantate*.[12]

Interviewed in the dressing room to which she had fled, Grégoire, a glass of scotch in her hand, had these eloquent words to say: "I was right—it's a hot topic." The group later justified its actions in a press release: "Homosexuals are sick of being a painful problem." The Front Homosexuel d'Action Révolutionnaire had been born.

〜

In the wake of the events at Salle Pleyel, a group of homosexual women decided to meet. Paradoxically, men were still absent when the women first took up arms, marking the birth of French homosexual radicalism. Initially, the revolution was women's work.

The Egeria of the movement was Françoise d'Eaubonne. An exuberant feminist, she had a simple plan: "You say society ought to integrate homosexuals. I say homosexuals ought to disintegrate society." Around her, united into a commando unit to confront Grégoire, were Marie-Jo Bonnet, Anne-Marie Fauré, her friend Marise, and an American whose first name was Margaret. There were also several personalities from the women's liberation movement, such as Monique Wittig, Christine Delphy, and Catherine Deudon; a few men, who were declared the "objective allies" of lesbians, joined a bit later. Of the men, the first actors in the French homosexual movement were Philippe Guy, who had returned from the United States; Pierre Hahn, an erudite journalist; and Laurent Dispot, then a student at Lycée Louis-le-Grand and, as others were, a fanatical believer in Chairman Mao.[13]

Men and women met regularly and, after the action, felt called upon to give their group a name. It was the era of "fronts." Thus they became the Front Homosexuel d'Action Révolutionnaire. Audacity has its limits, however: the name they registered at the Paris police headquarters was more moderate—the Front Humanitaire Anti-Raciste [Antiracist humanitarian front]—and the stated social goal of the group was altogether orthodox: "research."

Missing when the FHAR was formed was Hocquenghem, who soon joined the group. Until that time, his political choices had kept him at one remove from the themes of sexual liberation. In 1967, Pierre Hahn had attempted, unsuccessfully, to rally him behind the homosexual cause, and Philippe Guy tried to sensitize him to new forms of American protest, giving him texts brought back from the United States. But Hocquenghem was still a leftist and had been a militant for Vive la Révolution [Long live the revolution], or VLR, since September 1970.

VLR, a Maoist and libertarian branch of the left, created by Roland Castro and his friends, differed both from the Trotskyists of the Alain Krivine variety and from the orthodox Maoists of Gauche Prolétarienne [Proletarian left]. Hocquenghem was to say that the latter group was "sexually frustrated," characterized by a "clandestine homosexuality of machos among themselves."[14] The VLR was also a strange movement. Its ideological peculiarity within the far left went hand in hand with surprising contradictions and irreconcilable currents: a love of the masses, inspired by the Chinese Cultural Revolution; the individualism of French anarchism; an American-style communitarianism; and, soon, the eruption of the sexual liberation movements, which would splinter the organization. In VLR, Hocquenghem, who had been expelled from Jeunesses Communistes Révolutionnaires along with those who, somewhat later, were called the Maosspontex, completed his transition from politics (the class struggle) to homosexuality (the sex struggle).

In early 1971, Hocquenghem was attending the VLR's general meetings, which took place at a site already sanctified by May '68: the Ecole des Beaux-Arts, on rue Bonaparte—a place homosexuals would remember. During the same period, in April 1971, he finally went to one of the meetings of the FHAR. "I arrived in a little room with about thirty people in it," Hocquenghem later recounted:

There were some homosexuals there, pretty old ones, a little "fey," whom I didn't like being around, and lesbians. That was the first time I'd met any of them. Everyone told their life story, their dreams, their desires, who they had slept with, how, and why. And how they were dealing with it. . . . Some had been to the United States and had seen what the Gay Liberation Front was all about. Their dream was to do something like that in France.[15]

It was Jean-Paul Sartre who gave them the means to "do something like that." Beginning in September 1970, Sartre had overseen the biweekly newspaper of VLR, called *Tout!* [Everything!]. Its subtitle was a slogan in itself: "What we want: everything!"

In issue 1 (Sept. 23, 1970), *Tout!* published the declaration on homosexuality by the American "comrade" Huey Newton, who bore the high-flown title of Minister of Defense of the Black Panther Party. Newton wrote:

As we very well know, sometimes our first instinct is to want to hit a homosexual in the mouth, and want a woman to be quiet. . . . We must gain security in ourselves and therefore have respect and feelings for all oppressed people. . . . Homosexuals are not given freedom and liberty by anyone in the society. They might be the most oppressed people in the society. . . . The Women's Liberation Front and the Gay Liberation Front are our friends. They are potential allies and *we need as many allies as possible.*

This was an important declaration, since it authoritatively conferred "revolutionary rank" on homosexuals. The international authority and legitimacy of Newton's far left had a certain effect on French leftist militants; the leader of the Black Panther Party had gone so far as to assert that "homosexuals are not enemies of the people. . . . Quite the contrary, maybe a homosexual could be the most revolutionary."[16]

At the junction of VLR and the FHAR, Hocquenghem, who was responsible for publishing this text by Newton, proposed that the founders of the FHAR put together an issue of *Tout!* on homosexuality. This championing of "sexual issues" was a surprising move for the leftist newspaper, but Roland Castro and the editorial staff of VLR allowed it. The righteous struggle of the proletariat was shelved, and because the times and the "mass movement" required it, the articles appearing in issue 12 were "Our Bodies Do Belong to Us!" and "The Right to Homosexuality and Every Sort of Sexuality" and "The Right of Minors to Freedom of Desire and Its Satisfaction."

This issue, coordinated by Hocquenghem, appeared on April 23, 1971; nearly 50,000 copies were distributed. On the cover were male bodies that were nude or in skimpy underwear. Inside, the homosexual and feminist battles, as well as minors' right to desire, were combined. On the one hand, the newspaper addressed heterosexuals, asserting, "Deep down, everyone is more or less homosexual" and "Total revolution means not just carrying out a wildcat strike, or locking up a boss who pisses you off; it also means accepting sexual upheaval, without restriction. The harder that seems at first, the less you understand, the more you'll be able to tell yourself you're on the right path." In another typical article, "To Those Who Think They Are Normal," a militant from *Tout!* wrote:

You don't feel like oppressors, [and yet] your society has treated us like a social scourge.... You are individually responsible for the vile mutilation you have made us suffer by criticizing our desire.... Along with women, we are the moral doormat on which you wipe your conscience. We're saying we've had enough, you won't beat us up anymore, because we will defend ourselves, we will go after your racism against us, even in language. What's more, we won't confine ourselves to self-defense, we will attack.... You can do nothing for us as long as you do nothing for yourselves.[17]

The newspaper also addressed homosexual "brothers." The FHAR advised them to come out of the ghetto—the "noncommercial" ghetto (public toilets, street urinals) as well as the "commercial" one (bars and nightclubs): "A nightclub is the kingdom of cash. You dance there with other men, you size each other up as commodities: heterocop society exploits us there. Fear persists—regular raids by the cops, legal roundups." The message for homosexuals was radically new. It seemed to be: "You are ashamed because you accept the propaganda of the heterocops." Thus the theme of coming out appeared for the first time in France, unambiguously summed up in the title of an article: "Let's Stop Cowering in the Corner." The FHAR, "a saw for cutting up reality in a different way," in Hocquenghem's expression, had found its slogan.

In this historic issue, one manifesto has remained famous for its provocative nature: "We are more than 343 sluts. We have been buggered by Arabs. We are proud of it and will do it again."[18] This text was accompanied by a quotation from Jean Genet: "Perhaps if I had never gone to bed with Algerians, I would not have approved of the FLN [Front de Liberation Nationale]. I might have been on their side in any case, but it was homosexuality that made me realize that Algerians were no different from other men."[19] The staff of *Tout!* explained that this statement by the author of *Le journal du voleur* [*The Thief's Journal*] "appeared racist to certain nonhomosexual comrades." The debate began. Roland Castro was worried.

ϖ

Was his worry legitimate? Sartre, *Tout!*'s editorial director, was soon charged with "public indecency" and "pornography" by Raymond Marcellin, Jacques Chaban-Delmas's famous minister of the interior.[20] Ten thousand copies of the issue were seized, the offices of VLR were searched by the vice squad, and a vendor of *Tout!* was arrested in Grenoble.

Sartre, paradoxically, was happy about the charge, which, added to the recent banning of his organization La Cause du Peuple [The people's cause], publicly confirmed the absence of freedom of expression in the supposedly democratic France of Georges Pompidou. For the first time, Sartre would win a stunning victory against the justice system.[21]

Beyond this puritan reflex on the part of the authorities, who believed that Vive la Révolution had gone too far, the difficulties were even more obvious within the Maoist movement itself. The large leftist bookstore Norman-Béthune refused to distribute issue 12, and the proworker wing of VLR could no longer go along: How the hell could militants continue to sell that issue outside the Renault factories? Christian, a VLR typesetter, summed the situation up: "It's awfully hard to show up in front of a factory selling *Tout!* and shouting, 'Ask for issue 12 of *Tout!* Read our article "I Got Buggered by an Arab!"'"[22] As a result, the newspaper, after playing a role in the Constitutional Council's censure of the government, produced a rift in VLR. "The time has come to separate," Roland Castro announced at an emergency congress convened at Easter. Castro, an architecture student at Beaux-Arts, was both enthusiastic and worried about the consequences of issue 12 and was overwhelmed by the new demands of feminists and homosexuals, which in his view were too far removed from the preoccupations of workers. He decided on self-dissolution: "Change life!" must not be confused with "Change your life!"—that is, with "Freak out, get a rush, party down."[23] For orthodox leftists, homosexuality was only "petty bourgeois individualism," as *Lutte Ouvrière* [Workers' struggle] did not fail to remind readers, criticizing issue 12 of *Tout!*: "We may ask what could lead people who call themselves revolutionaries to publish a newspaper whose content sinks to the level of urinal graffiti. . . . So it is that petty bourgeois individualism, after embracing Stalinism, and then socialism in a single country, has managed to become the champion of 'socialism in a single bed.'"[24]

Despite these negative reactions, issue 12 retained its importance for thousands of French homosexuals. Many letters published in issue 13 confirmed the function of issue 12 as collective self-therapy, perhaps the main virtue of the FHAR: "Let me first express to you my joy, the fraternal joy that reading *Tout!* gave us. I say 'us' because when one feels the strength of comrades, 'I' becomes plural. And such inspired words galvanize the revolt of the lonely. . . . All men are women and all women are men. Abnormal? That's other people" (P.R., Grenoble). "It's the first time a newspaper has gone so far in tearing away the hypocritical veil of silence. I will have to reread your articles several times, they are so dense, innovative, and courageous: aren't you going to be prosecuted for them?" (C.D., Lyons). "When they managed to make me believe I was a monster, I wanted to commit suicide. But no more, because I know we are legion" (J.P., Paris). "I want to live as I am and without problems, even in my remote province. Unfortunately, it would be a real pain if you published my address" (L.C., Pas-de-Calais). "Can people in their forties join?" (P.C., Paris). "I am homosexual but I'm not sure I'm revolutionary. . . . In the end, I'm going to stop feeling sorry I was ever born. But I've never known how to become a revolutionary. By myself, I don't have the energy for that" (D.M., Reims).

Although VLR dissolved and *Tout!* folded in July 1971, the "deviants" who brought about the rift in the group were now moving ahead on their own steam.

"WE DON'T GET OFF INSIDE THE SYSTEM"[25]

The word quickly went out that an informal, coed movement of homosexuals, the FHAR, was meeting Thursday evenings in a classroom at the Ecole des Beaux-Arts. There were thirty people at the first meeting, half of them women and half men, but after the *Tout!* issue the crowd grew. There were about a hundred people the next Thursday, more and more of them men, and there were a thousand by the time the 1971 summer vacation was about to begin. "It's not a revolution, milord, it's a mutation."[26]

This transfer of sex into revolution needed a language, a new vocabulary for a new struggle. The FHAR, largely inspired by the women's movement, invented the terms of "dealienation." Homosexuals were now "queers," and heterosexuals were "heterocops." The *French-Homo Dictionary* of the FHAR defined other terms, such as "phallocrat," that is, "a heterocop who believes that having a prick gives him the right to oppress," or even "family cell" (for "family"), "the first source of neurosis and mental illness, as in the saying, 'family cell, the waiting room of prison (often for life).'"

Even though they borrowed most of the innovations of May '68—the idea of direct democracy, rap groups, consciousness-raising groups, rejection of the star system—the general meetings of the FHAR marked a momentous time in the history of the evolution of mores in France. They got homosexuals talking. "The image that comes to mind," a regular recounts, "is of the clubs during the Revolution of 1789, with loudmouths having shouting matches and women knitting on the rostrum and making comments between stitches. . . . What did we talk about? Everything that had to do with protest, the homo experience, and theoretical statements by stars and divas, but also bits of our lives were tossed out, sacks were emptied, in complete silence."[27]

A few tragic accounts alternated with more comical moments. "If bourgeois homosexuals think they can come here, they are mistaken," declared one speaker, who had no fear of overstatement. "Being reformist heterocops is out of the question," a lesbian confirmed. The FHAR faithful recall that several speakers, among them Françoise d'Eaubonne and the old anarchist writer Daniel Guérin, put theory into practice by boldly undressing in the middle of one general meeting, between two speeches on liberating the body. Hadn't a slogan in issue 12 of *Tout!* asserted, "Our bodies do belong to us"?

⤺

Daniel Guérin standing naked on a table in the amphitheater at the Ecole des Beaux-Arts? An astonishing image. His presence in the FHAR is nevertheless significant.

In a way, Guérin was the grandfather of the French homosexual movement. His life, described in 1971 in his *Autobiographie de jeunesse* [Early life], was representative of an era: early years tormented by "sexual dissidence," Platonic infatuations after World War I, and then masturbatory repression. Finally, "the explosion of a homosexuality raging because it had been too long contained." A reader of Sully Proudhon, Reich, and Fourier—the latter explains, in his *Nouveau monde amoureux* [New world of love], that homosexuality should be used to create social harmony—Guérin devoted several books to sexuality. In them he recounted his love of "oppressed young people" and explained how his association with "young fellows of the lower classes" had led him to socialism. He also compared the oppression of American blacks with that of homosexuals. Guérin was the oddest synthesis of anarchism and socialism, and he was converted by the grace of boys. "There is a formidable force in me, conferred on me by my homosexuality," he confirms. "That force had to be placed in the service of something much greater than debauchery or the struggle for homosexuality."[28] Beyond the singularity of his words, Guérin's presence at the general meetings at Beaux-Arts may be confirmation that a libertarian tendency was inseparable from the platform of the FHAR.[29]

⤺

On May Day 1971, homosexuals, including many women, marched for the first time as such in the streets of Paris. There were only fifty or fewer, but they did not go unnoticed. Born with the far left, the FHAR believed it was useful to join the traditional Workers' Day demonstration, but that intermixing was not considered natural by all the organizations present. Far from it. In the Communist Party, Pierre Juquin declared that "the issue of homosexuality . . . has never had anything to do with the workers' movement."[30] FHAR militants went to a meeting of the French Communist Party at the Mutualité and challenged Jacques Duclos, the party's secretary general, with the cry "Long live hysterical materialism!" Duclos replied, "You pederasts—where do you get the nerve to come and question us? Go get treatment. The French Communist Party is healthy!"

At the May Day march, as a result, homosexuals were sent to the end of the line, far behind the Communist Party, Michel Rocard's Parti Socialiste Unifié [Unified socialist party], or PSU, and the allies of Alain Krivine and Sartre. They marched between the Mouvement de la Libération des Femmes [Women's liberation movement], or MLF, and the Front de Libération des Jeunes [Youth liberation front], or FLJ. Along the way they picked up a few lesbian demonstrators from the MLF and made sheep's eyes at young men while chanting "High school students are cute." The anarchists, in a gesture of welcome, picked tulips at Père-Lachaise Cemetery and offered them to the "homos." By contrast, the stupefied Confédération Générale du Travail [General labor confederation], or CGT, pondered, "They're not so homosexual. Look, there are women with them." The FHAR militants retorted, "Run, comrades, run, the homos are in the rear!" The stage director Patrice Chéreau has a keen memory of Communist Party militants who turned and gawked at the "drag queens," declaring, "It's completely outside the tradition of the working class."

In the photograph published in issue 13 of *Tout!*, which immortalizes the May Day demonstration of 1971, one can make out the subversive Anne-Marie Fauré; Pierre Hahn, behind his glasses; Françoise d'Eaubonne, her fist raised; and Philippe Guy, attempting to hide behind a large banner, for fear of being recognized.[31]

"I decided to march," remembers Georges Lapassade, then professor at the brand-new Université de Vincennes. "I was the only academic to come out of the closet. I felt people were staring at me from all sides. I knew I would be recognized by leftist leaders, but I stayed in the procession."

On May Day 1971, the "girls" of the FHAR chose to sing, to the tune of Brassens's *La mauvaise réputation* [Bad reputation]:

> In the bland old world
> People don't want us
> To put our pricks in places they don't.
> Whether we love a girl or a boy
> Is none of your business.
> You'll have to resign yourself to the fact
> We won't wear the pink triangle anymore.
> We'll appear in broad daylight,
> And long live the revolution!

The Saint-Jacques is a little Maoist and Kabyle café at 69, rue Saint Jacques, very close to Lycée Louis-le-Grand. A few FHAR militants, with the unavowed idea of "fraternizing" with immigrant workers, met there after the May Day march—or later, in the evening, after the general meeting at the Beaux-Arts. There they prepared their commando actions: an expedition to rue Manin, against "queer bashers" in the public toilets; a trip to Tours, to take on Jean Royer [see note 20]; and a trip to San Remo, to sabotage a convention of psychoanalysts. Militancy and partying were not mutually exclusive: a parade was organized at the Tuileries, and a "witches' ball" was held in conjunction with the women's movement.[32] To celebrate Christmas, homosexuals in the FHAR composed another song, although a poorly rhymed one. It had been a fine year. The homosexual "comrades" of the FHAR were happy. They had fun, laughed uproariously, and made love.

⌒

"Making love" was in fact the new political platform of the post-'68 era. At the Université de Vincennes, where Guy Hocquenghem was appointed a lecturer in 1972, the FHAR met regularly every Friday (in the department of philosophy) and organized debates. The graffiti in the department's urinals illustrate the sexual liberation that was under way: "Come to room 217, building C, we're making porn movies." "Where is sex life?" "You're a queer." "'Desire' is not a reflexive verb, 'screw yourself' is." "Young revolutionaries: Make revolution, but above all, for pity's sake, don't make love, you don't know how" (in a female hand). "You shouldn't write with your left hand while jacking off with your right." "Come piss at our place; you're invited" (in a female hand). "Mao is only alienation of the individual. One solution: Bugger Mao (not restrictive: also Lenin, Trotsky, Bakunin)."

In 1971, the general meetings of the FHAR at the Beaux-Arts became a place for immediate sexual gratification. Militants put revolution into practice: they invented cruising relieved of its furtiveness, and, moving through hallways, surrounded by sculptures, or on the upper floors and in the attic, they experimented with Fourier's 36,000 forms of love. "The regulars went right upstairs," one observer recounts, "and crouched and clustered together in corners."[33] The general meetings, an early incarnation of the back rooms designed for quick, anonymous sex that were to spread throughout France in the late 1970s, replaced the Tuileries. People smoked Moroccan hash and black oils in little kohl bottles. In Hocquenghem's words, the FHAR became a "nebula of feelings."

This transformation of political platform into sexual space was not unanimously encouraged, however. Philippe Guy, cofounder of the FHAR, deplored this development: "In that subhuman cesspool of fucking, among those Deleuzian desiring machines, in that drunken boat, the FHAR could only sink." By 1972, Hocquenghem was also regretting the fact that "too often now, those who come to cruise at the FHAR are people unrelated to the mission of the FHAR. . . . Making love with someone also means wanting to transform him. We underestimated that, by reducing homosexual desire to the desire to sleep with other men."[34]

One American passing through Paris, confronted with the strange spectacle of an eroticized leftist movement and astonished by this enormous cruising spot distributed over six floors, had this telling question about the FHAR: "What is it supposed to be?"

FHAR militants had set themselves the task of "making war against normal people and love among ourselves." By 1972, it was clear which political activity they had chosen.

⌒

"Where's the beach? Where's the beach?" On May Day 1972, the surprise of the CGT tough guys reached its high point as mermaids—equipped with parasols, dressed in coats made of sponges, wearing jellyfish on their feet, and swishing as they threaded their way through the trade union procession—asked, "Where's the beach?" Never before had anyone thought to march in high heels, Chanel suits, or necklaces of trinkets. But the Gazolines—they dared. "Bring me my boa-a-a-a," one of them cried.

The Gazolines represented the "hysterical queen" faction of the FHAR. The most radical of all radicals, they were, in part, the dissidents of the homosexual movement, which they did not hesitate to make fun of: "Did someone say *fard?*"[35] Inspired as much by the Situationist Internationale as by Lesbiennes Se Déchaînent [Lesbians lash out], or LSD, they focused their attacks on the power struggles of the minor chieftains within the FHAR.[36] They insulted Guy Hocquenghem, Gilles Deleuze, and Michel Foucault. Nonetheless, they were tolerated by the FHAR "leaders" because they represented the quintessence of everything that heterosexuals hated. Outwardly, they chanted slogans that were disconcerting even to FHAR homosexuals who were still under the influence of leftism: "Nationalize the sequin factories" and (Hélène Hazera's invention) "Workers of the world, fondle each other!" That set the tone. In the May 5, 1972, issue of *L'Humanité*, Roland Leroy expressed his disgust: "This disorder does not represent the vanguard of society, but rather the rotting of a capitalist system in decline." In response, the Gazolines suggested that leftists and Communists take Mandrax, an aphrodisiac that, consumed with a great deal of alcohol, was supposed to turn heterosexuals into homosexuals.

Primarily composed of transvestites and a few transsexuals, the Gazolines, whose clothes came from flea markets, consisted of Hélène Hazera, Marie-France (future star of the Alcazar), Philippe Genet, Michel Cressole, Maud Molyneux, Jean-Michel Mandopoulos, Zelda, Dina, Pablo Rouy, and Griselda. Griselda recalls, "For us, political action meant wearing makeup, going down to Barbès or Café de Flore in bathing suits, and tottering on high heels with hair on our legs." Another challenged Jean-François Bizot, the owner of *Actuel*: "Don't be an idiot. Look at your mug, your long hair. . . . People are fed up with leftist metalanguage. The whole vulgar trip, the swear words, trading a packet of greasy french fries for an old roach—that's over. Now it's champagne, coke, and flounces."[37]

On March 4, 1972, the Gazolines were present at the funeral of Pierre Overney, a Maoist militant killed by a night watchman at Renault-Billancourt. Behind "Pierrot," 200,000 people clenched their fists in one of the last big demonstrations of May '68; simultaneously, a Gazoline dressed as a bereaved widow, complete with veil, took on the role of hired mourner while the other "girls" shouted a slogan that went unappreciated by the demonstrators: "Liz Taylor and Pierre Overney are fighting the same battle!" As a former Gazoline explains today, "We wanted to criticize the way the Maoists cashed in on their martyrs." Daniel Guérin, who fought to give the FHAR more structure, criticized this kind of action: "When the FHAR was created, I said to myself, Now, finally, I'm going to find what I've been looking for all my life: revolutionary homosexuals. And then, boom! I fall into something even worse than what I'd known . . . Completely unconscious creatures . . . Mooning the crowd the day of Overney's funeral—that was disgusting!"

Twenty-five years later, the leading figure of the Gazolines describes the group's influence as relative:

We were twelve peacocks; it was very marginal. You have to see the role of the Gazolines as relative. We put on lipstick and shouted provocative slogans. It was nothing to be proud of. We were twenty years old. Today I acknowledge my past as a Gazoline because you're supposed to if you were in the FHAR, but I'm not thrilled about it.

The person who spoke these words in 1995 was still a man in the 1970s. Since then, she has chosen to take hormones and become a woman. Beyond the sequins and makeup, political action remains a long-term commitment for the Gazolines.[38]

Contrary to how the Gazolines may have appeared, the work of the FHAR turned out to be surprisingly serious. Even issue 12 of *Tout!* went beyond mere provocation and remains a key document today. Revolution is a serious business. Nevertheless, the stars of the FHAR had very different approaches to homosexuality and to politics. There were so many contradictions, so many peculiarities, and so many forms of leftism. For Hocquenghem, it was Maoism transformed by the reading of Jean Genet. For Philippe Guy, it was Stonewall revisited by libidinal asceticism. For Françoise d'Eaubonne, it was libertarian feminism and heterosexual love with homosexual boys. For Hazera, it was hysteria tempered by hormones. For Guérin, it was anarchism in flirtation with Fernand Léger's *Constructeurs*. For Laurent Dispot, it was a hoary blend of Chairman Mao's thought and Madame Verdurin's.

This mixture of paradox and eccentricity produced Homeric free-for-alls, which the different publications of the FHAR reflected. In addition to the newspapers (*Le Fléau Social, L'Antinorm*), which show the various sensibilities of the FHAR, two essential collections give an idea of the theoretical work that was being done. In some ways, these collections serve as the movement's last will and testament. The first, titled *Rapport contre la normalité* [Report against normality], was published in late September 1971, reprinting texts published in *Tout!* The second appeared in March 1973, when the FHAR was already moribund. It was a special issue of *Recherches* titled "Trois milliards de pervers" [Three billion perverts] and devoted to the history of "homosexualities." Even though it had the backing of a great number of personalities (from Foucault to Sartre, and from Deleuze to Genet), the issue was seized, and its editorial director (Félix Guattari) was prosecuted in criminal court in May 1974.[39] The trial impelled Foucault to publish an opinion piece in *Combat* (April 27, 1974), in which he straightforwardly posed this question: "Yes or no: As a sexual practice, will homosexuality receive the same rights of expression and exercise as so-called normal sexuality?"

Nevertheless, the FHAR, the "libidinous antinorm," did not seek a response to this question. When the police were called in to the sixth floor of the Ecole des Beaux-Arts in February 1974, at the request of the administration, the general meetings of the FHAR were already long deserted. The political movement—a shadow of its former self ever since sex had replaced debate—was dead.

﹏

Now that the movement has left the stage, are we to believe that the FHAR had any effect at all in the remote regions of Pompidou's France? Despite the thousands of homosexuals who attended its forums between 1971 and 1974, and apart from attempts to create small regional groups and neighborhood committees in Paris, it seems that most provincial homosexuals hardly knew of the FHAR's existence.[40]

The exact influence of the movement thus remains difficult to evaluate. For Laurent Dispot, "the FHAR was virtually nothing but a catchphrase."[41] A regular prefers to use a different image: "The FHAR was a back room in broad daylight, adjoining a political agora." Alain Huet, another militant, remembers it as a space for free speech: "It was a permanent verbal logorrhea. All of a sudden, everyone started to talk, to recount his life, his life as an ashamed, closeted queer. The FHAR was a proliferation of speech." By creating social ties among homosexuals, the FHAR, a kind of peer group, opened the floodgates.

The symbolic importance of the movement is undeniable, even if it had no real impact on the French press. In this respect, it is surprising that such a disorganized group, which existed for so brief a time, did have so much influence. Even today it occupies a place in the collective memory of homosexuals. But had homosexual liberation come about in France?

In matters of individual rights, repression, and living conditions in the provinces, the FHAR had no influence; no political platform emerged from the spirit of revolt.[42] As proof of its futility, it even seems that the movement had little concern for the fate of people arrested for and then convicted of homosexual activity.[43] Moreover, "homosexual life" in the early 1970s was still far removed from the provocative militancy of the FHAR; to understand the era, it would be more helpful to consider the public toilets or the parks than the meetings at the Beaux-Arts.[44] The FHAR was the promise of liberation, not liberation itself.

The FHAR's accomplishments are nevertheless considerable. With the FHAR, homosexuality moved from private to public life, and this way of thinking managed to exert a lasting disruptive influence on the far left: "The revolutionary tradition maintains that the division between public and private is obvious. Homosexual militants' actions characteristically put the private, the shameful little secret about sexuality, on public view."[45] The repercussions of this ear-splitting entry of the homosexual issue into political discourse are still of key importance: "To make revolution," issue 12 of *Tout!* advised, "we will have to get rid of leftism." The FHAR attempted to carry out that ambitious plan, and the political parties, often reluctantly, had to take a position on the issue of homosexuality.

The leftist movement rested on general political theories with universal aims. The intrusion of irreducibly particular situations (the situations of women, young people, and homosexuals) could only destabilize it. In this respect, the FHAR managed to make leftist militants feel guilty, since tolerance of homosexuality became a litmus test of their repressive puritanism.[46] Some of the stars of the FHAR confirm that "all the great personalities of the left felt guilty"; even Jean Daniel desperately searched his memory to see whether he could find a homosexual relationship in his past. But could the marginal issue of homosexuality seriously claim to have revolutionized the revolutionary movements?

The FHAR was not free of contradictions in its relations with political groups. When homosexual battles were selectively co-opted by the "bourgeois press," the FHAR did not know how to confront critics on the far left. Moreover, the movement, calling itself revolutionary, rejected the assignment of a homosexual identity and championed polysexuality for everyone.[47] Guy Hocquenghem writes, "We attempted to define the attitude of the revolutionary homosexual as a homosexual vision or conception of the world."[48] Nevertheless, although the word "revolutionary" in the FHAR acronym was as important as the word "homosexual," the movement did not always keep its revolutionary promise or preserve its fear of identities. It even gave the impression that it was taking an autonomous path, leaving the feminists behind and championing a differentialist road, if not a right to difference—in total contradiction of polysexuality.[49] The final and most formidable contradiction was that FHAR militants were skillfully skewered by "conservative" homosexuals for defending, under Marxist, Maoist, or Castroist banners, political regimes that distinguished themselves on a daily basis by their hateful repression of homosexuals. Although the link between homosexuality and revolution was appealing at the intellectual level, the course of events quickly reduced it to nothing. Some will say that the era itself was contradictory, but that does not change the verdict.

The FHAR, apart from being a collective movement, allowed Guy Hocquenghem to emerge as the spokesperson for French homosexuals. Little by little, the young man asserted himself as the representative of the FHAR. This was an understandable process of identification in a wild, noninstitutionalized movement (it had no president, no agenda, and no membership cards). Hocquenghem owed this recognition to his intellectual authority, to his friendships within philosophical circles (with Deleuze, Guattari, Foucault, and Sartre), and to his eloquence.

With the bearing of a latter-day Julien Sorel, sporting fabulous red trousers that contrasted sharply with his disheveled hair, Hocquenghem, a combination of popular orator and diva, created his image through carefully monitored appearances. Others saw his intentions as more political—the art of infiltration and exploitation so characteristic of the Trotskyists, but also a "squelching of speech, a taste for the cult of personality." Laurent Dispot, who willingly would have played the role of political boss, claimed, "Guy Hocquenghem's arrival transformed what could have been a discussion forum into a media rocket subject to the gravitational pull of the star system."[50] This is a harsh judgment, and Hocquenghem seems to have responded in advance to this kind of criticism: "We are not a group, but a movement. . . . The FHAR belongs to no one. . . . It is merely homosexuality on the move. All self-aware homosexuals are the FHAR: any discussion between two or three of them is the FHAR. Jealousy, cruising, makeup . . . that's the FHAR."[51] In the fifteen years that followed, Guy Hocquenghem, who became by turns an essayist and a novelist, was able to remain the symbol of homosexuals in France. Here was his genius, and perhaps his imposture: to have anticipated, in the simple account of his life and his identification with the FHAR, all the hopes and impasses that lay in wait for modern homosexuality.

Despite the Brownian motion of the FHAR—less a product of organized leftism than the bastard son of feminism and the desiring machines so dear to Deleuze and Guattari—the first opportunity for homosexual liberation was missed. The 1970s had begun, but for many, in the provinces and in Paris, homosexuality was still an ordeal. Nevertheless, the cause now had its foundational myth: the commando action against Ménie Grégoire's broadcast "That Painful Problem, Homosexuality." Along the way, a militant score was composed in a well-known key (class struggle) and punctuated by felicitous wrong notes (desire, speech); the FHAR, not an identity movement or a reformist movement or an antidiscrimination movement, chose a revolutionary mode, rejecting the assignment of a fixed identity to homosexuals, but the homosexual movement in France could not always stay on pitch. Also along the way, the cause found its hero. For many he was the one who had "liberated homosexuals," and by the end of the "FHAR years" "Comrade" Hocquenghem had become the emblem of homosexuality in France.

2

Women's Liberation: Year Zero

Since the Arc de Triomphe [action], the women's movement has become widely known, or rather widely misknown, because the image of it that was disseminated was of hysterical shrews and lesbians.

— Simone de Beauvoir

The scene was the Arc de Triomphe. Several photographers were present, as well as a few cameras and microphones. One or another of the women had probably gotten overexcited and leaked the news to the media or deliberately chosen to make the event public. In any case, something was about to happen.

The story of this stunt has often been told, even though it was brief and a hopeless failure. On August 26, 1970, the fiftieth anniversary of women's suffrage in the United States, nine women who wanted to commemorate the event in their own way suddenly appeared on the loose gravel at the foot of the Arc de Triomphe, in Paris. Under the eyes of a few peace officers, easygoing at first, who would not allow them to carry out their plan, they attempted to unfurl banners on the central flagstone reading ONE MAN IN TWO IS A WOMAN and THERE IS SOMEONE EVEN MORE UNKNOWN THAN THE UNKNOWN SOLDIER: HIS WIFE.

In the photos published by the newspapers the next day, one can make out the writers Monique Wittig and Christiane Rochefort, but also women who were still unknown: Cathy Bernheim, Christine Delphy, Anne Zelensky, Monique Bourroux, Emmanuèle de Lesseps, Frédérique Daber, and Janine Sert. The feminists of the new generation were radical, spectacular, and funny. The journal *Partisans* ran the headline "Women's Liberation: Year Zero."[1] Through that action, the Mouvement de Libération des Femmes, or MLF, was born.[2]

↬

Cathy Bernheim, short, dark, and rather heavyset, was twenty-four years old in 1970. At a time when women wore long mauve dresses and black clogs, with henna-dyed hair falling straight past their shoulders, Cathy kept her curly hair short, wore overalls, and showed no interest in "threads."

In May 1970, Bernheim had an illumination. She learned that militant revolutionaries had dared to heckle some women simply because the women had wanted to debate the men at the Université de Vincennes.[3] A few days later, reading the issue of *L'Idiot International* [The international idiot] devoted to the "Battle for Women's Liberation," she felt she was reading her own thoughts: "Since time immemorial, we have lived as a colonized people within the people, so well domesticated that we have forgotten that our situation of dependence is not a matter of course. . . . If we resist [those who have made us mere sex objects], we are prudes, sluts, shrews, or hysterical feminists."

Reading these lines, Cathy relived images from her childhood. She recalled her male cousins, who claimed she was incapable of swimming as far as they could, of diving as long as they could, of catching crabs with her bare hands, of whistling through her fingers. One day, under the garden stairs, the eldest of these "little males," who had "learned to assess the importance of his penis," decided he wanted to "do it." To persuade Cathy when she refused, he asked what it would cost. "Childhood was over," she noted.

Then came her first period, and puberty. "Femininity seemed to be burdened with so many constraints that it did not take me long to decide I did not want to be a woman. . . . In fact, I would not have been able to tolerate loving men unless I had been a man myself." At sixteen, "with the impression that everything being played out at that moment could only be definitive," Cathy placed a tender kiss on the mouth of a pale-skinned girlfriend wearing "a black dress, like an adult": "I was reading *The Roman Spring of Mrs. Stone* and I took myself for one of the beautiful boys described by Tennessee Williams, who roamed palaces satisfying mature women in exchange for money."

Cathy resolved to be heterosexual, to lose her virginity "the way someone decides to go to the dentist": "I was not ugly, but I felt that I was, since it had been repeated to me so often." Then, one evening in August, she had dinner with a firebrand who proclaimed, with a laugh, that he could fuck any woman: "The memory I have of that evening is that the weather was very hot."

A poster from May 1968 showed a woman throwing a brick, with the slogan BEAUTY IS IN THE STREET. When Cathy read, on a wall, THEY'RE BUYING UP YOUR HAPPINESS, STEAL IT BACK, it was another "click": "They had taken our belongings, our lives, our bodies."

From then on, feminism was a part of her life, and when, two years later, she discovered the article in *L'Idiot International* and learned that women were coming together in groups, Cathy jumped up: "I must go see them right away!" She made contact with the women who had dared to write "We are the people," and, on August 26, 1970, she found herself among the nine women pioneers who placed a spray of flowers for "the wife of the unknown soldier."[4]

↩

The women's movement had various origins. There was a small group called "Féminin, Masculin, Avenir" [Feminine, masculine, future], or FMA, which since

1967 had been made up of a few friends from Andrée Michel's seminar, and which met with Anne Zelensky and Jacqueline Feldman.[5] Christine Delphy and Emmanuèle de Lesseps joined them. After May '68, FMA became "Féminin, Marxisme, Action": "Marxism" had replaced "masculine." Men were soon excluded from the group.

Parallel to the FMA, another circle (called the Vincennes group) formed around Monique Wittig, with Antoinette Fouque, Françoise Ducrocq, and Margaret Stephenson. Each group learned of the other by reading the newspaper: *Le Nouvel Observateur* published a letter from the FMA, and *L'Idiot International* printed an article signed by Wittig. Once the two branches had merged, it was decided that the group would be exclusively female: the women's movement would be homosexual in its structure.

The political history of these women was varied. Bernheim had never been involved in politics, but some of the women were Trotskyists or Maoists. Others had been activists in the Union Nationale des Etudiants Français (UNEF), the French student union, or in the Parti Socialiste Unifié [Unified socialist party], or PSU. Some on the barricades of 1968 were barely twenty years old; others were old enough to be their mothers: they had been militants during the Algerian war or, later, against the French involvement in Vietnam. More or less infused with leftism, all the women who came together in 1970 shared the desire to denounce the "machismo" of far-left militants—a position with which FHAR militants also agreed. In relation to the Trotskyists and, later, the men of Vive la Révolution, the women defined themselves as intrinsically political because "feminism in itself is political." They even criticized the leftists for getting the real battle wrong: "Your revolution is not ours."[6]

Feminists looking for a new identity now came together without any males present. At last they were "among themselves": they laughed, wrote songs, called one another by their first names. They could come to terms with their desires and speak of their bodies. This new experience was overwhelming.

In the issue of *Partisans* titled "Women's Liberation: Year Zero," one article did not escape anyone's notice: Anne Koedt's "The Myth of the Vaginal Orgasm." This American author maintained that the clitoris was the only zone capable of procuring an orgasm for women: "Men fear that they will become sexually expendable if the clitoris is substituted for the vagina as the center of pleasure for women," Koedt predicted. "Considering that the vagina is very desirable from a man's point of view, purely on physical grounds, one begins to see the dilemma for men." Some argued that women should seek out one another's company, now that the primacy of the vaginal orgasm had been called into question and clitoral orgasm had been recognized.

In the same journal, the writer Christiane Rochefort explained that there was no such thing as a frigid woman: clumsy and brutal men were solely responsible for sexual dysfunction. The author of *Printemps au parking* [Spring in the parking lot]—a novel in which she describes a relationship between two boys—denounced the macho slogan "Power is at the tip of the phallus," exclaiming, "So it's an instrument of power! And, what's more, you want us to think that's a good thing?" This writer, already famous, also skewered the "promotion" of vaginal orgasm, characterizing it as a "psychological war" whose goal was to valorize strictly heterosexual relations. From that point on, man was an oppressor: Marxism and psychoanalysis shed light on "exploitation by the penis."[7] The major themes of women's liberation were in place.

‮↝‬

In 1970, most activist women cited a single predecessor, either to follow her or to set themselves apart from her: Simone de Beauvoir. In April 1949, Beauvoir had published the first volume of *Le deuxième sexe* [*The Second Sex*]. In that dense theoretical work, she analyzed women's condition from a philosophical perspective (Existentialism), called the principle of vaginal orgasm into question, and dismantled Freud's theory that women—and even little girls—had "penis envy."[8] A quarter-century before the neofeminists, Beauvoir had brazenly addressed the burning questions of contraception, abortion, and sexual equality in the workplace, even if this ambitious, exhaustive, minutely detailed project became disconcerting in the end. Beauvoir, between demanding freedom of sexual pleasure for women and challenging their duty to reproduce, inaugurated the movement that would deliver sexuality from its shackles. In the MLF, children were nowhere to be found.

All the same, *The Second Sex* had no militant ambitions, and in 1949 Simone de Beauvoir still believed that feminism was outdated: "We are no longer combatants like our elders; on the whole, we have won." With no desire to seek revenge against men, Beauvoir wrote her overview in a distant voice, speaking in the third person as if the female condition, which she seems in fact to have escaped as an adolescent, could be analyzed from the outside. The book ends with words of peace: "Beyond their natural differences, men and women [must] unequivocally assert their fraternity."

Fraternity? It is difficult to imagine the hatred that so subversive an indictment elicited in its time. The critics had a field day, and, amid all the obscenity that followed, the best-known reaction is that of François Mauriac, who was bewildered by the book: "I'm learning many things about the clitoris and vagina of your lady friend. Confessions are becoming increasingly circumscribed."[9]

In the early 1970s, *The Second Sex* was reread in light of neofeminist events, and it became a classic. Hadn't part 4 of volume 1, with its premonitory title "Toward Liberation," proposed a model of action for the women "of the future"? In fact, the book provided the women's movement, especially its egalitarianist camp, with a theoretical foundation (the differentialist camp set itself apart from Beauvoir's

views). Beauvoir's theory analyzed social inequality between the sexes and showed
that woman is defined only in relation to man.

Nevertheless, this renewal of interest in *The Second Sex* is surprising. On the
one hand, it illustrates the need for predecessors among the neofeminists, who became acquainted with Beauvoir's work in late 1970. On the other, it shows, in the
expression of her principal biographer, how Simone de Beauvoir "abruptly ral-
l[ied]" behind feminism, having previously privileged theory and autobiographical introspection over collective action. Thus this book, which she aptly called "my
book on women," ripened for more than twenty years before achieving its full
force. We are even left with the impression that Beauvoir wrote it when she was
young (in 1949) but published it only when she was old (in 1970). From that date
on, the battle for the women's cause, condensed into the last fifteen years of her
life, occupied her completely. It made her the most famous French feminist, and it
played a role in eclipsing her literary works—something that might have appalled
her. This "rallying" gave her greater autonomy in relation to Sartre (he had been a
sponsor of leftism; she would be a sponsor of feminism). Beauvoir's slightly rau-
cous voice and rushed delivery were heard at all the meetings; her signature appeared at the bottom of all the petitions; her name figured in all the publications,
often as an editor in name only who could serve, if need be, as a backer. Behind the
feminist, however, it is never difficult to find Sartre, and, behind the woman who
sometimes defended the lesbian cause, a desire for men.

In volume 2 of *The Second Sex*, Beauvoir devoted a chapter to female homosexuality.[10] Although there is evidence of some valuable intuitions, this section has
troubled many women. "As a young lesbian of twenty," Bernheim explains, "I
opened volume 2 of Simone de Beauvoir's *The Second Sex* to the chapter 'The Lesbian,' read it, shuddered in disgust at so many generalizations piled one on top of
another, and shut the book." A missed opportunity. Nevertheless, Bernheim
quickly reconciled with Beauvoir, particularly through her more intimate writings,
her autobiography, and her novels, especially *L'invitée* [The guest, 1943].[11] She became a close friend, "a child in Simone de Beauvoir's big family," and recently
confided, "I was someone who did not just admire her, but loved her." The writer
Jocelyne Françoise is less harsh in her judgment of *The Second Sex*: "Despite its
somewhat one-sided, slapdash, laborious side, that big book counted a great deal
for me. It was a powder keg in the house. As for the chapter on the lesbian, Simone
de Beauvoir showed a lack of courage. She called homosexuality a sexuality of little
girls, though she later recognized her error." Finally, the literary critic Josyane
Savigneau still has reservations: "That chapter seemed a little ridiculous to me, a
word I don't like to use in connection with Simone de Beauvoir, since she triggered
something in me during my adolescence. Let us say I found it a little comical."

"As an 'erotic perversion,'" Beauvoir wrote, for example,

homosexuality elicits something of a smile; but, to the degree that it implies a lifestyle, it
elicits contempt or scandal. Lesbians' attitude is one of provocation and affectation, be-

cause they have no way of dealing naturally with their situation. "Naturalness" implies that one does not reflect on oneself, that one acts without representing one's actions to oneself; but the behavior of others leads the lesbian constantly to be aware of herself. It is only if she is old enough or enjoys great social prestige that she can go her own way with calm indifference.[12]

In spite of her blunders, Beauvoir was, in her own words, "inundated" with "love letters from women and queer men." She also explained that her book was called *The Second Sex* because "queers are called the 'third sex,' which must mean women come in second." Beauvoir always proved sensitive to the homosexual problematic, and until her death, in 1986, she never hesitated to defend homosexuals, both men and women. She signed a number of petitions and took the initiative in writing to certain foreign governments to ask them to decriminalize homosexuality. Beauvoir was not just Sartre's "charming Castor" or "dear little you"; she also guided the sexual liberation movements. With her beauty and, later in life, the artificial air of Goya's *Portrait of Marquesa de la Solana,* Beauvoir in her bright red turban—identifiable on every continent—was a beacon for feminists and their homosexual brothers in arms.[13]

ᔈ

"Since the Arc de Triomphe [action], the women's movement has become widely known, or rather widely misknown, because the image of it that was disseminated was of hysterical shrews and lesbians."[14] Does this observation by Beauvoir correct a false impression, or does it implicitly try to dissimulate a prevailing reality? Although it has rarely been acknowledged, a significant proportion of the women who launched the French feminist movement in 1970 found bisexuality appealing, and some were openly "homosexual."

It is not my intention to give a lesbian reading of the women's movement. The term "homosexual" itself seems altogether too reductive to define accurately what was happening in the MLF. In fact, this "brand name" masks very different relationships. For most feminists, homosexuality was an "experiential fact." If male domination had to be overthrown, could feminists continue having sexual relations with men? Christine Delphy recalls, "Feminists questioned their heterosexuality, which had become suspect." Lesbians were thus the only women who had not "made a pact with the enemy," the only ones to follow their new principles to their logical conclusion. Other women were in a situation of "compromise," at best, if not of "collaboration." For all feminists, heterosexuality was no longer a matter of course, no longer a model or an absolute; it was simply an option for those who were still practicing it. Every feminist now raised questions about her sexuality.

Issue 16 of *Tout!,* the same newspaper that brought the FHAR into existence, clearly raised an agonizing question: Can women still love men? A certain Vicky responded unambiguously in the negative: "One cannot be truly feminist and truly love men."[15] Others championed new solutions. In November 1971, a militant favoring abstinence proposed, "All you have to do is not screw." Other women had already adopted the refrain of an MLF song: "It's good, good, good . . . not to have a man on your back anymore!"[16]

The MLF was characterized, if not by the expression of a freely chosen homosexuality, then at least by a fundamentally monogamous women's culture in search of emotional intimacy and sharing, and by a female sexuality not exclusively focused on the genitals. Every nuance between homosexuality and heterosexuality was possible, and feminists seemed to run the gamut. Some, of course, were openly "homosexual." For others, lesbianism was an attitude chosen "situationally," in Beauvoir's expression. It was a particular moment of subversion against male power, a detoxification, at least temporarily. Some were distressed that they were not attracted to other women; others remained indeterminate; and still others had fluctuating practices. Some loved *a* woman but wanted nothing to do with a "lesbian identity": the emotional relationship was an act of liberation in relation to the male despoiler, a form of retaliation. Some no longer had any sexuality to speak of or were simply "desiring machines" (Deleuze) gone awry. Most simply felt no "need to define" themselves. And then there were the "clueless straight women" who quarreled with their husbands, forced them to share in household chores, and formed strange "leftist couples," which often did not survive women's liberation.

For Monique Wittig, "being in a movement that excluded men was a homosexual act, at least ideologically. Lesbianism is not only a sexual practice, it is also a cultural behavior."[17] Another feminist figure was even more frank: "Ninety percent of French feminists are lesbians. They come to the movement to cruise. But they refuse to talk about their homosexuality, even among themselves."[18] For a less subjective view, let us consider a detailed poll taken on this question by the political scientist Françoise Picq. A significant number (120) of women who joined the MLF between 1970 and 1972 were questioned about their sexuality in 1986. In 1970–72, according to the study, one-third of these women were homosexual, one-third heterosexual, and one-third bisexual.[19]

↩

"Not getting any?" [*Mal baisées!*][20] This was the supreme insult, hurled by a few phallocrats during the encounter at Vincennes in May 1970. Women stuck together. They closed ranks against such slogans. A leaflet distributed in front of the women's prison at La Petite–Roquette on October 19, 1970, summed up this "sisterhood": "Prostitutes, thieves, aborters, housewives, unwed mothers, homosexuals, heterosexuals, demonstrators, militants, we are all sisters. Whenever we are ourselves, we are outside the law." And in the police van that took them to the station in the eleventh arrondissement after that incident, during which they had chained themselves to the gate of La Petite–Roquette, they told the officers: "I have to pee!" "Me too!" "Me too!" "Me too!"

There were nine of them at the Arc de Triomphe. There were forty at La Petite-Roquette. There would soon be several hundred at the Ecole des Beaux-Arts.

BUT WHAT DO WOMEN WANT?

At Beaux-Arts on that Tuesday night in October 1970, there were already more than a hundred women taking part in the general meeting. The women of the MLF adopted the habit of meeting every Tuesday on rue Bonaparte, like the group Vive la Révolution, and like the FHAR homosexuals for whom they would serve, a bit later, as a model. At the first meetings, two conceptions of feminism stood opposed. Even though the women of the MLF claimed to hate theoretical models and philosophers, two personalities asserted themselves over the course of the months: Antoinette Fouque and Monique Wittig. "With all the disjointed comments and continual digressions," remembers Anne Zelensky, "it was difficult to understand the reasons for their [the two women's] antagonism."[21] This difference of opinion, not yet a rivalry between two great controversial figures, was to leave a lasting mark on the history of the movement.[22]

↩

A professor of literature on extended medical leave, she had arrived from Aix-en-Provence in 1960, her eyes hidden behind thick dark glasses that gave her an anxious look: this was Antoinette Fouque in the early 1970s. Still largely unknown within the women's movement, she compiled a reading list for women that combined the zephyrs of Lacanian psychoanalysis, the trade winds of classic women's literature, and the north wind of neofeminist theoretical thought (Luce Irigaray, and even Monique Wittig). About 1972, this intellectual mix led Fouque to a philosophy of her own, which would be crucial within the MLF, but which remains difficult to summarize. Fouque held that "the feminine" exists *in itself*. For her, "one is born a woman." She thus disagreed with Beauvoir's famous assertion "One is not born a woman, one becomes one." On this basis, Fouque gradually came to incarnate the "essentialist" camp of the MLF, the "féminitude" camp (she rejected the word "feminist"), which would be called "Antoinette's group" and then "Psychanalyse et Politique" [Psychoanalysis and politics]. Today it is known simply as "Psychépo." Two paths were perceptible from the beginnings of the movement, even though the rift became permanent only in the mid-1970s. On one side were the supporters of the "feminine all" [*le tout féminin*], many of whom were psychoanalysts, linguists, and artists (Irigaray, Fouque, and, later, Hélène Cixous). On the other, in the tradition of Beauvoir, were the Féministes Révolutionnaires.[23] They were more political, often sociologists and historians, influenced by Marxist materialism, class struggle, and a focus on domestic exploitation (Wittig, Delphy, Zelensky). This initial ideological difference eventually took the form of rigid positions, which led to a rift and was expressed in the founding of different networks, journals, and publishing houses.[24]

The homosexual issue played a central role in the difference between the two schools of thought, although there were lesbians in both groups. Fouque's position on homosexuality appeared vague if not murky to her detractors, but inspired if not ingenious to her followers. She had a broad interest in the issue, and in the fall of 1970 she organized a meeting on this topic in her private apartment. "It was the first political meeting of homosexual women in France," she says.

The organizer of Psychépo located homosexuality in the feminine and in the original relation between mother and daughter. For her, "every woman is homosexual, and there are only homosexual women." Female sexuality, Fouque believed, was grounded in emotional relationships between and among women and therefore ought to be a "showcase" for the culture she promoted. Although she emphasized the exemplary character of love among women, she was quick to condemn the asymmetry of lesbian couples. The enemy she was intent on battling was not man but masculinity. And this masculinity also existed on the part of women, particularly certain lesbians. Fouque endlessly denounced the dominating behavior sometimes seen in homosexual relationships; she made fun of "mannish women," "bull dykes," and "tomboys." She strongly condemned sadomasochistic practices among lesbians because these practices called the idyllic character of female culture into question and, more generally, because they gave the movement a bad name.[25]

Fouque thought the MLF was intrinsically homosexual: it was a "homosex movement," she said repeatedly. She was opposed to the "visibility"[26] of lesbians within it, however, even though she acknowledged that "women's homosexuality is the keystone of the MLF" and that "the marvelous family of homosexual women is the spice of the MLF."[27]

Guy Hocquenghem, who closely followed the beginnings of the MLF while remaining outside its quarrels, drew a striking portrait, not without irony, of the "Fouque method": "The fact that a woman, imbued with a mixture of political leadership and of affective, psychoanalytic submission, could unite around her a whole group of girls who had become her patients is not surprising, once you have felt the force of the MLF's ideological cement."[28]

In the spring of 1971, the differences on the lesbian issue between the two developing poles of the MLF made their appearance. At Psychépo, hurtful words were heard about lesbianism, controversies arose about the repression of homosexuality, and a difference emerged in analyses of experiences "among women" and of lesbian visibility. As a result, the women in the two groups no longer wished to have "joint meetings." At Antoinette Fouque's in February 1971, during a discussion devoted to the homosexual issue, one woman reportedly said, "We may have to resort to homosexuality; in times of war, people do eat rats." Another wondered about "homosexual orgasm." Christine Delphy, cutting them both off, voiced her opposition to this sort of analysis:

I would like the women here to worry about their heterosexuality before anything else. You talk about heterosexuality and homosexuality as if it meant preferring cabbages to potatoes. The important thing, the only important thing, is that one of these forms of sexuality is dominant and the other repressed. As for straight women's questions about "homosexual orgasm," they are indecent and out of place. The issue is politics, not tastes and colors. We are not circus animals.

Other meetings were soon organized around Wittig and Delphy.

~

Over the course of some months, Wittig emerged as the other great figure of the movement. In 1964, at twenty-nine, she had received the Prix Médicis for *L'opoponax*, a generational novel that explores the world of childhood—a time before sexual difference—from within. The novel attempts to move beyond sex determination, but it is ambiguous, and the future radical lesbian militant can already be made out behind the investigations into identity (the novel has been linked to the *nouveau roman* because it upsets chronology and alternates the use of the pronouns "one," "they," and "we"). At that time, Wittig was a prisoner of love for a man and freed herself from male power only in the late 1960s. Then, just as she was publishing what would be considered the cult book of the MLF feminists—the 1969 *Les guérillères* [*Women warriors, also titled Les guérillères in English*], because it depicted Amazons fiercely at war with men—she "tumbled" into homosexuality. As a result, Wittig flaunted her lesbianism and prepared a radical, raw book on the fantasies of homosexual women, *Le corps lesbien* [The lesbian body], which appeared in 1973. "The new converts are often the most radical ones," Anne Zelensky observes, amicably.

In the MLF, Wittig rapidly set herself apart from Antoinette Fouque by forthrightly responding, with Christine Delphy, that the "main enemy" was not masculinity but patriarchy. Very soon a lesbian subgroup of the MLF formed around that position, taking the name "Petites Marguerites" [Daisies], a tribute to the film by Vera Chytilova. This coterie became the Féministes Révolutionnaires, who, along with Psychépo, formed the second main camp of the MLF.[29] Wittig's and Delphy's group, keeping its distance from "féminitude," staged a good number of spectacular actions that drew on a strongly subversive discourse. The first was the one that had taken place at the Tomb of the Unknown Soldier; the second became known as the Calf's-Lung Lecture. Through this radical movement, essentially led by homosexual women, a new feminist militancy made its appearance in France.

~

"Look, Lejeune, I've had an abortion." Professor Jérôme Lejeune was stupefied: on his lecture table he had just received a viscous piece of calf lung. On February 10, 1971, at the Université Catholique de Paris, he had organized a meeting against the legalization of abortion. The name of his organization was "Laissez-les Vivre" [Let them live].

This coup, known ever after as the Calf's-Lung Lecture, symbolically inaugurated the debate on abortion in France. The feminists met again to oppose Lejeune on March 5, at another meeting of Laissez-les Vivre, at the Mutualité. This time, to illustrate his position, Lejeune brought in a woman (Denise Legris) born without arms or legs, who explained that she was happy to be living on welfare and thanked her mother for not getting an abortion. But the conference ended in a scuffle as the feminists clashed with the meeting's security forces—a combination of nuns and young people from the far right. On that day, FHAR militants united in the "sausage commando"[30] stood side by side with the feminists in the hall.

The first action by FHAR homosexuals, carried out a few days later against Ménie Grégoire at Salle Pleyel, was related, by virtue of its spectacular nature, to the actions against Professor Lejeune devised by the MLF. The proximity of the dates and the resemblance of the methods ought not to be surprising: some of the same individuals were involved in confronting, a few days apart, Professor Lejeune under the MLF banner and Grégoire under the FHAR banner.[31] Guy Hocquenghem explains this connection:

It is no mystery to anyone why women had a predominant role in the creation of the FHAR. ... The MLF was the inspiration for our movement at its beginning, and there might never have been a beginning if women had not themselves begun. We copied their style and mode of operation. We called each other brothers and sisters. ... We identified with the MLF even in our relations with leftism.

The FHAR thus adapted the themes of the women's struggle; like the women, the FHAR denounced the sexual roles of the heterosexual, reproductive family and championed freedom of desire. The FHAR organized general meetings at the Beaux-Arts, created its own songs, and organized weekends to make love "among ourselves," just as the women of the movement did. The FHAR was born of the womb of the MLF: in 1971, militants in the two movements were still lending one another a hand.

Feminists seemed very worked up in 1970–71. In November 1970, a group of "disturbing Amazons, the backs of their necks shaved," in the ironic words of *Le Figaro*, disrupted the "women's conference" organized by *Elle* magazine, with the cry "Women have nothing to do with a liberation conceded by Chaban-Lazareff-Moulinex-Delmas!" Shortly thereafter, they interrupted the Secours Rouge party at the Mutualité, stripping onstage and distributing an illustrated pamphlet that promoted female masturbation and autoerotic pleasure. That day, one of the feminists put up a poster with an enormous erect phallus and the slogan SO WHAT?

Evenings, after meetings, they came together to discuss the abortion issue, and sometimes they performed clandestine abortions in their homes. During the day, they read Chairman Mao or distributed the newspaper *Tout!* to workers at the Renault factory. "Yes," Anne Zelensky wrote, "little women were turning the establishment on its head. We were the new witches."[32]

The result of these first mobilizations in support of abortion is identified with the number 343, for the number of women who signed the petition—a bombshell—that was published on the cover of *Le Nouvel Observateur* on April 5, 1971: "One million women have abortions every year in France. ... Silence surrounds these millions of women. I declare that I am one of them." In addition to numerous unknown women, "the 343 sluts," as *Charlie-Hebdo* immediately called them, included Cathy Bernheim, Catherine Deneuve, Marguerite Duras, Françoise d'Eaubonne, Gisèle Halimi, Violette Leduc, Ariane Mnouchkine, Jeanne Moreau, Christiane Rochefort, Françoise Sagan, Marie-Ange Schiltz, Delphine Seyrig, Agnès Varda, Antoinette Fouque (who agreed at length to sign), and, of course, Simone de Beauvoir. Although Beauvoir may never have had an abortion, as some have said, she often agreed to have illegal abortions performed at her home. Anne Zelensky and Christine Delphy collected the signatures for the MLF, despite initial dissension from some feminists, and especially from women in the Psychépo camp. The success of this petition played a role in making the abortion issue central to feminist demands and in triggering activism within the movement. The Mouvement pour la Libération de l'Avortement [Movement for the legalization of abortion], or MLA, and then the organization Choisir [Choice], headed by Gisèle Halimi, attorney for the 343, were soon created.[33] In November 1971 the trial, at Bobigny, of an abortionist, a woman who had had an abortion, and their accomplices ensured that the issue of abortion would have a national audience.[34]

⤿

"I am homosexual as a political position," a good number of feminists asserted. "We are homosexuals all the time," Marie-Jo Bonnet replied. In May 1971, while preparing, as a second-year arts student, to compete for entry into the Ecole Normale Supérieure, Marie-Jo read issue "zero" of a "menstrual" [a pun on *mensuel,* "monthly"] called *Le Torchon Brûle* [The rag is burning].[35] "What I read between the lines," she explained, "was that something about women's liberation had to do with me." Marie-Jo, a lesbian, felt little affinity with the abortion struggle. At its headquarters on rue des Canettes, where she went after some hesitation, Marie-Jo discovered the existence of a mysterious group, the Polymorphes Perverses [the Polymorphously perverse]. The group, founded by one Margaret, was supposed to be limited to literary studies but included most of the lesbians from the FHAR. Soon the girls were singing, "We've had it up to here with getting fucked, and badly,/By guys full of their own superiority./Love among ourselves is equality,/And long live homosexuality." In this group, "we were soon overcome with desire," Marie-Jo acknowledges.

In 1971, like other lesbians, Marie-Jo was still hesitating between the militancy of the MLF and that of the FHAR. Lesbians, by turns exploited and rejected by both movements, and confused by their dual membership, sometimes chose to meet among themselves. They met in private apartments or created subgroups of the MLF. "Lesbian groups," Zelensky recalls today, "popped up like snails after the rain: someone would put up a poster with two names on it, and a new group was born."

At the Beaux-Arts, lesbians moved between amphitheaters: on Tuesdays, the general meetings of the MLF; on Thursdays, those of the FHAR. They had not yet decided between taking a critical position within the MLF, which they accused of being intolerant of them, and a dissident position within the FHAR, where they feared they would have to come to terms with men, even though they were homosexual men. This situation explains the development of numerous small unstructured groups, spontaneous and increasingly lesbian concentric circles, which formed and dissolved in 1971–72. Homosexual women called themselves "Polymorphes Perverses" or "Petites Marguerites," swelled the ranks of the FHAR, became Gouines Rouges, or created the enigmatic "drop of water" [goutte d'eau, a play on goudous, "lesbos"] camp. Above all, most of the time, they were the most radical faction of the MLF.

In addition to the alliance between feminists and lesbians, there was one between homosexual men and homosexual women. The joint meetings with the FHAR were not lacking in spice. Homosexuals of both sexes could toss off a line like this one without provoking general laughter in the amphitheater of the Beaux-Arts: "We can no longer tolerate having our mucous membranes, our anuses, our sex organs . . . made into cogs in the vile production machine of capital, exploitation, and the family." On the themes of marriage and the patriarchal system, "homos" and "lesbians" used the same language, engaged in the same battle. "Girls who kiss each other are powerful" was the emblematic slogan of one FHAR lesbian in issue 12 of Tout!

The same peaceful collaboration obtained during the debate on abortion, organized this time by Le Nouvel Observateur on April 26, 1971. On that day, in Salle Pleyel, women who had signed the petition of the 343 walked off the stage, accusing the newspaper of conducting an advertising campaign to "exploit" women's condition. Guy Hocquenghem, standing with the MLF, attempted to cool the dispute and, in the confusion, came onstage and calmed things down. The photograph of Hocquenghem as a spur-of-the-moment moderator has remained famous.

In the streets of Paris for the May Day march, during a week of meetings on patriarchy in Vincennes, or during a debate on sexuality and the family in Censier, male and female homosexuals again found themselves side by side. This cooperation had its paradoxes. In June 1971, to mark their disapproval of Mother's Day, the MLF and the FHAR decided to meet for a picnic on the lawn of Reuilly. Feminists rejected the idea of Mother's Day, established in France by Marshal Pétain, because it reduced women to their maternal function. They also criticized the appropriation of a holiday by "merchants," who had turned it into a purely commercial occasion. The men, for their part, hardly knew what justified their presence at the demonstration. Wouldn't Hocquenghem later write an article titled "Women Are Like Moms to Us"?[36] The times were contradictory in more than one way. Feminists declared, "We will not be mommies in the Europe of daddies," and a chorus of male homosexuals repeated the refrain.[37]

THE GOUINES ROUGES

"Down with the bourgeois order/And the patriarchal order/Down with the straight order/And the capitalist order/We are dykes, lesbians, depraved and foul/We love other women/We will break our chains/No more cowering in the corner/Let us love each other in broad daylight."

During the huge outpouring of the Days of Denunciation of Crimes Committed Against Women, organized at the Mutualité on May 13–14, 1972, this chant by a group of lesbians accompanied on the guitar by Marie-Jo Bonnet—between accounts of clandestine abortions and the difficulties of housework, between sketches and films—caught people off guard. There was even a "certain annoyance" in the audience: for some, the incident seemed out of place.

After all, wasn't desire a private matter, not to be exposed in public? Wasn't there a certain indecency, an unhealthy exhibitionism, in collectively declaring one's homosexuality? Cathy Bernheim and Marie-Jo Bonnet knew all that. Therefore, on that evening in May 1972, they hesitated before going onstage and taking this first step toward avowal.

Finally they went up, Marie-Jo with her guitar first, "because everyone else had stage fright," followed by Cathy, Christine Delphy, Catherine Deudon, and Monique Wittig. Then Cathy took the microphone and explained that, because it was so difficult to deal with and understand desires in their world, she could not swear that others in the room were not homosexual as well. Marie-Jo read the pamphlet of the Gouines Rouges, ending with the following words, which have remained imprinted on many memories: "Women who reject the roles of wife and mother: the time has come for us to speak from the depths of silence."

A small group of lesbians, for the first time in the history of the movement, had displayed themselves publicly in front of the MLF women who had gathered at the Mutualité. Immediately, on every side, lesbians began to speak; homosexual women were standing up and being counted: "Me too!" "Oh, you too?" "Yes, me too." Bernheim took the floor again and started a general debate on homosexuality and the political obligation of lesbian "visibility" as many others joined the little group of courageous women onstage.

"To prove that our battle was legitimate," Delphy explains today, "we had to avoid being denounced as homosexuals. This is why the movement refused to appear publicly for a long time. Men considered every effort at women's liberation to be an illegitimate revolt because it was the act of lesbians. Since lesbians were considered nonwomen, their visibility in the MLF would have invalidated the goal of the movement as a whole."

After the first years of battle, however, visibility had become more possible—and more desirable. Little by little, before the summer of 1971, the Gouines Rouges took shape around the writer Monique Wittig, as a reaction to the prevailing masculinity of the FHAR and to Psychépo's "féminitude."[38] Delphy named the group in memory of a passerby who had shouted at her, as she was selling *Le Torchon Brûle,* "Look, it's the red dykes." "Dykes" was a term of derision (similarly, the FHAR constantly used the term "queer"); "red" indicated that they were revolutionaries.

Nevertheless, this "tactical secession" was keenly contested within the MLF itself, and some women, sometimes even homosexual women, refused to rally behind it. With the first public appearances of the Gouines Rouges, homosexual women became more prominent in the MLF. "We are fundamentally subversive," they repeated while battling "the male phallocratic inseminators" and using the expression "Lesbienne, lèse-mâle" [Lesbian, outrage against the male] as a slogan.

↬

The action by homosexual women at the Mutualité in May 1972 clarified the position of lesbians within the movement. They had chosen to remain in the MLF. As the months went by, they even succeeded in acquiring a high degree of legitimacy within the women's movement.

As lesbians became more deeply committed to the MLF, relations with the FHAR further deteriorated. Each side was increasingly deaf to the other. The initial tactical alliance was superseded, and a rift opened.

Since the summer of 1971, in fact, the mixed nature of the group had become problematic within the FHAR. "The boys were supposed to be our allies," Bonnet explains, "but we found all the elements of male society within the FHAR. It was primarily a theater of male desire." The increasingly visible presence of the Gazolines within the FHAR increased the tension. "They were making a spectacle of themselves. The Gazolines liked to put on lipstick and high heels," Marie-Jo remembers. "We were tossing that oppressive stuff into the trash. We no longer existed for the men. We were being negated, when we should have been liberating ourselves together. Dialogue was no longer possible."

Bernheim does not share this point of view: "For me, the Gazolines were the ones who really smashed femininity. They took every image to its extreme. That really raised the problem of male desire. But I always appreciated their presence, since they seemed to be telling us: 'One is not born a woman, one becomes one.' They were more women than we were!"

"At the FHAR," Marie-Jo continues, "the boys were talking about active and passive roles, whereas we were destroying those roles. They had trouble following us in this critique of alienation. Then, too, we were very troubled by the fact that it was becoming a fuckorama." That was it: the boys were "fucking"!

Guy Hocquenghem acknowledges that the libidinous drift of the FHAR was a source of disagreement: "From the beginning, the FHAR distinguished itself as a sexual movement. We talked sex; in fact, we talked only about sex, to the point, some women told us, where love and human relationships hardly seemed to interest us at all. I tend to believe that's true: there is little place, or no place at all, in a homosexual movement for a psychology of relationships founded on 'truly human love.' If there is such a thing as an antihumanist movement, this is it, where the sex machine and organs plugged into other organs make up almost all the desire that is being expressed. We are come machines."[39] Some lesbians accused male homosexuality of being precisely that: "a concentrate of machismo." Thus Zelensky declared, "For the time being, *homosexualité mâle* [see note 40], as it richly deserves to be called, since it is obsession paired with systematic cramming, still produces precipitates of phallocracy that, from a naturalistic perspective, are of interest for the study of a dying ideology in its pure state."[40] This is a harsh judgment. Male homosexuals were unable to understand the term "sexual position" as a term designating women's oppression. Lesbians, by contrast, as women and as homosexuals, considered themselves doubly persecuted.

The rift between the MLF and the FHAR may show that, at the time, there were more differences between a homosexual man and a lesbian than there were between a homosexual woman and a heterosexual one. This oft-discussed position has not been unanimously accepted. American lesbians, for example, had a different experience. The history of their movement has been marked by the need to break loose from the women's movement and then from the male homosexual movement.[41]

Parisian lesbians, by choosing to remain in the MLF, also refused to disappear into the ghetto. At the same time, they set aside, consciously or unconsciously, any possibility of forming an autonomous lesbian movement. In fact, the Gouines Rouges, whose initial role in these issues was important, soon dissolved (in 1973). "We no longer see the necessity of a purely lesbian militancy," Marie-Jo Bonnet declared.[42]

In France, then, there was no lesbian movement parallel to the MLF, nor was there one in the margins of the FHAR. This French particularity, the absence of an autonomous lesbian movement, seems to have persisted to this day. It is one of the more significant consequences of the rift with the FHAR. Conversely, the homosexual issue became both a rallying point and a point of rupture within the women's movement, a thorn in French feminism's side. And there it may still be lodged, twenty-five years later.

3

"Down with Daddy's Homosexuality!"
(Before 1970)

Although the homosexual movements of the post-'68 era always referred to "revolution," coupling homosexuality with subversion and heterosexuality with capitalism, Arcadie was the only one to use the word "people."
—Michel Foucault, *Libération*, July 12, 1983

"Women's Liberation: Year Zero," feminists declared in 1970. "We are founding the homosexual movement," said the men of the FHAR shortly thereafter. In a revolt without a role model, men and women acknowledged no predecessors. Above all, they hated theoretical models and even claimed to be wiping clean the slate of the past in order to build the revolution.[1]

Without a doubt, the sexual liberation movements in France, which first appeared between 1968 and 1972, marked a break with the earlier homosexual world. Through antiestablishment slogans and spectacular actions, a "spontaneous generation" of militants, trained on the May barricades, turned traditions and lifestyles, almost unchanged since World War II, on their heads.

"Down with Daddy's homosexuality!" This cry, sent out by the lesbians of the MLF and by the first men of the FHAR during Ménie Grégoire's 1971 broadcast, was much more than mere provocation. It announced the collapse of an old world, even though no one could yet imagine the new one.

Rarely in the history of sexual mores in France had a rift been so brutal and so personalized. For more than twenty years, in fact, "Daddy's homosexuality" had been incarnated by one man, on whom all criticisms now converged. That man's name was André Baudry.

LITERATURE OF THE SHADOWS

In the late 1940s, when Baudry, about to appear on the scene, was gradually conceiving the project of Arcadie—the first real French homosexual organization—literature had already given birth to most of the cult books on homosexuality.

We may hypothesize that literature was, in various forms, the locus of homosexual militancy in France until World War II. The first militants of 1948 could find support in a field worked and prepared by writers. That situation is probably a French peculiarity.

Fiction, as a genre propitious for the expression of clandestine ideas, lets one express everything: marginality, revolt, even silence. If it was nice to learn that Virgil's shepherdesses were actually shepherds, it was no less comforting for prewar homosexuals to see some of the most famous authors of the era gradually unveiling themselves. The specific universes depicted by four writers played a role in forming a sort of "homosexual education": Marcel Proust, with *Sodome et Gomorrhe* [*Cities of the Plain*], 1922; André Gide, with *Corydon*, 1924; Jean Cocteau, with *Le livre blanc* [*The White Book*], 1929; and Jean Genet, with the "trilogy" *Notre-Dame-des-Fleurs* [*Our Lady of the Flowers*], *Miracle de la rose* [*Miracle of the Rose*], and *Le journal du voleur* [*The Thief's Journal*], 1946–48. For homosexual women, the Left Bank writers, especially Colette, played a similar role.

↬

Homosexual men can be broadly divided into two groups: those who have read Proust, and those who have read Genet. The lines of descent remain even today from Proust, the inventor of tolerance for homosexuality because it was worldly, and from Genet, the inventor of *homosexualité noire* [dark homosexuality]. A tradition reaching from the 1920s to the 1950s, from Proust to Genet, and including André Gide and Jean Cocteau, became imprinted on the collective memory of some of the homosexuals who found refuge in literature.

Proust's world in itself constitutes a social reference point for homosexuality. The character Charlus is its most visible hero. In *A la recherche du temps perdu* [*Remembrance of Things Past*], Charlus cruises the narrator, who, not understanding his strange demeanor with a drunken coachman, takes him for a madman. His true nature appears at last in *Cities of the Plain*. Charlus is an unsavory character who scarcely invites identification: he frequents Jupien's brothel, submits to flagellation, and wallows in sadomasochism. This scene from *Le temps retrouvé* [*The Past Recaptured*] was shocking, but it illustrated, perniciously, the suffering and guilt of the homosexual. "I angered many homosexuals with my last chapter," Proust said. "I feel very bad about that, but it's not my fault if Monsieur de Charlus was an old man; I could not suddenly make him look like a Sicilian shepherd."

Beyond the character Charlus, homosexuals applied themselves to decrypting numerous codes in the work: the narrator's doubts, the key to the character Albertine, and the beauty of Saint-Loup, who initially has a liking for women but reveals, in *La fugitive* [*The Sweet Cheat Gone*], sexual habits identical to those of Charlus.

Remembrance of Things Past also granted a place of choice to homosexual women: Albertine, who dances with Andrée at the Casino d'Incarville; Mademoiselle Vinteuil, who has a "bad reputation" in Combray; the actress Léa; and even

Esther Lévy, the paradigmatic lesbian of the *Remembrance*. Proust, in a letter to Natalie Barney, explained that in his writings "all Sodomites are hideous" but "all Gomorrhans are charming." Barney, not persuaded by the claim, drily replied that Albertine and her friends were not charming but implausible. "Not everyone who wishes to can plumb those Eleusian mysteries," she concluded.

At the end of his opus, in *The Past Recaptured*, all Proust's characters meet again for the final farewell and throw off their masks. It is time to move on to direct confession and to show, notably through the big scene at Jupien's bordello, the re-union of the Sodomites and the Gomorrhans. "No one was abnormal when homosexuality was the norm," is the famous saying from the *Remembrance*.

Although Proust, in his depictions, may have encouraged certain prejudices, certain naturalist theories about "shemales," or certain nineteenth-century phobias, he is still of capital importance, and his universe has left an enduring mark on the homosexual imagination.

⤺

"Will you never present us with Eros in young and beautiful forms?" Proust was asked by André Gide, who was disturbed by the representation of homosexuality in the *Remembrance*. In fact, Gide is diametrically opposed to Proust. In 1911, he drafted *Corydon*, four pseudoscientific dialogues on pederasty, which he finally decided to make public in 1924. "My friends keep telling me," he writes in his preface, "that this little book is of a nature to do me the greatest harm." Although aware of the risks of preferring man to nature, Gide did not want to lie.

Whereas Proust approached homosexuality in a series of novels that claimed to be the reflection of a world and an era, Gide, in this field strewn with land mines, chose to produce the work of a theorist and clearly criticized Proust for playing a role in "misleading public opinion."[2] *Corydon* claimed to be a serious work. At issue was natural history—hermaphroditic ducks and bisexual snails. Since homosexuality was widespread among animals, Gide concluded, it was natural. In this sense, although *Corydon* is now dated, it was the first effort in France to explain homosexuality, which at the time was called "uranism."

It is difficult today to assess the importance, no doubt considerable, of Gide's book—in the first place, his name itself was an asset. It is easier to evaluate the hostile reactions to which he was subjected as his public position affected his private life. A troubled Paul Claudel wrote to him, "If you are not a pederast, why this strange predilection for that sort of subject? If you are one, poor wretch, heal yourself and do not parade these abominations."[3] Some Vichy theorists, undaunted by even the most outlandish claims, went so far as to interpret the 1940 defeat of France by Germany as the result of the influence of Proust's and Gide's books on the population.

During Gide's travels in Germany and the Soviet Union, however, homosexuality may have led him to apprehend, at an early date, the reality of totalitarian regimes. He was one of the rare French personalities to visit Dr. Magnus Hirschfeld's institute in Germany; Dr. Hirschfeld, with his lectures, his library of more than 10,000 specialized volumes, and his sociological investigations, paved the way for Kinsey and established "the most important homosexual liberation movement ever organized on earth."[4] The institute was closed down by the Nazis in 1933. It seems, moreover, that the penalty of deportation inflicted on Soviet homosexuals contributed to Gide's disenchantment with Communism.[5] Finally, the author of *Si le grain ne meurt* [*If It Die*] went looking in North Africa for the contemporary descendants of Virgil's shepherds, which led him to denounce the violence of the French colonization. His imagination remained steeped in a desire that can be summed up, it seems, in one anecdote: in a city where he was looking for ship's boys, Gide explained, "I was promised a young boy, and what I saw coming was an old goat of fourteen."[6] Gide always hesitates between saying everything and asking forgiveness for everything.

ᴄ⁊

As for Jean Cocteau, "our sublime national queen,"[7] he played a symbolic role. Unlike Gide, he became "the resident invert," made cabaret singers snicker, and was the laughingstock of the Surrealists.[8] If he was indebted for some of his early recognition to Proust, with whom he corresponded at the age of nineteen, it was Gide who got him banned from the *Nouvelle Revue Française*.

In 1928, Cocteau anonymously published *The White Book*, a brief, limpid text about the love of boys (only thirty-one copies were printed). In 1930, he illustrated it with seventeen erotic drawings and added an accompanying letter—a clever way of signing the work, of which 400 copies were printed this time. "An anonymous effort toward the clearing of a field that has remained largely uncultivated," in his own words, *The White Book* oscillated between sensual poem and erotic text: "As far back as I go, and even at an age when my mind did not yet influence my senses, I find traces of my love for boys. . . . My misfortunes have come from a society that condemns the unusual as a crime and requires us to reform our penchants."[9]

Although *The White Book* ends with the famous words "But I do not accept being tolerated; that is a wound to my love of love and of freedom," the book, probably because of its secrecy, has not played an essential role in the collective memory of homosexuals. And although some of his poems, such as "Plain-Chant" [Plainsong] or "Un ami dort" [A friend is sleeping]—the friend in question was Radiguet—have often been cited, and though works like *Orphée* [the screenplay *The Testament of Orpheus*], or especially his films, may have played some role, it is less Cocteau's body of work than his personality that has left its mark. Moreover, Cocteau recognized, with disconcerting lucidity, that "the world accepts dangerous experiments in the realm of art because it does not take art seriously, but it condemns them in real life."[10]

Young men learned to recognize Cocteau's shock of silver hair and the stars that adorned his signatures. In film, as in drawing, song, and ballet (and even boxing and bullfighting), homosexuals recognized in Cocteau a lightness, grace, and elegance that were too mannered not to be equivocal. His relations with Diaghilev, Raymond Radiguet, and especially Jean Marais (from 1937 to 1950) contributed to this image. Of Radiguet, a prancing, myopic sixteen-year-old boy who would later write *Le diable au corps* [*The Devil in the Flesh*] and die at twenty, an inconsolable Cocteau wrote magnificently: "I saw immediately that Radiguet was a loan; he would have to be returned." The passionate loves of Cocteau, prince of frivolity, often intersected with those of Genet, prince of dark homosexuality.

↫

It was Jean Cocteau who, in 1943, discovered "a thief with a sackful of genius in his hand": Jean Genet. For his principal biographer, "Genet is the Proust of marginal Paris," and his five novels "can be read as a conscious response to Proust's seven-volume work, *Remembrance of Things Past*. Whereas Proust recorded primarily the lives of the upper-middle-class and aristocratic Paris ... , Genet documented the folkways of the underclass of Montmartre and elsewhere."[11]

In March 1946, Genet's *Miracle of the Rose* appeared in a limited edition of 475 copies. An advertising insert was signed by Sartre: "Proust showed pederasty as a destiny; Genet demands it as a choice." With its guilt-free tone and crude vocabulary, Genet's book stands opposed both to Gide's *Corydon* and to Cocteau's anonymous *The White Book*. For Genet, homosexuality must be "accommodated":

Pederasty was imposed on me like the colour of my eyes, the number of my feet. Even when I was still a kid I was aware of being attracted by other boys, I have never known an attraction for women. It's only after I became conscious of this attraction that I "decided," "chose" freely my pederasty, in the Sartrian sense of the word. In other words, and more simply, I had to accommodate myself to it even though I knew that it was condemned by society.[12]

Genet set himself apart from his predecessors. "What is a pederast?" he wondered in 1956, and then replied:

A man who, by his nature, goes against the current of the world, refuses to enter the system by virtue of which the entire world is organized. The pederast rejects one thing, denies another, disturbs still another, whether he wants to or not. For him, feelings are only dupery and foolishness; there is only pleasure. To live on surprises, changes, to accept risks, to expose oneself to affronts: that is the opposite of social constraint, of social comedy. . . . As a result, if the pederast more or less consents to play a role in that comedy, like Proust or Gide, he is cheating, he is lying; everything he says becomes suspect. My imagination is immersed in abjection, but in that respect it is noble, it is pure. I reject imposture; and if I sometimes exaggerate, pushing heroes and adventures toward the horrible or the obscene, I do so in the direction of truth.[13]

Genet belongs to the tradition of Rimbaud, anticipating William Burroughs, Truman Capote, and Pier Paolo Pasolini. "When I examine what I have written," Genet declared, "I can distinguish a desire, patiently pursued, to rehabilitate creatures, objects, and feelings reputed to be vile." His "school," if we can call it that, has the aim of "ennobling shame" and maintains a system of "vascular exchange" with bohemia, betrayal, and theft. In the 1970s, Guy Hocquenghem would define this universe as dark homosexuality.

Enamored of defeated Don Quixotes, "Juana la Maricona" ("Joan the faggot," as the Spanish writer Juan Goytisolo amiably called him) conducted numerous battles on behalf of marginal groups over the course of his chaotic, flashy life. A professional defender of the Black Panthers, the Palestinians, and prisoners, in 1973 he also supported the special issue on homosexuality ("Trois milliards de pervers") of the journal *Recherches,* lending his name to it. It would be wrong, however, to paint him as a defender of "the cause," since for him homosexuality was entirely bad.[14]

Genet's relationship, when he was forty-six, with Abdallah, an eighteen-year-old Arab boy, belongs to the writer's dark side. "What do I care whether he knows how to read?" asked Genet, who helped his new protégé become an acrobat. It was to him that he dedicated *Le funambule* [The tightrope walker], a reflection on the craft and solitude of the artist. But the young man, injured during a dangerous jump, let the writer down: "With Abdallah on the rope, I had achieved a kind of masterpiece. Now everything's all fucked up." Abdallah, adopted and then abandoned, committed suicide: his body was discovered in March 1964, surrounded by Genet's books, read and reread, annotated by the young man, who had secretly learned the French language from his lover's novels.

After this disconcerting suicide, Genet had the revelation, at once horrifying for the writer and reassuring for the human being, that every man is of equal value. Genet writes in *L'atelier d'Alberto Giacometti* [The studio of Alberto Giacometti], "Beauty has no other origin than the wound—unique, different for each person, hidden or visible—which every man keeps within himself, which he preserves, and to which he withdraws." For Gide, the writer's sources lie in his reasons for shame; for Genet, in his wounds.

↜

For homosexual women, the quartet of Proust, Gide, Cocteau, and Genet had a symbolic equivalent in the "women of the Left Bank."

Female homosexuality may be less shocking than its male counterpart because it is veiled in silence. It seems to have been marked by a great void since Sappho, if we except the "chatterings" of such writers as Théophile Gautier, Alphonse Daudet, Charles Baudelaire, and Guy de Maupassant, or even Honoré de Balzac (*La fille aux yeux d'or* [*The Girl with the Golden Eyes*] notwithstanding), who were often merely perpetuating an antiwoman discourse. In this way, the almost total silence of women themselves intensified the law's silence on the subject.[15]

Nevertheless, between 1905 and the 1960s, the salon at 20, rue Jacob, in Paris, presided over by Natalie Clifford Barney, an American nicknamed "the Amazon," became the center of "sapphic agitation" and has had no equivalent since. These flighty, wild women, who sported men's jackets, ties, and monocles, are legendary. The writers of the Edwardian era who had "tasted the forbidden fruit" met there: Renée Vivien, Djuna Barnes, Liane de Pougy. The salon was never empty. Canonesses and illegitimate daughters of grand dukes rushed to it, and Rilke, d'Annunzio, Gide, Paul Valéry, and Apollinaire, lost among enormous Valkyries, made occasional appearances. Pierre Louÿs and Rémy de Gourmont, for whom lesbianism was the height of dandyism, went more regularly. Proust went only once, in lady's scarves and furs, and immediately fled. Even in the 1930s, when baronesses and the czar's female cousins had vanished or at least lost their titles, the salon remained fashionable. Radclyffe Hall dropped by, as did Gertrude Stein and Alice B. Toklas.[16] "I can easily predict what a legend you will be," wrote Marguerite Yourcenar to Natalie Barney. "People particularly admire, without being able to explain precisely why, the calm duration of a free life, that tour de force. I told myself you had the good luck to live at a time when the notion of pleasure was still a civilizing notion; it is no longer so today."[17] Although Natalie Barney was not successful in producing what could truly be called a body of work, the Amazon represented, to the point of caricature, the emancipatory sapphism of the first half of the century.

Of all the women present at rue Jacob, Colette was certainly the most famous. Her writings, including the Claudine series, successfully addressed the theme of women's memory: the figure of the mother, childhood gardens, schoolgirl secrets, the initiation into perversion, the arrival in Paris, and, finally, the discovery of love among women. The world of Claudine-Colette was enveloped in sensual intrigues between young girls, and between young boys.

In parallel to her writings, the novelist's life served as a model of female independence, marked in particular by the revenge she exacted for her husband's unwarranted appropriation of her talent.[18] Her years of marriage, when she was just a "little village bride," were replaced by a completely new life after the divorce: she cut her hair short, smoked, and dressed like a man. From then on, her novels had to do with the lack of communication in love between men and women. Her love affairs with women, the scandal of the Moulin Rouge in 1907—she publicly kissed her partner, Missy, which led the police to intervene and close down subsequent performances—her friendship with Cocteau and Marais, her affair with Mathilde and then with her second husband's young son, forged her image as an iconoclastic woman. This new kind of femininity was one of the sources of her ardor and the spice of her writings. It was also the reason the church refused to give her a religious funeral in 1954.

Colette was censured by Catholics; Cocteau, mocked by the Surrealists; Proust and Gide, humiliated by backers of the Vichy regime. Homosexuals knew their enemies: the law, the church, ideology. It was not the last time these opponents would cross paths.

ARCADIE AND THE HOMOPHILES

In 1948, a young man of twenty-five, André Baudry, a former seminarian, appeared at the Paris home of André du Dognon,[19] who had a salon where a few homosexual poets and numerous friends met.

The young man had a thorough knowledge of Proust's writings and a passion for André Gide's. They were role models or "release mechanisms" that had made life easier for him when he "took up homosexuality." "I myself was very discreet, very secret," he explains today. Not knowing Genet, and mistrusting Cocteau, he took to making lists of famous artists and writers who shared his inclinations. Then, to reconstitute the hidden tradition of a "people" without memory, he added twentieth-century names to the classic ones (Socrates, Michelangelo, Montaigne, Shakespeare, Tchaikovsky). Did he find encouragement in the fact that so many illustrious personalities shared his condition?

Nevertheless, although "homosexual culture" played a decisive role in his life, Baudry was aware of how precarious that culture was. He knew it did not prevent loneliness, or shame, or the double life. He knew it was not enough.

↝

In 1948, when the seminarian first took his place in the history of homosexuality in France—he would soon create the first organized movement—the age of consent was still set at twenty-one. Any relationship between an adult and a minor was punishable by imprisonment from six months to three years, and an ordinance prohibited Paris establishments from admitting men wearing women's clothes, especially for drag shows, and imposed sanctions on places that allowed men to dance with one another.

Nevertheless, in 1948, the shock wave that had been produced in the United States by the Kinsey report [*Sexual Behavior in the Human Male*] hit France; the book was immediately translated. What did this pioneering book say? On the basis of a large-scale quantitative survey (11,240 individuals of both sexes were interviewed), Dr. Alfred Kinsey reported the results of his study on male sexual behavior (the volume on female sexuality appeared in 1953). His figures showed that 37 percent of white male Americans had had at least one homosexual experience during their adult lives. Of that group, 25 percent had had several experiences or at least one *accidental* experience; 8 percent had been more or less exclusively homosexual for at least three years; and 4 percent were exclusively homosexual during their entire lifetimes. Kinsey also cited the figure of 13 percent of white American males who had had "homosexual desires or temptations." Homosexuals, in keeping with the common phenomenon of overestimating the size of minorities, quickly calculated: 37 percent plus 13 percent made 50 percent!

Beyond the raw figures, which were the object of criticism,[20] the report, which had no militant aim, was important because it established a continuum instead of defining some dubious, fixed, essentialist "homosexual minority." Kinsey invented a kind of scale of homosexuality, representing it as a possible experience within an individual life history, and assigning a number from 0 to 6 to assess the intensity of desire. In its banality, homosexuality became one (fairly widespread) experience among others, an exceptional choice within a complex life journey— and not an identity. "In France, people had not read the report," Jacques de Ricaumont remembers, "but everyone vaguely retained the figure of 10 percent." Kinsey permanently shattered the image of homosexuality as "against nature," replacing the *why?* of psychiatrists, psychoanalysts, and even of Gide with *how?* and *how many?* In fact, an aging Gide is said to have read the book, trembling and overcome.

↩

In 1948, at twenty-five, the young philosophy teacher Baudry was an austere and tormented figure. He wore dark suits with double-breasted jackets and striped ties, and the serious glasses of an already responsible adult male. He was all business. Although he had been a student at a Jesuit high school, and then a seminarian, he had never been a priest, as it was later rumored. And yet he felt guilty for two reasons: because of his faith, and because of his sexuality. "The Jesuits had a considerable influence on me," he explains today. "That may be what gave me a certain ecclesiastical demeanor."

In the salon of the writer André du Dognon, where he went in 1948, Baudry found two acquaintances: Ricaumont, and the writer Roger Peyrefitte, who in 1943 had published *Les amitiés particulières* [Special friendships]. The Viscount Dognon, the Count of Ricaumont, and the erudite diplomat Peyrefitte: these three aristocratic musketeers deserve a snapshot. With Baudry, there were four: a new page in the history of French homosexuals could begin.

Peyrefitte was the most famous. *Les amitiés particulières* was a best-seller. Describing love between boys at a boarding school, it caused a scandal, despite the veiled sex scenes, an unnamed romance, and a concluding suicide against a backdrop of maudlin Catholicism. "I was a young diplomat," Peyrefitte recounts today, "and I wanted to show the origin of this kind of thing—that it was not simply under the influence of some disgusting adult that young boys feel that sort of attraction." Indeed, this was not the least significant contribution of the book, which in 1964 would be adapted for the screen by Jean Delannoy, to even greater acclaim. The same year, Peyrefitte took pen in hand to accuse François Mauriac, in the journal *Arts,* of keeping his own homosexuality quiet: another scandal ensued.[21] Peyrefitte defends himself: "I had proof of his hypocrisy." In 1976 he committed a further offense in *Lui*, claiming that Pope Paul VI had had relationships with boys when he was cardinal of Milan. The pope himself responded from Rome. Questioned today, Peyrefitte, the grandfather of outing, explains that it was necessary to "give homosexuality its pedigree: one had to name names." In 1977, when *Propos secrets* [Secret matters] appeared,[22] the literary critic Angelo Rinaldi settled his accounts with Peyrefitte:

Yesterday he was tallying up Jews and Freemasons—very useful work for future proscriptions—and today Roger Peyrefitte is working for the vice squad, in a book as engaging as a police report. . . . As for "advancing an accursed cause," . . . one has to be oblivious, at best, to make that claim. . . . If he did not exist, the "heterocops" would invent this collector of outdated gossip, this curly-headed septuagenarian whose adaptations for the screen make simple folk titter and reinforce prejudices.[23]

Baudry, Peyrefitte, Dognon: the fourth man was Jacques de Ricaumont. In 1948 he was already thirty-five and had just come to the capital to "seek [his] fortune in literature, love, and high society." Today, in his apartment on Boulevard Saint-Germain, where he lives surrounded by sculptures of Saint Sebastian and a signed photo of Jean-Marie Le Pen, he confides, not without humor, "But I succeeded only in high society." An aristocrat and a Catholic, a man of the far right if ever there was one, Ricaumont never recovered from the day his confessor scolded him for kissing his best friend on the mouth. After that, in the shadow of Sainte-Clotilde Church, he associated with counterrevolutionaries from Action Française, prelates as Machiavellian as in the novels of Eugène Sue, dowagers drinking Lapsang souchong; and, remembering "the delicious smell of incense, of candles with trembling flame, and of singers' frail voices soaring toward the nave,"[24] he decided to remain a virgin. Not totally, for—if it was possible, between two evenings spent pursuing "the battle that, even in the seventeenth century, set the ultramontanes against the Gallicans"—he chastely awaited ejaculation during erotic dreams, the only ejaculation that cannot be considered a sin, since it is involuntary. Such were the times in which he lived.

Since this ultramontane was also an aesthete, Ricaumont told the seminarian Baudry about a Swiss homosexual journal, *Der Kreis*. In the early 1950s, Baudry became its French correspondent and organized meetings for subscribers in his apartment on rue Jeanne-d'Arc. On the basis of that Swiss example, the success of these meetings, and his network of friends, in November 1953 Baudry had the idea of launching a homosexual review, *Arcadie*. It first appeared on January 15, 1954.

The first issue was fifty-four pages long and was fairly austere; 2,000 copies were printed. Peyrefitte, steeped in Greek sources, had the idea for the name *Arcadie*, but it was Cocteau who gave the review its real backing, offering a drawing and a letter of encouragement.

Within a few months, *Arcadie* had 1,300 subscribers. It had 4,000 in 1957, 15,000 in 1972, and 30,000 in 1975. They received the review in a "very discreet" envelope. The birth of *Arcadie*, in 1954, fit the times. In addition to Baudry, Peyrefitte, and

Ricaumont, the review was managed by a leading government official from Archives de France, who published under the pseudonym "Marc Daniel"; a former officer of the French army; a well-known magistrate; a few university professors; and former members of *Futur*, a short-lived, discreetly homosexual, secretly pederastic journal.[25] The entire philosophy behind *Arcadie* was present in these beginnings: honorability and respectability, and rejection of all eroticism or pornography.[26] A hidden life is a happy life.

What would they call themselves? In the 1950s, among themselves, homosexuals used coded expressions, such as "being one of them" or "having tendencies," whereas the general public, which disliked nuances and thrived on clichés, talked about "buggerers" or "bad news" (just as, in an earlier time, they might have spoken of men who were "limp-wristed," "light in the loafers," "Saturnians," "uranists," or "effete"). In this context, a great deal was at stake in the choice of a word.

It did not occur to Baudry to adopt "queer" or "dyke," with a healthy dose of self-deprecation, as militants would do in the early 1970s. What is more surprising is that he also ruled out "homosexual." The writer Roger Stéphane, a member of the organization Arcadie in its early days, explains, "The word 'homosexual' is completely foreign to me. I prefer the three categories articulated by André Gide in his *Journal*: the pederast, the sodomite, and the invert. The first loves young men, or, in any case, men younger than he is; the second likes to penetrate men; and the third likes to be penetrated."[27] Baudry, who would not have been unhappy with this classification, finally chose "homophile," a term tinged with hypocrisy. Nevertheless, according to Arcadie's founder, it had the virtue of not reducing the individuals in question to their sexual practices. "The homophile," explained Ricaumont, "had an inclination toward men but did not necessarily give in to that attraction." That said it all: in the early days, Arcadie championed the internalization of desire and encouraged the struggle against oneself—"sublimating one's sexual and emotional orientation into asceticism," in Baudry's terms, which were valid for everyone. Thus it is clear why the term "homophile" did not survive this movement.

Once the subscribers to *Arcadie* had been given their name, the review gradually became a movement, with "homophiles" as its members. Baudry's personality played a role in fashioning this organization, for which he become a kind of prophet. To kick off evening parties and banquets, the man nicknamed "the pope" gave regular sermons condemning homosexuals who frequented parks or public toilets. Everyone who remembers agrees: the former seminarian had enormous charisma and the dogged will of an apostle. In grand flights of oratory reminiscent of Charles de Gaulle, he addressed a "dispersed people, a lost people, a people without ritual, a people starving for love."[28]

〜

"Arcadie was the only [movement] to use the word 'people,'" Foucault has observed:

This was Baudry's prophetic madness: to make homosexuality acceptable within the value system that condemned it, somewhat in the manner of the prophet who dreams of bringing a sinful people into the bosom of the vengeful God. One might be surprised by how their leader was perpetually cursing the Arcadians for their bad morals. In fact, however, the "people" had to be sinful so that they would need a prophet.[29]

Despite its moralism and, in particular, its denunciation of homosexual vices, and despite Cocteau's drawings, when the review *Arcadie* was published, a decree from the minister of the interior prohibited its open display or sale to minors (the ban remained in effect until 1975). "We were blamed for our use of ellipses, that is, for things we might have thought but not written," Baudry confirms. As the sole person legally responsible for *Arcadie*—and one of the few who did not use a pseudonym—Baudry was prosecuted for public indecency in February 1955 (the charges were finally dismissed). In addition to this predictable hostility from the government, there was also criticism within the more circumscribed world of homosexual writers.

〜

Marcel Jouhandeau was one of the literary figures of the era. Although he increasingly alluded to his proclivities in his works (*De l'abjection* [On abjection] was published in 1939, at first anonymously), he was hostile to Arcadie. "I hope the police will close down that ridiculous shop you've opened," he wrote in the *Nouvelle Revue Française*. "Marcel Jouhandeau dealt with his homosexuality in private," Baudry explains today. "He did a brisk business with his books and did not want homosexuality placed on the public square. He was one of those people who saw only their own little self-interest." Ricaumont is more understanding: "For Jouhandeau, homosexuality had to be a purely individual matter. He did not accept the esprit de corps of Arcadie or the very idea of a homophile movement."

Jouhandeau produced a vast body of work, which includes many texts dealing with his particular weakness, beginning with *Ecrits secrets* [Secret writings]; it describes his discovery of sodomy late in life. Until his death, in 1979, "the puerilely scandalous old gentleman," who made amends for his antisemitism and believed he had been forgiven "for loving the Germans lying down rather than standing up," remained one of the most prominent figures of homosexuality. Over time, however, as the notion of sin has gradually disintegrated, his works have become less interesting. Rinaldi concludes that Jouhandeau "constantly went back and forth between boys—whose beauty damned him—and God, whose goodness absolved him."[30]

〜

The Arcadie movement took on a new dimension in March 1947, when it added a meeting place, discreetly called the Club Littéraire et Scientifique des Pays

Latins (The literary and scientific club of Latin countries), or CLESPALA. There was a complicated ritual required for acceptance: new members, accompanied by a "godfather," were introduced to Baudry, to whom they had to disclose their true identity. Once admitted, a new arrival could go to the banquets, the debates, and, above all, the Sunday-afternoon dances, which included the famous *danses du tapis*; he could also attend the Wednesday lectures on such themes as classical Greece, Plato's *Banquet*, or the trial of Oscar Wilde.[31] As a bonus, when the debate had to do with the Maghreb, for example, the lecturer showed slides of naked young Algerians but then immediately launched into a scientific exposition of the Berber language, circumcision, or Berber Algeria. Humor sometimes took unexpected forms in Arcadie.

With its 10,000 review subscribers in the late 1960s, its first "branches" in major cities in the provinces, and its specialized groups (of lesbians, Christians, pedophiles, married men), what Arcadie became was almost an extreme form of Freemasonry. Despite its discretion, Arcadie's focus on identity and—already—its communitarian strategy could not have been clearer.

A large number of personalities made their way to the private club: the writers Jean-Louis Bory, Daniel Guérin, Yves Navarre, Matthieu Galey, and Jean-Louis Curtis; the film critic Jacques Siclier; and perhaps even Foucault. Most of the founding members of the FHAR were members of Arcadie: Françoise d'Eaubonne, Anne-Marie Fauré (who was even a salaried employee), Pierre Hahn. It appears that Guy Hocquenghem attended one meeting.

"Above all, Arcadians told one another how lonely they were," one member of the club recalls. Another member, a renowned journalist, confirmed that, for him, "the club played a decisive role." For many, Arcadie was a refuge.

↝

Although the record crowds confirmed the success of the "Baudry method," two episodes disturbed Arcadie's underground operation, two scares that would gradually discredit the movement.

On July 18, 1960, Paul Mirguet, the leftist deputy from Moselle, proposed to the National Assembly that homosexuality be classified as a "social scourge" like tuberculosis, alcoholism, and prostitution. The proposal (the law of July 30, 1960) was passed without discussion. The government was now free to adopt as ordinances "all measures designed to fight homosexuality," and the penalty for public indecency increased considerably when it involved "an act against nature with an individual of the same sex."

One sign of Arcadie's influence with the government is that Mirguet immediately wrote to Baudry, explaining the reasons for the law. Yet, despite the good relations that Baudry maintained with the police and the justice system—"Every police commissioner, every precinct captain knew me"—this was a considerable setback. Arcadie's militancy had proved ineffectual. For the first time, its viability was in question, and Baudry's moral authority was in doubt. The club suspended its afternoon dances, and the journal its personal ads. Some people claim to have considered exile.

But let's not exaggerate: homosexuals survived the Mirguet law, which never had any great impact on daily life. This much is certain, however: it was the end of an era for Arcadie.

The second big scare was May '68. "There was one Arcadie before 1968 and another one after," one interview subject explains. This time, the difficulties no longer came from the government but from within the organization. Just as they now considered the allusions to homosexuality in Marcel Carné's films inadequate, and found Louis Aragon's innuendo too timid when he sang "Les yeux d'Elsa" [Elsa's eyes], some members of Arcadie wanted to put an end to the era of camouflage. In the winter of 1969, things were further stirred up. "Right now, you're being challenged," one of Baudry's faithful told him. A magnanimous Baudry explains today: "Given the life I had led, it was obvious I was not at all prepared to understand and accept the excesses of a certain number of homosexuals."

What followed is part of the early history of the MLF, and then of the FHAR. In November 1970, Baudry allowed an autonomous group of young Arcadians to organize. The first meeting was a success, and many lesbians and feminists met—to denounce André Baudry's misogyny.[32] The leader of Arcadie remembers that meeting today: "From my room on the third floor, in our offices on rue du Château-d'Eau, I heard violent, sharp, intense discussions, almost shouting. At the end of the meeting, I went downstairs and asked for an explanation: it was indescribable, the yelling, the threats." Led by Eaubonne and Fauré, the group of homosexual women was close to splitting off from Arcadie. The women met to plan several actions of the MLF and, in particular, they gathered at Fouque's apartment to discuss homosexuality. For Baudry, they were simply a group of irresponsible people. "That group degenerated into leftist politics," he comments even today. As a result, the disruptive elements, who at the time he felt had "no future," were expelled from Arcadie. This time, however, what followed would prove him wrong.

In 1971, the lesbians of Arcadie embraced the revolution of "queers and dykes," railed against the "heterocops" and their accomplices, "the apologetic homosexuals," and resolved quite simply to throw the old choirboy Baudry overboard. In a sense, that is what happened at the tumultuous debate organized in March 1971 by Ménie Grégoire. The lesbians who had been expelled from Arcadie shouted, "Down with Daddy's homosexuality!" "Arcadie will die soon!" they predicted, making the split final. One of the lesbians even slapped the "pope," and his glasses ended up on the floor. Red with anger, he turned on one of the Arcadie renegades, Pierre Hahn: "Are you the one who brought all these girls here?" But he chose to slip out of Salle Pleyel through a secret door.

At Christmas 1971, a chorus of militant FHAR women sang a song written by Eaubonne, to the tune of *Il est né le divin enfant* [The divine child is born]:

> Depuis dix-neuf ans Arcadie,
> Où André Baudry jouait au prophète,
> Depuis dix-neuf ans Arcadie
> Nous promettait le paradis.
> Mais il est né le mouvement du FHAR,
> Chantons pédés et jouons tapettes,
> Mais il est né le mouvement du FHAR,
> Nous pouvons laisser tomber ces mauviettes.

> For nineteen years, Arcadie,
> Where Baudry played the prophet,
> For nineteen years, Arcadie
> Promised us paradise.
> But the FHAR movement is born,
> Let us sing, queers, let us play, pansies,
> But the FHAR movement is born,
> We can drop those weaklings.

Children are always ungrateful. The 1970s militants, born from the womb of Arcadie, made the former seminarian their whipping boy. "Arcadie had a perfectly despicable image of respectability," recalls Alain Neddam, a militant from the Lyons chapter of Groupes de Libération Homosexuelle [Groups for homosexual liberation], or GLH. Jean-Pierre Michel, a deputy in the camp of the Socialist Party's Jean-Pierre Chevènement, takes an even harsher view: "A bunch of moralizing old grandfathers, the protectors of beautiful young men." Another fellow traveler of Arcadie today defines the movement as a gathering of "little model children who became perverse by producing a journal on repression." Finally, a member of the Council of State, even more critical, explains that Arcadie "was okay until 1970, but after that it was Pétainist."

Pétainist? Judgments of Arcadie were passionate and overblown. Nevertheless, chronology alone can explain how an undertaking that was courageous in the beginning elicited only derision and sarcasm in 1968. In the FHAR era, Arcadie had become anachronistic.

Arcadians called themselves "homophiles," but FHAR militants declared themselves queers and lesbians. Arcadians had lived through the postwar period; FHAR militants, through the post-'68 period. Arcadie cloaked itself in respectability and tried to manage the original sin of homophilia. The FHAR built a revolutionary theory of desire, demonstrating side by side with drag queens and the Gazolines. Before 1968, homosexuality located itself on the political right; now it was part of the left. Was dialogue still possible?

↩

If literature is any indication of the state of society, the labored tribute that *Arcadie* paid to Henri de Montherlant in 1972 (issue 228) may allow us to compare the fate of one body of work with the fate of the Arcadie organization. Montherlant, who had just committed suicide, surely belonged to a world that was collapsing. For leftists, Montherlant was a closet queen, not a part of their history. A Catholic writer who celebrated the ideal of a heroic and virile life (in *Les olympiques* [The olympics], about sports, or in *Les bestiaires* [The bullfighters], about bullfighting), he remained an aristocrat, the sort who was "incapable of calling his housekeeper anything but 'the girl.'"[33] And, to fuel his imagination while remaining discreet, he simply disguised his Arab youths as "ladies gathering branches" (as in *La rose de sable* [The sable rose]).

Inducted into the Académie Française in 1960, Montherlant had long since announced his intention to publish a book on homosexuality—his final revenge for being expelled from high school for pederasty in 1913, or a self-defensive reaction after hoodlums left him beaten and almost blind, for reasons that can only be imagined. In 1969 he made up his mind and published *Les garçons* [*The Boys*]. But the confessions were not very explosive: now that more intimate apparel had been removed in public, the critics were harsh. Marred by his scruples, Montherlant had lost some of his haughtiness; and his books, no longer fueled by shame, lost much of their power. Gide's terrible comment is still true: "Montherlant? The yellow belly shows through the purple mantle."[34] But this judgment may have been rendered null and void, for the first time, by the circumstances of Montherlant's death.

↩

Baudry found memories of his own life in the universe of the Christian writers and, in particular, in Montherlant's stories of a Catholic youth. The founder of Arcadie chose to remain faithful to the path on which he had set out in the early 1950s, still rejecting "visibility" and even the idea of coming out. More than ever, the Arcadie movement mirrored an unpolished Freemasonry, divided between self-loathing and the cult of the self.

In 1969, the Arcadie Club had just set up its headquarters (they were to be its last) in a former theater on rue du Château-d'Eau: André Baudry was going to stay the course. He published a periodical called *Aghois*, intended for Spanish homosexuals who were victims of Francoism. He held many gala evenings and banquets but continued to reject, as he put it, the "risqué photos, frivolous articles, and making whoopee" that some hoped for.[35] As a sign of his newfound largesse, he turned a blind eye to little kisses in public.

The specialized groups within Arcadie that had been created during the 1960s now began to attract larger crowds. This was the case for the religious group, which brought priests and laypeople together; it had grown since May '68. For December 15, 1971, Baudry organized a roundtable discussion on Christianity and homophilia, calling on an Arcadian, Gérald de La Mauvinière, to lead the debate, in which a Catholic priest, an Anglican reverend, a Protestant pastor, and an Eastern Orthodox deacon were also supposed to participate. But the religious group later left Arcadie, less because of disagreements than because of the wish to be autonomous.

In January 1972, Gérald de La Mauvinière created the David and Jonathan Society for Christians of different religions who were seeking to reconcile their homosexuality and their faith. Throughout the 1970s, the society played an important role; it had nearly 700 members in 1978, among them a significant number who continued to subscribe to *Arcadie*. Militants proclaimed their sexuality as well as the authenticity of their faith. They were not obsessed with the Old Testament, but they were not unaware that Sodom and Gomorrha are destroyed in Genesis, and they were always deeply troubled by these words from Leviticus: "If a man also lie with mankind, as he lieth with a woman, both of them have committed an abomination: they shall surely be put to death; their blood *shall be* upon them."[36]

For the most part, the David and Jonathan Society came to the aid of coreligionists, and especially of clergymen in trouble, some of whom were mistreated by the church's "inhospitality." The society used the intricacies of casuistry to argue the difference between *chastity* (mastery of carnal pleasure) and *continence* (rejection of carnal pleasure). Wondering whether someone could set aside continence without forsaking chastity, members held passionate debates throughout the 1970s, attempting to reach agreement on abortion, pedophilia, and sadomasochism. La Mauvinière, the society's Vincentian founder, was associated with the lay religious organization Saint Vincent de Paul; its best-known spokesperson, Father Jacques Perotti, was a close associate of Abbot Pierre. Both were emblematic figures. Together, they epitomized the David and Jonathan Society's Christian affiliation. Today the society's 500 members, organized into about fifty distinct groups, seek to know themselves and, according to Jacques Cougnaud, one of its leaders, "to accompany all those who have lost their bearings or need help breathing."

↬

As one particular path, one unique response, the religious life has sometimes served as an alternative for male and female homosexuals alike.[37] The words of Brother Jacques Laval, who frequented Arcadie, may illustrate this complex link between homosexuality and religion. They demonstrate the uneasiness characteristic of homosexual believers and allow us to understand the importance of such collective movements as Arcadie's religious group and the David and Jonathan Society.

Brother Laval, a Dominican living in the monastery on rue des Tanneries, in Paris, is today eighty-five years old. His life history is typical of an entire generation:

When I was very young, I believed in the love God has for all men. At twenty-three, I discovered love and suffering with a seminarian. I loved that boy, but I also loved God. Then I began to suffer: Does the living God prevent those who serve him from being happy? This suffering guided me, made me grow, led me to understand many poor souls, who, like me, were in anguish. Were my intentions always pure? I don't believe so. I was often attracted to the people I wanted to help. Nevertheless, physical desire creates a color, a human vibration, and it can be beneficial. I had to deal with strange and difficult situations involving the dregs of society, boys abandoned by everyone. They moved me because they were so vulnerable. I couldn't let them get too attached to me, or myself to them. Some were no choirboys! Compassion is something I feel and, though it is beautiful, it is also dangerous.

Laval entered the seminary at eighteen and became a curate, then a hospital chaplain, before joining the Dominican order: "Everywhere, I suffered from the lack of a love life, a sex life." Later, he was sent on missions to Rome, Mexico City, and Calcutta: "Most of the time, I was alone, and to travel alone is to travel with the devil." Since then, he has lived communally in the Dominican monastery, where the friars lead a religious life, usually as theologians or, less often, as teachers. A passionate reader of Mauriac and Gide, Laval adds, "In the church, homosexuality plays an important role; it is hidden, or it is shameful, and people have a hard time dealing with it. The question is dismissed in silence. Confusing attractions can be dulled through prayer. I never felt guilty because of my difference; not even the idea of sin made me feel guilty."

Laval's view of the self-declared homosexuals of the early 1970s is similar to Baudry's. "Sexual life is not as simple as is often claimed," Laval says. "Sexuality by itself precludes love. Love is an art, a masterpiece. The sexual act is very commonplace on its own: if one whole person wants to meet another whole person and walk with him part of the way, that is not so easy. I love fidelity very much: you can be engaged to be friends just as you can be engaged to be married."[38]

$\hookrightarrow$

In the late 1970s, despite the times and the criticism from the new homosexual militants, Arcadie, paradoxically, attracted its largest crowds. Between 1972 and 1975, the review picked up 15,000 subscribers, and the movement now had 30,000 members.[39] Provincial branches multiplied, and the organization became a virtual special-interest lobby. And, surprising though it may seem, Baudry, who still had the upper hand in Arcadie, was until 1980 the only one to engage in discussions with trade unions, parliamentary groups, and political parties.[40]

Between the two rounds of the 1974 presidential election, Baudry questioned François Mitterrand about his intentions. Mitterrand, first secretary of the French Socialist Party, sent him a particularly cordial letter in response: "I am against all sorts of oppression, whether economic, social, or sexual, whether they attack the fundamental right of certain social groups to exist or whether they attack the most complex and intimate reality of individuals. I have also said throughout my campaign that I recognize the right to difference, and, of course, the right to live that difference." After pronouncing himself in favor of lowering the age of civil majority, and of making the age of consent the same for heterosexuals and homosexuals, Mitterrand went on: "As you see, I am completely different from my opponent [Valéry Giscard d'Estaing], who, unlike me, voted for the July 1960 bill that declared homosexuality a social scourge. Permit me to add that I personally understand the tragedy, especially for a young man or young woman from a modest background, of feeling rejected by society, and sometimes by peers. It is also against this discrimination that I am fighting."[41]

During the 1978 legislative elections, Arcadie again represented the homosexual movement, and Baudry, though publicly on the right, entered into dialogue with the Socialist Party, asking that legislation be modified—something that no militant group of the 1970s, even this late in the decade, had yet thought to do.

But the great success of Baudry's career was the congress, in May 1979, celebrating Arcadie's twenty-fifth anniversary: at the Palais de la Porte Maillot, in Paris, more than 900 participants and various personalities (Jean-Paul Aron, Robert Merle, Dominique Fernandez, Yves Navarre, Gabriel Matzneff) discussed homosexuality. The presence of Foucault at the demonstration, surprising though it might appear, contributed to its success.[42]

↤

Despite this success, Baudry decided to dissolve his organization on May 13, 1982. Wounded by critics, bitter since the victory of the Socialists, and lonely, he wrote in the final issue of his review, in an impassioned style that aptly sums up his history, "As for myself, far from the commotion of my people, whom I have loved in every individual who has come unto me, I shall await death somewhere, expressing one wish only: that you all be made happy through the demands of a homophile life composed of courage and dignity."[43]

Since 1982, Baudry has, as he puts it, "withdrawn from that homophile world." Now over seventy, he lives in Naples with Giuseppe, the love of his life.[44]

4

Drifting

We are not unstable, we are mobile. No desire to be anchored. Let's drift.
— Guy Hocquenghem

In spite of the militant movements—respectable before 1968, and revolutionary in the early 1970s—homosexual lifestyles seem to have been marked by a great deal of continuity, something the overused expression "homosexual liberation" seems unable to reflect.

The meeting places and love circuits of homosexuals, as common threads running through several periods, illustrate this continuity. Until the late 1970s, homosexuality was characterized by a dissymmetry between night and day, combined with a dichotomy in the ages and social backgrounds of partners, whether they met in bars or in public toilets.

The term "drifting," coined to sum up this dichotomy, became a fetish expression among French homosexuals, and the activity it denoted became a commonplace of male cruising.[1] With connotations ranging from fluid sexuality to the experience of marginality, the term characterizes the frankly sexual quest and the harsh, somber world of males; it marks the borderline between daily dissimulation and anonymous desire, between constraint and risk. Guy Hocquenghem writes, "Queer sexuality—encounters at the Tuileries, at nightclubs, on Moroccan beaches—none of that is any substitute, any desperate search aimed at filling a void. We are not unstable, we are mobile. No desire to be anchored. Let's drift."[2] In a similar vein, Hocquenghem distinguishes between an easygoing, everyday, visible, diurnal, bright homosexuality and a dark homosexuality, or *homosexualité noire* —dangerous, nocturnal, almost sordid. Pier Paolo Pasolini's death on a beach in Ostia in 1975 may well be the emblem of dark homosexuality.[3]

The history of these lifestyles, these cruising spots, probably has no identifiable beginning. The period between the pre–World War II era—the *années folles*—and the late 1970s provides us with subjective parameters for uncovering these love circuits, but the borderlines remain indeterminate. Homosexuality is a different way of "being in the world," regardless of the era.[4]

DAY AND NIGHT

"In the legendary times before 1968, the nice 'homophiles' of Arcadie fear-fully rejected the promiscuity of the bars, which they saw as an insult to authentic love. Post-'68 leftists proclaimed that earlier homosexual lives had been marked by persecution. It had been a kind of Middle Ages, when fags were locked up in Louis XI's iron cages. Both visions are false. Homosexuals became freer and freer in their lives between the 1930s and the 1970s." With these words, Bernard Minoret, who lived through the postwar period, seems to be thumbing his nose at the homosexual militants, giving a completely different picture of lifestyles before 1968.

Three Paris locales can serve as illustrations: Chez Graff, the restaurant and bar in Pigalle; Le Fiacre, in Saint-Germain-des-Prés; and Le Sept, on rue Sainte-Anne. Three locales, three eras, three pictures of homosexual nightlife, three neighbor-hoods; but, beyond their differences, they belong to a single universe and display a great deal of continuity.

Before the war, the first homosexual "axis" was on the Left Bank, stretching from Place de Clichy to Place Pigalle. Chez Graff, on Place Blanche between these two crossroads, was the hot spot of the neighborhood from the 1920s to the late 1940s. A theater of stock characters, it was characterized by a great deal of social mixing. For example, people went there after the premiere of Cocteau's 1921 ballet *Les mariés de la tour Eiffel* [The Eiffel Tower wedding party]. After they had taken their wives home, men in tuxedos flocked to the restaurant in search of young men wearing pendants and leg-of-mutton sleeves.

The ease of homosexual relations seems to have been a typical feature of the *an-nées folles*. "The sexes were much more separate than they are now, and that of course favored unusual love affairs," André du Dognon explains.[5] At Chez Graff, this social differentiation led to odd couplings: ephebes in flat caps and Jésus la Caille types[6] in wide corduroy pants became smitten with the last representatives of the impoverished aristocrats, whose names ended in *-ski, -ska,* or *-skof.* "Lackeys" not even familiar with the names "Diaghilev" or "Nijinsky" took to commenting on the latest Swedish ballets. Young men in the know adopted endless red flannel belts, which they wound about their waists by spinning around with one end secured to a door handle. A French Algerian pimp might accost a Moroccan soldier on leave; an old philatelist, slightly dotty, might take himself for Max Jacob. The Spanish *infante* might dally with the little bellhop from his hotel; a spry hussar might call himself the Duchess of Bouillon. People drank mint or cassis cordials. A charming lady might tell you she used to be a man; a black woman, that she is actually white.

The Magic City Ball, which reflected, almost to the point of caricature, this at-mosphere of the *années folles,* was one of the high points of homosexual history. Held every year until 1939 in a dance hall on rue Cognac-Jay, the ball placed an as-tonishing array of boys in plumes and pearls on display; some of them were naked except for a bunch of artificial grapes at their middles. Twice a year, for Mardi Gras and for the Thursday of the third week in Lent, Parisians stood in front of Chez Graff after the ball, to consider—or mock—the unparalleled transvestism of the celebrated milliners Mimosa and Peaches and of Divines straight out of Genet's *Notre-Dame-des-Fleurs*, all photographed by Brassaï.

The shady Pigalle of the 1930s, as the first pocket of homosexuality in Paris, included numerous mixed-sex cafés, showy piano lounges, and specialized dance halls: Chez Ryls on rue Frochot, La Taverne Liégeoise on rue Pigalle, Le Palmyrium on Place Blanche, Chez Ma Cousine on rue Lepic, Tonton on rue Norvius, and even, after the war, Mon Club, La Licorne, and L'Hélicoptère, three bars near Place de Clichy. Homosexuals applauded Edith Piaf at the Bar du Rugby—it was there she fell in love with a legionnaire—while at the Clair de Lune the ineffable Bijou, a madame in pancake makeup, distributed her boys on the basis of the gentlemen's calling cards. Outside, under the blue fog of gaslights, Boulevard de Clichy allowed for all sorts of encounters.[7]

The neighborhood also had its less dissolute arteries to the south, near Place de la Madeleine, with the famous Boeuf sur le Toit on rue Boissy d'Anglais. This artistic, high-society bar and dance hall was characteristic of the prewar period. People listened to jazz and compositions by "The Six" and rubbed shoulders with Picasso, Radiguet, and especially Cocteau, who passed for the owner of the place. Le Boeuf changed addresses three times, and with each move its clientele became more homosexual.[8]

⤳

During those years, the *gousses* and *beautés d'azur*—homosexual women—went to Le Monocle, a lesbian cabaret that had been open on Boulevard Edgar-Quinet since the 1930s. Women in three-piece suits played a hilariously funny saxophone or trombone while hostesses, always with one hand behind their backs, asked the ladies to dance. Some evenings, the women accompanied Suzy Solidor, who, with a cap covering her long blond hair, invited people to sing along with her song *Escale* [Port of call]: "The sky is beautiful,/The sea is green,/Leave the window open a bit." Customers responded, "Leave your fly open a bit!"[9]

Other women preferred Smith's Tea Room, on rue de Rivoli, the picture of "lesbian elegance"; or, in the late 1940s, Caroll's, on rue de Ponthieu. There the proprietress, Fred, argued with the painter Hélène Azenor as dairymaids dallied with women from the Left Bank. Women also frequented Le Fétiche, in Montmartre; the mixed-sex Chez Elle et Lui; the cabaret Entre-Nous, on rue Laferrière (opened in 1946 and still frequented today); or the Sunday afternoon tea dances at Chez Moune, in Pigalle (established in 1930). At such spots they sang *Mon petit copain d'abord* [My little pal first] with Nicole Louvier in the 1950s, or *A ta santé madame* [To your health, madame] and *Mathias* with Gribouille in the 1970s. For the men, Montmartre was the neighborhood of choice, and social and cultural differences gave cruising its spice.

⤹

After World War II, Paris seemed to be the European capital of homosexuality, and Saint-Germain-des-Prés became its heart. The cafés, all with their particular codes, played their part as typical spots for encounters.[10] The second floor of Le Flore was a "sensitive" (read "effeminate") spot, despite the resistance of its owner, Boubal, who for a long time was intolerant of his homosexual clientele, even though they paid top dollar for his espressos. L'Apollinaire was chic but macho. Finally, La Reine Blanche, a perfectly innocent-looking alleyway where Madame Blanche held court, was working-class and attracted hustlers. Insomniacs from every social class met there all night long. But these places, which were not openly homosexual, soon had to compete with more specialized spots.

Le Fiacre, in Saint-Germain-des-Prés, was the most mythic one. This bar and restaurant was opened in the early 1950s by Louis, called Loulou, a mustachioed Basque with the look of a grande dame and a studied effeminacy, who greeted you with a ritual "What will you have, my delicious friend?" Situated at the foot of rue du Cherche-Midi, this typical mahogany-paneled bar was enveloped in ornamental molding hung with velvet and covered with engravings of carriages. On the second floor, a mixed-sex restaurant welcomed Roland Petit and Zizi Jeanmaire, Jean Marais, Maria Callas, and Alain Delon, all coming in from the theater. On the ground floor, a narrow stairway linked two different worlds and allowed anyone to engage in conversation or let his hands wander with impunity. "Talking was a way of cruising," Paul remembers nostalgically. "There was always someone offering a glass of champagne." At the bar, which opened at 7 P.M., the social mix was absolute: writers and circus hands, bankers and elevator operators. Beyond its folksiness, Le Fiacre made dialogue possible: the music was discreet, and there was no dancing—a godsend for many young people. In a sense, Le Fiacre allowed adolescents to apprehend, if not come to terms with, their "second birth," since, by introducing young people to homosexuality, it played the same role as the traditional "ferrymen": an old uncle, an eccentric female friend of the family, a woman professor of French, or, in André Téchiné's *Les roseaux sauvages* [Wild reeds], set in the early 1960s, a shoe salesman whom the young hero, François, discovers to be an "invert" and resolves to question about his fate.

Although it allowed all its customers to discover people like themselves, Le Fiacre was an invitation to eccentricity. Homosexuals grew bolder: they smoked "Virginias"; they dared to wear ankle boots with pointed toes, bracelets, fur coats. People dressed up to go to Le Fiacre, and customers in blue jeans were rare and frowned upon. Hustlers were regulars there; no ill-tempered doorman barred their entry. "In the summer, we were often out on the sidewalk because of the crowds," Jacques recalls simply. When Le Fiacre closed, after Louis's death, in 1967, Saint-Germain-des-Prés continued to have a high concentration of homosexuals until the mid-1970s, thanks in particular to the Boîte aux Chansons and to the bar Le Nuage, frequented by queens and German highbrows.

Relationships with hustlers were commonplace at that time for a certain social class. With an air of being on safari, as some said, ironically, the "bourgeois" cruised the "proles." It was the era of Yugoslavian male escorts, which precipitated the Markovic affair.[11] There were 300 male prostitutes in Paris in 1970.[12] The Café des Sports on rue de Rennes, the Speakeasy on rue des Cannettes, the Sherry Lane on rue des Ciseaux, and the Royal Saint-Germain, replaced by the Drugstore in Saint-Germain-des-Prés (opened in October 1965), had long brought in regulars.

The brothel run by Monsieur Jean was in Pigalle, a neighborhood that remained "hot" even after the war. Jean, a hotel owner who supplied partners at a fixed rate, supposedly had been "trained" by Albert Le Cuziat, who is depicted in Maurice Sachs's *Le sabbat* [*Witches' Sabbath*]. In Proust's *The Past Recaptured* he appears under the name Jupien, owner of the Temple de l'Impudeur, where Charlus goes to have himself flagellated. Upon "retirement," Monsieur Jean was kind enough to pass the torch, teaching the trade to Madame Madeleine. A worthy heiress to so prestigious a line, she is remembered by all as the last manager of the brothel on the dead-end rue Guelma. A whole ritual existed at the time: audacious johns made their choices on the corner of Boulevard de Clichy, in a café called La Nuit, and then discreetly followed their conquests to Madame Madeleine's. The most timid, or most notorious, clients waited in Madame Madeleine's "salon" until she introduced their future cavaliers to them. About 1967, on evenings when he was less tormented by his faith, Marcel Jouhandeau regularly went there—and, it is said, not only because he craved conversation with "Madame Made." In one of his *Journaliers* [Dailies], he recounts how he made dates by telephone with the young man of his choice, some little telegraph operator or sewer worker in high rubber boots. He does not tell us, however, whether Madame Madeleine was able to groom her successor.[13]

DARK HOMOSEXUALITY

Homosexuals recall that, apart from the restaurant bars and brothels, the best place for cruising until the late 1970s was the public toilet. "The more distinguished people said 'urinal,'" Jacques de Ricaumont corrects. Others, preferring slang, spoke of "tearooms" or "glory holes."

Although "inverts" had cruised the public parks since the ancien régime, the creation of public toilets in the nineteenth century gave them a new place of worship.[14] The group urinal, "a narrow half-stone kiosk where I go astray" (Rimbaud), became the place of choice for all those who—from timidity, bad conscience, or lack of money—could not act on their desires in a more social manner, not to mention the perverts who satisfied their eroticism and exhibitionism in these public conveniences, in choreographies that sometimes became a game of hide-and-seek with the police. The public toilet outside the Trocadéro cemetery was even nicknamed "the glory hole of the departed." This proximity to peril and sordidness

made the public toilet the temple of dark homosexuality, to use Guy Hocquenghem's phrase.

Certain latrines have remained famous: those on Boulevard Haussmann,
where homosexuals went before and after the opera; the ones, very busy, on Avenue Gabriel and Boulevard Malesherbes; those on rue de la Chapelle, which was
more working-class and attracted truckers. Proust described the three-seated public toilets; the middle seat was the place of choice for voyeurs.[15]

An enchanted symbol of urban nightlife, the public toilet held a central place
in the imagination of Genet, the preeminent author of dark homosexuality. In *The
Thief's Journal* his hero, Java, follows the "sacred path," three street urinals at the
far end of the Champs-Elysées, and René goes there for "queer bashing." "Show a
little surprise that he is proposing love to you," the narrator advises. For Genet, the
public toilet is the universe of rough cruising, of faceless, nameless, wordless shadows under broken streetlights. Kenneth Anger's *Pink Narcissus* (a cult film for the
FHAR), Stephen Frears's [film] *Prick Up Your Ears* [adapted from the stage play by
Joe Orton], and Patrice Chéreau's *L'homme blessé* [The wounded man] also depict
cruising in public toilets, where the hustler, the tramp, the queer, and the lout rub
shoulders in an amazing cocktail of stinking filth and Vaseline.

In the provinces, where homosexual spots were rare, public toilets played a
greater role. In every city, the "poufs" had their particular customs: in the public
toilets on rue Henri-IV and Place Renaudel, in Bordeaux; along a *via dolorosa* in
Lyons stretching from the urinal on the Lafayette Bridge (nicknamed "la Lafon")
to the one called "Our Lady of the Arabs," and including "the Wilson" and "Our
Lady of the Temples." Everywhere else, it was urinals in train stations and on
wharves.

Many people have alluded to the presence of immigrants in the public toilets.
For Philippe Guy, cofounder of the FHAR, "love with Arabs is an encounter between two sorts of sexual poverty. Two sorts of poverty plugged in to one another.
. . . It is my sexual poverty as well. Because I need to find a guy right away. You have
to because you're in a lousy situation. . . . And sometimes I tell myself: in such a
situation, good God, you have to get fucked over to get off!"[16]

You could also meet all sorts of people, openly homosexual or not, in public
toilets: a few hustlers, the rare transvestite, office workers, local celebrities, masons,
heads of companies. "You could have relations with people from every social
background," Jean-Pierre confirms. Again, in addition to the dissymmetry between diurnal and nocturnal homosexuality, there was a dichotomy in the ages
and social backgrounds of sexual partners. "There were drag queens and college
professors," Jean-Paul Montanari of Lyons recalls today. "I am terribly nostalgic
for that time."

Nostalgic? On January 28, 1980, the Paris city council authorized the first three
Decaux *sanisettes:* automatic, sterilized urinals for a single person; they rapidly became ubiquitous (City Hall ordered 400 models for the capital in January 1981).

The old public toilets, now judged unseemly, were collected in a vacant lot outside Paris, where they have been rusting away ever since. A cemetery of street urinals has become the sepulchre of "a certain way of experiencing homosexuality."

↩

The persistence of the forbidden in homosexuality accentuated the separation between sexuality and feelings.[17] The norms of social respectability led to marriages of convenience, which allowed individuals to keep up appearances and avoid sinking into an out-of-control single life. These "front" marriages remain common among French homosexuals. Because homosexuality, like any other clandestine practice, required a system that minimized risks while optimizing efficiency, men sought out quick, anonymous relationships. The public toilet was part of this problematic, but not the only part. All my interviews with homosexuals allude to other atmospheres that were similar to that of the public toilet: an adventure in the high school john, encounters in the *jardin vert* of Angoulême, at the Penbrom beach near Nantes, around the "packing crates" in Bordeaux, or on the Gravier promenade in Agen. In 1970s Paris, as many as 150 people may have gathered every evening in the Jean-XXIII Gardens, or behind the cathedral of Notre Dame, or in the gardens of the Trocadéro, or around the tennis courts in the Tuileries.[18]

"My sexuality was hygienic," Jean-Pierre explains. "I collected little packets of adventures. Encounters were extremely quick, in parking lots, vacant lots, deserted places. You never saw the other person again." Some mentioned experiences in the street. Charles claims, "In those days, you didn't need an access code to get into buildings; at night you could fuck in entryways."

Men also began to meet in working-class neighborhood movie theaters, which were not yet porn houses.[19] On the pretext of seeing a Western or an adventure film, homosexuals discovered specialized spots in Pigalle, which was still the neighborhood of working-class homosexuals. "In the darkened theater" at the Louxor, in Barbès, Serge recalls, his eyes followed "the people who were changing seats or going to the toilet: it was a regular walking bordello, with an extraordinary Egyptian decor." The Trianon, on Boulevard de Rochechouart, had magnificent china urinals. On rue du Faubourg-Saint-Martin, the theater management itself kept a lookout. "When the vice squad made its rounds," Henri recalls, "the usherette went up to the balcony and switched a flashlight on and off three times. Then we kept still."

During this time, informers for the vice squad, who were sometimes homosexual themselves, caused outrage by allowing themselves to be fondled in public toilets or movie theaters until the police wagon arrived, at which time they would point out whoever had touched them.[20] Arrests, police checks, and the knowledge that they would be put "on file" mark the collective memory of homosexuals. Even today, homosexuals often have an irrational feeling of insecurity.

"I became interested in marginality when I was thirteen years old," explains Jean, a young man from Marseilles whose journey through the 1970s can be reconstructed. "Marseilles was a city of colors, climates, and sweat. There were a lot of fairies there. I lived at night and slept during the day. I was a hair stylist in the Turkish baths on rue Thubaneau, when the place was teeming with drug addicts, prostitutes, burglars, and cops. It was very theatrical, a very cinematic world, girls getting dressed up and coming to get their hair done by me. There were a lot of foreigners."

"In Marseilles," Jean continues, "people cruised in the Goudes creeks" (FHAR slogans are still visible on the Callelongue blockhouse). His friends preferred to drive around Gare Saint-Charles, or, in the summer, to go to Mont Rose, a rocky nude beach on Pointe-Rouge. There was also Le Cancan, "a queer nightclub for straights," and La Mare au Diable, reputed for its garden full of bushes, where on Saturday night butch men turned out in tank tops and mustaches. The homosexual disco was lighted up all the time: "We thought it was run by the underworld," Jean adds. "In the 1970s, homosexual life in Marseilles was a bit sordid: there were the public toilets, the movie theaters, the dark places with hoodlums hanging around. One day, they assaulted me and messed me up pretty good."

Since then, Jean, the little hairdresser of rue Thubaneau, has become Guidoni, carving out a shadowy kingdom for himself in French song. The ambiance of that era nurtured the dark angel who cried alone at midnight, the writer of "Carnet de Griselidis" [Griselidis's notebook], about the famous Swiss prostitute by that name; of "Drugstore, 18 heures" [Drugstore, 6 P.M.], about streetwalking in Saint-Germain-des-Prés; of "Eros Palace," about peep shows; and of "Je marche dans les villes" [I walk in the cities], about homosexual cruising. Guidoni sings about the world of starving hustlers, hoodlums with pale lips, stumbling over the sticky pavement. He sings in high heels, if necessary, as a tribute to Judy Garland: "I was a voyeur, something of a sociologist, but I was unaware of it: they were the human material for my future songs."

⤬

The drag queen, a colorful figure immortalized in song by Guidoni, was the hero of the night in the 1970s. The transvestite, marginal within marginality itself, represents for the sociologist Michael Pollak "the species that has lived through and survived a situation of social oppression, in which the homosexual does everything possible to conform to the stereotype invented by his oppressors. He attempts to defuse hostility by making people laugh."[21] Sporting wigs for a night, or on hormones for life, Divine, Dina, Zaza Napolie, Marie France, Lady X, and the "Transvestite Transsexual of Transylvania" (TTT) went to all the parties.[22]

RUE SAINTE-ANNE

Although Saint-Germain-des-Prés and Pigalle continued to attract crowds, nothing in the history of homosexual lifestyles was more striking and mysterious than the appearance of specialized clubs, discos, and restaurants on rue Sainte-Anne. In the early 1970s, this short artery between the Opéra and the Palais Royal, a rather dreary business district that was deserted after working hours, became a pocket of homosexuality at night and attracted the whole of the Parisian clientele.

The homosexual hot spot of the neighborhood, Le Vagabond, which catered to elderly gentlemen, opened in 1956 at the future strategic crossroads of rue Thérèse and rue Sainte-Anne. A stone's throw away, on rue Chabanais, Le César, a late-night bar run by a lesbian couple, opened in 1959. Spanish domestics and Portuguese transvestites were still regulars in the 1960s, despite constant police raids. Le Vagabond and Le César were thus the origin of the homosexual ghetto on rue Sainte-Anne.

At the end of the street, on Avenue de l'Opéra, is Le Royal Opéra, a heterosexual café. It is open all night, and for that reason it has been frequented by hustlers since the 1950s. Finally, not far from there, the Tuileries have been a cruising spot since the ancien régime.

At the conjunction of these various elements, and probably more by geographical accident than deliberate choice, rue Sainte-Anne became specifically homosexual when Fabrice Emaer opened Pimm's.

↩

Twenty years later, Emaer, a stellar personality with exaggeratedly blond hair, has succeeded Louis at Le Fiacre and, like his predecessor, has become the new luminary of homosexual night life in Paris. Back in 1964, this beautician-turned-bartender set up Pimm's on his own and invented a new way of being homosexual: chic and mod, to the beat of American music.

With this first experience of Pimm's under his belt, Emaer—on December 18, 1968, at 7, rue Sainte-Anne—opened the place of his dreams, which he named, simply, "Le Sept" [Seven]. This club, whose opening coincided with sexual liberation, combined a basement nightclub with a restaurant and played a role in popularizing the new disco music. Until the mid-1980s, it was the obligatory entryway into gay life in Paris. Le Sept's great innovation, by comparison with Le Fiacre, was to give priority to dancing. There had been dancing at the Arcadie Club since 1957, of course, and at Le Métropolis and Le César, but dancing in such places was a constantly threatened privilege. At Le Métropolis, everyone danced with one eye fixed on a little light above the entrance. "When it blinked, you had to stop dancing and go sit down," a regular remembers. "The police were on their way."[23] At Le Sept, there was no need to worry: homosexuality was becoming calm, bourgeois, and cheerful. It was dealt with "in the French way," with an "embarrassed indifference," in the words of the journalist Franck Arnal.

Michel Guy,[24] Valéry Giscard-d'Estaing's minister of culture, publicly organized dinners at Le Sept, under mirrors with geometric motifs, inviting to his table the cartoonist Copi, or famous choreographers and dancers. Yves Mourousi met Iggy Pop there.

In the mid-1970s, rue Saint-Anne was so crowded at night that you couldn't even drive on the street. Several bars, all with their own clienteles, had opened, and they ranged from the most chic (Le Sept) to the most working-class (Le Bronx, a kind of parking lot where even sex was served up on the premises). As in other gay areas, prostitution, with its convenience and its harmful effects, became compartmentalized on rue Sainte-Anne. The most "decent" male escorts were welcomed at Le Sept, and, before leaving with you (a rich foreign client) for a nearby room at Hôtel Meurice, they closed the deal with a bottle of champagne. Other escorts, if they were presentable enough, could line up along rue Sainte-Anne (with Le Bronx nearby, in case of rain) but could not enter Le Sept before taking you to the brothel on the corner—provided you could pay cash. Not to worry about the antibiotics left lying around the room: it had nothing to do with gonorrhea, they said—which was moderately reassuring. Hustlers, who were downscale escorts, often foreigners, boasted a price that was a tenth of what their counterparts at Le Sept charged. They wore stolen basketball shoes—to outrun you—and were relegated, while waiting for their gullible clients, to a place in front of the Royal Opéra and were asked—*porca miseria*—to ply their trade out in the open. The social dichotomy characteristic of the postwar homosexual setting, and of which Le Fiacre had been a symbol, continued. Social mixing remained, although divisions began to appear among the different spots and among homosexuals, but also among their paid counterparts, the male escorts.

In this subtle geography, every spot soon acquired a distinct character: Le Piano Bar, opened by Emaer, was quickly taken over by Isolde Chrétien, one of the first airline stewardesses, who began a new—nocturnal—career of making people feel welcome. People went there very late at night. Le Colony, a restaurant at 13, rue Sainte-Anne, was pseudo-chic; Le Bronx was working-class. On adjoining streets, Le Club 18 was chic and rightist, whereas Le Scaramouche was working-class and leftist. Le Bec-Fin offered improvisational theater after the meal. Later on, Le Brooklyn, an American-style bar, but without a liquor license, also opened.

According to which spot it was, the owner might organize *danses du tapis*, where everyone could kiss the person of his choice on the dance floor. "To enter the homosexual world of the 1970s," explains Maurice McGrath, a bar owner, "was to aspire to climb up a rung in the social hierarchy: to go to the most expensive bar you could afford, the most chic bar your appearance allowed, the most snobbish bar you wanted. Homosexuals and hustlers were always thinking about being selective." In this way, rue Saint-Anne marked the origin of the ghetto. Women were gradually banned from Le Bronx: male sexuality intensified and blossomed, far from indiscreet glances.

A joyful neighborhood, a place for parties and laughter, rue Sainte-Anne was not safe from police raids. Hôtel Sainte-Anne, in the heart of the cruising district, never accepted the "invasion" of homosexuals and regularly summoned the law.[25] The writer Yves Navarre recounts, somewhat disabused, "I saw nine guys hauled out of a club ten days ago, about half past midnight. At random, like in some nasty lottery. Two minutes later, everybody in the bar was drinking as if nothing had happened. I have to confess my beer tasted a little bitter."[26]

In spite of these raids orchestrated by the vice squad, the police tolerated rue Sainte-Anne because, in the memorable words of one police superintendent, it had the advantage of "containing the homosexual problem."

The commercialization of cruising symbolized by rue Sainte-Anne was decried by homosexual militants. Paradoxically, among those who denounced this "ghetto" there were as many respectable homophiles from Arcadie as there were revolutionary queers from the FHAR. Arcadians deplored these loci of perversion, criticizing those who gave in to their instincts rather than trying, in cruel struggles with themselves (a constantly recurring theme of Baudry's "monthly message," which championed fidelity), to overcome the plural desire that enslaved them. The FHAR radicals were disturbed by the extreme secrecy in matters of love and by the social hierarchies that remained, and they criticized the formation of a "commercial ghetto": capitalism had "swallowed up sex." Leftist militants organized a demonstration on rue Sainte-Anne against commercialization. "The libido has been subjected to the law of value," wrote Alain Fleig, an FHAR leader. He announced his intention to place a bomb at Le Sept, since, according to him, the establishment had betrayed both the homosexual cause (by exploiting sexual suffering) and the revolution (by exploiting its clientele economically).[27] The homosexual rank and file, less mindful of dogma and the orthodoxy of revolutionary struggle, and no longer heeding Baudry's "messages," flocked to the short street, whereas attendance at the FHAR's general meetings became increasingly sparse. "If there had been no FHAR, there would have been no rue Sainte-Anne," another historical figure of the FHAR explains without rancor.

These criticisms of the "commercial ghetto" are more than anecdotal, and they remain significant. The objective alliance between members of Arcadie and theorists of the FHAR shows that the militants did not understand the new homosexual lifestyles. It also shows that sexual "liberation" could not emerge from liberation movements but only from ways of life.

On November 1, 1975, the filmmaker Pier Paolo Pasolini was murdered on a beach in Ostia, just as his *Salo, or the 120 days of Sodom* was being released. Had the one-night stand with a *ragazzo* he had picked up at the Stazione Termini gone bad? Like Mishima, Pasolini became, through his death, a symbol in the homosexual imagination: "One sordid (Pasolini) and one showy (Mishima) act of hara-kiri," the writer Dominique Fernandez concludes.[28]

When Pasolini died, Hocquenghem wrote a fiery article on the murder for *Libération*. The director's films, which depict homosexuality marked by guilt and repression, could only fascinate him: boys sometimes did look at or accost each other in these films, but they did not necessarily desire each other.[29] His death, which partook of dark homosexuality as defined by Hocquenghem, could serve as an emblem of "drifting." The incident illustrated only too well the relationship between the homosexual libido and marginality, the crossroads between delinquency and danger. If Hocquenghem is to be believed, Pasolini finally found the executioner he had been seeking, since, for the hero of the FHAR, homosexual destiny was inseparable from a "specific quality of danger."[30] "Pasolini took the risk of getting murdered," Hocquenghem wrote. Thus Pasolini, killed by his paid hustler, "was as guilty as the murderer": "In the eyes of the courts and the police, there is no difference between victim and murderer in this case, only a seamy environment teeming with mysterious associations, a Freemasonry of crime where queer and murderer meet." For Hocquenghem, this was certainly a scandal, but it was nevertheless "a distinctive mark of the homosexual condition." The queer libido is "a libido attracted to objects outside the laws of ordinary desire," and "the criminal aspect of homosexuality is actually a lucky chance for us."[31]

On this slippery slope, where Hocquenghem found common ground with Genet, the founder of the FHAR met a great deal of opposition. Feminists condemned this view of things. At the MLF, Anne Zelensky, disgusted by the bestiality in the film *Salo*, was undisturbed by the murder: "Because Pasolini was paying, he thought, just like some straight guy who goes to prostitutes, that he was entitled to dominate and bugger, with no discussion. Except that on the night of the murder he ran into a stubborn little piece of ass."[32] Just as critical, but for the opposite reasons, the younger members of the FHAR spoke out against their predecessor: "Guy Hocquenghem confuses the taste of sperm with the taste of blood"; "By conflating homosexuality and criminality . . . by attacking the far left's new awareness of homosexual repression, Hocquenghem has produced a bourgeois discourse"; "Isn't his machismo the mirror image of assault? Isn't his guilt the guilt of the moral order? Doesn't his taste for transgression serve to maintain repressive laws?" For the young homosexual militants, Hocquenghem pointed out "the dangers of denouncing homosexual repression in the very name of the components of homosexual desire itself": "When you're being tortured," they said ironically, "get off unfettered!"[33]

Hocquenghem had now been superseded—passed on the left—on the field of identity politics, as he soon would be on the field of lifestyles by the new homosexual militants of the late 1970s.

5

The Militant Explosion

A homosexual man is just a heterosexual man who likes men.
— Jean-Louis Bory

"I am the one who will bring change." On May 19, 1974, the evening of the second round of the presidential election, Valéry Giscard d'Estaing, with youthful ardor, felt he could announce, "This day marks the beginning of a new era in French politics, the era of rejuvenation and change in France."

Change is not revolution, of course. But, with that term, Pompidou's France awoke from its slumber. On July 5, the new president of the republic, as a goodwill gesture, decided to lower the age of majority to eighteen.

For the changing fortunes of homosexuals, Giscard's election was a turning point. The FHAR had closed its doors, and women now had an official representative in the government. Militancy was also forced to change. The sexual liberation movement had lost its unity. Among women, the struggle for abortion rights soon gave way to a battle aimed at criminalizing rape. In a parallel movement, men attempted to achieve the decriminalization of homosexuality. Although the finest pages in the militant battle for sexual liberation were to be written in the second half of the 1970s, men and women were now going their separate ways.

"WHEN WOMEN SOW SEEDS OF LOVE AMONG THEMSELVES, MEN DO NOT REAP"

In May 1974, after feminism had become organized—when it had its reviews, its bookstores, even its own publishing house—there were two women in the government who were responsible for women's issues. Françoise Giroud, named secretary of state, had already come out in favor of abortion on demand, the most sensitive of these issues. Nevertheless, the legislative bill lay with Simone Veil, the new minister of health. Her predecessor, Michel Poniatowski, had commented ironically, as he handed his minister's portfolio over to her, "At this rate, there will be an abortion taking place in your office."

The question of abortion had been central to women's demands since the petition of the 343 and the Bobigny trial. The debate on abortion now had a national following, and pressure had intensified from the Mouvement de Libération de l'Avortement et de la Contraception [Movement for legalized abortion and contraception], or MLAC, and from Planning Familial. The law was being flouted, and the government could no longer evade the issue.

Simone Veil wanted legislation. She managed to convince Giscard, who was already persuaded that mores ought to be liberalized. Prime Minister Jacques Chirac remained cautiously beyond the fray. The parliamentary majority, with little concern for the new president's reformist spirit, was not ready to follow blindly. The debate was broadcast on live television. France was already in an uproar; the social issue had taken on the aspect of a religious war. "It was impossible not to take such ad hominem attacks personally," Simone Veil remembers. "There was the mail, a vast quantity of mail downstairs in my building every morning, swastikas in the elevator, obscene slogans on our car. When I went outside, people came up to me and made gestures, the way witches were pointed at in the Middle Ages ... Not to mention the accusation of genocide."[1]

The Veil law was finally adopted by the National Assembly on the night of November 28, 1974, thanks to an unusual alliance among fewer than one-third of the deputies in the majority party, the Union des Démocrates pour la République [Union of democrats for the republic], or UDR, half the centrists, and almost all the socialists, leftist radicals, and communists. "You are paving the way for a traffic in death," shouted Jacques Médecin, shortly before the law took effect on January 17, 1975.

When the abortion issue reached a political settlement in France, obstacles in other areas were removed.[2] No-fault divorce had been passed a few months earlier, and legalized contraception was part of the Veil law. Now contraceptives were available to everyone, even underage women, and costs were reimbursed by Sécurité Sociale. "All women were officially invited to pleasure," concludes Jean-Paul Aron.[3]

Homosexual women participated in the battles of 1974, even though they were little affected by the abortion and contraception issues. The struggle against rape was completely different and became a sensitive issue in September 1975.

    ↩

Luce was a psychoanalyst. Hélène was a playwright. Michèle was a writer. Anne was a Spanish professor. Four symbolic women, engaged in different ways in the same struggle, were considering the problematic of feminism. These four complementary faces show the diversity of paths in 1975, the International Year of the Woman.

In that year, Luce Irigaray published *Speculum de l'autre femme* [*Speculum of the Other Woman*], an overview of psychoanalysis and a meticulous, critical reading of Freud. "Female homosexuality has escaped the psychoanalyst's notice," she concluded in a sort of response to Deleuze and Guattari's *Anti-Oedipus*, in which she flushed out the male imperialism hiding under the claim of neutrality and universalism. For her, "female pleasure does not have to choose between clitoral activity and vaginal passivity," since "woman has sex organs all over." In August 1975, in a theoretical article on lesbianism titled "Les marchandises entre elles" ["Commodities among themselves"], she wondered, "What if the 'commodities' refused to put themselves on the market? Maintaining among themselves an 'other' sort of commerce? Exchanges without identifiable terms, without reckoning, without end ... gratuitous pleasures, *jouissance* without possession." Reconciling her theoretical work with her commitment to militancy, Irigaray had begun to offer courses at the Université de Vincennes in late 1969, courses attended by the future representatives of the Psychépo camp of the MLF. Ousted from the Université de Vincennes in 1974 because she disagreed with Jacques Lacan (for whom "woman," in the famous expression, did "not exist"), Irigaray gradually became the principal theorist of the feminism of difference and thus, in many respects, of the Psychépo camp.[4]

In 1975, Hélène Cixous published *Souffles* [Breath] with Editions des Femmes—which was enough to mark her proximity to the Psychépo camp. Moving back and forth between militancy and research, in 1971 she participated in the Groupe d'Information sur les Prisons [Information group on prisons], or GIP, where, standing beside Michel Foucault and Daniel Defert, she discovered the existence of police arrests and billy clubs. She also participated in the women's movement, and although, like Irigaray, she chose a "feminism of difference," she pursued, in her art and research, struggles begun in the street. Calling the female libido "cosmic," Cixous, like other women theorists, questioned the notion of penis envy: "It's all just tales about Tom Thumb, *Penisneid*, whispered to us by kind old grandma ogresses, servants of their paternalistic sons. The fact that men, to feel good about themselves, think they have to believe we're dying of envy, that we're this hole surrounded by envy of their penis, well, that's been their problem since time immemorial." She conducted research on bisexuality, which she attempted to define, and on the dark continent of woman: "We, the disruptive ones ... nothing requires us to deposit our lives in this bank of lack, to understand the constitution of the subject as a tragedy of repeated wounds, to keep the father's religion constantly afloat. Since we do not want it."[5] Cixous has produced an important body of work—about forty books—particularly in theater, in a regular collaboration with Ariane Mnouchkine at the Théâtre du Soleil. She crossed paths with the French philosopher Jacques Derrida and became one of the most influential theorists of differentialist feminism, especially in the United States, where her writings, like those of Irigaray, have a large following.

"I am not a feminist, I am not a homosexual, I am a radical lesbian," explains Michèle Causse, the third symbolic woman of the mid-1970s. On the margins of the MLF, for which she felt no affinity, she published *L'encontre* [Contrariwise] in 1975, an autobiographical fable that is hardly readable today. "The women's movement is sustained by lesbians in every country; it is a lesbian movement, profoundly lesbian," she explains today. In France, Causse became associated, although against her will, with Monique Wittig's ideas, and she exalted a "lesbian worldview": "I am allergic to groups. I find them necessary but castrating. For me, feminism is a collaboration with the patriarchal system. And the women's movement mutilated lesbians: to admit one's lesbianism was to *compromise* the women's movement!" Causse's reservations about the MLF also extended to its battles: "Abortion is a false debate: the problem is male insemination. I am all for getting to the root of things: the sexual act. Abortion, parity . . . those are lesser evils." Of prostitution, she says: "Prostitution is the worst thing for me. The body is fragmented, purchased, mutilated. . . . At least they are paid to do what others have to do for free." Causse emigrated to Quebec and taught a course at the University of Montreal titled "Lesbianism and Writing: Lesbian Writing?" In it, she said, she discussed such "authoresses" as Djuna Barnes and Wittig. It is clear that Causse represents the radical branch of lesbian militancy.

The last individual chosen to represent the paths taken by women in the mid-1970s is Anne Zelensky. She was at the Tomb of the Unknown Soldier in 1970 and, during the same period, edited the issue of *Partisans* titled "Women's Liberation: Year Zero"; Zelensky was thus a feminist from the early days. Like the heroine of *One Sings, the Other Doesn't*, the film by Agnes Varda (1976), she says, "Not a floozy, not a homebody, not a dullard. I am a woman, I am myself." The MLF led her to lesbianism, and she tells of her conversion in her fictionalized *Histoires d'amour* [Love stories]: "Then I lived with a woman. I wonder how people can live any other way than with a woman. It's so simple and yet so difficult at the same time. You have to be weeding constantly, pulling out the crabgrass they planted in us."[6] In 1975, Zelensky, with Simone de Beauvoir, founded the Ligue du Droit des Femmes [League of women's rights] while at the same time preparing her own history of the MLF.[7] "At first I was a little frightened by a kind of homosexual terrorism in the movement," she remembers today. "You felt guilty if you were still in a relationship with a man. As in any group, there was a hierarchy of radicalness: living as a homosexual had a great deal of legitimacy. But the corporatism bothered me. Feminism is about reconciliation, whereas lesbianism is exclusionary." By 1975, Zelensky had completed her "intimate revolution"—she "assumed" her homosexuality, in Beauvoir's expression—and threw herself into new public issues: the struggle against rape and sexual harassment.

    ↜

The scandal that triggered the mobilization against rape went back to the previous year. In 1974, two Belgian girls, Anne Tonglet and Aracelli Castellano, were practicing nudism and primitive camping in the Morgiou inlet, between Cassis and Marseilles. It was learned during the trial that they were homosexual and thus "liberated." "As a vacation prank," three "boys from the area" took advantage of the isolation of the locale and the marginality of the two young women and, despite some "fleeting resistance," raped them for most of the night. "The two girls were very happy about it," a lawyer for the defense said.[8]

On October 15, 1975, after a first conviction for assault and battery, the lower court considering the matter in Marseilles declared itself unqualified to try the case. That was a first.[9] A few months later, the appeals court confirmed that the acts merited a criminal charge and sent the rapists to a court for more serious offenses, for what would become the famous Aix-en-Provence trial. On behalf of the two homosexual victims, Gisèle Halimi won her case in 1978: one of the men was sentenced to six years at hard labor, the two others to four years in prison. "Rape is a crime!" feminists chanted. The justice system had nodded its approval.

Until that time, like Sir Stephen in the 1975 erotic film *Histoire d'O* [*Story of O*], a man could force a woman to have sex and then claim she had enjoyed it. Leftists had been able to say, like the "black comrade" who in 1973 raped Louison, a Vietnamese MLF militant, "She was not a virgin, she was not a nun, I had the right."[10] The Aix-en-Provence trial closed this loophole.

For a time, the women's movement recovered its unity. Homosexual women led the march in the fight against the battering of women and in demonstrations against the film *Histoire d'O*. They were extremists on the rape question: Wasn't cruising attempted rape? Didn't pornographic images degrade and torment women's bodies?[11]

Soon militant women invaded the sex shops, burning pornographic books and inflatable dolls. A few moderate feminists, alone and isolated, wondered whether the damage caused by banning pornography was not greater than that resulting from its free distribution. Nevertheless, most militant women preferred to shout, "We are all prostitutes," standing side by side with women who trafficked in their charms.[12] The most radical women translated these new demands into slogans: "Women are fair game in the street," "It's open season on women all year long," "Every man is a potential rapist." Others avoided this confusion. A poster confirmed the tendency in 1981: THIS MAN IS A RAPIST, THIS MAN IS A MAN.[13]

"For men, the line is so thin between sexual extortion by persuasion—which is part of the concept of romantic conquest—and extortion by violence, that they sometimes find it difficult to understand what rape is," commented a militant Frenchwoman.[14]

Theorists provided new arguments for activist women. Thus, in 1976, Susan Brownmiller's *Against Our Will* declared, "Man's discovery that his genitalia could serve as a weapon to generate fear must rank as one of the most important discoveries of prehistoric times, along with the use of fire and the first crude stone axe." Ti-Grace Atkinson, in *Amazon Odyssey*, declared the same year: "Men must, at the very least, cooperate in curing themselves."[15]

Homosexual women found much of interest in these books and invented new slogans, which soon became those of the women's movement as a whole. Such slogans ranged from the enigmatic line, so reminiscent of Ionesco, "A woman without a man is like a fish without a bicycle" to the Laroussian "When women sow seeds of love among themselves, men do not reap"[16]

⤸

The struggle against rape, now at the center of feminist demands, was widely taken up in the provinces, where public activism proliferated in 1976. That year, in most of France's large cities, the women's movement, present since the early 1970s, grew in importance. In Lyons, the MLAC attracted feminists, and the Centre des Femmes [Women's center], for women only, opened after the Veil law passed and clandestine abortions ended.[17] In February 1976, a lesbian group formed at the women's center, eliciting "reactions verging on hysteria," especially since no feminist had yet declared herself homosexual. Nevertheless, it rapidly became a success, with meetings every week, beginning in 1976. It soon included about forty lesbians, and an autonomous journal was published, its title a nod in the direction of the MLF slogan *Quand les femmes s'aiment.*[18]

The debates and conflicts that emerged within the Lyons women's movement in 1976 were reminiscent of those within the Paris MLF in 1972. The disagreements centered on whether to have mixed-sex or all-female groups, and whether lesbian militancy ought to be made public or remain silent within the movement. There were debates about "féminitude" versus radical feminism, and about cooperation versus noncooperation with male homosexual groups.[19] These questions were resolved in various ways. Some women participated in national lesbian meetings, which began to spring up about 1977–78. Others—the majority—preferred to stay with the Centre des Femmes and continued to attend the lesbian group, which grew in size. A few were part of mixed-sex groups and worked with the male homosexual group in Lyons. Summing up a recurring problematic within the MLF, militants from the Centre des Femmes in Lyons wrote, "In the lesbian model as incarnation of a more perfect feminism, lesbians found a valorization that was refused them on the outside, and feminists found an image reflecting all their ambivalence."

Female homosexuals in Lyons were particularly involved in the struggle against rape, and their radicalism led to heated discussions. With the most dogmatic women opposed, the decision was made to omit the line "Every man is a potential rapist" (the line that had caused so much debate in Paris) from the Lyons pamphlet.

In Nantes, where a women's group was created in 1970, the issue of rape was also a topic of much debate. "We had a lot of mistrust for the judicial system," explains Maryse Guerlais of the Centre Simone de Beauvoir. "Some women, who rejected recourse to bourgeois justice, proposed that we become vigilantes!" Like the women in Lyons, the Nantes feminists did not adopt the slogan "Every man is a potential rapist," choosing instead a more cryptic phrase: "Have you ever been raped by a woman?"

Cautiously, but with determination, homosexual women and feminists in Paris and in the provinces made the struggle against rape a high priority of women's liberation, taking the battle as far as they could.

↩

Did they go too far? This question kept returning within far-left organizations, particularly among the new staff at *Libération*. On February 28, the criminal court in Beauvais sentenced an immigrant convicted of rape to twenty years in prison. On March 12, in another case, the criminal court in Isère was even harsher: twenty-five years. Françoise Picq comments, "The judicial machine was set in motion, it couldn't be stopped. Women wanted to use the justice system, and it used them. The campaign against rape served as an excuse for repression, fueled the discourse of law and order."[20]

But, beyond these causes célèbres—the topic of many debates—and despite the divisions that reemerged after the mass demonstrations, women had made a great deal of progress since the day in 1970 when they placed a spray of flowers for the wife of the unknown soldier. Some of them, during a preplanned demonstration in May, still asked, humorously, "Where May we place ourselves?" [*Où est-ce qu'on se mai?*]; nevertheless, everyone was aware that women had found a real place in society. In the words of President Giscard d'Estaing, who took credit for their progress, their presence on the world stage was now a reality.

Militant women could now open the *Petit Larousse* dictionary and read with satisfaction the evolution in the definition of *woman*: "companion of man" in 1906, "female human being" in 1959, "human being of the female sex" in 1971.

The Veil abortion law was reaffirmed and expanded in 1979. The 1970s ended with the adoption, on November 19, 1980, of a law against rape, a law also recognizing marital and homosexual rape. This time, homosexual men could not go along.[21]

"TO HELL WITH THE GHETTO: HOMOS ARE IN THE STREET"

"They said on television that it was allowed." The historian Paul Veyne reported these words, heard in his village in Vaucluse, at the foot of Mont Ventoux, a few days after an Antenne 2 broadcast of *Les dossiers de l'écran* [Screen files] devoted to homosexuals.

Long delayed, and banned for a time, the most famous broadcast of the era brought the homosexual issue to the small screen on Tuesday, January 21, 1975. Nineteen million viewers tuned in.[22]

It was no simple matter. On September 25, 1973, the *Dossiers de l'écran* broadcast devoted to homosexuality had been canceled "at the request of the Elysée Palace." The reason cited was the president of the republic's official visit to China, with no perceptible link between the two events. A first failure: blame Pompidou.

On December 2, 1974, the broadcast was again canceled for fear that, according to *L'Aurore* of December 3, "the provocative presence at the debate of Roger Peyrefitte and Jean-Louis Bory would make it look like a crusade for homosexuality." A second failure: blame Arthur Conte, the pusillanimous president of the Office de la Radiodiffusion et Télévision Française [Office of French radio and television broadcasts].

The broadcast finally took place in January 1975, preceded by the film *Les amitiés particulières* (based on the novel by Peyrefitte). Armand Jammot and Alain Jérome's forum had invited writers, for the most part: famous writers, such as Bory; young and recently recognized writers, such as Yves Navarre; and already passé writers, such as Peyrefitte. The other personalities were part of the large social organizations theoretically opposed to homosexuality: the church (represented by a very conciliatory Father Xavier Thévenot), medicine (represented by an endocrinologist and a neuropsychiatrist), and the law (represented, inevitably, by Deputy Paul Mirguet, author of the bill classifying homosexuality as a social scourge). André Baudry, the head of Arcadie, was also there—lonely, taciturn, and speaking to "homophiles." The only dark shadow in the portrait was the absence of women, which was immediately denounced by an irritated Bory, who brought up female sexuality several times.

The long-awaited debate was polite. Bory won support with a calm argument that clashed with his strident, loud voice; Navarre, who had just published *Les loukoums* [Turkish delights], was more self-effacing; and Peyrefitte retreated behind his childhood memories, classical Greece, and Plato. Surprisingly, during the debate all the guests, including the priest and the two doctors, joined forces against Deputy Mirguet. Mirguet, floored, spoke about the support he had received from "heads of families" and about the reasons behind his struggle (defense of white civilization, fear of the falling birth rate) and then finally acknowledged that he was not opposed to homosexuals *as such*.

The conclusions to be drawn from the broadcast were that one is not born a homosexual but becomes one, that the problem of pedophilia is not specifically linked to homosexuality, and that you cannot cure homosexuality but also cannot catch it (all of Deputy Mirguet's arguments that adolescents are "easy prey for adult homosexuals, who seek them out" were dismissed). Alain Jérome did not hesitate to cite as self-evident the statistic that 7 percent of French people were homosexuals.

With *Les dossiers de l'écran*, in 1975, the first live television battle on homosexuality was won. The era was aiming for greater freedom, as demonstrated by the interest that French music took in the subject, alongside the liberalization of the visual media.

During this time, some homosexuals gathered at Café d'Edgar to see Sylvie

Joly. In *Starmania*, the rock opera by Michel Berger (1977), Fabienne Thibeault sang *Un garçon pas comme les autres* [A boy unlike the others], about Ziggy's nightly adventures: "Every night he takes me to dance / In very very gay spots / Where he has lots of friends. / Yes, I know he likes boys / I should resign myself." In 1978, in *L'abbé à l'harmonium* [The abbot with the harmonium], a delightfully hypocritical tune, Charles Trenet laid mischievous stress on the line "My God! how he pedaled, how well the abbot pedaled!"[23] A few years earlier, he had jovially sung *La flûte du maire* [The mayor's flute]: "He invited me to his shed / And, showing me his flute, / He greedily said, / 'I very much want you as my son-in-law, / But first you have to learn / To play this instrument.'"[24] Trenet loved ambiguity, as can be seen in *La folle complainte* [Fairy's lament], and equivocation, a likely element of *Le jardin extraordinaire* [The extraordinary garden], which some have said is about the Tuileries. Homosexuals also confirmed their passion for divas, from Dalida to Juliette Gréco, and, rightly or wrongly, felt an affinity for Claude François, François Valéry, Dave, and Hervé Vilard. Everyone understood the suggestiveness of *L'amour au téléphone* [Love on the phone], by Sheila, the images of love disincarnate in songs by Barbara, and, of course, Patrick Juvet's clear allusions: "Where are the women?" and "I have immoral dreams about boys intertwined."

The complicity between homosexuals and show business extended, sometimes at the risk of caricature, to drag shows. The idea was not new: in bars and in the first discos, touring "stars" of variable talent put on women's clothes and lip-synched "J'aurais voulu être un artiste" [I should have been an artist], Claude Dubois's *Le Blues du businessman* [Businessman's blues], Patachou's *Le tapin tranquille* [The quiet hustler], or Dalida's *Il venait d'avoir 18 ans* [He had just turned eighteen] and *Mourir sur scène* [Dying onstage]. Homosexuality was amused with itself: feathers, costume jewelry, and sequins. Tante Agathe, Speedy and Raphaël, Joy, and the transvestite Coccinelle, who was in a car accident with Charles Trenet, were all part of the legendary nightlife. As dinner theater, the Pédalos, with a show called *Essayez donc nos pédalos* [So try our pedal-boats], also had their hour of glory. It was fun; people laughed.

One troupe, distinguishing itself from the mass, raised the genre to the level of live theater. "In the 1970s," Denis Bernet-Rollande recalls, "I felt like homosexual militants were in a tight spot because we, with our shows, were much more effective, and we were funnier." Denis, alias "the hooker Germaine," was one of Les Mirabelles, a troupe (created in 1974) that performed drag shows. Dressed in feathers, lace, and gaudy clothes, five cheeky boys claimed to be producing art. It was Jean Digne, director of the Théâtre du Centre in Aix-en-Provence, who welcomed Les Mirabelles for their first show, called *Fauves*. In a cage—exhibited, whipped, subjugated, and sometimes nude—were Loulou Bonheur, Marie Bonheur, Nini Crepon (in a bathing cap), the hooker Germaine, and Ginette Plumetis. At night the Mirabelles paraded, exuberant and wearing makeup, on Cours Mirabeau in Aix-en-Provence, at the outdoor café Les 2G, an unacknowledged homosexual spot. "I was teaching in the literature department," Denis recalls. "I showed up in pigtails. . . . We were completely in tune with the times." The shows proliferated in that era, from the official Avignon festival to the Ranelagh Theater in Paris (1975), and were on numerous programs at art houses: *Les guerrillérose* [The lavenguerillas], *Blanchisserie blanche* [White laundry], *Passage hagard* [Wild side], *Les oiseaux de nuit* [The nightbirds]. Félix Guattari devoted an article to the Mirabelles in *Libération*. It was titled "J'ai même rencontré des travestis heureux" [I have even met happy transvestites]. This homage gave the troupe a place in the atmosphere of the time.

⤳

A Lacanian psychoanalyst commenting on a drag show in *Libération*! An unlikely story, perhaps. In reality, this example shows that the Maoist daily was now the haven for the militant battles of sexual minorities.

Jean-Paul Sartre and Serge July had introduced the newspaper on January 4, 1973: *Libération* would be what its readers made of it. *Libération, or Libé,* was situated at the crossroads of the sexual liberation movements and Maoism—which had not aged well, but which, it was said, had performed miracles in its youth. And that year, the newspaper claimed to be the daily of sexual mores.[25] But the formula that assured the success of *Libé* came only in 1975. The paper printed its columns and headings upside down, perfumed itself with incense when the pope came to France, left copyright notices off photos, stole election results (Mao: 0.3 percent), and allowed itself to be overrun by the notorious "Notes from the Compositor."

For the French press, *Libération* was an event; for homosexuals, it was a minor revolution. The name associated with *Libé*'s transformation into a media link for homosexual militancy was Jean-Luc Hennig. This grammarian, who held an *agrégation* certificate, arrived at the daily in 1974 after being suspended from the national education system because he had told his students to read the "Trois milliards de pervers" number of *Recherches* and had offered a psychoanalytic interpretation of *Little Red Riding Hood*.[26]

Glancing through the first issues of *Libé*, we discover the day-to-day homosexual life of the times: news items on the formation of militant groups, demonstrations, nudist camps, new discos, public indecency. A few article titles sum up how difficult the homosexual condition still was: "Five Truck Drivers 'Tease' a Homosexual" (April 4, 1977); "Godfather Is Homosexual—What a Nightmare, the Parents Didn't Know" (July 18, 1977); "The Tuileries: Looking for Friendship, Finding Cops and Muggers" (Dec. 23, 1977); "Hard Love: A Homo Gets Sucked Off and Mugged in a Movie Theater John" (Jan. 27, 1978); "The Nasty, Brutish Story of an Auvergnat Clan Dealing with Homosexuality: Homo Murdered by His Brother" (Feb. 24, 1978).

The paper kept an eye on all the sex scandals and covered all the trials: Christian Hennion, a former member of the FHAR, had a column called "Flagrante Delicto" in which he sought out guilty parties in the police's stead. Above all, however, it was the notorious "Chéri(e)" personal ads, initially published free of charge, that accompanied homosexual liberation.[27] Despite intensifying censorship, the ads, which began in 1975, had a rapid success. The vogue also had its limits: "More than a hundred men at the Métro Richard-Lenoir for a date from one personal ad," one bored reader commented (Jan. 14, 1978). This new form of cruising led to a charge of "public indecency and debauchery" (March 15, 1979). Beginning that year, the ads were published in *Sandwich*, the weekend supplement to *Libération*: "*Sandwich* was my idea of dark homosexuality," comments Hennig, inventor of the gay personals. At the same time, letters from readers served as an outlet: everyone spoke of his sexuality, his loneliness, his problems.

In 1976, Hennig brought Guy Hocquenghem in to work at *Libération*; Hocquenghem in turn brought in Michel Cressole, the former Gazoline from the FHAR. The two then took charge of the television listings. For example, between the names of two broadcasts they inserted this, because they had dined the previous evening at Foucault's: "Michel is not as good a cook as she thinks!"

With Alain Pacadis covering music, Serge Daney and Louella Interim on film, and the former Gazoline and transsexual Hélène Hazera on theater, the "homo" team at *Libé* was complete. Under the two pseudonyms "Bayon" and "VXZ 375," an "apologetic heterosexual" wrote such fiery columns as "How I Lost My Virginity, by VXZ 375" (Feb. 24, 1979). In "In Praise of the Male Member" (March 3, 1979), he wondered, "Do you have to scream when you 'do it'?" And he spoke frankly of his love for a rock 'n' roll reporter (Apr. 26, 1980) at the newspaper: "How I Buggered Pacadis!" In one effort, speaking as a confused observer, he even reported the homosexual cruising in the *Libération* john.

"There was a kind of coming out of the closet," explains Serge Daney, *Libé*'s film critic:

It was a lively place for people like Michel Cressole, Hélène Hazera, and Guy Hocquenghem, who fearlessly pursued their furious, provocative cultural agitation. And the newspaper went along with them. I remember that when I arrived at *Libération* Cressole and Hocquenghem had a great attitude, which consisted of looking at everything, with no concern for consistency. Their only criterion was, Like it or not, take it or leave it; you hate some announcer, you dismiss him. It was an extraordinary time at *Libération*, it was just an indescribable mess, but I was able to sell my ideas about film. . . . I have to say that the film crew I managed to put together was 80 percent homosexual.[28]

This testimonial from the "film guy" at *Libé* shows a magnanimous spirit. Daney, a Maoist, was discreet about his homosexuality and was openly accused by former FHAR Gazolines of being a "closet queen." The first time *Libé* suspended publication, in 1981, Franck Arnal, one of the most prominent French homosexual militants, claimed, "*Libération* published more information on homosexuality in eight years than the daily French press as a whole had done since 1881." This observation, valid or not, is significant.

↜

Among the contributors to *Libération* there was one who had total freedom.
That was Copi. A cartoonist, he went to the press bed before the paper was printed
and drew pictures wherever he liked: in the middle of an article, at the top of a column, or beside a photo. Copi was to the iconography of the paper what the "Notes
from the Compositor" were to the text. With Libérett' and Kang, his *Libération* heroes, Copi adopted a controversial style, provocative enough to eventually get him
ousted from the newspaper.[29]

Copi had arrived in France in 1963. He was Argentinian, and the pseudonym he
chose for himself means "little chicken" in his native language. "In 1964, I saw this
guy arriving at my office, a tiny, skinny, rather gloomy little man who looked like a
bird," Christian Bourgois, the publisher, remembers. Copi had begun to make
chalk drawings on the Paris sidewalks and was selling collages in the street, sometimes on the Pont des Arts or even at the Coupole. "He came to see me," Pierre
Bergé recalls, "with plays, drawings, handbills." Bergé sent the young man to
L'Express, thinking he might be hired there. But Françoise Giroud did not take
him. In 1965, the man she had not seen fit to hire would become the most famous
cartoonist at *Le Nouvel Observateur*, with his "seated woman" talking to a duck or a
gastropod at her feet.

In the spring of 1966, Copi appeared onstage for the first time, sitting in a
bathtub and sprinkled with talcum powder. It was *Sainte Geneviève dans sa
baignoire* [Saint Genevieve in her bathtub], directed by Jorge Lavelli, his life partner, also an Argentinian. "At that time," recalls Bourgois, "Copi was a complete
lunatic, wandering through the world. He got high a lot. He was smoking these
enormous reefers. It was before 1968. It was 'natural' homosexuality."

As a contributor to *Le Nouvel Observateur*, thanks to Claude Perdriel, or as an
artist for *Vogue* or a staff member at *Hara Kiri*, Copi gradually felt welcome
enough in France to stay: he chose exile. In October 1971, as the first militants were
finding their voice at the FHAR, Copi performed *L'homosexuel ou la difficulté de
s'exprimer* [The homosexual, or the difficulty of expressing oneself] in fishnet
stockings at the student residents' hall. At the first performance of *Loretta Strong*,
at the Gaîté-Montparnasse Theater, in 1974, he took off his canary-yellow suit, exposing a haunting thinness that made him look like the raw-boned chicken of his
cartoons. He was green all over, completely naked, and his penis was painted red.

Copi met Guy Hocquenghem during those years. Lovers for a short time, they
even lived together. "Copi was madly in love with Guy," Christian Belaygue remembers. "That's true," Hennig confirms, "Copi and Guy were very close. Copi's
world was an extravagant world of the night, of intermixing, of queens, all the
things Guy Hocquenghem also supported." "Oh! I'm a fairy!" Copi is reported to
have said, like Rimbeau in *Une saison en enfer* [*A Season in Hell*].

In an Yves Saint-Laurent evening gown, surrounded by transvestites and by
queers cruising public toilets, painted black, or drunk on zubrowka, the author of

the slogan "Perrier: it's crazy, no?" added his "almost nonexistent humor" to the battle between the sexes and to the issues of virility, transsexuality, drifting. Although not a militant, Copi probably did more to shape the homosexual imagination than the Groupes de Libération Homosexuelle [Homosexual liberation groups], or GLH, which came into being in 1974.

↪

In 1974, Jean-Paul Montanari was twenty-seven years old and living in Lyons. A half-Jewish French Algerian and a homosexual, he was, as the progeny of Genet, Pasolini, and Maurice Béjart, a child with an impressive lineage: *The Thief's Journal*, *Teorema*, and *Symphonie pour un homme seul* [Symphony for a lonely man]. As for his actual parents, he had the usual hostile relationship with his father, and he had a Jewish mother of the "Italian mama" type: he and his mother idolized each other. A classic family, verging on caricature.

In 1968, like everyone else, Montanari made revolution: "Gradually, homosexuality emerged." In 1971, he ran halfheartedly for the departmental council as a candidate of the Parti Socialiste Unifié [Unified socialist party], or PSU: "I came to homosexuality through politics, not through homosexual organizations." Very quickly, the idea of forming a Groupe de Libération Homosexuelle took shape. Was this the typical route to homosexual militancy?

In the mid-1970s, some homosexuals in Paris but especially in the provinces joined the homosexual fight. Where were they when women were fighting for freedom of abortion and, soon after, against rape? Who were the men who created the GLH chapters in most of France's large cities?

"In Lyons, we were reading *Arcadie*, we were going to the first demonstrations in Paris," says Montanari, "and sometimes to the women's demonstrations on abortion. If we were going to change society, we didn't think the homosexual struggle could be separated from other struggles."[30] With a pal, Alain Neddam, he decided to organize "meetings of queers," and the GLH was born. Soon a few men were meeting in an alternative restaurant, Les Tables Rabattues in Croix-Rousse, Lyons's "Prole Hill." Every Saturday afternoon, about ten of them met, like the early feminists, in "rap groups." "Our idea," Neddam recalls, "was to come out in the open, to seek visibility." Then, to attract attention, they staged publicity stunts, a privileged method of small organizations. "We were a group of bigmouths, totally out of control, terrorists," Neddam explains. Fairly quickly, they enjoyed some local success. There were now Michel, Pierre, Graham, René, Bruno, Bernard, and Christian. Around 1976–77 there were few commercial homosexual spots in Lyons: a discreet restaurant (Les Feuillants), some dance halls (Le Milord, La Bohème). Homosexuals in Lyons thus found a place for talking—and cruising—in the nascent group. Militants from the Lyons GLH chapter were sometimes "card-carrying members" of the PSU, of the Ligue Communiste Révolutionnaire [Communist Revolutionary League], or LCR, and sometimes of charitable organizations and organizations for human rights. They distributed "Trois milliards de pervers," which they stacked on makeshift tables, and they soon created their own review, *Interlopes*.

Twenty years later, *Interlopes* seems to offer a snapshot of the debates taking place at the time in one of France's large cities. The issue from the autumn of 1978 expressed as much concern about the growing Americanization of the homosexual movement as about the appearance of a "commercial ghetto" and the persistence of violence in cruising spots.[1] What was the point of it all? "It was not what you might think," Neddam explains today. "It was useful in itself. GLH–Lyons was a milestone. There were things about it that were too obscene, but there were also very theoretical things: it was the desire to survey the complex reality of homosexual experience in several voices, and out loud." Today, Montanari is director of Montpellier's international dance festival, created with the choreographer Dominique Bagouet, and Neddam is a theater director.

In the 1970s, Montanari and his pals at GLH–Lyons sometimes went out to Villeurbanne, fifteen minutes from Lyons, where a young producer, Patrice Chéreau, was codirector of the Théâtre National Populaire. "We met at Patrice Chéreau's plays," Montanari remembers. At the time, Chéreau was directing Marivaux's *La dispute* [The quarrel]. "*La dispute*," Chéreau explains today, "was a moment of incredible erotic fulfillment. A touch of madness wafted through the troupe in Villeurbanne, and at one point everyone wanted to sleep with everyone else. *La dispute* is a play about the mechanics of adolescence, and I had chosen to stage it in terms of polymorphous desires: men love men who love women who love women who love men." The precocious student Chéreau had directed his first plays at the Lycée Louis-le-Grand, with Jean-Pierre Vincent, and at the time supported Brechtian theater "with a dose of libertinism." Very early, in 1969, he confessed that "we intellectuals are a bit like Molière's Don Juan: we have developed a progressive morality, but we still side with the master." Some mornings he hawked *La Cause du Peuple* with Samy Frey, Sartre, and Simone de Beauvoir, and at night, in 1970, played the role of Shakespeare's King Richard, in full makeup and surrounded by cute little transvestites. Over the public address system, Maria Callas sang *Suicidio*. "I discovered my homosexuality late in life," Chéreau confides, "at an age that would be laughable today. At the time, I went through a great frenzy of sexual discovery, the discovery of men's bodies and of my ability to seduce: I had thought I would never be able to seduce anyone. Adolescence was a sad time for me, with no prospects, especially because that's when you find out that life is much more complicated than you thought. I think there was all that in my shows of the time, especially in *La dispute*."

Chéreau recalls that during his plays in Villeurbanne a homosexual group sometimes heckled the actors from the back of the theater: "The homosexual militants were annoying. I knew Guy Hocquenghem, but there was no love lost between us. Hocquenghem had a kind of self-importance, which meant I had little desire to join his fight. I don't think you can lay claim to matters of private life, of the intimate. In my shows, I was simply trying to get as close as possible to my own life. I don't know how to do otherwise, and my works are steeped in homosexuality." Needless to say, Chéreau was not a member of GLH–Lyons.

⇥

Between April 20 and 26, 1977, most of the Groupes de Libération Homosexuelle, including the Lyons group, met in Paris at the Olympic Theater for a week of films. On November 11 and 12, the GLH met at Saint-Germain-au-Mont'd'Or, near Lyons. Thus, in late 1977, there were GLH chapters nearly everywhere in France.

The FHAR had been gone since 1974. Between 1974 and 1976, sometimes later, the Groupes de Libération Homosexuelle were gradually built on its ruins. The main groups were in Marseilles, Lyons, Lille, Nantes, and Bordeaux. Were they a success? Each GLH chapter had about fifteen to thirty members at most, about fifty during demonstrations. Most militants came from modest provincial backgrounds, and their emancipation had come at the cost of a break with their original environments. People from comfortable Parisian backgrounds, by contrast, seemed less inclined to be militants: their view of homosexuality was more optimistic; social acceptance would come to them by virtue of their "birth," and they were less aware of the political issues involved in militancy.[32]

The Paris GLH chapters attracted renegades from Arcadie, who had been ousted in 1973 for being too political, and former "spontaneist leftists" from the FHAR, who had become regulars at La Buvette, a bar in the fifth arrondissement. The spot was not specifically homosexual, but the bartender was none other than Gérard Vappereau, future managing editor of *Gai Pied*. The bar was frequented by Hocquenghem and Christian Hennion as well as by such magistrates and jurists as Dominique Charvet, Jean-Pierre Michel, and Louis Joinet, future figures in the leftist government.

Not all the GLH chapters followed the same political line. There was an openly revolutionary camp, often associated with the LCR, which denounced bourgeois and patriarchal society. That was the case for the main GLH in Paris[33] and for the GLH chapters in Caen and Rennes. The latter was headed by Gilles Barbedette and his friend Jean Blancart, who were intransigent on the question of "class struggle." In Aix-en-Provence in the late 1970s, the local GLH sported the provocative nickname "Mouvance folle lesbienne" [Lesbian queen movement]. Headed by Patrick Cardon, these "queens" claimed to be as seditious as Copi and were reminiscent of the Gazolines or the eccentric Jean Lorrain.[34] "We were sick of queers; we wanted to be queens," Cardon remembers. This ideology of "follitude" rubbed off on the movement as a whole. "We all had a feminine identity," Mélanie Badaire explains.

"We used feminine pseudonyms, said 'girl,' and 'sisterhood' instead of 'brother-hood.' We were revolutionaries, subversives, hence queens."

Another camp called itself reformist and egalitarian. More distant from the far left, it sought to inform, to organize political parties, and to create a minimal plat-form of demands.[35] That was also the case for the GLH in Marseilles, where the group, created in November 1976, welcomed a large number of participants and entered into dialogue with trade unions and even with Arcadie. At the GLH in Or-léans, Jacky Fougeray refused to make common cause with the leftists.

Nevertheless, whatever their political lines, all the GLH chapters had nearly identical activities. The militants responded to mail, lonely messages sent to SOS Amitié, for example; they formed consciousness-raising groups, created journals (*Libido Hebdo* and *Agence Tasse* in Paris, *Strasse* in Rennes, *Fil rose* in Marseilles). The subversiveness of homosexuality was put forward in most of the groups: "We would go do our knitting in tough-guy bars in Canebière, with mascara on," recalls Jacques Fortin, president of the GLH in Marseilles. "We liked to do our crocheting there." In the "joyful, garrulous task" proper to the GLH, the ideas most often de-veloped were those of the FHAR: coming out, "flaming," avowal without guilt or blame. Nevertheless, some of the militants, who sometimes dogmatically champi-oned the need to come out, refrained from doing so in their private lives. "Most of the militants," Pierre Kneip explained in 1995, "continued to hide their lifestyle from their families."[36] On the basis of this collective philosophy, however, certain GLH militants went so far as to run for office in the municipal elections of March 1977 or the legislative elections of 1978, which required that they appear publicly. A campaign poster designed by Copi ("Let's play with the queers") reflects this short-lived effort, but the candidacies were usually rejected, and their share of the vote was tiny.[37]

ↄ

In the late 1970s, many artsy and experimental film houses organized small festivals of homosexual films in collaboration with the GLH: at the Cinémato-graphe in Lyons and in La Rochelle, in 1977; in Marseilles, in 1978 (*Quiet, Some-one's Talking*); in Rennes and Tours, in 1979. In Paris, the GLH's biggest success was the week devoted to homosexuality in film at the Olympic, a theater run by Frédéric Mitterrand, who had already had occasion to schedule pornographic films. Between April 20 and 26, 1977, a different theme was addressed each day: transvestites, the ghetto, latent homosexuality, pederasty, female homosexuality.[38] *Libération* devoted two pages a day to the event and published the list of all the GLH chapters—something the newspaper continued to do on a regular basis. More than 1,000 people attended "homosexual week" (5,000 film tickets were sold, according to *Libé*) and frequented the bookstore Atmosphère and the tea room L'Eléphant Rose, which adjoined the Olympic (the theater has since become L'Entrepôt).[39]

There were many women's festivals as well. In 1978, Jackie Buet and Elisabeth Tréhard, continuing a March 1974 experiment called "Musidora," created the Festival International de Films de Femmes [International women's film festival] in Sceaux. It quickly attracted a female audience. Although it had a high level of participation from homosexual women from the beginning, the festival directors wanted to avoid making it a lesbian festival. "Our point of view was obviously feminist," Buet explains today. "We decided to open the festival to female identity in general. We wanted to avoid constructing a ghetto, and for that reason we did not make it a strictly lesbian festival." The festival was so successful that in 1984 it had to move to a more suitable place (Créteil). Each year, the Créteil venue gave carte blanche to one woman: Monica Vitti, Bulle Ogier, Bernadette Lafont, Delphine Seyrig, and, more recently, Catherine Deneuve. The festival has gained momentum and has managed to present authentic films by original voices and to reconcile the irreconcilable: professionalism and militancy, films made by women and films for women, women's films and lesbian films. "It's a relic of historical feminism," Buet confirms today. Like the men's festival, the international festival has had its imitators, such as Ciné-femmes in Nantes, Ciné-nanas in Nice in 1980, Cinéna...na in Rouen in 1979, and, since 1987, Quand Les Lesbiennes Se Font du Cinéma [When lesbians make films].[40]

This proliferation of homosexual film series and women's film festivals during the 1970s, sometimes scheduled on the spur of the moment by owners of movie houses, has played a major role. Films make possible the development of a "specific culture," especially for minorities, and they supplement literature. Just as homosexuals in Arcadie drew up lists of writers in the 1950s, militants in the 1970s compiled lengthy filmographies and organized screenings.

This was not a new role for film, of course. In a shift away from a period of camouflage, when comic or transvestite homosexuality had a "Laurel and Hardy" aspect, incarnated in Michel Simon's high-society queen, homosexuals were soon being moved by the likes of Cary Grant, Gary Cooper, Clark Gable, and even the blond, romantic Pierre-Richard Willm. "To become a film lover," Serge Daney explains, "means to identify, in an entirely conscious manner, with *something else*. In the 1950s, all you had to do was see Cary Grant and James Stewart, Robert Ryan and Henry Fonda, with their graying temples, to recognize the charm there, the seduction, the desire to get yourself kidnapped."[41] A few of the great film legends, with the angelic Greta Garbo and the stunningly erotic Marlene Dietrich in the lead, were idolized by male homosexuals. For women, the Swede Zarah Leander—high priestess of Nazi film—the more masculine Katerina Edburg, and the poisonous beauty Jany Holt were also attractive.[42] Jacqueline Audry's films—*Minne l'ingénue libertine* [Minny the libertine ingenue], *Huis clos* [No exit], *Olivia*, *La garçonne* [Bachelor girl]—stayed in step with the movement.

"Things really began to fall apart after World War II," the film critic Jacques Siclier explains. "Four guys projecting ambiguous images appeared in American cinema: Marlon Brando, Paul Newman, James Dean, and Montgomery Clift. Men now appeared vulnerable, divided, seductive. Pretty soon, you could count on the fingers of one hand the Hollywood actors who had not had homosexual relationships." Such films as Kenneth Anger's *Fireworks* or Joseph Losey's *The Servant* impressed those who were paying attention, even before Italian films began to appear that maintained a special relationship with homosexuality (those of Visconti, Pasolini, and even Fellini). "Beginning in the 1970s," Siclier continues, "there was almost always one homosexual character in films." Fassbinder confirmed this tendency with *Fox and His Friends* (1974) and *The Year of Thirteen Moons* (1978). In *A Special Day* (1977), Ettore Scola depicted a homosexual character (Marcello Mastroianni) as being politically on the fringe. In France during the same period, Edouard Molinaro's *La Cage aux Folles* (1978) repeated the success of the stage play of the same name.[43] In that film, despite the appealing character of Zaza, homosexuality is depicted in a stereotypical manner; *La Cage aux Folles II* (1980) and especially *La Cage aux Folles III* (1985) sank definitively into the grotesque. At the opposite extreme, Wolfgang Peterson's *The Consequence* (1977) was a moving depiction, set against a prison backdrop, of an adult man's destructive relationship with a minor. Derek Jarman's *Sebastiane* (1976), a film in Latin about Saint Sebastian, was made in a mannered, erotic style. It features the naked bodies of young Roman soldiers, with scenes of persecution by fourth-century Christians as a pretext. Although Jarman did not have the power and influence of Pasolini, who challenged Italian society, he did attempt to provoke his English audience. In a similar movement among women, filmmakers made movies "in the feminine": Nelly Kaplan (*La fiancée du pirate, Nea*), Nina Companeez (*Faustine et le bel été* [Faustine and the lovely summer]), and Yannick Bellon (*Quelque part quelqu'un, La femme de Jean, Jamais plus toujours* [Someone somewhere; Jean's wife; Never again forever]).

↩

"In those days, we were full-time queers. We didn't do anything professionally," recalls Pablo Rouy, a former Gazoline of the FHAR and a militant in the Paris chapter of the GLH. When homosexual militants were not organizing film festivals, they were getting together to demonstrate. On May Day 1977, at the traditional unionist march, they rallied around a symbolic and contradictory slogan: TO HELL WITH THE GHETTO: HOMOS ARE IN THE STREET! On June 25 they mobilized again, this time on their own, for what would become the first French Gay Pride parade. The call went out from homosexual women in the MLF, and especially from Christine Delphy, the former Gouine Rouge, who tried to get Simone de Beauvoir and Jean-Paul Sartre involved. Instead of marching shoulder to shoulder with 400 homosexuals, they agreed to circulate a petition. What set the autonomous mobilization off came, as always, from the United States, in the person of Anita Bryant. The former Miss America—now mother of a large family, and a

singing spokesperson for a brand of orange juice—had just launched, Bible in
hand, an antihomosexual crusade in America.[44]

Several days earlier, a few homosexual militants, standing beside Michel Foucault and André Glucksman, had spontaneously gathered during an official trip to
Paris by Leonid Brezhnev, president of the U.S.S.R., to demand that the Russian
filmmaker Sergei Paradjanov be set free.[45] That day the militants shouted, "Free the
homos, East and West!" In its way, this first mobilization against a "socialist" regime that repressed homosexuality was an indication of homosexual militants'
disenchantment with leftism.

In the mid-1970s, most militants were sympathetic to Maoism, to Fidel Castro's brand of communism, and often to Marxism. When Aleksandr Solzhenitsyn
was expelled from the U.S.S.R. in 1974 and *The Gulag Archipelago* was published,
criticism of the Communist regime—attacking both its philosophical pedigree
(Marxism) and its latest incarnation (Trotskyism)—began to stick. The militants
of sexual liberation, orphaned by Stalinism in May 1968, had forestalled disaster by
appealing to Maoism, not understanding that it was all a mask: Maoism was simply
an anti-Soviet Stalinism.

In 1975, Jean Pasqualini, with *Prisonnier de Mao* [Mao's prisoner], an account
of seven years in a work camp, delivered a second blow: not all the camps were in
the Soviet Union; they also existed in the China of the Cultural Revolution. In
particular, Pasqualini raised the case of a homosexual prisoner who was made an
example of by being executed. Maoist homosexuals blanched, Guy Hocquenghem
foremost among them. The enchantment with Chairman Mao, who was popular
in the West because he set young people against the party apparatus, evaporated.
Only Fidel Castro, whose Marxism had the charm of the tropics, still remained.
Then came the final blow. Information reached France about Fidel Castro's persecution of homosexuals in Cuba. Between 1965 and 1969 Castro had opened "reedu-
cation camps" to "treat" homosexuals: photographs of naked men were projected
on a screen as the "patients" were given electric shocks. Leftist militants were hor-
rified. A few years later, Reinaldo Arenas, an exiled Cuban homosexual, described
these persecutions in his autobiography.[46]

This series of disillusionments, which required constant damage control, gives
an indication of the new militants' lack of political role models. And these revelations did not affect the homosexual movement alone. Most of the social movements, including feminism, felt the repercussions. Feminists believed they had
found a women's paradise in the U.S.S.R. (Simone de Beauvoir), in China (Julia
Kristeva), and even in Cuba (Gisèle Halimi).[47] The sense of well-being among progressive homosexuals was only the illusion of children spoiled by capitalism. Faced
with the brutal reality of totalitarianism, they had to rethink their plan. The prospect of a victory by the Union de la Gauche [Leftist union], beginning with the
municipal election of 1977, favored more pragmatic reflection. Homosexual discourse, losing its revolutionary veneer, struggled toward an organized and strictly

antirepressive militancy of protest: it became "strategically political."[48] But you don't switch ideologies with a mere patchup job. This evolution took several years to complete, and so the battles of the late 1970s still had the revolutionary ambiguity of the early days, but now at the cost of unforgivable concessions, and they were still contaminated by subversiveness and infatuated with controversy. Total haziness prevailed.

Some still brandished slogans like "Worker, under your overalls, you too are a transvestite" or supported a kind of "Gay is beautiful" ethos inspired by the "Black is beautiful" of militant black Americans. Others, still under the charm of an apocryphal Marxism, anachronistically fought a final battle against the "commercial ghetto"—business establishments saddled, naturally, with the "bourgeois" label. Finally, some homosexual men spewed quotations from Chairman Mao at lesbians, thus showing that their divorce from women, unlike their divorce from totalitarian China, had become final.

↪

In the late 1970s, the criminalization of rape was at the center of debate. But debate was not engaged in with the most serious intentions; it seems that the skirmishes between male homosexuals and feminists did not meet the measure of the issues. Women of the MLF explained that they did not want to be whistled at by (heterosexual) men in the street. Homosexual men replied that this was all they dreamed about, and this was why they went to Morocco. In *Libération*, Guy Hocquenghem attacked "mothers" who protected their children too much, keeping pedophiles from doing what they liked undisturbed. Some homosexual men fought openly for pedophilia, whereas others defended the right of same-sex couples to marry. All of this baffled feminists, who still wanted to destroy marriage in any form.[49]

These differences in interpretation increased with the issue of rape. Journalists "on the left" noted, ironically, that "a little penetration is not Dachau, after all."[50] On rape, Hocquenghem himself proved to be a radical, recovering the verve he had displayed upon Pasolini's death. "Women have never had the secret complicity with their attackers that queers have with the worst of the thugs who beat them up," he commented. When the feminist movement sued a rapist who happened to be an Arab student, Hocquenghem called the trial "odious," and added, in the same article:

Vengeance, it seems, is served up by raped women. They are ruthless. They become Amazons, they steel themselves against any vain male ruse of humanism! . . . I can't get it into my head how a slight wound, inflicted with the blunt instrument called a prick, could be more serious than painful burns or dangerous assaults.[51]

Hocquenghem also reminded readers that women's recourse to the justice system raised an ethical problem for leftists, and he denounced the tactical alliance between the feminists and the virtue leagues: "You do not have the right to resort to bourgeois justice."[52] Echoing Hocquenghem's position, an editorial in the newspaper *Agence.Tasse*, which was associated with the GLH, also blamed women for wanting to criminalize rape:

The issue of rape has no specificity. To want to privilege rape over other kinds of assault is to suggest that it is not only violence but also profanation, and thus that a woman's body is a sacred vessel. In short, it relies on Judeo-Christian values that are the exact opposite of revolutionary struggle. ... Queers are bad citizens; that is an opportunity for them. And women want to ruin that? ... The criminal courts seem to be a rather poor solution for people who claim to be revolutionary.[53]

Foucault's initial position on the matter was vague and betrayed a surprising ignorance of feminist analyses.[54] Later, he eliminated all ambiguity in an American interview:

As for the political objectives of the homosexual movement ... , we must first consider the question of freedom of sexual choice. I say freedom of sexual choice, and not freedom of the sexual act, because certain acts, such as rape, should not be allowed, whether between a man and a woman or between two men. I do not believe our objective ought to be a kind of absolute freedom, total freedom of action in the realm of sexuality.[55]

On the issue of rape, women were rightly intransigent. Thus Cathy Bernheim, a former Gouine Rouge, immediately replied to Hocquenghem and criticized the "false brothers" who took them for "female hostages":

They write, they talk: liberation, they know what that is. ... They write it, digest it, and deal with it among other men, their brothers, with the same contempt for women and at that price. ... As for us, we women who have been called lesbians, we women who have been called mothers, we women who have been called whores, we women who have been called women, and because of it sold, raped, mortified, we know very well that we are somewhere else. We've gone, and we've left them no forwarding address.[56]

During this period, militant homosexual women, with the exception of a few who went to the GLH, usually met at the Groupe de Lesbiennes Féministes [Group of feminist lesbians], or GLF, a first, short-lived, effort to find homosexual expression on the margins of the women's movement and away from the homosexual men's movement: a "chosen ghetto."[57]

The sexual liberation movements had lost their unity. In many respects, that unity was only tactical to begin with and did not rest on a solid foundation: the movement had established alliances and formed pacts that were based on the theory of the so-called main enemy, at the cost of compromise. Revolution came at this price, but it was only a strategic illusion. Dialogue was difficult between homosexual women and heterosexual feminists, and between pedophiles and militant homosexuals. Generational conflicts intensified, and contradictions were made into a system.

One man remained outside these entanglements, apart from revolutionary movements and utopian ideas. Independent but not isolated, he may have been the only one who could have led militant homosexuality out of its impasse. But Jean-Louis Bory had decided to check out.

JEAN-LOUIS BORY: THE RIGHT TO INDIFFERENCE

The solitary life path of Jean-Louis Bory, who fought tirelessly to banalize homosexuality, can serve as a guiding thread in summing up the decade that Guy Hocquenghem had ushered in. The dialogue between Hocquenghem and Bory, who stood at opposite ends of the decade, is among the most interesting ones.

In 1977, the two men collaborated on and published an essay on homosexuality, *Comment nous appelez-vous déjà?* [What do you call us again?], but their respective experiences of homosexual life, although sometimes intersecting, bore no resemblance. True joint authorship of this work thus proved impossible, and the project became the mere juxtaposition of two irreconcilable points of view.

The differences that arose between Bory and Hocquenghem on the issue of homosexuality were played out by other minorities as well. Among immigrants and Jews, the same cleavages existed between a revolutionary camp, exemplified among homosexuals by Hocquenghem, and a reformist camp, whose objective was equality and integration, and for which Bory was probably the most illustrious homosexual representative. The two authors cannot be reduced to this schematic conflict, but most militants situated themselves between these two positions.

Jacques Fortin, president of GLH–Marseilles, understood his platform as a reformist one: "At the GLH in Marseilles, we defended Bory against Hocquenghem." Albert Rosse, a homosexual militant in the PSU, makes the same observation: "We at the PSU were very influenced by Bory, primarily because he was a socialist but also because he placed his battle within a political perspective and did not isolate himself within the militant homosexual movement." Montanari (GLH–Lyons) is more divided, explaining that Bory's role "was at least as important as Hocquenghem's, especially if you lived in the provinces." The more radical militants naturally felt closer to Hocquenghem.

Bory, the representative of a faction of the intellectual left that had existed before May 1981, was a former member of the Maquis who fought for the Resistance in the Orléans forest and was one of the signers of the Appeal of the 121 (for that reason, he was dismissed by the national education system), as well as a "'68er" from the Cannes festival. Above all, however, he was a writer. He won the Prix Goncourt when he was still very young, at twenty-six, for *Mon village à l'heure allemande* [My village on German time] (1945) and then published a series of novels in which the latent homosexuality of his characters became increasingly clear and, in the end, all-encompassing.[58]

After his masterpiece, *La peau des zèbres* [The zebra skin] (1969), a roman à clef about homosexuality, Bory published an unambiguous confessional autobiography, *Ma moitié d'orange* [My half an orange] (1973). In it he developed two opposing themes that sum up his position on the subject fairly well. First, there was a wrenching and repeated cry: "I'm hurting." Bory had an obsession: to find his soulmate, whom he called his "half an orange." But this quest included "emotional collapse," since he believed it was more difficult to establish a lasting relationship with a man than with a woman. Thus, drawing inspiration from Simone de Beauvoir, he was able to conclude, "One is not born a homosexual. One becomes one. There is no innate queerness."[59]

Bory also defended a more optimistic, contradictory thesis: the banality of homosexuality, its relative simplicity. He evaluated the friendships often associated with it: "I make friends the way I make love," he said, in an expression that would not have displeased Foucault.[60] He remembered his mother, who had discovered his homosexuality through a letter, "as in a bad novel," and he reported his father's words when Bory introduced his first lover: "Whoever or whatever you are, don't be scared. If you don't hurt anyone, you have nothing to be ashamed of. Take a hard look at yourself, that's the main thing. It may well be that the choice you make, based on what you know you are, will make life difficult for you. Good luck!"[61] Bory's entire future battle on behalf of homosexuals, who sported the pretty names "zebras" or "horses in pajamas," was already present: the desire to take responsibility for himself, without shame but also without aggression. "No shame, no recruiting" was Bory's slogan.[62]

Bory's considerable influence can be measured by the new militancy whose representative he would become, almost in spite of himself. Bory forged a path between a revolutionary homosexuality strewn with leftist logorrhea—from the FHAR to the GLH—and the respectable, slightly apologetic homophilia of "Arcadian choirboys monitored by the Reverend André Baudry." Beginning in 1954, Bory was a member of Arcadie, where, along with Pierre Hahn and Daniel Guérin, he represented the leftist sensibility.[63]

René Schérer, a close friend of Guy Hocquenghem, sums up the issues under debate: "Jean-Louis Bory was living within the logic of Arcadie and was fighting for integration and tolerance, whereas Guy always insisted on marginality: he wanted integration with exceptionality, integration within marginality." Therefore, Bory mistrusted the radical visibility championed by Hocquenghem and his cult of marginality; he favored a militancy on behalf of banalization: "There is a homosexual reality, and I am here because homosexuality exists," he said in 1975 on *Les dossiers de l'écran*. "I do not confess my homosexuality, because I am not ashamed of it. I do not proclaim my homosexuality, because I am not proud of it. I say I am homosexual because it is so."

Bory thus claimed homosexuals' "right to indifference," an expression that he seems to have been the first to apply to the cause, and which he continued to embrace. Bory battled obsessively for this cause throughout the 1970s. "I do not plead, I inform," he repeated constantly. On March 18, 1970, before the FHAR had come into being, he had already participated in the first mass-audience radio broadcast on this theme (Michel Lancelot's *Campus*, on Europe 1). That day, in the company of Baudry, he rejected any idea of a "homosexual movement" but defended the fight for freedom and declared that he was obviously a homosexual and a "model citizen," and that the two were necessarily linked in his mind. In April 1973, in the Swiss review *Accord*, he published a text titled "Oui, je suis homosexuel" [Yes, I am a homosexual]. He talked about himself more openly in this manifesto, aptly explaining, "Like the riding horse that stumbles from fear before an obstacle, I did a little dance at the edge of the river. And then I jumped in. Never mind the splash." In this text he defined the objectives of the battle he intended to wage: "I cannot continue to wave the gleaming red banners of happiness and freedom if I refrain from writing about what brings me happiness and about why I am demanding freedom." Situated between Arcadie and the FHAR, but also between the right and the far left, Bory rejected both scandal and the watered-down label "homophile," since "in our society, scandal often goes hand in hand with amused contempt."

Bory became, in his own words, "queerness on the left." With a "look"— turtleneck and corduroy pants—that made him immediately recognizable, he was a film critic for *Le Nouvel Observateur* throughout the 1970s. He was one of the French critics who discovered Fassbinder, Forman, and Woody Allen. Above all, he was the key personality on *Le masque et la plume* [The mask and the pen], a broadcast from Paris Inter (later France Inter). As "the horrid leftist," he went head to head with the right-wing Georges Charensol in all the oratorical (and still memorable) jousting matches. During these mock-heroic quarrels, he gave his traditional greeting—"Bonjour, mes cocos jolis" [Hello, my pretty little darlings]—and then made homosexuality one of his favorite topics for jokes, thus securing a national audience for the issue.[64] As the literary critic Angelo Rinaldi recalls with a laugh, "On Sunday afternoons, in order not to miss his duel with Georges Charensol, we would not linger in bed—not necessarily our own bed— even when much remained to be done there."[65]

In broadcasts and in novels, Bory claimed above all to be the spokesperson for a silent majority and spoke in the name of all who could not identify with the militant movement. He thus directed his battle toward the "homosexuality of the poor," in his words, concerning himself with those who were "rejected by their families, scorned by their neighbors, fired by their employers, mistrusted or even expelled from their unions, and manhandled by the police." He spoke for all those who did not have the privilege (or the excuse) of an education. On *Les dossiers de l'écran* he read a letter from a young homosexual living in a small village and explained what homosexuality was like for a worker or a mason. He also evoked the memory of Patrick, a twenty-year-old man who had committed suicide because he was homosexual. Bory read an excerpt of a letter from the boy's mother. "As far as I am able," she wrote, "with the meager means at my disposal, I am trying to prevent too many more Patricks."

Busy with this constant battle, Bory did not join the homosexual militants, either those in the FHAR or those in the GLH. He criticized the activists for sometimes committing "blunders" or engaging in counterproductive actions. He added, "That's their problem," even though he understood and, on the whole, approved of the militants' actions. "It's a question of generations," he concluded magnanimously.[66] Bory's battle was an individual one.

Bory—constantly approached, questioned about the topic on Jacques Chancel's *Radioscopie* broadcast, thrown into the ring with an intolerant psychiatrist, called upon to justify some current event, attacked on all sides—understood that he had become (in the words reported by his friend Jean-Louis Curtis) "the nincompoop of militant homosexuality." "Why," his friend Angelo Rinaldi wondered, "did he need to set off on that crusade, when public opinion—without his help, and with the assistance of May '68—would have evolved in the direction of tolerance anyway?"[67]

As for his own battle on behalf of homosexuality, Bory confided to a journalist in April 1978, "I have had enough. ... Leave me alone. I paid with my person. I went to the front and came back covered with wounds and decorations."[68]

"It's true, applause sounds like falling rain," Bory wrote at the end of *L'odeur en herbe* [The budding aroma]. He was worn out by his exhibitionism, and when a good-looking young man came into his life in 1977, it was the death blow. The boy wanted to be an actor; Bory fell in love. Believing he had found the "rare bird" he was seeking, Bory set out to realize Pygmalion's dream: he wanted to take this "hustler who wasn't even his type" (as Rinaldi would write) and make him famous. But the boy had no talent, and his relationship with Bory was unhealthy. Like Oscar Wilde, Bory might have written:

I blame myself for allowing an unintellectual friendship, a friendship whose primary aim was not the creation and contemplation of beautiful things, entirely to dominate my life. ... The gods are strange. It is not our vices only they make instruments to scourge us. They bring us to ruin through what in us is good, gentle, humane, loving. But for my pity and affection for you and yours, I would not now be weeping in this terrible place.[69]

The young man's reply to Bory might have been the following: "Is it the fault of the river that it is beautiful and that someone jumps into it and drowns?"

Bory—a wounded man caught in the cogs of the psychiatric machine, mourning the recent loss of his mother, abandoned by Paris's "in crowd" for whom "the clown was no longer funny"—committed suicide on June 11, 1979.[70]

In the chorus of eulogies delivered by the press on June 13 for this symbol of sorrowful gayness, one false note may illustrate the path that remained to be traveled. Renaud Matignon, a journalist at *Le Figaro*, wrote:

Along the way, [Bory] fought a bit in the Resistance. He was probably not responsible for the "Reich" division's retreat. But he discovered fine virile chests and drew one conclusion: he was homosexual. He would become the Pancho Villa of ephebes. . . . [Bory] perverted a whole pseudointelligentsia, manufacturing . . . leftists of buffoonery . . . buffoons of leftism, recruiting little boys. . . . He petitioned, stamped his feet, grinned.

Rinaldi asked that the publication of *L'Express* be delayed so that he could reply to this insult, and *Le Canard Enchaîné* reacted forcefully to Matignon: "Some little guy got himself a corner of the office and a few sheets of toilet paper to soak up a few lousy, fascist lines about Jean-Louis Bory. . . . This little guy wouldn't have found work at *Je Suis Partout*: at least Nazi collaborators required their snitches to have talent. All this little faker found was *Le Figaro*, which left him free to blubber in the company of the Überidiot, Michel Droit."[71]

⤳

With Bory's death, the radical years ended: homosexuality had been a moral problem; it was now a social problem. But the man who had fought so hard for the banalization of homosexuality did not live to see his work bear fruit. History, however, would soon prove him right. Guy Hocquenghem was marginalized, and the radicalism of the GLH, still provocative, disappeared into a smaller common denominator: antidiscrimination. With socialization under way, the homosexual of the early 1980s was Bory's progeny.

In Dominique Fernandez's *L'étoile rose* [The pink star], which some have said is a fictionalized version of the conflict between Hocquenghem and Bory, the older hero, contemplating his young lover making revolution, declares, "As he was talking to me, I was thinking about everything that would have been different in my life, in my character, if at eighteen I had realized I was a gay man rather than a pariah." The primary change brought about in the 1970s was that one was now "gay" rather than having "tendencies" or being a "homophile" or even a "homosexual." Rarely has the evolution of a minority been so well summed up in a single word, a word Bory chose not to use.

From the first getups of the FHAR Gazolines in 1971, amid stress and Situationism, to the last gasp of censorship and vice squad surveillance, from the ideologue Hocquenghem's "queers" to the "zebras" depicted by Bory—the *other* militant of "the cause," who ushered in the end of the revolutionary repertoire and the 1970s—a first evolution was complete. Homosexuals had become gays.

PART II

The Era of Socialization (1979–84)

"We Must Be Relentlessly Gay"

> To be gay, I believe, is not to identify with the homosexual's psychological traits
> and visible masks, but rather to seek to define and develop a way of life.
>
> — Michel Foucault, "De l'amitié comme mode de vie"

"To be gay, and for kicks. Not to sink back into the wasp's nest of the ghetto."[1] With these words on its cover, an odd monthly, *Gai Pied,* made its debut in kiosks in April 1979. "The 1980s will be active, technological, and gay," prophesied *Actuel* in its new slogan. The term "gay" set the tone.

"Our purpose," declared the editorial in *Gai Pied*'s first issue, "is to give gays, the homosexuals of today, a place to express themselves." By putting together a staff of young journalists and surrounding them with well-known names, *Gai Pied* intended to become the most prominent "homosexual showcase." Some of the leading figures of the sexual liberation movements were on display: Guy Hocquenghem and Pierre Hahn (FHAR), the writer Dominique Fernandez, the philosopher Jean-Paul Aron, the cartoonist Copi, the photographers Jean-Daniel Cadinot and Patrick Sarfati, and, with issue 13, Jean-Paul Sartre.[2] The small staff was enlivened by "the seven dwarfs," as Hocquenghem nicknamed them because of their small stature. Among them were Gérard Vappereau, Yves Charfe, and Jean Le Bitoux, editorial director.

The life path of Jean Le Bitoux, a substitute music teacher and son of an admiral, sums up the spirit of the staff and the nature of the project. A former member of the FHAR, Le Bitoux was one of the directors of the Groupe de Libération Homosexuelle in Paris, which he had represented as an ill-fated candidate in the 1978 legislative elections. The staff of the first truly homosexual periodical in France formed around GLH–Paris after a time of reflection in communities—of "brief, hoary, provincial ideologies" (Hocquenghem). Although *Gai Pied* still had a certain militant look (it was printed on the Ligue Communiste Révolutionnaire presses and distributed at the GLH meetings), it became a true business enterprise. In opposition to the militant scene, *Gai Pied* was launched as a limited corporation and not as an association. It was sold in kiosks and took many of its ideas from its predecessor *Libération*. "We did not want to be the *Humanité* of queers or the *Obs* of homosexuals," Vappereau recalls today, "but rather the *Libération* of gays."

Thus the "Notes from the Compositor" made their appearance in *Gai Pied*, as they had done in *Libé*; personal ads, a kind of "novel in fragments" in Roland Barthes's words, were published in the "Rézo" supplement. They resembled the "Chéri(e)" personals so closely that one set could easily be mistaken for the other.

Gai Pied drew inspiration from its predecessor, and several contributors were shared by the two newspapers. It claimed to be practical and playful: it published legal notes, health reports, a "report on the psyche"—a space for parapsychoanalytic confession—and a media survey that tracked "homophobia." Although erotica was not its specialty, *Gai Pied* dared the occasional erotic photo, a niche market that would be further exploited by other publications (*Hommes, Off, Jean-Paul, Man, GI,* and *Honcho*).

Its playful and sensual side, more than its militant aspect, ensured the paper's success. From the beginning, the classified ads and the parties organized at Le Bataclan made *Gai Pied* self-supporting. Homosexuality was becoming fashionable: *Gai Pied* intended to adapt to the new market.

The establishment of a forum that was culturalist in nature (one, that is, that embraced the notion of a minority culture) also played a part in the project's initial logic. Hugo Marsan, a former literature professor, emerged in 1980 as the cultural critic for the paper, alongside the writers Gilles Barbedette and René de Ceccatty. He increased the number of pages devoted to literature and created an erudite column, "Gai savoir" [Gay science].[3] In 1982, the writer Renaud Camus kept an "Achrian journal," Tony Duvert regularly signed articles (including "crossword puzzles"), Frédéric Loiseau (the pseudonym of Frédéric Edelmann, journalist for *Le Monde*) had a monthly column called "Night Solo," Alain-Emmanuel Dreuilhe was a New York correspondent, and Yves Navarre and the anarchist Daniel Guérin contributed for a brief period of time. "Nearly everyone was a contributor to *Gai Pied*," Marsan concludes.

On the cover of the first issue, surprised readers found an article titled "Un plaisir si simple" [Such a simple pleasure]. Its author was not just another militant. This curious article on homosexuality and suicide was signed by Michel Foucault.

Among other legends, one tenacious rumor attributes the paternity of the name *Gai Pied* to Michel Foucault.[4] The philosopher certainly welcomed the cofounder Le Bitoux into his kitchen and is said to have been enthusiastic about the title, preferring it to other suggestions, such as *Outrage* and *Guet-apens* [Gayambush]. Nevertheless, it seems that the name *Gai Pied* was discovered earlier, probably as an allusion to Jean-Louis Bory's *Le pied* [The foot]. Foucault may have liked the expression because of its irony and its play on *guêpier*. Though not necessarily valid, the idea that one of the most famous philosophers invented the title of what was to become the first French homosexual weekly is certainly appealing—and Foucault never contradicted the anecdote.

In any case, the philosopher liked the word "gay."[5] He defended the use of the term on several occasions, preferring it to "homosexual" because it contributed to "a positive assessment of a consciousness in which affection, love, desire, and sexual relations are valorized."[6] For Foucault, "homosexual," a term of medical and legal origin, reduced individuals to their sexual behavior, whereas "gay" reflected a way of life and a self-definition. Hence the slogan "We must be relentlessly gay." As Foucault explained, "Sexual choices also ought to create ways of life":

> To be gay means that these choices involve every aspect of life; in a certain sense, it means rejecting the usual ways of life. It means making sexual choice the impetus for a change in one's mode of existence . . . I say, we must use our sexuality to discover, to invent new relations. To be gay is to be ever-changing. Let me add that we must not be homosexual; we must be relentlessly gay.[7]

The term was probably only a lesser evil for Foucault, but it seemed less "fixed" to him and not inevitably associated with an "identity."

From its beginnings, Foucault's notoriety assured *Gai Pied*, if not a certificate of respectability, then at least the protection needed in the later Giscard years. In March 1977 and March 1978, Michel Poniatowski, minister of the interior, had prohibited several erotic publications (*Lui*, for example) from being sold to minors. This ban also covered the very few homosexual publications already in existence (*Man, Dialogue homophile, Andros, Gaie Presse*).

Foucault's presence among the "founders" of *Gai Pied* was not accidental, given the philosopher's life history. And in 1979 he was at the height of his glory.

⤶

As much a man of action as a man of reflection, Foucault participated in most of the battles of the 1970s: he stood beside Sartre, founding *Libération* and aiding the boat people; walked with Genet at the head of immigrant marches; stood by André Glucksmann in support of the filmmaker Paradjanov; and demonstrated at the gates of prisons with the Groupe d'Information sur les Prisons.

Tormented by homosexuality in his adolescence, Foucault seems to have had difficulty coming to terms with it even as a young adult. "In 1950, at twenty-four years of age, Foucault was torn apart by homosexuality," his friend Paul Veyne recalls today. "'I'm a hysteric,' he told me. He spoke of the profound comedy of homosexuality." According to Didier Eribon, one of his biographers, "His wish to commit suicide, his exile in Sweden, and his break with the French Communist Party were so many events linked to his homosexuality."[8] In October 1960 Foucault met Daniel Defert, with whom he would have a relationship from 1963 until his death. Gradually, he dealt with his desire with greater serenity. "By the 1970s, he had completely accepted his homosexuality," Veyne recalls. "'I'm a good old queer without any problems,' he told me. He considered homosexuality harmless, normal in a certain way." Later, when he participated in launching *Gai Pied*, Foucault agreed to give interviews on the issue, especially in the United States, where he had gone to teach.[9] He frequented homosexual neighborhoods in San Francisco at the time and, in that California paradise, became interested in sadomasochistic establishments: "laboratories for sexual experimentation," in his own words. He found them captivating.

Yet Foucault was not a gay militant, for several reasons—first of all, because he was critical of any "homosexual identity." Although Foucault was particularly interested in categories of "the excluded" (the madman, the delinquent, the pervert, the homosexual), his concern was to fight against power as much as to dismantle the logic that drew a line between the "normal" and the pathological. In the end, his objective of "inventing" individuals was more important than that of leading an insurrection against the forces of power.

And where was power in the case of homosexuality? In identity. For Foucault, sexual acts did not lie at the foundation of a "nature" that produced a fixed identity. Such essentialism implied the alternative between "repression" and "liberation." He was intent on deconstructing the two terms of that alternative. But the philosophy of the French gay liberation movement (FHAR, GLH) was based on a problematic of liberation. This partly explains Foucault's absence from the general meetings of the FHAR in 1971 (at the time, he himself was founding the Groupe d'Information sur les Prisons).[10]

Foucault's presence in the first issue of *Gai Pied* was thus paradoxical in more than one respect. A new context for demanding rights? An evolution in his thinking? A new strategy? Or simply a fondness for the *Gai Pied* employee who had solicited the article? In any case, the philosopher contributed a piece to the first issue of an "identity-based" homosexual monthly (though he did not commit himself to any great extent).[11] Foucault quickly became critical of the paper, which he chided for conveying a single image of homosexuality and perpetuating a youth cult. "What I might ask of your newspaper," he responded in an interview with *Gai Pied* in 1981, "is that, when I read it, I should not have to consider the question of my age. But reading it forces me to consider that question; and I have not been very happy with the way I've been led to do so. Quite simply, I had no place in it."[12] In another interview he said, "I am sure that, as a man of fifty, when I read certain publications by and for gays, I have the impression they are not addressing me, that in some sense my place is not there."[13]

Apart from this "incident" in the philosopher's nonmilitant history, does Foucault's relative proximity to the Arcadie movement allow us to understand the path he chose? In May 1979, he participated in Arcadie's twenty-fifth-anniversary congress at the Palais des Congrès at Porte Maillot. He was accompanied by his friend Paul Veyne and by the writers Robert Merle and Jean-Paul Aron.[14] Invited by André Baudry to speak at the opening of the debates, he apologized that he had not joined Arcadie, adding that he had been "wrong not to do so." Why did Foucault respond to the invitation, when for ten years Baudry's movement had been judged outdated and conservative?

Foucault's appearance that day seems to have been the result of relations that he had maintained with certain "Arcadians" and sometimes with Baudry himself.[15]

On one or two occasions, the philosopher may even have participated in the homophile movement, which he learned of in 1955. "Michel Foucault was always extremely affable toward me," Baudry explains today, clearly seeking assurance. "He never criticized me in any way." In 1982, in an article for *Libération*, Foucault felt called upon to comment on the dissolution of Arcadie. In that text, which is surprisingly gentle toward the homophile movement, Foucault notes that Arcadie wanted to have homosexuality accepted "by the established values" and that it would therefore be "naive, perhaps, to criticize it for its conservatism," since, on reflection, this was "an infinitely more difficult, infinitely more queer enterprise than wanting to set up spaces of freedom outside institutions."[16]

Does Foucault's interest in Arcadie reveal an ideological affinity between the philosopher and the "Baudry method" [see chapter 3]? We need only read Foucault's North American interviews on homosexuality to be disabused of this notion. In those interviews, in fact, the philosopher defended a certain right to "visibility," spoke of "gay culture," and seemed to have forgotten all concern for discretion. In 1982, Foucault even participated in a Gay Pride parade in Toronto.[17]

Foucault's thinking on homosexuality remained complex in many respects, and the philosopher probably would have claimed the right to contradiction. For one thing, context and chronology shed light on the philosopher's inconsistent positions; he defended Arcadie in 1982, for example, both because he found the belated attacks of gay militants unfair and because he recognized what Arcadie had been in 1955. In spite of the uncertainties and the different eras, several of his positions do seem to have been consistent. First, the philosopher was always critical of the logic of "liberation," whose theoretical and practical effects he called into doubt. Second, he rejected the logic of confession, which he never valorized. He demonstrated how it functioned in concert with the very mechanisms of repression and shame that it claimed to be fighting. Finally, Foucault mistrusted any effort to translate sexual conduct of any kind into an "identity."

Beyond the consistency of these three essential points, it would be possible to give a double reading of Foucault's writings. Some readers, on the basis of the philosopher's North American interviews, might argue that he supported a certain radicalism, and that he was tempted to take a multiculturalist approach, even to support a gay culture.

Others might find that Foucault's writing—and particularly *La volonté de savoir* [*The History of Sexuality*, vol. 1]—thumbs its nose at any form of revolutionary militancy operating through subversion (in the style of Guy Hocquenghem) or identity politics, and thus at militant homosexual movements. In this sense, beyond the philosopher's uncertainties and, probably, his own internal conflicts, Foucault may well have had a philosophy of homosexuality, a philosophy that privileged the emancipation of individuals through the rejection of norms and the liquidation of identities.

Homosexual militants, who were more influenced by Gilles Deleuze's philosophy, discovered Foucault only later, after *The History of Sexuality*. Because they were themselves rethinking their platform at the time, they turned their attention to his discourse and to a body of work that found them lacking. Were they ready for change? In the late 1970s, Foucault became the center of debates and of appropriation, a kind of "statue of the Commendatore" for the French homosexual movement. Today, fifteen years after his death, he still haunts that movement.

AN ERA OF SCISSION FOR FEMINISTS

A woman dressed by Yves Saint-Laurent, a large white silk shawl covering her hair, surrounded by "bizarre magistrates in green tails," became a legend on January 22, 1981. The designer, *féminisme oblige,* had set aside his severe straight skirts and tight gold lamé pants. There were no opulent jewels from Loulou de La Falaise, nor was there the traditional sword—a necessary breach of protocol. Marguerite Yourcenar had just become the first woman named to the Académie Française.

In the speech she gave under the Coupole, carried live on FR3 and in the presence of Giscard d'Estaing, president of the republic (two exceptional situations), Madame Yourcenar explained that she was entering the academy "surrounded, accompanied, by an invisible band of women who ought to have received this honor much earlier, so that I am tempted to step back and let their shadows pass through." She then spoke of Colette and George Sand, "an admirably womanly woman" who "caused a scandal because of the turbulence in her life" and who, "as a person, even more than as a writer, was ahead of her time."

Although Grace Frick, with whom Madame Yourcenar lived for forty years, had recently died, and although the novelist was beginning a romantic relationship with a man who was himself gay, no one had any doubt—and especially not the members of the academy, hungry for gossip—that Yourcenar was homosexual. Because she had the shortcoming of being a homosexual and, moreover, a woman, it had been particularly difficult for her to be named to the academy. "The 'company,'" explains her biographer, Josyane Savigneau, "never welcomed women. Nevertheless, for certain members of the academy, Yourcenar had the advantage of that notorious 'male talent' so long attributed to her. But for the majority, this supposed 'virility' was a major obstacle: she was not 'woman enough,' to be precise. They hinted at what they thought they knew about her sexual preferences."[18] Albert Cohen, for example, had not hidden his view that she could not be a good writer because she was "so fat and ugly."

It may have been the tenacity of Jean d'Ormesson, the nod from Alain Peyrefitte, minister of justice, or perhaps the encouragement of President Giscard d'Estaing that got her named. But that honor was above all the result of a pathetic and hypothetical bargain: Yourcenar was named on the condition that Michel Droit, De Gaulle's sidekick—but a writer who had long since given up literature—

be named on the same day to the other free chair. Paying no attention to such dealings, Yourcenar, who had never in her life taken any interest in honors or even, really, in men, refused to bow to the ritual of attending the academy's meetings at 23, Quai Conti [the Institut de France]. She said of Quai Conti, "I went there once. They're overgrown kids who play together on Thursdays. I don't think a woman has much to do there." The malice of the academy's members toward this woman was tenacious: not one of them attended the funeral service held in her memory on January 16, 1988.

Her writings are still the most important thing, as Savigneau explains:

Male homosexuality fascinated Marguerite Yourcenar to the point where it became an ever-present subject in her books, but this was not a way of dissimulating her love for women while at the same time speaking of it, as she has often been wrongly accused of doing. Nor was it because she secretly wanted to be a man—men will never be convinced of that, but what does it matter? It was because male homosexuality was *in the weave* of her life.

Yourcenar's writings seem to center on this theme, from *Alexis* (1929), a long letter written by a homosexual man to the wife he is leaving, to *Mémoires d'Hadrien* [*Memoirs of Hadrian*] (1951), which describes the passion of the Roman emperor for Antinoüs's curls, and even *L'oeuvre au noir* [*Zeno of Bruges*, 1968], which introduces us to Zeno, an alchemist who also likes the occasional *mignon*. Nevertheless, she did not embrace her "sexual problem," or for that matter her femininity, in an exhibitionistic or militant way.[19] The expression she chose to define her relationship with her translator, Grace Frick, remains a model of sobriety and an example: "The woman with whom I share my home."

Although Yourcenar's election to the Académie Française may appear symbolic of the ten years of women's protests that preceded it, the years 1979–80 in fact marked the last gasp of the women's movement.

By 1979, debate had replaced action. The major figures of the movement were succumbing to the temptation to write "their" versions of the history of feminism, and new journals proliferated. Women's publishing houses were founded, and a "women's" bookstore opened in Paris. A few women set up the Répondeuses, a telephone recording of feminist news. The Babouches, a soft-rock group, played evenings at women's celebrations. Some women studied mechanics or plumbing. To conquer fear, classes in self-defense were set up, particularly for survivors of rape.

Some homosexual women discovered the works of an American feminist, Kate Millett. In her broadly autobiographical *Flying* (1975), she describes a community transformed by lesbian love. In *Sita*, translated into French in 1978, the narrator openly acknowledges her homosexuality and decides to live with a woman, despite some jealousy. In *Sita*, lesbian daily life has become natural and positive.

Although feminism retained its radical appearance, it gradually became institutionalized. There were a few relics from the heroic era, of course, but the movement was losing steam. Some women still fought against pornography, "the supreme instrument of women's oppression." Lesbians were particularly interested in this issue, since they were constantly the object of fantasies in heterosexual pornographic films. "Did the rapist read porn?" the Groupe de Recherche Féministe sur la Pornographie [Feminist research group on pornography] asked. Some feminists also attacked the notorious "Chéri(e)" personal ads in *Libération*. Dialogue with male homosexuals was impossible at a time when commercial eroticism and the classified ad market were becoming more significant among gay men.[20]

During this period, some homosexual women experimented with new spaces for dialogue; lesbian communities, built on the model of mixed-sex leftist communities, prospered for a time. Marie-Jo Bonnet, the former Gouine Rouge, speaks of this atmosphere in the mid-1970s: "There was a terrible loss of steam. We were supposed to have assimilated the MLF: some women opted for alternative medicine, vegetarianism, and acupuncture, others for self-knowledge, art, creative endeavors. As for myself, it was during this time that I began my thesis on the history of lesbians." Lesbian communities, presented as a solution to the alienating relationships of coupled heterosexuality, appeared at the same time as pacifism and the vogue for nude beaches. They did not always avoid stereotypes: women playing guitars around campfires and living off the land. Jackie Buet confirms this trend: "The move toward communities played an important role. There was a collective dimension to them that satisfied many utopian desires in the 1970s. Communal life was supposed to blow the couple apart: there would be a sharing of chores, of sex, the absence of a private life, collective daycare." Women's houses, reserved for use by lesbians, offered a room or a bed to rent and, sometimes, camping in the summer; they proliferated in Gers, Les Landes, and Cévennes. "That gave rise to the Greens," Buet concludes.

Within these communities, the "lesbian experience" had to confront the difficulties of daily life. The result was a mitigated success. As the feminist Evelyne Le Garrec has observed, "If two women can have a sexual relationship from which relations of domination and power are excluded, but cannot live together without one or the other party becoming alienated, without a power relation being created, this may very well be because a power relation is created any time two people share the same territory, and one party ends up imposing power on the other." The communities of the 1970s, proposing themselves as a solution to the patriarchal model of oppression, may have been unable to survive these contradictions.[21]

⤸

At the tearoom La Souris Papivore on rue Sainte-Croix-de-la-Bretonnerie, or, in the evening, at Carabosses et Barcarosse, a bookstore and all-woman pastry shop, militant women met to assess the years gone by. They observed that the golden age of feminism had passed. "The movement had fallen like a soufflé," concluded Thérèse Clerc, a grassroots militant.

The first reason for this demobilization was the ratification, in 1979, of the Veil law [legalizing abortion], initially passed for a trial period in 1974.[22] The second reason was the construction of a more moderate discourse on women, which appropriated radical feminism's victories—the better to detach itself from radical feminism—and which marginalized the lesbian aspect of the movement. The word "feminist" began to be an insult.

F Magazine, a shining example of this new trend, was launched in January 1978 by the group L'Expansion. Claude Servan-Schreiber and Benoîte Groult were the editors of this serious magazine, which attracted former contributors to *Elle* and a few young journalists just starting out (Christine Ockrent, Catherine Nay, Anne Sinclair, Michèle Cotta). This moderate feminist discourse for the young managerial set enjoyed a rapid success, and its circulation reached 450,000. It was a long way from the subversive journals, from the time when women discarded their bras. "Feminism—popularized, cleaned up, and watered down—was no longer frightening," Françoise Picq comments. "It had slipped away from those who, using provocative means, had brought it into being."[23]

This evolution was also noticeable in the Parti Socialiste [Socialist Party], or PS. In the heyday of the MLF, women's groups had been organized within the PS. A small national collective had formed under the aegis of Marie-Thérèse Eyquem, Colette Audry, and Cécile Goldet. "Like the other parties, the Socialist Party was misogynous," François Mitterrand has explained. "I constantly had to fight against that tendency."[24] At the Pau congress (1973), the PS decided that, at a minimum, 10 percent of the committee seats should be set aside for women. Denise Cacheux, named a national delegate for Mitterrand, established the first Commission Nationale à l'Action Féminine [National committee for women's action]. At the Nantes congress (1975), the Secteur Femmes [Women's sector] achieved the status of a leading organization in the party, and Yvette Roudy was designated national secretary—a first. In 1978, women from the PS formed an autonomous camp and presented a motion to the Metz congress (April 1979) titled "L'autre moitié du chemin" [The other half of the road]. This time, when feminism asserted its radicalism and autonomy, it had no significant effect on the PS. The women (Françoise Gaspard, Anne Le Gall, Edith Lhuilier) who wished to defend a "different relationship to life" were not taken seriously, and their proposal received only 1 percent of the vote at the congress. Between 1979 and 1984, they published *Mignonne, allons voir sous la rose* [Darling, let us go look under the rose; an allusion to Pierre de Ronsard's "A sa maîtresse" and its line "Mignonne, allons voir si la rose" . . .]. A more moderate path prevailed, and it was personified in particular by Denise Cacheux in Lille, by Renée Dufourt in Lyon, and by Renée Broustal in Nantes. This reformist feminism was successfully exploited by Yvette Roudy.

Now that feminism had become reasonable, it began to dissolve from within.

In an influential article, Marie Antonietta Macciocchi announced "the death of historic feminists," and, in *Lâchez tout*, Annie Le Brun, an antifeminist militant, openly attacked the movement's "muddled" and somewhat Stalinist discourse. The MLF, weakened and torn apart by its new contradictions, went through a twofold internal rift that crippled it, in the end.

࿚

The two breaks that affected the feminist movement in 1979–80 had nothing in common. One, centering on the issue of lesbianism, was unexpected; the other was simply the umpteenth confrontation between two opposing camps dating back to the beginnings of the MLF.

Even in the Pompidou years, Antoinette Fouque had opposed the Féministes Révolutionnaires. According to Françoise Picq, this quarrel resulted in "a double impasse" for the women's movement: naturalism and "féminitude" on one side (Psychépo), sociologism and cultural conditioning on the other.[25] At the time, however, the disputes took the form of sometimes virulent debates, which in the end contributed to the vitality of the movement. They were settled the first time in 1977, at the *prud'hommes*, the board governing industrial disputes, after the firing of a strike leader.[26] The second time, however, the civil war between the two "legitimate" camps of the French feminist movement was of much broader scope.

In October 1979, the group Psychépo registered the by-laws of an association called "Mouvement de Libération des Femmes/MLF" at the Paris police headquarters; in November, they registered a commercial trademark of the same name. The official logo was the very same one that had adorned the issue of *Partisans* in 1970. One camp of the MLF had appropriated, legally, the name, image, and history of the movement as a whole. Women who opposed Fouque denounced these new "political commissars" and cried, "Thief!": "A social movement cannot be registered at police headquarters!" In 1980, the dispute entered a new phase: an association was created that proposed to prohibit any unapproved group from using the acronym. Fouque, as if pronouncing the magic words of femininity, denounced the Féministes Révolutionnaires for contributing to "gynocide." A legal war was inevitable.

In this confrontation, feminists discovered at great cost to themselves that power issues were not specific to men, that they were not necessarily a male schema. The illusion of happiness among women, built on the absence of authority and power—the exclusive privilege of men—was shattered. This sudden appearance of power relations within the MLF represented the end of a dream. Fouque and the Psychépo camp, because they had shattered that dream, now inspired tenacious hatred on the part of their opponents.[27] The dupe in this affair, the Féministes Révolutionnaires and others making up the movement, had to console themselves by declaring, with irony and disappointment, that they were the "MLF-*non déposé*" [MLF, unregistered trademark].

↫

It was now the turn of the "survivors" in the "MLF–*non déposé*," the last relic of a movement in decline after the rift with Psychépo, to come unraveled. The review *Questions Féministes*, founded by Christine Delphy in 1977, was where this final confrontation took place, and this time lesbian separatism served as the detonator.

Delphy, a stunning woman with medium-length hair, was a historic figure of feminism, one of the nine women who had placed the spray of flowers at the Tomb of the Unknown Soldier in 1970. Full of extreme leftist ideas, she was also a homosexual and did not hide the fact. She participated with the FHAR in sabotaging Ménie Grégoire's broadcast and, at the MLF, invented the name "Gouines Rouges." Since then, she had played a part in all the feminist battles. In 1977 she founded *Questions Féministes*, a journal headed by Simone de Beauvoir, and proposed a theory of radical feminism, defending the idea that women were a "social class." It was in these circumstances that the second internal conflict within the movement emerged. In February 1980, in issue 7 of *Questions Féministes*, two points of view stood opposed. In an article titled "La pensée Straight" [Straight thought], Monique Wittig developed the idea that feminism could now exist only within the framework of lesbianism. For her, heterosexuality was not a life choice; it was a constraint, the result of social conditioning. It was an ideological and economic system, a logic that oppressed all women. Only lesbianism allowed women to escape men's exploitation. "If we—lesbians, homosexuals—continue to tell ourselves that we are women, to conceive of ourselves as such, we are supporting heterosexuality." The radical Wittig ended her article with a phrase that has remained famous: "Lesbians are not women." On the opposing side, Emmanuèle de Lesseps wondered in her article, titled "Hétérosexualité et féminisme," "Can a person be both heterosexual and feminist?" She forcefully criticized the idea that "social duty entails the repression of heterosexual desires." Her argument was just what some homosexual women had been waiting for; cozy inside a movement of polymorphous desire, they had difficulty understanding why they were suddenly being called upon to label themselves.[28]

Between these two lines of argument, Delphy chose continuity over scission. She indicated her preference for the position of "Mano" de Lesseps, refusing to give a *uniquely* lesbian direction to the movement. Delphy wanted the homosexual cause to remain a women's cause and was thus surprised that some lesbians were meeting separately at the Jussieu secondary school: "I rejected scission and the opposition between a lesbian movement and a feminist movement, since I thought— I still think today—that feminism must *also* take lesbians and lesbianism into account, but not exclusively. It cannot claim to be exclusively heterosexual. But, at the same time, I was unwilling to see that Monique Wittig had evolved and that she sought separatism. All of a sudden, I became the devil incarnate for her, a lesbian who had made a pact with the enemy." Delphy was not tempted to renounce the movement: she could affirm her lesbianism within the MLF and was not going to risk joining a hypothetical "lesbian, chauvinistic, sexist nation, the incarnation of an *other* place, the *sectarian sect* (already seen in Psychépo)."[29] Some fifteen years after this final rift, a magnanimous Delphy attempts to explain the separation: "In spite of everything, the feminist movement was responsible for this split because it never wanted to acknowledge lesbianism. The oppression of lesbians is an integral part of women's oppression."

↩

Why did this debate, which had existed since the origins of the MLF, provoke a rift this time? The issue is all the more curious in that most of the militant women of *Questions Féministes*, whether they favored Wittig's article or Lesseps's position, were in fact homosexual.[30]

Young lesbian militants had joined the MLF during its final years. They were embarrassed by the transformation of radical feminism into an easygoing feminism broadcast through government-sponsored TV spots. Their disappointment was echoed in the accumulated resentment among lesbians from the early days, with Wittig in the lead. She had been hit hard by the failure of both her book *Le corps lesbien* (1973) and her efforts to create the Front Lesbien International [International lesbian front] about 1975. She had chosen a first exile in the United States to lick her wounds.

As Christiane Jouve, future cofounder of *Lesbia Magazine*, explains, young radical lesbians agreed with the homosexual women who

had taken an active part in the women's movement, rightly believing that nothing affecting women was unrelated to them, including contraception and abortion, which they did not really need. . . . Militant women began to chafe when they realized that their own concerns were not part of the platform, and that solidarity worked only in one direction. . . . Tired of talking to the wall, many left a movement that was losing steam, with the bitter feeling of having been swindled.[31]

This may explain the revival, in the early 1980s, of an anachronistic-looking radicalism. For lesbians, the MLF, which had been content to "adjust to heterosexuality," was a reformist movement in the worst sense of the word. As "the last combatants against male power," they accused nonlesbian feminists of being "collaborators": A WOMAN WHO LOVES HER OPPRESSOR, THAT'S OPPRESSION; A FEMINIST WHO LOVES HER OPPRESSION, THAT'S COLLABORATION.[32] For her part, Wittig explained in the last issue of *Questions Féministes*:

The aim of our battle is to eliminate men as a class, as part of a political class struggle—not as genocide. . . . [A] lesbian is not a woman, not economically, politically, or ideologically. What makes a woman a woman is a particular social relationship to a man, a relationship . . . of serfdom . . . which lesbians avoid by refusing to become or to remain heterosexual. We have defected from our class.[33]

What a bewildering about-face! Wittig's militancy began with the struggle against Psychépo's "féminitude," out of concern for equality and universalism; it ended in lesbian essentialism, which is neither egalitarian nor universalist. In essence, hers was an exclusively lesbian Psychépo. The author of *Les guérillères*, inspired by her American experience, now defined herself as a radical lesbian—neither man nor woman—out of political choice. Separatism had won out over the belief that it was "better to live together."

Inspired by Wittig, who had returned to France in the winter of 1979, the most radical women—to cries of "Apologetic lesbians!"—resigned from the staff of *Questions Féministes*, provoking its dissolution. In 1981, Delphy, along with Emmanuèle de Lesseps and Claude Hennequin, revived the journal with an only slightly modified name: *Nouvelles Questions Féministes* [New feminist questions] and asked Simone de Beauvoir to head it once again. She accepted and even donated 20,000 francs to the collective. Radical lesbians sued over what they saw as a usurpation of the name. During the trial, Delphy's friends were able to count on the support of Beauvoir, who had a letter read in court. That unpublished document remains essential. It confirms the fact that part of Beauvoir's legacy was to reject the autonomy of the lesbian question. After confirming that she had participated in launching the journal and that she was regularly associated with it, Beauvoir explained that she had been kept informed of the demands of homosexual woman and that, in this respect, she was firmly opposed to the epithet "collaborationist" in describing heterosexual women: "I found and still find it scandalous that these people [the radical lesbians] have allowed their sectarian interests to come before the interests of feminism as a whole."[34] The radical lesbians' suit was dismissed.[35]

Disabused, the secessionist women now wanted to sever all ties with feminists, and they proposed "spaces of resistance" and "alternative lifestyles." The "radical lesbian" movement, which had begun within various groups in 1980, became organized in March 1981 under the name Front des Lesbiennes Radicales [Radical lesbian front], or FLR. It was composed of a portion of the former staff of *Questions Féministes*.[36] "All women must become lesbians, that is, they must stand together, resist, not be collaborators," one woman declared in a mimeographed pamphlet.[37] The front intended to attract "resisters to heterosexual power, without whom feminism could never have taken place."[38] It created a review, *Espaces*, housed in the homosexual bookstore Les Mots à la Bouche, that was short-lived; the quarterly and the all-female gathering place managed to hang on a bit longer.

Most homosexual women did not accept this development, however. That was true for Evelyne Rochedereux, a former Gouine Rouge, who criticized dogmatism and the idea of lesbian purity: "I have sometimes noticed that the women who are most intransigent about homosexual purity, especially radical lesbians, are those who have a particularly weighty heterosexual past." Others quite simply rejected the term "lesbian," which the radicals wanted to impose on them: "The word 'lesbian' has been thrown in my face," commented Cathy Bernheim (another former Gouine Rouge). "I insist on the fact that homosexual women are also 'gays.' We must not abandon this word to the men, as the radical lesbians wanted to do, piling ghetto upon ghetto. I am a gay woman, not a lesbian."

Cut off from its traditional feminist cocoon, resolved to avoid any collaboration with gay men, the ghetto chosen by the Front des Lesbiennes Radicales had no real support in the provinces and was soon deserted in Paris. Lesbian militancy could not overcome its own internal conflicts, nor could it avoid dogmatism. The front finally collapsed in the summer of 1982. Feminism itself barely survived it.

Disappointed that she had been unable, for the second time, to create the Front Lesbien that she dreamed of, Wittig persisted in thinking that "one must be relentlessly lesbian." Unlike Foucault, however, she was filled with resentment. She left France for good and went to Gualala [some 160 miles north of San Francisco, on the California coast] and then to Tucson, Arizona, a veritable "paradise" of gay and lesbian studies, where she lives today. There, it appears, one can call oneself a "writeress" or an "authoress" in peace.

↜

An optimistic alternative to these cleavages might be imagined: feminist groups pursuing their struggle in the political realm, and lesbian militancy centering on cultural, emotional, and lifestyle questions. Even if this hoped-for division of tasks had come about, the feminist movement and the hypothetical lesbian movement would still have had difficulty finding their bearings in the 1980s.

In France, the issue of lesbianism—as the feminists of the early days assumed—could not exist outside the women's struggle. By causing a rift within *Questions Féministes*, lesbians simply confirmed the fact that the issue of homosexuality was at the center of the MLF's origin and evolution. And that in itself is not insignificant.

With the presidential election, homosexual militants, feminists, and lesbians could take a breather. They were now obsessed by an odd couple, Simone de Beauvoir and Michel Foucault, who they believed would get them through the 1980s, which looked full of promise. In 1981, the new faces of the sexual liberation movement (*Gai Pied, Nouvelles Questions Féministes*, the Front des Lesbiennes Radicales) were confidently waging the last battle of May '68.

"Seven Years of Happiness"? (May 1981)

Homosexuality must cease to be a criminal offense.
—François Mitterrand, April 28, 1981

"Look, something has changed, the air seems lighter, I can't define it./Look, the sun has broken through the clouds, and everything has begun to glimmer./A man with a rose in his hand has shown the way toward a different tomorrow." This tune, written just after the May 1981 Socialist victory by Wicked Fairy Barbara, stooped under her classic Lanvin velvet tunic, sounded like a party song.

Five days earlier, Alain Pacadis, in his *Libération* column on Paris nightlife, had been the only one to note a significant happening: "The most important event of the evening was the categorical stand taken by Fabrice [Emaer] for the candidacy of François Mitterrand, a stand taken as a gay man and as the owner of the largest nightclub in the capital." Pacadis had a keen eye for the telling anecdote: Emaer, owner of Le Palace and known to be "on the right," had felt the tide turning and called on people to vote for Mitterrand.

On May 10, during a gay tea dance, Emaer announced the Socialist victory, to thunderous applause. He then threw together a special evening, and he himself sang the Grace Jones version of *La vie en rose*. People danced all night long.

Outside, on the Place de la Bastille, homosexual militants were partying and mingling with the huge crowd, waving tricolor flags, and warmly greeting the mayor of Marseilles, Gaston Defferre, as one organization unfurled a banner: HO-MOS HAVE CHOSEN FREEDOM. A sudden cloudburst: "It's a good luck sign," murmured a drenched feminist. "At Last the Adventure Begins!" was the headline of the new *Libération*.

After the Socialist victory, polls revealed that the women's vote, for the first time, was farther to the left than the men's. The MLF-*déposé*, in the first round of voting, and the MLF–*non déposé*, in the second, urged women to vote for Mitterrand. As for homosexuals, an unsigned news item written by Frédéric Edelmann appeared in *Le Monde* on May 12, 1981: "It was claimed on Sunday evening that the homosexual vote contributed to the president's victory, either directly or by abstention." Real or not, this "homosexual vote"—a protest vote—must not be overestimated.[1] *Gai Pied,* unruffled, ran the front-page headline "Seven Years of Happiness?" in the next issue. The cover carried a single photo—of the president of the republic—with this caption: "Homosexuality must cease to be a criminal offense." It was, despite the cliché, a "pink" victory in every sense of the term.

↩

"Homosexuality must cease to be a criminal offense." History, surprisingly, has remembered this brief sentence, which Candidate Mitterrand never actually uttered. Invited to the meeting held at the Palais des Congrès by Gisèle Halimi and the organization Choisir on April 28, 1981, François Mitterrand was questioned about the issues of mores and homosexuality by Josyane Savigneau, a journalist from *Le Monde*.[2] Mitterrand, then first secretary of the Parti Socialiste [Socialist Party], or PS, replied, "Personally, I cannot accept the fact that homosexual cases [of indecency] should be punished more severely than others. That seems unfair to me. It goes against the equality of citizens before the law; we should not get involved in judging other people's morals."[3] In a second attempt, Halimi questioned the candidate more directly: "On one precise point—if you are elected, will homosexuality cease to be a criminal offense?" And Mitterrand, wavering between a strategy of cooperation and one of rift, and drawing on an infinitely varied array of tones and body language, replied:

Oh, absolutely. . . . There is no reason to judge a person's choice. It's the law of nature, following one's inclinations, whatever. The choice of each person must be respected, that's all, but within a normal framework of relations between men and women, or between men, or between women, within laws, which, all the same, ought to organize a society. But no discrimination because of the nature of one's morals; for me, that goes without saying. I have assumed responsibility for this, but I know very well that, if you poll people about it, I know very well what response would be given me, but I have assumed responsibility for this in writing.[4]

As on the question of capital punishment, Mitterrand said he was not waffling about antihomosexual discrimination, whatever the electoral cost of his position. It is significant that these words were uttered within a feminist space, which confirms both feminists' particular interest in the subject and Mitterrand's greater freedom of expression when he was speaking of female homosexuality.

In spite of the courage shown by the Socialist candidate, some have maintained that his position catered to the electorate, since it was simply echoing the demands of homosexuals in 1981.

↩

On Saturday, April 4, 1981, nearly 10,000 homosexuals marched from the Place Maubert to the parvis of Beaubourg, responding to the call from homosexual organizations. Along the way, gays—spontaneously, it seems—tore down posters for Candidate Giscard, chanting, "Giscard, diamonds for our lovers!" At the head of the procession in this special Gay Pride march were the writers Jean-Paul Aron[5] and Yves Navarre and a shadowy figure who still had not received much attention from the media, someone who would claim the title "minister of desire": Jack Lang, draped in the blue, white, and red sash of a Parisian municipal council member. That evening, demonstrators met at the Mutualité for a recital by Juliette Gréco, who performed *Les pingouins* [The penguins] and received a standing ovation when she sang, "A little bird and a little fish loved each other tenderly, but how could they manage, when one was in the air and one was in the sea?"

The next week, on April 13, at a celebration marking the two-year anniversary of *Gai Pied* at Le Palace disco, Navarre took the microphone. Flanked by Aron and Emaer, he read a telegram received from Candidate Mitterrand:

With these few words, I want to tell you that I share in the obvious and necessary fervor of your national march and in your celebration this evening. Celebrating must go hand in hand with defending the cause. And I ask Yves Navarre to convey the respect and attention I bring to the way of life you desire, and which ought to be made possible by removing obstacles, both by abolishing laws and by creating new laws. Sincerely yours, François Mitterrand.

Navarre, a messenger for Candidate Mitterrand? The authenticity of this telegram is doubtful, at the very least, especially because the public relations office of the Socialist Party refused at the time to confirm the message for news agencies. It is possible that this telegram never existed. Given his connections, Navarre, a member of the so-called Writers' Committee of the PS, may have asked the candidate for a message for the *Gai Pied* celebration in which he was taking part. An agreement on principle may have been reached, but Navarre, seeing that no message had arrived, and with Aron's complicity, may have taken the initiative at the last minute, drafted the telegram himself, sent it to himself, and then, later, read it, to thunderous applause at Le Palace.

"I do not remember that telegram to Yves Navarre," Lang explains today. "François Mitterrand knew Navarre. He did a thousand and one things for us. If that telegram is a fake, it is only a venial sin, since it was a good reflection of François Mitterrand's thinking. And if the public relations office of the PS did not want to confirm the text, they were idiots." Mitterrand, naturally, never contradicted the story.

⌒

This apocryphal telegram sums up the climate of the time, and it also illustrates the free hand that Navarre enjoyed. Nevertheless, Navarre's career cannot be reduced to his association with Mitterrand.

Navarre had joined the PS in 1974. He remained flawlessly loyal to the Socialists. In 1980–81, after first supporting the idea of having homosexuals turn in a "blank" ballot and then asking, with a certain naïveté, that these ballots bear the logo of the pink triangle, he finally urged people to vote for Candidate Mitterrand.[6]

Divided between his struggle on behalf of homosexuality and his battle for the leftist victory, Navarre sought the support of Jean-Louis Bory and became his clear successor. In 1971, in *Lady Black*, Navarre grappled with the theme of sexual marginality; in 1973, in *Les Loukoums*, homosexuality appeared more directly, with violence and candor. From the beginning, the book's success was more than respectable. In 1975 he was invited to *Les dossiers de l'écran* and was seated between André Baudry (Navarre was still a member of Arcadie) and Bory. From then on, he continually supported the homosexual cause, although he had reservations about the word "homosexual," preferring "homosensual." In 1980 he was awarded the Prix Goncourt for *Le jardin d'acclimatation* [The zoological gardens]. "Was it a victory for homosexuality?" he was asked the same evening by Patrick Poivre d'Arvor on the eight o'clock news.

Underneath his success, Navarre nursed the sensibility of a wounded man, and his writings, which are similar to screenplays, depict characters who destroy what they have created (the hero of *Killer*, Sevy in *Niagarak*) or fail to express themselves (Pipou in *Je vis où je m'attache* [I live where I am rooted], Quentin in *Kurwenal*, Bertrand in *Le jardin d'acclimatation*, Roussel in *Le temps voulu* [The time needed], or Rasky in *Les Loukoums*). Obsessed by the impossibility of dialogue between men, by aging, and by memory, Navarre presented an inventory of his own life in his novel *Biographie* (1981).

He also suffered from the militant image he had acquired:

Militancy is an odd forum. I've never seen so much hate or discerned so many rivalries in people's eyes or flitting across their lips. Before May 10, I found myself on the front lines many times, and alone, terribly alone. Jean-Louis [Bory] spoke to me as an elder brother, told me to watch out: "I've already been knocked around, you haven't," he said. We are much more racist with one another than other people are with us.[7]

Like Bory, Navarre gradually collapsed. Publishers rejected his novels, and his torment overcame his desire to live. "He told me I had saved him twice," Michel Tournier recalls. "The first time by giving him the Prix Goncourt, the second time by giving him my cat, which he named Tiffauges." But, in the end, could Navarre be saved? After a difficult exile in Quebec and a period of wandering around Paris, a lonely Navarre chose on January 24, 1994, to take his own life.

↬

In 1981, Navarre had taken part in a whole series of initiatives on behalf of Mitterrand. Appreciative of this support, the candidate's entourage, with Jack Lang in the lead, managed to convince Pierre Bérégovoy, at the time Mitterrand's director of public relations, to make a public statement.[8] Bérégovoy did so in early April, in an interview with *Gai Pied* that confirmed the Socialist Party's interest in the issue of sexual liberation and the party's opposition to any inequality or discrimination against homosexuals.[9]

For his part, Giscard d'Estaing knew that he had to demonstrate his goodwill on the subject. Therefore, he proposed a revision of the discriminatory ordinance aimed at homosexuals, even though this ordinance had been passed the previous year—that is, during his presidency. To make his position known, on the day of the *Gai Pied* celebration he simply sent a short letter to Arcadie in which he explained that he would no longer interfere with any possible suppression of discriminatory ordinances.[10] The letter had little effect.

During this time, other activities were being organized in support of the Socialist candidate. A petition, circulated in late April, urged homosexuals to vote for Mitterrand. It was signed by Gérard Depardieu, Michel Piccoli, François Truffaut, Edmonde Charles-Roux, Dalida, and Roger Hanin.[11] Gilles Barbedette, for *Gai Pied,* and the senior editorial staff of the journal *Masques* collected more signatures for the petition and held a joint press conference with Editions des Femmes (Psychépo)—with the American writer Kate Millett in attendance—to get out the vote for Candidate Mitterrand.

All these elements demonstrate that the "homosexual" vote had to be reckoned with, and they partially explain the warmth of Mitterrand's words at the meeting of Choisir. Was it conviction, or was it political calculation? The candidate's personality and his personal life shed some light on his cooperation with homosexuals.

↝

"François Mitterrand," Jack Lang explains today, "was a man with a passion for human beings in all their complexity, in all their diversity. It's true. I found he was interested in unique, original human beings, homosexuals, perhaps even more than in so-called normal people." Everyone interviewed on the question confirmed that President Mitterrand spoke very freely on the issue of homosexuality. "We never talked about homosexuality, he and I," explains Pierre Bergé, who spent time with Mitterrand, especially before 1986. "We talked about homosexual individuals. He sometimes asked, 'Is so-and-so homosexual?' But for him, in fact, homosexuality did not exist, in the good sense of that expression." Lang is cautious, however, in speaking of Mitterrand's commitment to homosexuality in 1981: "François Mitterrand was not the type to flaunt it. Personalities and groups came to him, and he was invited to express his views." According to Thierry de Beaucé, one of Mitterrand's advisers at the Elysée Palace, "He was not very interested in male homosexuality. He sort of joked about it. He had a tendency to dodge the issue of male sexuality in general, not to see the social dimension of the problem. The lesbian question, on the other hand, fascinated him."

Although we cannot reduce Mitterrand's political choices to his intimate secrets or to the people with whom he associated, let us note that Mitterrand was extremely close to a succession of homosexual women, including some who were legendary.

In 1943, when Mitterrand was a fugitive and, by his own account, "a bit of an outlaw," moving "from one safe friend to another, to take advantage of their hospitality," he went to the home of the American writer Gertrude Stein[12] and her companion, Alice B. Toklas, who had both sought refuge in Culoz, a village in Ain.[13] In addition to this odd wartime meeting between Mitterrand and this pair of "naughty ladies," as Marlene Dietrich called them, there was his relationship in the 1950s with the British novelist Violet Trefusis. A fervent royalist, and a friend of E. M. Forster and Natalie Barney, Trefusis spent part of her life in France, where she was involved with Jean Cocteau. Their relationship illustrated, in Baudelaire's expression, that "loving a woman of wit is one pleasure of pederasty." Trefusis, "a winged huntress," made no secret of her homosexual relationships, as was amply demonstrated by her love affair with Vita Sackville-West (for whom she and Virginia Woolf were rivals).[14]

Mitterrand, then a minister of the Fourth Republic, met Trefusis in the 1950s. Invited to the Ombrellino, her villa in Florence, Mitterrand stayed with her while preparing a book on Laurent de Médicis. There he kept company with the great aristocratic and aesthetic pederasts of England (Lord Acton and the rest). He later visited Trefusis in Paris, at her apartment on rue du Cherche-Midi or at the so-called Saint-Loup house. Mitterrand and Violet saw each other regularly in the 1960s. As Thierry de Beaucé confirms, "He was a member of the National Assembly, and very early on she discerned that he was statesman material. She was a rather decadent English Egeria, with stormy love affairs. The relationship could not help but work out." Mitterrand subsequently wrote a preface to a biography of Trefusis and, after becoming president of the republic, remained loyal to this friendship by writing another preface, this time for one of Violet's books.[15]

In addition to having had these close ties to Stein, Toklas, and Trefusis, Mitterrand did on one occasion express his views on homosexuality. In 1954, as minister of the interior, he had to reply to attacks on officials high in his ministry. It was a complex situation. Under the government of Pierre Mendès France, in a closed meeting at the Elysée Palace, informers divulged secrets that involved the Department of Defense to the benefit of the Parti Communiste Français [French Communist Party], or PCF. During a tumultuous session of the National Assembly, associates of the minister of the interior came under suspicion because they belonged to the "currently fashionable homosexual brotherhood" and because "their habits" made them "particularly vulnerable in the posts where you [Mitterrand] have kept them, or to which you have named them." Mitterrand replied, "Regarding the sexual habits you have mentioned, if one of the officials placed under my authority has a dubious record, I ask that it be communicated to me. How can you expect me to tolerate such high officials' being slandered, attacked, and decried in this way?"[16]

I do not wish to engage in a debate about the past of the former president of the republic, but the words just quoted show a certain ambivalence on Mitterrand's part about the subject of homosexuality. He equivocated in 1954, and yet one of the themes of his 1981 campaign was the abrogation of discriminatory laws aimed at homosexuals. Thus Mitterrand displayed a sinuous but, in the end, clear approach, even though, on this subject as on many others, the "Mitterrand enigma" remains.

In May 1981, after Mitterrand's victory, the National Assembly was dissolved, and legislative elections were scheduled for June. Many intellectuals took up the pen to urge in a petition that gays vote for Socialist deputies, since, if gays were to gain their rights, "the defeat of the antihomosexual parliamentary majority" had to be secured. On the front lines, as signers of this new petition, were the writers Yves Navarre, Jean-Paul Aron, Guy Hocquenghem, Simone de Beauvoir, Dominique Fernandez, and Françoise Sagan, as well as the philosophers Gilles Deleuze, Félix Guattari, and Michel Foucault, but also Jack Lang, Frédéric Mitterrand, Fabrice Emaer, and the attorney Gisèle Halimi.[17] On June 21, the Socialist Party obtained an absolute majority in the assembly (285 seats)—a state of grace.

With the "pink wave" of May and June 1981, the new Socialist government now had the political means to keep Candidate Mitterrand's promises. The key negotiator with the government on the issue of homosexuality was a coalition: the Comité d'Urgence Anti-Répression Homosexuel [Emergency committee against homosexual repression], or CUARH. A kind of loose federation, it had been created in the context of the "Université d'été homosexuelle" [Homosexual summer school] of July 1979[18] and assembled most of the homosexual groups and associations, with the exception of Arcadie, around the lowest common denominator. Truly organized in February 1980, the CUARH chose a political agenda, favoring dialogue with political parties and trade unions. With each of these interlocutors it denounced the repression of homosexuals and protested police raids of cruising spots and the banning of homosexuals from certain professions. A mixed-sex group, the CUARH maintained relations with the women's movement, welcomed the writer Geneviève Pastre, and established a lesbian association, the Mouvement d'Information et d'Expression des Lesbiennes [Movement for lesbian information and expression], or MIEL.[19] The coalition published a monthly review, *Homophonies*,[20] compiled reports, and drafted manifestoes. The culmination of the "unionist" mobilization led by the CUARH was the large gay march of Saturday, April 7, 1981. With the victory of the Socialists, the CUARH asked for a meeting with Gaston Defferre or with the prime minister's adviser on human rights, Louis Joinet.[21]

The CUARH's mode of operation and the nature of its commitments symbolized, within French homosexual militancy, a shift from minority culture to political culture. The struggle of homosexuals, once confined to consciousness-raising and rap groups, was now oriented toward pragmatic demands. This slow process of emancipation was not specific to homosexuals; the shift from one form of militancy to the other can also be found among most other minorities (Jews, immigrants, and so on) and among feminists. After a period of identity politics—

centripetal, introverted, and introspective—the discourse evolves, and militants turn to defending the rights of the minority group in a quasi-unionist, centrifugal movement.

By focusing on discrimination, by fighting for normalization, integration, and public recognition of homosexuality, and by making itself into a lobby, the CUARH established itself as the exact opposite of the FHAR. Thus, paradoxical though this may seem, it returned to a task on which only Arcadie had placed importance until 1980. In this domain, a turning point was marked in the early 1980s by the shift from a revolutionary movement, built on the theory of class struggle, to a reformist movement, built on the ideology of human rights.

↩

This evolution in the homosexual movement also intersected with the evolution of political forces, which were increasingly interested in the issue of sexual mores—and this explains why dialogue was initiated between the two camps. Until the 1981 election, homosexuality even seems to have been a significant measure by which it was possible to trace the stand taken on social issues by the Ligue Communiste Révolutionnaire [Revolutionary Communist League], or LCR, the Parti Socialiste Unifié [Unified socialist party], or PSU, the PCF, and the PS.

About 1980, the LCR, a Leninist-Trotskyist organization, was still the most active group on the far left and the one least opposed to homosexuality; hence the presence in the group of several CUARH members.

And yet the party of Alain Krivine [former leader of the Jeunesse Communiste Révolutionnaire (Revolutionary communist youth), or JCR] had not always been understanding of homosexuality's political expression. Only in 1977 did the militants of the LCR, who had vigorously opposed the FHAR in 1971–73, create the Commission Nationale Homosexuelle [National homosexual commission]. A second commission was established in 1980, one that maintained links with the CUARH.[22] For all these militants, each of whom used several pseudonyms,[23] the desire to fight on behalf of homosexuality came into being within the commissions of the LCR, and these inroads led them to the CUARH. This shift from political militancy to homosexual militancy, and not the reverse, was crucial.

Conversely, the LCR's interest in homosexuals (but also in the women's movement)[24] can be explained, according to its detractors, by its tactic—familiar to the Trotskyists—of infiltrating "mass organizations." It was often claimed that nonhomosexual LCR militants—"moles"—had taken control of a GLH chapter in Lille, or of an FHAR newspaper (*Antinorm*), with the sole aim of urging members to vote for Alain Krivine in 1974. "On the contrary," retorts Hervé Liffran, now a journalist for *Le Canard Enchaîné*, "it was the homosexuals who absorbed the LCR. Do I have to provide a list of my lovers to prove I was not a straight infiltrator?"

Infiltrators or not, the militants of the CUARH and of the LCR were victims of a mutual banning, a characteristic sign of the perpetual unrest in small far-left groups.

    ↪

Along with the LCR, the PSU was on the front lines in the battle for homosexual rights. Led by Huguette Bouchardeau after Michel Rocard joined the Socialist Party, the PSU produced numerous initiatives, created a homosexual commission, welcomed gays as candidates for legislative elections, and organized, at La Courneuve, celebrations that became ritual gatherings for homosexual militants.[25] In 1981, Bouchardeau jumped into the fray as a presidential candidate and, to support the gay cause, even gave over a portion of her air time on France Inter to the writer Dominique Fernandez. But this sequence was censored by the campaign control commission, and in its place, a furious Bouchardeau had to be content with repeating, for six minutes, "This is Huguette Bouchardeau's broadcast on freedom, bleep-bleep, a censored broadcast, bleep-bleep."

Notwithstanding her undeniable courage, Bouchardeau demonstrated her commitment to minorities in order to form a federation of interest groups (an aggregation of minorities), like Marco Panella's Partito Radicale in Italy or, later, the Reverend Jesse Jackson's Rainbow Coalition in the United States. Her share of the vote in 1981—1.1 percent—suggests that she did not succeed.

    ↪

The Communist Party, the Confédération Générale du Travail [General confederation of labor), or CGT, and Lutte Ouvrière [Workers' struggle]—unlike the PSU and the LCR—opposed homosexuals' demands, paradoxically positioning themselves alongside the right-wing parties, which in 1980 still favored discriminatory laws.

For Lutte Ouvrière in the late 1970s, and for Arlette Laguiller in particular, homosexuality was still a defect of the capitalist world and a petty bourgeois problem: as one sign of a utopian world, the future classless society would have no homosexuals. This theoretical view was combined with a strategic position: do not "torment" the working class with such a touchy subject. Naturally, dialogue with homosexual militants was impossible.

The PCF, which initially adopted a line similar to Lutte Ouvrière's, as attested by its difficult relations with the FHAR, evolved in the late 1970s. The ambiguity remained in 1976. On the occasion of the twenty-second congress "on freedom," the PCF even reaffirmed its hostility to homosexuality and to feminist discourse, declaring, in the tradition of Lenin ("no monk, but no Don Juan either"), "The revolution is not a barracks, but it is also not a brothel." Nevertheless, in October 1976 a homosexual commission was created at the Centre d'Etudes et de Recherches Marxistes [Center for Marxist studies and research], or CERM, and Danièle Bleitrach, a member of the editorial board of *Révolution* and an associate of Guy

Hermier, produced numerous initiatives. Despite this evolution in "the system," the most significant advances came from such isolated Communists as Jean Ristat (a writer and friend of Louis Aragon), *L'Humanité* journalist Michel Boué, and *La Marseillaise* journalist Emmanuel Guallino, who declared their own homosexuality within a fairly hostile environment.[26]

It was another grassroots Communist, Jan-Paul Pouliquen, a member of the CUARH—skillfully claiming to speak in the name of the party—who took a very tolerant position on homosexuality, which the PCF could not contradict. Pouliquen also persuaded Pierre Juquin to revise his position on the issue.[27]

Nevertheless, in 1980 the Croissant affair placed this evolution in doubt. What was at stake? In an open letter to *L'Humanité*, Marc Croissant, a member of the PCF, and particularly of the homosexual commission of CERM, had protested the media's treatment of a news item about an underage homosexual. After receiving an indignant response from the writer Roland Leroy, Croissant learned that he had been banned from his cell in the PCF and that his work contract at the Communist town council in Ivry was going to be terminated. Ultimately he was dismissed, but, given the scope the affair had taken on,[28] the PCF's image in connection with sexual mores did not improve, to say the very least.

⤳

During the period before 1981, the PCF was in fact outdistanced by the Socialist Party, which pursued an intelligent policy of gradual change. Shortly after the Epinay congress (1971), the PS adopted Rimbaud's words for its political platform, words that had been a slogan of May '68: "Change life." Still, the PS rapidly came to be seen as a government party, and hence as relatively cautious on a subject that was considered difficult for the public to accept. In 1974, Giscard d'Estaing was quick to appropriate moral issues (abortion, contraception) for himself. To attract any attention, the PS, thus deprived of the major themes of sexual liberation, had to depend solely on the legalization of homosexuality. In 1976, in *Liberté, libertés*, a book prefaced by François Mitterrand, the PS fixed its position once and for all: "Homosexuality is a sexual behavior like any other. It is an expression of the fundamental freedom of the body. Homosexuality must not be the occasion for imposing any form of inequality or discrimination."[29] From that point on, the PS regularly reminded everyone that it advocated the pure and simple abrogation of discriminatory ordinances targeting homosexuals.[30]

This change was even more explicit in certain large municipalities. In Rennes, Edmond Hervé—a young Socialist who had enjoyed a brilliant victory in the municipal elections of March 1977—was conciliatory, offering his aid to the local GLH. Meanwhile, in Marseilles, even more unexpectedly, Gaston Defferre also proved to be understanding.[31]

One of the more outstanding paradoxes concerning Defferre, a macho personality if ever there was one, was that he turned out to be open to this issue at all. In

1979, he offered the campus of the School of Architecture in Luminy for the first "Université d'été homosexuelle" and proposed that homosexual militants coming for the sessions be housed in the residence halls. "That made waves," recalls his wife, Edmonde Charles-Roux. During the same period, he welcomed militants from GLH–Marseilles to the Fête de la Rose and went so far as to introduce them to Mitterrand, who was head of the PS at the time. He also asked his wife to attend a debate with Dominique Fernandez about the latter's novel L'étoile rose, as much to avoid an incident as to indicate his solidarity with the cause.

"It was his Protestant blood," claims Charles-Roux, explaining this liberal side of Defferre. "He was a man who could not accept any form of ghettoization or marginalization, for any reason. Even today, I'm stunned by his fierceness. He had a clear position in his city as the protector of homosexuals. . . . When he died, they found books on his work table that he had regularly read and annotated: there were L'étoile rose and Mère Méditerranée [Mediterranean mother], by Dominique Fernandez, as well as Jean Genet's Le balcon [The Balcony]."[32] Jacques Fortin, who was president of GLH–Marseilles at the time, has a more narrowly political explanation: "Defferre's success came from the fact that he had always had his Armenians, his Greeks. . . . When there got to be queers, he had his queers."

"HOMOSEXUALS, YOU'VE GOT A NEW BOSS"

Once Mitterrand was elected president of the republic, in 1981 (with Pierre Mauroy as prime minister, Gaston Defferre as minister of the interior, Robert Badinter as minister of justice, Jack Lang as minister of culture, and Yvette Roudy as minister of women's rights), things began to move very quickly for homosexuals.

The new government's speed in responding to the demands of gays was striking. Less than a month after being appointed minister of the interior, Defferre had a note sent by his chief of staff (the famous Prefect Grimaud from 1968) to the general director of the national police force. It was disseminated to all the police precincts. The note read as follows:

My attention has been drawn to the attitude of police squads toward homosexuals. In particular, I have learned that, within the drug and prostitution squad of the Paris police headquarters, there is a special group of inspectors engaged in the surveillance of establishments frequented by homosexuals. I also believe that during identity checks at public gathering places, people are being put on file as "homosexuals." It is certainly the mission of the police to monitor establishments open to the public that may represent a threat to law and order; nevertheless, in accordance with the guidelines set by the president of the republic, no discrimination, and, above all, no suspicion, shall be brought to bear upon people solely as a result of their sexual orientation.[33]

Foucault heartily applauded: "The fact that a minister has such a memo sent around is very important, even if the memo is not being applied. This is a political act."[34]

On June 12, Jack Ralite, the Communist minister of health, announced that France would no longer recognize the World Health Organization's classification of homosexuality as a mental illness. On August 4, 1981, presidential pardons were extended for certain homosexual offenses: on August 6, the sentences of approximately 150 homosexuals were commuted, and those who were in prison were set free.[35] On August 27, Robert Badinter, minister of justice, sent the public prosecutor's office a memo to announce that the National Assembly would soon vote on the abrogation of laws discriminating against homosexuals and to ask, therefore, in the interest of harmony, that the public prosecutor's office no longer institute proceedings based on article 331 of the penal code. Finally, in February 1982, the law on housing eliminated the requirement that renters be "good family men."

In spite of these measures, both rapid and unprecedented, one issue persisted after May 1981: the abrogation of paragraph 2 of article 331, which banned homosexual activity before the age of eighteen, even though the "heterosexual age of consent" was fifteen. President Mitterrand committed himself to take action in the name of equality before the law.

Surprisingly, this antihomosexual article was of relatively recent origin. It dated from the Vichy government and had originated in an order given by Marshal Pétain on August 6, 1942. Before that time, one would have had to go back to the ancien régime to find the "crime of sodomy" in the penal code: in 1783, a monk who had committed a sexual act with another man was burned alive, after his limbs had been broken. The revolutionary law of 1789 and the Napoleonic Code were silent on the issue of homosexuality—thanks to Jean-Jacques Régis de Cambacérès, himself a homosexual, whose nickname was "Tante Hurlurette" [Little Miss Eccentric]. It was under Pétain that laws limiting the rights of homosexuals reappeared in France.

With the Liberation, the government of the Fourth Republic sought to eliminate all anti-Semitic laws, and yet the orders given by Vichy concerning homosexuality were integrated unchanged into the penal code. Article 331–3 stipulated that any homosexual act with an individual younger than twenty-one was punishable by imprisonment. If two minors of the same sex were caught together, they could even be charged under case law with "mutual assault and battery." In 1960, this inequality between homosexuals and heterosexuals was exacerbated when homosexuality was listed as one of the "social scourges" in a bill by the Gaullist deputy Paul Mirguet. In June 1974 the age of civil majority was lowered, and this automatically changed the "homosexual age of consent." There was still a difference between the age of consent for heterosexuals, which was set at fifteen, and the age of consent for gays, set at eighteen. It was on this basis that militants mobilized in the early 1980s.

Several legislative bills, particularly the one by Senator Henri Caillavet,[36] in March 1978, and those by Michel Crépeau (MRG), Jean-Pierre Chevènement (PS), and Michel Rocard (PS), in 1979, advocated equality before the law for homosexuals. Giscard d'Estaing was favorable at the time, and, on behalf of the government, Monique Pelletier, secretary of state for the minister of justice, proposed suppressing paragraph 3. But the debates in the National Assembly proved more delicate than the government had expected, especially since the bill was presented during sessions devoted to rape, a circumstance that distorted the bill's intent. On November 19, 1980, homosexual public indecency was decriminalized; it became a misdemeanor, and article 330–2, which had made homosexual indecency a more serious offense, was abrogated. This key vote marked the end of discriminatory measures related to homosexual acts between adults. The same day, however, a bill by Deputy Jean Foyer was adopted to maintain the "offense of homosexuality" for relations with a minor between fifteen and eighteen years old. "All the same, this High Assembly will not vote to reestablish a law that comes from Pétain!" proclaimed Senator Cécile Goldet (PS) at the session. (Ordinarily, to indicate her boredom, Goldet preferred to sit and knit on the benches of the Palais du Luxembourg.) "Homosexuality is not a criminal offense, even when those who commit it are not Gide or Pierre Loti or Cocteau," the senator added in a firm tone. Despite the offensive led by certain Socialist deputies in the name of equality—with Raymond Forni and Joseph Franceschi in the lead—paragraph 3 of article 331 survived a third vote in the National Assembly.[37] Philippe Marchand, a Socialist, summarized the debate as follows: "Is it natural that, in our country, an old man of eighty-five can have sexual relations with a girl who is fifteen years and one day old and risk nothing if she gives her consent, whereas a young woman of twenty, who has relations with a girl of seventeen years and eleven months, risks three years in prison?"[38] Once again a petition circulated[39] while the Socialists referred the bill to the constitutional council, invoking the principle of equality before the law. The council rejected the appeal.[40]

The parliamentary majority and the constitutional judge thus agreed on the issue of maintaining a form of homosexual discrimination, which had strong symbolic value, although it may have had little real effect. Six months later, in June 1981, the parliamentary balance of power had shifted, and the issue immediately came up again. These successive jolts to an evolving citizenry pointed more than ever to the paradoxes of French political life.

In this last, post-1981 homosexual battle for equalizing the legal age of consent, Gisèle Halimi, a key feminist figure, orchestrated the debate. Homosexuals and feminists crossed paths one last time.

᠆

Gisèle Halimi was the most famous advocate of women's cause. Her life history was closely linked to the history of the women's movement, even though, being something of a reformist, she deviated somewhat from the movement. Founder and copresident of Choisir, in 1972 she defended Marie-Claire, the sixteen-year-old girl at the Bobigny trial. Through her defense, she shifted the legal system's views on abortion, and soon the views of the country as a whole. In 1978, at the Aix-en-Provence trial, she also supported the two homosexual women who had been raped in the Marseilles inlet, this time exposing the issue of rape to public view. Finally, in April 1981, she organized the meeting of Choisir where Mitterrand unambiguously pronounced himself in favor of eliminating discrimination against homosexuals. Elected as a deputy (PS) from Isère in June 1981, Halimi found herself responsible for drafting the report on homosexuals on behalf of the legal commission, "because nobody else wanted to do it."[41]

The abrogation of article 331–2 would not be easy, given the guerrilla war being conducted by the senate and by Jean Foyer in the National Assembly. His argument was unsurprising: legislation that was too tolerant would "exert a gravitational pull" and would end up promoting homosexuality. He was also worried about the influence such liberalization might have on "young people who are not yet completely mature."[42] Here again was the grand tradition, in legislation and law enforcement, of claiming that homosexuality could be encouraged.[43]

Thus there was serious resistance, "tougher than for the abolition of the death penalty," as Robert Badinter, minister of justice, would say. As a result, between the senate and the National Assembly, the abrogation dragged on from the winter of 1981 to the summer of 1982. "According to them, I wanted to turn France into a huge brothel," Halimi recalls today. One member of the assembly shouted at her, "You are nothing but a beast of pleasure!" The newspaper *Présent* was even more direct: "It's open season on little boys for one fine summer in the Sodom and Gomorrah of advanced Socialism" (June 26, 1982). Despite these heated debates, Halimi was backed without reservation by Badinter.

Addressing the National Assembly, the minister of justice launched into a history of homosexual repression that Foucault himself could have written: "Nineteenth-century legislators knew very well—by long experience, as I dare not say— that repression never had the slightest effect on homosexual practices." Adorning his speech with free quotations from Jean-Louis Bory and jokes drawn from "dragqueen mythology," which had now attained the status of official resistance, Badinter explained that "if there is any perversion here, it is perversion of the law." Finally, in response to Jean Foyer—who asked, gravely, "Can you stand the idea of a lecherous old man sodomizing a boy of fifteen?"— the minister of justice fixed his eyes on him and said simply, "To use your expression, I am no more capable of standing the sight of a lecherous old man sodomizing a little girl of fifteen."[44] The caryatids and atlantes of the Bourbon palace shuddered.

Beyond its anecdotal value, Badinter's speech to the representatives of the nation had considerable symbolic importance. Indeed, on that day the minister of justice replaced "denial of recognition" with an unprecedented word of acknowledgment, perfectly summed up in the preamble to his speech: "It is high time that we say how much France owes to homosexuals, as to all other citizens, in so many areas."

On July 27, 1982, thanks to the overwhelming Socialist majority in the assembly, Badinter and Halimi won on the fourth vote.[45] The bill that passed consisted of a single article: "Paragraph 2 of article 331 of the penal code is abrogated."[46] *Le Monde* ran the headline "The End of Homophobic Law."

➦

In one year, the Socialist government had purged French law of most of its archaisms in matters of sexual mores. This "cascade" of measures, which must be set in a more global context of increasing individual freedom, remains without precedent in the history of French homosexuals. "Homosexuals, you've got a new boss," Guy Hocquenghem concluded in *Libération* on December 22, 1981, in a long article with that title.

All the same, the new forces in power took care not to replace repressive laws with legislation favoring homosexuals as a category or special-interest group, something that might have proved contrary to the freedom and interests of the people concerned.

As the first geraniums were blooming on Jean-Louis Bory's grave in Méreville, the left he had embraced came to power. In a public tribute, Gisèle Halimi, Robert Badinter, Louis Joinet, and Gaston Defferre had not forgotten his lessons and his relentless battle for the "right to indifference."

8

Swan Song

> I do not believe our objective ought to be a kind of absolute freedom, total freedom of action in the realm of sexuality.
>
> —Michel Foucault (1982)

On December 12, 1983, Jean Genet was awarded the Grand Prix National de Littérature. Masterfully turning the tables, the author of *Querelle de Brest* [*Querelle of Brest*] chose to be represented at the ceremony by a black fifteen-year-old ephebe. A smiling Jack Lang good-humoredly accepted the writer's whim and handed the prize over to the handsome proxy.

During the same period, Gaston Defferre, minister of the interior, made a bet with his friend Genet that the Republican Guard would honor him. In a totally Felliniesque scene, the little man in a black leather jacket, walking beside the old Protestant minister, climbed the main staircase of Place Beauvau between two lines of military men standing at attention.

And so it went in the 1980s. Homosexuals seemed to be "winners" on every score and could even allow themselves a few fantasies. Gays played a role in fashion trends, at a time when couturiers were redesigning men's underwear. Jean-Paul Gaultier paraded Boy George and dressed Régine Chopinot's dancers.

In this context, the end of the "Chéri(e)" personal ads in *Libération* may have been simply an epiphenomenon. And yet. . . .

⟿

The last homosexual demands were gradually being met: Lang lifted the ban on certain films and books in 1983, and the article of the penal code requiring public employees to be "of good moral character and conduct" was abrogated in the new universal statute on public employees (July 13, 1983). As for Defferre, on February 7, 1984, he received a delegation of militants on the delicate question of police files and named a parliamentary attaché for homosexual affairs to his office.

Nevertheless, the euphoria surrounding Mitterrand's victory was followed by a large-scale demobilization within all the social movements. In mid-March 1983, the Socialists negotiated the key economic turning point of the leftist government, and public opinion did not see that a certain kind of socialism was on its last legs. The right and the left were now to be distinguished primarily on moral or cultural grounds: economic liberalism became the chosen government, and the national consensus on political institutions was reaffirmed.

It was in this context—the end of utopian thinking (paradoxically marked by the emergence of the Front National in Dreux, on September 4, 1983)—that Yvette Roudy's "antisexist" legislative bill appeared. It was supposed to be the culmination of feminist and homosexual demands and of the public battle against discrimination.

↬

Jean-Pierre Michel is one of the Socialist figures who best sums up that period. A magistrate from Nîmes who frequented La Buvette with some former members of the FHAR in the mid-1970s, he was now a member of the Syndicat National de la Magistrature [National union of the magistracy]. There, and within the Mouvement d'Action Judiciaire [Movement of legal action], or MAJ, he established ties with homosexual militants, first those in the GLH and then those in the CUARH. These friendships explain how leftist jurists (Louis Joinet and Jean-Pierre Michel, but also Dominique Charvet and Robert Badinter) were able to mobilize so quickly in favor of homosexual demands after May 1981.

When François Mitterrand became president of the republic, Jean-Pierre Michel was forty-three years old; he was elected deputy from Haute-Saône on the "pink wave." He later became vice president of the National Assembly and a member of the Commission Nationale Informatique et Liberté [National computer and freedom commission]. He headed the session of the National Assembly during debates on the abrogation of article 331-2, ably backing Robert Badinter and Gisele Halimi in their final confrontations with Deputy Jean Foyer. In March 1983 Michel again found himself chair of the legal commission, for the "antisexist" bill defended by Yvette Roudy. This time, however, the government would retreat from the feminist struggle.

THE CHOSEN GHETTO

Since the early 1980s and the rifts within the MLF and *Questions Féministes*, the women's movement had not found its hoped-for second wind. Despite the activities of the MLF-*déposé*, stemming from the Psychépo camp of Antoinette Fouque, and despite the activities of organizations associated with feminism, such as Halimi's Choisir, it seems that the Ministry of Women's Rights, headed by Roudy from 1981 on, took the place of the women's movement. "Women have not gotten up off the couch that Antoinette Fouque and Luce Irigaray put them on," the writer Anne Garreta comments harshly.

Homosexual women were also trying to find their way. "I thought feminism was going to solve my problems," Catherine Deudon, a former Gouine Rouge, explains today:

But, as an individual, I feel like I got a raw deal. After the movement, I was all alone with my problems. Seventies feminism made the mistake of confusing the legitimate demand for sexual equality with homosexuality. Somewhere, we had a totalitarian system in our heads: everyone was supposed to be bisexual, if not homosexual. The result was that only homosexual women stayed in the movement. An insidious aristocracy of homosexuality was set in place—a lot of hierarchies characteristic of small tribes—but it was never made explicit. In the end, that upset everyone, including homosexual women like me, who found they were back in the same ghetto they had fled when they joined the movement. Part of that mistake was to make feminism exclusively female from the beginning. I miss the time when people looked for an ideal of freedom and rejected confining labels and definitions, a time when we did not need to define ourselves as homosexuals or heterosexuals.

The Maison des Femmes [Women's house] was created in Paris in 1982 as a meeting place, at the initiative of feminists and homosexual women; it was subsidized by Roudy's ministry. The house was the creation of the MLF–*non déposé*: pluralism triumphed for the first time, and the different feminist camps—with the exception of Psychépo—all met there. But, unlike identical spots in the provinces (for example, the later Centre Simone-de-Beauvoir, in Nantes), the Maison des Femmes chose to be exclusively female—surprising for a place financed by the government. Various lesbian groups attracted by this exclusivist space "appropriated" the Maison des Femmes, becoming its principal users. Situated on a seedy dead-end street lined with the carcasses of wrecked cars, the Maison des Femmes soon became the focal point of all the tensions within the declining MLF. Today, privately operated and deprived of government subsidies, it is threatened with closure.

In the realm of homosexual militancy, two sensibilities have struggled to survive since the early 1980s. The first located itself on the fringes of the movement and, even while preserving its autonomy, did not rule out participation in actions alongside the last troops of feminism or even the male homosexual movement. These women attempted to move beyond the opposition between feminism and lesbianism; they claimed to be "lesbian feminists." For the most part, they emerged from a series of organized meetings in Paussac, Dordogne (July 1979), in Marcevol in the Pyrenees (July 1980), or in L'Euzières, Cévennes (July 1981).

Two new groups that appeared in 1981 and are still in existence today have placed themselves in the "lesbian feminist" tradition. MIEL [see chap. 7] was created in conjunction with the CUARH in the summer of 1981 at the meetings (with 600 participants) in L'Euzières. Housed at the Maison des Femmes, and one of its most active components, in 1983 MIEL created a "lesbian cafeteria" called Hydromel. The MIEL girls—who kissed in public, shouted "Down with straights," and rejected lesbians with children—learned moderation as they came into contact with feminists. Françoise Renaud explains, "We still believe that lesbians' problems are also women's problems. But it is clear we will never again fight for such issues as contraception/abortion, because we feel this entails working for other people, that is, it entails accommodating heterosexuality."[1] Since 1994, MIEL has been gradually disappearing and has no real social base.

In the "lesbian feminist" tradition, an autonomous journal, *Lesbia*, was created in December 1982 by Christiane Jouve and Catherine Marjollet. It fancied itself rather convivial, culturally oriented, and not particularly militant. *Lesbia* organized disco parties, which were unlike the celebrations in the feminist movement (guitars slung over shoulders, and protest songs). During homosexual demonstrations, the *Lesbia* girls appeared with bare breasts, to indicate the evolution of the lesbian look. But, unlike *Gai Pied*, *Lesbia* did not become professionalized. The work of volunteers and the absence of a real financial market is probably still the main difference between female and male homosexuality. As for the classified ads, which had appeared in *Lesbia* from the beginning, they had a "soft," sentimental tone, which also distinguishes the sexuality of lesbians from that of gay men: "F who has seen 32 springs," "A shoulder offered for big kisses," "Young F, still in high school, seeks friend, 30 to 40 years old, masculine build, you perhaps," "Young F seeks F for biking weekends." An attempt at an "erotic superposter" went nowhere. The girls of MIEL insulted the editors of *Lesbia* in 1983 with the slogan "That's not what being a lesbian means." When the writer Hélène de Monferrand became a regular contributor to *Lesbia*, some homosexual women interpreted this as a move to the right on the journal's part. "No," replies Catherine Gonnard, the current editor in chief. "We are trying to allow for the coexistence of all political sympathies, from Michèle Causse to Hélène de Monferrand." *Lesbia*'s monthly circulation is now close to 10,000.

The second camp of lesbian militancy liked to believe it was the heir to the Front des Lesbiennes Radicales, which was inspired by Monique Wittig, and which had fallen apart in the summer of 1982. An antifeminist movement, it considered women who were nostalgic for the MLF to be "heterofeminists." The label "radical lesbian"—not "lesbian feminist"—defines them perfectly.

The Archives Lesbiennes [Lesbian archives], or ARCL, belongs to this tradition. A kind of documentation center, the archives were created in 1984 by Claudie Lesselier for the exclusive use of radical lesbians. "It was absurd," its founder acknowledges today. Then the archives became integrated into the Maison des Femmes, with nonfeminist lesbians taking over and toning down their radicalism. "Lesbians have a particular relation to archives," explains Catherine Gonnard of *Lesbia*. "We have such a need for memory, history, because it has been completely concealed from us." Concealed? The archives, a ghetto within the ghetto, are open fewer than three hours a week and, naturally, are closed to men. As a result, "radical lesbianism," of its own accord, has slipped into secrecy.

⌇

After 1981, the new Socialist government took on the task of improving women's condition. Mitterrand entrusted ministerial responsibilities to a number of women; Parliament voted to have Sécurité Sociale reimburse costs for voluntary interruption of pregnancy (December 1981) and adopted a law on professional equality between men and women (June 29, 1983).

In spite of this, a symbolic bill from the Ministry of Women's Rights, quickly named the "antisexist" law, languished for a long time. To Yvette Roudy's mind, it was a question of setting up deterrents, on the model of the 1972 antiracist law, and enacting "positive discrimination." The idea was to protect women's image, especially in advertising and the media, and to allow women's organizations to file civil suits.

The bill, when it was adopted by the Council of Ministries on March 9, 1983, caused an outcry that included sarcasm, derision, and personal attacks on Roudy, who was compared to an "ayatollah" (*Le Matin*, March 18, 1983) and to a "nun stupefied by young breasts under tight sweaters" (*Minute*, March 16). People attacked Roudy's "dreadful, outdated pants" and then her new "Chanel-style suits." They made fun of the interview she granted to *Lui*, and several journalists (*Le Matin*, March 18) wondered who could legitimately lodge a formal complaint: the lesbian movement? the movement of housewives? In *Le Nouvel Observateur* (March 18), Katherine Pancol reproached feminists for producing "generations of homosexuals" through such laws: "Madame Roudy, we are grownups. We take the pill, we earn our keep, we throw fits. We can settle things with the guys all by ourselves." *Gai Pied Hebdo* had an ambivalent reaction: at first it thought the "fig leaf" bill was puritanical; then, realizing the law could be extended to homosexuals, it changed course and supported it, envisioning an antihomophobic law (April 2, 1983).

Simone de Beauvoir, for her part, energetically defended Roudy and appreciated her style. At Roudy's invitation, she agreed to participate in several meetings at the ministry: "I did not think there was such a capacity for male chauvinist hysteria in France" (*Le Monde*, May 4). In *Marie-Claire* (June 1983), a more disillusioned Anne Zelensky, whose opinion piece had been turned down by *Le Monde*, explained, "We knew this bill was explosive. ... We felt we had reached the limits of what we could do within a male chauvinist system."

Roudy's bill was opposed by everyone; it made strange bedfellows of those who wanted to weaken the government for political reasons and those who harbored a certain misogyny without admitting it publicly. Moreover, the bill was the object of numerous attacks by journalists who were less sensitive to their moral obligations than to the possible legal ramifications for the press's advertising revenues.

Roudy herself committed a number of blunders; in particular, she sided with feminists, and especially with lesbians, to raise the stakes and fight for a more radical text. Thus, the day before the government adopted the Roudy bill, feminists in the women's movement and lesbians in MIEL demonstrated, announcing that they would boycott the 1983 municipal elections. They brandished the slogan "Yvette, you've been hoodwinked, that's not what we want!" ["*Yvette, poudre aux yeux, c'est pas ce qu'on veut!*"] The radical lesbians, MIEL, and the CUARH subsequently proposed broadening the antisexist bill to include discrimination against homosexuals.

Today, the writer Annie Le Brun has a harsh analysis of these developments:

With the Roudy law, neofeminists confirmed in 1983 that sexual liberation had never been their objective. They set up the equivalent of new virtue leagues, and in so doing they demonstrated their desire to "eradicate desire," a sign of their hatred for the body— which is so present in Simone de Beauvoir. What is a liberation movement if its only aim is to prohibit, purge libraries, control school curricula? A long time ago, the neopuritans of the MLF lost sight of the essential need for freedom in love, which was defended by their predecessors, the libertarian feminists at the turn of the century. Neofeminists have exacerbated the isolation of men and women, at a time when our societies are opting for separation in all its forms, in order to put an end to what remains of our individuality.[2]

Inundated by passions on both sides, in 1983 the government finally gave up the idea of submitting Roudy's bill to Parliament. "And the macho sky came down on my head," the minister commented simply.[3] The failure of the "antisexist" law confirmed the fact that a certain kind of feminist intransigence no longer had support within the government, or even in public opinion. This failure also indicated the distance that now separated zealous feminists from the watered-down left. For feminists, the era of scission was succeeded by an era of disillusionment.[4]

In the 1970s, militants in the sexual liberation movements had lived under the illusion that "everything" was possible; they justified their excesses by the cause they were defending. Irresponsibility, disproportion, and the carefree life were integral parts of this utopia. After 1981, the Socialists learned, at their own expense, that it took moderation and rigor to "change life."

⮑

Just as the failure of the Roudy law shattered the feminist dream, the Le Coral scandal played a similar role in putting an end to the pedophiliac dream. Within this overall logic—despite some essential differences, if not complete antagonism—the Roudy law and the Le Coral affair put a definitive end to the idea of boundless utopias.

Until the legal age for homosexual relations was lowered, in 1982, the pedophiliac and gay causes seemed to go hand in hand. From Situationist leaflets in the Strasbourg of 1966 to the "let's learn to make love" documents distributed in 1971 by Dr. Carpentier at the Lycée de Corbeil, and from the scandal surrounding the philosophy professor Nicole Mercier (who was criticized for an unorthodox course) to the creation of the Conseil Supérieur de l'Information Sexuelle [Higher council on sexual information] recommended by Lucien Neuwirth, issues of sexual liberation regularly intersected those that had to do with the sexuality of minors.[5]

In the late 1970s, a number of scandals involving homosexuality and education demonstrated the importance of the subject. In addition to the issue of sexual relations without consent—that is, rape or sexual assault (the new names for public indecency)—the issue most often raised by the mounting scandals was the possibility that a homosexual might be teaching young people or otherwise be in contact with them.

Foucault, questioned on this point in 1982, gave a response that has the merit of clarity:

Do you think the instructors who told children for years, dozens of years, centuries, that homosexuality was unacceptable, and the school manuals that purged literature and falsified history in order to exclude certain kinds of sexual behavior, have not caused at least as much damage as what can be imputed to a homosexual instructor who talks about homosexuality, and whose only sin is to explain a given reality, a lived experience? . . . A homosexual instructor should not pose any more problems than a bald instructor, a male professor in a girls' school, a female professor in a boys' school, or an Arab professor in a school in the sixteenth arrondissement of Paris. As for the problem of the homosexual instructor who actively seeks to seduce his students, all I can say is that the possibility of this problem is present in every pedagogical situation. There are many more examples of this type of behavior among heterosexual instructors—quite simply because they make up the majority of instructors.[6]

Added to the issue of education was the issue of the age of consent. In 1977, intellectuals published an appeal in *Le Monde* on behalf of three men imprisoned for nonviolent public indecency with consenting fifteen-year-old minors. A petition, asking that children's right to a sexual life be acknowledged, asserted forthrightly, "Three years in prison for kissing and fondling: that's quite enough!"[7] The petition attracted emblematic personalities on the left, many homosexual militants (particularly former FHAR figures), and the most famous supporters of the pedophiliac cause.

Some, skirting censorship and repression, found it exciting from that point on to cause outrage and shock the self-righteous. A few writers wanted to fight for pedophilia and make the cause fashionable. "My pedophilia takes an interest in impubic boys," wrote Tony Duvert in *L'enfant au masculin* [Child in masculine form]:

But when does impuberty begin? Babies are not yet appealing to me; little boys of two or three are wildly attractive to me, but this passion has remained platonic; I have never made love to a boy younger than six, and this lack of experience, although it breaks my heart, does not really frustrate me. At six, however, the fruit seems ripe to me: he's a man and lacks nothing. This ought to be the age of consent. That day will come. So much for children. When your lovers reach puberty, you cease to be a pedophile: you become a pederast.

In 1980, two courageous books appeared to denounce "pederasty, [which] has often taken on the trappings and prestige of social nonconformity and sexual liberation."[8] In response to these attacks, Duvert replied ironically, "I don't dare count up the hundreds or thousands of years of prison my love affairs ought already to have earned me."[9]

⌐

With respect to this well-worn subject, the scandal of Le Coral, which broke in France in October 1982, was almost a caricature, combining the issues of education, troubled childhood, and pedophilia.

Le Coral was a "group home," established near Montpellier, where mildly disabled adolescents were placed. It all began when several well-known personalities, photographed in the company of these minors, were accused of having had sexual relations with them. This somber affair, a veritable legal conundrum, was immediately exploited by the far right, which attempted to show that the leftist government was inevitably lax and immoral. The coincidence of dates is striking: the Le Coral affair came to light only weeks after the abrogation of article 331–2; thus it appears to have been an attempt to pursue, on the field of public denunciation, a battle lost in the parliamentary arena. *Présent*'s interpretation of the affair (on October 20, 1982) confirms this analysis: "Whoever legalizes or normalizes sin (the pill, abortion, homosexuality, lewd behavior) commits disgraceful attacks on the innocent. ... Here it is, then, the new liberationist therapy of our leftists. It serves, odiously, the neurotic resentment of sexual impotents, repressed living detritus, authorizing them to commit every sort of crime against innocence." Increasingly large concentric circles were targeted by way of Le Coral: pedophiles, group homes, homosexuals, the leftist government. To add a sensational aspect to a scandal that was already sordid, the names of members of the government and of intellectuals, notably Pierre Mauroy, Jack Lang, Félix Guattari, and Michel Foucault, were cited and appeared in falsified documents. One hysteric and pathological liar even went so far as to release photos of the minister of culture at Le Coral: "We were dealing with a madman," Lang concludes.[10] Although these four personalities were immediately exonerated, the establishment's two directors were incarcerated; the philosopher René Schérer was brought up on charges, but the charges were later dismissed.[11]

At the beginning of the affair, some homosexual militants, supported by a few intellectuals, had attempted to defend Schérer by taking advantage of the Socialist presence at the head of the government. But their actions, unlike the abrogation of article 331–2 of the penal code, found no support. In the first place, *Libération*, which had published a number of articles in favor of pedophilia in the late 1970s, now refused to take up the fight. Christian Hennion, who at the time was covering the Le Coral issue for *Libération*, recalls today, "I wanted to mount a campaign. But the pedophiles wanted a militant leftist position and apologies to the people who were being harassed in this scandal. We were doing spin control; we were no longer fighting." Neither *Libération* nor, a fortiori, Minister of Justice Robert Badinter nor even *Gai Pied* continued to support pedophiles. Only the CUARH and its journal *Homophonies*, which made pedophilia one of its themes of choice, took up the fight.[12] As for the writer Gabriel Matzneff, then a columnist at *Le Monde*, he attempted to mount a campaign but was disavowed by the newspaper's editorial board, and he left shortly thereafter.[13]

The consequences of these events, which received a great deal of media attention, were enormous, and the Le Coral affair—despite its mysteries, which were
never elucidated—may have been a turning point. On the one hand, some homosexuals, through a clear concern about liability, chose to distance themselves from
the issue of pedophilia and now refused to combine it with the homosexual struggle. On the other hand, a few diehards (for example, the CUARH) raised the
stakes, rejected all social standards, demanded legislation that would set the age of
consent at thirteen or even eleven, and denounced the "totalitarianism" imposed
by mothers on their children. For René Schérer, "the Le Coral affair was an important moment in the modern legal system's general mobilization against pedophilia." The photographer Bernard Faucon, whose works illustrate almost exclusively the "theology of childhood," explains today that in France "pedophilia has
become a subject on which debate is no longer possible." By contrast, Hervé Liffran, a prominent figure in the CUARH and today a journalist for *Le Canard Enchaîné*, looks back critically on the matter: "For the most part, the homosexual
movement was on the wrong track about pedophilia. The free consent of children
was an error."

A great deal of bitterness remained in 1983 among the supporters of pedophilia,
who could argue, not without some truth, that their struggle had contributed to
homosexual liberation and to the implementation of true sex education for the
young. Nevertheless, the growing distance between homosexuals and pedophiles
could not be separated from the abrogation of article 331–2. Beginning in the
summer of 1982, consensual homosexual relations were considered legal after the
age of fifteen, and so the domain of pedophilia shifted to below that age. The stakes
had changed, and the pedophiles were necessarily marginalized. From that point
on, pedophilia was judged more and more severely, eclipsing the day when Gide
could publicly sing the praises of "little Moroccans."

Homosexual militants and pedophiles no longer circulated joint petitions.
Gays had succeeded in untangling their own cause from the pedophiliac cause,
which was now judged hopeless. The more positive attitude toward homosexuals
came with a new requirement: that they no longer have relations with boys under
fifteen. Even as they abandoned their marginality in the early 1980s, homosexuals
saw, with satisfaction and not without a certain ingratitude, a minority group
within their own sexual minority—and, as a result, their Bluebeard image—fall
conveniently away from their new lives.

⌒

Among pedophilia's supporters in 1983 and 1984 was Guy Hocquenghem,
standing side by side with Schérer, his old professor and mentor. What, since the
heroic era of the FHAR, had become of the most famous French homosexual
militant?

After making a controversial amateur film with Lionel Soucaz in 1979, titled

Race d'Ep ("pederast," in back slang), Hocquenghem continued to produce an original and much discussed body of work that depicted a xenophobic and chilly France (*La beauté du métis* [The beauty of the wog]). What was even more significant, in 1979 he published a survey of the "new right," with which he apparently shared an admiration for Pasolini, and for his death; that survey supported the "right to difference" and the "rejection of universalism." Because of this article, which was judged too ambiguous, he was forced to end his association with *Libération*.[14]

When the Le Coral affair surfaced, Hocquenghem, who had already had difficulty coming to terms with the May 10 election, claimed to have been betrayed by the Socialists for whom he had got out the vote, and he denounced them for going back on their word. Like Baudelaire and Renan, both disenchanted with the 1848 revolution, Hocquenghem chose to retreat, after his disillusionment in May 1981, as in May 1968, into aesthetics and literature. But first he took care to settle the score with the "little Socialist Rastignacs" by authoring two pamphlets, cries of incomprehension from a man abandoned and cornered by a form of homosexuality that was now socially acceptable. In 1983 he published *Les petits garçons* [Little boys], which discreetly depicted the Le Coral affair. In it, under cover of pseudonyms, was everyone, from Lang to Foucault,[15] who had not wanted to defend "Stratos," alias Schérer, against the Socialist ministers. For Hocquenghem, their actions symbolized the first waffling of the leftist government. The message was clear: Schérer was Dreyfus, and Foucault had not been Zola.

In March 1986, Hocquenghem made public his *Lettre à ceux qui sont passés du col Mao au Rotary Club* [Letter to those who have gone from the Mao collar to the Rotary Club]. This time he attacked ex-leftists by name: "For you, the important thing is not to be on the right or on the left, but on the winning side. . . . Co-opted, wearing your turncoat medals around your necks, you are the Legion of Dishonor, the decorated veterans of the about-face." Criticizing the consensus party, which had "Glucksmann's nose, Serge July's cigar, Coluche's round glasses, Lang's tan, Bizot's long hair, Debray's mustache, BHL's open shirt, and Kouchner's voice," he also attacked Patrice Chéreau, "the Andromache of the outhouse," and Laurent Fabius, "Normale grad . . . experienced in every sort of treachery."

Angelo Rinaldo commented immediately:

Mr. Hocquenghem is a shooter who wastes his bullets, spraying them every which way until, running out of ammunition, he picks up whatever he can from the gutter. We no longer tolerate people's use of physical shortcomings to disparage individuals, like prewar barking dogs on the far right. . . . With all the inaccuracies and all the excesses and all the long-windedness that mar his talent . . . , Mr. Hocquenghem has proved that he belongs irremediably to his native tribe. . . . Leftism has produced no writers.[16]

Questioned today, Jack Lang, who associated with Hocquenghem and Schérer in the 1970s, attempts to explain this evolution: "He is a very odd character, with whom I had a very difficult relationship. Anyone who was politically close to him was by nature an enemy. I had hardly got myself settled on rue de Valois when Guy Hocquenghem criticized me in *Libération* on the issue of film censorship. I had not yet done anything, and he already suspected me of not taking action. Of course I abolished censorship."[17]

Disgusted with the Socialists, Hocquenghem was also fed up with homosexual militancy, as he confided in 1984 to Hugo Marsan, editor-in-chief of *Gai Pied*: "Does this have anything to do with what used to be called revolution? I don't think so. . . . In general, the typical homosexual militant is an extremely slow, frustrated person, someone with a shriveled, hard, touchy psyche, who gives advice about morality and wants to secure safety, an identity."[18]

In a way, the writer Marcel Jouhandeau had seen things clearly when he shouted at the May '68 militants, "Go home! In ten years you'll all be notary publics." Hocquenghem, because he refused to repudiate his own views[19] and become a "notary public," gradually became marginalized and isolated and finally chose to turn in on himself and devote himself to writing fiction. But first he predicted an inevitable backlash: "Mitterrand played the queer card in the election. If he is made to regret it, he will not hesitate to change course. He did it with the economy and with the immigrants, and he can do it with the queers, with less damage."[20]

What is disturbing about Hocquenghem's development is the shift from an initial indeterminacy—an indifferentiation of the sexes, which constituted the FHAR's theoretical power—to a homosexual particularism, raised to the level of race. Homosexuality as a "worldview": for the first time, Hocquenghem was taking his own words seriously.

ART: ANOTHER FORM OF MILITANCY?

On September 4, 1984, ten years after the first *Dossiers de l'écran* devoted to homosexuality, Antenne 2 did it again. The symbolic broadcast, titled "Etre gay en 1984" [To be gay in 1984] no longer included priests and doctors among its guests, nor did it include old Deputy Mirguet [see chap. 3]. Now the legal system, the church, and the medical establishment were replaced by writers (Dominique Fernandez, Renaud Camus, Jocelyne François), the historian Paul Veyne (a specialist in the classical age), and Hugo Marsan, managing editor of *Gai Pied Hebdo*. Although there was still one psychiatrist (Didier Seux), he had experience in the treatment of homosexuals, who made up the greater part of his practice. The times had changed: "Queens are no longer caged" [*Les folles ne sont plus en cage*] was the headline of *Le Crapouillot*.

Self-styled militant spokespersons had apparently been replaced by writers; art had once more become a particular form of militancy. As in Gide's day, but with new methods and an updated discourse, writers appeared on television to delineate the gay life, with its codes, its prescribed refrains, its leitmotifs. The discourse on homosexuality became plural and voluble, redundant and nonstop.

"All in all, the role played by culture in the evolution of homosexuality has re-placed the one played by militancy," Jean-Pierre Joecker observed in 1985. Joecker had launched the review *Masques*, putting his money on a forum for reflection and culture.[21]

The parallel lives of two writers, Jocelyne François and Dominique Fernandez, who both participated in the 1984 *Les dossiers de l'écran* broadcast, shed light on this evolution. François had been awarded the Prix Féminina in 1980; Fernandez, the Prix Goncourt in 1982. Both contributed to the review *Masques* and repre-sented the new face of homosexuality in France.

In *L'étoile rose*, published in 1978, Fernandez contrasts two characters be-longing to different generations. The younger one calls himself "gay," whereas the older thinks of himself as a "pariah." They begin an intermittent romantic rela-tionship, with a new conception of the homosexual couple serving as backdrop. The relationship is based on deep love and, at least for one partner, on fidelity—a departure from the militant discourse of the time. "I received a very large number of letters," Fernandez recalls today. "All the readers told me they were like the older hero of the book, that they had trouble dealing with their homosexuality in the provinces." Initially, the book was supposed to have been called *La lie de la terre* [The dregs of the earth].

"For me," Fernandez says today, "it was a way of being a politically committed writer. I no longer had the right to keep quiet." Speaking out was part of the author's life history, which can be read as a long coming-out process made up of a series of victorious battles waged one after another. It was an attempt to gradually live an authentic life.

Through the narrator of *L'étoile rose*, Fernandez also evoked what the enigma of homosexuality had been for him as an adolescent: "Knowing nothing of the evil that tormented me, deprived of an internal oracle who could have done no more than choose among so many portents, I was constantly ill at ease. I didn't feel safe anywhere, not in a deserted street, not in the middle of a crowd. A passerby asked me what time it was: I pretended not to hear." As a student preparing for entrance to the Ecole Normale Supérieure in 1946, Fernandez tried to write a paper on Vautrin, Balzac's great homosexual character: the paper was rejected. "I went home to my mother a little more depressed each time," adds the narrator of *L'étoile rose*. "Hiding from her, lying to my friends, desert as far as my eye could see, re-morse and shame to be suffered between escapades for a whole school term, the specter of old age already beckoning, vague plans of marriage broken, less from scruples than from cowardice. That was all I could expect from life."

Once he had earned his *agrégation*, Fernandez taught at the French Institute in Naples but was dismissed for giving an unorthodox lecture on Roger Vailland. He then chose marriage to the very understanding Diane de Margerie, who was perfectly well informed of the situation, and he had two children with her. "I was persuaded that homosexuality was a dead end," Fernandez explains today. "My image of love between men was life as a scoundrel, as the dregs of society, a life in ports with sailors. I wanted to be like other people. So, not being a misogynist, I got married." Married until 1971, Fernandez did not really begin his homosexual life until 1972: he was forty-three. "We had our first experiences abroad," he recalls. "I was rather obtuse, but the fact that we were away from France removed our inhibitions." He fell in love with opera, Italy, and *ragazzi,* and he liberated himself from an emotional life that did not totally satisfy him. He began to publish various novels, especially *Porporino,* the story of two Neopolitan castrati (Prix Médicis, 1974). He still had to tell his mother. He wrote *L'étoile rose* in 1978 precisely for that purpose: "For over twenty years, the world forced me to lie. One day, I wanted my mother to know; I didn't want her to die without knowing who I was. I wrote the book and sent it to her." His mother responded: "Now I understand why you turned away from me at eighteen." Fernandez adds, still obviously moved nearly twenty years later, "I became much closer to her until her death: she was happy I had stopped lying to her."

In 1982, Fernandez published a fictional autobiography of Pasolini, *Dans la main de l'ange* [In the angel's hand], and this time *Gai Pied* ran the headline "Our Goncourt 1982." "My militancy always passed through the filter of literature," he says. "But I was never altogether at ease with militants, because they did not understand that the most important thing is not the gay cause. As a result, they never totally adopted me."

↬

Jocelyne François is even more atypical. Her relationship with a young woman she met at the end of her secondary studies blossomed into love during her university years. A priest's interference separated the two. Like Fernandez, François got married (to a man she did not love) and had three children (whom she did) but divorced seven years later to return to the woman who was waiting for her. *Les bonheurs* [Good times], her first novel, published in 1970, was burdened by the weight of this "disrupted passion." François, who categorically objects to the word "lesbian," explains, "What is unique to homosexuality counts less than the joining of two people who have chosen each other. Every life is unique."

Why, then, did she agree to appear on *Les dossiers de l'écran?* "It was not to aid the cause of homosexuality in any way, but rather to talk about reality—my reality, of course." For the same reason, she rejects the expression "homosexual writer" as an "absurd conglomerate": "I am one of the writers who think that literature is not in the service of any cause, that it is supremely free. Literature is a different path. The goal is not to militate but to write, to write things that get at the truth of being." Her own books, which are autobiographical in nature, include *Les amantes* [The women lovers] and *Joue-nous España* [Play "España" for us] (Prix Féminina, 1980). In them she attempts to live up to this definition of writing.

↪

Was homosexual militancy superseded by a "homosexual culture"? This phrase is rejected by both François and Fernandez, who find it unsatisfactory in that it encompasses only works that depict the rituals, lifestyles, and practices of homosexuals, without reaching the general through the particular. This supposed literary genre, which has its obligatory *exercices de style* (the acting out of desires or fantasies, the habits and customs of the tribe, the confession), has been aptly skewered by the critic Angelo Rinaldi as the genre of "regional specialties."[22]

The description of the sex act is another requisite scene in these works, a fact Foucault has attempted to explain: "The wink in the street, the instantaneous decision to seize the adventure, the speed with which homosexual relations are consummated, are all results of a prohibition. From the moment a homosexual culture and literature began to take shape, it was only natural that they would concentrate on the most burning and exciting aspect of homosexual relationships."[23] All the same, the philosopher had reservations about "homosexual culture." Although he called for gay publications that could make "a homosexual culture possible, as instruments for polymorphous, varied, individually modulated relationships," he found the idea "of an agenda" dangerous: "As soon as there is an agenda, it becomes a law, a ban on inventiveness. There ought to be an inventiveness characteristic of a situation such as ours, of the desire that Americans call 'coming out.'"[24] Foucault returned to this issue in another interview a few months later: "We need to understand that with our desires, through them, new forms of relationship take shape, new forms of love and new forms of art. Sex is not fatality; it is a possibility for achieving a creative life." But he added, "I am not sure that we have to create *our own* culture. We *do* have to create a culture. We have to produce cultural creations. In doing so, however, we come up against the problem of identity. I don't know what we would do to produce these creations, and I don't know what forms these creations would take."[25]

The refusal to form a "homosexual culture" in France seems to be part of a movement contrary to the one that emerged in the United States in the 1980s, where programs in gay studies have multiplied. The American writer Edmund White explains:

In the United States there is a very lively homosexual culture, and there is no mainstream literature. When you go into a bookstore that isn't specifically gay, there are shelves: black, Jewish, feminist, queer. . . . We don't have literature in itself, we have only special-interest groups, we have only ghettos. It's a reflection of our culture: we also have no average citizen or universal politics, we have lobbies.

The philosopher Alain Finkielkraut is skeptical about this movement:

The adolescent who discovers his homosexuality endures the ordeal of solitude: that is always painful. To break through this isolation there are books, of course. Your homosexual library normalizes you and, above all, gives you companions. But it is possible and necessary to go beyond these initial comforting words, and to read these authors in a different way. One must be intransigent on this point. If you classify Proust as a gay writer, you insult literature. Art exists to build a bridge between men, to make our world habitable, to clarify existence. It is a space for friendship, not for closed identities. If, under cover of an indispensable acknowledgment [of homosexuality], one submits literature to a ghetto mentality, things become dreadful.

Michel Tournier also sees the limits of the genre: "From the moment the writer is prisoner to a certain sensibility, he is diminished. At that moment, homosexuality becomes a disadvantage." The author of Le roi des aulnes [The ogre] likes to quote this line from a famous musician: "There are three sorts of pianists: the Jews, the homosexuals, and the mediocre." He compares the issue of homosexuality today to the issue of Jewishness:

When Albert Cohen uses Jewishness without calling attention to it, he produces masterpieces such as Le livre de ma mère [My mother's book]. But Mangeclous, with its society of stereotypical Jews, is not interesting. What had been a literary advantage has become a handicap. Although there may be a Jewish culture, there are countless Jews whose works are not part of Jewish culture. There is no homosexual culture: there are homosexuals who write books, but to claim they have something in common is a mistake. Tchaikovsky did not make homosexual music, and to claim that a single thread can be traced from Oscar Wilde to Gide to Proust is nonsense. There are dozens of kinds of homosexualities: Gide despised Proust's sexuality, and Cocteau despised Gide's.

Nevertheless, Tournier concludes, not without humor, "Homosexuality may not be an advantage in literature. But heterosexuality is definitely a disadvantage."

We might observe a similar evolution among feminists and homosexual women who attempted to produce a certain kind of art but could not avoid getting locked inside the ghetto. In a famous letter, Rimbaud wondered, "When woman's immemorial bonds have been shattered, when she lives for herself and through herself, when man—abominable until now—has sent her on her way, she too will be a poet! Woman will find the unknown! Will her world of ideas be different from our own?—She will find strange, unfathomable, repulsive, delicious things; we will take them, we will understand them."[26] These were premonitory words: since Rimbaud, numerous women writers have achieved international renown.

This new women's art can also be found in the live theater that has developed along the lines forged by Ariane Mnouchkine and the munitions factory in Vincennes, which since 1973 has organized a "women's fair."[27] An entirely new kind of art has emerged, ranging from Karine Saporta's choreographies, with their femmes fatales demanding the heads of the men they love (Carmen, Les taureaux de Chimène), to Odile Duboc's work on the female body.

These original paths have sometimes led to dead ends, however. "Every word must pass through the sieve," Monique Wittig urged in *Les guérillères* (1969), sending her troops to fight the misogynistic rules of grammar. Reform language to make room for the feminine: "That was an interesting idea, provided we worked subtly, step by step, as Hélène Cixous did in *Dedans*," says Jocelyne François. "But along the way some women started to produce raving mad texts." Josyane Savigneau, literary critic for *Le Monde*, shares this opinion: "Hélène Cixous's work had an impact, and then, gradually, she got mired in the avant-garde. In fact, I never thought it was possible to sex writing."

Some homosexual women, as a last resort, have wanted to transform vocabulary. Thus Geneviève Pastre created the word "Octavian," which echoes "Achrian," a word invented by Renaud Camus because he was fed up with "being called queer" by his landlady and "homosexual" by his "shrink." Some also imposed the use of "auteure" [authoress] or "écrivaine" [writeress], believing that only what is named exists.[28]

Despite an apparent continuity, cultural feminists have not pursued the same objectives as the radical activists of the 1970s. The idea is no longer to denounce discrimination but to create an autonomous identity grounded in a homogeneous culture. It is clear why, in France, these debates were launched by the Psychépo camp of the MLF—Antoinette Fouque always maintained that writing was "absolutely sexed"—and by Luce Irigaray and Hélène Cixous. Their ideas were then enthusiastically taken up by a number of homosexual women. And yet most Frenchwomen—with the exception of Monique Wittig and Michèle Causse, who no longer have much influence—seem to oppose such terms. The figure of Simone de Beauvoir still haunts feminists: the author of *The Second Sex* was always hostile to the notion of "feminine writing" and denounced all efforts to glory in menstruation:

I absolutely despise the idea of locking woman in a female ghetto. . . . I also do not accept the idea that every coitus is a rape. . . . I do not believe there are qualities, values, or lifestyles that are specifically female: that would be to admit the existence of a female nature, that is, to embrace a myth invented by men to lock women into their condition as an oppressed people. The issue is not for women to affirm their nature as women, but rather to become human beings through and through.[29]

Faithful to the Beauvoir tradition, Savigneau feels no attachment to neologisms: "Frankly, I don't give a damn. The fact that people said *institutrice* [instructress] did not advance the condition of teachers. As for *écrivaine*, it's a horrid word. You need to have an aesthetic sense . . . and it would better to say *romancière* [woman novelist]."

The experiments of male and female homosexuals have bogged down, and originality has collapsed under the weight of exclusivity. The project of a specific kind of art, even when it did not directly champion purges, required the use of a French-Achrian or French-Lesbian dictionary to make itself understood. Given this high level of hermeticism, a kind of writing that claimed to be "completely other" became simply "completely opaque."[30] It is not clear, however, whether these hypermodern experiments are completely extinct. They remain particularly robust in the United States, and the debates center, as they often do, on the theme of childrearing.[31] These discourses, by members of minority groups claiming to find some consolation in exalting their own cultures, call the very status of value judgments into question. At the same time, a new antiheterosexual radicalism has emerged, with the backing of subjectivist theories (from Foucault's to Derrida's) that are sometimes made to serve instrumentalist purposes. This radicalism proclaims that value judgments, in the last analysis, are grounded in criteria imposed and then reinforced by power structures. Only the future will reveal whether this new radical militancy, taking new forms and using new weapons, will be exported, and whether it will find a following in France.

"WHAT IS LEFT OF OUR DREAMS?"

Between 1982 and 1985, militancy was disappearing as writers, sometimes in spite of themselves, became mouthpieces for homosexuality.

The "Chéri(e)" personal ads in *Libération* had been suspended for some months. "Serge July no longer wanted to develop that sort of ghetto," comments Jean-Luc Hennig.[32] In 1982, Arcadie, which had battled "human and religious stupidity" in its serious, homophile way, closed its doors. As for the CUARH, it saw its following drop off and the readers of its monthly, *Homophonies*, dwindle away. The CUARH had no successor.

"One day," says Jean-Paul Montanari, former head of GLH–Lyons, "we decided that the 'L' in 'GLH' had become a reality. We were liberated." "It was a rather naive time," a circumspect Jacques Fortin (GLH–Marseilles, CUARH) explains today. "You have to be indulgent with us: we were, on the whole, nice people."

Marie-Jo Bonnet, a former Gouine Rouge, declares, "I do not repudiate anything. It was a phase. I acquired a freedom in the women's movement, the ability to deal openly with my love for women. Homosexuality was an ordeal of initiation, and straights also have their ordeals. For me, thanks to the MLF, I am today a lesbian at peace with the woman I am."

Cathy Bernheim, another feminist figure, says, "It is time for me to retrace my steps and find my old footprints. To see what is left of my dreams. No, not 'my dreams,' but 'our dreams': since May '68, I have been in the habit of universalizing my personal experience!"[33]

↩

In 1983–84, a certain kind of homosexual militancy disintegrated for lack of themes to mobilize around. Soon the mouthpieces, for lack of militants, found themselves without troops. Homosexuals now preferred discos to the working-class balls of the CUARH: they went to the new ghetto and discovered modern ways to talk about love. "In the CUARH, you weren't a good militant if you didn't leave the general meetings with a guy," Albert Rosse recalls. To explain the end of militancy, he adds that the "gathering places" provided by the 1970s organizations later faded away in favor of commercial cruising spots. People still laughed, but they were laughing somewhere else.

"Collective struggles" lost some of their legitimacy, and the battles for freedom that have been won since 1981 stripped the militant organizations of part of their reason for being. The "commercial ghetto" now exploited the space left vacant by the militants' departure. Although some new experiments were ventured, they were more a swan song than a recomposition. The militant groups—ranging from an openly vote-rustling militancy on the fringes of the Socialist Party (Gais pour les Libertés [Gays for personal freedoms]) to political groups opportunely focused on a struggle against discrimination (Projet Ornicar, Homosexualité et Social-isme) to (unsuccessful) efforts to form a right-wing militancy (Mouvement des Gais Libéraux [Movement of gay liberals])[34]— were unable to fend off the rise of individualism, which was now evident on all sides.[35]

Context and chronology probably come close to explaining this demobiliza-tion, which appears oddly universal. But is that enough to make the phenomenon intelligible? This end to militancy was so abrupt, so collective, and so lasting that its origins must have been more essential and more profound. What happened in the early 1980s after Mitterrand's election? What major phenomenon managed to shake so much of homosexual militancy to its very foundations, to reduce it to a devastated landscape? In many respects this swan song remains, curiously, myste-rious.

↜

Gai Pied also underwent a rift in 1983. Minor though it was, this split per-fectly sums up the developments under way during that period, and yet it offers no explanation for them.

From the beginning, Gai Pied was a slightly crazy endeavor, but it rode the wave of sexual liberation that brought Mitterrand to the Elysée Palace, and it rap-idly proved successful: 30,000 copies per month were printed in 1982.[36]

Every prominent personality, homosexual or not, from Dalida to Jean-Paul Sartre, expressed a view in the paper, which within a few years became the "Elle of homosexuals," in the words of the cartoonist Copi. Yves Mourousi posed for Gai Pied in an advertisement for Look, a gay bar he had opened in Les Halles in May 1984. Jack Lang, minister of culture, allowed himself to be interviewed by the paper in November 1984: "Historical necessity requires that you rally around a flag, a banner. But, like you, I know that, fortunately, within this community, behind this flag, there is an infinite richness of differences. . . . [Gai Pied] is a well-put-together paper that I read regularly. It is intelligent, subtle, and courageous. I have found original articles and facts in it. ... In this way, it is cultural, in the full and robust sense of the term."

Despite this success, two trends gradually crystallized within the staff of *Gai Pied*, which became a weekly in January 1983 under the name *Gai Pied Hebdo*. The discussion focused on ads for the gay business establishments of David Girard, who did not allow foreigners or anyone over forty to enter his bathhouse, Le King Night. One portion of the staff did not want to accept his ads, which betrayed the battle for sexual liberation by creating a new form of exclusion. As can be imagined, the dispute was expressed in a large number of skirmishes, with some cowardice on one side and a great deal of betrayal on the other. In short, it was a regular soap opera. Like many such rifts in both the homosexual movement and the women's movement, the split could also be traced to couples who were not handling their breakups very well.

The managing editor, Gérard Vappereau, prompted by a legitimate concern for the paper's survival, took control of *Gai Pied* during a confused and disorganized general meeting on July 9, 1983. Some of the original staff members resigned, led by Jean Le Bitoux, one of the founders. They filed a lawsuit that was eventually dismissed. A bitter Le Bitoux observed, "Militancy vanished in favor of a discourse of seduction and pretty pictures. What does a twenty-year-old who buys *Gai Pied* get out of it? If he is not urged to analyze his situation socially, it's all over. If he is simply shown portraits of cute twenty-year-old guys, or how to dress stylishly, it's pretty paltry and demagogic."[37]

After the rift, Franck Arnal, a former FHAR militant who passed for a radical and was remembered by all for coming nude to meetings at the "Université homosexuelle d'été" in Marseilles, put his clothes back on—and became editor in chief.

In its own way, *Gai Pied* followed the same path to professionalization as *Libération* and the leftist government. The 1983 rift at *Gai Pied* was, in a way, the second death of the FHAR and the victory of the baths, the disappearance of the "queen" and the public toilets and the triumph of the commercial ghetto, the end of a radical militant adventure in the context of everyday life. Thus the new weekly reflected the new face of homosexuality in France.

9

Happiness in the Ghetto

> The lover's discourse is today *of an extreme solitude.*
> —Roland Barthes

In the high-tech drabness of the 1980s, when militancy seemed to be vanishing, new lifestyles spread: new kinds of relationships, new sexual practices, new meeting places. This evolution became particularly visible in France in the late 1970s. Nightowls went to the strangest parties, homosexual discos and disco music proliferated, independent radio stations appeared with gay broadcasts, and soon gay computer networks emerged. A sexual marketplace was established, to accompany homosexual emancipation. A homosexual community was already appearing, not as the reflection of a gay identity or a political minority group, but simply as a community of shared desire: sex was becoming communalized.

This evolution was essential, since it allowed the homosexual movement to survive and to become a concrete reality as it entered the marketplace. But coming out of the closet also had its limitations: it meant entering the ghetto.

In this new world under construction, Le Palace, a decadent temple of homosexual parties, which reflected the 1980s universe of easy money and easy sex, was a minor revolution—the second revolution for Fabrice Emaer.

⤚

Fabrice Emaer had a knack for the right mix. He had already demonstrated that when he opened Le Sept on Rue Sainte-Anne in 1968, a spot that set the tone for the homosexual nightlife. It was in that restaurant and disco that Giscard's former minister of culture, Michel Guy, knowing Emaer was looking for a new location, told him about an old music hall, built in 1895 on rue Montmartre, where Maurice Chevalier had sung "Le chapeau de Zozo." Thus the theater and nightclub that opened on March 5, 1978, combined several different styles. It joined modernity, with the new lasers and disco style of John Travolta in *Saturday Night Fever*, to the world of champagne and divas, which had spelled success for Régine, Castel, and Chez Michou. Its aggressive bouncers seemed to be saying, "Dictatorship at the door, democracy inside." And it incorporated the style of artists and couturiers: Thierry Mügler designed the waiters' outfits, Gérard Garouste painted the scenery, Karl Lagerfeld held his Venetian Ball there, Paloma Picasso got married at Le Palace, and Yves Saint-Laurent was a regular. Added to all this was the style of politics and culture: Louis Aragon and William Burroughs came, and Michel Guy and Jack Lang moved from Le Sept to Le Palace. Finally, it had the seriousness of a professional and commercial establishment, like a real theater company, giving the undertaking a unique style.

In many respects, the running theme that made Le Palace a success—but without making it a ghetto—was homosexuality. Love between men was the rule. The place was reminiscent of Andy Warhol's Factory: photo exhibits by Robert Mapplethorpe, concerts by Patrick Juvet or Prince, a showing of Genet's 1950 film *Chant d'amour* [Love song], and a historical reconstitution of Magic City's famous Mardi Gras Ball, which had been forgotten since the war. Le Palace was the paradise of transvestites, whores, models, and Casanovas, a place that combined easy sex and cruising as a mode of socializing. A certain homosexual narcissism was omnipresent, symbolized to perfection by the long hallway at the entrance, with its combination of storefront windows and mirrors, and the dance floor, situated in the orchestra pit of the old theater. Michel Foucault commented, "One may observe a whole series of behaviors on the order of 'homosexual theater,' where people come to show off their beauty or that of their lovers, or to better display their contempt in front of other people."[1]

Frédéric Edelmann, in *Le Monde*, ran the headline "Gay Power of Nightlife at Le Palace." A blunter Dr. Claude Olievenstein declared, in *Façade*, "The First Meat Market of Dance." The fact deserves notice: Le Palace became the symbolic site of a new bisexual lifestyle, which also spread to the provinces and to the nearby Les Bains-Douches (this spot, following close behind, had opened on December 21, 1978). This lifestyle soon spelled the success of Piscine, and then of Boy and Queen. Le Palace was an integral part of homosexual integration, even though the famous gay tea dance on Sunday afternoons, beginning in 1979, and the Wednesday evening party, beginning in November 1980, were still exclusively gay. It was at these tea dances that disc jockeys like Laurent Garnier became famous. They got nearly 1,500 men dancing every Sunday to the tune of the Village People's "YMCA," the Weather Girls' "It's Raining, Man," Miguel Brown's "So Many Men, So Little Time," Gloria Gaynor's "I Will Survive," Donna Summer's "I Feel Love," and Aretha Franklin's "Think." With Grace Jones, Amanda Lear, and Eartha Kitt, these singers formed an eclectic mix of Egerias for Planet Gay.

The evening parties at Le Palace displayed all Paris's divas and crowned heads, all its nightowls for an evening, its megalomaniacs for life. "When I used to go there," the choreographer Daniel Larrieu recalls, "people would always tell me it had been better the night before." Beyond such anecdotes, two figures familiar to the place may have marked those years better than anyone else. The two were a study in contrasts. They characterized the different faces of Le Palace and of homosexuality. They had been regulars at Le Sept, and they cruised rue du Faubourg–Montmartre. Nothing predisposed them to meet except homosexuality, with its oft-celebrated virtue of bringing different social classes together. Alain Pacadis and Roland Barthes ran into each other, stared at each other, and recognized each other. Both took pen in hand to comment on the nightlife at Le Palace and to describe through it the lover's discourse and its caprices.

⤸

In May 1978, a little article appeared in *Vogue Homme*, titled "Au Palace ce soir" [At Le Palace this evening]. It was signed "Roland Barthes."

"In our time, theaters are quick to die. . . . Le Palace is a rehabilitated theater," Barthes wrote. "Would Proust have liked it?" he wondered, evoking the simple pleasure he took in this place of "light and shadow," where he could "move up and down, change location at a whim." Barthes seemed as transfixed as a child by the sight of the "intelligent laser, with its complicated and subtle mind." He enjoyed watching "young bodies coming and going in the shadows, among rows of seats and in open loges, making a sort of rounds."

Barthes, a meticulous observer, probably gleaned part of his subject matter— the "intrigues" and snatches of dialogue needed for his book *Fragments d'un discours amoureux* [A Lover's Discourse: Fragments]—from Le Sept and other homosexual spots.[2] In his engaging book, which had a resounding success, he describes the lover, who "struggles in a kind of lunatic sport" and hunts the "loved being" (in this case, neither male nor female). He recounts the waiting, the quest, love at first sight, the words "I love you," jealousy, memory . . . all the sweet nothings that make up "the lover's discourse." All of a sudden, "not managing to name the specialty of his desire for the loved being, the amorous subject falls back on this rather stupid word: *adorable!*" This fictional affirmation, in which love proves to be at once improbable and joyous, proposes a unique ethics of solitude. It whispers homosexuality, even though the issue is not even mentioned.

Barthes had known Emaer since the days of Le Sept, and the latter had the habit of calling him "my philosopher." Barthes was even the first visitor to Le Palace, when it was still being renovated. The author of *Mythologies* discovered, like a prefiguration of the parties to come, the enormous empty room ringing with the sounds of an Italian aria that Fabrice, to please him, had put on the turntable. Once Le Palace opened, Barthes seems to have taken up residence in this "rehabilitated theater," particularly in the superb room on the second floor, reached by the main staircase, where he was somewhat protected from the loud music. There, standing motionless, he became part of the decor, and for nights at a time watched from the corner with the tormented voyeurism of Dirk Bogarde in *Death in Venice*. "Le Palace is a 'nightclub' unlike any other," Barthes wrote:

It gathers together, in a single spot, pleasures that are ordinarily dispersed: the pleasure of the theater in a building lovingly preserved, the pleasure in seeing, the excitement of the modern, the exploration of new visual sensations resulting from new technology, the joy of dance, the charm of possible encounters. All that combined produces something very old, called Fête, which is very different from Distraction: a whole range of sensations designed to make people happy for one night.

Few nightowls at Le Palace recognized this man with the serious look and white hair—he was sixty-three years old—who had just been named professor at the Collège de France. He was a semiologist of international renown, at the height of his glory in 1979. All the same, Barthes remained fairly discreet about his private life and was very upset by the rumors circulating about him. He said he was ready to sue those who accused him of being a "closet queen" and who attempted to make his homosexuality public.[3]

In 1977, Barthes lost his mother, his "dearest." He wrote, "What I have lost is not a Figure (the Mother) but a being, and not a being but a quality (a soul): not the indispensable but the irreplaceable."[4] Did her death make it possible for him to be more visible on the issue of homosexuality? In any case, Barthes began to express himself more easily on a subject he had taken care not to make public.

In 1979, Tricks, a daring story about homosexuality, appeared in bookstores—a little event that thrilled intellectuals, especially Parisians. Tricks is the systematic description of forty-five homosexual relationships, rapid and often anonymous. Neither vulgar nor sociological, this book, written by a young novelist named Renaud Camus, describes tricks, which progress from "I want you, you want me" to the act itself. Each sequence, almost invariably, ends with the words "never seen again." By writing Tricks, Camus helped to create a new gay imagination, that of homosexuality at peace with itself. At the same time, in the "Achrian chronicles" he wrote for Gai Pied Hebdo, he criticized gays for their excessive femininity, attacked the disturbing image that Genet had given homosexuality, vituperated against "queens," and made himself the "theorist" of the back room. "There is no social danger in the trick," explains Jean-Luc Hennig:

It's a video game. You can exchange X for Y at any moment. They are identical before the trick and even after it. This is what Hocquenghem calls "bright" homosexuality, the opposite of "dark" homosexuality, which is a whirlwind that calls the subject's situation, its identity, into question. Hocquenghem could not stand Renaud Camus because he made homosexuality banal.

The preface to Camus's Tricks was signed "Roland Barthes."

The interest that the author of A Lover's Discourse took in Camus's book is hardly surprising, even though it was written by one of the many "pains in the ass" who asked him to write prefaces.[5] "Homosexuality is less shocking, but it continues to elicit interest," Barthes wrote in the preface to Tricks, in March 1979. "It is still at the stage of excitation—it produces what could be called feats of discourse. To speak of it allows those 'who are not like that' (an expression already skewered by Proust) to prove they are open-minded, liberal, modern; and those 'who are like that' to bear witness, to make demands, to be militant. Everyone works himself into a lather, but in different ways." Barthes describes the trick and admits he prefers the "preparatives": "walking around, taking notice, playing little games, approaching, talking, going for a room, noting the domestic order (or disorder) of the place." He also likes the encounter, with its "mixups," evokes "the stubborn movement of a quest that will not be discouraged," and concludes:

A trick is an exchange that occurs only once. It is more than cruising, less than a love affair, an intensity that passes without regrets. As a result, for me, the trick has become a metaphor for many adventures that are not sexual: the exchange of a look, of an idea, of an image, a short-lived, strong camaraderie, which one agrees to let go of easily, an unfaithful act of kindness. A way of not getting mired in desire, but of not eluding it either. A kind of wisdom, in short.

Because of these confessional texts by Barthes, homosexual militants and advocates of gay studies have maintained that it is possible to read all of Barthes's writings in a new light.[6] Some have reread, at times with a bit of disillusionment (since he speaks of perversion), the magnificent passage from *Roland Barthes par Roland Barthes [Barthes by Barthes]*:

The pleasure potential of a perversion (in this case, that of the two H's: homosexuality and hashish) is always underestimated. Law, Science, the *Doxa* refuse to understand that perversion, quite simply, *makes happy*; or to be more specific, it produces a *more*: I am more sensitive, more perceptive, more loquacious, more amused, etc.—and in this *more* is where we find the difference (and consequently, the Text of life, life-as-text). Henceforth, it is a goddess, a figure that can be invoked, a means of intercession.[7]

Such after-the-fact interpretations are pointless, however, since, with few exceptions, there is little relation between Barthes's homosexuality and his early writings, where the question is treated almost exclusively in a playful manner.[8]

By contrast, homosexuality may have played a role in the drift into pathos that seemed to afflict Barthes in the late 1970s, a tendency that can be summed up by the opening words of *A Lover's Discourse*: "The lover's discourse is today *of an extreme solitude*." This observation echoes Philippe Sollers's portrait of Barthes in *Femmes* [Women]: "He did not deal with his homosexuality the way most people do now, in a triumphant, aggressive, militant, hard, decisive manner ... I saw [him] again at the end of his life. . . . He was letting himself slip more and more into complications with young men. That was his inclination, and it suddenly accelerated."[9] We learn along the way that the world-famous linguist got slapped while cruising on a beach in Biarritz. And, with the publication of *Incidents*, which has a crudeness inconsistent with his usual discretion, readers discovered a Barthes tormented by the issue of homosexuality.[10] In a chapter titled "Paris Soirees," Barthes reveals a "separate piece" of himself—how he "loves to be quite alone in a café, looking this way and that," and why he goes to the homosexual porn theater Le Dragon and down to the back room: "I am always sorry afterward for this sordid episode, where each time I submit to the ordeal of my forlornness." He also describes his solitary walks in Paris, which no longer elicit desire: "Though tired, I still wanted to see boys' faces; but there were so many young ones that it was unfriendly." And then, one last entry, dated September 17, 1979: "A kind of despair has taken hold of me. I wanted to cry. I saw altogether clearly that I had to give up boys because they had no desire for me, and I was either too scrupulous or too clumsy to impose my own desire ... what a sad life I have. Finally, I am bored, and need to get this interest, or this hope, out of my life. ... I'll be left with only hustlers. ... What will the spectacle of the world become for me?"

On February 25, 1980, Barthes was hit by a truck and gravely injured not far from the Collège de France, shortly after a luncheon with François Mitterrand and Jack Lang. He seems to have gradually had "less of a desire to live," according to his biographer. Some have said he let himself die, a plausible thesis, though Foucault refuted it, considering it absurd.[11] Barthes passed away in a hospital a month later, on March 26.

↩

He was called "the nightclubber." Alain Pacadis, the second familiar face at Le Palace, and who regularly haunted the club, had nothing in common with Barthes. They were different in every way, but this spot often brought them together.

In 1971, Pacadis was more or less associated with the Front Homosexuel d'Action Révolutionnaire (FHAR) and venerated the Gazolines. In his journal, *Un jeune homme chic* [A nice young man], he spoke of his transvestite pals whom he ran into at a costume ball for the review *Façade*:[12] "Marie-France is dressed as an old-fashioned movie star with an enormous cigarette holder; Maud, as a plasterer, with a bucket and trowel: she's whitewashing the walls, which, however, have just been repainted." In 1976, Pacadis discovered the punk movement and contributed to its popularity in France: "A key year in the history of our life. ... Now we'll be able to show the world our pallid faces and our hearts the color of darkness." In 1977, he attended the homosexual film week at the Olympic Theater, the homo ball that followed, and the May Day march with the Groupes de Libération Homosexuelle (GLH), "more from habit than anything else." That year, he abruptly shifted to "disco" and in 1978 became the "official poet" of Emaer's Le Palace. "Disco is the music of big cities, of night, of sex," Pacadis comments in his journal. In that world, he found a universe to suit him: after meals, he pilfered tips from the Le Palace restaurant (Le Privilège) before falling asleep, belly up, in an armchair or a seedy hotel in Pigalle. In the morning, his things were sent back in garbage bags, and the hotel bill was delivered to *Libération*. Yes, he had found refuge at Serge July's newspaper, where he became a journalist and had a running column, its name borrowed from Iggy Pop: "Nightclubbing." He also did work for *Gai Pied*, with "Filatures" [Tailing], in which he gave his account of the nightlife and the stars he met. Sometimes he submitted the same article to both newspapers, a way to get paid twice. But his "Vaseline journalist" style made some people unhappy: readers of *Libé* petitioned to have him fired.

Pacadis, a notorious homosexual and confessed heroin addict, might have borrowed Andy Warhol's words to describe Paris: "One thing is certain: most people who are doing something in New York are homosexual."[13] Pacadis became the symbol for a slightly shady and funny homosexuality. As a gag, he appeared in *Les enfants du rock* [The children of rock], Philippe Manoeuvre and Bernard Lenoir's broadcast on Antenne 2. "This broadcast is definitely becoming gayer and gayer!" he shouted, looking like an alcoholic Droopy.

Pacadis was also a friend of Félix Guattari, who invited him to La Borde, and of Serge Gainsbourg and Alain Souchon. For a time, he became one of *Libération*'s mascots, even passing for Serge July on occasion, if that helped him get into some very selective spot. "The officials," Jack Lang recalls, "found it strange to have him wandering from office to office in the ministry." In one of his columns, Pacadis gave a good overview of the nighttime spectacle, its codes and disappointments: "You have to go out, appear at all the parties, laugh at nothing, kill with a look, seize the moment, and that's all very real. A moment of inattention and you're dead."

In a suicide he ordered up and announced beforehand, in the wee hours of December 12, 1986, Pacadis allowed his "little brother," a young man of twenty-four—his last cruising buddy, whom he loved hopelessly—to strangle him. That act earned the young man nine years in prison.

Le Palace's merit lay in its invention of a new mode: homosexuality in a heterosexual spot, or vice versa. Henceforth, in France's large cities, and even in other Paris discos, gay soirees would be scheduled. This was also a triumph for new kinds of music.

Beyond Le Palace and Pacadis's columns, disco stars, and soon funk stars, made homosexuality a fashionable aesthetic. Even in the 1970s, there were frequent allusions in certain songs by Elton John ("All the Girls Love Alice" and "Daniel") and Simon and Garfunkel ("Keep the Customer Satisfied"), or, to an even greater extent, in the repertoire and cross-dressing of David Bowie ("Queen Bitch," "The Jean Genie," "Rebel Rebel"). The provocative look of Divine, and of the Village People's gang of mustachioed men dressed in leather, became symbols.

With the 1980s, hints turned into obsessions and keys to success, especially in British music, where such groups as Bronski Beat ("Smalltown Boy," "Why," "I Feel Love") did not allow women backstage during their concerts. Freddie Mercury cultivated the image of a mustachioed sex symbol, and Frankie Goes to Hollywood that of sadomasochistic practices (the "Relax" video). As the stakes were raised, the allure of Prince, a seducer in makeup, and the innuendo of Depeche Mode ("Boys Say Go," "What's Your Name," "People Are People") and the romantic Morrissey ("William, It Was Really Nothing") quickly paled in comparison to groups whose songs were manifestoes: Boys Town Gang ("Cruisin' the Streets"), the Communards ("Never Can Say Goodbye," "You Are My World"), Culture Club ("Miss Me Blind," "Karma Chameleon"), and especially Boy George, emblem of the transvestite ("No Clause 28"). These disguised protests by the British groups belonged in part to a reaction against Thatcherism, which continued to enforce laws against homosexuality. Dance music became a form of militancy.[14]

French singers also conveyed the image of a confused male sexuality, from Taxi Girl's "Cherchez le garçon" to Axel Bauer's video of "Cargo de nuit" [Night cargo] (produced by Jean-Baptiste Mondino in the style of *Querelle*) to the ambiguity in some of Marc Lavoine's or Etienne Daho's songs. Serge Gainsbourg suggested in an interview with *Gai Pied* that homosexuality "has already been done, m'lad."

⮑

They called themselves *Mauvaises fréquentations* [Bad company] in Lyons, *Voyage en petite lesbianie* [Journey to little lesbiania] in Nancy, *La voix du chat* [The cat's voice] in Toulon, *Cuir et dentelles* [Leather and lace] in Clermont-Ferrand, *La vie en rose, Antenne rose,* or *Canal rose* [Life in the pink, Pink station, Pink channel]. After May 1981, local radio stations and homosexual programs were created to broadcast gay hits nearly everywhere in France. This liberation of the airwaves, secured by the law of October 2, 1981, played a major role for homosexuals, especially in the provinces.

Illegal homosexual stations had been created in the 1970s. In 1978, Radio Mauve in Paris had broadcast during a homosexual festival. Radio Fil Rose, the progeny of Radio Mauve, was a short-lived, pirate homosexual station, at a time when censorship required the greatest prudence.

All the same, it was not until Mitterrand's election that more than fifty gay broadcasts were created in France, between 1981 and 1984.[15] These homosexual radio stations, whose audiences grew throughout the 1980s, replaced broadcasts in which listeners freely confided (until 1981) in Ménie Grégoire. Later, listeners turned to France Inter (*Allô, Macha*) and confided in Macha Bérenger, who had a weakness for male homosexuals, or in Jean-Charles Aschéro, who was very fond of lesbians (*Les choses de la nuit*). Broadly established in the provinces, independent radio became a forum for homosexuals to come together: announcers on gay programs read mail on the air from regional listeners and mentioned the gay spots being created and the books being published. People were talking.

In Paris, Carbone 14 and the announcer Jean-Yves Lafesse opened their microphones to homosexuals until the signal was jammed. Radio Gilda created *De quoi sont faits les garçons* [What boys are made of], and La Voix du Lézard broadcast homosexual classified ads. But the most decisive action was the creation of Fréquence Gaie, in September 1981.

⮑

The adventure began on Paris rooftops. From the hills of Belleville, where a transmitter with a weak signal was installed in a private apartment, Fréquence Gaie began broadcasting on September 10, 1981. It was still the era of amateurism: records were played at the wrong speed, static was common, and budding technicians used chicken wire to counteract the Faraday effect. But the listeners were a good audience. By late November, when the power of the transmitter was increased tenfold and the station became audible thirty kilometers from Paris, nearly 120 announcers—most of them under thirty—had already taken turns at the microphone. Misti, who worked for *Gai Pied*, was moderator for the broadcast *Action!*; Yann offered *Gay Parade*, which devoted a great deal of time to "gay men's divas." On a more serious note, Patrice Meyer offered *Le Magazine de la Santé* [Magazine on health], and Alex Taylor delivered the news. But the hit show on Fréquence Gaie was moderated by Guy Hocquenghem and Jean-Luc Hennig. Every Monday and Thursday evening, they presented *Double Face*, broadcasting classified ads in a live version of the "Chéri(e)" personals.[16] In the studio, anonymous individuals came to flaunt themselves and do a striptease, which was immediately described on the air, while the reporter for the program would invite himself into listeners' homes and comment on their sexual exploits live via telephone linkup. Those were the days. . . .

There was a whole series of station directors: Patrick Oger, Luc-Olivier Bézu, the writer Geneviève Pastre, and then Manuel Lherbet. Finally, in early 1987, this frequency fell into the hands of *Gai Pied*. It was renamed Futur Génération in 1988 and FG in 1990. "What I liked," recalls Marc Epstein, an announcer who was twenty years old at the time, "was that we were not militants." "It's my baby!" Pastre cried. Like other activists who participated in the Fréquence Gaie adventure, she has a unique life story.

A militant lesbian and dedicated feminist, Pastre participated in feminist lesbian groups and in Gisèle Halimi's movement, Choisir, where she represented the homosexual viewpoint. Defending a mixed-sex homosexual movement, she collaborated with gay men, first in the CUARH, where she rejected the Trotskyist infiltration, and then actively in Fréquence Gaie, where she served as president for a time. She called herself a poet and was the author of several scholarly works, including *De l'amour lesbien* [On lesbian love] (1980): "I began with the idea that lesbians are so poorly regarded, so hidden, so little understood, that they have everything to gain by coming out into the open. Radio is a fabulous experiment. . . . Fréquence Gaie is not the mouthpiece of the homosexual community but an autonomous group, the radio station of homosexuals, of lesbians, and of their friends."[17]

Fréquence Gaie quickly attracted a large following and was ranked fifth in popularity in Paris, with more than 100,000 listeners.[18] But the independent station did not enjoy unanimous support. On July 16, 1982, the Holleaux commission—to which Georges Fillioud, minister of communication, had assigned the task of authorizing radio frequencies, "monopolies notwithstanding"—refused to grant a license to Fréquence Gaie. The blunder was cleverly exploited by the radio staff, which denounced the return of the moral order and "homophobia," even though booby traps set by other homosexual groups seem to have been behind the decision as well. The day after a mass demonstration on July 20, 1983, when 3,000 listeners marched, draped in miles of pink fabric, a radio frequency was finally located.[19]

THE CRUISE MACHINE

On Fréquence Gaie and in discos, homosexuals appeared publicly via transparently coded songs while "Planet Het" danced to the beat of man love.

A new look, originating with the Village People and Queen, took root. Leather, supermale looks, army fantasies, and boot cults all shaped a new aesthetic that became broadly established through the legendary "comic-trip" of Tom of Finland, whose drawings were widely distributed in the 1970s.[20] Sexual differences diminished within heterosexual couples as men took a liking to aftershave lotion, emollients, cologne, and shower gel. Men's toilet cases became more important than their tool cases. Men liked the new brightly colored underwear by Jil, Eminence, and Hom. They even began to do some of the housework. At the same time, paradoxically, gay men chose a new, even excessive virility. Some homosexuals, who had chosen the androgynous look and been the first to use such perfumes as Habit Rouge, created by Guerlain in 1960, or Brut, by Fabergé, seemed to rediscover a strictly male imagination. The typical homosexual now sported a mustache, an earring (right ear), Levi's 501s and, already, a green bomber jacket accompanied by army boots. The younger ones, before the rest of society, adopted Calvin Klein boxers, ripped jeans, Doc Martens, and sometimes G.I. medals, all of which confirmed that the "aesthetic strategy" of gays was becoming "a presentation of the male body in such a way that the potential partner could presume the sexual act as much as possible" and anticipate the relation to come.[21] Gays drank tequila on the rocks. They smoked Lucky Strikes and Philip Morris. They chose uniformity and virility. Every homosexual believed he was unique and showed himself to be run of the mill. The sexual revelation of the late 1970s was the clone.

This was also the beginning of the era of the body, a narcissistic wave and cult. It affected heterosexuals as well, with the opening of the first Vitatop Club (Porte Maillot) in March 1974. But it took on specifically homosexual dimensions in the new Paris gyms and weight rooms. A certain tendency toward sadomasochism also found expression. Enthusiasts specialized (there were clubs and stores), and the names of accessories entered the vocabulary: there was talk of piercings, Ben Wa balls, golden showers, penis rings (or prince alberts), slings, and fisting. "For me," said the American photographer Robert Mapplethorpe, "S&M does not stand for sadomasochism. It stands for 'sex is magic.'" The new homo had arrived, in Speedo or jumpsuit. The queen was gone; the "sissy" was on her way out.

But didn't the homosexual appear even more subversive when he was no longer easily recognizable? Foucault observed a shift in the United States in the mid-1970s and attempted to understand its meaning:

It's a great myth to say that there will no longer be any difference between homosexuality and heterosexuality. I think this is one of the reasons homosexuality is a problem right now. And the claim that to be a homosexual is to be a man—the claim that one loves oneself—this search for a lifestyle goes against the ideology of the sexual liberation movements of the 1960s. It is in this sense that mustachioed "clones" have a meaning. It's a way of responding: "Have no fear, the more liberated we are, the less we love women, the less we blend into that polysexuality where there is no longer any difference between one group and another." And that is not at all the idea of some great communal fusion.[22]

The sociologist Michael Pollak has also attempted to explain this evolution, noting homosexuals' redefinition of their image at a time when oppression was relaxing: "In reaction to the stereotype that made the homosexual an effeminate man at best, a failed woman at worst, a new ideal of man was forged in the 1970s."[23]

By contrast, Guy Hocquenghem, more a militant than an observer, expressed regret about this new identity:

The traditional queen, nice or nasty, lover of thugs, aficionado of public urinals—all the colorful types inherited from the nineteenth century have vanished before the reassuring modernity of the (young) homosexual (between twenty-five and forty) sporting a mustache and attaché case, without neuroses or affectations, cold and polite, the ad executive or department store clerk, the enemy of outrageous behavior, respectful of authority, lover of enlightened liberalism and culture. Gone are the sordid and the grandiose, the odd and the nasty; sadomasochism itself is now only a clothing style for proper queens. ... The stereotype of a state homosexual ... is progressively replacing the baroque diversity of traditional homosexual styles. The time will come when the homosexual is no longer anything but a tourist of sex, a polite member of Club Med. ... A homosexuality that has finally become bright, or white, has been set in motion. ... Homosexuals have become indiscernible, not because they hide their secret better but because they have become uniform in body and soul, deprived of the saga of the ghetto. ... And everyone will fuck within his own social class; dynamic middle managers will catch a delightful whiff of their partners' aftershave. ... The new official queer will not go seeking pointless, dangerous adventures in the interstices between social classes.[24]

In *Comment nous appelez-vous déjà?* Hocquenghem returned once more to this theme:

All queens realize they have only to buy a leather jacket to discover the eroticism of blue jeans—of their own blue jeans, which is a more serious matter. But in return, this virility is drained of all conflict, and not only among ex-queens. There are no real men left anymore—nothing but Levi's models. ... Let us be consoled by the fact that the Pyrrhic victory by which the homosexual stereotype was abolished has been the privileged instrument of an enormous transformation of norms. We had to go through it so that the masters could remain where they are. From disorder to particularity, and from particularity to generality, the integration of what is today only one component of man is reaching its culmination.[25]

This new, more prosaic virility, disseminated through specialized reviews, fed the public's imagination. It created images that were conveyed through actors in a proliferation of porn films—films that were "unnoble," to use Serge Daney's expression—as exclusively homosexual movie theaters opened.

Two events seem to have marked the shift in the porn business, the scope of which is sometimes underestimated by the public at large: first, the new legislation of 1975; and, second, the advent of video. Before 1975, porn films did not follow any particular formula; they ran in mainstream theaters, which simply prohibited entry to anyone under eighteen. There were few French producers, and they most often specialized in soft porn with heterosexual subjects. But between 1968 and 1975 the audience greatly expanded, and the market in erotic films came to represent as much as 20 percent of the total market share, thanks to such hits as *Emmanuelle*, in 1974, and *Histoire d'O*, in 1975. An "irreversible erotic escalation," in the words of the critic Jacques Siclier, was part of the sexual revolution. In 1975, Giscardian liberalism legalized hard-core films, in which the sex was no longer merely simulated. This audacity was checked, however, by a law of December 30, 1975, which established the X rating, forced producers of films so classified to book them in a network of specialized theaters, and imposed heavy taxes with no possibility of obtaining aid from the state. The consequences of the law were significant: a concentration of the industry, the birth of French production companies (since the high taxes limited imports), and a profusion of specialized theaters. Paradoxically, the law also made it possible for a circuit of homosexual porn theaters to come into being: three movie theaters existed in Paris as of 1976 (Le Dragon, La Marotte, and Le Vivienne), and the real show was as much in the audience as on the screen. The disjunction increased between heterosexual and homosexual distribution of X-rated films, with the exception of lesbian porn films, which gave the voyeurs a thrill.

The second porn revolution occurred in the 1980s with the appearance of the VCR, and this had an effect on the specialized distribution system. Rentals created a surge in the homosexual porn market, which had been on the decline. Now it was possible to borrow a film without having to keep containers in one's home that might eventually cause embarrassment in front of families, wives, or housekeepers.

In the market for gay films in France, the name of Jean-Daniel Cadinot came up often. He had a reputation for the French touch—a departure, it was said, from the American scenarios and their too perfect models, such as Peter Berlin or, more recently, Jeff Stryker and Brad Stone. "My erotic dreams are contagious," explains the filmmaker, who knew how to capitalize on the new homosexual imagination. A former photographer of nudes (Yves Navarre on the cover of the journal *In*, for example), Cadinot produced nearly forty films in twelve years. With porn, homosexuality no longer raised the problem of guilt. "It was a dream world from which sin had been eliminated," Cadinot confirms. Nevertheless, beyond the "sad monotony of necessary repetition" in the sex scenes, to use Serge Daney's expression,

Cadinot said he wanted to create real stories with plot lines, developments that, according to him, differentiated him from "the U.S. armored cavalry." The French pornophile paid more attention to shots and the sequence of scenes. His films were called *Voyage à Venise* [Journey to Venice], *Harem*, *Gamins de Paris* [Paris kids].[26]

As it shaped the public imagination in the 1980s, Cadinot's world was soon much more poetic than real life.

⤷

A few working-class homosexual bars still existed in Paris, combining a jovial atmosphere and pleasant company. There were also a few cabarets with drag shows, and dance halls for men in their forties who wanted to try out a paso doble or a tango with their life partners. But the main novelty of the late 1970s was called the "back room," and it originated in the United States.

The homosexual nightclub that served as the trigger for the phenomenon was not so much Saint Mark's Baths or the Eagle's Nest as the Mineshaft in New York, a hallucinatory place for immediate pleasure and sadomasochism, in a meatpacking neighborhood of the West Village. Foucault, having spent time at the Mineshaft, described this new world:

In cities such as San Francisco and New York, one finds what might be called laboratories for sexual experimentation. They can be seen as the equivalent of medieval courts, which set very strict rules of propriety in courtly rituals. It is because the sex act has become so easy and so accessible to homosexuals that it runs the risk of rapidly becoming boring. Thus everything possible is done to introduce innovations and variations that intensify the pleasure of the act.[27]

The writer Hervé Guibert also spoke of the atmosphere of these spots: "San Francisco homosexuals lived out the most extravagant fantasies in these spots, replacing urinals with old bathtubs where victims lay all night long waiting to be soiled, going upstairs to cramped floors of smashed-up trucks, which they used as torture chambers."[28]

The back-room phenomenon became a reality in Paris in the late 1970s, and in the French provinces in the early 1980s. The sexuality that developed there, a kind of "experimental delirium," was very different from the cruising in public toilets or parks, which was still marked by fear and guilt. The novelty lay less in sexual promiscuity, already a tradition in the public baths,[29] than in its "institutionalization" and "systematization," less in sex than in the creation of specific, visible, commercial places "for fucking."

In 1975, in the side room of Le Bronx on rue Sainte-Anne, Parisian homosexuals discovered pleasure consumed on the spot. The owner had the idea of showing porn films and installing iron beds. Le Bronx was the first sex bar—the first back room, though the term was not yet used. Appearing in the same neighborhood at the same time was Le Continental–Opéra, an immense, chic bathhouse whose opening seems to have been tolerated by the police. The former movie theater included a swimming pool and a natural maze in the basement (it served as the set-ting for Copi's novel *Le bal de folles* [The drag ball]). The next year, a back-room bar (Le Villette) opened in the former café of the La Villette cattle market, in a neighborhood deserted at the time because of the Grande Halle construction proj-ect that was under way.[30]

Institutionalized sexuality, begun by Le Bronx, Le Villette, and Le Continental, seems really to have taken off with Le Manhattan. This American-style bar was di-rectly inspired by the Mineshaft in New York. It opened in Paris at 8, rue des Anglais in late 1976. Thus the back room was an American phenomenon before being imported into France in the late 1970s. Le Manhattan was the first French "sex disco." A regular summed it up: "You dance and you fuck." Renaud Camus set his story *Tricks* at Le Manhattan. Women were not allowed in, and great quan-tities of alcohol and poppers were consumed. It is remembered for a major police raid: all the customers who were engaged in activity in the back room, in a state of undress, were arrested, and the place was closed for a year.

Although, from a militant standpoint, Le Manhattan did not have the same symbolic value as the Stonewall Inn—the New York gay bar where police were pelted with rocks in 1969—it was nevertheless the beginning of the back-room phenomenon in France. Between shortly before 1979 until just after 1984, a number of bars based on the same model opened: the Bistrot des Halles (BH), on rue du Roule (opened in June 1981); Le Transfert, on rue de la Soudière; Le Trap, on rue Jacob; Le Broad (1982), on rue de la Ferronnerie; Le Haute Tension, on rue Saint-Honoré (opened in December 1983); and even Le Keller, a former coal merchant's operation in the vicinity of the Bastille that was converted into a bar.

Collective sex became the "banquet of joy" and the "systematic disordering of all the senses" desired by Rimbaud. Some have analyzed the back-room phe-nomenon as a return to the traditional orgy, with a multiform sexual promiscuity allowing people to satisfy a physiological need and giving them the sense that they belonged to a community. Pollak confirms this: "Far from signifying the desire for sexual satisfaction alone, cruising and the quest for many anonymous partners must be interpreted as a ritual of belonging."[31] According to this view, the back room communalized sex, which had been unduly privatized, and the community emerged reinforced by these orgies, which in their own way celebrated social and community bonds. Rarely has liberation sprung from so much sweat.

A private dialogue, a "round" as in Arthur Schnitzler's *Reigen* [*The Merry-Go-Round or Hands Around: A Cycle of Ten Dialogues*], the back room was a coded, highly ritualized universe with its own unspoken laws of anonymity, silence, and complicity within its walls and denial of its existence without: the law of lawless sex. A new scenario and new rules of the game were established: a steam room where you lay on benches arranged end to end, a purely pro forma bathrobe, individual booths with or without curtains, with or without movie screens. An atmosphere was created: a swarming mass of men, sighs, bodies in ecstasy, the hunt, potential prey, silence, the glow of burning cigarettes, sweat, sometimes a burst of laughter.

In this precise setting there was no longer any place for the words "What's your name?" A letter signed "Anonymous," *Libération*, letters to the editor (1977): "We no longer have faces; it's completely dark. Are our bodies perceptible?" Sometimes, in an atmosphere where everyone seemed "drunk on pleasure," snatches of affectionate conversation emerged, to the great astonishment of the American writer Edmund White, who arrived in Paris in September 1983: "The French are romantics; even in back rooms, Frenchmen kiss strangers." But White, who had trouble cruising because he still had an imperfect command of the French language, admitted with humor that back rooms "were unusually attractive to me: you don't need to talk there."[32]

The success of the back rooms illustrates the demand for immediate sex that characterized a precise moment in sexual liberation. "The whole social problem of homosexuality is magically forgotten in that enclosed place" ("Anonymous," from *Libération*, letters to the editor). By keeping the secret, by abbreviating the seduction phase and the preliminaries, back rooms allowed a large number of people, often provincials or married men, to avoid the visibility of cruising in public places even while increasing the "sexual yield." Darkness also allowed them a sexuality that was no longer based on physical attractiveness but rather on manner, touch, and shape; thus pleasure was offered to those who, because of their age or physical appearance, were most likely to have been deprived of it. Some regulars of the back rooms in the provinces noted that when the owners left a little night-light on, it was regularly broken. "Desire must have been censored, denied, and castrated, politically, socially, culturally, and morally, in order for it now to be incapable of being expressed in any way other than this form, and with such frenzy" ("Anonymous," from *Libération*, letters to the editor).

The back room was secretiveness within secretiveness, anonymity within anonymity, as Foucault has observed: "I think it is politically important that sexuality be able to function as it functions in the baths. There, without being imprisoned in your own identity, your own past, your own face, you can meet people who are for you what you are for them: nothing but bodies from which pleasure combinations, the manufacture of pleasure, are going to be possible. And it is too bad that such places for erotic experimentation do not exist for heterosexuals. Wouldn't it be marvelous, in fact, if they could enter a place, day or night, that has all the comforts and all the possibilities imaginable, if they could encounter bodies there that are both present and fleeting? It is certainly an extraordinary opportunity to desubjectify oneself, to desubject oneself—perhaps the most radical opportunity, but in any case intense enough to be important." For Foucault, this bathhouse ambiance, where you leave "your calling card" at the door and where all sorts of "pileups [are] possible," is a "phenomenon of desexualization," a "kind of deep-sea diving so complete that you come out of it with nothing left of that appetite, nothing left of the throbbing, that is often still with you after all, even after you have had satisfying sex."[33]

In Paris, the back-room phenomenon took on an aspect of commercial defiance. David Girard, a resourceful hustler and the son of a male prostitute, made his first moves on rue Sainte-Anne, turning 13,000 tricks there. His case would be merely anecdotal if he had not become the patron saint of organized cruising and, like Jean-Daniel Cadinot in film, had not specialized in hard-core spots. In his way—and perhaps in spite of himself—Girard became the symbol of the 1980s. Where Loulou invented the chic homo restaurant (Le Fiacre, in the 1960s) and Emaer thought up the gay nightlife (Le Sept and Le Palace, in the 1970s), Girard catered to the taste for immediate sex and the "cult of youth." Within a few years, he was in charge of a small "empire," which included two bathhouses (Le King Sauna and Le King Night) and a disco (Le Haute Tension) made up of long passageways with a back room and screenings of X-rated videos, and had soon published several companion books and magazines. Yves Mourousi went so far as to show Girard's magazine GI on the one o'clock news, and Girard was invited to be on Bernard Pivot's Apostrophes in April 1986 for his book Cher David, Les Nuits de Citizen Gay [Dear David, the nights of citizen Gay].[34] "I did not invite you for the literary qualities of the book," explained Pivot, "because, as far as style is concerned, it's not worth a darn. But your book is none the less incredible. Because of your sincerity, your cynicism, and your arrogance." Beyond the person of Girard and his extravagant cult of personality, his life history says a great deal about the state of venality on rue Sainte-Anne in the early 1980s, and the state of emotional abjection among the clients he serviced (the letters he published are edifying in this respect). Nicknamed "the little Bernard Tapie of homosexuality," Girard, championed as a guru for a time, raced madly ahead, finally foundering in the late 1980s.

Guy Hocquenghem, who nicknamed Girard "the little barkeep," harshly attacked Le Haute Tension, his new sex club, but, through it, also the back-room phenomenon as a whole, as in the February 23, 1985, issue of Gai Pied Hebdo:

Threading through the crowd, swishing along, pressed up against one another, single file, along the sewer lines of Le Haute Tension . . . , swarming by the hundreds in the same glaucous clubs, scampering along in line and squealing at the moon on Saturday night, queers have often made me think of rats. . . . At bottom, the psychology of the rat is superior to that of the homosexual . . . and rat society does not exude Kapos.

Philippe Guy, cofounder of the FHAR, confirms Hocquenghem's view: "We were the ones who set things off, but we never wanted that. We were wrong because we created ghettoes, and Guy told me, the last time we saw each other, in the mid-1980s: 'We went too far.'" Echoing the same sentiment, the writer Tony Duvert also spoke of the back rooms in L'enfant au masculin: "These haggard debauchees, fallen into animality, lose all self-respect . . . pant, moan, and groan: a view of the pigsty and of hell, a frightening, subhuman symphony, Lautréamontesque dementia!" This time, the champions of homosexual liberation were outpaced on their own territory by the new liberated homo.

In the late 1970s, the back-room phenomenon took on an unexpected scope in Paris; its development in the provinces was just as spectacular. In the early 1980s, every city of more than 50,000 had a bathhouse, discreet or run-down in appearance, rarely identified as homosexual, around which a varied clientele congregated. It was a boon for the homosexual in Dax or Sénas, who was otherwise isolated, tangling with "queer bashers" and police roundups in perilous outdoor cruising.

As the baths were being created in the provinces, disco clubs proliferated as well, sometimes even in remote rural areas. In these spots, several "businesses" could be combined: a heterosexual swingers' room, a homosexual dance floor with drag show, *danses du tapis* in the morning to encourage the formation of couples, and, all night long, a continuous "self-service" sex café in a back room behind the bar or in the basement, a discreet and freely accessible place where the owner was "kind" enough to set mattresses on the floor. "We often went to Le Phébus," a homosexual from Montpellier, Michel, cheerfully recalls. "We liked to go to the back room, since that meant we didn't have to order drinks. Otherwise, we had to dance continuously on the floor so we wouldn't get caught at the bar." Dozens of spots of this type existed in France in the early 1980s: Le Blue Boy in Nice, La Petite Taverne in Lyons, L'Esclave Bar in Avignon, La Mare au Diable and Le Cancan in Marseilles (Le Cancan later became Le New Cancan), La Chimère in Aix-en-Provence, Le Zanzibar in Cannes (one of the oldest), and Le Tison (Titio) on the way to Arles, in southern France.

ٮ

In parallel to the back-room phenomenon in Paris, rue Sainte-Anne, more and more given over to prostitution, was soon supplanted by a new, increasingly important gay destination. The Opéra–Palais-Royal axis was replaced by the Les Halles–Marais axis. Les Halles was demolished in July 1971, and architect Renzo Piano's blueprint for Beaubourg was adopted the same year. The Centre Georges Pompidou, inaugurated in January 1977, gave a boost to the neighborhood. Between rue des Lombards and rue Vieille-du-Temple, homosexuals rediscovered a spot that, unbeknownst to them, had been dear to "sodomites" in the past. As early as May 1871 it had been frequented by all the graying tutors and old students of Paris, as described by Julien Gracq. That ended when the Hôtel de Ville burned to the ground in the last fires of the Commune.

In December 1978, the neighborhood welcomed its first gay bar, Le Village, on rue du Plâtre. It was a little American-style coffee shop, open in the afternoon, similar to a corner café, where the owner, Joël Leroux, welcomed "homos who had become run-of-the-mill gays" (he opened Le Duplex on rue Michel-le-Comte in

July 1980). Following close on its heels was the opening of Le 10 du Perche (November 1979), Le Central (September 1980), Le Piano Zinc (June 1981), Le Coffee Shop (October 1981), and Le Swing (spring 1983), which has since become Amnésia Café.[35]

Every bar opening was joyfully celebrated as a new milestone in the triumphal march of desire. This explains the immediate success of the Marais and confirms the fact that it satisfied a hope closely linked to the process of coming out. New establishments have continued to appear in the Marais since then: Le Quetzal (April 1987), Le Subway (1989), Le Bar Bi (June 1995), L'Open Bar (July 1995), Le Cox Café (December 1995). In the last few years, the area has also developed along two new axes: toward Les Halles, along rue de la Ferronnerie, and, more recently, toward the Bastille, along rue Keller.

These homosexual spots, grouped together in clusters on a street "appropriated" at night, exert a certain fascination. Succeeding Pigalle, Saint-Germain-des-Prés, and rue Sainte-Anne, the Marais has become a trendy neighborhood, a kind of gay urban village, even though the people who frequent it do not necessarily live there. It is difficult to explain its genesis, however. As Maurice McGrath, owner of Le Central, explains, "The Marais is a historic neighborhood that gays found exciting, and rents were still not too high in the early 1980s. The neighborhood recovered its nightlife and was restored, thanks to the arrival of gays."[36] All the same, the birth of the Marais was not simply a matter of relocation, a notion that implies a continuity of style. It was a profound change whose success rested on an almost point-for-point contrast with earlier sites. The rue Sainte-Anne market was built on three principles: "It is impossible to get homosexuals to come out before midnight," "They have only one drink" (therefore, it must be expensive), and "One must be selective in admitting people, to avoid hustlers." The daytime bars in the Marais set out to demonstrate that these three hypotheses were false, establishing a clever policy of low prices (coffee cost two francs and beer five at Le Central in 1982, whereas, at the same time, a glass of wine was thirty francs at Le Sept on rue Sainte-Anne). They valued visibility, which met the new public demand, at a time when coming out of the closet was prevalent (in the Marais, bars were well lit, with a view of the street, but on rue Sainte-Anne they were still equipped with reinforced doors, buzzers, peepholes, and bouncers). It was now possible to cruise in well-marked amorous circuits and to kiss in greeting on the street. In addition, the Marais spots were militant bars where gay journals could be found; most of the clubs on rue Sainte-Anne did not accept pamphlets or posters from organizations. And, finally, the birth of the Marais was part of a shift from nightclub to bar, from loud music to background music, from elitist club where you remained seated to bars where you stood up so you could talk to everyone around you. Thanks to the Marais, the hierarchies and compartmentalization of Le Fiacre and Le Sept disappeared.

This intrusion of gay life into the historic neighborhood met with some difficulties, however. In the beginning, Jews—rue des Rosiers was close by—seem to have been intolerant of the transformation, particularly with the opening of Le Swing in 1983, which replaced the only Jewish bar and tobacco shop in the neighborhood, on the corner of rue Vieille-du-Temple and rue des Rosiers.[37] But coexistence gradually improved, and the two communities even formed an alliance during a period of attacks in 1986.[38] Since then, Madame Trottier's pastry shop, on rue Vieille-du-Temple, has brought them together: she welcomes without discrimination, and with the same smile, Jews and homosexuals from the neighborhood.

Jean-Pierre Meyer-Genton's bookstore, Les Mots à la Bouche, opened in the heart of the new chosen ghetto in August 1983.[39] This symbolic site, open until eleven o'clock every evening, brought the nascent phase of the gay neighborhood to a close and cemented the community by offering it the cultural legitimacy and valorization of a gay identity that had been lacking.

↩

Were happiness and the ghetto now synonymous?[40] Since recent history had made the Marais a gay neighborhood, everything conspired to make it even more homosexual. In the 1980s, a symbolic and certainly marginal fringe of homosexuals appeared, wearing a "gay uniform" (leather, mustache), and became "Citizens Gay." They had breakfast listening to Fréquence Gaie, went to work at a gay business (there were more than a hundred in Paris), got their news from *Gai Pied Hebdo*, had dinner in a homosexual restaurant in the Marais, and then danced till morning in a gay disco. For some homosexuals, this lifestyle existed within a closed circuit, which transmitted fixed images of their identity. It had its own temporality, that of the gay community, which, so to speak, no longer ran by the national clock. Nevertheless, these new lifestyles did not reach the intensity that they had in specific regions of the United States (Manhattan's West Village, San Francisco's Castro District, Boston's South End).

According to the rare polls in existence, the clientele that frequented businesses in the "commercial ghetto" in France seems to have been composed of homosexuals from the urban middle classes. They were economically independent, often led their lives openly, and publicly declared their homosexuality. People in this group (which, of course, is not representative of male homosexuals as a whole) typically had a very high number of sexual partners and very few heterosexual friends. "This is how the gulf between the heterosexual and homosexual worlds comes about," Michael Pollak explains. "The liberalization of mores made the existence of a homosexual universe official. For lack of something better, it could be called a *destiny group*. Forged by affinities and a shared memory of discrimination, this homosexual world settled into a *freely consensual segregation*."[41]

As this erotic commerce in all its forms (films, videos, back rooms) was spreading in France, an "international homosexual dialogue" was also growing. By lowering the price of charter flights, airlines brought homosexuals closer to America, the land of enchantment par excellence. The novel *City of Night*, by John Rechy (1963), and images of the young athlete Joe Dallesandro in *Flesh*[42] fed the myth of a gay America and encouraged homosexuals to visit the famous sex shops on Forty-second Street, with their hypnotic neon. Although there had always been homosexual tourism, at least since colonial times, the number of destinations multiplied in the 1970s; it came within reach of the middle classes for the first time in the early 1980s. As reports from the American ghetto multiplied,[43] a significant number of gays began to travel: to the Maghreb with Tony Duvert's books, to Asia with Gabriel Matzneff's, to southern Italy or Budapest and its baths with Dominique Fernandez's. During the summer, many homosexuals tanned on nude beaches in Sitges, Spain, or on the Greek island of Mykonos. The rest of the year, some of them spent their weekends in the specialized neighborhoods of Amsterdam or in the new gay nightclubs of London. The homosexual had become a citizen of the world.

THE WOMAN CRUISER

Three anecdotes, three significant quotations, may serve as vignettes to illustrate the lesbian problematic of the 1980s.[44] The first is a (notorious) retort by Léna's husband in Diane Kurys's 1982 film *Coup de foudre* [*Entre Nous*]: "You know what you are? Dykes!" The second is a line from a song ("Sans contrefaçon") by Mylène Farmer: "Tell me, mama, why am I not a boy?" The third is from Catherine Lara, who, when a journalist asked her, "What's the first thing you notice about a man?" replied, "His wife!"

In the 1980s, homosexual women more or less followed the same movement of liberalization seen among the men, and, in their own way, discovered "happiness in the ghetto." Nevertheless, a study in 1984 showed that gay and lesbian lifestyles no longer had very much in common.[45] As differences between men living in Paris and those in the provinces were disappearing, the distance between male and female homosexuals was growing. For the most part, men met their partners in places within the "ghetto," whereas women met most of theirs within a traditional social life: the workplace, or a network of friends.

"Lesbian cruising," the writer Hélène de Monferrand explains, "is like women's cruising generally. We are not programmed to cruise. From Perrault's fairy tales to 'Sleeping Beauty,' our upbringing has kept us passive." Michèle A. confirms this tendency: "There is no sense of adventure. Lesbians have a more settled side, a stronger desire to form into couples, a greater sentimentality." Thus women met at friendly dinners: in many cases, couples broke up and got together with other people in their autonomous group, nearly cut off from society. Whether as cause or as effect, the main difference between male and female homosexuals lies in the small number of commercial sites for women. "We are not accustomed to going to cafés," declares Catherine Gonnard, editor in chief of *Lesbia*. "Commercial spots are not a habit with us."

All the same, some specialized establishments did appear, though their number remained small and their existence often little known. "Discos for women," the writer Anne Garreta explains, "always functioned behind closed doors, so that no one would see what was going on inside." The writer has personal knowledge of the subject: she was a disc jockey at Le Katmandou, and her novel *Sphinx* was set in that disco.

⮌

"The 1970s were truly the best nightlife years," recalls Elula Perrin. Originally from Vietnam, and a former professor of African dance, in May 1968 she opened Le Yéti, a lesbian club in Saint-Tropez. The next year, after the success of this first experiment in the provinces, she launched Le Katmandou. Opened on December 2, 1969, on rue du Vieux-Colombier, in Paris, the disco was for twenty years the most famous lesbian spot in France.

Le Katmandou maintained a delicate balance between the VIP tables at the entrance (where all sorts of famous women were welcomed, from Alice Saprich to Mélina Mercouri) and a working-class "nightclub" with more affordable prices. Until the mid-1970s, the disco also offered lip-sync shows, performed by the club's exclusively female staff, and *danses du tapis*, which were gradually replaced by gay tea dances. "But a women's nightclub is very hard to keep going," explains Perrin. "Girls don't hold their liquor as well, and so they drink in moderation. Arguments break out here, but there are never any brawls in gay men's clubs. I notice the girls often come in as couples and tend to go out on the town only on special occasions." In an attempt to give nightlife a certain prestige, Perrin, in her own words, "led all the rear-guard actions": "First, I tried to prevent lesbians from coming to Le Katmandou in jeans; then I just wanted to ban running shoes, then just leather jackets. ... Gradually, I had to resign myself, to give up my illusions. Girls now come to dance at Le Privilège–Kat with backpacks on!" Le Privilège–Kat is the new disco whose management Perrin assumed when Le Katmandou closed, in March 1990. Perrin is a throwback to the time of a female nightlife, just as Fabrice Emaer is to the time of a male nightlife. She refused to join the MLF, preferring to be a member of Arcadie. She published several fairly successful books. Thirty years of nightlife, she says, have made her an "avid bourgeoise" who votes on the right. "What purpose did Socialism serve," she insists, "since none of the promises made by the left were kept?"[46]

⮌

In parallel to Le Katmandou, commercial businesses proliferated in France, even though feminism was losing strength and such reviews as *Lesbia* were becoming widespread. The names of these places were quite different from those of gay men's bars: La Théière [The teapot], in Les Nuages (rue Cloche-Perce); Elles Tournent la Page [Women turn the page], formerly on rue de la Roquette; Nini Peau de Chien [Nini dogskin], a restaurant run by Claire and Cristine on rue des

Taillandiers; La Fourmi Ailée [The winged ant], a bookstore and tearoom. In these places, the atmosphere was often more "feminist" than homosexual. El Scándalo (on rue Keller) and La Champmeslé were the exception. La Champmeslé was a specifically homosexual bar. Opened by Josy on rue Chabanais in 1979 as a women's bar, it became more lesbian—though she does not like the term "lesbian," preferring to define La Champmeslé as a "gay bar." Nevertheless, men were allowed only into the main room, not the back.

This development also occurred in the provinces. In 1993, a lesbian phone book listed nearly 200 specialized spots throughout France, either businesses or organizations. Among them, a few convivial places achieved a certain notoriety: La Lune Noire, in Strasbourg; Le Bilboquet, in Caen; Le Gay Tapant, in Lille; La Rose Noire, in Rennes; Le Café Chantant (which became Le Damier, and then Le Village), in Lyons; and La Gavine and Le Bagdam Café, in Toulouse. La Gavine and Le Bagdam combined concerts, painting exhibits, women's balls, and art films.

A more marginal but still significant phenomenon was a new toughness in lesbian lifestyles during the 1980s, as illustrated by the photographer Duane Michals in *Femmes violentes* [Violent women] (1983). A masculine view of things spread in certain places, and women sometimes adopted the "truck driver" or "tough guy" look. Replacing the three-piece suits of the 1950s "bull dykes," images spread of women dressed in checked lumberjack shirts, army surplus clothing, and flat-heeled shoes, sporting tattoos and cropped hair. "It was a radical response to Barbie dolls," Hélène Monferrand comments. Butch women liked to have people call them "Monsieur." In the United States, radical lesbians, choosing to be called "dykes," discovered the pleasures of sadomasochism: the "happiness of sharing a good thrashing with the woman you love," says Cathy Bernheim, ironically. There were also a lesbian sadomasochistic spot in Pigalle and lesbian prostitution and porn magazines in the United States (the most famous of the magazines was called *On Our Backs*). Certain unambiguous personal ads in *Le Nouvel Observateur* belong to that trend, as do Denise Brial's broadcasts on Fréquence Gaie.

Women's practices lagged behind men's homosexual liberation, but the change was still unprecedented. "Speed and violence—the girls came to adopt the habits of men; they were *phallicized*," writes Michèle Causse with regret. "I expected something different from women," says Rachel, a disappointed feminist.[47] Would the new lesbian lifestyles negate the reality of feminist battles, and, more than that, the female essentialism preached by feminists of difference? "What seems interesting to me about lesbian S&M," concludes Foucault, "is that it allows us to get rid of a certain number of stereotypes about femininity."[48]

↬

Homosexual women banging on a computer keyboard in search of a "trick" for the evening: here was a new image of femininity. But lesbians' use of the computer service Minitel was no small matter, nor was the new demand for an "immediate sexual yield," a demand that, reviving—and dethroning—the technology of desire's deferred expression, as represented by the personals, became a real social phenomenon in the mid-1980s.

Nothing predisposed Minitel to become the forum for gay electronic communication. History tells us that conversations via Minitel originated when Strasbourg's *Dernières Nouvelles d'Alsace* was pirated by the electronic news service Gretel (created in October 1982). The pirated version even bore a peculiar pseudonym: Big Panther. Little by little, users spontaneously, and therefore illegally, appropriated these networks (thus sparing France Télécom from having to shift to a smutty format), in which users with names like "Peggy Piglet" and "Shameless Glans" emerged. Housed within media enterprises, as the law required, electronic information services rapidly made room for the exchange of personal messages: Elletel, BDI, Stel, Funitel, PL (the service of *Le Parisien Libéré*). The success of these services was secured primarily through the creation of the "Kiosque" on February 6, 1984 (special rates on exchange 3615, the result of a surtax that allowed electronic publishing enterprises to be remunerated).[49] Homosexuals found a new form of conviviality that suited them, a new sociability of desire. Cruising on Minitel, with its combination of secretiveness and invisibility—since it required the use of pseudonyms—allowed for every sort of transvestism. It replaced the personal ads, which declined from then on. Sexual difference could be abolished; role playing thrived within a permanent carnival where masks were required. "M or F?" was the first question on the computer service at *Libé* or on Service Médical (the name of a service that was a front for the famous S&M service beginning in 1984). In 1985, the first openly gay service offered by David Girard's organization appeared (3615 Code Gay), followed by 3615 Code Graffiti and then by the services of the *Gai Pied* organization (3615 Code GR in June 1985, 3615 Code GPH in January 1986).

The lover's discourse of gays adopted the language of Transpac and produced a peculiar kind of writing: "Do you want to make love via Minitel?" "Fuck?" "Active? Passive?" And a moment later: "Thank you, you made me come. See you tomorrow." The success of this verbal swinging, which occurred in the wee hours, when boredom strikes, was enhanced by the fact that on-line data-processing companies hired the unemployed, in a form of "workfare," to serve as paid moderators of electronic bulletin boards and then replaced them with actual data banks that could digitally handle nearly 30,000 ready-made sentences. Reduced-rate codes making different servers compatible with one another were also disseminated parsimoniously. The possibility of searches by geographical region emerged, and e-mail became widespread as advances were made in electronic communications. A few years later, cruising on phone networks partially replaced the use of computers, as 3665 and 3670 numbers, which charged a fee for every call, became more accessible.

In every city, and often among people who did not acknowledge their homosexuality, it was possible to find, via Minitel or telephone, at any hour of the day or night, someone for a brief encounter or for a lifetime.[50] Minitel's role as a meeting place was a major development in the history of homosexuals in France. A cruising place "outside the ghetto," it allowed them to find companions. It put gays in touch with one another. In the provinces, the homosexual emerged from his isolation.

☞

The new love codes, all part of the same phenomenon—words without voices (Minitel), voices without images (phone networks), or bodies without voices or images (the back room)—made "queer sexuality" more homogeneous and systematic. Timidity, social propriety, and convention were forgotten. This unprecedented socialization, the proliferation and commercialization of gay establishments, was related to something that might be called homosexual "emancipation" rather than "liberation." Sex acts took precedence over militant discourse; in the early 1980s, for lack of a gay political community, a sexual community appeared in France.

The struggles of revolutionary, reformist, and protest groups (the FHAR, the GLH, the CUARH) had a concrete effect on homosexual emancipation only after they had been appropriated by business, and when sex itself became communal.[51] The slogan "Our bodies belong to us," championed by MLF-FHAR in 1971, became "Every body belongs to those who want to take pleasure in it." Now homosexual militants found the doors to David Girard's bathhouses closed to them.[52]

In less than five years, between Le Palace in 1978 and Le Haute Tension in 1983, gay lifestyles had undergone an enormous transformation. This change came about within an extremely short period of time.

"Sexual flitting," sweaty, anonymous bodies, the new madness that seized the gay community, the "detergent love" recommended by Rimbaud in *Album Zutique*, did not of course constitute the lifestyle of all homosexuals. There were many who now went "outside the ghetto"—an expression destined for great success—to define themselves. In many respects, for many gays in the early 1980s, homosexuality was a problematic situation. As a result, the notion of an exuberant or polyvalent sexuality is only an imperfect representation of the reality. Some men and women, without necessarily rejecting their homosexuality, complained about their unstable love lives, which were limited to relations as numerous as they were short-lived. Their lovers, picked up at Saturday-night discos or tendentious Sunday-afternoon walks in the park, became merely a series of fading shadows. For others, homosexuality was a desert as far as the eye could see.

This serves to explain why many felt that homosexual liberation had not taken place. "If there was a revolution, I for one didn't notice anything," explains Didier, a thirty-five-year-old homosexual interviewed in Strasbourg. We find the same opinion in Claude from Le Mans: "I've been alive a long time, seventy-one years, and I've never encountered sexual liberation."

↝

What is the source of homosexuals' difficulty—so often contemplated—in maintaining stable relationships? The classic but now dated argument put forward by Alain Girard in Le choix du conjoint [The choice of a mate] provides valuable information on love relationships.[53] It asserts that for heterosexuals love at first sight does not exist, meetings are not the result of chance, and all couples have a large number of factors in common: geographical region, social and cultural background, tastes, professional choices. . . . These objective criteria are not determining factors, and there are many exceptions; statistically speaking, however, couples build on important similarities. A man meets his wife at the village café (but not just any café), in a university lecture hall, at a friend's party, on a beach. The illusion of randomness in the first meeting and of an imagined love at first sight inevitably collapses under the coolly realistic eye of the sociologist. So many random events are programmed!

This logic of heterosexual relationships is disrupted by the particularities of homosexuality: the relatively low number of individuals in the gay population, the timidity that being gay produces in adolescence, latent or patent repression. "I have the impression," says Hervé, who was born in Marseilles, "that I did not have the love problems of adolescents at fifteen; rather, I'm having them now, at twenty-five." The writer Vaclav Jamek echoes this comment, wondering, "As I approach forty, am I only now at my Werther stage?" He worries, "You see, they promised you'd end up cruising outside high schools."[54] Thus the homosexual only rarely meets his partners in school, within his family circle, or among friends. He is often forced to move away from his traditional social milieu. "You go into the homo area to cruise because you're a little fed up with knocking yourself out for straights," explains Pascal from Lyons. The homosexual then frequents gay discos and bars, sometimes even public parks and train-station toilets. And he exiles himself to these places by cutting himself off from the heterosexual world and from traditional forms of meeting sociably.

In these new situations, the homosexual finds himself in the presence of many potential partners. Although a one-night stand can be based on attraction alone, it is difficult to build a lasting relationship simply on sex. The other criteria necessary for an encounter are immediately apparent: age is increasingly a determining factor, though all combinations are possible; there are also physical criteria (good-looking/not good-looking), which translate into one of the criteria for having sex (fuckable/not fuckable).

In the "homosexual marketplace," therefore, chance plays a more important role than it does in the choice of a heterosexual mate. Although princes no longer meet shepherdesses in the heterosexual world, they still do in the homosexual universe.

In addition to the difficulty of forming a lasting relationship based on sexual desire, there is the difference in the *rhythm* of heterosexual and homosexual sex.

The habit of brief encounters leads to a perpetual and unending quest.[55] In fact, there are probably many encounters before a real love connection is made. In addition, partners are chosen on the basis of visual criteria alone. Relationships are more quantitative and, some claim, more intense: "fucking" a stranger seems much more exciting than "making love" with one's mate. Since encounters are so easy in an accessible and almost inexhaustible market, and since no social pressure "disciplines" homosexuals and guides them toward stability, separation seems just as simple and immediate: "Release the specimen back into nature after ascertaining that our lives are not compatible."[56] The prospect of nurturing love disappears in favor of Don Juanism and the perpetual quest. Daniel Larrieu of Tours says, with regret, "They are relationships between people who do not look at each other, who do not really meet. I was like that as well. However, when you suffer, you can't bear it anymore when all someone has to do to meet you is to come up and ask what time it is." Once more, there may be all sorts of exceptions: various combinations, a rigid and often acknowledged distinction between sexual partners and life partner, "open couples." "We made two agreements," explains Pascal from Marseilles. "First, we agreed we could have relationships outside the couple. Second, we decided not to be in love." Homosexuality can lead men to break the rules, to transgress sociological givens and statistical norms. But the difficulty of stable homosexual relationships is increased by the fact that traditional meeting places are abandoned.[57]

"The persisting prohibition against homosexuality," Michael Pollak explains, "has reinforced the separation between sex and emotions. Hence the search for anonymous and multiple relationships. Homosexuality, like any clandestine practice, compels one to find an arrangement that minimizes risks while optimizing efficiency."[58] A humorous remark by Michel Foucault illustrates this situation: if for heterosexuals "the best moment of lovemaking is when you head up the stairs," for homosexuals it is instead "when the lover disappears from view in a taxi."[59]

It is probably possible to explain the greater stability of lesbian couples in a parallel manner.[60] As we have seen, homosexual women seem to meet their partners in daily social life (at work, within a network of friends), while men are more likely to frequent specialized spots. The male couple is thus more vulnerable. In the absence of a model of social life, and outside the stability procured by a child, a union may deteriorate as the partner's "power of enchantment" declines. The happy couple may gradually move from the symbolic realm of "community" to that of "community property"; the relationship may evolve into simply a successful friendship. "We get along very well together," Christian of Marseilles explains. "But we stopped having sex with each other fifteen years ago."

Thus the "à la carte" homosexual couple can sometimes take the form of a mere refuge where, independent of his sex life outside the relationship, each partner returns to lick his wounds, store up shared memories, and build a safety net in case of future difficulties. Each partner may have emotional security without being strictly faithful; he may continue to hold on to the possibility of breaking the loose association if a "more advantageous" situation presents itself. "It will last as long as it lasts," is an expression often repeated within homosexual couples who have adopted this "relaxed" morality, to use Pollak's expression.

By contrast, heterosexual stability, though relative, can be explained by the fact that the partners give up certain illusions about passion. The habit of living together on friendly and social terms, and the need to raise a child, may complement love or take its place. The homosexual couple is less likely to embrace all these elements and seems to have more difficulty coming to terms with the "disenchantment" of love. The partners may even categorically refuse to allow an emotional relationship to take the form of heterosexual "pathos." "One is bored, the other unhappy" might sum up the situation as it deteriorates. The specific precariousness of the homosexual couple, which, for lack of social bonds, weathers the years badly, can be attributed to all these factors. At the same time, it attests to a greater frankness and emotional genuineness.

In many respects, the homosexual couple, a social entity where all the contradictions of gay life converge, may also be the site where the love relationships of the future are being invented. As the 1980s got under way, a new kind of social life was being invented, and homosexuals served as the vanguard in the new dialogue about love. Might not heterosexuals come to imitate them?[61]

⌐

In May 1983, *L'homme blessé* [The wounded man] was released in French theaters. It illustrated the difficulties in homosexual relationships but also depicted a certain happiness within marginality.[62] It took a certain courage for Patrice Chéreau, its producer, and Hervé Guibert, who collaborated with Chéreau on the screenplay, to choose this difficult subject, which was initially supposed to be a film adaptation of Genet's *Thief's Journal*.

Chéreau's camera shows the descent into the gutter, the quest for love in exchange for hard cash. Cruising at dusk, a pursuit that does not always keep its promise of pleasure but can cost a person his life. Drifting in the toilets of some train station, where perverse-looking boys cling to life. And always Chéreau's "universe": "How people manage in life, or don't manage, have trouble living, sometimes have trouble dying."[63]

Henri (Jean-Hugues Anglade), the young hero, discovers "the desire for homosexuality." Then, suddenly, "he wants a guy." That turns out to be Jean, a pimp and drug dealer. Later, back at his parents' house, he has doubts, "dreams of normality." Chéreau's themes emerge: the complex evolution from adolescence to adulthood, the first adolescent crush, the difficulties of love, the trafficking in feelings, a jarring, hard, violent love, but love in spite of everything, passionate love in the world of prostitution.

Is this a depiction of the difficulty of homosexual relationships? Henri is picked up as a hustler by a voyeuristic doctor, Bosman (Roland Bertin). Brought to a parking garage that serves as a spot for "hetero" prostitution, Henri discerns couplings behind car windows plastered with newspaper, and the sound of these couplings combines with the creaking of car suspensions. "It's music," his client tells him. "Listen. And you see, those are couples. Normal couples."[64]

"When I made *L'homme blessé*," Patrice Chéreau reminisces today,

I wanted to make a film that would speak clearly about the passion of one boy for another. You know, these are things that exist in your own life. In theory, you put your own experience into it, and so, in a certain way, you talk about yourself, but most of the time you do it in the disguise of a heterosexual situation. And then, one day, I decided to stop. To tell what I wanted to tell and what was close to me. I made this film with great peace of mind, but after shooting it I had the impression I had put so much of myself into it that I felt ripped open. To have come so close to what made up my life, in a way, without any transposing, I had the impression I was spilling my guts. Ten years ago, it was not easy. I was never ashamed or even guilty, and I never had problems about normality, but it wasn't easy.

To those who criticized him for his dark universe, and *L'homme blessé* for not showing a satisfying homosexuality, Chéreau replied, "Have *you* ever seen a satisfying homosexuality? And even if it happens sometimes, you don't make a film about a happy homosexual situation. In general, you don't make films of happy stories. No one ever criticizes unhappy heterosexual stories for showing heterosexuality in a bad light. If a situation is satisfying and fulfilling, there's no point in creating a film or novel about it." Chéreau continues, "On the other hand, I have little admiration for people who deal unproblematically with their homosexuality and are absolutely at peace with it. Anyway, the experience is different from heterosexuality, to say the least. Maybe because I have always experienced it as the remains of a necessary marginality or rebellion, as something that at times involved some unhappiness. But there is unhappiness among heterosexuals as well."

↬

In the early 1980s, *L'homme blessé* (with its astonishingly premonitory title), a last nod to a world that was disappearing, as if to get on celluloid memories that were becoming blurred, was the culmination of the repertoire of marginal homosexuality. But neither Patrice Chéreau nor Hervé Guibert nor any other homosexual in France could have guessed then that, in reality, two stories were ending at the same time. The first, Pasolinian, dark, sometimes sordid, the story of public toilets, of hard cruising, and of "drifting," had ended with commercialization and communalized sex. It was then that the queen took her leave and the bull dyke went away. "Seven years of happiness?" was the headline in *Gai Pied* in 1981. Life had changed. Time was on your side, you had only to bear witness to what you had endured. Homosexuality was no longer an illness. The carefree life had finally arrived. Laughter as well.

When *L'homme blessé* was released in French theaters, however, another page of history, the homosexual revolution and socialization—timidly begun in 1971, completed in the late 1970s, and celebrated in the early 1980s—suddenly came to an end.

"Are you ready for the eighties?" the Village People sang. Homosexual liberation, barely under way, was over.

PART III

The End of the Carefree Life (1981-89)

10

The Conflagration

At the beginning of scourges, and when they are over, people always employ a little rhetoric. In the former case, the habit is not yet lost, and in the latter, it has already returned. It is at the moment of misfortune that one gets used to the truth, that is, to silence. Let us wait.
—Albert Camus, *La peste*

There is only one thing the FHAR taught us that has become part of the new homosexual movement, and that is a distrust of medicine. I do not see many others.
—Guy Hocquenghem, interview in *Masques* (Summer 1981)

"A cancer that afflicts only homosexuals? No, it's too good to be true, I could die laughing!" Michel Foucault fell off his sofa, contorted by a fit of uncontrolled laughter, when Hervé Guibert brought him this news, which he had heard in the United States.[1]

The American writer Edmund White witnessed a similar scene: "In 1981, shortly after François Mitterrand's election, I had dinner with Michel Foucault and Gilles Barbedette. I talked to them about the 'gay cancer.' They found it so funny they burst out laughing. In fact, they felt it was a typical expression of my American puritanism, and, in the end, they did not believe me."

↪

A disease specific to gays! It was a hilarious joke at a time when the new Socialist government was decriminalizing homosexuality. A joke history played on homosexuals as the century ended.[2]

In 1981, Willy Rozenbaum, always looking a little angry, his hair disheveled, was only thirty-five years old. Assistant to the head of the medical clinic for infectious and tropical diseases at the Claude-Bernard Hospital in Paris, he was just beginning his medical career. The doctor still had a taste for adventure and militancy, left over from his recent days as a medical student and Trotskyist: putting his principles to the test, he had gone to help the young Sandinista regime.

In the June 5, 1981, edition of the journal of the U.S. Government's Centers for Disease Control, a journal to which he subscribed, Willy Rozenbaum learned of five serious cases observed in California hospitals. The shared symptoms were fever, weight loss, respiratory infections, and homosexual practices.[3] The homosexuality of the five patients was underscored, but no causal link to the disease was made.

The same day, in Paris, Rozenbaum saw a patient in his office. Vincent M. was thirty-eight and had a persistent fever. He was an airline steward and a homosexual. He had spent two weeks in the United States in February 1980 and declared that he had had about forty sexual partners in the previous year.[4]

In July, the second article in the American journal extended its observation to twenty-six cases of homosexuals; meanwhile, Vincent was suffering from a series of different ailments. "We had hardly pulled him through one infection when another, even more serious one jeopardized our earlier success," Rozenbaum recalls. "Could Vincent have lost his immunity?" wondered the practitioner, who had grown fond of this atypical patient who came to visit him with his boyfriend. In August, Vincent had pneumocystis pneumonia, then hepatitis B. Hospitalized again by Rozenbaum, this time he developed tubercular pneumonia, cancer of the mucous membranes, and a cytomegaloviral infection. He died in late 1982.

After observing the clinical signs of his patient for several weeks, after much trial and error and despite the skepticism of his colleagues, Rozenbaum noted a resemblance between his patient Vincent and the cases reported in California. The "gay cancer" had been diagnosed in France.[5]

〜

In the early 1980s, homosexuals who had numerous partners sometimes sought regular medical attention because of sexually transmitted diseases.[6] These diseases, whose names are taken from zoology or botany, hold a major place in the collective consciousness: vegetations, papules, genital warts, fungus, crabs. The Institut Vernes (site of the STD clinic), the old Tarnier Hospital, the Red Cross clinic in Paris, and the STD clinic on rue de Pressencé, in the heart of the Arab district of Marseilles, all had a largely homosexual clientele. Faced with the increase in STDs in the late 1970s, *Gai Pied* created a medical column ("Gai Toubib" [Gay doc]), written by Serge Hefez and, later, by Claude Lejeune. The idea for the Association des Médecins Gais, or AMG [Association of gay doctors], was conceived at the same time. That organization, run by homosexual doctors, formed gradually between 1979 and 1980 (hence before the first cases of "gay cancer" were observed) around *Gai Pied* and, especially, Dr. Claude Lejeune. Its bylaws were registered on May 5, 1981, and its stated ambition was to "facilitate dialogue, the way a foreigner might ask to consult a doctor who speaks his language" (*Gai Pied*, November 1981). Clients were happy to find understanding interlocutors to whom they could speak of their difficulties with anal sex or their gonorrhea. Occasionally, they found someone who could do a piercing or put on a penis ring. Transsexuals could get hormone prescriptions. For member practitioners, the AMG had the advantage of providing a clientele. It was openly corporatist, and its ethical practices were slightly shady: it provided the addresses of gay doctors on its telephone service.

The AMG chose as its emblem a narcissistic version of the caduceus (a snake admiring its own reflection in a mirror), a symbol that was a perfect representation of the primacy granted to homosexuality, at the expense of medicine.

Despite the new virulence of viruses such as herpes and cytomegalovirus in the late 1970s, and despite the resistance of certain strains, which could make the genitals look like a cauliflower or an upside-down mango (condylomata), medical treatment was a mere formality, and underlying causes were almost never addressed. A careless attitude prevailed.

"I had gonorrhea every three months," recalls Denis. "Nobody cared in the slightest." Michel Canesi, a dermatologist who worked at the Institut Vernes on rue d'Assas, recalls the atmosphere: "Homosexuals came in saying they had the clap again, raving on because it was the third time within a month." The institute, directed by Dr. Dominique Lachiver, a homosexual member of the AMG, had a predominantly homosexual clientele (close to 70 percent, according to several observers). The rest of the patients were female prostitutes. "At the clinic, an old Catholic granny ruled with an iron fist," Michel Canesi continues. "She spent her days giving antibiotic shots to unbelievable creatures: she felt she was a missionary in the jungle." The men being treated continued the hunt nevertheless, cruising the clinic waiting rooms.

༄

The first mention of "gay cancer" in the monthly *Gai Pied* dates from September 1981. It took the form of a short informative article signed by Antoine Perruchot and titled "Amour à risques" [At-risk love]: "The American gay community is in an uproar. In the last several weeks, about forty cases of the very rare Kaposi's sarcoma have been recorded in the United States. All the patients are queer." A few months later, the AMG's president, Dr. Claude Lejeune, "Gai Toubib" columnist and, in this capacity, codirector of the editorial staff at *Gai Pied* (a dual post that combined militant legitimacy and backing from the medical community), reacted in an article titled "US gai cancer" (*Gai Pied*, January 1982): "Haven't we fallen victim once more to the puritanism that clings to our chromosomes, and that American gays have not managed to leave behind?" That year, the newspaper reconsidered the "strange disease" five times, even publishing the first interview with a patient, on the front page in July. The context in which the disease appeared serves to explain the reactions of gay journalists:

Since the beginning of the year, not a week has gone by when the mainstream press has not reveled in sensational headlines about a disease that is preying on us poor queers. More virulent than the plague and gangrene combined. . . . Wait and see. In the meantime, live, do not panic. So fucking is dangerous? What about crossing the street? [Claude Lejeune, *Gai Pied*, April 1982]

"So, as a result of a disease specific to them, queers are now going back on the list they had unfortunately dropped off, that of social scourges." [Albert Rosse, *Gai Pied*, June 1982]

In November 1982, Dr. Lejeune announced that "the gay cancer" was not homosexual at all, and that poppers, implicated for a time, were exonerated, "along with sexual vagrancy." "Thus," he continued, "you can again without fear . . . go from one man to another, you'll catch something different from AIDS!" He concluded his article with this line: "From gay cancer to acquired immune deficiency, it's the aborted birth of a metaphor."

This first phase, denial of the disease or, at the very least, a belief that it was unlikely to come to France, can be easily explained: no one knew how the disease was spread. The virus had not been discovered, nor had the means of transmission; seropositivity and the test for it were equally unknown. In addition, there was a real fear of renewed discrimination (police brutality or segregation), as certain headlines in the mainstream press might suggest. These headlines were rare but were still perceived as threatening: "Homosexuals punished . . . by cancer" (*Le Matin de Paris*, January 2, 1982); "Mysterious cancer among American homosexuals" (*Libération*, January 6, 1982). It is understandable why gays fought to rid themselves of their new image as "biological assailants."[7]

⇆

In 1982, Jacques Leibowitch, who had just turned forty, seemed like a kind of mad genius, a former leftist and a brilliant immunologist on leave from medicine. "In 1974, I had broken away from the profession," Leibowitch recalls. "I had become a kind of court jester." During this period, traveling in film circles (he lived with Carole Bouquet a few years later), Leibowitch was also in contact with the homosexual milieu. One of his filmmaker friends, André Téchiné, even took him to Le Bronx, a disco on rue Sainte-Anne, where the first Parisian "back room" had been created: "Visiting that back room, I became very anxious: it was hallucinatory. I was terrified, and at the same time it was like a childhood dream come true. I told myself we ought to create that kind of place for straights. I had just discovered the extraordinary homosexual revolution."

In late 1981, Leibowitch, along with Dr. Odile Picard, followed the cases of two young homosexuals and, like Rozenbaum, established a link between their symptoms and American information on Kaposi's sarcoma. "Before AIDS, like all males, I was afraid of homosexuals," Leibowitch confides. "After that, I returned to medical practice, and I immediately made my peace with them."

In February 1982, Willy Rozenbaum and Jacques Leibowitch met and brought together a "small group of friends" in an attempt to gather information on the "gay cancer." Rozenbaum's particular commitment to this new disease eventually cost him his position at Claude-Bernard because too many homosexuals were flooding in. "They said things insinuating that if I wanted to involve myself with queers I would have to go elsewhere," Rozenbaum recalls. "The person in question apologized a few years later." From Claude-Bernard he went to Pitié-Salpêtrière, from which he was also dismissed a few years later. "A lot of people are still convinced I am homosexual," he says with a smile.

The profile of doctors, from Rozenbaum to Leibowitch, who fought the "gay cancer" seems quite atypical. One of these mavericks sold *La Cause du Peuple*, another was nicknamed "The Great Helmsman," and the women involved called themselves feminists.[8] "We were outside the mandarin circuit," Professor David Klatzmann confirms. "We were not part of the system but were rather like free electrons." "The generation of doctors concerned with AIDS," explains Professor Michel Kazachkine today, "were often veterans of May '68. The medical establishment of the 1970s, with its emergency ambulance services and heart transplants, was living with the illusion that you could cure anything, but the sixty-eighters were necessarily receptive to a mysterious disease that was perceived as incurable from the beginning." When the "gay cancer" was diagnosed in France, the epidemic had the odd distinguishing trait of mobilizing more practitioners and epidemiologists—albeit "novices"—than there were patients.

The informal group of friends established by Rozenbaum, which was to become the famous Groupe Français de Travail sur le Sida [French work group on AIDS], met at Claude-Bernard Hospital every two weeks, then at Pitié-Salpêtrière.[9] Thanks to the help of Claude Weisselberg, who assumed the risks of an unusual request, the group was financed by the Direction Générale de la Santé, or DGS [General office of health], which provided a half-time salary for an epidemiologist (Jean-Baptiste Brunet). With the notable exception of Weisselberg, however, these clinicians were so inexperienced at administrative and political procedures that medical institutions had a tendency to marginalize them, thus keeping them from having any real political influence. Yet the form of the group favored the discovery of the virus: it put clinicians, immunologists, and researchers in contact with one another.

It was during one of the meetings of the "gay cancer"–alert group that the doctors considered what name to adopt for the new disease. Always inventive, Leibowitch proposed *cité-syndrôme* [city syndrome], which was not adopted, and Rozenbaum, remembering that one of his Brazilian lesbian friends was named "Sida," proposed to simply reverse the letters of the acronym AIDS. The future acronym SIDA was chosen.

"I had the feeling," says Leibowitch, "that we were making history somehow. But I did not know we were in the middle of the most important medical story of the century." Leibowitch's words might appear grandiloquent. In reality, they are almost humble. The participants in the Groupe Français de Travail sur le Sida were already writing the history of the virus's discovery.

↪

One of the important facts about the AIDS epidemic was the rapid awareness, with the first cases, that it specifically targeted homosexuals. This early observation was made possible by the greater visibility of homosexuals in the early 1980s and the high level of medical treatment given to that population (especially in the United States, where there were specifically gay clinics).[10]

In fact, AIDS appeared soon after the homosexual liberation movement. Thus, as the historian Jean-Noël Jeanneney explains, a very short time had elapsed between the "reduction of social blame and the 1980s, when homosexuals were hit by the virus." Its initial progression occurred at a time when homosexual lifestyles had become widespread in France: there was organized cruising, there were baths and back rooms in the provinces, and there was the new specialized neighborhood of the Marais in Paris. In many respects, the homosexual "theater" of the early 1980s was a boon for a new virus. The way AIDS was spread, via networks and relays fed by the high level of sexual promiscuity and the intermingling of partners, set off a chain reaction that grew exponentially. For homosexuals, the conflagration had started.

"I quickly perceived what the reality of homosexual practices was," Rozenbaum recalls. David Klatzmann, who visited sites of sexual promiscuity in New York in 1981, has the same memory. What was new about the AIDS-alert group was that it got in touch from the beginning with homosexual organizations, a rare public health measure. In what was probably an unprecedented move, medical and administrative agencies warned homosexual "leaders" in France. This was the beginning of the darkest chapter of this dark history: the efforts of a pioneering group of doctors to warn homosexual militants, the staff at *Gai Pied*, and the owners of commercial spots were thwarted by self-proclaimed representatives who did not take them seriously, who laughed, dismissed the problem, and finally lost interest.

Thus Rozenbaum and Leibowitch made contact with Paris homosexual networks early in 1982, to warn them but also to obtain information.[11] Their initial concern was not so much prevention as research. "I called everyone," recalls Leibowitch. Klatzmann warned former acquaintances in the FHAR. In March 1982, Rozenbaum alerted the Association des Médecins Gais. "I called Claude Lejeune, who headed the AMG," he recalls. "He replied, 'Let us die in peace.' We had a lively but not mean-spirited debate." A few weeks later, the AMG organized a "training seminar" and decided at the last minute to include a session with the title "Kaposi's Sarcoma, Immunity Deficiencies, and Homosexuality" (April 24 and 25, 1982). The mere existence of this roundtable at such a surprisingly early date might lead us to reassess the AMG's initial denial.[12] During this colloquium, however, gay doctors took it upon themselves to completely disassociate the new pathology from homosexual lifestyles. Rozenbaum and Leibowitch, invited to give their views, expressed reservations about this approach and recommended taking very seriously the risk factors associated with homosexual practices. At this roundtable, gay doctors also opposed the media attention to the disease; one of them even went so

far as to evoke, despite Rozenbaum's futile objections, the classic militant argument concerning "the inopportuneness of information that can be exploited by
the forces of moral repression."[13] This surly encounter between the group of gay
doctors and the Groupe Français de Travail sur le Sida already contained, in embryo, an irresolvable conflict between the glorification, romanticization, and corporatism of the gay groups, on the one hand, and the starkness of the medical facts,
on the other: the two groups simply talked past each other. The gay journalist
Gilles Barbedette, who had just returned from a stay in the United States, unquestionably belonged to the first group. He made an ambiguous presentation at the
AMG colloquium,[14] criticizing the "gay cancer" metaphor but incidentally giving
information to Leibowitch. He provided the immunologist with all his contacts at
Gay Men's Health Crisis (GMHC) in New York (the first American [nonprofit]
AIDS organization) and with press clippings from American gay newspapers. In
August 1982, Barbedette gave Leibowitch an extremely valuable article from *Medical World News*, in which Robert Gallo's name was mentioned and his hypothesis—that an HTLV retrovirus might be the source of the epidemic—was made
public for the first time.[15] Thus Leibowitch could advance the hypothesis that there
was an infectious agent from the retrovirus family, and not simply a virus. Thanks
to Barbedette, the link between the Groupe Français de Travail sur le Sida and
Professor Gallo's team was established in August–September 1982.[16] A giant step
had been taken in France toward the discovery of the retrovirus.

At this meeting of the AMG, Rozenbaum and Leibowitch, despite some disagreements with gay doctors, took stock of their knowledge, speaking very frankly
about their concerns but also about their areas of ignorance. The reactions of
doubt, perceptible in articles by homosexual militants, were therefore a response
to the uncertainties and enormous confusion on the part of practitioners.

↜

The president of the Association des Médecins Gais was invited to participate in the Groupe Français de Travail sur le Sida. Vaguely concerned about the
new epidemic, he finally agreed at the April roundtable to send a representative.[17]
In May 1982, this representative was Dr. Claude Villalonga; later, it was Dr. Dominique Lachiver, director of the Institut Vernes. In spite of the early—though irregular—presence of these two "gay doctors," information was not disseminated.
"At the Association des Médecins Gais, every member was divided within himself
between two tendencies: good cop and bad cop," Rozenbaum explains. "There was
the doctor who paid attention and the homosexual who refused to see AIDS."
Thierry Gamby, chief of STD services in Marseilles and a former member of the
AMG, is even more harsh: "We had a very bad image of the Paris AMG. Their idea
of the homosexual milieu was false; to us, they seemed to be homosexual militants
more than doctors." The comments of Leibowitch, who had to talk with the militants, are equally unforgiving:

I immediately thought, Who are these damned fools who think they're better than other people because they're both doctors and gay? They were queer, granted. But as doctors, they were nobodies. I therefore found them very suspect. People tried to explain to them what was happening, even though we ourselves did not understand much of it. When I told them, in September 1982, that it was a virus, they took it very badly and wrote that I had problems with anal sex.

Rozenbaum and Leibowitch began to frequent gay spots "for the good of the cause," and got in touch with Fabrice Emaer, who ran Le Palace, and David Girard, owner of several gay businesses. Girard refused to see them: "We had no effect on him," Rozenbaum confirms. The leaders of the work group, which was not discouraged by these failures, gave more and more interviews to homosexual journals in 1982–83 and were invited to speak about the disease on Fréquence Gaie.[18] Very quickly, they invited the Comité d'Urgence Anti-Répression Homosexuelle (CUARH) to participate in the work group. This unusual move was met with caution by the CUARH, which reluctantly sent a representative. He came very sporadically and then disappeared, without making sure that the information obtained was passed on.[19] Here again, Leibowitch is very critical:

The CUARH were clowns. Their thinking was antiscientific, antimedical. They took a malign pleasure in saying the exact opposite of what we were telling them: we said 'virus' and, on principle, they responded 'castration.' In fact, they were not in a position to want to understand. They were opportunistic homosexual activists, and they all thought a great deal of themselves. Once they felt truly in danger and understood their mistakes, they vanished into thin air.

Daniel Defert, future founder of Aides, confirms that neither the CUARH nor the AMG did its part: "Those two organizations did not create real links with the gay milieu, or even stay in the work group."[20]

Between February 1982 and September 1984, Rozenbaum and Leibowitch's group, lacking effective relays, did not succeed in alerting the homosexual population.[21] A few individuals, however—foremost among them the psychiatrist Didier Seux—did manage to convey valuable information. In 1982, Rozenbaum, who knew Seux, sent his patients to the psychiatrist to get appropriate psychological support. "Didier Seux had no authority," Rozenbaum remembers. "He was a homosexual agitator. At the time, he had an iconoclastic position on the disease that was very disturbing for the homosexual establishment, which was trapped in denial. He immediately championed radical action in the gay environment, especially in the back rooms." Leibowitch also remembers, with a certain romanticism, which might make us forget Seux's equally important levelheadedness and seriousness, that Seux "was in an impossible position, trying to reconcile extremes. He immediately apprehended the horror the epidemic was going to become. Just as quickly, he came up with a messianic discourse and recommended radical but fair methods. He was fueled by a mortal anguish, sublimated into debonair extroversion." After joining the Groupe Français de Travail sur le Sida on March 8, 1983, this prophet was murdered by one of his patients, in April 1987.[22]

↩

In stark contrast to the Frenchman Seux stands the French Canadian Gaetan Dugas. Among the once-anonymous figures made famous by the epidemic, Dugas will probably remain the international symbol for a certain irresponsibility on the part of gays. A flight attendant with Canadian Airlines, he was the archetype of the modern homosexual of the early 1980s: blond, mustachioed, twenty-nine years old. Every year he accumulated an estimated 250 sexual partners. In June 1980 he learned that the blotches on his body were due to a very rare form of cancer, Kaposi's sarcoma. Rapidly informed by doctors that he had contracted the "gay cancer," he agreed to give them the names of seventy-three of his recent lovers. The epidemiological research, conducted by a method similar to police cross-checking, showed that in 1982 at least forty of the 248 cases diagnosed in North America were among former partners of Gaetan. Duly warned, he nevertheless rejected advice to be careful and to take protective measures, saying of the disease, "I got it; they can get it, too!" He died on March 30, 1984. This "sex kamikaze" was nicknamed "Patient Zero."[23]

In late 1982, twenty-seven cases of AIDS were reported in France: eight of the patients were homosexuals who had spent time in the United States around 1980, and there was no question that they had been infected there. Four others were also homosexual but seem to have been infected in France; the rest were heterosexual and had traveled to the Caribbean (Haiti) or to equatorial Africa. The disease gradually progressed from being the "gay cancer" to being the "4H" cancer: homosexuals, heroin addicts, Haitians, and hemophiliacs.

The lack of professional respect suffered by the doctors in Willy Rozenbaum's AIDS-alert group was confirmed in late 1982, when key French virologists refused to begin research on the causal agent for AIDS. Rejected by medicine's mandarins and new stars, Rozenbaum tried to find a research laboratory that would confirm the hypothesis that the AIDS agent was a retrovirus. Finally, in late December 1982, Françoise Brun-Vézinet of Claude-Bernard Hospital put him in touch with the virologists Jean-Claude Chermann and Luc Montagnier.

On January 3, 1983, Willy Rozenbaum removed a lymph node from a French homosexual patient who had spent time in New York. Frédéric Brugière, thirty-three years old, worked in the fashion industry. He has since become internationally known under the name RUB, or BRU.[24] That afternoon, Montagnier placed the sample in a culture under a hood at the Institut Pasteur. "We had decided to do a probe, as we call it," recalls Françoise Barré-Sinoussi, who worked on the Montagnier team. "We had an extraordinary stroke of luck because the first probe was the right one."

On the fifteenth day, with the initial culture still alive, Dr. Barré-Sinoussi detected the presence of weak but significant "reverse transcriptase" activity.[25] It took another few days for the retrovirus to be definitively identified (gradually, between January 17 and January 26). On May 17, 1983, *Libération* announced on its front page, under the headline "Gay Cancer: Contagion via Blood," that French researchers at the Institut Pasteur had isolated a virus that might be responsible for AIDS. On May 20, the American journal *Science* announced the discovery of the retrovirus possibly responsible for AIDS (it was named BRU, after the name of the patient, and then LAV).[26] The paper in *Science* carried the names of twelve coauthors sharing credit for the discovery of the virus and included, in prescribed order—the discoverer, then those also responsible for the discovery, and, finally, the head of the department where the experiment was conducted, who in that capacity was credited with the discovery—Françoise Barré-Sinoussi, Jean-Claude Chermann, Christine Rouzioux, Françoise Brun-Vézinet, Willy Rozenbaum, and Luc Montagnier.[27] Montagnier later summed the discovery up as follows: "In February 1983, it appeared this was a new virus. In August 1983, a cluster of experimental proofs made it the prime suspect as the causal agent of the disease. In November 1983, the growth of the virus in cells of tumoral origin allowed it to be produced on a larger scale, for the purpose of doing blood tests."[28] The discovery of the retrovirus, whose causal link with AIDS was not actually confirmed until April 1984, gradually provided details about the disease's modes of transmission. Above all, it confirmed the fears of the epidemiologists.

↬

"I told myself, Son of a bitch! Son of a bitch! It's serious! This time it's serious. It's no laughing matter now," Leibowitch recalls today. "The discovery of the virus confirmed the fact that it was really very serious. AIDS had begun like a Hollywood film, with stars and homosexuals. Then, all of a sudden, a very nasty virus appeared. Thinking again about the back room of Le Bronx, where André Téchiné had taken me, I said to myself, They're all going to die."

Christine Rouzioux, a codiscoverer of the virus, has the same memory: "In 1983, an American researcher from the Centers for Disease Control in Atlanta came to see us. His name was Harold Jaffe. He told us the number of partners some homosexuals have had: over 3,000. We thought we had misheard, and made him repeat it twice: 3,200. . . . We were stunned and terrified because we had just discovered a virus."

Until mid-1983, the researchers' worries met with no response from the affected milieus. Even after the denial phase (1981–83), the editors of *Gai Pied* took it upon themselves to minimize the epidemic's importance both quantitatively (there were few cases, and there were errors in diagnosis) and qualitatively (it was not very contagious and could be cured). Militants believed they were the victims of an antigay paranoia, illustrated, in their view, by headlines in the national press.

In particular, there was the famous "Epidemic of Gay Cancer" (*Libération*, March 19–20, 1983), but also "New York Fights, Paris Dances On" (*Le Nouvel Observateur*, June 7, 1983), "Panic Among Gays" (*Le Nouvel Observateur*, June 17, 1983), and "AIDS, the Gay Plague" (*Parisien Libéré*, August 31, 1983).

Nevertheless, although the causal link between the disease and particular behaviors on the part of homosexuals was virologically false (the virus was not specific to gays), the truth is that this link was epidemiologically well founded (most of the people infected in France were homosexual). Some of the articles in the mainstream press were tactless, but homosexual reactions appear to have been disproportionate, given the proved statistical correlation. This was also true in the case of the recurring debates about the expression "gay cancer," debates that, in essence, indicated a desire to mask the gravity of the disease, if not its existence. "Gay cancer is going away," Jean Le Bitoux wrote in a *Gai Pied Hebdo* editorial published on April 9, 1983. "We are not the only ones affected. It's a more complex matter than simply divine punishment for our lifestyle. It's a way to dismiss the issue of homosexuality: the homosexual environment, they say, causes not only cancer but also crime." In a *Gai Pied Hebdo* article from the same period, published on July 9, 1983, Dr. Claude Lejeune denies the idea of a "gay cancer" while denouncing "the constant exaggeration of a phenomenon that, numerically speaking, is extremely minor." It was as if the militants were speechless in the face of catastrophe, incapable of articulating ideas. They invented artifices, including the denunciation of a "gay cancer." For homosexual militants, denying the correlation implied by the expression "gay cancer" was a handy expedient: it allowed them to avoid self-criticism, which was proving difficult; it also obfuscated the deadly nature of the epidemic and, even more, its spread according to laws and probabilities that were, unfortunately, linked to the number of sexual partners. By denouncing the idea of a "gay cancer," however, militants fell victim to the same identity trap they claimed to be fighting. They confused AIDS, which attacks homosexuals for "what they *do*," with a disease that would attack them for "what they *are*." When AIDS struck, the only strategy compatible with the militant past seemed to be denial of the correlation. Disputes about a "gay cancer" were an easy way out of a tight fix.

The Gay Pride Day festivities of June 18, 1983, made no reference to AIDS. But when, in August 1983, the singer Klaus Nomi became the first famous person with AIDS, editorialists at *Gai Pied* took the subject up.[29] Le Bitoux mentioned "AIDS hysteria" and concluded his July 2, 1983, editorial with this enigmatic line: "We are sick only from being acted upon, not from being actors."[30] *Gai Pied*, along with militant organizations (CUARH, AMG), also denounced the "alarmist position of the French media." Even after the viral agent had been discovered, militants saw no reason why homosexuals should not donate blood. *Libération* rallied behind their protests: an unsigned article on June 16, 1983, was headed "Queers: An Undesirable Blood Group?"

The discovery of the virus led to the distribution of a questionnaire intended to exclude blood donors who belonged to "at-risk groups" (ministerial memo of June 20, 1983). Since the tragedy of the contaminated-blood scandal, we have learned that this memo's instructions were rarely followed. It is less well known that homosexual militants were among the most virulent opponents of donor exclusion, which at the time was the only possible way to avoid catastrophe, since the test for exposure to the virus did not yet exist.[31]

⌐⌐

It is understandable why homosexuals felt that any administrative action designed to keep them from donating blood—a social act and a civic duty—was (in Françoise Héritier-Augé's words) "a threat of the pink star." The first questionnaires that were distributed, particularly those of the Centre de Transfusion Sanguine [Center of blood transfusion] in Paris, included an awkwardly phrased question regarding the private lives of donors: "Over the last three years, have you had sexual relations with multiple homosexual partners?" And the exclusion of "queers" and Africans from blood drives may have appeared rather incongruous in 1983, if not racist on both scores. All the same, there was never any question of putting homosexuals on file, as a rumor claimed. And the ministerial memo of June 20, 1983, written by Drs. Habibi (Centre National de Transfusion Sanguine, or CNTS [National center of blood transfusion]) and Brunet (undersecretary at the department of health), in collaboration with Willy Rozenbaum's work group, showed much more tact: the notion of multiple partners referred not to homosexuals exclusively but rather to "homosexual or bisexual persons having multiple partners." This new formulation might also appear unfortunate, but in 1983, in the absence of a test or technological procedure for inactivating the virus, the safety of the blood supply could be ensured only through the screening of donors. The administration's strategy, which was to exclude anyone who posed a potential risk, was therefore proper, since contaminated blood could not be separated out once the donation had been made.[32] In these conditions, the reaction of homosexual organizations to the plan for excluding homosexuals with multiple partners from donating blood can be understood as particularly irrational.

Some CUARH militants joked, "We'll donate blood anyway." They sent out numerous press releases and letters of protest. One press release quoted by *Le Monde* denounced "the medical ineffectiveness of the measure applied by the Centre National de Transfusion Sanguine, which consists of asking blood donors if they have had sexual relations with multiple homosexual partners. This measure tends to reintroduce the old racist idea of contagion by homosexuals."[33] In another open letter from the CUARH, sent to the state secretary at the Department of Health and reprinted in *Le Monde*, we read, "The CUARH warns against the danger of using a biological phenomenon for moralizing, particularly against homosexuals."[34] For Hervé Liffran, one of the leading figures in the CUARH and today a journalist at *Le Canard Enchaîné*, "Those press releases were stupid. But they cannot be compared to the administrative and political errors. It must also be remembered that, at the time, many in the media were referring to AIDS as the 'gay cancer.' Hence the hypersensitivity on the part of organizations like the CUARH, and this reaction, which was extreme and stupid." Reacting to the debate, Jean-Pierre Soulier, director of the CNTS, explained in a public response solicited by *Libération* on June 17, 1983:

Homosexuals do not belong to a particular blood group. They are individuals who are potentially at risk, whose blood, until further notice, ought not to be used in direct transfusions or in the preparation of clotting factor for hemophiliacs. . . . To maintain [that homosexuals] represent the primary risk group is simply an observation of fact and not a matter for debate. If there have been any "serious blunders," they lie in the desire to transform a problem of public health into a problem of "racist discrimination," to repeat the words of the CUARH.

In a follow-up letter,[35] Professor Soulier also confirmed that the CNTS would not dodge the question of homosexual relations in its questionnaire as long as it was not "clear that homosexuals with multiple partners [were] duly and accurately informed by special reports or committees . . . of the potential risk they represent[ed] to recipients of blood products." A press release from the AMG in July 1983 criticized the memo from the CNTS, and an article published in *Gai Pied* on May 28, 1983, carried the headline "The Blood of Subhumans."[36]

Did the reaction of homosexual militants delay the implementation of the memo on selection of donors? The question is important, especially since it was raised on several occasions during the various lawsuits associated with the contaminated-blood scandal. Blood banks used this argument in their own defense[37] and entered documents from the period into evidence, to illustrate the state of knowledge of the time.[38] Unfortunately, these press releases may have reinforced the decision of the blood banks not to screen donors; it also seems, however, that the opposition of homosexual leaders, who were few in number after all, could not have played a major role. "The problem with the memo," the sociologist Michel Setbon confirms today, "is that no one took it seriously. The reactions of homosexuals were too insignificant to have played a role."

The contaminated-blood scandal, which arose from this notorious 1983 memo, sheds light on a serious malfunction of the health administration and the French blood-transfusion system. Militants, however, by refusing to instruct homosexuals to refrain from donating blood, did not demonstrate any great civic responsibility. In this matter, a comparison with other countries does not show the French militants in a good light.

In the spring of 1983, for example, the powerful Swedish homosexual organization RFLS itself alerted the Swedish health ministry, urging it to take charge of the fight against AIDS. At the same time, gay Swedish militants became the primary source of messages recommending that homosexuals stop donating blood: in Sweden, gays decided on self-exclusion.

Gai Pied expressed ironic surprise when it learned of these "Viking practices" and of the zeal shown by Swedish homosexuals in collaborating with their minister of health. The newspaper found an explanation in the Swedish mind-set, a "supersophistication in matters of security," and in the preoccupation with death already apparent in the works of Strindberg and Bergman (Patrick Cabasset, *Gai Pied Hebdo*, September 14, 1985).

A comparison with Great Britain is no less revealing. At the time, the Thatcher government was practicing legal moralism, and the result was a stronger repression of homosexuality than existed in France. Despite this "state homophobia," however, homosexual militants raised the warning flag early, without worrying about the expression "gay cancer."[39] In the United Kingdom, the homosexual community's first awareness of AIDS occurred in 1982, at a time when the number of patients was markedly lower than in France, and when there were no baths or back rooms in that country.[40] The relatively structured network of organizations (the Gay & Lesbian Switchboard, the Gay Medical Association) immediately responded as a community and, in early 1983, established the Terrence Higgins Trust (Higgins had died of AIDS). This AIDS organization, composed primarily of homosexuals, then made an important political decision: it opened its doors to everyone and rejected a strictly homosexual image. It established a telephone hotline and, in late 1983, distributed brochures in gay gathering places. It also alerted the government, and the administration took immediate action: all blood donors were informed, and those who were homosexual were told to refrain from donating. English homosexual militants stood behind this warning and played a key role in the decision.

In light of these elements, we might think that the reaction of homosexual militants was linked to the community structure of organizations. The purely communitarian model (the ghetto and American-style multiculturalism) initially proved ineffectual in dealing with AIDS. The republican model—the French one, for example ("Be yourself only in private")—was also incapable of reacting. Only mixed, open models that harmoniously combined the special interests of minorities and the interests of the nation as a whole fostered the proper reaction (the English model, to a certain extent, and the Swedish model par excellence).[41]

In many respects, on the issue of blood donation but also on the issue of homosexuals' mobilization against AIDS, French militants were conspicuous for their flightiness. In the end, they fell two years behind the English and the Swedes.

If homosexuals in France had simply been warned of the risk they might pose to the rest of the population, they would have exercised more caution. After all, why would homosexual donors have stubbornly persisted in giving blood if they had been informed of the potential danger to recipients that their actions might represent? But the information did not get through—not via blood banks, which refused to alert their donors or even to screen them, nor via gay militants, who did not take the initiative in informing gays. Failure to implement the 1983 memo on the screening of donors (homosexuals, drug addicts, prisoners), combined with blood drives in prisons, turned out to be directly responsible for the contamination that occurred in France over two years' time.[42]

⎨

Whether because they feared being publicly identified, refused to acknowledge a permanent link between AIDS and homosexuality, or feared a return of homophobia, gay militants refused to believe in the reality of the risk. This was probably unavoidable and is easily explained. One must remember the context: at the time, mortuary employees sometimes refused to cremate the bodies of those who had died of AIDS; they put on gloves to carry the caskets and, for fear of contagion, even burned the leather jackets of dead AIDS patients. There were cases of stones being thrown at patients and of nurses leaving hospital meal trays outside doors. Various individuals have described how infected people were excluded from hospitals and from gay establishments. The homosexual was perceived as a leper; he would soon become a scapegoat once more.

To avoid any retrospective mental reconstructions, let us consider two interviews that Willy Rozenbaum gave to *Gai Pied* during this period. On October 8, 1983, he explained that the number of sexual partners was the determining factor in the AIDS risk and confirmed that "AIDS is a slow virus that becomes active only after a very long period of latency," estimated at the time to be between six months and three years. All the same, Rozenbaum tried to underplay the seriousness of the situation: "I think it is high time to put things in their proper perspective: homosexuals would be very wrong to get worked up." He also mentioned the fact that the disease might have a benign form and that some people "recovered from AIDS." On January 7, 1984, he gave another interview to *Gai Pied Hebdo*, this time to speak of "false AIDS cases," the notorious cases called "AIDS-related complex," or ARC. For him, the patients in question did not have AIDS, and only about 1 to 5 percent of them would eventually get it. ARC subsequently proved to be a preliminary phase of AIDS.[43]

"You had to balance two concerns," Rozenbaum recalls today. "You had to warn without causing panic." The year 1983 was still the prehistory of AIDS in France: medical hypotheses were vague and contradictory, but the great majority of patients were homosexual and Parisian.[44] There was no biological test at the time to determine whether a person was infected. The doubts of militants reflected those of doctors.

⎨

In a pacifist demonstration in late October 1983, a group of homosexuals displayed a banner: BETTER AIDS THAN HIROSHIMA! In an editorial commenting on this slogan, Franck Arnal, editor in chief of *Gai Pied*, criticized those who found his newspaper too timid on the AIDS risk: "This impression is due to our desire not to be too dramatic. ... To sound the alarm would have been the best way to make AIDS a disease of homosexuals." He added, "We know that most of our readers have something less than a wild sex life. Do you talk about the chances of winning the lottery with someone who doesn't even play?" As for those who did have multiple partners, Franck Arnal said in *Gai Pied* on October 29, 1983, "It's their job to assume the responsibilities. Excess sometimes has its disadvantages. Those who are too fond of tobacco, alcohol, fast cars, or even passionate love know they may be condemning themselves, without wanting to. They have made the choice, however. All men are mortal."

The figures for 1983 were nevertheless troubling. Among patients of French nationality, homosexuals represented more than 80 percent of cases, and the numbers were growing rapidly. Despite this increase reflected in the epidemiological data, the debate had less to do with prevention (which was nonexistent) than with the validity of the figures. For Dr. Lejeune, "AIDS was not at all a disease specific to homosexuals"; conversely, Jean-Baptiste Brunet of the Ministry of Health criticized the figure cited by Lejeune (62 percent) as too low, defended the 80 percent figure, and called for mobilization: "I don't think we should wait until there are 1,200 cases in Paris [as there were in New York] to sound the alarm."[45] In a virulent article from the same period, Dr. Lejeune declared, "What is happening is very serious. Homosexuality is at issue, not because of the disease but because of the people who risk destroying its [homosexuality's] very existence." On that occasion, he again denied the scope of the disease and declared, in *Samouraï* in September 1983, "The number of sexual relationships has nothing to do with the chance of catching it."

On January 23, 1984, *Gai Pied Hebdo* and the Association des Médecins Gais organized the first French benefit gala to support research on AIDS. This early action is interesting: it shows that these two organizations oscillated between denial and a growing awareness. Singers slated to appear were announced (Renaud, Jean Guidoni, Diane Tell, Nicole Croisille, Sapho, Nicoletta); Jean Marais and Pascal Sevran were to come; the choreographer Daniel Larrie would dance in honor of Klaus Nomi. But, despite the fact that Yves Mourousi announced the gala on a televised news magazine, it was a failure. Many of the personalities (Renaud, Jean Marais, Nicoletta) canceled, and the public did not mobilize. In early 1984, neither homosexuals nor the general public were ready to combat AIDS.

In 1984–85, it was confirmed that LAV (the future HIV) was the virus responsible for causing AIDS. In December 1984, a test (called "Elisa") was developed to detect antibodies to the virus, and its distribution began in July 1985.[46] These developments changed the way the disease was viewed: on the one hand, condom distribution began to be considered a means of prevention (1984); on the other, anyone could find out whether he had been exposed to the virus. In 1985, the test revealed that there was a phase of seropositivity, a latency period during which the person was infectious but not ill. The epidemiological prospects took on a new dimension: so-called healthy carriers were now renamed "asymptomatic carriers." The scope of the tragedy became clearer. Current patients were only the tip of the iceberg: AIDS was truly a pandemic of enormous proportions.

"BETTER TO DIE OF AIDS THAN OF BOREDOM"

The 1984 issues of *Gai Pied Hebdo* give us a significant point of reference. There were now many editorials and articles on AIDS, and notable differences appeared. Although the editor in chief, Hugo Marsan, was still claiming (in an editorial of April 21) that "the virus of fear" was "much more pernicious" than AIDS itself, a first turning point occurred in late summer. In September, Dr. Lejeune finally sent out a warning. His forcefulness at that time was a departure from his earlier attitude; it was as if he were eager to liberate himself from the denial he had played a role in perpetuating. His earlier arguments had been contradicted by the facts, and the statistics were increasingly troubling. Therefore, in *Gai Pied* on August 25, Dr. Lejeune abruptly appealed to homosexuals "with multiple partners" to "wake up." AIDS was "about to become an almost exclusively homosexual disease" (September 8); its "course [was] deadly most of the time"; and, as a result, "we can no longer bury our heads in the sand" (press release published on September 15, 1984, in *Gai Pied Hebdo*). Dr. Lejeune's metamorphosis was astounding. Thus we can say, without hesitation, that the AMG finally woke up to the problem in August–September 1984. The journalist Eric Conan, who had regularly targeted the serious blunders of homosexual spokespersons, commented on this conversion: "The position of Dr. Lejeune symbolizes the confusion of French homosexuals. ... He has suddenly and stereotypically moved from self-inflicted blindness to panic."[47] In fact, after this sea change, Dr. Lejeune sent out numerous press releases and gave many interviews. One interview, published on September 6, 1984, in *Le Matin de Paris*, can be taken as typical. Dr. Lejeune declared, "I cannot escape the following observation. ... It is practically a homosexual disease." From then on, Dr. Lejeune presented himself as a knight on a mission to make up for the delays of French homosexuals, who "are more fatalistic or individualistic than the Americans." He promoted changes in gay lifestyles, since "this way of life is dying out." He also defined the new rules of prevention, designed to cut the losses. His message was dramatically simple: "Since the number of partners is a risk factor, we must lower that number. Obviously, the virus must be in the blood: let us therefore refrain from donating our blood. Finally, the virus may be in sperm, so we must use condoms. ... Every aspect of sexuality is affected by AIDS." Admitting for the first time that the risk of contracting the virus increased with the number of sexual partners, the Association des Médecins Gais chose to depart from its earlier line. September 1984 marked a turning point.

All the same, these new positions were not unanimously accepted. Because he dared to question homosexual lifestyles, Dr. Lejeune, who had come a long way, was chided by other gay militants, who disputed his legitimacy and criticized him for his "homophobia-generating publicity stunt." Hervé Liffran, an emblematic figure in the CUARH, acknowledged that the progression of the disease was troubling but publicly denounced the "fantastic and antiscientific concepts" of a "homosexual disease" promoted by Lejeune: "There would be no reason to grant much importance to these words if they came from a person renowned for his homophobia. But there you have it: Dr. Claude Lejeune is president of the Association des Médecins Gais." Liffran also criticized Lejeune for his "perorations on the supposed irresponsibility of homosexuals."[48] In the same spirit, a certain Jean Boyer denounced "the alarmist articles *Gai Pied* has been printing since September 1984," accused its journalists of being "worn-out Casanovas," and criticized them for getting bored "with monotonously repetitive fucking; perhaps AIDS [provides them with] a pretext to take a break. Other gays reply that it is better to die of AIDS than of boredom" (*Masques*, winter 1984–85). That last line made history.

The positions of the CUARH and of the homosexual periodical *Masques* appear to have been more rigid than those of the AMG.[49] The persistent, determining influence of Trotskyist rhetoric, and especially the rejection of medical treatment, were the key differences between the first two organizations and the AMG. They also marked a dividing line within the staff of *Gai Pied*, which did not unanimously adopt Dr. Lejeune's new line. Despite Lejeune's about-face, the more "political" editorialists of *Gai Pied* continued to tilt at windmills. Their initial denial had made AIDS an invention of American puritanism; now these writers denied that the virus had reached epidemic (pandemic) proportions: a new phase; a new form of denial.

In the second half of 1984, Franck Arnal made repeated comparisons designed to reduce AIDS to its "proper" proportions. In his editorial of August 25, he compared the number of cases identified to the number of car accidents. A month later, on September 22—repeating the same errors as Dr. Lejeune, but with a two-year delay—he declared, "In terms of statistics, it seems that the homo Parisian runs as much risk [of AIDS] from having multiple partners as he does of developing lung cancer from smoking two packs of cigarettes a day." A little later, on October 27, he again declared, "At the moment, one homosexual per week is murdered in France after an encounter. . . . If you're living in Limoges, that's a threat more real than AIDS!"

↬

It was in this context that the police decided to turn the lights back on in the darkened back rooms. For gay militants, the back room, poppers, and multiple partners were the signs of homosexual liberation. With the threat of closure hanging over the back rooms, all the familiar trappings of the 1970s fell apart, and all the victories seemed to be called into question. Could the militants do anything besides shout at the return of the moral order?

From September 1984 to February 1985, the drug and prostitution squad of the Paris police (formerly the vice squad) proceeded to close some of the back rooms, a measure also taken in the provinces (for example, at Le Blue Boy, in Nice, in the autumn of 1985). This decision, which was not motivated by the AIDS epidemic, was an application of article 334, paragraph 6, of the penal code, whose aim at the time it was adopted had been to prohibit "public debauchery." The same measure had already been adopted to deal with the many heterosexual swingers' clubs.

"There are no back rooms left in Paris today," Roland Surzur lamented in *Gai Pied Hebdo* on February 23, 1985. The journalist concluded his long article by writing, "The closing of the back rooms may be only the prelude to a reactionary movement on the part of the police, the return of the old discriminatory methods used against queers ... It has a name: backlash!" "Why did they close *our* back rooms?" *Samouraï* wondered with sorrow in May 1985. "The police have launched the battle of the back rooms; but we must not let them win," replied Gérard Bach in the April issue of *Homophonies*. "Let us praise the back rooms. ... [They] were a new possibility for homosexual expression in the 1970s." Bach added, in the May issue of *Homophonies*, "We must not allow them to be jeopardized."

In reply to Hervé Guibert, who hypothesized in 1983 that there was probably no one left in the San Francisco bathhouses, Foucault reportedly said, "Don't kid yourself. There have never been so many people in the baths, and it's really extraordinary. This threat hanging over everyone has created a new complicity, a new tenderness, a new solidarity. Before, you hardly exchanged a word; now, everyone talks. Everyone knows precisely why he's there."[50]

Was it wise to close the back rooms? At one time, the Americans thought it was.[51] Despite the debates, in 1985 closing the back rooms was undoubtedly not a high priority. Given the incredulity of the time, the decision would have been perceived as a sign of the moral order's return rather than as an epidemiological necessity. Despite their symbolic power in sounding the alarm, such methods probably would have proved counterproductive. "If you close the baths, you open the bushes," was Daniel Defert's amusing line.[52] The only solution would have been to use these available sites to distribute solid information. But in the early years, the owners of the back rooms did not want that, either. "They were small-business owners," Jacques Leibowitch recalls. "The owners of the back rooms criticized us for wanting to kill them off by depriving them of customers. In fact, the reverse happened: *they* killed the homosexuals. For them, business was more important than militancy. They were engaged in collaborationist profiteering on behalf of the epidemic."

What is significant about this debate over the back rooms is that it seems to have been a distraction, to avoid preventive measures. The delay in getting information out, even more than the question of closing the back rooms, was a determining factor in the death rate at a time when AIDS was spreading in France.

While the condom was emerging as the only effective measure of prevention (the impermeability of latex to the LAV virus was confirmed only gradually, between 1984 and 1985), nothing was more striking than the homosexual community's delay in accepting the idea. The government shared this reticence about the subject: it was not until 1987 that condom advertising was authorized.

"Sexual liberation kept us from understanding the condom issue," explains Jean-Marc Choub, who at the time headed the medical committee of the CUARH. "Those who were disseminating the first prevention messages upset us, and we pretended not to hear them. For us, using a condom and reducing the number of partners was a return to a bygone era, a crime against love."

On their own, homosexuals began to desert the back rooms. The disappointment of the militants, who thought their struggles had contributed to the opening of these sites of pleasure, was in proportion to their past involvement. If a comparison is needed, their disillusionment was equaled only by old André Baudry's feelings when, after twenty years of solitary homophile battles, he was cast out by "the queers" of the FHAR. The bitterness of the grandfather of the homosexual movement, accused after 1968 of being an old killjoy, was echoed in the anger of the last heirs to the gay revolution, who found the doors to *their* back rooms locked.

↬

One scandal followed another, and the closing of the back rooms was supplanted in 1985 by fears concerning the test. This was the second act, as it were, of the contaminated-blood scandal.

In late 1984 and early 1985, in fact, the possibility of a test for detecting exposure to the AIDS virus led to a debate. "This long-awaited test has just been developed by the Institut Pasteur," wrote Franck Arnal in a *Gai Pied Hebdo* editorial of December 8, 1984. "We fear the Institut has thought only of potential gains. But this test means we'll all be on file."[53] Laurent Fabius's announcement, on June 19, 1985, of mandatory testing of donated blood for the AIDS virus met with a fresh response from *Gai Pied*.[54] It is true that many uncertainties persisted about the reliability of the test, and guarantees about the confidentiality of the results were not satisfactory. But it is astonishing to note that Roland Surzur, a journalist at *Gai Pied*, still feared even on June 28, 1985, that this test would allow the state to keep track of homosexuals.[55] Clearly, *Gai Pied*'s objurgations of the government reflected a major confusion between ensuring the safety of blood transfusions and submitting to the vagaries of security measures.[56]

In the first results of the testing conducted by blood banks after the 1985 Fabius decree, the rate of infection among blood donors was extremely high—"the highest rate in Europe," Michel Setbon confirmed.[57] Three hypotheses are possible. First, homosexuals may have come to the blood banks in the summer of 1985 to find out whether they were infected, thus increasing the rate of contamination in the blood collected. Second, homosexuals may have given blood more often than the population at large because of the social benefits of donating blood. Or, third, the contaminated blood may not have come from homosexuals carrying the virus. In this connection, we have known ever since the sensational trials and published studies on this question that blood drives among drug addicts in prisons and in "sensitive" neighborhoods of Paris played a major role. This was the epicenter of blood contamination. Nevertheless, given the higher prevalence of the virus in the homosexual population at that time, these blood drives among high-risk groups cannot fully explain the extent of the damage (every week between March and July 1985, between fifty and one hundred people who received transfusions were infected).

The high rate of contamination observed in the lots of blood in 1985 probably resulted from a combination of the three factors just noted, but we cannot say how much each one contributed. Nevertheless, homosexuals probably started coming to be tested in the summer of 1985. Some may even have made a second donation, to confirm that they were seropositive. To avoid this eventuality, the administrative and political authorities ought to have opened anonymous testing centers specifically for homosexuals, so that people concerned about their HIV status could have been screened without having to donate blood.[58] This poor screening of donors, responsible for most cases of infection between 1981 and 1985, played a significant role in infection via blood until August 1, 1985.[59]

↜

It is possible to see the history of homosexuals' mobilization against AIDS between 1981 and 1985 as an almost uninterrupted series of grave misunderstandings, delays, and self-imposed blindness. The "flighty" way in which homosexual leaders treated the AIDS problem took various and contradictory forms, from denying that the disease existed to denying its importance, from refusing to take preventive measures to refusing to be tested for exposure to the virus. Their reactions were almost always marked by significant delays and lack of foresight. Beyond errors that were committed, it is difficult to assess the weight of sins of omission and of the absences, delays, preventive measures not taken, and overall passivity that prevailed until 1985. If we add all the silence, these delays take on even greater importance, and the blame is mind-boggling.

Willy Rozenbaum offers the following explanation:

Truths have to be placed in their original context. In 1985, a diagnosis of AIDS meant a very quick death. In July 1985, testing was widely available. At the time, we thought that 10 percent of all people infected would develop AIDS five years after becoming infected.[60] So we said that being HIV-positive was not the same as being sick, since thousands of people with the virus were likely to perceive it as a death sentence in the very short term. Today I am sorry that we made this distinction between having the virus and being sick, since it reinforced denial.

Gai Pied is the best barometer of the times by which to measure the internal contradictions of the French gay milieu, which refused to choose between alarm and denial. Yet the growth of information in this periodical was enormous, in quantitative if not qualitative terms: there was one article in 1981, with five in 1982, thirty-four in 1983, fifty-one in 1984, and 170 in 1985.[61] This progression strikingly sums up the scope that AIDS gradually assumed in the homosexual world.

　　⌐⊃

What were the reactions of other newspapers? In the first half of the 1980s, the gay press, *Gai Pied* included, probably had a total circulation of about 50,000 in France (its readership probably exceeded 100,000).[62] Thus, for all periods combined, the influence of the information disseminated in homosexual papers was not insignificant.

Homophonies, the militant monthly of the CUARH, seems to have followed *Gai Pied*'s evolution quite closely, despite a marked delay in mid-1984. "No Danger in Delay" was the newspaper's headline in June 1982. In February 1983, the headline for one article was a play on words: "Pas de cancer gai" [both "No gay cancer" and "Gay cancer makes inroads"]. In September of the same year, the editor of *Homophonies* commented, "AIDS was recently the cancer of journalists in need of a story. On the pretext of giving information, through second-rate sensationalism, they have revived homophobia and given it new prospects. . . . [These] irresponsible journalists would like to force us into a hasty retreat to our closets." In the same issue of September 1983, *Homophonies* put together a dossier that included an interview with Luc Montagnier and a very competent interview with the dermatologist Michel Canesi, who encouraged readers to rethink gay sexuality and "advised against any form of anonymous sex."[63] But the attitude of *Homophonies* remained ambivalent. For example, it published a letter from Charles A., a gay doctor in Nantes: "Even though I'm a doctor, I am proud to know almost nothing about the 'gay cancer.' The glut of information about a disease I will probably never see in my office makes me sick" (letter to the editor, November 1983). In February 1984, *Homophonies* accomplished another feat: it published a survey, running for more than ten pages, on San Francisco, "the gay El Dorado," which completely obfuscated the question of AIDS. Beginning in early 1985, the monthly embraced the positions of doctors but failed to take preventive measures on its own. Willy Rozenbaum, without eliciting any reaction, could declare in February that "in the matter of preventing AIDS, sexual promiscuity is the main issue. . . . There are objective reasons to be afraid: for myself, I'd be afraid to go to the back rooms today." Although *Homophonies* remained consistently ambivalent, neither sounding the alarm nor giving clear instructions regarding prevention, it did give doctors a forum. This fact is essential. It is amazing, though, that militants in the CUARH and at *Homophonies*, so lacking in vigilance in the fight against AIDS, were at the same time so focused on the pedophile cause. After 1985, *Homophonies* could not survive such contradictions.[64]

The review *Masques* seemed even more hesitant than *Gai Pied* and even *Homophonies*—no small feat. The first mention of AIDS dates from the autumn 1983 issue and carries the limpid headline "The Golden Chains of Gay Liberation." The article was written by Alain Sanzio. But it was Jean Boyer who really distinguished himself, and with disconcerting tenacity, in his denial of the AIDS risk. His attitude may be explained by the fact that he lived not in Paris but in Dijon. For him, AIDS was an "antigay racism" (*Masques*, spring 1984): "So people who risk death a hundred times driving a car reject the small supplementary risk of a viral infection?" In the same article, he attacked American gays, who were reacting "as if AIDS were a disease . . . when it is in fact a political phenomenon." A few months later, he concluded, with a keen sense for prognostication: "American fantasies are without foundation," and he sharply attacked Leibowitch and Rozenbaum (*Masques*, summer 1984). "No, the U.S. does not foreshadow France's future," he insisted again six months later. In the same article, he used the startling line already cited: "Better to die of AIDS than of boredom" (*Masques*, winter 1984–85).

As for the homosexual review *Magazine*, founded by Didier Lestrade, it quite simply ignored the AIDS question. And yet this periodical, which targeted Paris high society (with interviews, photographs, and erotic news), was published between 1980 and June 1986. When it folded, AIDS had still not been mentioned. This silence had no equal in the rest of the French homosexual press.[65]

Because homosexual women were not a population at risk, lesbian newspapers did not mention the AIDS question in the first years of the epidemic. Like gay men, however, the female agents of sexual liberation were caught off guard by the mysterious disease. This may explain an article by one of the key lesbian militants of the time, Christiane Jouve, then editor in chief of *Lesbia*: "The evolution of the 1980s remains incomplete, and above all very fragile. Public opinion is still lagging behind, laws may still be applied, and people cannot see the forest of unanswered questions for the trees of AIDS."[66]

The treatment of the AIDS issue in *Libération* is also a reliable reference point. Despite the opposition of militants, *Libé* did not hesitate to make frequent use of the misleading expression "gay cancer." Serge July, the newspaper's editor, quickly saw the importance of the subject, asking that it be granted a key place. In an article titled "Homosexuals and the AIDS Effect," published on October 20, 1984, the journalist Eric Conan wrote, "Homosexuals, attacked biologically by this disease and socially as a cultural ethnic group, have long denied the threat, sometimes in a manner verging on hysteria." A year later, in an article published on December 12, 1985, Conan wrote, "The homosexual intelligentsia and the press [have preferred] to bury their heads in the sand. They choose denial so as not to drive the Marais to despair." *Libération* always claimed to be sensitive to the gay cause, but it was not a homosexual newspaper. It had neither the tone nor the corporatist manner, especially once a new editorial policy was established, just after May 1981. At that time, *Libé*'s "homo lobby" was marginalized: Guy Hocquenghem and Jean-Luc Hennig quit the paper. All the same, Conan's articles became the object of much criticism. The AMG, the CUARH, and the RHIF (a splinter group of the CUARH), in letters addressed to Serge July, expressed indignation about information on AIDS published by *Libé*. "You have done the homosexual community a bad turn," wrote Alain Leroy (RHIF), who objected to the term "gay cancer." For him, this "choice of term [was] racist." In 1983, Dr. Lejeune asked to reply to Serge July: the title of his article was "*Libération* Is Panicking for You."

In addition to these reactions from militants outside the newspaper, it is interesting to observe that the staff of *Libération* harbored various opposing positions. Medical journalists who chose to sound the alarm found themselves face to face with a virtual "internal front" led by *Libération* homosexuals (Christian Caujolle, Philippe Hoummous, and especially two former Gazolines, Michel Cressole and Hélène Hazera), all former members of the FHAR. During staff meetings at the newspaper, and especially "in the hallways"—a privileged forum for discussion—Cressole and Hazera expressed indignation about the excessive importance accorded articles on AIDS and the hygienics related to the disease, and they openly criticized Conan for his hysteria. To them, he was "homophobic." When Conan mentioned condoms or other modes of prevention, they protested—even in 1985—against such alarmism. "Stop talking about us," "Leave homosexuals alone," "It's not serious," Hazera and Cressole repeated. "Some homosexuals at the newspaper, and certain pedophile militants at *Libé*, ranted constantly about our articles, which were sounding the alarm," recalls Dominique Couvreur, former city editor at *Libé*.[67] "I often found myself alone on two fronts," Conan explains. "But Serge July always defended me without reservation, and I also received the consistent though isolated support of Serge Daney, the paper's film critic, who was lucid and clear-sighted from the beginning." We might legitimately wonder whether *Libération*'s use of the expression "gay cancer" was not misguided, since the term is doubly inaccurate (AIDS is not cancer, and it is not intrinsically homosexual). In reality, however, the debate had less to do with questionable headlines than with the perceived need to accord the disease importance. Thanks to numerous articles, and despite criticism from former members of the FHAR, *Libération* succeeded in sounding the alarm. In this way, it was significantly different from the gay press.

&

"Homosexual denial" is an important fact in the history of the epidemic in France, and the fear of being stigmatized yet again is not an adequate justification for the irresponsibility of homosexual militants.

How can we understand this enormous blunder if we opt to observe and explain this disconcerting blindness rather than look for responsible or guilty parties?

One hypothesis is that the profile of homosexual militants in France in the early 1980s played a large role in the delays. The staff at *Gai Pied* was a perfect reflection, if not a distillation, of the state of mind at the time. Former leftists accustomed to slogans (FHAR, GLH) and fearing medical treatment ("Doc, heal thyself" was a platitude used by the FHAR), the editors of the homosexual periodical evolved a great deal in the early 1980s. They converted to professional business practices but still embraced the symbols of homosexual liberation: the defense of free love, multiple sex partners as an emblem of militancy, rejection of the coupled life (which mimicked the institution of the family), an obsession with homophobia. In various forms, Renaud Camus's "Achrian chronicles," published in *Gai Pied* in 1982 and 1983, and texts by such former heroes of the FHAR as Laurent Dispot and especially Guy Hocquenghem, were characteristic of this inadequate and rigid ideology.[68] Further exacerbating this tendency was the fact that, after the split in 1983, the most fervent representatives of the need to maintain close ties with advertisers (corporatism with respect to the owners of the baths and the back rooms) remained at the newspaper. Several former *Gai Pied* journalists have confirmed that by 1983 it had become impossible to criticize the owner of a gay establishment, and that the newspaper's new managers too often yielded to the injunctions of advertisers.[69] *Gai Pied* combined two major handicaps, which prevented it from seeing the reality of the epidemic at the time: a militant identity politics obsessed with homophobia, and a pecuniary chumminess with commercial spots. Despite contradictory and, often, even fiery debates among the staff at *Gai Pied*, whose editorial board was less unanimous than it appeared, the staff could not shift abruptly from a discourse focused on pleasure, excess, and irresponsibility to a discourse requiring moderation and responsibility. Nor could it face, shortly thereafter, the prospect of bodies slowly deteriorating and often dying. Could the people who had invited homosexuals to "unfettered pleasure" become evangelists for the condom? Even apart from *Gai Pied*, homosexual groups in the France of the early 1980s were unable to move (as groups had done in the United States) from the discourse of an oppressed minority to the provision of lifestyle-based services. In 1982–83, France, unlike Sweden and Great Britain, had no homosexual community: the only bond was sexual; it was a community of desire.

In the 1980s, there were few homosexual militants, and they had no legitimacy and no troops. The militants were probably also still profoundly steeped in a far-left ideology rooted in a fundamental anti-Americanism. The Ligue Communiste Révolutionnaire's influence and anti-imperialism during the Vietnam War were essential factors. In this sense, the fact that AIDS had made its appearance in the United States led to a dual error, at least at the unconscious level. First, militants

saw the disease as a symptom of the puritanism of a society that was at bottom reactionary; and, second, they believed there was no chance that AIDS would spread
in a comparable manner in France.[70]

Within this general context, one of the initial errors of Willy Rozenbaum's
AIDS-alert group was to entrust the dissemination of information within the gay
community to organizations like the AMG and the CUARH. The surface respectability of these organizations concealed the fact that they were hardly representative, and their corporatism made them oblivious to information. They were only
the illusion of a community. "We did not effectively raise the question of our interlocutors' legitimacy," Rozenbaum says today. Jacques Leibowitch concludes,
sadly, "We screwed up. The information did not get through. The will to live was
secondary to homosexual desire."

The phase of denial observed among homosexual leaders also occurred in associations for hemophiliacs. This comparison is instructive. With the progress of
medical science, hemophiliacs, who before World War II almost never lived to be
twenty, saw their hopes for life grow, thanks to supplementary transfusions of
simple cryoprecipitates. From the 1970s on, decisive improvements were made
through the use of concentrated blood products obtained by the so-called pooling
method.[71] Just as homosexuals ceased to be pariahs, hemophiliacs lost their handicap. "We no longer needed to go to the hospital," explains Edmond-Luc Henry,
vice president of the Association Française des Hémophiles [French association of
hemophiliacs], or AFH. "We could go abroad with our stable concentrated factor,
which we kept in a standard ice chest. We could play sports." "Before, hemophiliacs had been handicapped. They became normal citizens," Willy Rozenbaum concludes. The life of hemophiliacs had changed in the late 1970s. Could they easily accept returning to the past? "Hemophiliacs refused to consider AIDS. There was an
attitude of denial," Henry confirms. Although the facts in no way attenuate the
government's responsibility, it is interesting to note that, in parallel to the tragic
political delays illustrated by the contaminated-blood scandal, the AFH and its
journal, *L'Hémophile*, adopted a reassuring attitude. They constantly minimized
the risks associated with antihemophiliac products, encouraged hemophiliacs to
increase nonessential perfusions, and denounced journalists who included hemophiliacs in the famous "4H" AIDS-risk groups.[72] Of slightly more than 3,000 hemophiliacs living in France, nearly 50 percent were infected by the virus between
1981 and October 1, 1985.

༄

The errors of homosexuals, some of them probably inevitable, went hand in
hand with those of medical bodies and politicians. How could it have been otherwise?

Albert Rosse, a journalist at *Gai Pied*, still regrets writing certain articles; he recalls, "We didn't believe in AIDS for a second. They couldn't restrain us with mo-

rality, the church, or the law: we told ourselves they *had* to invent a virus. AIDS was little green men coming to punish homosexuals once the laws no longer repressed them. We burst out laughing." Alain Sanzio, cofounder of *Masques*, gives a rather similar analysis: "During a trip I took with Jean-Pierre Joecker to Fire Island, in the United States, in 1982, we felt something was happening. There were a few banners, people were cruising less in the bushes. Our immediate attitude was not to talk about it. We buried our heads in the sand. We had left the provinces for Paris in about 1975: we were finally living. We would not, could not, shatter our dreams because of a disease."

Patrick Cardon, a former GLH–Aix-en-Provence militant, has another explanation:

AIDS came along at the precise moment when doctors and homosexuals had stopped talking to each other. Some parents took their children to psychiatrists when they learned they were homosexual. It was doctors who treated homosexual attraction with a radical procedure: lobotomy! Our image of medicine was that it was repressive. And just then, doctors wanted to reestablish dialogue, to announce the appearance of a new disease, at a time when we had managed to get homosexuality off the list of psychiatric disorders. Doctors were no longer credible.

Jacques Fortin, head of GLH–Marseilles, also pleads guilty: "When AIDS came along, it negated everything we had lived through, and it marked our difference in an even more visible manner. That called everything into question again. We were sick about it. We did not believe in it. The homosexual hecatomb caused by AIDS is partly our own fault."

Thierry Gamby, a homosexual who became a leading member of Aides in Marseilles, is very critical of the militants: "There was an enormous amount of denial. People engaged in demagoguery. *Gai Pied* spread AIDS for five years." A more moderate Didier Heller, former contributor to the homosexual newspaper, claims to be just as lucid: "It's bitter to observe that *Gai Pied* did not do its part. What was at stake in the fight against AIDS cannot be calculated. So what if they had lost money from the personals or from advertising? Prevention was a huge issue." Also pleading guilty, Jean-Marc Choub, head of the CUARH's medical committee and of *Homophonies*, offers this self-criticism: "I am not proud. What makes me indulgent toward the parties deemed responsible for the contaminated-blood scandal is that it's easy for me to measure the inadequacy of my own assessment and of the positions I took at the time." Gérard Bach, one of the key figures of the CUARH, echoes this sentiment: "I have regrets. There were real risks of major blunders: panic and the resurgence of homophobia. That was avoided, but at the cost of an inadequate appraisal of the gravity of the epidemic in the homosexual milieu. That is probably what Georgina Dufoix's verdict of 'responsible but not guilty' reflected."

Jacky Fougeray's observation is even more unusual. The former GLH militant, copy chief at *Gai Pied* until 1982, explains today, "Those militants wanted the disease not to exist. And why not? They felt that their dream, homosexual liberation, was disappearing. So they didn't believe it. I find this denial romantic, almost touching."

↪

This chronology, which has traced the hesitant birth of the fight against AIDS in the homosexual milieu between 1982 and 1985, allows us to refute certain analyses written in the 1990s. These studies have attempted to demonstrate that homosexuals were victims of a particular form of ostracism and that the government remained totally indifferent, despite their heartrending pleas. "My explanation," writes Franck Arnal, "rests essentially on the premise that a French moral order, refusing to make homosexual reality visible, was unable to establish a real policy of prevention directed at homosexuals."[73] Although this situation may have existed in the second phase (1985–89), Arnal is guilty here of an anachronism. Can one criticize the government in hindsight for its well-established passivity in the period between 1981 and 1985, when gays themselves, during the same period, refused to see the importance of the disease? "You can't win against the interested parties," Rozenbaum confirms, "even if you have political power. You couldn't go into the back rooms and practice prevention against the will of individuals, organizations, and gay business owners. Nothing was possible without the consent of homosexuals."

The spokespersons for militant homosexuality thus refused to see the scope of the pandemic and were unable to respond to the formidable challenge of alerting homosexuals without increasing the stigma. Since they preferred to sacrifice crucial health imperatives in favor of a blind defense of sexual liberation, new organizations had to emerge to fill the void.

↪

On November 17, 1984, a long letter signed "Jean" appeared in the letters to the editor of *Gai Pied Hebdo*. It launched a virulent attack against the editorials in *Gai Pied*, targeting editor in chief Franck Arnal in particular:

Your last editorial flabbergasted me. I don't understand what you're doing. Right now in Paris, there are three or four new cases of AIDS a week. . . . 90 percent of them are homosexuals. More than 25 percent of gays, who have not taken a vow of chastity, are now carriers of the virus, according to an epidemiological study published this summer by Dr. Jacques Leibowitch. . . . So stop the paranoid fantasies that crop up whenever someone talks to you about AIDS. It's a disease that is threatening our bodies, but also our way of life. . . . In the face of the facts, you and your newspaper seem to oscillate between burying your heads in the sand (the disease is minor and inflated by the nasty "heterocops") and engaging in moralizing alarmism (those who are sick are horrible perverts).

Jean added, "After abandoning gay activism in 1979, I have returned to service so that a chain of true gay solidarity can be established."

The man who wrote this critical letter, and who did not want to give his name, was in fact Jean Blancart. A former GLH militant, he was already weakened by the disease in 1984. He lived for several years with the writer and journalist Gilles Barbedette. At the end of his letter, Blancart announced that he was participating in a new organization, of which he later became vice president. That organization was called Aides.

11

Aides: The History of a Social Movement

I have never been a militant of homosexual identity because identity politics is
not my style.

—Daniel Defert

I n a heavy silence, his voice cracking and husky with sorrow, the philosopher Gilles Deleuze, fellow traveler of the sexual liberation movement,
read an excerpt from Michel Foucault's *Histoire de la sexualité* [*The History of
Sexuality*] in the small courtyard of the Pitié-Salpêtrière Hospital. Foucault was
well acquainted with this former gunpowder factory, which had been turned into a
hospital for the poor, then into a prison for female prostitutes, and then into an
asylum before finally becoming part of the Pitié Hospital under the name Pitié-
Salpêtrière. He had described its role and evolution at length in his *Histoire de la
folie* [*Madness And Civilization: A History of Insanity in the Age of Reason*]. And it
was here that he had just died, on June 25, 1984.

For this last tribute, at which Deleuze had been invited to speak by Foucault's
partner, Daniel Defert, a mixed crowd gathered: his friends from the Collège de
France (Paul Veyne, Pierre Bourdieu, Pierre Boulez), such illustrious professors as
Georges Dumézil and Georges Canguilhem, Minister of Justice Robert Badinter,
but also Simone Signoret and Yves Montand, Hélène Cixous and Bernard Kouchner, among several hundred others. There was also a spray of roses from his close
friends, whose three given names appeared behind a lavender taffeta ribbon:
Mathieu, Hervé, Daniel.[1]

Mathieu Lindon, a journalist for *Libération*, the writer Hervé Guibert, and Deleuze were among the very first paying members of the organization that Defert
created.[2] Foucault's death can thus be seen as the founding act in the birth of Aides.

↪

"I lived for eighteen years in a state of passion toward someone, for someone. Perhaps at a given moment that passion turned to love," Foucault explained.
"I do not believe there is anything in the world, whatever it may be, that can stop
me when I need to go find him, talk to him."[3] Foucault met Defert when the young
Burgundian (he was born in Vézelay, Yonne) entered the Ecole Normale Supérieure in Saint-Cloud, after an adolescence spent in Lyons. Their relationship
lasted nearly twenty-five years.

A politically active student, Defert fought against the Algerian war, particularly in his role as delegate to the Ecole Normale coalition. He participated in the
anticolonialist committees and, in 1970, joined the (Maoist) Gauche Prolétarienne
[Proletarian left], or GP, after it was declared illegal by the government. In the
1970s, however, Defert's life history became virtually indistinguishable from that
of Foucault. As the Front Homosexuel d'Action Révolutionnaire (FHAR) was
forming, the two of them established the Groupe d'Information sur les Prisons, or
GIP [Information group on prisons]. The concordance of dates is striking, and, in
spite of an obvious political proximity, Foucault and Defert did not join in the
homosexual struggles.[4]

They preferred the battle against political and social discrimination to identity
politics. At that time in particular, they fought discrimination affecting prisoners.
With Jean-Marie Domenach, who directed the review *Esprit*, and Pierre Vidal-
Naquet, Foucault and Defert led a vast campaign in the GIP denouncing living
conditions in French prisons. On the basis of a philosophy of "rights," they proposed to let prisoners speak, a first step toward recognition. The justice system deprived prisoners of their freedom, but, for Defert and Foucault, prisoners still had
rights within the penal institutions. Defert and Foucault were also concerned with
living conditions in prison, from the frequent suicides to health problems to poor
access to the press, all signs of the system's brutality.

Foucault and Defert led a true movement of solidarity, creating focus groups
and several committees in the provinces. Deleuze, Jean Gattegno, Hélène Cixous,
Claude Mauriac, Jean-Paul Sartre and, at times, the former prisoner Jean Genet,
among many others, participated in the enterprise. Defert acquired a reputation as
a good organizer, planning many demonstrations and mobilizing doctors, monks,
nuns, and lawyers. He was in contact with the medical corps and the Mouvement
d'Action Judiciaire [Movement for judiciary action] and established ties with
professional groups involved in the medical or prison systems. To raise the public's
awareness, original events were staged: skits were performed in front of prisons by
actors from Ariane Mnouchkine's Théâtre du Soleil, and a trial was reenacted in a
housing project in Créteil. The indisputable successes, however, ought not to mask
the enormous spontaneity of the GIP, which was characterized by an almost deliberate lack of organization. As one might imagine, the GIP was a valuable apprenticeship for Defert and, in many respects, became the model for Aides.

In the winter of 1971–72, the GIP had to deal with more than thirty revolts and
hunger strikes in French prisons. In a number of these cases, attention was focused
on a young prisoner, H.M., who had been thrown into solitary confinement for
engaging in "homosexual acts" and who then had hanged himself. Foucault
worked to get H.M.'s moving prison letters published and accompanied them with
an unsigned commentary: "Certain people are directly and personally responsible
for the prisoner's death."

Once the goal of giving prisoners a voice had been set, the logic of the GIP required the organization's self-dissolution. That occurred in late 1972, but Foucault and Defert consistently pursued similar militant actions in the Groupe d'Information Santé [Health information group] (aspects of which were also found in Aides), in the Djellali committee (with Genet), in the Comité de Défense des Droits des Immigrés [Defense committee for the rights of immigrants], and in actions against the death penalty. The purpose of all these activities was to drive out "oppression," which, wearing different masks, was expressed toward prisoners and immigrants, that is, toward the "other," the outsider.

He was robbed of his death, he who had wanted to be its master, and he was robbed even of the truth of his death, he who had been master of truth. Above all, the name of the plague could not be uttered. . . . Even before he was dead, the family for which he had always been a pariah reclaimed his body. The doctors said despicable things about the law and blood relations. His friends could no longer see him, except by breaking and entering. . . . And, upon his death, it was [his lover] who negotiated with the family, struck a bargain that allowed him to choose the shroud, on the condition that his name not appear in the death announcement.[5]

This account by Hervé Guibert was confirmed in a short, unsigned article in *Libération* the day after Foucault's death (June 26, 1984), which challenged the "rumor" that was already circulating. "Since his death, rumors have spread," said the article. "Foucault is said to have died of AIDS. As if an exceptional intellectual, because he was homosexual—though extremely discreet about it—represented an ideal target for the disease currently in fashion. . . . We are embarrassed by the virulence of this rumor. It is as if Foucault had to die in shame." This extraordinarily unseemly article shows how difficult it still was to speak of AIDS in 1984: connotations of "shame" were still attached to the disease. It seems to indicate as well that the doctors did not clearly inform Foucault of his illness. Defert explains, "The doctors acted on the assumption that, if the patient did not ask about his diagnosis, there was no reason to tell him."[6] He adds, "I asked one doctor what he had. She replied: 'If it were AIDS, I would have examined you as well!'"[7]

We will never know whether Foucault was aware of the nature of his illness. There are few witnesses, and they disagree. According to his friends Paul Veyne and Georges Dumézil, there is no doubt that the philosopher knew he was infected with AIDS. Veyne reports in his book that Foucault, seven months before his death, wrote in his journal. "I know I have AIDS, but I forget, thanks to my hysteria."[8] Defert disputes this version of things, but it is true that the doctors lied to him about his friend's fate. Hervé Guibert speaks of Foucault's knowledge of his illness as the "dual discourse of lucidity and delusion."[9]

In 1987, the question of Foucault's silence about AIDS became the object of a lengthy debate when Jean-Paul Aron attacked Foucault by name, criticizing him for keeping his illness quiet and accusing him more broadly of being ashamed of his homosexuality. Defert replied immediately:

The more ashamed one is, the more one confesses! The notion of confession belongs to the wider arena of guilt and shame. . . . I shared twenty-three years of Foucault's life and his moral choices. If we had been apologetic homosexuals, as Aron says, I would not have created the Aides. In his writings, Michel Foucault placed the confession within a problematic of power. He never valorized confession as such but always demonstrated its policing aspect. . . . There is no obligation to confess; there are several different courageous strategies.[10]

No one is entitled to judge the personal choices of an individual facing illness, and we ought to rejoice that, in France, medical confidentiality continues even after death. Nevertheless, in the interest of prevention, we may regret the fact that Foucault's illness was not made public. The impact of such an announcement might have played a key role in alerting the population, especially homosexuals.

⤺

Beyond his own fate, however, Foucault was not unaware of the disease's importance. In 1982, he even foresaw the social consequences of AIDS, as demonstrated in an unpublished document uncovered by one of his biographers. Using a pseudonym in an article for *Libération*, Foucault mentions the situation in the United States:

The American homosexual community is in the midst of a grave crisis and is having guilt heaped upon it once more, from two directions. From the outside, new repressive legislation is appearing in several states. From within, on the basis of the "gay cancer" (an undeniable medical phenomenon), the entire movement and its newspapers, and the entire dynamic operating for the last ten years as the driving force in intensifying sexual relations, have all shifted into reverse and become the main instrument for spreading slogans about monogamy and the couple, about the need to engage in sports rather than sex, and this in a voluntary, organized manner.[11]

Foucault made this observation about America in 1982; after his death, in 1984, Defert made the same observation about France. The philosopher, having become a "statue of the Commendatore" for the homosexual movement, now haunted the AIDS movement.

⤺

In the summer of 1984, after Foucault's death, Defert visited the island of Elba, where Hervé Guibert had gone to live. He had just sent out a mailing to a few lawyer and physician friends, reflecting on medical practice and, more particularly, on the fact that the diagnosis of AIDS was not being communicated to the patients who were affected by it. From Elba, Defert left for London. There, while reading *Time Out*, he discovered by chance the existence of the Terrence Higgins Trust, the first English AIDS organization. The Terrence Higgins Trust was run entirely by homosexuals and had been inspired in part by Gay Men's Health Crisis (GMHC), created in New York in January 1982. In London, Defert, who had not lost his interest in research (at the time, he was a lecturer in sociology at the Université de Vincennes), was spending time in the medical section of the British Library and reading all the books available in English on the virus.

Back in Paris, on September 25, 1984, he sent out another mailing to about ten people, including some representatives of the gay press, this time with the firm intention of creating an AIDS organization. In this decisive letter, adopting an eminently Foucauldian tone and turns of phrase reminiscent of the GIP, Defert explained that AIDS could not remain a strictly medical issue: "AIDS is a crisis of sexual behavior for the gay community; the majority of the victims it has struck are from this population, whose culture has recently been built around gymnasium values, perpetual youth and health. We have to face and institutionalize our relation to illness, infirmity, and death." Defert, whose first objective was to make the grieving of homosexuals public, went on to explain in the letter, "Gays have not assessed the moral, social, and legal consequences for themselves. Sexual liberation is not the be-all and end-all of our identity. It is urgent to conceptualize our ways of loving until death, something straights institutionalized long ago. I will not go home to Mama to die." The future president of Aides, whose platform was already clear, further declared:

Let us sever our deaths, like our sexuality, from family life. The gay movement offers only sexual alternatives. . . . There are other intense ways of loving to be promoted within gay culture. I say that [AIDS] is a cultural problem; thus it has psychological, material, and legal aspects. We must face them head-on. That is better than panic and moralizing. In the face of a clear medical emergency and a moral crisis, which is also a crisis of identity, I propose a place for reflection, for solidarity, and for transformation. Do we want to create it?

This founding letter is amazingly rich. All the future projects brought into existence by Aides appear in it; homosexuality is placed at the center of the organization's problematic, but with arguments that mark a departure from gay militancy, which is discreetly criticized. Aides would continue to ruffle the feathers of homosexual organizations.

A name still had to be found. Defert explains:

When we created the Groupe d'Information sur les Prisons—GIP—with Michel Foucault, he indicated to me that the "I" was there to mark the iota of difference that intellectuals needed to introduce into the practice of the Gauche Prolétarienne, . . . which dominated the social movements of the time. As a nod in his direction, I therefore made every effort to find a name that could have two meanings. That is how "Aides" came about, a word that encompasses both the word "aide" [support] and AIDS.

Foucault's influence on the birth of Aides, and the line of descent from the GIP, could not be clearer.[12]

〜

Despite its foresight, Defert's letter outlining his platform did not inspire enthusiasm. Most of the doctors and lawyers who were contacted did not reply. As a result, only homosexual militants attended the first informal meeting of Aides, which took place in Defert's apartment on October 4, 1984. In addition to Gilles Barbedette (a member of the GLH and an ex-journalist for *Gai Pied*) and his friend Jean Blancart, who was already ill, there were Franck Arnal, editor in chief of *Gai Pied Hebdo*, and Jean-Pierre Joecker, director of the journal *Masques*. Arnal had reservations about Defert's project. He argued for the idea that the readers of *Gai Pied* had vicarious sex lives. A few weeks later, in an American interview, Defert described this decisive meeting: "I brought together representatives of the gay press and asked them if any of their contributors could lend me a hand. The attitude of the gay press was rather mistrustful: 'Our readers don't like to hear about this disease. They like fantasy, pretty boys on the cover. If we start to talk about AIDS, sales will go down.' So I adopted a broader approach and presented my project to *Libération*."[13] More recently, Defert took the opportunity to recall the atmosphere of that meeting:

Franck Arnal told us, "The problem has to do with the people who go to the bars, and those people rarely read *Gai Pied*. Our readers are primarily provincial, and they like to use our newspaper to imagine a sex life they don't have." Jean-Pierre Joecker offered two militants from the newspaper to help us, but they never showed up.[14]

Arnal's and Joecker's reactions seem all the more surprising in that Jean Blancart, a former militant from GLH–Rennes, was there; he was already very frail, and his presence indicated that the illness had crossed the Atlantic. The curious lack of receptivity on the part of the two foremost gay publications deeply disappointed Defert. It probably illustrates an unprecedented example in Europe of gay militants refusing to be associated with the creation of an AIDS organization.

〜

On October 20, 1984, the journalist Eric Conan, who was writing an article for *Libération*, decided to interview Defert about his project.[15] He wanted to provide a resource for his readers, at the very least an address. Defert was thus led to open a post office box and to register the bylaws of the organization at the Paris police headquarters, which was done on November 28, 1984.

The true founding meeting of Aides came on the heels of that interview, on Tuesday, October 30, 1984. In addition to Defert, Barbedette, and Blancart, who had all been present at the first, informal meeting on October 4, there were Alain Siboni (an old pal of Foucault's and a former member of the FHAR), Jean Stern (formerly of *Gai Pied* and soon to be a contributor to *Libération*), but also the American writer Edmund White (cofounder of Gay Men's Health Crisis in the United States), who came with a young doctor whom he had invited "because he was the best-looking boy at the gay tea dance at Le Palace." All the same, notable for their absence were Franck Arnal and the representatives promised by Jean-Pierre Joecker.[16]

In 1984, Frédéric Edelmann was thirty-three years old. A journalist, he had been writing the architecture column in the newspaper *Le Monde* since 1976. His open Protestantism may explain the reluctance he felt about the homosexual organizations whose meetings he had sporadically attended. In May 1971 he had gone "by chance" to the general meetings of the FHAR at the Ecole des Beaux-Arts, where he got to know Alain Siboni. Edelmann later attended Foucault's classes at the Collège de France with Siboni, and they sometimes had dinner with the philosopher, "inevitably" running into Defert afterward. The editorial board of *Gai Pied* also got in touch with Edelmann in 1979, and his first article, published under the pseudonym Frédéric Loiseau, was a column called "Solo de nuit" [Night solo], in which he described his sadness after being left by a young man (Jean-Florian Mettetal) with whom he had been in love since 1973. He hoped that Mettetal, knocking about Montpellier with his new boyfriend, would read his column, not knowing he was its author. A Shakespearean comedy.

In 1983, Edelmann left *Gai Pied* during the rift that centered on the question of the newspaper's independence with respect to gay businesses: "I was convinced that in France, but not only in France, homosexual militancy had become archaic, inoperative, abandoned by every reliable personality, thus by every strong voice, and in the end, not credible."[17] On December 12, 1984, Edelmann received a request from Siboni, who, on the advice of Defert, invited him to join Aides and informed him that Jean-Florian Mettetal had already attended one meeting of the organization. This last argument finally convinced Edelmann, since the separated lovers constantly sought each other out.[18] The fight against AIDS allowed them to reestablish a relationship that had lasted "long, good years" but had ended stormily. In early January, before they had time to ask why, Edelmann and Mettetal were side by side at Aides.

Defert, Edelmann, and Mettetal, three complex and complementary personalities who worked well together, thus took their places as the founders of Aides. Defert had thought the project up and, according to Edelmann, remained a sort of "reptile with revolutionary tactics" who was the embodiment of the organization for nearly ten years. Edelmann conceived of the organization as "the constitution of a discipline" and gave priority to gathering information.[19] Mettetal was an urban doctor (a geriatrician). A close friend of Hervé Guibert, he had begun to have reservations about the capacity of the homosexual movement to fight against AIDS, as a result of his contact with the Association des Médecins Gais [Association of gay physicians], or AMG, which he frequented timidly. He quickly left "because of our incompatible viewpoints." In Aides, it was he who tempered Defert's initial project, which called the medical profession to account. Mettetal gave the organization its strongly medical orientation.[20]

Around this nucleus, thanks to the article in *Libération* and then to the first actions in homosexual bars, others joined the organization: the anesthesiologist Philippe Le Thomas, Dr. Jean-Michel Mandopoulos (formerly of the FHAR and a member of the AMG, which he also abruptly chose to leave), Didier Seux (a psychiatrist), Dominique Laaroussi (a psychiatric nurse), and Jean-Pierre Derrien, a contributor to *France Musique*. Other notable names soon appeared: Gérard Pelé (who later oversaw Minitel), Dr. Denis Samdja, Marc Imbert (an actor who ran the hotline), Pierre Kneip (a French professor), Christine Rouzioux (a virologist), Françoise Barré-Sinoussi (also a virologist), and the sociologist Michael Pollak. "In many respects," Defert explains, "the organization represented a group of mourners. We must never forget that the volunteers who became involved in Aides were also dealing with their own problems."

What linked these pioneers in the struggle against AIDS in France was their awareness of a state of emergency. Nevertheless, "we had every possible problem on our hands," Edelmann recalls. The organization immediately chose to move in several directions: it formed a telephone hotline with a recording (a privileged mode of communication on sexuality—initially, it was the famous 804 00 99), distributed brochures and pamphlets, staged debates and public lectures, but also, already, provided a service destined, unfortunately, for a long future: "aid to the sick." Everything was set in place in early 1985, with no financial means except gifts from the first volunteers. They juggled their personal telephone lines for the first hotlines. Edelmann offered his apartment on rue Michel-le-Comte, in the Marais, and it virtually became the office of Aides. Defert offered to sell one of his paintings.

AIDS specialists—Willy Rozenbaum, Jacques Leibowitch, Jean-Baptiste Brunet—were immediately contacted and were relieved to learn of the creation of Aides, which finally allowed them to have a credible interlocutor among homosexuals.[21] Their initial feeling in 1982, that it would be best for information to be given by peers, had finally been heard. "Our first encounter with Aides was a real stroke of luck," Brunet explains. "We finally had people ready to bring up matters of importance, people who were not hobbled by homosexual militancy." Leibowitch makes the same observation, even more precisely: "We were very happy. In fact, they were our first interlocutors, because before then all we had run into were the old harpies of homosexual activism. The founders of Aides had the incredible courage to tell their little home truths to their homosexual brothers." As a sign of confidence, Aides immediately decided that any medical documents produced by the organization would be distributed only after they had obtained a kind of imprimatur from Professors Rozenbaum, Leibowitch, Brunet, and Lachiver. Defert was invited by Luc Montagnier to participate in the Pasteur work group—an offer he declined. At the same time, all the doctors specializing in AIDS were frequently invited to public debates organized at gay spots by Aides.[22] Relations were now cordial—and reciprocal.

HOMOSEXUALITY IN AIDES

Although their life histories were varied, the founders of Aides were for the most part homosexual. Critical of the initial denial on the part of their peers, they were aware of how urgent the situation was. Contact was established with *Gai Pied*. Some of the newspaper's "editorials devoted to Aides," Edelmann recalls, "characterized it as an organization of angels of death, antiqueers who understood nothing about reality and who were spreading the fantasies of heterosexuals."[23] After Defert's initial disappointment with Arnal of *Gai Pied* and Joecker of *Masques*, caution became a necessity. As a result, by the time the representatives of *Gai Pied* finally made the offer of a telephone line and an office, Aides leaders preferred to maintain their independence.[24] In January 1985, however, Edelmann and Mettetal made another attempt and tried to get *Gai Pied* to insert the organization's first brochure into the paper. This time, they met with a polite refusal: Arnal hesitated, fearing that AIDS would take over his newspaper. There was even more hostility on the part of gay establishments. David Girard still had the upper hand in the baths and discos; on two occasions, January 24 and 30, 1985, when the founders of Aides tried to see him, he refused to receive them. Fearing that the fight against AIDS would cost him customers, Girard shortly thereafter explained to a journalist from *Gai Pied*, "I don't really want to put up condom dispensers or information boards about AIDS. People come to the baths to relax, not to get all upset." In his book, published a year later, in April 1986, he added, "For us, the time to choose has come. While we wait for the final cure, everyone must make his own decision. To stop doing everything (raise your finger if that is your decision), to stay with a single partner (*bonjour tristesse*), or to act as if there were nothing to it, telling yourself that Russian roulette must be a very exciting 'game.'"[25]

In 1985, neither prevention nor solidarity was the order of the day in gay bars. There are several reports of AIDS patients being kicked out of commercial spots, of homosexuals being deprived access to certain gay restaurants because they were suspected of being infected, and, even more frequently, of situations in which one partner in a relationship abandoned the other the moment the latter was struck by the disease. There was the same reluctance on the part of gay establishments toward Aides volunteers. Mettetal explains, "We were perceived as a new Protestant moral league, as if we were preventing those who were making money on the backs of gays from continuing to operate their businesses."[26] "Some even threw us out," Defert confirms, "as if our brochures were carrying the virus." Gay business owners, having no reason to pass on the bad news about a disease that directly undermined the base of their enterprises, began to look more and more like swindlers—and got unlisted numbers. Added to the initial denial on the part of homosexual militants, there was now often rejection of any and all preventive measures in commercial homosexual establishments. The many forms of this rejection persisted until the 1990s. "Total ignorance seemed to predominate. There was enormous skepticism everywhere," Edelmann recalls. "Among homosexuals, the issue did not exist."

It is striking to observe that in 1985, three years after Willy Rozenbaum's and Jacques Leibowitch's Groupe Français de Travail sur le Sida [French work group on AIDS] had attempted to warn homosexuals, the first measures taken by Aides drew similar reactions. The similarities between 1982 and 1985 (despite the critical new epidemiological data), and the history of fits and starts, which followed the same immutable cycle, from denial to underplaying of the statistics, and from doubt to silence, remain incomprehensible. It was the history, in short, of a disconcerting, never-ending denial.

&

Given the context of 1985 and the urgency of the situation, the pioneers in the fight against AIDS in France decided to venture into gay bars, beginning with those whose owners were more receptive, either because they had recently spent time in the United States or because they already knew people who were infected. A first excursion was made on February 13, 1985, to the gay White Party at Le Palace. In particular, however, beginning on March 10, 1985, it was at Le Piano Zinc, the piano bar opened in 1981 by Jürgen Pletsch, that Aides activists distributed brochures about AIDS. They quickly set up weekly meetings on AIDS at the art bar Le Duplex, also in the Marais, thanks to the immediate actions of Joël Leroux, the owner.[27] The same actions were taken at the disco Le Broad Side (which has since become Le Banana Café), where they were welcomed favorably, and at Le Central. Of a total of more than a hundred gay spots in Paris, however, fewer than ten establishments accepted the Aides prevention information in 1985–87.

In February 1985, the organization mounted another offensive targeting *Gai Pied*. Aides published a first information brochure (55,000 copies) and distributed it in gay establishments. After delicate negotiations, *Gai Pied Hebdo* finally consented to insert it into one of its issues (February 16, 1985).[28] Reread today, this brochure, made up of several panels, with a drawing of Oedipus and the Sphinx on the cover (find the answer or die), seems prophetic, despite medical gaps easily explained by the context. This first document was a radical departure from the waffling of the editorials in *Gai Pied*. "The vast majority of people infected with AIDS, over 80 percent, are male homosexuals," Aides declared frankly. Set in a box in bold type were the words "Caution: AIDS is contagious. AIDS is sexually transmitted." Regarding protection, the brochure explained that "as sex with different partners increases, you raise by the same increment the risk of coming into contact with a partner who is already infected." The baths and back rooms were clearly singled out, but without moral judgment, as places that facilitated the transmission of the virus. The writers also explained, "We're talking about elementary precautions: use a condom, and limit the number of your partners." The brochure concluded, "If you belong to a risk group, do not donate blood." In February 1985, the new

AIDS organization, which was challenging the prejudices of some and the hesitation of others, was characterized by a new discourse on prevention.

The entry of Aides onto the homosexual scene was the beginning of a great upheaval. But in 1985 *Gai Pied* was still ambivalent. Olivier Poivre d'Arvor published a crazy text in the paper titled "Sida, mon amour" [AIDS, my love], in which he compared AIDS to imagined illnesses and denounced the obsession with it. He explained that the AIDS virus was "the disease of the press," that "AIDS [was] only an artifact," and expressed regret at the fact that "homosexual coming out [might be] really and truly crushed" (*Gai Pied Hebdo*, March 2, 1985). Franck Arnal, editor in chief of the newspaper, began to acknowledge what was first called "safe sex," and which rapidly became "safer sex." Yet his editorial was still written in the conditional: "The homosexual knows he must invent his future at every moment. This necessity tends to make me think that the majority of gays would have little difficulty modifying their behavior if it turned out that the threat of AIDS obliged them to change their sexual practices" (*Gai Pied Hebdo*, May 4, 1985).

Although it pretended to engage in a new discourse, in 1985 *Gai Pied* remained the newspaper of the personals, published without prevention messages, and of ads for bathhouses extolling the merits of unprotected sex with multiple partners.[29] During the summer of 1985, the whole issue of safe sex was still dominated by fantasy. Roland Surzur even accomplished the feat of proposing an interview with an unknown doctor from Quebec who had reservations about safer sex and at the same time twisting the words of Daniel Defert, with whom he had requested an interview.[30]

In the same issue in which Defert gave his first interview to *Gai Pied*, Guy Hocquenghem, historically the most famous militant of homosexuality in France, chose to express his views on AIDS for the first time. The article he signed was as disconcerting as it was anachronistic: published in July 1985, Hocquenghem's piece would not have been out of place among the error-strewn writings of 1982. Although such errors had been understandable at that earlier time, repeating them three years later was a sin. If a humorous metaphor were needed, we might say that this document is "worth a special trip"; in reality, it is with sadness that we reread this piece from the summer of 1985. Hocquenghem began by alluding to "that thing—you know, the thing most talked about this year" and acknowledged that he had "more or less avoided the issue until now." Not content to criticize "journalistic prose, which smoothes things over and promotes a disgraceful, self-sufficient, hygienic ideology of safety," Hocquenghem also chose to attack Aides and Daniel Defert, but without naming them. He denounced "unlicensed sermonizers and advisers, [who] are breeding like mushrooms—nothing like an epidemic of fear to bring out the little chiefs draped in ignorance and presumption" (*Gai Pied Hebdo*, July 13, 1985). Hocquenghem mentioned AIDS again in an article of the same year (*Gai Pied Hebdo*, September 21, 1985): "Tobacco causes cancer, we all know that. Have we stopped smoking? Sex causes illness. Must we stop making

love? Modern life causes cancer. Should we retire to Ardèche? . . . How can we believe in a medical establishment that discourages us, that announces nothing but
catastrophes of contagion, that marches only to the tune of fear and despair?"[31]

   ↜

    In light of these forgotten pieces by Hocquenghem, and given the context, it
is easy to understand why the entire strategy of Aides consisted of refusing to become a homosexual organization. This choice is also explained by the life history
and personalities of the three founders of Aides. None claimed to be a homosexual
militant; for each of them, homosexuality was not the essential component of life,
nor was it an identity. Defert's reply to a journalist at *Gai Pied Hebdo* perfectly
summed up this view: "Battles of a moral nature are very important to me; I have
never been a militant of homosexual identity because identity politics is not my
style. But the fight against discrimination is something that involves me deeply.
Identity politics puts up barriers."[32]

    True to this logic, Aides made every effort not to give the appearance of being a
homosexual organization. "Our strategy at the time," Edelmann recalls,

was designed to transform an organization that sounded homosexual, one having to do
with a disease that had something of a stigma attached to it, and to quickly confer upon it
public notoriety and power. AIDS was considered a disease of queers. Therefore, we
chose to defend the sick and not homosexuals as such. It was obvious that, in order to do
battle in the social arena, Aides could not be assimilated to an organization for supporting homosexual rights.

Defert shared this view:

In 1984, with 294 AIDS cases in France, not many people had mobilized, and most of
them—both AIDS victims and those who had mobilized—were homosexual. A major
problem for those who were infected was how to live publicly with AIDS, which also
meant living publicly with homosexuality. In the majority of cases, individuals had not
been open about their homosexuality with the people around them. I commissioned the
first Aides prevention poster from Bastille, a very well known homosexual artist, who
made a particularly bold and violent poster. The organization was all set to distribute it,
even though it was not the image we wanted to project. I asked people with AIDS in the
organization for their opinions. They had a very clear reaction: they said that, given the
state of their health, for them life was not in the baths, not in the bars, but in the hospital.
They wanted their image to be respected in the hospital. So we killed the poster.[33]

In addition to this notion of sobriety and responsibility, there was a desire for
credibility. Defert explains, "If we had a certain number of Parisian hospital executives on our board, we could take measures. That was the strategy we adopted."

    Since then, some homosexual militants have criticized Aides for its "respecta-
bility" (rather as if the AIDS organization resembled the defunct homosexual organization Arcadie). Others have been tempted to take Aides to task for its rejection of gay visibility, its "hygienism," or even its delay in forming an autonomous
prevention group in the gay milieu.[34] Such recent criticisms may appear anachro-

nistic, but they are not gratuitous. They are probably based on splits whose persistence in the age of AIDS can only be explained in terms of deep ideological differences. What is the best way to fight an epidemic? Should the model of an American-style coalition be adopted, one based on identity and multiculturalism? Or should it be the universalist and, as necessary, republican model?

Defert opted for a mixed model that he calls the "communitarian approach," which mobilized people who had been infected or exposed to AIDS within a collective logic of solidarity. It consisted of privileging, in the tradition of Foucault, a discourse of technique and not a discourse of norms ("refuse to normalize behavior in the name of prevention"). A search through the history of Aides for a hygienist ethic, or even for the slightest effort to close the back rooms, would be fruitless, and yet homosexual militants were probably threatened by what they saw as Aides's mistrust of identity movements. Not knowing where exactly to situate Defert and his friends within their homosexual interpretive grid, they took the communitarian approach to be a problematic of "apologetic queens." They thought they were witnessing the return of André Baudry, even though Foucault was the tutelary figure of Aides. As a child of the GIP, Aides quite simply took the epidemiological risk seriously. Since the disease was affecting areas where the legal infrastructure intersected with the political realm (homosexuality, prostitution, and soon drug addiction and incarceration), the organization's leaders chose to privilege "invention" and proposed taking certain measures (condoms, needle exchanges). In reality, the word that best characterizes Aides is less "respectability" than "responsibility": it ardently sought legitimacy. Was any other path possible in 1984?

If homosexual visibility in Aides is compared to homosexual visibility in the other AIDS organizations that existed in 1987, Defert's organization was similar to the Terrence Higgins Trust in London,[35] to Aids Hilfe Schweiz in Switzerland (which had never been homosexual), and to the Deutsche AIDS Hilfe in Germany, which was initially homosexual but evolved into a form of organization that resembled Aides. The choice to build Aides around a problematic divorced from any category of individuals thus replicated other examples abroad, though such examples were not the general rule.[36] Aides was not at all unique; on the contrary, it seems to have anticipated the configurations to come, because in the late 1980s, with the epidemic affecting the general population, organizations outside France generally moved toward an all-inclusive model.

⌒

In July 1985, when Aides was formed in Paris, its founders decided to take a trip to Marseilles, where the "homosexual summer school," organized by militants from the GLH and the CUARH, was taking place. The summer school had been created in 1979 by GLH militants in Marseilles. Meeting every two years, thanks to the support of Gaston Defferre, it took place until 1987 and attempted to bring together all the homosexual organizations in France, as well as gay businesses and newspapers.

Aware of the continuing reluctance with regard to prevention, Defert and Edelmann were accompanied to Marseilles by Dr. Jacques Leibowitch. There, this very motivated little "commando" of AIDS activists confronted the last bastion of homosexual identity. "We were very poorly received, as bearers of bad news," Edelmann recalls. "Our strategy was to show the pale intellectuals from the gay community that the men concerned about AIDS were young and in good health, tanned, swimming and laughing! On that occasion, we certainly managed to upset the community. For those who were in Aides, that trip to Marseilles is our happiest memory."

Two images may sum up the Marseilles trip. First, a smiling Edelmann, bare-chested and wearing shorts, being roundly hissed for shouting out in the middle of a plenary session, "Three years from now, we'll have the same terrifying percentage of infected gays as in the United States. That may mean a very large proportion of the people in this room. Do the math!" Second, there is the image of Defert, nick-named "Miss Rubber," going into the back room of a disco in Marseilles to pass out condoms. He was soon surprised to see the club's owner, furious that someone was "insulting the sexuality" of his customers, coming down to the back room to reclaim the condoms one by one from his customers' hands.

⌐

In 1985, Thierry Gamby was a dermatologist and department head of the cancer center in Marseilles, specializing in STDs. He was the local representative for the Association des Médecins Gais and was already a member of Willy Rozen-baum's AIDS-alert group, and he no longer felt comfortable with homosexual militancy.[37]

In Marseilles, gay doctors had a standing committee in the local GLH office. "I was terribly ill at ease in the GLH," Gamby recalls. He, too, was at the summer school and chose to break ranks with identity politics (the GLH and the AMG) and to join Aides. Defert and Edelmann soon assigned him the task of creating an Aides chapter in Marseilles.

The history of Aides in the provinces thus began in late 1985. "Neither Defert nor Gamby had a very precise idea of federalism," explains Alain Molla, current president of Aides–Provence. "Along the way, the federative idea took hold on its own, both at the national level and at the local level." The Marseilles project is in-teresting in that it shows the birth of one of the principal committees of Aides in the region of France that, after the Paris region, was most affected by the epidemic. Aides–Marseilles was created on November 5, 1985. In late 1986, it had 130 mem-bers and fifty-six volunteers, as well as a telephone hotline that took more than thirty calls a day.[38] A network of representatives was put in place in most of the cit-ies in the south of France.

How was the epidemic perceived in the provinces in 1985? An anecdote recalled by Gamby may illustrate. During a public medical meeting, a participant made passing mention of prevention in homosexual bathhouses. At the podium, a dermatologist and university professor reacted indignantly, as Gamby recalls:

[She] protested this sort of prevention because, according to her, it involved a serious misunderstanding about the modes of infection, since AIDS was not transmitted via bath towels or dirty objects. "How do you expect wooden boards to transmit the virus?" concluded the specialist, who was obviously ignorant of the fact that gay baths were places to have sex.

This telling response is probably one key to understanding the delays in prevention. No one knew about homosexual lifestyles, and no one found it useful to alert gays. In Marseilles, as in Paris, the heavy silence of homosexual militants was the mirror image of this "institutional" ignorance.

In 1983–85, militancy was still keen in Marseilles, especially around a former bakery on rue de Bruys, which had become a homosexual center. In June 1983, a local spokesperson declared:

We are mature, whatever some people may say. We are perfectly aware that homosexuals are a high-risk group for this illness, but ... its magnitude is grossly exaggerated. About fifty cases in all of France! ... Given the current state of affairs, we don't see the need to stop donating blood, for example. The whole current campaign is disturbingly reminiscent of the attitude of the Nazis, who used scientific theories to get rid of homos, Jews, and gypsies.[39]

The initial mobilization against AIDS occurred around Gamby, who had a falling-out with local gay militants. As a result, he created Aides–Marseilles, based on Defert's national conception, the aim of which was to divorce homosexuality from AIDS. "For those of us in the provinces, Aides could not be a homosexual organization," Gamby confirms. "We wanted to build a partnership with [public agencies], and looking like a gang of homosexuals was out of the question. As a result, the birth of our organization was poorly received by young, messed-up homosexuals in the GLH. For them, we were apologetic bourgeois who refused to declare their homosexuality and who possessed medical power. For them, we were Arcadie." The relations between Aides–Paris and *Gai Pied* were now being replicated by the relations between Aides–Marseilles and homosexual militants. "The stars of the GLH," Gamby recalls, "thought that a discourse of prevention was incompatible with militant discourse. They criticized our persecuted-homosexual paranoia and even called me a 'homophobe.' In fact, the whole difference between us was that we were not demagogues; we could not agree to adapt the truth to fit the circumstances."

Questioned ten years later, the militant homosexuals from Marseilles have a different reaction. Christian de Leuse is still head of a homosexual collective:

I experienced AIDS as a destroyer of the homosexual movement. In Marseilles, everyone demobilized; we were vaporized. As for Aides, they built up a kind of mistrust for the

GLH and never paid any attention to the struggles of homosexuals. Until 1994, they re-fused to march with us on Gay Pride Day. There's something not quite right in Aides with regard to homosexuality, and at the same time they see us as competitors in the fight against AIDS.

Jacques Fortin, former president of GLH–Marseilles and founder of the ho-mosexual summer school, has an entirely different reading. "No one is a man for all seasons," he argues. "Two worlds met at the summer school, but we couldn't talk to each other. We didn't want to listen to the Aides representatives. One world was vanishing, the other was dawning." Fortin, thoroughly aware of these mis-takes, abandoned militancy to live in a little town in the Vaucluse: "In the GLH, the first case of AIDS came shortly after the summer school. He was a hustler who came to our meetings. We didn't want to believe in his illness. Later on, when we did believe it, we resigned. We resigned our mission because we could no longer be responsible for it." Today, moved by the work of Aides–Provence, Fortin feels re-morse and no longer has any desire to fight for the gay cause: "Our successors are the people who have fought against AIDS. They are the heirs, not of the militant homosexual movement, but of homosexuals as a whole in this country."

↵

It might be imagined that militants in the battle against AIDS would have rallied around the Groupes de Libération Homosexuelle or around gay militancy (the CUARH, *Gai Pied*, the homosexual summer school, *Masques*). With a few ex-ceptions, in Paris and in the provinces, that was not at all the case before 1989. The suddenness with which AIDS appeared, and the terminal diagnosis it entailed, were too complex to be dealt with, the issues were too serious, and the reasons for mobilizing were too different. Apart from a few people who were affected from the very start (Jean Blancart, for example) or had traveled to the United States (Gilles Barbedette), and a few militants who had "obligations" (Patrice Meyer lost a close friend in 1983), those who had participated in the gay liberation movement were missing from the fight against AIDS during the 1980s.[40] As the sociologist Michael Pollak confirms, "Among those who are engaged in the fight against AIDS, there are former militants who converted to the new cause, but only a limited number of them. I think that, for most people, AIDS was the beginning of their involve-ment."[41]

In France during the 1980s, then, the "AIDS movement" was not established by homosexual militants but rather by homosexuals who were not involved in iden-tity politics. That made all the difference. On the one hand, such an observation allows us to explain the specifically French delay in mobilizing organizations, a delay that, despite the arrival of Aides in 1985, puts France in the next-to-last posi-tion on the list of European countries.[42] This observation also helps to illuminate the mysterious disappearance of homosexual militancy in the mid-1980s.

Some have said that, for civil society in general and for homosexual militants in particular, François Mitterrand's election had the paradoxical result of depriving social movements of themes around which to mobilize. Some have also expressed the belief that the individualism of the 1980s, along with the new lifestyles, weakened militancy by depriving it of troops. Finally, it has been assumed that the disappearance of certain actors, as a consequence of AIDS, made the task of organizations difficult. These elements played a role, but they are probably insufficient to explain the great retreat from militancy in the 1980s. And this retreat was particularly spectacular: all the GLH chapters closed their doors before 1987, the CUARH disappeared about 1985, the homosexual summer school vanished in 1987, *Homophonies* folded in 1985, and *Masques* and *Samouraï* folded in 1986. After 1985, the Association des Médecins Gais vegetated when it might have played the role of Aides, whereas *Gai Pied*, whose sales rose until 1985, took five years to die, losing about a thousand readers a year between 1986 and October 1992. Only one hypothesis can make such a wide-ranging phenomenon intelligible: in the mid-1980s, homosexual militancy shut down in France when it saw that it had missed the great tragedy of the century's end.

According to the sociologist Michel Setbon, "The irruption of AIDS into the homosexual world was an essential factor in that world's reorganization on a new basis." His thesis, based on a comparison among Sweden, Great Britain, and France, underscores "the relation between the problem AIDS posed for gay organizations and their degree of structure in the early 1980s." It seems that AIDS as a problem specific to homosexuals placed these organizations on the horns of a dilemma that was painful, if not impossible, to address: either adopt the epidemiological definition of AIDS as a "gay cancer" and demand attention and protection, at the risk of being stigmatized, or deny its reality and avoid homophobia ("AIDS is a myth"). "Only the powerful and highly structured Swedish homosexual organizations could choose the first strategy," Setbon explains today,

by demanding aid directed at gays even while reinforcing their homosexual identity, without excessive fear of being stigmatized. British homosexual organizations quickly accepted the heterosexual definition of the disease, which was a major factor in their restructuring around AIDS. The phenomenon was even more pronounced in France than it was in Great Britain, and we can hypothesize that the inability to choose one strategy or the other forced organizations into aphasia and thus led to the disappearance of the homosexual movement. The unresolved dilemma condemned them to silence, and dissolution was the logical consequence.

Thus it is possible that at a time when the cards were being reshuffled, when things could not simply be patched up, and when men ready to take up the slack were already in place, the inability of militants to respond to AIDS, their initial "flightiness," was in large measure what caused the French homosexual movement to disappear in the early 1980s. Jean-Florian Mettetal of Aides makes the following observation: "There is no longer any homosexual liberation movement. Nevertheless, to a certain extent, I think we are one."[43]

In its way, this revival demonstrates that the arenas of competence and activism were distinct, and that all new problems produce and require new actors to solve them.[44] It may well be that, through an unprecedented collective resignation, a new generation of homosexuals took the place of the previous one, to which it bore no resemblance. In light of these contradictions and refusals, but also these silences, it may also be possible to understand, in part, the specifically French AIDS hecatomb in the homosexual milieu.

⤶

Aides, a far-reaching, all-inclusive organization within the epidemic, as Hervé Guibert explains, "hit the ground running."[45] "I had the feeling," Jean-Florian Mettetal explains, "that we were advancing in seven-league boots. . . . I felt we were like the doctors in the Middle Ages, depicted during epidemics with those big beaks that made them so mysterious."[46]

In an atmosphere often marked by the violence of illness and grief, activists from Aides, often HIV-positive themselves, took care of a family of Haitians, then a Zairean drug dealer, a sixty-year-old female prostitute, and a transvestite without identity papers. They passed out condoms in the Verrières woods, an outdoor cruising spot on the outskirts of Paris, or in the Tuileries. Defert's and Edelmann's apartments again served as the organization's offices (later moved to rue de l'Abbé-Groult in Cité Paradis, then to rue de Belleville, and finally to rue du Château-Landon, where the office is today). As proof of the new notoriety of Aides, foreign television crews came to cover the Le Duplex bar during public debates, and in March 1985 the organization even received a letter from Professor Patrice Debré of Pitié-Salpêtrière, asking for a grant from Aides. "Taking out the garbage is also doing something to fight AIDS," said a volunteer. Aides had 1,200 volunteers in 1985. Small checks arrived from all over France,[47] sometimes accompanied by words or accounts like the one—packing a great emotional charge, and often cited by volunteers from the early years—from a sixteen-year-old butcher who sent fifty francs because he was "homosexual with Jean-Pierre."

By creating a broad movement of solidarity, Aides met with enthusiastic reactions from the beginning, especially from the mainstream press, as demonstrated in another article by Eric Conan in *Libération*: "Everything comes to the one who waits. . . . Avoiding the pitfalls to which the intelligentsia and the French homosexual press have succumbed, as they have moved hysterically from a discourse of denial to a discourse of panic, Aides focused on the essential (but until now neglected) task of bringing aid and counsel to the sick." The journalist then hailed the publication of the first Aides brochure, "which is one of the most honest and cool-headed texts devoted to AIDS" (March 8, 1985).

Gradually, the Aides hotline was set up, twice a week at first, in one home or another, and then in Edelmann's apartment on rue Michel-le-Comte. "We spent whole evenings answering the phone in the john, getting out of the way when someone wanted to use it," recalls Sophie Chamaret, codiscoverer of HIV and an Aides volunteer. The hotline became a daily one in June 1985. It was then run in a collegial and familial manner by the "seven dwarfs" (each leader was responsible for it one day a week). It was set up around Marc Imbert and Sophie Chamaret at first, and then, after 1987, around Pierre Kneip and France Uebersfeld. "The hotline was a human voice among mechanical voices," Kneip concludes.[48]

SEXUAL CONTAMINATION: ANOTHER AIDS "SCANDAL"?

In 1983–84, homosexual militants' denial of AIDS may have reinforced political leaders in their desire not to act. The politicians' reluctance to intervene in what was considered the delicate matter of homosexuality, combined with the denial of militants, easily explains the silence of this early period.

The situation changed in 1985, however. Of course, *Gai Pied* still showed evidence of flightiness. Hugo Marsan, its editor in chief, persisted in underestimating the numbers when, after a terrible earthquake hit Mexico City, he concluded his editorial of September 28, 1985, with a baffling analogy: "Like the 18 million residents of Mexico City, gays now know that in a few minutes an earthquake can produce a number of victims that makes the number of AIDS patients seem laughable." Despite such blunders, information spread. After the World Congress on AIDS in Atlanta (May 1985), which resulted in numerous medical articles, Rock Hudson's death, on October 2, inspired a great deal of commentary. It was particularly important in France, since Hudson had been hospitalized there. In July, the actor and archetype, with a reputation for being healthy in body and mind, had braved hordes of movie cameras and proclaimed loudly and clearly from the Hôpital Américain in Neuilly that he had come to France to be treated for AIDS.[49] (Hudson was a friend of Elizabeth Taylor; she had starred with him and James Dean in *Giant* and eventually took over the AIDS foundation that Hudson had established.) Suddenly Hudson looked like a frightened homosexual, so unlike the good-looking boy from Illinois that he was. We should probably see this man, whose now pale body stood in stark contrast to the Yankee male he depicted in *The Tarnished Angels*, as a symbol likely to leave an impression. Marsan paid tribute to him in an editorial published on October 12, 1985, in *Gai Pied Hebdo*: "Let the French people heed this well: a great American actor died because he loved men. He died of homosexuality. That, of course, is the message with which the media are assaulting us." Even as the airplane used to transport him was disinfected, and even as a famous actress said publicly that she was appalled that he could have kissed her on the mouth for the purposes of a shoot, many newspapers issued reports and articles on AIDS in conjunction with Hudson's death. A general broadcast on Antenne 2 seized the opportunity to invite Willy Rozenbaum and Luc Montagnier to speak.

In France, there was probably one history of AIDS before Rock Hudson's death and another after it. The year 1985 seems to have been the time when the illness appeared in the media. Gradually, the large number of individuals who were HIV-positive took their place beside patients with full-blown AIDS (of which there were 573 identified cases by late 1985). Only in 1986–87, however, was the estimate made that there were about ten individuals with HIV for every person with full-blown AIDS. The profile and significance of the disease changed. Faced with the facts, *Gai Pied* could no longer hesitate: it sounded the alarm, accompanied by a certain amount of hysteria, and regularly published inserts from Aides.[50] A condom was even inserted into the issue of November 16, 1985, with financing from Aides, and in spite of a law that prohibited it.[51] This calm in the stormy relationship with Aides attested to a desire to fight the scourge—which was now taken seriously—to fight it, if not jointly, then at least facing in the same direction. The truce was also based on the fact that many homosexual leaders—at *Gai Pied*, the AMG, and elsewhere—had just discovered, thanks to the new testing, that they were themselves HIV-positive. This in turn led them to abruptly revise their positions.

During the same period, the modes of transmission became clearer, and it was confirmed that the virus could not permeate latex. This marked the real beginning of widespread condom use.[52]

How did the government react during this period? To answer this question, we need to backtrack a bit. On February 15, 1982, Jacques Godfrain, a deputy in the Rassemblement pour la République party, drew the attention of the minister of health (Jack Ralite of the Communist Party) with a written inquiry to the government about the growing number of cases of Kaposi's sarcoma. He used the opportunity to ask the minister whether "he [did] not therefore judge it necessary to develop an advertising campaign designed to inform youth of the dangers of homosexuality." This vicious question received a well-informed response from Ralite. On May 3, 1982, the minister of health replied, with remarkable foresight, "If the [epidemic's] reality is confirmed in France, the Ministry of Health will take the necessary measures to curb its growth, measures that will include informing the homosexual population."[53]

And yet, before 1987, none of the French administrations implemented this commonsense recommendation, which dates from 1982. This places France's governmental campaign in the second-last position chronologically within the European Community.[54] What is even more serious, the first governmental campaigns specifically targeting homosexuals did not begin until 1989. According to several homosexual militants, this peculiar delay constitutes what could be called, for lack of a better term, another "scandal" of AIDS contamination.

⌣

Among the new protagonists named in July 1984 were names already mentioned in the contaminated-blood scandal: Laurent Fabius (prime minister),

Georgina Dufoix (minister of social affairs and spokesperson for the government), and Edmond Hervé (undersecretary at the Department of Health, working for the minister of social affairs).[55]

Aides leaders approached Hervé in 1985. Their goal was to sensitize the minister to the problems caused by AIDS. In particular, they sought a change in the law against condom advertising and proposed installing condom dispensers in the baths. In addition, they wanted financial aid. Seeking credibility, they waited to ask for a first meeting until their concrete actions and the early documents on prevention that they had published could attest to the group's effectiveness. On April 3, 1985, Edelmann and Alain Siboni were received by Dr. Claude Weisselberg,[56] who had been designated to head up the effort against AIDS (Hervé himself could not see them). Weisselberg was very happy that Aides had been created, felt very positive about the actions envisioned, and was sensitive to the issues associated with AIDS, with which he was well acquainted. He arranged for Aides to hold its conferences at the Ministry of Health—symbolically, this was very important—and promised to see Aides leaders again soon, after he had considered the question of financing. "I had the impression I was being very bold for supporting an organization with strong connotations of homosexuality," Weisselberg recalls today. On June 5, a second meeting took place with Daniel Defert present, but again without Edmond Hervé. This time, Weisselberg explained that, having consulted Hervé and his counterparts in Fabius's cabinet, he could not really promise financial aid. Edelmann recalls the discussion as follows: "'They're stupid,' Weisselberg told us, 'but the department of the prime minister thinks that if we were to fund Aides, that would create the impression that we were helping queers.'" Nevertheless, Weisselberg encouraged Aides to present a formal request for a grant. Edelmann made this request on July 20, 1985, in a letter to the Direction Générale de la Santé [General office of health], or DGS. The grant was finally approved, with the agreement of Hervé's office, and in November 1985 the sum of 250,000 francs was handed over in its entirety to Aides. For the times, the sum was not negligible, though it might be considered perfectly ridiculous today.[57]

Weisselberg also referred Aides leaders to the Comité Français d'Education pour la Santé [French committee for health education], or CFES, whose delegate-at-large was Jean-Martin Cohen-Solal.[58] The CFES was an organ of public health under the supervision of the Ministry of Health and was responsible for official state campaigns. During this period there were campaigns to prevent heart disease, nicotine addiction, and drunk driving. Edelmann approached the CFES on several occasions in early 1985 and was finally received by Cohen-Solal in June. On his desk, Cohen-Solal displayed a portrait of himself next to François Mitterrand. Cohen-Solal had the generous affability of a debonair Socialist militant but the cautiousness of an apparatchik. He was a young technical adviser, ill at ease with the sensitive subject of AIDS and clearly embarrassed about the issue of homosexuality. He had his own reservations about the urgency of the fight against

AIDS, and until 1986 he refused to direct any prevention campaigns targeting the general public. It goes without saying that no campaign targeting homosexuals was outlined.[59] It was only at Michèle Barzach's urging that the new director agreed to mount the first national CFES campaign. It adopted the following oft-criticized slogan, which made no mention of condoms: "AIDS won't get by me."[60]

Franck Arnal, already suffering from AIDS, took a legitimately aggressive stance. He wrote:

One day the CFES may know the will of the interested parties, all of them taxpayers, who wonder what purpose such a chilly public bureau of prevention can be serving. . . . This bureau chose to ignore the tragedy of the many homosexual adolescents who were infected at that time. They now lie near death in hospitals, scandalized that they were not warned at the time about the risk they were taking or advised about the protective measures that might have allowed them to avoid it.[61]

The position of the French government at the time is even more significant than the position of the CFES, whose freedom was limited. Political leaders, although sensitive to the problem, feared what use the opposition and the press might make of a commitment to fight against AIDS (the upcoming 1986 legislative elections looked to be a delicate matter). As a result, although the Fabius government took relatively quick action in 1985, when it required an HIV screening test for blood donations, it refused in the same year to authorize condom advertising and the legal sale of syringes. These decisions had grave consequences. Instead of acting, Georgina Dufoix, already drawn to alternative medicine, chose to announce loudly at a hasty press conference on October 30, 1985, that cyclosporine was an effective treatment.

The most urgent measure taken to prevent the sexual transmission of AIDS—somewhat comparable to the decision authorizing the legal sale of syringes for drug addicts—was the legalization of condom advertising. Yet that decision was made, not by the Fabius government, but only two years later, by the Barzach law of January 27, 1987.

Was the decision necessary, given the French epidemiological situation in 1985? And, if so, does the state's inaction in the matter of preventing sexual transmission of the AIDS virus constitute another contamination scandal in France?[62]

⌐

"The problem was never put to me, Fabius."[63] Former prime minister Laurent Fabius has no other explanation for the refusal to legalize condom advertising. Nevertheless, this refusal is one thing for which his government has been criticized, and it is seen as being parallel to the so-called contaminated-blood scandal. Thus the question should be posed differently: Is sexual transmission of a disease a public responsibility or a private one?

This question must be raised if we are to understand the obstacles that served to maintain the status quo. The ministers involved made the decision that it would not be useful to authorize condom advertising or mount a campaign targeting the general public.[64] Of course, the disease was not yet perceived as an epidemic that could affect society as a whole; AIDS remained a disease with strong homosexual connotations. Above all, the lifting of the ban required a parliamentary debate, which promised to be stormy.[65] Some have also alluded to the importance of the upcoming election. "To my way of thinking," Fabius explains today,

those were not obstacles. In matters of public health, all of that is secondary. You can explain [things] to people—and I've always thought the role of politics is to make people privy to knowledge about the decisions we make. In addition, a political decision always has advantages and disadvantages, unless it happens automatically. If you establish that there is a real public health problem and that a measure is useful, you take it. It's simply that this measure was not proposed at a certain point, so you can't invent it. I think that if the question of condom advertising had come up, the measure would have been taken. So the question is, Why did it come up at one moment and not another?

Huguette Bouchardeau, then minister of the environment in the Fabius government, and in this capacity a participant in the Council of Ministers every Wednesday, replies with her own version: "In 1984 and 1985, there was a conjunction between leftist goodwill, which refused to assimilate AIDS and homosexuals, and resistance to any action that might be upsetting, which was so characteristic of the Fabius government. A desire for respectability, a concern with mere electoral expediency. The left had a fear of frightening people."

Apart from these opposing explanations, some of the people infected between 1984 and 1987 think the inaction of the three ministers concerned, but also of the administrations overseeing them, was "criminal." Some AIDS patients and some militant gays have spoken of a deliberate refusal to intervene "on behalf of a marginal population whose survival mattered very little." Of course, as Willy Rozenbaum recalls, "In France the real scope of the epidemic was realized only in 1986, thanks to the testing of a large number of people. Anyone who says otherwise is a liar." Nevertheless, since the government recognized the disease in mid-1985 with respect to the issue of blood transfusions (Fabius's decision in July of that year), it is legitimate to wonder why, on the heels of a ministerial order that came relatively early, a true comprehensive policy was not established to reduce the risk of AIDS everywhere it might exist. The government's response was thus only a limited commitment (testing and testing alone). As a result, we cannot dismiss the question of the absence of public campaigns and the refusal to legalize condom advertising between 1985 and 1986.[66] Also in this area, it is disconcerting to observe that France's early epidemiological knowledge of AIDS (via Willy Rozenbaum's AIDS-alert group), as well as the prodigious advances to which it attested at the virological level (the discovery of HIV), had no noticeable effect on the administrative and political response.

It is difficult now to know at what level arbitration took place, what the precise reasons were (lack of time or lack of political will), and who, exactly, played a role in blocking particular measures. Hypotheses have been offered with respect to every level of the hierarchy. At the lowest level, the delay could have come from the DGS, whose employees were sometimes embarrassed about AIDS-prevention measures. On this question, Defert recalls that he saw "timidity" at the DGS, especially when he suggested state financing for condom dispensers in the back rooms. "We are not supposed to know there is sexual activity," he was told. "That's the same attitude as toward abortion!" he replied. Nevertheless, the internal hierarchy of the DGS seems to have accepted the idea of legalized advertising, as an unpublished document demonstrates. A note from the DGS proposed revising the law and confirmed that the absence of condom advertising "represents an obstacle to the increased sale of these products and a constraint in informing the public."[67]

A different hypothesis is that the delay came from Hervé's ministerial office or from Dufoix's. The names of Weisselberg and Cohen-Solal are also often cited in this context. Did these individuals perhaps reject all debate about prevention? Or did they simply lack the time to act? At a meeting with Aides in June 1985, Weisselberg, adviser to Hervé, mentioned the government's reluctance on the issues of prevention and legalization of condom advertising. Defert reportedly replied to Weisselberg, "Remember that the left votes for you, and don't think only of the right."[68] Weisselberg again justified this position in an interview with Gai Pied on November 16, 1985: "If we had been sure, or had even strongly suspected, that the way condoms were sold at the time was a factor limiting their distribution, we would have given a great deal of thought to changing the law. But, even so, it's very easy to get condoms." In spite of this significant public response, there is every reason to believe that the debate on the need to legalize condom advertising took place in Hervé's office, at least belatedly (late 1985 or early 1986). In early 1986, a note from Weisselberg to Jacques Roux, general director at the Department of Health, even urged his administration to "think about" legalization.

There is one final hypothesis, namely, that the decision was blocked at the interministerial level, that is, by a technical adviser to Laurent Fabius. Several observers confirm that it "was improper to mention the legal sale of syringes and the authorization of condom advertising" in the offices of the prime minister.[69] In the absence of a precise response, it seems probable that this refusal to legalize condom advertising resulted from a whole series of uncertainties and hesitations, from a certain amount of self-censorship, and from explicit refusals. Added together, these factors constitute a prime case of irresponsibility, the essentials of which have already been brought to light in the contaminated-blood scandal.

Is the sexual transmission of AIDS a public responsibility or a private one? According to the response, these delays and "government waffling," to use Defert's expression, can be interpreted in two different ways. Those who believe that the issue is a public matter may understand it in polemical terms. They may regret the fact that administrative and political agents refused to adopt the necessary preventive measures, probably because these measures were associated with homosexuality and required a certain political courage. These individuals may conclude that public officials were singularly lacking in lucidity, if not in judgment, or that they were simply incompetent. And this incompetence was perniciously served by an epidemiological situation that was difficult to interpret.

Those who believe that sexuality ought to remain within the confines of private life may have a more contextual reading. They may find it surprising that, even as the Fabius government was worrying about the possible political repercussions of distributing information to the most vulnerable group, even as it was refusing to place the fight against AIDS on the political agenda (and, in particular, to mount a campaign and authorize condom advertising), organizations emanating from the Fabius camp of the Socialist Party were adopting a policy aimed at courting the homosexual vote.[70] As the (difficult) legislative elections of 1986 drew near, the Socialists apparently made their choice: the homosexual vote rather than information for gays.

↩

In 1985, Michael Pollak was already working with Aides volunteers. The young Austrian sociologist with a solid scientific reputation had moved to France the previous year. In the tradition of Pierre Bourdieu, whom he had discovered during a first stay in Paris in 1971, Pollak had already published numerous articles on nuclear power, the Nazi deportation, and the Vienna society he had come from. Although a cosmopolitan, he remained very discreet about his private life, and it was difficult for him to publicly acknowledge his homosexuality. Therefore, he refused to fight within gay organizations, although, in the interests of scientific rigor and banalization of the issue of homosexuality, he agreed to publish several important articles on the subject.[71]

It was AIDS that led Pollak to orient his research decisively to homosexual lifestyles and practices. "I quickly understood," Pollak explains, "that this was an important and tragic phenomenon. ... My involvement is the reaction of a sociologist who is also homosexual."[72] From the beginning, Pollak was a maverick, interviewing patients in Willy Rozenbaum's practice because he sensed that homosexual identity and the fear of AIDS were indissociable. "You must help us reach the silent majority of homosexuals," Rozenbaum told him on many occasions. Convinced of the urgency of this approach, in December 1984 Pollak came up with the idea of doing a study on gays. From that point on, as a precursor of the AIDS pollsters in France, Pollak played a determining role in the fight against the epidemic, especially among homosexuals.

Throughout 1985, the sociologist spent time with the first Aides volunteers: he participated in training sessions, questioned hotline operators, and, in the end, joined the organization's administrative council in March 1987. But how could he reach that "silent minority," as Rozenbaum had suggested? The homosexual "population" was very difficult to target and question because of underreporting of homosexuality in surveys, difficulties in constructing a sample, underrepresentation of homosexuals in the provinces, and the existence of "intermediate" individuals (bisexuals, people who had infrequent homosexual encounters) whose practices were neither wholly homosexual nor heterosexual. Pollak had no other solution but to ask *Gai Pied* to distribute a questionnaire to its readers (despite the inevitable statistical skewing, which he perceived immediately), especially since the Association des Médecins Gais did not want to help him.

In early 1985, he met with Franck Arnal to present his proposed questionnaire. Arnal was interested in the idea but refused to have the newspaper assume financing for the survey. Pollak then turned to the Centre National de la Recherche Scientifique [National center for scientific research], or CNRS. In an absurd dialectic, reflecting the academic world's hesitations about a homosexual forum as much as *Gai Pied*'s mistrust of institutions, the CNRS was slow to accept the plan,[73] and Arnal now bristled at seeing the CNRS interfere with financing.[74]

After delicate negotiations, Pollak managed to convince both parties, and a questionnaire was published in two issues of *Gai Pied* in the summer of 1985. The sample thus obtained (a thousand responses) was, as it were, the first AIDS survey in France.

The results of this 1985 survey uncovered a fairly universal refusal to use condoms but an already very high level of information among homosexuals. The individuals surveyed seemed to have confidence in *Gai Pied* as a source of information on the disease, but nearly 60 percent of the readers who were surveyed were still only "a little" or "not at all" worried about the epidemic. These results were difficult to interpret, and the sociologist lacked perspective. In 1986, Pollak changed the questionnaire and took precautions: those surveyed had to agree to take the HIV antibody test and to report their reactions if they were found to be HIV-positive. The survey proved to be unexpectedly rich, allowing Pollak to follow the evolution of those surveyed as they recognized the risk and adopted safer-sex practices. This allowed Aides and, later, the government to adapt their campaigns to these results.

In 1986, Pollak observed the gradual widespread use of condoms and the increase in medical follow-up among gays. Initially, Pollak explains, "homosexuals felt they were being accused, not for their practices, but as homosexuals, for what they were. Thus they could only react by denying and denouncing such a situation." But in 1986, the most open homosexuals—they were also the first to lose loved ones—began to consider the risk as more a medical one than a social one, and they rapidly took precautions. It is significant that safer sex was broadly adopted before the government mounted any sort of information campaign. All the same, those who "had trouble dealing with their homosexuality" continued to refuse preventive measures, "projecting onto AIDS the discomfort they felt in their families." Pollak then demonstrated that the main taboo surrounding AIDS was not death but sexuality. He concluded, "The degree to which homosexuality is socially acceptable is very important in understanding the fear of AIDS."[75]

THE RIFT

In early 1987, the history of Aides, an organization that was not yet three years old, appeared to be an enormous chain of solidarity marked by sequences of exemplary action and, already, by a series of deaths. The silence of the government and the health agencies was still deafening, and the homosexual "community" still appeared hesitant about which line to adopt. At the same time, individuals who had no financial interests (unlike gay business owners) or militant options (unlike the CUARH, the AMG, and *Gai Pied*) or professional obligations (unlike the government or medical leaders) were mobilizing full-time to fight against AIDS. We may say, without exaggerating, that Aides can be understood as an extraordinary and salutary initiative.

But this mobilization was not free of tension. In fact, there was a tendency for Aides to be paralyzed for months at a time by disputes. Rumors of rifts, divisions, and banishments finally crystallized in March 1987. The groups divided into two camps, with Defert on one side and with Edelmann and Mettetal on the other.[76] Called on to choose during the general meeting of March 7, Aides volunteers took a vote. It is this rift that Guibert recounts in *A l'ami qui ne m'a pas sauvé la vie* [*To The Friend Who Did Not Save My Life*], barely concealing the protagonists under pseudonyms. The following passage, although completely fictionalized and rather cynical, deserves to be quoted for its evocation of that difficult time:

Stéphane devoted himself body and soul to the organization he had founded ... upon Muzil's [Foucault's] death. ... AIDS became the social existence of many people, their hope for position and public recognition. ... Dr. Nacier [Mettetal], who had joined Stéphane's organization, also enlisted his crony Max [Edelmann], who had been my colleague at the newspaper. Muzil had said he looked like "the insides of a chestnut." Dr. Nacier and Max formed an unholy alliance, which some called a criminal conspiracy. I think Stéphane fell in love with the couple, especially the insides of the chestnut. Max and Dr. Nacier became his right hand. At the same time, Stéphane was singing the same old tune: "It won't be long before I pass the reins on to you." In fact, Stéphane created Max and Dr. Nacier's treason, like one of those old ladies who take an unwholesome pleasure in nurturing the greed of their heirs, tempting them with fabulous things—some exceptional diamond rivière or dish cupboard—only to will them, at the last minute, to the masseur or the garbage man. Since I was seeing both Stéphane and Dr. Nacier at the time, it amused me to hear Stéphane tell me: "My impression is they're ambitious and hungry for fame." Then Dr. Nacier would say: "We have two plagues to combat: AIDS and Stéphane." [I took] care to report to Stéphane all the plots to unseat and plunder him that Dr. Nacier was hatching with Max, and Dr. Nacier confided them to me in all innocence. So Stéphane was able to plan a vote designed to blackball the ambitious couple. Max wrote him a fatal letter, in which he told Stéphane he was giving "the organization too homosexual an image."[77]

Despite Guibert's fictionalized version, this rift was probably not so tragic, given the context. In 1987, it gradually came to light that for every identified person with AIDS there were between ten and fifteen people with HIV. To face the long term, it was now necessary to institutionalize the fight against AIDS. And the break within Aides occurred along strategic lines. Should an AIDS organization turn to professionals, especially the medical establishment, and acquire information, as Edelmann thought? Or should it be "communitarian" in nature, a mass movement of infected or exposed individuals, a kind of family where one fought for others as much as for oneself, as Defert wanted? Ought it to be a paramedical organization, with all this might imply in terms of salary and research, or a social movement of support and solidarity, made up of many individuals with HIV? It was an eminently political rift, but it occurred between two historical sensibilities that probably deserved to find expression independently, at a time when Aides was increasing in importance and growing into a national federation.[78]

"We had a hard time dealing with the rift in Aides," recalls Thierry Gamby, then president of the Marseilles committee and future vice president of the national federation of Aides:

It was a struggle between different styles but also a struggle between stars, since all three were very big personalities to whom we were very attached. But for us the history of Aides was one of personal grief, Daniel Defert's grieving for Foucault, which had been transformed into a collective phenomenon. For us, Aides meant a father, Daniel, with our two big brothers, Frédéric Edelmann and Jean-Florian Mettetal. We voted for Daniel.

The Aides dissidents, Edelmann and Dr. Mettetal, were welcomed into another structure, Arcat-sida, created in 1985. Its activities had been confined to clinical research.[79] With these new activists, Arcat got its second wind and oriented itself to spreading knowledge among medical and paramedical personnel (physicians, nurses, dentists, insurance companies, trade unions). It remained faithful to the strategy backed by Edelmann at the time of the rift. Arcat's image was less homosexual than that of Aides, and its strategy was to rely on existing professional channels, in a spirit of public service. Arcat-sida chose the path of professionalism and social action. In 1988, Edelmann and Mettetal created a specialized monthly publication, Sida 88, which became Sida 89, Sida 90, and then Journal du sida [AIDS journal]. Arcat-sida remains one of the principal AIDS organizations in France.

↩

Thus the birth of Aides was exemplary. Even as the organization radically distanced itself from traditional gay militancy, Defert, Edelmann, and Mettetal made Aides the first large-scale, communitarian homosexual network in France. In their own way, they corrected the initial errors of the gay militants they had replaced. In part, Aides even wrote the history of homosexuals in France during the 1980s. "One day," Pollak writes,

when historians write the social history of AIDS, the most notable fact, beyond the shadow of a doubt, will be the mobilization of organizations outside the medical field.

And in Western industrialized countries, the contribution of homosexuals and bisexuals (primarily men) to that struggle will be an obligatory chapter.[80]

The pioneering years of Aides ended with the rift, in 1987. In view of the new epidemiological data and the new political context, a chapter in the history of AIDS in France was also coming to an end.

12

Backlash

I admit there must be homosexuals in the National Front, but there are no fags.
—Jean-Marie Le Pen

"No one has adequately recognized the degradation in our culture and in the media that took place in the 1980s. These young people were between eight and fourteen years old in 1981. They are the children of idiotic rock music, the pupils of pedagogical vulgarity ... fed on the infra-ideological soup cooked up by show business, stupefied by the saturnalia of 'Touche pas à mon pote' [Don't touch my pal], and above all, the products of Lang culture. ... They are afraid not to have loose morals. That's their only understanding of revolution. The young are infected with mental AIDS. They have lost their natural immunity; all festering viruses infect them."

So it was that Louis Pauwels, an editorial writer for *Figaro magazine,* symbolically introduced AIDS to the political scene on December 6, 1986, in the midst of student demonstrations that would lead to Minister Devaquet's fall, even as *Libération* was publishing a complete account of AIDS, with many drawings of fisting and analingus.[1]

Although Pauwels's article was not specifically devoted to AIDS or to homosexuals, the tone and hatred emanating from it were not harmless. A few days earlier, on November 27, Michèle Barzach, the new deputy minister at the Department of Health, had declared AIDS the "great national cause for 1987." Pauwels's notorious expression "mental AIDS" can thus be interpreted as a response by the "true right" to this decision. The right had already criticized the Chirac government for, as Pauwels also wrote, wallowing in "the dregs with which Socialism made its vinegar." "Cohabitation," skewered by the famous deputy Jean Foyer as "an AIDS of institutions," was also targeted by Pauwels. The year 1987 was just beginning; every possible blunder would be committed over its course.

᠈

French homosexual militants' denial of AIDS between 1981 and 1985 seems incomprehensible unless we take into account their fear of a return to the "moral order" and to repression. From the delays of *Gai Pied* to the press releases of the

CUARH, from Guy Hocquenghem's hysteria to the reactions of "gay writers," spokespersons for homosexuals said nothing else: it's not the illness that's dangerous, it's homosexual liberation they're trying to attack through it.

The founders of Aides also saw the threat that the clock would be turned back, under cover of AIDS prevention. "For me," explains Daniel Defert, "one of the important issues in 1984 was to prevent homophobia from surfacing via the disease. I believed it was essential to create a context that could avoid or prevent the rejection of AIDS patients directly, but also of an entire social group."[2]

Probably not since syphilis had an illness elicited "as much anxiety and fascination as AIDS, churning up the age-old fears and taboos of epidemics, homosexuality, and death."[3] And even syphilis was not intrinsically associated with homosexuality except in a mix condemning decadence and a certain image of debauchery, regardless of the kind of sex involved.

The sometimes obsessive fears of gay militants were confirmed in 1987 in the discourse of exclusion advanced by two moral-political forces whose motivations were probably at odds but whose results proved to be identical: the church and the far right. A large number of individuals closely allied with them also seized on the AIDS theme, the gravity of which put a damper on extravagant behavior. "Homophobia," announced six years earlier in all the homosexual forums, sprang up. With it came a rhetoric of hatred, exclusion, moral depravity, and fear of the other. A backlash?[4]

⌐

In March and April 1987, in reply to Pauwels's criticism of "the democratization of disorder," Minister of the Interior Charles Pasqua took a series of measures to regulate immoral behavior. A public prosecutor in Paris was assigned to investigate gay computer networks, which he did under the still famous pseudonym "Slip dodu" [Bulging briefs]. Dominique Latournerie, director of public liberties at the Ministry of the Interior, was asked by Charles Pasqua to monitor periodicals and publications.[5] On March 9, Latournerie wrote to Mathieu Lindon's publishers and asked them, on the basis of an article of the law of July 16, 1949, concerning publications intended for young people, to stop marketing Lindon's novel *Prince et Léonardours*. Lindon's book, a homosexual novel in which young love is illustrated with drawings, repeated a certain number of themes from his *Nos plaisirs* [Our pleasures]—prostitution, rape, drugs—but in a watered-down version.[6] "I was delighted with that threat," Lindon remembers today. "I never for a moment envisioned prison. It was so stupid that people who heard about it were more envious than anything else."

After this first harmless blunder, Pasqua repeated the offense on March 16. But this time it was more serious. *Gai Pied Hebdo* was presented with a similar letter; everyone knew that, for such a publication, the strict application of the law protecting minors meant certain death. The value-added tax was increased to 33 percent, sale of the paper to minors and advertising posters was prohibited, and its distribution channels were restricted.[7] The next day, *New Look*, *L'Echo des Savanes*, and a dozen other glamour magazines were honored with the same letter.

Apart from the real risk to *Gai Pied Hebdo*, the threat was received with good humor. "In all things related to minors, I have no intention of being either tolerant or liberal-minded," remarked a boastful Pasqua, while Dominique Latournerie proclaimed to anyone who would listen that no one would hit him with "a Madame Bovary." Pasqua announced that the "Musée de l'Horrible" [Museum of the horrible], an exhibit displaying the debaucheries of the press, would be held in April. Jack Lang, along with several hundred celebrities, immediately gave his support to *Gai Pied*; at the National Assembly, he offered the minister of the interior the complete works of Rabelais (in the Pléiade edition, with dedication) and delivered a reproduction of a pornographic drawing by Picasso to the Musée de l'Horrible. "I did not offer an original, of course," Lang confirms today with a wink.

The response to Pasqua's "bans" was unanimous within the political class, including the majority party—everyone was against them. President Mitterrand went so far as to break his cohabitational silence, asserting in particular, "I am against any form of censorship. I am necessarily in step with everyone who loves liberty."

The huge blunder of the republican state ended a few days after the scandal broke, with a ludicrous letter from Latournerie to *Gai Pied*: "I have decided that the proceedings currently under way will not continue."[8]

⌐

It is still amazing that *Gai Pied* was threatened with a ban at a time when several thousand homosexuals in France were already afflicted with AIDS. The most amazing aspect has to do with AIDS prevention. During this period, the weekly newspaper had become a critical forum in the strategy to fight the disease. In February 1987, its directors learned of the results of a new survey by Michael Pollak, and the weekly announced that one-third of its Paris readership was HIV-positive. The time of doubt had passed; it was time to sound the alarm. Everyone realized that a tragedy was taking shape.[9] Charles Pasqua's action thus indicated less a deliberate desire to take on homosexuals than an obvious misunderstanding about the importance of AIDS prevention. It would be useless to look for the senior staff of the Rassemblement pour la République (RPR) party behind this absurd decision, and for good reason: there was nothing but petty prejudice and dilettantism. Some might wish to find electoral ambitions behind the decision, but one finds only bureaucracy, not a new hatred of homosexuals but instead a collection of petty hatreds, ordinarily kept in check by an equally widespread resistance.

Shortly thereafter, however, another politician took the same path, engaging in a new "homophobic" fight that, this time, had nothing at all funny about it.

The political media event took place on May 6, 1987. On that day, the president of the National Front broke the political silence with a clamor, devoting a long section of his *Heure de Vérité* [Hour of truth] to AIDS. The etiological doubts surrounding the conditions for infection now fed the self-serving imaginings of Jean-Marie Le Pen.[10] On Antenne 2, the AIDS patient was presented as "terribly" contagious "via his perspiration, his tears, and his saliva, a true modern leper." In the same broadcast, Le Pen called AIDS patients *sidaïques* (a term analogous to *judaïques* [Jewish]), insisted on the need to create *sidatoria* (analogous to "sanatoria"), and called for the systematic screening of at-risk populations and resident aliens. This political turning point in the history of AIDS in France was announced by the loyal Dr. François Bachelot, a scientific adviser to the far-right leader and a new deputy, who believed that AIDS was proof "of the decadence of society, of lax morals, drugs, homosexuality, and the drop in the age of first sexual experience."[11] Amazingly, the virus attacked Haitians (thus immigrants), homosexuals, and drug addicts: Could the far right of our time have dreamed up anything better?

"AIDS," Dr. Bachelot wrote, "has destroyed the sexual fantasies of aging sixty-eighters. ... Distinguished sodomites snickered at the archaic ways of half-wits who continued to make love the natural way, and, moreover, with a single partner—a woman. Today, many of them must be thinking that over on their deathbeds."[12]

AIDS became a major theme in the repertoire of the National Front during the first six months of 1987 (it did not come up before December 1986, and this theme did not last long after the summer of 1987). The consequences of this campaign of misinformation, as sudden as it was short-lived, were varied. Foremost among them was that information was garbled in extravagant slogans and in the subtle use of intimations (never spelled out) about concealed modes of transmission, which left doubts in the minds of the population well after 1987.

Nevertheless, Le Pen's campaigns seem to have played a fairly limited role in marking homosexuals as scapegoats. Although the leader of the National Front exploited uncertainty, working in "the realm of worry and reassurance," as Michel Foucault might have said, he did so in a way that contradicted the epidemiological data on categories of risk. He did not denounce gays so much as immigrants as a target population of the epidemic. He often neglected the SOS Racisme button "I Love Who I Want" in favor of "Touche pas à mon pote." Homosexuality rapidly disappeared from the discourse of the National Front, drowned by a litany of xenophobia and racism of all kinds.

Another consequence of the National Front's discourse was that it upset the government, Michèle Barzach in the first place, who was forced to distance herself from its slogans. The screening of at-risk populations, which was considered for a time, could no longer be done so objectively once it had become one of Le Pen's themes. Thus Barzach's entire policy was built around an ethical view of politics (fighting discrimination) and expressed in three key decisions, which since then have legitimately formed the basis of her popularity: the lifting of the ban on condom advertising, the creation of anonymous and free testing centers, and, above all, the legal sale of syringes.[13]

In the essential area of public discourse, the deputy minister had the great virtue of clarity: "The Most Intelligent Right Wing in the World" was the headline in *Gai Pied* on October 24, 1987, announcing the government campaigns. In spite of important decisions, and probably because of this purely political logic, Barzach was unable to establish a real strategy to combat AIDS.[14] Her courageous political reactions have made us forget her minimalist policy, which did not translate into proposals or aid for AIDS organizations. On the means of implementation, the health administration hesitated between a piecemeal approach and improvisation.

After the confrontation between Barzach and Le Pen, AIDS became one of the key points distinguishing the RPR from the National Front, especially in the context of the 1988 presidential election. Although politicians, journalists, and health professionals now worked to stigmatize stigmatization—sometimes reveling in their work—paralysis "due to the fear of fear itself" was the result.[15] Although Le Pen's malicious digressions had the unexpected effect of allowing AIDS to emerge as a problem in the political field, they also showed the limits of politics.

↩

Reviews and politicians were swallowed up in the gulf opened by Le Pen, and, like him, they manipulated hatred of "the other." As always, it is in circles like these that we must seek the use of discriminatory words that are less dressed up in circumlocutions than were those of the leader of the National Front. *Minute*, for example, published an astonishing science fiction account in which *sidateux* [AIDSers] conquered the "healthy" and a stark-naked madman paraded alone on the Champs-Elysées with a billboard: STOP ANTIHOMO RACISM![16] Later, the nationalist daily *Présent* wrote of *Gai Pied*, depicting it as a "lobby of sodomites," "With its recruiting, with its classified ads for 'encounters,' [it] first favored the spread of the evil [AIDS]! Everything leading to homosexual practices contributed, and still contributes, to spreading the epidemic."[17] This view was not far from the one heard recently from Ernest Chénière, RPR deputy and former principal of the Lycée de Creil, who spoke against Philippe Douste-Blazy's AIDS policy: "A remarkably organized minority of fringe elements—homosexuals and drug addicts—launched a powerful campaign to obtain an unwritten law, under pressure, which would objectively legalize their perversions and deviance."[18] Implicitly echoing the declarations of the National Front, Jacques Médecin attempted to have the municipal council in Nice pass a measure stating that everyone with HIV would be required to register with the police.

Beyond the issue of AIDS, the far right recovered its usual tone after 1987 and denounced the "homosexual lobby." The modern criticism made of homosexuals is no longer that they are unsociable people on the fringe but precisely that, like the Jews, they have become too sociable. Thus Pierre Gendron, a leading National

Front figure, declared, "Culture is the last bastion held by the left. It establishes the reign of intellectual terrorism via three lobbies: Jewish, Marxist, and homosexual."[19]

Such clarity is rare. Two reviews, Le Crapouillot and especially Gaie France, have established a more equivocal link between homosexuality and the far right. Le Crapouillot has already published close to a dozen special issues devoted to homosexuals and pedophiles, chock-full of clichés but also with unprecedented revelations and the addresses of numerous gay spots. Gaie France, a pedophile publication created in 1986, is a despicable mixture of photographs of Boy Scouts, scholarly articles on antiquity (Roger Peyreffite is a contributor), and fascistic allusions, which have earned it a ban on several occasions.[20] Because of its ambiguous nature, which brings together apologetic "fascists" and apologetic "queers," it has many readers who simply enjoy the pictures. The same readers once read nudist journals that concealed virtual networks of pedophiles behind libertarian and ecological aims.

The links between homosexuality and the far right are not altogether accidental and cannot be dismissed as anecdotal. One might think that the hard reality of nationalism, love of order, would disintegrate in the face of homosexual experience—the experience of social disorder par excellence—and, by negating that experience, would serve as its foil. On the contrary, the attraction/repulsion that these journals exhibit with respect to the far right is testament to the galvanizing role that homosexuality can play; oddly enough, this attraction/repulsion can also be an expression of self-loathing.

༄

Self-loathing? A recent news item may illustrate this point. On August 29, 1995, Jean-Claude Poulet-Dachary, chief of staff to the new National Front mayor of Toulon, was murdered after spending the night at Olympe, a gay establishment where he was a regular. He was a bewildering figure, and his death shed light on his atypical life. A photo of Marshal Pétain discovered at his home, side by side with the international homosexual guide Spartacus, was a telling sign of what he was all about.

Convinced of his calling to the priesthood in his youth, at twenty Poulet-Dachary joined the fundamentalist Catholics of Monseigneur Lefebvre after three years of studying canon law. He wore a cassock at the time. For obscure reasons—he may have been expelled from the seminary because of a relationship with a boy who had "spoken [about it] at confession"—at twenty-six he joined the Foreign Legion under a pseudonym. The cult of virility? An attraction to the uniform and the "very strong camaraderie"? He became editor in chief of the review Képi Blanc [White kepi] before being forced to return to civilian life because of his "homosexual recruiting." He then became active in Action Française, where he enjoyed the clandestine complicity and the secret signs of recognition that joined readers of

National Hebdo and readers of *Gai Pied*. Finally, he came out into the open, becoming the strongman for the National Front in Toulon, where some claim they
saw him give the Nazi salute or shout "Heil, Hitler!" This glorified militant from
the National Front was criticized within his own party for the "sick propositions"
he made to young militants. During the municipal elections of 1995, Jean-Marie Le
Chevallier was elected National Front mayor, and Poulet-Dachary became his
chief of staff. More than ever, his life was a partitioned juxtaposition of several
personalities: the "soldier monk" for Le Chevallier, "Poulet" for his friends, "La
Poulette" for his detractors in the National Front, and above all "Gloria," his pseudonym after nightfall in the gay establishments of Var. At his death, the local National Front tried to capitalize on the scandal by alluding to a political crime, and
Présent denounced "the jackals" of cosmopolitan France who were spreading
"abominable rumors." Le Pen, declaring "there [was] no zipper patrol" in his
party, had this telling comment: "I admit there must be homosexuals in the National Front, but there are no fags. They are invited to go elsewhere."[21]

Poulet-Dachary loved lost causes to the point of caricature: he was a distant
echo of the obscure French writer Maurice Sachs, the ex-seminarian, Jew, homosexual, and collaborator with the Gestapo who was probably killed by the SS in
1944, taken down beside a trench with a bullet to the back of the neck. The unthinkable, in short.

⟳

In 1987, AIDS became a political theme for the National Front and, more
broadly, served as a sounding board for society's problems. Several debates involving morality surfaced by way of a disease that carried with it irrational fears:
the legal sale of syringes reintroduced the problem of drug addiction; the question
of abortion for HIV-positive women raised the issue of voluntary interruption of
pregnancy; and the legal sale and advertising of condoms reintroduced the issue of
birth control and sex outside marriage. Once the far right entered the fray, could
the church be far behind?

AIDS quickly became a matter of conscience for the Catholic Church, probably one of the most problematic it had to face. Pope John Paul II and the bishops of
France, tempted at first to sidestep the issue, could not remain silent indefinitely or
agree to divorce sexuality from fertility. "The church was paralyzed," sadly observes Jean-Michel di Falco, spokesman for the bishops of France.

In this battle more than any other, the church had many faces, and the pope's
line was often called into question, explicitly or implicitly. In the case of the
church's official position, however, there is no doubt that the judgment of future
historians will be harsh, as it is for Leo XII, who in the early nineteenth century
condemned vaccination for smallpox. John Paul II did not in fact confine himself
to silence—which is always possible—or to a strictly ethical role. Instead of inventing a new casuistry, an art of accommodating rules in "matters of conscience"

and a "situational ethics" to "limit the damage," instead of drawing on the tradition of Vatican II (1962–65), which wanted to understand the modern world and
its anxieties, John Paul II repeated, "The end never justifies the means." In so doing, he became a militant in the fight to ban condoms. He chose to conduct his
new religious war even in Poland and Africa. In February 1993, he pronounced his
famous Kampala homily in Uganda, one of the countries most affected by AIDS.
By such actions, John Paul II fought not against AIDS but against the condom,
which is to say that he unquestionably fought on the side of AIDS. Through an
objective complicity with the epidemic, an entire faction of the official Catholic
Church probably found itself discredited, especially as people with AIDS became
more accepted by society.

As the church in France moved from state culture to "counterculture," Monseigneur Lustiger turned the pope's words to his own account and began his crusade, using AIDS to build a new human rights ideology in opposition to the tradition of the French Revolution. This crusade elicited no more than indifference to
his message, and an ironic smile from André Santini, the deputy who declared,
"Lustiger doesn't understand a thing about the condom because he puts it on his
index finger!" During the *Heure de Vérité* on December 1, 1988, Cardinal De-
courtray, president of the Conférence Episcopale in France, confirmed his opposition to the condom. He persisted on this path during comments on the eight
o'clock news on TF1. "The use of condoms is an easy solution, a contemptible and
contemptuous solution," he said on November 1, 1992. Monseigneur Vilnet had
this comment regarding the condom: "In trying to put out fires, you are creating
more drafts." Through Monseigneur Lefebvre, in disgrace with the Vatican, the
fundamentalist far right even embraced the position of Le Pen's far right.[22]

It would be wrong to underestimate these intransigent discourses: although
they probably had no great consequences for the individual behavior of French
people, they allowed the mobilization of social forces close to the church (Catholic
family organizations, the trade union of private schools). These organizations used
the church's discourse as a tool and made anathema their instrument. The influence of the Catholic vote probably played a role in maintaining the ban on condom advertising until 1987 and in delaying the installation of condom dispensers in
high schools. Thus, in France, the choices that the church made mattered when
they had an effect on legislation, and when, through go-betweens, religion became
a lobbying machine and dictated a temporal order. Its actions affected even those
people whose spiritual life was not guided by the church. "In France, on the issues
of condoms and contraception," Daniel Defert explains, "the church exercised
temporal power, abused temporal power."[23]

In the ranks of the church itself, however, other voices gradually made themselves heard and gave a different shading to Catholic positions. Let us acknowledge
that the church in France, unlike Rome, always refused to invoke AIDS as a divine
punishment and never wavered on the imperative of solidarity with the sick. The

archbishop of Toulouse, Monseigneur Collini, finally came out in favor of condoms: "There is my discourse as a bishop, but there is also my discourse as a man, which says clearly that if you cannot change your sexual behavior, you have no right not to use a condom, since you would be behaving as a carrier of death, and the fifth commandment says: Thou shalt not kill."[24] Others were even more courageous, but also more marginal. In Germany, for example, there was the theologian and psychoanalyst Eugen Drewermann; in France there were Bernard Besret, former prior of Boquen, and the theologian Xavier Thévenot in addition to Monseigneur Gaillot, former bishop of Evreux. These men went even farther, causing trouble and finding themselves called to account or simply suspended from giving sermons.[25]

Out in the field, a number of monks, nuns, and lay believers, active in ministering to and caring for the sick, also did not follow the discourse of exclusion. Christians were involved in the regional branches of Aides and, more marginally, in the David and Jonathan Society. At the center of all these groups, two figures in particular showed that dialogue was still possible.

↵

Antoine Lion, a Dominican and former member of Aides–Alsace, became president of Chrétiens et Sida [Christians and AIDS]. "The virus had the vulgarity to show the world that the ideal of the Catholic church was not being practiced," he explains today ironically. "You see, if everyone came to marriage as a virgin and remained faithful, it would be a lousy time for AIDS. So, confronted with such a rude virus, a virus that scoffed at the church, a virus, you might say, that was so un-Catholic, I can see very well why the thinking of the Vatican went awry." Crisscrossing France, this man of conviction seemed to be mounting a dual battle, against AIDS and against the Vatican's position. "I was sometimes stung by criticism insinuating that Christians 'would do better to keep quiet.'" Brother Lion continues:

I understand these reactions, because the church has a real responsibility on such issues as AIDS and homosexuality. This was already true before the epidemic, since it's probably complicated to be both Catholic and homosexual. Since AIDS, however, it was inevitable that the church would be challenged, given the seriousness that homosexuality had assumed and its new relation to death. The response of the Catholic Church, which continues to be the chief purveyor of rites, cannot simply be to remain psychologically rigid, to undermine all human relationships, or to offer a few brief dry words. One might argue for compassion, for example, which is a beautiful Christian term that has been devalorized today. As for me, I think the condom can have a certain ethical value because it introduces notions of responsibility and respect for the other person, which are authentic Christian values. But what most strikes me among the Vatican clergy, in addition to the difficulties they have dealing with their own sexuality, is the incompetence of these people with respect to AIDS. For me, "Judge not" is one of the essential precepts of the church. That has been somewhat forgotten.

Another face in a more nuanced portrait of the Church is that of Father Gérard Bénéteau, head of Solidarité-Sida–Saint-Eustache (Saint Eustachius–AIDS solidarity). Almost one-third of the funerals occurring in the Paris parish where he has conducted his ministry since 1984 are those of AIDS victims. "For many homosexuals, AIDS has revealed the failure of their lives, and homosexuality may appear to be the cause of that failure. Some, wishing to spend the end of their lives with a woman, seem to deny their homosexual condition—which indicates a great uneasiness." Father Bénéteau is very critical of the usual discourse on homosexuals inside the church:

The church has a great responsibility. We should allow people to be able to say anything. Yet people who did not choose to be different are being asked to consider themselves sinners from the outset. At best, if someone takes notice of what they are, they are asked to abstain from any physical relationship, thus being deprived of the fundamental right to realize their total personalities. For me, the only way out of the impasse is to acknowledge certain realities and accompany them with moral precepts.

Father Bénéteau belongs to the post-'68 generation of priests and has met with many homosexuals during his religious mission, which allows him to look differently on those who have come to ask for his help. Although he brushes aside the new rules of love, he refuses to imprison man in alienation and guilt. "The sexuality of a homosexual cannot develop in the same way as other people's," he explains:

Because his personality is awakened under unusual circumstances, the homosexual has the sense of a taboo in adolescence. The conditions surrounding the first encounters, which are often concealed from the family, create habits and an uneasiness, and traces of these remain for a long time. These experiences take on a terrible weight in the sequence of events. The fragility of the couple, the high number of partners, the separation between sexual life and emotional life seem to me to be consequences of this fact.

In his mission as a priest, he has met few happy homosexual couples. "I am still persuaded that this difference is a source of suffering," he asserts, "and that many feel deprived of certain conditions allowing them to pursue happiness." Might homosexuality still be a "painful problem"?

Through Solidarité-Sida–Saint-Eustache, Father Bénéteau attempts to reestablish ties between AIDS patients and the church, to promote reconciliation, and to create spaces for dialogue. In the parish where he serves as a priest, he has encouraged ecumenical wakes in memory of AIDS victims. These wakes show that some priests are energetically fighting the illness in their own way.

ↄ

Brother Lion and Father Bénéteau, critical of the discourse of John Paul II, have noted a link between the pope's position on AIDS and his position on homosexuality. The Catholic Church's discourse of exclusion toward homosexuals returned in force in 1986, at a time when the AIDS epidemic had begun to worry the public at large as homosexual visibility in western Europe was growing.

Although relations between the church and homosexuality historically have been problematic—especially for homosexuals, who were sometimes burned—silence has often been the rule.[26] Under Paul VI, in 1975, a distinction was made between the "condition of homosexuals" (a tendency that is not acted on) and their "acts," which alone are considered "intrinsically dissolute" and "in any case, not subject to approbation." Since the beginning of John Paul II's pontificate, which began on October 16, 1978,[27] homosexuality has again become a neurotic fixation of the church. In addition to the ethical goal of condemnation, there is also a political goal: to oppose all legislation in favor of homosexuals.

Thus, from apostolic letters to papal encyclicals, at large-scale masses abroad that took the form of shows reminiscent of Pink Floyd concerts, or in "little phrases" skillfully dropped from the chair of Rome, in the mid-1980s John Paul II worked to develop his "jurisprudence" of homosexuality. Far from being confined to "intrinsically dissolute" acts, in 1986 homosexuality itself, including inclinations that are not acted on, became "dissoluteness."[28] Relying on the recommendations of Cardinal Ratzinger, who had become supreme judge in the matter, in 1992 the pope approved of certain specific measures of discrimination related to employment, housing, and social protection for homosexuals, going so far as to tolerate limiting the rights of AIDS patients.[29] More concretely, he fought all forms of decriminalization of homosexuality in eastern European countries; in reference to the "legal approbation" of homosexuality by the European Parliament, he maintained that it was not "morally admissible," since no one could "confer institutional value on behavior contrary to God's design while favoring man's weaknesses."[30]

Although they embraced the principles supported by Rome, the bishops of France said that they were more concerned with individuals. A certain number wanted to stay in touch with reality, and Monseigneur Albert Rouet, bishop of Poitiers and president of the Social Episcopal Board, is even trying to put forth a different discourse:

I am trying to understand why the church is so misunderstood. We should have spoken about the meaning of sexuality, created places for dialogue, pointed out that there is enormous emotional and sexual poverty in our societies. We must speak of the suffering of homosexuals, the pain of couples. But the church must also teach people to live at peace with themselves. In this respect, Christian homosexuals, like those in the David and Jonathan Society, have the right and probably the duty to meet. Every priest prefers the homosexual who comes to tell him he is a homo and that he can do nothing about it: "Go about your life, I will help you" should be his response. But if someone declares that he embraces the choice as a matter of pride, one might wonder whether he is not simply justifying his tendencies. A person is greater than his inclinations.

Beyond such words, faith may have as much importance for homosexuals in France as for heterosexuals; attendance at religious services is comparable for both groups.[31] The most rigid positions of the Catholic Church thus remain problematic for believing homosexuals, introducing a serious gap between faith and private life and excluding them, with no possibility of "reconciliation."

In contrast to these positions, which go against the grain of society's evolution, the Protestant Church in France has demonstrated a great deal of indulgence, precisely in the name of "reconciliation." It has gone so far as to champion tolerance for homosexuals: "There are forms of productivity in the homosexual condition that can surface in domains other than sexual reproduction. Happiness and mutual respect can also exist within homosexuality. Homosexuality presents itself as a fate and is experienced as a wound ... which calls one to take the road leading to reconciliation."[32]

> ↩

As for the far right, we may advance the hypothesis that one of the keys to the church's "homophobia" is its attraction / repulsion with respect to homosexuality. This issue, like sexuality as a whole, has been poorly grasped by the church. The choice of the priesthood and the religious life has always been conceived as a solution for repressed and guilt-ridden homosexuals.[33] Until the 1970s, Christian literature was the primary place where homosexual inclinations were mentioned. There have been countless scandals involving pedophile priests in the United States,[34] though in France such affairs are usually hushed up, and the offending priest is transferred to a different parish. Priests' vows of celibacy are regularly held responsible.

It would be easy to establish a parallel between the most "homophobic" discourse pronounced in the parish of Monseigneur Lefebvre (a far-right fundamentalist) and the homosexual "scandals" in the Catholic community. An HIV-positive homosexual sexton at the Eglise Saint-Nicolas in Chardonnet was dismissed in 1987, the choirmaster of the same parish was ousted for homosexuality, and several members of the choir confessed to having had relations with men. In this case, too, there is attraction / repulsion.

The Catholic Church's view of homosexuality, especially at this view's most extreme, oscillates between two poles: punishment and fantasy. On the one hand, there is excommunication and, whenever possible, stoning. On the other, there is Umberto Eco's *The Name of the Rose*. In this novel, the abbey's Franciscan friars court one another and exchange favors until one day the young monk Adelme, overcome with remorse, throws himself from a tower. Everything is for the best in the best of Sodom's worlds, as long as there is mercy.

> ↩

In the second half of the 1980s, then, AIDS gave rise to a "homophobic" discourse in France, which was particularly perceptible in the positions of the far right and the Catholic Church. Nevertheless, this discourse came relatively late (1987), and its effects probably would have been more devastating if it had been put forward at the very beginning of the disease, at a time when the combination of medical uncertainty and weak AIDS organizations might have prevented an effective, well-reasoned response.

This return of a repressive discourse was hardly translated into action, however. We may regret that it played a role in blocking preventive measures for several more years—it was not until 1989 that prevention became widespread—but this was still distinctly the discourse of a minority.

Of course, homophobia cannot be measured solely by public expressions of exclusion. Hostile attitudes toward homosexuals are more widespread and, we dare say, more commonplace. They frequently cause difficulties in daily life. News items attesting to them are legion: a blackmailed teacher or instructor, a neighborhood up in arms, a rent dispute, questioning by the police, complaints met with ironic replies, discrimination in employment, wrongful dismissals, an obvious imbalance in a family inheritance. In the provinces more than in Paris, homosexuality has led to astounding scandals, and although homosexuality is not a crime, a homosexual involved in a neighborhood dispute can easily be labeled the guilty party. How can we fail to adapt Sartre's famous saying about anti-Semitism, that being homosexual is not a fault, but being homosexual with a fault means having two faults?

On a more mundane level, homophobia manifests itself in rumors or in gossip from the mailman, the next-door neighbor, or the neighborhood scandalmonger, all of which wears one down. Even more often, the silence about homosexuality within the family suddenly subjects the homosexual adolescent to the experience of social prejudice: the announcement of his specificity can trigger irrational reactions in his parents. In any case, their reaction is absolutely unpredictable: it may be hostility or it may be acceptance.

～

Beyond the many forms—new or traditional, recurring or infrequent—that denunciations of homosexuality can take, despite the far right (joined on this point by the "official" discourse of the church), despite the words of Philippe de Villiers (which combine these discourses in a joyful "fight for values"), despite the murder of Pastor Doucé (which remains fairly mysterious),[35] homophobia is not anti-Semitism or racism. It is an expression of uneasiness in the face of the inscrutable, equivocal other whose practices are "a little like mine."

The great fear of homosexuality and illness combined was not focused on homosexual individuals except in very rare cases. These cases elicited very calm reactions from political and health leaders, and from domains that had a clear pedagogical function with respect to society at large. Thus the main effect of the claims that AIDS was a divine scourge come to punish immorality (according to certain Catholics), or that AIDS was a sign of moral depravity and an occasion to crack down on practices characteristic of a degeneration of the species (according to some supporters of the far right), was the discrediting of those who made such claims. The return of a hatred of homosexuals? Hardly. It was only the old, well-known trappings of conservatism if not of stupidity, and of bygone if not archaic exercises in style by moralists and killjoys who believed that, thanks to the new disease, they could once again make themselves useful.

In the end, with respect to AIDS, Le Pen, terrified by disorder, remained a simple man of law and order, faithful to himself. Through the pope's voice, the Catholic Church is still a stubborn old lady, less frightened of the world's moral drift than of its own demise. In the end, Louis Pauwels and Charles Pasqua are only bogeymen. The resurgence of "homophobia" during the 1980s was visible only in the familiar repertoire of the old morality, which its advocates used in their effort to stage a comeback. They succeeded only in confirming how little influence they still have, even in difficult circumstances.

"The concept of homophobia appears in the West when homophobic attitudes recede," explains the philosopher Alain Finkielkraut, reminding us, in the tradition of Foucault, that "all the same, homosexuals do not need homophobia in order to live."[36]

Paradoxically, then, the obsession with repression, which was central to homosexual militants' interpretive grid, and which fed their discourse and obscured the illness between 1981 and 1985, has hardly been revived by the advent of AIDS. The brief blunders of Le Pen and the pope do not preclude a return of repression in the future, possibly in many different forms—a hypothesis that should not be ruled out—but the great wave of homophobia that was noisily anticipated did not occur. Therefore, it can neither justify, after the fact, nor account for the denial on the part of militants.

⤳

Almost nothing remains of homophobia but a few backward-looking individuals, who are comical, and, in their recurrent obsession, almost touching. It was Pauwels, an inconsolable curmudgeon in the face of the world's mad progress, converted to a hard-right discourse and illuminated by faith, who wrote an editorial for *Figaro* magazine on "the democratization of disorder." Having once alluded to "mental AIDS," he now attempted to confront the devil in person. His name? Arthur Rimbaud:

It sometimes happens that genius combines filth and diamonds or takes pleasure in creating pigs with wings. . . . In the face of a mad genius, judgment sometimes goes astray. . . . But in the collapse of values and the errant behavior that afflict our society, it [is] troubling to make Rimbaud a popular hero. . . . For the weak, the obtuse, the uneducated—and they are legion—it is pernicious to give official sanction, even with the best of intentions, to the sense that license and liberty, dissolution and illumination, moral anarchy and great art, rebellion and excellence naturally go together. . . . They claim that by universalizing the Rimbaud myth, they are expanding taste [*le goût*]. Without fail, they are expanding the sewer [*l'égout*].[37]

13

The Hecatomb

I feel an immense pity for us.
— Hervé Guibert

Enormous photos were projected onto the wall of the main courtyard of the Palais des Papes on July 27, 1993. There, at the Avignon festival, where the choreographer Dominique Bagouet had dreamed of staging one of his productions, the dancers in his company, together one last time, performed *Jours étranges* [Strange days] with a frantic desire to do it justice. The set consisted of a gigantic assemblage of loudspeakers. The music of the Doors was playing in the background; Bagouet used to say it put him in mind of "a vague, ill-defined desire to rebel against established norms and codes." In the second part of this unusual homage, the dancers performed *So Schnell* from Bach's Cantata no. 26, whose chorus, marked by a Puritan fatalism, repeated, "How vain and uncertain is human life! ... Dust and ash do not spare those who are the equal of God." This chorus was interrupted by sounds emanating from industrial hosiery-making machinery, the same machines that Bagouet had heard in the little textile factory of his childhood. All Bagouet's dancers (Fabrice Ramalingom, Bernard Glandier, Catherine Legrand, Olivia Grandville, and the rest), all the members of this extraordinary galaxy of stars, his friends (the designer Alain Neddam, the journalist Raphaël de Gubernatis), choreographers he had trained or who had collaborated with him (Michel Kelemenis, François Raffinot, Angelin Preljocaj), were gathered together. Here, too, was his "brother in arms" Jean-Paul Montanari, a former militant from GLH–Lyons, who had become director of the Montpellier Dance Festival. With Montanari, Bagouet had waged many battles for contemporary dance but also, in a way, for homosexuality. Even so, it had been very difficult for Bagouet to come to terms with his sexuality, and he certainly had not been a militant. As if better to forget the photos projected onto the walls, the performers, one last time before the Bagouet company was dissolved, broke open a bottle of champagne onstage while the huge crowd filling the courtyard applauded without letup. A page had been turned in the history of contemporary dance in France. But this time Bagouet could not attend his own triumph.

↜

Rudolf Nureyev, wearing a nightcap, came onstage at the Palais Garnier, carried by two principal dancers, Isabelle Guérin and Laurent Hilaire, like the giants in Patrice Chéreau's *Ring*. The members of the audience fell silent. They understood. After about fifteen seconds of heavy silence, there was thunderous applause that lasted more than twenty minutes. Minister of Culture Jack Lang felt called upon to come onstage and embrace the choreographer. That night, October 8, 1992, was the premiere of *La bayadère*, which was to be the last ballet choreographed by this young tartar who had become an exile at twenty-three, and who, with his turban and high-heeled boots, swore like a Russian sailor. Nureyev was not afraid to declare his attraction for men, but he preferred to keep his illness quiet. He died on January 6, 1993, a few months before Paolo Bortoluzzi, with whom he had performed the famous *Chant du compagnon errant* in 1971.

↜

Nureyev. Bagouet. Two images, two sets. Two symbolically important moments in the collective tragedy of AIDS in France.

What had happened? Why had it happened? How was it possible? AIDS is "a specific tragedy that has massively affected only one community and which is fairly reminiscent of the plague in the ghetto," the historian Jean-Noël Jeanneney explains today. Within a very few years, AIDS became for homosexuals the symbol of collective death. Particularly for those between the ages of thirty and forty, a whole generation was decimated.

The director Patrice Chéreau explains today, "It took what seems like an inordinate amount of time for me to understand that AIDS was not just another illness, because it had begun to affect all my friends in particular. It is only now that I am beginning to understand it, now that we all have address books filled with people whose names we don't know whether to leave, cross out, or tear out."

"It's hard," echoes Arnaud Marty-Lavauzelle, the new president of Aides. "Sometimes you have to go to Père-Lachaise Cemetery three times in the same week."

↜

The cycle of homosexual liberation, set in motion in France between 1971 and 1981, shifted into reverse, and the stream of history flowed backwards. The procession of the Front Homosexuel d'Action Révolutionnaire (FHAR), which first marched on May 1, 1971, shouting loudly in front of Père-Lachaise, seems, in an unbelievable twist of fate, to have been recomposed and repeated in misfortune. This was no longer the time for makeup and wigs; now it was a procession of mourners. Today, those active in the groups, movements, and publications constituting the history of "homosexual liberation" gather to count their dead.

Most of the Gazolines from the 1971 FHAR are dead: "Wanda" Colson, Jean-

François "Blédine" Briane, Jean-Michel Mandopoulos, and Michel Cressole. Of the twelve militants who belonged to GLH–Lyons in 1975, half are dead or suffering from AIDS. Among the seven founders of GLH–Marseilles, Alain Julien, Roland Thélu, and Marco have passed away. Of the four transvestites from the celebrated Aix-en-Provence troupe called the Mirabelles, "Marie-Bonheur" is dead, and another is ill. Of the leaders of the religious David and Jonathan Society, founder Gérald de La Mauvinière, treasurer Pierre Delrieu, André Bec of the southwestern chapter, and Gilles Chiano and Frédéric of the Marseilles chapter are all dead. From the 1979 Comité d'Urgence Anti-Répression Homosexuelle (CUARH), Alain Leroi (nicknamed "Joan of Arc"), Vincent Legret, and Gérard Maison are dead. Well-known personalities of the gay nightlife, among them the businessman David Girard, have died off. In the respectable land of Arcadie, the deaths are equally numerous and began with one of the organization's founders, the writer André du Dognon, dead of AIDS at the uncommon age of seventy-nine. There are also many dead among the staff members of *Homophonies* and *Masques*, among them Jean-Marie Combettes. Of the 1979 *Gai Pied* staff members, nearly half the contributors, freelance journalists, and photographers have died or are now ill— Franck Arnal, Antoine Pingaud, Marco Lemaire, Luc Coulavin, Alain-Emmanuel Dreuilhe (a correspondent for the paper), and Michel Gilles—but so are layout artists, switchboard operators, and the bookkeeper.

The AIDS movement has been hit even harder than the homosexual organizations. Of the five people Daniel Defert brought together in October 1984 to create Aides, four are dead: Jean-Pierre Joecker (founder of *Masques*), Franck Arnal, and Jean Blancart and his partner, Gilles Barbedette, both of whom moved from *Gai Pied* to Aides—that is, from the homosexual struggle to the fight against AIDS. Among Aides volunteers, the list of the dead is too long even to be compiled. As always, it is the most famous names that return: Jean-Florian Mettetal, cofounder of Aides and then director of Arcat-sida; Michael Pollak, the brilliant sociologist who can be given credit for analyzing, with scientific objectivity, an illness that was affecting him personally; Denys Bucquet, an epidemiologist; Jean-Michel Mandopoulos, Yvon Lemoux, and Jean-Paul Baggioni, all former presidents or vice presidents of Aides–Paris–Ile-de-France. More recently there has been Pierre Kneip, a volunteer from 1985 on and founder of Sida Infos Service. Many less well known members of Aides have "gone to their glory": Dominique Le Fers, Mark Anguenot-Franchequin, Jean-François Gagnieux. Even from the narrowly medical AIDS-alert group established in 1982 by Willy Rozenbaum, four participants have died, among them Dr. Claude Villalonga, who represented the Association des Médecins Gais. At *Libération*, the "homo department" of the newspaper, as Serge Daney called it, has been deeply affected: Daney, of course, the film critic; but also Philippe Hoummmous, the "flaming" media critic; Christian Martin, who wrote the column "Moi et mon sida" [My AIDS and me]; the cartoonist Copi; and Michel

Cressole. The few journalists in the Communist press who frequently mentioned homosexuality are all dead: Michel Boué and Rémy Darne at *L'Humanité*, Emmanuel Guallino at *La Marseillaise*.

"It's terrible, all the friends of ours who are dying," confides Michel Guy, former minister of culture to Valéry Giscard d'Estaing and a regular at Le Sept and then at Le Palace. Guy also died from complications of AIDS, as did Maurice Fleuret, director of music and dance for Jack Lang; Bernard Dort, a theater actor; Gérard Guyot, fine-arts adviser to the Ministry of Culture; and Jacques Garnier of the choreography research group at the Paris Opera. The death of so many artists and writers has made a particular impression in France, since they had the most visibility. Think of the actors Rock Hudson, Anthony Perkins, and Brad Davis (the star of *Midnight Express* and *Querelle*); the filmmakers Derek Jarman and Cyril Collard; the female impersonator Thierry Le Luron, of course; the painter Keith Haring; vocalist Freddie Mercury of Queen; and Klaus Nomi. But there are also many names that are recognized within their own specialized fields: the pianist Yuri Egorov; the harpsichordist Scott Ross; the set designer Lou Goaco; the publisher Jean-Luc Pinard-Legry; the actors Alain Salomon and Richard Fontana; the filmmaker Michel Béna; the playwright Bernard Chatelier; the photographer Claude Bricage; Thierry Juno, director of the deaf troupe of actors in Vincennes; the writers Bernard-Marie Koldès, Reinaldo Arenas, Conrad Detrez, and Pascal de Duve; Gilles Dusein, who ran the gallery Urbi et Orbi; Louis Bercut, set designer for Copi's *Une visite inopportune* [An inopportune visit] at the Théâtre de la Colline; and "Pinpin," the most illustrious of the makeup artists at the Opéra. As an indication of the particular importance of this disease for the cultural arena, in 1987, for all age groups combined, AIDS was the cause of over half the deaths among men working as professionals in the news media, the arts, and the theater.[1]

In the field of dance, AIDS seems to have made dying of old age a utopian dream. And if the deaths of Dominique Bagouet and Rudolf Nureyev were symbolic in France, these men also served as painful torchbearers for the entire profession, which mourns Michael Bennett, the Broadway choreographer; the principal dancer Clark Tippet; Jorge Donn, one of Maurice Béjart's dancers; Poonie Dodson of Chez Chopinot; the choreographer Alvin Ailey; Alfonso Cata, director of the Ballet du Nord (and Bill T. Jones's life partner); Arnie Zane; and the young choreographers Philippe Tressera, Lari Lcong, and Hideyuki Yano. Because dance is an art without memory, and because homosexuals are a minority without history, AIDS is one reason why recording and retranscribing performances and notating choreography have become matters of urgency.

In addition to these deaths, covered at length in the press, there was of course a flood of anonymous lives taken by AIDS. How many bartenders and professors, students and hairstylists, transvestites who had sung in provincial clubs? How many men who, since the mid-1970s, had engaged obsessively in sports in order to be virile and muscular, and whose bodies, skinny as Giacometti statues, were thus an even more radical departure from what they had once been? How many hustlers who, at the end of their incredible misfortune, met up with their old tricks in the hospital? André Baudry, head of Arcadie, who left France around 1982, was stunned to learn, little by little, that "almost all the boys who worked at the club—bartenders, secretaries, porters, cloakroom workers—are dead." "You have to admit," he adds, "it's absolutely extraordinary that I left Arcadie at exactly the point when a new era of homosexuality was beginning. The mystery of fate. I often wonder, if I were to come back to Paris one day and send out a letter to the members of Arcadie, inviting them to get together, how many of us there would be. And how many deaths would we learn of?"

Robert Mapplethorpe did a self-portrait (1988) in which he holds a cane with a death's-head handle and seems to say, "Look, I'm in deathly company." "Bad blood," Rimbaud would have said.

⟿

"AIDS clearly marked the return of people dying young in our culture," Daniel Defert notes. "When you're a homosexual, it's not easy to deal socially with mourning the death of a friend. . . . Everyone needs new rites, ways to share emotions that otherwise do not find expression or legitimation. Through this recognition of dying and this display of the dead—and not of death—I think a great cultural transformation is under way."[2]

With the specific and collective AIDS hecatomb, which often affects a young population, new representations of death have been put in place. That is true for the Names Project, founded in the United States in 1986 as a revival of the American quilting tradition, a means of expression for black slaves.[3]

In France, the "patchwork of names," modeled on the Names Project, was created in 1989. On a rectangle of cloth measuring one meter by eighty centimeters, the loved ones of a person who has died of AIDS honor their friend by stitching together a set of symbols that evoke his or her personality. These collective patches, joined end to end, become virtual monuments that can be spread out during ceremonies on the Mall in Washington, D.C., or, in Paris, under the Eiffel Tower. Defert explains, "Who doesn't feel how much more violent their presence is in the heart of a city, on the esplanade at our shows, in our stadiums, at our fairs, than in the confines of the cemeteries? The quilt allows us to visualize the new relationship our civilization is stitching together with death. But its gentleness and its violence affirm, in all their names, that we still want to have at life."[4]

Paradoxically, the first "political" AIDS funeral was for Fabrice Emaer, the former owner of Le Palace, on June 11, 1983: the crowd applauded his coffin as it came out of the church.[5] Since then, ceremonies using candles or "blank pages," as well as new rituals within the church itself, have multiplied. Death notices in the papers and death announcements began to mention the notorious "longtime companion"; the traditional expression "died following a long illness" has gradually been replaced by the clarity of "death from complications of AIDS." More discreetly, but unambiguously, death notices in *Libération* and *Le Monde* often include the request "no flowers or wreaths; donations may be sent to Aides." The writer Edmund White, HIV-positive for a decade, bought a double plot at Père-Lachaise Cemetery when his last partner, Hubert Sorin, died, "so that, at my death, visitors will see two men's names side by side, will see a homosexual couple."

Cremation has played a major role in these developments. Although cremation was initially a response to health concerns, which in the United States brought special governmental regulations to bear on the body of a person who had died of AIDS, cremation has become so frequent in France that there must be other reasons for choosing it. Nevertheless, as Arnaud Marty-Lavauzelle of Aides notes, "it's a horrible ceremony":

For this secular ceremony, you gather under a canopy studded with junk jewelry. In the best case, there's recorded music selected by the deceased, which is generally enough to make you scream in horror. You wait for the chicken to roast, and, after an hour and a half, an urn comes out: nothing has been said, nothing has been shared, the people have not been honored. That's why we're trying to rethink homosexual mourning, to avoid that, to create new memorial ceremonies.

At Aides rituals for grieving have been established, along with moments of "memory and solidarity" on behalf of the deceased. They allow the organization's volunteers to take stock, but they also serve as a memorial. "The entire history of homosexuals is a history of denial," Marty-Lavauzelle continues:

You might say that the history of homosexuals is written in sand. For me, the appearance of AIDS was a replica of the Vietnam war: generations of people began to fight a traumatic event that was bigger than they were. But what will we do with this event? We must be able to retain traces of this collective struggle and find the tools to write this history.

Two key dates, two opposing paths, may say a great deal about this "unbelievable" history. In 1972, Guy Hocquenghem's stunning public "confession" of homosexuality in *Le Nouvel Observateur* came as a response to "unspeakable homosexuality"; fifteen years later, in 1987, Jean-Paul Aron responded to "the unspeakable disease" by "confessing" "his AIDS" in the same newspaper. Two intersecting fates, two lives at odds with each other, two dates in opposition. Both men succumbed to the same virus eight days apart, Aron on August 20, 1988, and Hocquenghem on August 28.

Aron was not a militant. A dilettante intellectual and dandy, an imp with large pointy ears, a member of Jack Lang's cabinet beginning in 1981, this cousin of the famous Raymond Aron timidly mentioned his "specificity" in the early 1980s, remaining marked by a half-Baudry, half-Bory influence despite the clarity of his audacious 1978 book *Le pénis et la démoralisation de l'Occident* [The penis and the demoralization of the West] and several lucid interviews in *Gai Pied*. In 1987, Aron decided to make his illness public, a decision that necessarily entailed the announcement of his homosexuality.

What does he say in this decisive interview, titled "Mon sida" [My AIDS] and published in *Le Nouvel Observateur* on October 30, 1987? It is an extraordinary document, executed with the skill of a tightrope walker over an abyss, and, miraculously, it avoids morbid voyeurism. In the first place, Aron bluntly distinguishes himself from Michel Foucault, whom he blames from the outset for concealing his illness, an act out of character for the philosopher of truth Foucault claimed to be: "Foucault was a man of language, knowledge, and truth, not of lived experience and meaning. He was also a homosexual. He was ashamed of it, and he sometimes dealt with it irrationally. His silence about the illness disturbed me because it was a silence of shame, not the silence of an intellectual. It was so contrary to everything he had defended! It seemed ridiculous to me!"[6] Beyond this settling of accounts, the interest of "Mon sida" lies in the simplicity with which Aron recounts his life and illness. This magnificent narrative must be quoted at length.[7]

Even three months ago, when my loved ones asked me if they could tell somebody I was HIV-positive, I answered that there was no point [I would not have spoken publicly about my homosexuality, as I am doing today, for anything]. It took the illness to produce this recent spontaneity in my words. Does the change come from the presentiment of death, the inevitability of my death? . . . Mythically, magically, I believed I was safe. The reigning atmosphere of freedom—political values finally coincided with contemporary moral values—reassured me. It was at that time, in about 1982–83, that I started to show up at demonstrations where homosexuals were defending their rights and freedoms. I knew photos would be taken of me: I accepted this implicit admission. The liberal atmosphere, created by the left, also led me to visit—though with moderation—places I had hesitated to go until then, gay moviehouses, for example. I remember that Roger Kempf, with whom I had an exemplary and significant relationship for thirty years, beginning in 1947—it's over now—phoned me one day in 1983 and warned me: "Watch out for AIDS! Be very careful!" That seemed absurd to me. I told him, "Listen, I hardly do anything!" But that warning, the only one I got, those premonitory words, greatly irritated me, and for a long time. You see, I still think about it. I couldn't accept his advice because, with *Le pénis et la démoralisation de l'Occident,* published in 1978, a book Kempf and I wrote together, a process of liberation began, as the title of the book indicates. Even though I did not reveal myself in it, and even though the theme of homosexuality remained peripheral, it was still present. I didn't want to admit that AIDS posed a threat to me and that I posed a threat to others. I acknowledge that it took me some time before I started taking precautions during sex. I didn't consent to be tested until the first warning signs. And today, since I have decided to speak truthfully, I admit that I don't feel any retrospective remorse at the idea that I may have infected someone before I knew I carried the virus [at my request, my brother administered the test to me]. Because of his position [he's a renowned physician], he was very quickly informed by the laboratory, and he himself told me by phone that I was HIV-positive. That was a revelation . . . a cataclysm. . . . Then I received a dry, precise report on my blood analysis. Under the label "LAV" they had written "positive." No accompanying letter. Nothing. Nothing but this "positive," which had to be dealt with. And I had even been warned!

From this stark confrontation with death, a kind of serenity gradually came into being. In daily life first. . . . And then, there's celibacy. As soon as I discovered I was HIV-
positive, I immediately chose total celibacy, and without particular suffering. In fact, although I had great love affairs, intense desires, I didn't do very well in life, in love or in desire. I believe, however, that I was a success at friendship. . . . You know, in terms of contracting the illness, I'm very suspicious of an American I met in Florence in December
1981. Because after that, I had so few sexual relationships! Well, if I saw him where you're
sitting, in that chair, I would be nice to him. I have no anger. I often tell myself I was very
unlucky, given the life I have led. . . . In all frankness, I am incapable of admitting to you
that I experience AIDS as a punishment. This just seems scandalous to me, this terrible
bad luck. . . .

The truth about me is that I'm a bundle of guilt. Homosexuality is a big part of that, but
not everything. If I had not found the determination—though it was not easy—to declare
myself in a book, I could not have taken it, psychologically. I am sixty-two years old. . . . I
believe I have remained faithful to the outlook of Les modernes: lived experience and
meaning, as opposed to theory and structures.* This is what I'm leaving behind, since I have
no children. I have never experienced this lack as a tragedy. I've had moments of regret, I
may have told myself it was too bad not to have an heir, but the pneumocystis didn't change
anything. I must say, I've always felt very different from other homosexuals. My connection
with religion, with God, with my family [key and problematic], with marriage, with children, with social marginality, hardly resembled what I observe in homosexual society,
where in fact I spend very little time. This was probably silly, maybe inauthentic, but I've
never felt homosexual. Only the illness forces me to concede that I belong, essentially and
socially, to that category. I denied my specificity [not because I was ashamed but] because I
didn't have the desire to be "one of them." There was a skittishness in me about being part
of that community because I had no knack for it.

Of course, the more alone, the poorer, and the more anonymous you are, the harder it
is to deal with this curse [AIDS]. Social class, professional background, and material
means change the experience of AIDS a great deal. Also, I understand very well that some
may wish to remain anonymous, from the time they take the test to the time they become
ill. But I understand less well the embarrassment, the shame, of people who have little to
fear. Many of them will tell you they do not want to hurt their parents, to abruptly reveal
to them both their lifestyle and their misfortune. That is their absolute right, and I respect
it. I will never have peace of mind, either. Homosexuality is not solely about physical or
emotional contacts. It governs the whole structure of existence. No one can claim to be
happy living on the fringe. Very simply, you can sometimes take pleasure in it, and I think
I have sometimes felt that.

In France, the repercussions of this "confession"—Aron himself uses the
word—were great. The interview, first published in 1987, broadcast on Antenne 2
(as "Sida, après l'aveu" [AIDS, after the confession]) on June 21, 1988, and then republished in book form, was rebroadcast by Antenne 2 and published yet again by
Le Nouvel Observateur when Aron died, in August 1988. This media attention
played a key role, allowing the illness to be demystified at a time when Jean-Marie
Le Pen had latched onto it. Nevertheless, it is difficult to say whether this eminently symbolic announcement led to a beneficial change in the social climate surrounding people with AIDS, and it is even more difficult to evaluate whether it

changed individual attitudes and behavior in relation to AIDS. In a word, did Aron get people to use condoms?[9] The death of Rock Hudson, in 1985, played a major role in sounding the alarm, but the disease was still seen as American, distant, the illness of an actor who had come in a private jet to be treated. Unlike Hudson, Aron, in his elegant suit and tie and his starched collar, was stereotypically French and clearly identified as a homosexual. His tone—for example, the restraint he used in speaking of his initial reservations about the disease—probably played a role in making AIDS lose its American associations and become more common-place.[10] For French people, the disease, though it remained Parisian, now had a human face and bore a name. This is not insignificant.

Gai Pied Hebdo harshly criticized Aron for this interview, judging that the writer had not rid himself of his characteristic feelings of shame about being homosexual, and finding it deplorable that he had waited until he got the disease himself before making his confession.[11] This reaction shows an odd insensitivity to the remarkable courage of a sixty-two-year-old man who had spent his entire life keeping quiet, and who, between one day and the next, had agreed to be the embodiment of AIDS.

In August 1988, eight days after Aron's death, Guy Hocquenghem also died. The proximity of the dates invites comparison. Just before their deaths, the paths of these two men crossed a second time.

Hocquenghem, a leading FHAR figure, was the symbol of homosexual liberation in France and a rather flawed—but also tormented and already mythical—representative of homosexual denial in the face of AIDS.[12] When *Libération* devoted its front page to "the gay cancer," Hocquenghem, for the first time in his life, threw *Libé* into the trash, criticizing the newspaper for its hysterical alarmism about AIDS.

For a long time, Hocquenghem refused to be tested and reportedly learned he was HIV-positive only after he was already ill. He supposedly even refused for some time to be monitored medically, an extreme form that the denial sometimes took in the first years of the epidemic. As a result of his first run-ins with doctors, he had an unyielding bitterness toward them, which led him to write his novel *Eve*, an icy, sometimes fantastic diary of his months in the hospital. In this novel, genetic clones cross paths, and Hocquenghem alludes to AIDS without naming it, but with an astounding frankness and cruelty.[13] "You feel yourself being transformed into a thing, a mannequin, an eviscerated toy whose springs strike the explorer in the face because it is forced to submit to such explorations." Like a child seeking revenge, Hocquenghem dedicated this book, with its overtones of science fiction, to Willy Rozenbaum. The hero of *Eve* meets his doctor's "X-ray mania" with stoicism: "I am afraid of aggressive treatment; my body, my poor crucified body in pain, will ask for peace. 'Let me die in peace' is a Japanese prayer."

Might the hero of gay liberation have played a role in raising the consciousness of homosexuals by insisting on "warning" them or, like Aron, by making his own illness public? Hocquenghem did not believe so.

The American writer Edmund White recalls that he "quarreled" a great deal with Hocquenghem: "Even in 1985, even though he had gone to the United States, he still thought AIDS was a conspiracy invented by heterosexuals."[14] Others have given different explanations: for example, Laurent Joffrin asserts, "Admitting he had AIDS would have been emphatically conferring on it the status of a shameful disease, and at the same time denying twenty years of battles for recognition of homosexuals."[15] René Schérer, a lifelong friend of Hocquenghem, has another interpretation:

Guy thought that it was just another illness, and that you could recover from it. He did not want to accept, or did not believe, that his words could have a real influence on the behavior of other homosexuals. He was slightly embarrassed by Aron's article: he found "Mon sida" a strange way of embracing a misfortune coming from the outside—as if it were his own, as if he were boasting about it. In fact, he disliked the "confessional" tone in general, and in that respect he was in agreement with Foucault. It was a completely different matter to speak of his homosexuality in a context of provocation and collective struggle. But talking about "his" AIDS did not seem likely to excite anything but an unhealthy curiosity and, in the end, pity.

Finally, his friend Roland Surzur explains in the preface to a posthumous work by Hocquenghem:

Certain people, specifically those in what we are accustomed to call the homosexual community, have been surprised by the fact that Guy Hocquenghem did not publicly acknowledge his illness. Had he taken advantage of whatever notoriety he might have had, the public at large might have put a face and a name to AIDS, a disease that was still rather misunderstood in 1986–87. . . . There was no "confession" from him simply because he wished to live his remaining years in peace and quiet. He did not see himself as a role model for what he certainly did not consider a cause. For him, it was a strictly private matter. He feared the media frenzy that would have constantly surrounded him, as happened to Jean-Paul Aron during the same period and, later, to Hervé Guibert.[16]

Despite these efforts at exoneration, the history of the first ten years of struggle against AIDS in France may serve to contradict Hocquenghem's view: Is it possible that AIDS was precisely and indisputably a cause, and that it was homosexuality that became a simple question of private life?

Hocquenghem's silence can be interpreted harshly or in militant terms according to whether it is considered an indication of great social irresponsibility, of incomprehension at the end of a path that AIDS came to negate, or, on the contrary, as a rare example of serenity based on his capacity to distance himself, a capacity acquired through twenty years of militancy. His assessment of the exact importance of what he called "Rozenbaum's disease" for the history of homosexuals will probably remain as mysterious as it is debatable. And to understand his denial, we probably must link it to his notion of dark homosexuality, the drifting that he championed and that led him to celebrate Pasolini's death in exalted tones.

The curly-headed imp who arrived one fine day in 1971 will remain the principal theorist of the "new homosexual world," which he played a key role in founding, and from which, as an ascetic who had found peace of mind, he was taken away in the midst of the storm.

↩

In discos, the music became wooden. New homosexual fashions—repetitive house music and convulsive techno-pop—replaced the dance funk and disco fever of the early 1970s. Men danced bare-chested on immense floors while drag queens, flamboyant transvestites with silicone breasts, set the tone. Beyond the commercial exploitation of the AIDS phenomenon (compilations, films, press offices), there were probably both too much derision and too many sequins in the drag queens' fashions for these not to have been a reaction to AIDS. Men high on ecstasy, crystal meth, and K, combined with acid and crack, played at being robots and tried to pick up the beat.[17] Gays now needed "love pills." Fog machines invaded the dance floor; homosexuals played at being epileptic dancers and drug addicts.

House music, popularized in France in 1987 by Didier Lestrade, music reporter for *Gai Pied* and *Libération*, and brought to gay clubs by Laurent Garnier, a deejay, began to spread in 1989. Then, in the early 1990s, Fréquence Gaie, the homosexual community's radio station, made house music its regular format, simultaneously increasing its audience tenfold.[18] "House music and ecstasy appeared at a time when the homosexual community was attacked full force by AIDS: this is no coincidence," Lestrade explains:

House music liberated gays who were alienated by illness and who were going to clubs to let off steam. The lyrics of this music linked the disease to the liberation of American blacks and the rights of queers in a society that denied their presence. The music paid tribute to the dead. In the same way, ecstasy replaced cocaine, the drug of competition and of the 1970s. Ecstasy put you in touch with the world, made you talk to other people; it's the perfect communal drug for suffering queers.

Divisions among groups became more entrenched in the 1980s; sexual identities became fixed, and this led to all-out war. Consider the words of Maurice McGrath, owner of the Marais bar Le Central: "We realized quite late, in about 1988–89, that something serious had happened. Gay nightlife was still very active in 1987. Everything collapsed in 1988, the customers came out less, the bar owners had to create happy hours to attract them with lower prices. It was then we understood that AIDS had moved into the neighborhood for good; since then, we've been waiting for the cloud to pass over and for the sun to come out again." Homosexuals became experts at safer sex. Some wore safety pins (the short-lived emblem of safer sex around the summer of 1986), and, shortly thereafter, many adopted the red ribbon. Aides "buddies," incongruous volunteers in 1984, became familiar figures. Disc jockeys became the notorious "Deejays Against AIDS" at Fréquence Gaie. "One morning," Didier Lestrade explains, "we woke up to the realization that psychedelic socks and gaudy Lycra shorts might not be the ideal outfit for visiting a friend in the hospital."[19]

We should not exaggerate. The epidemic's consequences for lifestyles were slow to appear and are still difficult to measure. The only certainty is that the best years of gay nightlife ended in the 1980s, between the deaths of Fabrice Emaer and David Girard. The carefree times were over.

⤙

The illness did not spread uniformly within the homosexual population. As in an electrical circuit, the virus was transmitted from one group to the next through individuals serving as relay points.[20] It appears to have first affected people in the most sexually active group, those between the ages of twenty-five and forty-five, spreading within the limited circle of regular visitors to places for brief sexual encounters, such as the baths and back rooms, and then gradually infecting occasional visitors.[21] Paris and, later, the vacation spots served as "switch points." AIDS got its start among fairly specific socioprofessional groups: intellectuals who traveled abroad, employees in communications, art, and theater, and then personal-service staff (in hotels, restaurants, bars, cafés, and hair salons), men in the liberal professions, and, finally, senior executives. Only after 1986 did significant numbers of working-class homosexuals turn up in the statistics. There was also a strong urban concentration, with the Parisian region alone accounting for 90 percent of cases until 1983, 68 percent in 1987, and still 47 percent in 1995. After the disease had struck the Parisian middle classes, in 1987 it moved on to six regions of France: it was strong in the Provence–Alps–Riviera region, then in the Rhône–Alps, the Midi–Pyrénées and Aquitaine region, and, finally, in Languedoc–Roussillon and Alsace.[22] Gradually, it hit homosexuals living in cities of fewer than 20,000 inhabitants, and then those living in midsize cities in the provinces and on the outskirts of Paris.

Since the beginning of the epidemic, homosexuals have represented the majority of the cases recorded in France: an absolute majority in 1988 (between 52 and 66 percent), and a relative majority after that (between 45 and 49 percent). Even this gradual drop is only a reflection of the more rapid increase in the number of cases in other transmission groups. The last surveys of the *Bulletin Épidémiologique Hebdomadaire* show that, of the 37,000 total cases of AIDS recorded on June 30, 1995, 46.5 percent (17,200) were homosexuals. Given the problem of underreporting, this figure may be closer to 20,000 homosexuals.[23]

LIVING WITH THE DISEASE

Homosexuals learned to make the presence of AIDS an element of their daily lives. The ordeal of being tested, a common experience, is one of the rituals of the new gay life: one day, everyone becomes Agnès Varda's protagonist in *Cleo from 5 to 7* (1962), who awaits the results of her biopsy. The free and anonymous screening center, where everyone looks for signs of homosexuality in the other people present; the delay before learning the results of the test; the moment the "verdict" comes in—these are so many elements of the new homosexual fate. For those who are "negative," there is an immediate and disturbing return to indifference; life resumes its course, as before, with its tragic, pesky little problems, even though everything might have been turned upside down.

Among those who find they are HIV-positive, once the brutality of the announcement has registered, some say, "I'm a different person," as if they have radically changed identities. "My time is no longer the same, my body is no longer the same, my body is a little unfamiliar to me, my relation to others is no longer the same; my emotional and sexual relationships and my relationship with my parents have changed."[24] This sort of reaction has been observed frequently at conferences held for people living with HIV. One patient, Michel Pelegrin, declared (attracting criticism from other patients), "I am going to say a monstrous thing: I am very lucky. In the end, this illness is the best thing that ever happened to me. It's strange; it's bizarre to say so, but I wouldn't change places with anyone."[25]

Michel Cressole, a former Gazoline from the FHAR, said a few months before his death, "Of our group of friends in the 1970s, Copi was the first to get sick, the first to die, and then it was Guy Hocquenghem's turn. Gradually, the 1980s became a real nightmare. Now it's my turn. AIDS is the culmination of my life."

For those who are HIV-positive, a new life seems to be beginning, sometimes marked by a double secret: the secret of AIDS and the secret of homosexuality. In some cases, the person who has been diagnosed chooses a "period of silence," becomes a stranger to his family and friends, none of whom know anything about the major aspects of his life.

Nevertheless, it is helpful to announce to loved ones that one is HIV-positive, since, as seemingly everyone affected by it claims, it is important to "talk about" one's illness. Moving beyond this silence, which so closely resembles the experience of the "unspoken" in homosexuality, an individual often chooses to confide in an extremely limited number of family members. He informs his lover, and then other homosexual friends. In 1986, however, only half of a sample of asymptomatic patients with HIV had informed their regular partners.[26] Only later, after a silence that is rarely broken, do they inform, in an often immutable order, their heterosexual friends and then their sisters, their mothers, their employers, their brothers, and, finally, their fathers. When HIV develops into full-blown AIDS, this change often serves as the trigger for informing the family. After all, is it even possible to continue hiding such an illness when your bathroom is a pharmacy and your overnight bag is full of remedies? In 73 percent of cases, the mother is informed during the AIDS phase. It seems that she is both the first person you want to tell about the disease and, at the same time, the one you most want to spare such an announcement. The fact that fathers are almost always the last to be told is in itself emblematic of the tumultuous family romance, which is full of twists and turns, thanks to homosexuality, but never reaches a denouement.[27] A survey of interviewees confirms that in some cases parents find the disease easier to accept than a son's homosexuality. Such disconcerting reactions are also significant.

"I have the impression that I don't have interesting relationships except with people who know," writes Hervé Guibert. "I would have liked to have the strength, the crazy pride, the generosity as well, not to admit it to anyone, to let friendships live free as the air, carefree and eternal. But what can you do when you're exhausted and the illness even manages to threaten friendships?"[28]

Difficulties can also arise within groups of friends who have been informed. Jean-Noël Pancrazi, in Les quartiers d'hiver, has his hero say, "They leave my house with a clear conscience: they'll be able to tell one another how they handed me a glass or a spoon without hesitation. And yet they're a little uneasy: What if they've gone too far?"[29] As Michel Pelegrin recalls, sometimes a friend will blurt out, "You're boring us with your problems. You're no fun anymore!" "An illness is so boring," Gilles Barbedette confirms.

Having HIV is a completely new condition in the history of incurable illnesses simply because of the asymptomatic phase, which can last several years. All sick people are afflicted with a sense of vast destitution and the deep-seated feeling that a great injustice has been done them. AIDS, however, adds something more to that sense. "I am ashamed of the failure my life is coming to symbolize," Gilles Barbedette writes. The fact that the illness still has connotations of divine or even societal punishment, and that it affects individuals belonging to a small number of marginal groups, further increases the bewilderment of the people affected. "To die of an acronym only adds to the horror," notes Renaud Camus. "I'm paying tribute money to my homosexuality," one AIDS patient explained to his doctor, Christine Katlama. Hervé Guibert writes, "I'm a dung beetle on its back, struggling to get back on its feet. ... I feel like an elephant with its feet bound." For many, AIDS seems to confirm the fact that their lives are failures, and their homosexuality may appear to be the cause of their failure.

People with AIDS become trained in all the ins and outs of the illness: T4 lymphocytes, platelets, speed of ribosomal sedimentation, results of the Western blot. With full-blown AIDS, you start using a timer to tell you when to take AZT or ZVD, those little blue-and-white capsules. "What regimen are you on?" Cyril Collard is asked by his girlfriend's mother in Les nuits fauves [Savage nights]. "AZT," the hero replies. Results of blood analyses often nourish hope, which can easily vanish: "Four months ago," Michel Pelegrin recalls, "I suddenly lost my capital of a year of immunity. My partner began to cry. I told him he was right: it really was a terrible sorrow."

The inexorable illness is perceived as a collective and limitless tragedy. Each patient finds his own fate written on other people's faces. In groups of infected friends, each follows a path already taken by the one before him. Thus Pascal, after Luc's death, says, "I'm next on the list. That really sucks." "I see patients in the hospital at every stage of the disease," Hervé Guibert says. "You see yourself the way you were two years ago, and you're sitting next to somebody who's dying, as you soon will be in turn."[30] AIDS is "an illness of steps, a very long staircase [leading] surely to death, but in which each step [represents] an unparalleled learning experience; [it's] an illness that [gives] you time to die," Guibert writes. Guy Hocquenghem expressed his surprise when a priest came to the hospital ward: "I thought he was coming to bring me comfort. Not at all: he was a patient."

The disease has attacked networks of close friends, reminding some homosexuals of grandfathers who lost many friends during World War I. But this new accumulation of deaths usually takes place over several years, so that some homosexuals have done nothing since 1985 but visit the hospital and have not had time, as they say, to "mourn" those who have died. For these men, the appropriate comparison is not World War I but the Hundred Years' War.

↬

And so the need for love reappears, its intensity increased by worries about one's fate. Meeting emotional needs seems to be an essential quest and a new form of hope. The hero's mother in *Les nuits fauves* says to her son, "This virus may make you capable of loving." That emotional search is made difficult by a puzzling obstacle course; personal ads often include the term "HIV+." "I've always hated December the first, International AIDS Day" says Michel. "I didn't buy the newspaper that day. ... I forced myself to watch the broadcasts, I cried, I would have liked to be with somebody." Pancrazi's hero says, "Desires go away, too. I have only one left, and I know it cannot be satisfied: it is that someone will agree to lie beside me for a night, just one night." There are also many HIV-positive couples (sometimes one has infected the other) who have linked their fates "till death do us part." The relationship becomes a magical and painfully illusory refuge. When one of the partners dies, the survivor remains "without direction," to borrow Cocteau's words after Radiguet's death.[31]

Gille's Barbedette's posthumous words about the death of his partner, Jean Blancart, are a good illustration. These excerpts from a love story between two emblematic figures of the French homosexual movement, and then of the history of Aides, deserve to be quoted: "No one will ever know how lonely I have been. ... I think the major turning point in my life with Jean has been this return of loneliness. ... Jean was my whole family. ... Jean often told me: 'My poor Gilles! How alone you will be!'"

After Jean's death, Barbedette writes in his journal:

I will never be truly happy again, I know it. Too many deaths have marked my meager fate. ... I sometimes wonder: What if I did not have time to write this story? Who would know how extraordinary Jean was? ... Terrible nightmares last night about Jean. I was looking for him everywhere. I was waiting for him, and he didn't come. He was curled up next to me. . . . I have forgotten what a kiss was like. . . . Jean's been gone for almost six months, and I still can't manage to believe it. I still wonder how to live without him, without his presence. His ill presence, his bedridden body, were the best thing I had in the world, when I no longer had anything else. . . . How to love someone new when you love someone else too much? . . . In fact, I have recently begun to live like a widower. I am a widower. . . . I went to the cemetery to gather my thoughts in front of Jean's gravestone. . . . I am sure . . . he is protecting me, that he is overseeing my destiny and that he is thinking of me. And, in fact, this has a certain effect on my morale.[32]

The emotional relationship within "mismatched" couples, serologically speaking—within "mixed" marriages, to use an apt metaphor—seems even trickier. For some, the announcement that one partner is HIV-positive precipitates a breakup. For others, by contrast, it intensifies the relationship. "There are three of us in this relationship," Damien explains, "him, me, and the virus":

But it's hard to remain honest. We don't have the same spontaneity in our relationship. He wears religious medals out of superstition and has a frenetic pace I can't keep up with. He lives beyond his means, orders fine wines in restaurants, the most expensive extras. Sometimes I have the impression he's testing me by switching our drinking glasses, even though I know for a fact I'm not running any risk. He plays with my toothbrush, my razor. I don't know what to tell him; he thinks I'm selfish whenever I react. In our sexual relationship, he's less spontaneous than before. I'm afraid the condom will break: it's so stupid, like a blind spot in the relationship. Socially, he doesn't want to make the effort anymore. He wants to go for the essential, rush through things. He's quick to quarrel with my friends. As one who has gone through difficult ordeals, he looks down from on high on those who haven't had to endure them. He harbors an everlasting hatred for one of his friends who wasn't sick and who committed suicide. He thinks when you're homosexual and HIV-negative, you don't have the right to commit suicide. And then, you know, it's so easy to make blunders with someone who's HIV-positive, so easy to hurt him. I often make slips like "You look good in black," and once I said *trépas* [death] instead of *prépas* [comprehensive exams]. At the same time, he has a romantic ideal I can't live up to. He's sometimes very quiet. Maybe I like him that way.[33]

HOMOSEXUALITY IN THE HOSPITAL

Homosexuals are generally dealing with this illness, with its "tinge of vespers and cold springtime," to use Pancrazi's expression, in the hospital. For years, people who were HIV-positive, "asymptomatic carriers," had to go to specialized wards for checkups, which might occur every six months, sometimes more often. Some waiting rooms thus became "annexes to gay bars." Doctors and nurses got to know the ways of homosexuality during periods of hospitalization. Thus they spoke of homosexuals with a new, unprecedented regard.

"For me, the first cases of 'gay cancer' were a curious anomaly," Professor Michel Kazatchkine explains. "It took me two years to realize the role that homosexuality played in the matter." Then, like other doctors, Kazatchkine visited homosexual establishments and began to read *Gai Pied*. At the hospital, like many other doctors and nurses, he began to write "homosexual" on the medical chart. "In the beginning," recalls Nadine Balcon, head nurse in the Rozenbaum ward of Rothschild Hospital, "I wanted to know whether they were transfusion patients, drug addicts, or homosexuals." But that lasted only until about 1986 or 1987. Today, neither Kazatchkine nor the nurses on AIDS wards ask patients how they were infected. "Kaza," as he is called, prefers to see his patients in the evening, at ten o'clock, and to talk to them about opera.

"With AIDS," Kazatchkine recalls,

we saw homosexual couples for the first time. The men come to office visits together. At first it was disconcerting. And then we saw how broken up one was when the other was dying. That made a big difference. We were not expecting that: lovers who screamed, who held each other in their arms. The staff was overwhelmed by how strong love could be between two men. These relationships totally contradicted the image of the disease, which is linked to multiple sexual partners. We realized homosexual love could be just as strong as heterosexual love.

All the doctors who were questioned confirmed their initial amazement at such scenes: "I saw loving relationships, extravagant demonstrations of love, with a power I rarely see among heterosexuals," Professor Christine Rouzioux explains. Very quickly, in all these wards on the front lines of the illness, nurses created discussion groups.

"We began to learn about homosexual practices," Balcon explains. "The patients themselves talked about them a great deal. It flustered you. They were very normal-looking. In six years on the ward, only once did I see a genuine queen in a veiled hat. . . . The men had frequently left their families very young, and reunions often occurred at the hospital, when they were thirty-five, with the boyfriend at the foot of the bed and the father taking off his cap and not understanding, even in an infectious ward, why there was a man crying in his son's room."

The hospital staff had to decode the nature and importance of the ties the patient had with other visitors. "We quickly saw tribes showing up," says Kazatchkine. "We got to know groups in which many members had been lovers. A self-limiting little society, they had all loved one other and broken up, and all with a great deal of solidarity when one of them lost his nerve." Some doctors also describe love affairs between two end-stage patients and talk with amusement about how men brazenly cruised the wards.

Kazatchkine continues, "We often saw a woman with these patients—the mother, the sister, a female friend." The mother, as all the interviews confirm, plays a central role in the hospital phase. "We often see a couple: the mother and her ill son," Christine Katlama remarks. "These are men of forty who suddenly become little ten-year-olds again, as soon as their mothers are there." "The mothers often have to make a choice between their husbands and their sons," Kazatchkine explains. "And at the hospital, we've seen mothers meet the lovers, sometimes learning of their sons' homosexuality at the same time. I have seen very painful fights: I was asked to serve as arbitrator, for example, during the last nights of one man in the end stage, to decide which one, the mother or the lover, had the legitimate right to sleep in his room."

Many doctors agree that their greatest surprise came from observing the silence that their patients had kept about their homosexuality. "Many parents found out at the hospital what was going on," Katlama notes, and Christine Rouzioux laments, "The family is sometimes completely absent. Homosexuals have to deal with horrendous intolerance from the family."

An amazing complicity often develops between professional caregivers and patients. "There are patients," says Katlama, "who tell me they have been living together for ten years." "I remember one patient," adds Françoise Baranne, "who fell in love with his doctor. He now lived only to talk to the intern, who had just arrived and was very handsome." Balcon describes the very special relationships that develop: "I've had nurses who got depressed because patients died soon after they had formed relationships of friendship or love with them. They defended the patients when the doctors got on their backs."

These varied comments suggest how the thread of homosexuality runs through individual lives, yet it is also true that the disease sometimes strikes those who have no network of homosexual friends. Many have said that they never heard of anyone with HIV, never heard anyone mention the disease. This allows us to understand all those homosexuals who declare that AIDS is not part of their collective memory.

DEATH AS PROPAGANDA

"And to top it all off, AIDS!" This succinct remark by the francophone Czech writer Vaclav Jamek may give some indication of how abruptly the illness made its appearance in the little world of writers and filmmakers.[34] AIDS, visible in the hospital and discernible in homosexual lifestyles, also became a theme for artists, who gradually recognized the extent of the hecatomb.

AIDS is consonant with the repertoire of the artist, already wounded and intrinsically tragic. The first to translate AIDS into literature was Dominique Fernandez, followed by Yves Navarre, Edmund White, Guy Hocquenghem, Renaud Camus, and Copi. They became what I am reluctant to call "homosexual writers," a reductionist and inexact label. In a way, these writers came together again to combat the disease, just as they had supported sexual liberation, and some came forward one last time to address the world under the "gay" rubric. Only Matthieu Galey, taken by multiple sclerosis, and Jean-Louis Bory, who had committed suicide, were missing from the parade. Other, younger writers—Alain-Emmanuel Dreuilhe, Christophe Bourdin, Vincent Borel—felt the need to publish a first novel with AIDS as the theme.[35]

For artists, AIDS was an illustration both of daily suffering and of extreme loneliness, but it was also the return of "early" death. The specters of Rimbaud, Radiguet, Büchner, Huguenin, and Crevel emerged between the lines. When existing forms of literature seemed too cramped to accommodate lived experience, a few writers were tempted to create a new literary style, as Hélène Cixous had done in *La ville parjure* [The faithless city]. This new ghetto quickly proved to be a dead end. Despair, in fact, was not enough. To borrow Genet's words, "Genius is despair overcome by rigor."

There is nothing positive about a tragedy, but one must nevertheless tell the history of this suffering. Take Alphonse Daudet's *La Doulou*, on his own syphilis; Thomas Mann's *The Magic Mountain*, on tuberculosis; Arthur Schnitzler's *Dying*; *La Dame aux camélias* [*Camille*], by Alexandre Dumas *fils*; Zweig's *Beware of Pity*. The writer is face to face with his reader, the filmmaker with his viewer. He translates the reality that he lives every day with his "brothers," who are experiencing the same thing in a nearby hospital. All these stories complement one another. There is, as it were, a shared unity of place (the French hospitals of La Pitié, Rothschild, Broussais, Claude-Bernard). The heroes are also sometimes the same— Michel Foucault, who appears in the works of Hervé Guibert, Gilles Barbedette, Jean-Paul Aron, and René de Ceccatty; or Dominique Bagouet, to whom both François Raffinot and Michel Kelemenis pay tribute.

All the same, every writer, every choreographer, every artist remains who he is, with his own style, his own way of doing things. To take one example among others, AIDS was introduced into Copi's dramatic writings in 1988, with *Une visite inopportune*. With sublime humor, Copi integrated AIDS into his universe, and the disease did not blot out the landscape of mass murders, transsexualism, and the Argentinian tango. "I have AIDS," Copi told Facundo Bo, one of his favorite actors. "I pick up on all the fashions." A few months later, he confided to a flabbergasted Jorge Lavelli, "You know, I was very sick with AIDS. Now I'm okay. I'm cured." *Une visite inopportune* was part of the tonic (sometimes macabre) humor that Copi used to "amuse" himself with the illness. The hospital room becomes a burlesque theater, where various characters cross paths in front of the dying hero: the actor, abandoned by his public; a former lover, who has bought the patient a mausoleum at Père-Lachaise, between Oscar Wilde and Montherlant, and shows him aerial photos of the construction already under way; a nurse, hysterical because the patient has told her off; a doctor with whom the patient plots and schemes; a diva in high heels who yells, "What a sublime illness! What an apotheosis . . . and what a fate for a widow!"

As for film, AIDS appeared in *Encore* [*Once More*], by Paul Vecchiali (1987), who idealized the illness as a life choice. In that film, an actor, Louis, declares, "AIDS is life!" There is also Norman René's *Longtime Companion* (1990), whose title is borrowed from the discreet phrase used in American obituaries to designate the partner in a homosexual couple. Other films met with varied fates: François

Margolin's rather eye-catching *Mensonge* [The lie] (1992) was a commercial failure; Jonathan Demme's *Philadelphia* (1994) was a turning point and managed to become a mainstream film.[36] Above all, however, it was Cyril Collard's *Les nuits fauves* that became a true social phenomenon. The success of the film was ensured by a love scene, as brutal as it was unprecedented, between Cyril Collard (Jean) and Romane Rohringer (Laura).

"What's the matter?" Laura asks.

"You know," Jean answers, "I've been with quite a few men. Not always choirboys. Maybe the two of us should be careful."

"Careful about what?"

"I was tested for AIDS. I'm HIV-positive."

Laura steps back. "You knew it the first time we made love?"

"Yes."

"And you didn't say anything! You knew it and didn't say anything! How can that be? How could you do that and not tell me anything? Nothing! That's monstrous! You're a monster!"

Collard, who died on March 5, 1993, received four César awards on March 8 for his film. François Mitterrand declared him a "youth hero." A total of 2.8 million French filmgoers saw *Les nuits fauves* between the time the film was released (October 21, 1992) and the summer of 1993. Here, at its most basic, is the "mystery" of Collard, and the film's success is unprecedented, whatever one's opinion of it may be.

    ↬

AIDS changed the views of writers and artists who earlier had written about or filmed their homosexual love affairs. This evolution was significant. AIDS brought a new dimension to the history of homosexual literature, complementing the silence-breaking works of Proust, Gide, and Cocteau, the confessional writings of Fernandez and Navarre, and the body of work celebrating recently acquired pleasures (Camus, White). Although there was no debate in France, as there was in the United States, about the appropriateness of continuing to describe pre-AIDS gay lifestyles, at the end of the 1980s it was no longer possible to write a book like *Tricks* or make a film like *L'homme blessé*. Patrice Chéreau explains, "*L'homme blessé* is a film I wouldn't make the same way today; it's a pre-AIDS film, a film impossible to make now. Now I wouldn't film the Gare du Nord john. That has become impossible."

People who write or dance are people who suffer, directly or indirectly. Whatever the level of their talent, they bow to the same necessity. With the weapons of art, they may believe they can withstand the virus—at least for a moment. Still, the writer's sources are varied and mysterious: illness is a theme, but inspiration can also come from the experience of exclusion, solitude, the suffering produced by illness. Every writer and every artist integrated the "AIDS theme" into his own world, "used" it and made it a character or a metaphor—not a backdrop. This capacity for distance (for transcendence), not the reductive, hypothetical, and probably erroneous label "AIDS art," is what defines the quality of a work.[37] Beyond this (dubious) new genre, the novels, films, and shows about AIDS, proliferating at the same rate as the number of cases in the *Bulletin Epidémiologique Hebdomadaire*, serve primarily to introduce an essential social phenomenon of our time into the realm of art:

Suddenly, because my death was imminent, I was seized with the desire to write all the books possible, all the books I had not yet written, even at the risk of writing them badly—a funny, nasty book, then a philosophical book—and to devour these books almost simultaneously in the little time left me, to devour time with them, voraciously, and to write not simply the books of my anticipated maturity but also, as if shooting arrows, the slow-ripened books of my old age.[38]

Hervé Guibert became the most famous of the writers who chose AIDS as a theme. When he moved to *Apostrophes*, he was promoted to spokesperson for the illness, and his death at thirty-six, on December 27, 1991, made him its standard bearer.

The precocious Guibert had thrown himself into literature, photography, and journalism in such a rush and with such frenzy that some feared he was just another dabbler. With *To the Friend Who Did Not Save My Life* and then *Le protocole compassionnel* [*The Compassion Protocol*], a stark record of final despair, the reason for this ardor became clear: Guibert had worked himself to death as if through prescience, to foil the designs of the death lying in wait for him. "Guibert always gave the impression he knew his death was near," his friend Agathe Gaillard says. "He tried to put that day off through the vitality and abundance of his artistic creations. Probably, unconsciously, he accepted premature death and wanted to be its master. He 'chose' the illness and the death of his generation. A slow death, which he could make a subject of his writing."

Guibert was not a gay militant. He always refused to write for *Gai Pied*, even after he had fully acknowledged his homosexuality. "Deep down, I do not feel homosexual," Guibert explained. "Rather, I'm a completely heterosexual homosexual. I dream of conquering the missing part of myself."[39] Yet his writings were marked by persistent, often acute, homosexual preoccupations. Such themes as child love, pornography, and sadism surfaced. In late adolescence, Guibert was already writing stories in which his heroes, still children, devoted themselves to rather "curious" occupations. *La Mort propagande* [Death as propaganda], in 1977—with its amazingly premonitory title, which would be the front-page headline of *Libération* the day Guibert died—is an erotic book in which acts of love turn criminal, a kind of "magnificent bordello," written in an "anal-phallic" style.[40] In *Les aventures singulières* [The curious adventures], the reader rediscovers Guibert's particular interest in defecation—another recurrent theme. *Fou de Vincent* [Mad about Vincent] deals with passion in the raw and—an obligatory exercise for "the homosexual writer"—a gay man's desire for a straight man who wants nothing to do with him.

Before AIDS, Guibert recounted "fantasies," in the sense in which Genet used that term. A writer who feels no gratitude for his "paid" leave at the Villa Médicis is the setup for *Incognito*, just as a son's ingratitude toward his family provides the scenario for *Mes parents* [*My Parents*]. A novella, *Mauve le vierge* [Lavender the virgin], tells of an erotic pleasure confined to the creaking of joints. In the novella *Le baiser à Samuel* [Samuel's kiss], a john agrees to pay 5,000 lire simply to be kissed by an adolescent parked at a train station. In *Les chiens* [The dogs], Guibert writes a lewd, vivid sentence that sums up his universe: "Later, with every thrust, I crammed him deeper into her, and it was then, in the stream of our sperm, passing from me to him, up to his balls, and from him to her through spongy tissue, it was at that instant that she became pregnant."

Guibert recreated his own little world. It is composed of about fifteen characters, famous personalities as well as anonymous friends, engaged in a "war of insects."[41] All of them played a role in the real world of AIDS: Foucault and all Guibert's other characters, bearing transparent pseudonyms, reappear in *To the Friend Who Did Not Save My Life*, a novel of grand reunions and anticipated funerals. Irreverent meanness and exhibitionism permeate *My Parents*, and these aspects return in *To the Friend* and in *Cytomégalovirus, journal d'hospitalisation* [*Cytomegalovirus: A Hospitalization Diary*]. Sadomasochism was present in *Les chiens*; it becomes the guiding thread in *Mon valet et moi* [My valet and I]. And fantasies recur: a famous painter who must sign works he has not painted is at the core of *L'homme au chapeau rouge* [*The Man in the Red Hat*]; a wine cellar in which Guibert is imprisoned symbolizes AIDS in *The Compassion Protocol*.

Even though he sometimes relates the story of Foucault's death or the birth of Aides and describes Claude-Bernard Hospital transformed into a ghost town, we should have little faith in the authenticity of what the writer reports, even about his own illness. "Only false things happen to him," Foucault would have said.[42] Guibert the narrator, for example, his throat still numb from the anesthetic for a biopsy, calmly goes to eat oysters at La Coupole and cruises the waiter, a "handsome boy" (*The Man in the Red Hat*).

In many ways, the illness allowed Guibert to "fulfill himself," and the virus only confirmed the fact that life was tragic, on the whole, and nothing more. "I told myself we both had AIDS. That changed everything in an instant. . . . It paralyzed me and gave me wings at the same time, reduced my strength and increased it tenfold. I was afraid and inebriated, calm and crazy; perhaps I had finally achieved my goal."[43] His friend Patrice Chéreau confirms this approach: "At a certain point, and this is the scary thing, in a certain way Hervé found—what I'm saying is horrible—he found in the illness a little of the transcendence he was seeking."

This idealization of the illness, which, as we know, enjoyed great success (200,000 copies of *To the Friend* were sold) became a sort of bullfight for Guibert, with its beauty, its passes, the *faena* that characterizes it, and finally, the death-blow.[44] For Guibert, the illness was fulfillment, an anticipated, romantic death, which was completely inscribed within homosexual destiny, as Guy Hoc-quenghem had said of Pier Paolo Pasolini's murder.

Might AIDS give meaning to homosexuality? The attraction/repulsion that Guibert, like other homosexual writers and artists, implicitly felt for the illness soon exasperated the new AIDS militants. In the homosexual ruins of the late 1980s, in the face of a series of deaths, this idealized discourse about the illness seemed intolerable to patients who found in such a quest little to please them, even in fiction. These militants rejected the individual epic because they were all too conscious of the collective torment they were enduring, and they perceived the hecatomb not as a fatality that could be idealized but as a broadly planned opera-tion, one that had been fomented by a whole series of protagonists, if not collabo-rators, of routine decisions, if not sins. Jean-Paul Aron's "Mon sida," Guibert's "thanks to the illness, I have finally recovered the arms of a child," and Collard's cult of the self gave way to a new militancy. Militants stood up to denounce those responsible for the hecatomb. AIDS, they said, is no more consonant with a ho-mosexual destiny than are AZT or Rozenbaum's hospital ward.

In 1989, "the year of DDI," the new militants—opposing Guibert but especially the epidemic's abettors—rediscovered the political approach. The biological sub-ject no longer sought heroism and literary fulfillment, but rather survival.

PART IV

The Era of Contradictions (1989-96)

14

ACT UP: The History of a Political Movement

AIDS: If you liked the first decade, you'll love the second.
—Slogan of ACT UP–Paris

He looks like an Old Testament prophet. Bearded and Jewish, he is, like Woody Allen, always between two appointments with his psychoanalyst. He is middle-class, rumored to be rich—maybe because he went to Yale. He is homosexual, supposedly sentimental and moody—maybe because, like many people, he is entangled in a frantic quest for true love, which he seems never to find. In 1981, Larry Kramer, Jewish and stereotypically American, was forty-five years old.

Kramer's life history was atypical, a long process of coming out: first guilt-ridden and tormented by his homosexuality, he chose clarity in 1978 when he published a novel called *Faggots.*[1] With new life breathed into him by homosexuality, Kramer painted a rather humorous portrait of the New York gay life, a teeming fresco peopled with Rastignacs newly arrived from the Midwest. But he acquired a sulfurous reputation by denouncing, in his prophetic novel, promiscuity, back rooms, and the obsession with sex. Because he criticized what was at the time the very essence of the homosexual lifestyle, Kramer was viciously taken to task in 1978 by gay activists, who denounced his persistent guilt, "gay homophobia," self-loathing, hidden moralizing, and proselytizing hatred of sex. A missed opportunity.

↩

On August 11, 1981, just a few weeks after the first information about the "gay cancer" had become public ("Rare Cancer Seen in 41 Homosexuals," *New York Times*, July 3, 1981), a group of New York gay friends including the writer Edmund White met in Kramer's living room. In January 1982, on the heels of that meeting and despite the lack of support from traditional gay leaders, six of them created the first American AIDS group, which became Gay Men's Health Crisis (GMHC). "Larry Kramer immediately had a realistic view of the epidemic and of the scope of the tragedy," White recalls. The organization quickly received the support of such personalities as the painters David Hockney and Andy Warhol and the writer Susan Sontag. The task at the time was to respond to the difficulties of the first people with AIDS in a country without a universal social safety net, even though the epidemic was still affecting only "yuppies," for the most part. The homosexual male was muscular, healthy, athletic; he worshiped virility and belonged to a private gym. It was said that he was buying the American dream.

The United States, to an excessive degree, is a country where it is possible to be promoted to full professor at almost any university because you are gay and, for the same reason, to get your face bashed in on almost any street. Reactions at the start of the epidemic—radical and fanatic for certain homosexuals, conservative and marked by withdrawal for others—mirrored these paradoxes.[2] Two camps faced off from the beginning: those who feared stigmatizing themselves, who believed that the "gay cancer" did not exist in itself but was the result of circumstances, and that sexual freedom was more important than the fight against AIDS; and those, like Kramer, who wanted to impose morality on the gay lifestyle and close the baths and the back rooms in the interest of public health. A familiar opposition: freedom or death, on the one hand, prevention or death on the other. Kramer attacked the lack of awareness in homosexual newspapers, even adopting the line of some doctors who advised homosexuals to stop having sex completely. "In the entire history of homosexuality, we have never been so close to death and extinction," he wrote. "I am sick of guys who moan that giving up careless sex until this blows over is worse than death."[3]

Apart from Kramer and the pop singer Michael Callen, the writer Randy Shilts, a reporter for the *San Francisco Chronicle*, was the most famous representative of the camp that was critical of the gay community. In fact, Shilts denounced the inertia of the government, on the one hand, and, on the other, the complicity of gay establishments in the epidemic and the lack of perspicacity on the part of homosexual organizations. He asked the government to close the baths—a decision often made by big-city mayors at the request of homosexual doctors and some gay leaders. In 1987, he published the ironically titled *And the Band Played On*, a chronological account of the epidemic. He died of AIDS on February 17, 1994.

All the same, Kramer's and Shilts's ideas were far from unanimously shared within GMHC, and it took a relatively long time for homosexual groups to rally behind prevention. The evolution was obvious: in 1982, Gay Pride Day was still a carefree carnival; in 1984, it was already a symbolic parade of coffins. That year, the principal gay newspaper, *The Advocate*, decided to suspend its personals. The "total body" was set aside: the body had betrayed. The model of the yuppie homosexual went up in smoke.

During the Reagan years, given the peculiarities of the social welfare system in the United States, GMHC rapidly became an immense network of solidarity. It provided the sick with masseurs and male nurses; it arranged home visits and psychological support. It invented the "buddy system," pairing a healthy homosexual with an AIDS patient.

About 1985, the illness became a national problem in the United States (in

France, this occurred in about 1987 or 1988). As the virus spread into the heterosexual population, the government became more vigilant in the fight against
AIDS. The New York GMHC and the Shanti Project—an organization providing
similar services in San Francisco—began to receive government aid, at least indirectly. Their members became experts in the fight against AIDS, which, now that it
was institutionalized, became less militant. In the 1990s, GMHC owned a six-story
building on Twentieth Avenue and had 130 salaried employees, 1,800 volunteers,
and a budget of over $15 million.

In 1985, Kramer, who discovered he was himself HIV-positive, published *The
Normal Heart*, a play about the epidemic, and then *Reports from the Holocaust*, in
which he dared to compare the immobility of American officials to the complicity
that had made Jewish genocide possible. Claiming to draw on the ideas of Hannah
Arendt and Primo Levi, Kramer developed the comparison at length. For him, a
holocaust is not simply a question of numbers; it is also related to society's indifference to death. "AIDS is an intentional genocide on the part of our government,"
he claimed. "Gays, like Jews, sometimes give the impression they are going to the
gas chambers without reacting or fighting back."[4] Kramer, amazingly, expressed
regret that gays had not planted bombs or formed terrorist organizations the way
Jews had done. According to him, such acts had played a role in the creation of Is-
rael. "They killed and shot people. Gays will never have that," he sighed.[5]

On the basis of this logic, with 20,000 Americans already dead of AIDS,
Kramer hoped for a return to radical grassroots militancy. On March 8, 1987, he
created the AIDS Coalition to Unleash Power, known by the acronym ACT UP.
The organization adopted the slogan "AIDS is our holocaust"; it chose the pink
triangle as its emblem, but, symbolically, inverted it so that the tip pointed up-
ward, like a weapon that has been turned upside down. An openly homosexual organization, ACT UP chose provocation, as indicated in such slogans as "The government has blood on its hands." "ACT UP is a rude, nasty, irritating organization,
like the virus that is killing us," wrote Kramer, who called for civil disobedience at a
time when individuals with HIV were being turned away at U.S. borders: "George
Bush, you're a murderer!"[6]

In spite of this aggressive stance toward the government, Kramer relentlessly
continued to look critically at gays who were oblivious to the emergency and at
those who, by contrast, had "settled into" the fight against AIDS, making a brilliant
career of it. He condemned the bureaucracy, which had misled the "overly polite"
GMHC. Hence what was original about Kramer and ACT UP–New York was primarily a spirit of self-criticism and the capacity to protect gays against their own
community.

In conjunction with ACT UP, American homosexuals invented the practice of
"outing," publicly revealing the homosexuality or HIV status of a person reputed
to be a "closet queen" or a conservative.[7] The gay journalist Michelangelo Signorile
was the inventor of outing: he revealed the homosexuality of a very rich, very influ-

ential leader on the American right. The spokesperson for the secretary of defense was also outed, shortly before the debate on discrimination against homosexuals in the military got under way. Outing flourished and became widespread: posters with photographs of politicians or show business figures, boasting the words AB-SOLUTELY QUEER, covered the walls of some cities. This was a way to announce that queers were everywhere.

In the late 1980s, following an approach similar to that of ACT UP, American gay activists had chosen to call themselves "queer," appropriating an insult hurled at them by heterosexuals. In late 1990, queer groups gathered informally throughout the country, forming Queer Nation. The activists of Queer Nation adopted outing and provocation; for example, they organized "kiss-ins" (reminiscent of sit-ins) during which gays and lesbians kissed publicly.

Like Stonewall, which had made possible the birth of the FHAR, these developments, characteristic of the American homosexual groups of the 1980s, necessarily crossed the Atlantic. More than ever, America exerted a magnetic force over gay movements abroad, exporting its particular forms of protest. The shape of the epidemic at the turn of the 1980s can explain the emergence of ACT UP–New York; by contrast, it is the French *political* context of the years 1989–91 that accounts for the birth of ACT UP–Paris.

↵

At the end of an interview, the writer and journalist Naim Attalah noted that in English-speaking countries most men prefer the company of other men, to which his subject replied:

Yes, but most of those men are homosexual—maybe not the majority, but in the United States a full 25 percent of them are, and in England and Germany it's nearly the same thing. . . . I don't know whether that's a biological or cultural fact, but I remember noticing in London—and all girls make the same observation—that men don't look at you in the street. . . . Anglo-Saxons are not interested in women as women. . . . It's a problem of upbringing, and I consider that a kind of illness.

This interview, published by *The Observer* in England (June 16, 1991), was shocking, especially since the interview subject who made these remarks was Edith Cresson, the new French prime minister.

"What are they dragging out that old thing for?" In Matignon, Cresson was furious. In London—where, according to the old adage, the House of Commons can do anything "but change a man into a woman"—the British press, with the *Financial Times* in the lead, was hysterical, and the two countries were on the brink of a diplomatic incident. To redeem herself, Mitterrand's new appointee claimed she was the victim of a conspiracy, since the interview published in *The Observer* dated from 1987. The press office decided to deny everything: "The words attributed to the prime minister regarding homosexuality are false." Things ought to have remained at that point.

Nevertheless, after a general policy declaration failed before the National Assembly, after her remark that she was "in the dark" about the stock market, and after her comment that the Japanese worked "liked ants," Cresson stood in the crosshairs of newspaper editors. It was then that she agreed to give an interview to the American television network ABC. After a classic political overview, reporter Chris Wallace ended his interview by returning with feigned nonchalance to homosexuality. And Cresson stumbled a second time: "A man who is not interested in a woman, that seems bizarre to me. . . . I think [heterosexuality] is better. Homosexuality is different and marginal. It exists more in the Anglo-Saxon tradition than in the Latin tradition. Everyone knows that. It's a fact of civilization."

This time, ABC had the scoop and carefully sold this single sound bite to French stations.[8] The interview was broadcast in mid-summer. The outcry was so great that Mitterrand remonstrated with his prime minister. Even today, Cresson is astonished by all the fuss: "I gave my point of view because I was asked for it. It involved only myself. Someone must have really wanted to bludgeon me at all costs to turn my words into an antigay charge."[9]

The scandal, which may seem laughable, was, in its way, of a piece with homosexuals' disillusionment with the Socialists. In 1988, however, the presidential election had persuaded homosexual newspapers and organizations to campaign for Mitterrand's reelection, since the return of the left had, it seemed, brought new hope.[10] It is true that the Socialist Party had not abandoned a certain vote-rustling stance toward homosexuals and continued to evade criticism. Everyone still remembered Charles Pasqua's attempt to ban *Gai Pied* and Jean-Marie Le Pen's comments aimed at reviving the theme of moral decadence by exploiting doubts about the etiology of AIDS.

With a baffling sense of timing, *L'Express* ran this front-page headline on November 4, 1988: "AIDS: This Time, It's an Epidemic." That year, the Rocard government chose to come up with an overall plan to combat AIDS. This plan privileged the "exceptionality" of the illness and, for the first time, provided substantial funding. In late 1988, Claude Evin, the new minister of health, announced that new organizations were to be created. Following recommendations in the report that Professor Claude Got had submitted to him, he proposed a research agency, an ethics council, and, above all, a "publicity superagency," the Agence Française de Lutte contre le Sida, or AFLS [French agency to combat AIDS].

The program was favorably received, but it quickly deteriorated. Dominique Coudreau, the first director of the AFLS, resigned for a better-paying job; the agency became involved in "territorial battles" with AIDS organizations and embroiled in quarrels with the administrative office overseeing it (the General Office of Health). In April 1990, the prime minister's Service d'Information et de Diffusion, or SID [Information and distribution service], came out against a poster campaign promoting condoms, which had been planned for the subways in Paris, Marseilles, and Lyons: 72% OF FRENCH PEOPLE DECLARE THEY ARE IN LOVE. HOW

MANY PROVE IT? The unbelievable decision to kill the poster was made at the highest levels of the state, by SID director Jean-Louis Missika. "The Left As Censor" was the headline in the May 17, 1990, issue of *Gai Pied.*

Apart from this blunder, it is also amazing that Claude Evin did not propose that Rocard personally go to bat for the issue. Between 1988 and 1991, the prime minister—faithful, in a sense, to Rocardian logic—privileged technical matters concerning the epidemic (Claude Evin, Claude Got, the AFLS) and probably underestimated the political importance of the fight against AIDS.[11]

At Evin's request, however, Dominique Charvet, deputy director of the agency, launched a campaign targeting homosexuals, which soon flooded gay spots in Paris, and especially in the provinces, with slogans like THE MOST IMPORTANT THING ABOUT "SAFER SEX" IS THE WORD "SEX" and I LOVE MEN WHO LOVE MEN WHO LOVE SAFER SEX. These messages were accompanied by pamphlets that took a resolutely direct approach (the collection titled "Hommes entre eux" [Men among themselves]) and were complemented by prevention messages in the personals of specialized newspapers. Questioned today, Charvet remembers this era:

I had the feeling, the intuition, that when a group is affected by an epidemic, there is not only the medical or physiological cause but also the issue of social recognition or nonrecognition. As with drug addicts, the fact that homosexuals were ill could be partly explained by the fact that they were not citizens. It seemed immediately obvious to me that if we wanted to combat AIDS, homosexuality had to be part of common law. HIV also attacks the state of governance in a society.

It is clear, however, that the issue of AIDS continued to cause upheaval in the government, particularly among Socialists. By 1988, it had already cost Léon Schwartzenberg his job in the short-lived ministry because he proposed decriminalizing drugs—he did not say which ones—and making screening tests universal. Created eight years after the first AIDS cases appeared in France, the agency was never able to make up for its late start. Dominique Charvet resigned in 1991; of his two successors at the head of the AFLS, one (Patrick Matet) made numerous blunders, and the other (Jean de Savigny) made numerous errors. At the same time, Ministers of Health Bruno Durieux and Bernard Kouchner, lacking in courage by comparison with Michèle Barzach or even Claude Evin, with his wide-ranging technical procedures, inexplicably lost interest in the fight against AIDS.[12]

To complete the picture, in May 1992 Pierre Bérégovoy "personally" made the decision to ban a television campaign by the AFLS, whose "clever" slogan, judged "pointlessly shocking," was supposed to be "Contraception, so you'll think only of love."[13] This accumulation of new delays, errors, shredded pamphlets, and misleading slogans has assumed an added dimension in light of the revelations surrounding the contaminated-blood scandal, which erupted in 1991–92. There was total disillusionment with the Socialists, who proved incapable in their second term, as in their first, of assessing the epidemic's scope. The critical stage in the fight against AIDS in France had arrived.

"AIDS IS DISCO"

In 1989, flying back to France from the United States, where he had spent as much time as he could in recent years, Didier Lestrade wondered whether it might be a good time to create an ACT UP organization in Paris. Lestrade was a reporter for *Gai Pied Hebdo* and *Libération*, where he wrote a column on dance music, and he was also a friend of the English singer Jimmy Somerville. He marveled at American homosexual life, with its chosen ghettos and communitarian political culture, and even more at the strong-arm tactics of ACT UP–New York:[14] "I went through the 1980s like the queers of that time: going out, having fun, cruising, fucking, not thinking. We had an irrational side when it came to the disease. Until very late, I was looking the other way." Lestrade was infected with HIV at a late date—in early 1987, when, as a contributor to *Gai Pied*, he was perfectly well informed of the risks. He awaited the signal from his friends to launch the ACT UP venture. He was thirty years old.

Pascal Loubet, a writer for *Rock & Folk*, and Luc Coulavin, a reporter with whom Lestrade shared his office at *Gai Pied*, were interested in the project and agreed to help him import the slogans, "philosophy," and methods of ACT UP to France. The word "import" is no exaggeration: from New York Lestrade ordered fifteen T-shirts printed with the pink triangle and the slogan "silence = death." He and a few friends wore these shirts during the Gay Pride parade of June 1989. The first action of the group stunningly combined its two main lines of descent: the American influence, and the homosexual nature of the movement.

After that, the organization was launched, and it was registered at Paris police headquarters on July 26, 1989. "ACT UP was created for the media by journalists, in an agitprop vein," Lestrade confirms. "Use the media, sell them events lock, stock, and barrel."[15] Militants picketed in front of the National Assembly, manipulating powerful images and words. Their signs were translated into French: "silence = mort" and "action = vie." On December 1, 1989, they demonstrated against the church's opposition to condoms, making catcalls and shouting "Condoms are life, but the church forbids them!" They hung a banner reading OUI À LA CAPOTE ("Yes to rubbers") between the towers of the Cathedral of Notre-Dame de Paris.[16] Later (May 28, 1990) the prime minister's Service d'Information et de Diffusion was "zapped" because it had censored the AFLS subway campaign. The city of Paris was hit (June 16, 1990) for its "AIDS plan," which was judged too timid. The Senate was zapped (May 6, 1991) for trying to make it a crime to transmit the virus and for reinstating homosexuality as a criminal offense.

In many ways, the scenario set in motion and the methods used were similar: speed, technology, media visibility, brief and explosive slogans, all accompanied by catcalls, the throwing of blood, and pictures of cadavers. ACT UP–Paris's modes of operation were largely borrowed from ACT UP–New York. "Zaps" (rapid actions against a person, a media outlet, or an organization), fax or phone zaps (the purpose of which was to flood an administrative office's phone lines) die-ins (where militants simulated death by lying silently on the ground), and "political funerals" were all methods characteristic of ACT UP, whose "general philosophy," according to the militants, was based on nonviolence.

The organization used slogans that were Manichean ("AIDS: Mitterrand is guilty," "Got HIV? France prefers you dead"), political ("Infected under Mitterrand, dead under Chirac"), oddly demanding ("Give me T cells, Balladur!") [a reference to Prime Minister Edouard Balladur], provocative and vulgar ("Proud to exist, proud to fist"), and even morbid (at Père-Lachaise Cemetery, militants spray-painted "Look, the state is investing in your future!" or shouted "Make way, we're coming!").[17] The watchwords were often amusing, vaguely Dadaist ("Eat apples to fight AIDS!"), or bordering on self-ridicule ("AIDS is disco"). They could also be sentimental, as in this moving slogan on Gay Pride Day 1992: I WANT YOU TO LIVE!

On October 3, 1990, Mitterrand was zapped by ACT UP in front of his home on rue de Bièvre. The president of the republic was a favorite target of the organization, which criticized him for his silence. "Your country is no longer our country, Mr. President. You have excluded us from it," ACT UP declared in one of the many open letters to the president, to which he never replied. Certain militants went so far as to propose the slogan "Mitterrand, the silent AIDS," and on April 2, 1995, a poster asked ironically, 330,000 CASES OF HIV AND 1 OF PROSTATE CANCER: WHAT COULD BE BETTER? That day, an enormous black banner concluded a march against aids: GOOD-BYE, MITTERRAND.

Beyond the debates and the tone adopted by ACT UP, the former president of the republic's silence on the AIDS issue remains incomprehensible. All in all, the disease, which appeared when he was elected in 1981 and increased tenfold during his two seven-year terms, was never the object of the slightest assessment on his part. Thus Mitterrand failed to address one of the key issues of the century's end, an issue encompassing both exclusion and discrimination. And there is nothing to explain this blunder.

On September 17, 1987, during Christine Ockrent's broadcast *Le monde en face*, President Mitterrand agreed to appear live for a dialogue with Jean-Paul Baggioni (future president of Aides–Paris–Ile de France), who was HIV-positive. In essence, the twelve-minute discussion turned out to be a monologue. The president simply took notes and made one or two remarks: "You have said the essential thing. No exclusion. Be aware." Even so, at the end of the interview, Mitterrand promised: "I will take up this problem [of HIV] very, very soon."

At the end of his second term, Mitterrand still had not kept his promise. Worse, invited on three different occasions by medical reporters from *Le Monde* to mention in interviews the various health and ethics problems raised by the AIDS epidemic, the president declined. An exasperated Ségolène Royal, one of his advisers at the Elysée Palace, finally replied to the reporter Jean-Yves Nau, "It is not up to the president to talk about AIDS."[18]

President Mitterrand did send a written message to *Gai Pied* in 1989, on the occasion of the paper's tenth anniversary:

Gai Pied, which today is celebrating its tenth anniversary, is a place of words first of all. I salute these past ten years. A courageous anniversary. One can never fight hard enough against taboos and scorn. There can never be enough information about a disease that is striking everyone, male and female, and your *community* more than anyone else. For all that, I salute your tenacity and your efforts.[19]

Apart from these rare words, how are we to understand Mitterrand's significant absence? One of his former advisers at the Elysée has a fairly convincing explanation:

There was, I will say, a delay in getting started. He never realized the importance of exclusion, of marginality, in the disease. Once that political mistake was made, it was too late to go back and try to catch the moving train. From that point on, if he had wanted to visit the offices of Aides in 1992 or 1993, he would have been greeted with tomatoes!

Even Laurent Fabius was astonished by this silence: "I could not explain why François Mitterrand did not express himself more. Was it embarrassment? Did he personally know or not know people around him who were infected with the disease? I don't know."

⤺

A hybrid movement of complex filiation, ACT UP borrowed some of its methods from the far left of the 1970s, its slogans from ACT UP–New York, its denunciation of homophobia from the homosexual movement, and, finally, its sense of urgency from Aides. ACT UP–Paris thus stands at the crossroads of this fourfold filiation—but, as usual, there are breaks as well as continuities between it and its predecessors. In fact, although ACT UP–Paris looked to the past for its inspiration—from the proletarian left to the FHAR, from the leftist dream to disillusionment with the Socialists, from Malcolm X to ACT UP–New York—it reshaped these influences into a new, resolutely modern form. Hence, from its birth, Lestrade's organization was a departure from its four predecessors.

From the traditional French far left, ACT UP borrowed its style of protest, its general meetings (renamed RHs, for *réunions hebdomadaires*, "weekly meetings"), its direct democracy, and even its anonymity (as had been the practice in the Mouvement de la Libération des Femmes, articles in the ACT UP newspaper were not signed). The humor and self-deprecation of ACT UP are also reminiscent of May '68 slogans; even then, the Ligue Communiste Révolutionnaire thought up the idea of pouring blood from slaughterhouses into the holy water at Notre-Dame. The profile of the ACT UP militants also resembles that of the protesters in leftist political movements: they were young, and many of them were college-educated,

urban, single, far-left, and atheist. Despite some earlier involvement in homosexual militancy, or, more rarely, in SOS Racisme, the ecology movements, and Sections Carrément Anti–Le Pen [Committees squarely against Le Pen], or SCALP,
most of the ACT UP militants had little or no militant past or history of political
activism. Students, teachers, and the unemployed predominated: the fight against
AIDS was probably their primary commitment. ACT UP also had a significant
number of women, lesbians among them. According to a recent study, 62 percent
of ACT UP members were homosexual (11 percent bisexual, 27 percent heterosexual), but 68 percent were HIV-negative (17 percent were HIV-positive, 4 percent
had full-blown AIDS, 9 percent did not know their HIV status, and 2 percent chose
not to respond).[20] Nevertheless, about sixty militants from ACT UP–Paris have
died since 1989.

Like its predecessors, which, under the leaden mantle of the Pompidou years,
had chosen provocation, ACT UP reintroduced a "capacity for indignation" that
had often been lacking in the France of Pierre Bérégovoy and Edouard Balladur.
Two postulates provided the organization's theoretical foundation: AIDS was a
war, and AIDS was a political disease ("Conquer AIDS: A question of political
will"). "Total war" was declared, and any means possible would be used to win it.
ACT UP militants joined campaigns against the Gulf War and in favor of legalized
drug use, and they headed the push to have condom dispensers installed in high
schools ("When I grow up, I'll be HIV-positive"; "Bayrou, minister of fate"). They
demanded that the Bois de Boulogne and the gay Minitel networks be reopened;
they formulated proposals for drug addicts, prisoners, and homeless people, and
they denounced Simone Veil's passivity when the government to which she belonged expelled foreigners with AIDS from France (the militants called the policy
"deportation").[21]

Because of this affinity with the golden days of leftism, many newspaper editors
who had been Trotskyists, Maoists, or Castroists had an immediate bias in favor of
ACT UP, which allowed them to recapture the spirit of their youth. Some journalists thought this new face on the far left radiated utopian dreams and the revolutionary spirit, at a time when the leftist government was in the midst of a grave
ideological crisis. "The emancipation of HIV-positive people will come from the
HIV-positive themselves," ACT UP seemed to be saying, plagiarizing Marx. Journalists approved of this "uprising of the sick," this noble anger. This may explain
why the discourse of ACT UP was received so sympathetically and why it resonated
so deeply in the media and in French society. In other words, ACT UP came at just
the right time.

Although ACT UP placed itself in the tradition of the far left, which it revived, it
also had plenty of novel elements, both in its organization and in the nature of its
struggles. ACT UP was an ultraorganized FHAR in the age of house music.[22] Although it adopted classic methods, such as phone trees that allowed it to organize
events at very short notice, the organization belonged to the 1980s and adopted its

technology, from fax machines to the many uses of the personal computer. In addition, for its normal operations, ACT UP adopted a complex organizational chart, with management levels (coordination committees, weekly meetings), several specialized vice presidencies (for lobbying, communication, and public action), and a number of technical committees. It also devised a rigid protocol for public meetings, which were run by aggressive "facilitators."[23] These debating methods, sometimes denounced as undemocratic despite the appearance of direct democracy, were the subject of internal disputes and sometimes led to resignations.[24]

In its discourse, ACT UP also introduced a change that would have been unthinkable on the far left of the 1970s: technology. With ACT UP, the sick "seized power" and stood up to doctors: the AIDS patient became a political actor. "We are the experts," proclaimed the militants who played a role in implementing treatment methods and putting medications on the market.[25] In January 1993, Parisian militants revealed that a laboratory was using a blood-pooling method in its antibody testing and forced the lab's temporary closure. Finally, ACT UP believed in the role of the state and became its permanent critic. That was enough to distinguish it from the many leftist camps of the 1970s and, above all, from the entire far-left fringe, which was under the sway of anarchism.[26] Thus ACT UP remains a profoundly original and hybrid movement, and its impenetrable, unclassifiable nature has contributed to its strength. "ACT UP is a group based on anger," explains one of its members, Mathieu Potte-Bonneville, a Foucauldian and student at the Ecole Normale:

This means constantly shifting the front lines, because otherwise anger becomes paralyzed, turning to indignation—"AIDS is not good"—or despair—"Nothing more can be done." It then loses its productivity and no longer disturbs anyone: indignation always inspires condescension, and despair, sympathy. This is why ACT UP, by constantly shifting its front lines, is always on the move.

ACT UP's relationship to the French homosexual movement is also marked by breaks and continuities. It seems obvious that ACT UP is a homosexual organization. Everything seems to confirm this: it first appeared on Gay Pride Day in 1989, and several of its founders were on the staff of *Gai Pied*; several of its members had a militant past (especially in the Mouvement des Adolescents Gais and in Gage—Association des Etudiants Gais), and its new headquarters is the old office of *Gai Pied*. In addition, ACT UP includes former members of the FHAR. "ACT UP is certainly the embryo of a queer community," confirms Michel Celse, its former vice president. "ACT UP is a very fragile organization, and it's always the issue of homosexuality that keeps us from breaking apart, that allows us to reestablish ACT UP." Cleews Vellay, who became ACT UP's second president, was a caricature of homosexual visibility. A former pastry chef, then the operator of a kennel, he was the emblematic figure of the organization until his death, on October 18, 1994. He made people call him *la présidente* [Madam President], used feminine forms of speech to refer to himself, called his partner, Philippe, "my husband," embraced the word *folle* [fairy], and appeared in drag at the Gay Pride parade. During Sidaction [AIDSaction] in April 1994, he was broadcast live on all the TV channels dissolving in tears in the arms of Line Renaud, all at once fragile and angelic, the child abandoned by his father.

But, once again, ACT UP's affinity with the French homosexual movement is combined with an essential discontinuity: "AIDS: Queers, lesbians, wake up!" proclaimed the ACT UP slogan at the Gay Pride parade in June 1991. In contrast to the discourse of gay militants who, in the early 1980s, tirelessly repeated that people "are talking too much about AIDS," ACT UP established a new, radically different discourse in the early 1990s: "You can never talk enough about AIDS!" In addition, ACT UP militants quickly distanced themselves from their elders. "When I created ACT UP," Lestrade explains, "I thought the people active in the homosexual movement, cultural leaders such as Renaud Camus, Michel Cressole, and Jean Le Bitoux, would join us. They didn't come. It's fascinating to note how many leaders of the gay movement refused to join ACT UP. I think the explanation is simple: those who were in leadership roles in the 1970s didn't do their job fighting AIDS in the 1980s." "We are very far from the internal debates of the gay community," explains Christophe Martet, current president of ACT UP. "As for the pains in the ass, the sourpusses in the queer movement, we have nothing to do with them because we are dealing with an emergency."

Some members of ACT UP disapprove of the idealized discourse of homosexual leaders and gay writers, and some criticize even Hervé Guibert. "I came to ACT UP to oppose Hervé Guibert," says Philippe Mangeot, former director of the organization:

For Guibert, AIDS is the best possible scenario for homosexuality—AIDS is programmed, it's an epiphany. Guibert's whole strategy was to give a meaning to AIDS. All of a sudden we were dealing with a purely sacrificial logic and, for the sacrifice to be complete, the victim had to consent. So there it was: Guibert was the consenting victim. That really disgusted me. Guibert told me that a good queer is a dead queer: for myself, I need other fictions.

Following the logic broadly inspired by Larry Kramer in the United States, ACT UP–Paris adopted a discourse intended to energize the homosexual ghetto and mobilize it in the fight against AIDS. This serves to remind us that the movement was an import. What breaks and continuities did this importation produce? The Paris movement, like ACT UP in the United States, used the comparison between AIDS and the Holocaust. It is symbolized in ACT UP's logo itself, the same in France as in the United States: a pink triangle, the same triangle—though inverted—that homosexual deportees wore in Nazi death camps.

ACT UP–Paris appropriated the stance of the emblematic victim of oppression, if not of repression, substituting the pink triangle for the yellow star. The French organization has intentionally used ideologically charged images: "In 1940, they watched the trains go by: today, they contemplate the hecatomb." Along these lines, ACT UP called for an "AIDS Nuremburg," compared Georgina Dufoix and Laurent Fabius to Eichmann, and placed coffins with the slogan FROM ONE GENO-CIDE TO ANOTHER at the Mémorial de la Déportation.[27] Lending credence to the comparison between AIDS and the Holocaust, an article in ACT UP's newspaper claimed, "If those who are doing nothing [in the fight against AIDS], or who are doing things poorly, are not (always) Nazis, they are at least collaborators." In the same paper, another article on homosexual visibility concludes, "They would rather see us dead than hear us alive. ... Will the day come when the only image they have of us will be ... thousands of HIV tests hanging from barbed wire and blown about by the winds that blow through the camps?"[28]

We should not overestimate the power of this discourse, which in its polemical exaggeration is probably too outlandish to have any effect on French society. It is likely that it was designed for internal use only, to strengthen the ranks of the emerging "homosexual community." The success of ACT UP–Paris might lead us to believe that the organization essentially has achieved its goal of mobilizing and valorizing the fight against AIDS within the homosexual movement.

Although Larry Kramer's influence is important whenever the Holocaust is at issue, in this area, too, a significant break has occurred. Apart from its discourse critical of the Reagan administration and U.S. politics, the true originality of ACT UP–New York was its capacity for self-criticism, its critical stance in relation to gay agencies and businesses. When the organization crossed the Atlantic, it lost this self-critical element. With respect to gay establishments refusing to practice prevention, one would seek in vain any action by ACT UP, any zap, any article in *Action*, any criticism. By erasing this fundamental principle set down by Kramer, ACT UP–Paris deprived itself of a valuable ethical justification. As Michael Pollak writes, it is now condemned to be seen as a structure that does not defend a "noble cause in the name of a common humanity" but rather the "particular interests of those who are already touched by the epidemic."[29] How can a group build the credibility needed to criticize the government's delays and silences if at the same time it dismisses the problem of financial scandals within certain gay organizations for which the fight against AIDS was a "cash cow," in the infamous words of one gay leader? or remains silent about the refusal of gay newspapers and bathhouses to promote prevention? or does not note the signs of a fresh outbreak of high-risk practices in the reopened baths and back rooms, and this despite an overabundance of information? Paradoxically, ACT UP denounced as "criminal" the ministers of national education and the principals who refused to promote or install condom dispensers in high schools, but it refrained from making the same argument about owners of gay businesses, where the prevalence of HIV is incommensurably higher. In this sense, ACT UP has passed on the most infamous bias of the far left: the repeated claim that "everything is political" applies only to "politicians," as ACT UP calls them, and "bureaucrats," not to the complex mechanisms and psychological causes behind denial in the affected populations. In addition, the weakness of ACT UP's discourse on prevention is telling: it lends support to Pollak's argument that ACT UP functions primarily as a lobby for people with AIDS and homosexuals rather than as an organization for combating AIDS.

"We were wrong," Didier Lestrade explains today:

There was a real lack of courage on our part. We distributed ACT UP pamphlets at the entrances to gay bars, even though we knew very well that people inside were fucking without condoms. We should have gone in and cleaned out the fucked-up mess inside. For my part, I have always supported a minority position, which was and still is to have the back rooms closed down. But I was not followed on this point by ACT UP. Our idea was to have the gay community acknowledged, and it was difficult to ask simultaneously that the back rooms be closed. Then there was ACT UP's strategy, which always privileged big targets: there was a greater advantage and more recognition in beating up on Mitterrand than in criticizing some little owner of a back room where prevention wasn't being practiced. I also think most queers in ACT UP liked going to those places too much. The result is that for ten years no one did any prevention in the back rooms, and, on the pretext of freedom, the infection rate remained high. Today we have to tell the owners of these places and the homosexuals who go there, "If you can't be responsible, we'll be responsible for you, and we'll shut down places that allow you to be irresponsible."

In spite of Lestrade's "minority" position, ACT UP–Paris did not promote this line with respect to gay spots. It short-circuited any self-criticism of the homosexual community, and, in an act of repression, dismissed, behind catcalls and shouts, the errors of the homosexual identity movement of the early 1980s. And yet ACT UP–Paris adopted an extremist attitude toward the contaminated-blood scandal. In March 1992, militants covered Dr. Bahman Habibi with red paint and chained him to a radiator. In July 1992, they showed up every day in front of the Paris courtroom where the (first) blood-scandal trial was unfolding. They set up a permanent picket line. Through its intensity and duration, this "political ballet" played a role in keeping the scandal in the news. One slogan declared, "Fabius, you murderer! You have blood on your hands," and a poster added, FABIUS, RESPONSIBLE AND GUILTY. At the same time, ACT UP militants demonstrated in front of the headquarters of the Socialist Party after Fabius was elected to head it: AIDS: THE SOCIALIST PARTY HAS A SHORT MEMORY! A joke circulated at the organization's weekly meetings: "Don't say, 'He's an infected hemophile.' Say, 'He's a Fabiusian, it's in his blood.'" Gradually, the organization even usurped the role of the justice system: after the verdict was announced for Drs. Garretta, Allain, Netter, and Roux, on October 23, 1992, ACT UP threatened, "This trial is not over!" Whenever there was a request that legal sanctions be revoked—when the Conseil National de l'Ordre des Médecins [National council of physicians] proposed allowing Drs. Garretta and Habibi to practice medicine again, or when Willy Rozenbaum signed a petition on behalf of Garretta and Allain—ACT UP militants inevitably replied with zaps, threats of boycotts, and press releases. Thus the organization went looking for guilty parties and scapegoats and even, in its fashion, handed down and enforced its own sentences—signs clearly indicating a need to purge itself of its own sins, its share of blame in underestimating the risks.

Michael Pollak has attempted to analyze this phenomenon. Shortly before his death, he expressed his views in a discreetly autobiographical and particularly harsh passage on the ACT UP militants:

Those who were infected during the first phase, before 1985, were infected by "fate," as it were, in the absence of widely shared awareness. Later, information was available to everyone. . . . But, though understood, [methods of safer sex] were still not widely practiced. Young people who were beginning their sexual lives at that time arrived perfectly well informed of the risk of infection. . . . They no longer had any "excuse," they could not invoke some fatality that permitted them simply to "live with it." The self-blame at having destroyed their own lives in a moment of negligence—this feeling was combined with bad conscience and guilt and then found an outlet in the search for the "guilty party." The result was that they turned their resentment against the "government," supposedly responsible, in the last analysis, for every evil.

Pollak adds:

To go from the feeling that you're submitting to biological destiny to the sense that you've endured an injustice, you have to name an enemy who is responsible, a human being, something other than the virus. Then the virus no longer seems to be the only agent of the epidemic. Along with the virus, politicians were accused of being responsible for the current situation.[30]

Frédéric Edelmann shares this view:

The rage of the ACT UP militants was directed at institutions first of all, and, in fact, these institutions had not done a great deal, had perhaps done nothing, at the beginning of the epidemic. But, to me, it also seemed to be a rage directed at themselves, because more than one militant had not wanted to take AIDS seriously and was infected in full possession of the facts.

It is nevertheless true that ACT UP, along with transfusion recipients, played a major role in "constructing" the contaminated-blood scandal.[31] This scandal led to the investigation of a number of individuals and escalated from a civil to a criminal trial. At its apogee, it was marked by charges of "complicity in poisoning" filed against three former Socialist ministers, and—an extremely rare event—by a revision of the constitution on the part of the highest court in France.[32] "We had to find victims," Lestrade explains today:

ACT UP was the pressure group that made the scandal erupt, and the scandal became huge because of us. It was just too good. If we had been able to finish Fabius off, I would have been very proud of ACT UP. It's a political way of thinking: if a small group like ACT UP manages to bag someone as big as Fabius, that shows it has a lot of power. The end justifies the means. And if you manage to hit this hard, it also means it's fundamentally legitimate. So even if it was proved that Laurent Fabius was not responsible, I'd go on thinking we were strategically right to attack him: we had something to prove in political terms. We had to create an AIDS Watergate.

Christophe Martet, president of ACT UP, thinks they may have been innocent. "But, given the way they defended themselves, they had no honor." Emeric Languerand, a former member of ACT UP, has reservations about this way of thinking: "These repeated actions had a perverse effect: some people, even within ACT UP, wanted to drag us into the legal system: demanding trials, incarceration, increased penalties. ... The danger was that, little by little, we would come to be defenders of prison." Jean-Marc Choub, former medical director of the CUARH, who remembers the errors committed by homosexuals at the beginning of the epidemic, says he is "dismayed by how easily ACT UP agreed to play the blood-scandal game." Interpretations of the state of knowledge about AIDS between 1981 and 1985 are probably the major division between the militants of ACT UP and traditional homosexual militants. ACT UP members tried to demonstrate that "people were perfectly well informed, they knew everything," and they felt the need for a personalized, very localized guilt. They probably viewed the contaminated-blood trial and hearings the way the Corsicans viewed the Furiani trial: as an ideal pedagogical tool. Traditional homosexual militants, by contrast, were altogether ready to "understand" the blood scandal, provided that no one came around to bother them about their own mistakes, and so they preferred to allude to some anonymous, diluted responsibility that could be explained by a context where everyone had contributed, in his own way, to the silences, the careless little acts and daily cynicism. This lack of short-term memory may be one of the major features of the history of AIDS in France: homosexuality may have been a link between ACT UP and its predecessors, but henceforth the generation gap would make all the difference.

    ↩

Two powerful images may serve to sum up the final discontinuity—ACT UP's break with the AIDS movement—that marked the organization's arrival in France. On May 21, 1994, a few hundred militants from ACT UP–Paris lay on the ground on the parvis of Beaubourg for "the day of despair," among pictures of coffins, slogans about the hecatomb, and, in ACT UP's newspaper, many reproductions of death's heads. A week later, on May 29, Aides organized "the march for life" from the Palais Omnisports in Bercy to the Eiffel Tower. There were several thousand marchers in a joyful, easygoing, familial atmosphere; in the end, several million francs in donations were collected. These two demonstrations in themselves mark the distinction between ACT UP and Aides.

ACT UP, following the same evolution as in the United States, appeared in France eight years after the first AIDS cases, and five years after the birth of Aides. Protest took root among young people with HIV, the second generation of patients, often infected late, who still had several asymptomatic years ahead of them, given HIV's long latent phase. The epidemic was now part of the long term, more visible and protracted.

"And so here we are, all of a sudden," Lestrade recounts, "a gang of angry queers in action. We have a rhythm, effectiveness. The image of HIV has changed profoundly. We've been able to sell AIDS as show business."[33] The fight against AIDS underwent a shift, from a defensive to an offensive movement. Aides said, "It's not your fault you're sick." ACT UP upped the ante: "It's other people's fault you're sick." Aides said that the risk of infection was linked to what individuals *did*. ACT UP tried to show that homosexuals had been infected because of a political choice, because of what they *were*. As a result, individuals with HIV who came to ACT UP could no longer identify with institutionalized and supposedly respectable organizations. "Despite their laudable work," Lestrade wrote in 1989, "these organizations are *managing* the epidemic, whereas they should have made the government *stop* it."[34] Even today, Lestrade repeats his criticism: "Aides nauseates me sometimes. Their hegemony in the fight against AIDS, their life centers, which cost a fortune and produce nothing but hot air.[35] All that revolts me. Aides revolts me." In 1989–90, ACT UP militants reproached Aides as much for its professionalization (primarily its salaried employees) as for its elitism—its "cushiness"—and its fundraising, which, they say, served primarily to fund the organization's internal operations. ACT UP's political logic stands in opposition to the communitarian logic of Aides, which claimed to be personally taking care of every aspect of the epidemic. According to ACT UP, it is the state's responsibility to combat AIDS. The militants' battle was no longer to be limited to requests for grants: it was up to the government to take action. As a result, ACT UP wanted to limit its overall costs and maintain financial autonomy by turning down grants. Initially, however, Lestrade seems to have employed a different tactic: "I thought we needed to take the money wherever it came from. I was extremely cynical: we needed to get money from the state so we could use it against the state! But I wasn't followed in this way of thinking by ACT UP, and we didn't ask for a grant." In spite of everything, Lestrade criticizes the AFLS for "playing with fire by privileging its relations with Aides and Arcat. The grant system is necessary, but, at the moment, it is generating most of the tension between organizations"[36] As a result, the AFLS became a key target for ACT UP: "The AFLS is dancing on our graves!" militants shouted. One of their zaps targeted the agency's director, Dominique Charvet, whom militants tried to handcuff and finally managed to knock to the ground. This new strategy in the fight against AIDS was immediately criticized: "New, more radical organizations with less 'diplomatic' approaches are arriving on the scene," Michael Pollak said with surprise. "Let's hope they know how to identify the virus as the real enemy, and not this or that person who has great symbolic value. Criticizing bad decisions is indispensable. But to attack the person of Dominique Charvet, as ACT UP has done, is a tactic of psychological terrorism, which I strongly question."[37] Pollak would return to this zap: "For the first time in France in the fight against AIDS, a line was crossed: the line leading to physical violence."[38] Questioned today, Charvet remembers that day, April 13, 1991: "I found it inadmissible and intolerable. I fought for freedom, and they wanted to handcuff me. It was a philosophical error. I resisted like hell, but I'm no hero. There are times, after an act of violence, when you feel a need for other people." Today, touched by the show of solidarity that met him when other large AIDS organizations, Aides among them, broke ranks with ACT UP for the first time, Charvet displays a certain leniency: "The violence I encountered personally is only too understandable, given the violence of the disease." His resignation a few weeks later, however, was not totally unrelated to the event. We now know that Charvet was probably the best director the AFLS ever had.

Aware of these criticisms, Lestrade proposes his own explanation: "There is a great deal of violence within ACT UP because of the despair, the anger, and the grief. This despair was put to use, channeled somewhere. Militants were told: 'You're scared, you're angry, you can do something with that anger.' ACT UP is the only organization that channels that anger outward."

ACT UP also distinguishes itself from Aides in its strong declaration of homosexual identity, transforming a social stigma into a positive identity. Aides may have appeared more "apologetic"—something for which it has naturally been criticized by ACT UP.[39] In ACT UP, as in Aides, the majority of members are homosexual; the difference is that ACT UP makes that fact known. In Aides, people are homosexual. In ACT UP, they are queer. This stance is reminiscent of the FHAR, which made using the term "queer" a matter of principle. There were two advantages to this use of the term: first, it effected a "strategic reversal"; and, second, it rejected identity (the word "pédé," like the English "queer," does not denote a single identity).

This rehomosexualization of the fight against AIDS, in which ACT UP played a role in the early 1990s, appealed to many young homosexuals whether or not they were personally affected by the epidemic. They were attracted to gay militancy, which was rarely being practiced elsewhere. This also explains the arrival of women at ACT UP. "Very early on," Lestrade says, "I noticed a strong presence of women, and especially of lesbians, in ACT UP. We had to take their demands into account, since the struggles of homosexuals and women are joined at a certain number of points. But we sometimes have to remind ourselves that we are primarily an AIDS organization, and that we shouldn't mix it all together." In spite of its founder's caution, ACT UP–Paris has provided the framework for various militant utopian undertakings. The attraction exerted by the organization at a time when, paradoxically, AIDS is becoming more "democratic," moving into populations not previously designated as "at risk," may represent one of the chief ambiguities of ACT UP. It is a homosexual organization for combating a disease that has become heterosexual as well.

Paradoxically, ACT UP, despite its criticisms of Aides, has had a tendency to strengthen the positions of that organization, which, though still fairly moderate, has established a new relationship of power with the government. "If you don't talk to us, you'll have to talk to ACT UP," Aides seems to be saying. If the tension between Aides and ACT UP served to energize the AIDS movement, or even to bring it into existence in the first place, one might assume that greater consensus between the organizations could weaken the movement as a whole, though it would also make possible a true battle plan, a unified and collective one.

Philippe Mangeot, a student at the Ecole Normale and an activist against the Gulf War, is one of the significant figures in ACT UP–Paris. "I'm the brains at ACT UP," he jokes; he is writing his thesis on Jules Verne.[40] He has been HIV-positive since 1986, and, surprising though this may seem, is the son of the CEO of Glaxo-Wellcome–France—the pharmaceutical company that produces, notably, the notorious AZT. "People do not necessarily come to ACT UP because they are angry," Mangeot explains. "Anger is something that is learned. ACT UP is a machine for producing anger. As for me, I came to ACT UP because I was queer." With something of a minister's demeanor and a surprising sense of humor, Mangeot, who says he is in love with structure, like the old leftists, enjoys deconstructing the ACT UP machine:

Of course we're a far-left group, but we're also a group of queers. I have a tendency to think that in France the two major political innovations of the last ten years have been Aides and ACT UP. All the ACT UP groups throughout the world are collapsing. I think ACT UP–Paris has remained the most powerful one because there is no gay activist group in France. ACT UP takes its place. Maybe ACT UP is even preventing the creation of a gay activist group. Or maybe all the gay activists are in ACT UP? Sometimes I tell myself I'm going to leave ACT UP and create a radical fag group. But I won't do it, because gay militancy is a pain in the ass. The queer militancy of ACT UP excites me: a fairy in front of the minister, that's funny; pom-pom girls from ACT UP chanting—no gay group would dare do that!

Is ACT UP a fashion trend or a social movement? "ACT UP is obviously a fashion trend, and it's a strategy," Mangeot continues:

I find ACT UP slogans like "AIDS is disco" exciting because they show that AIDS is trendy, that AIDS has become all about high-fashion designers, galas, parties. This is the only slogan that [Minister of Health] Philippe Douste-Blazy can't appropriate. And then, I like the fact that people say: "They've gone completely nuts." So it's a fashion trend, a glamour movement. It's undoubtedly a political movement, and I hope it's also a social movement.

In the face of numerous criticisms regarding ACT UP, Mangeot is understanding, and he acknowledges that the organization has sometimes gone too far. But he places these errors inside a more comprehensive logic: "ACT UP has to constantly push the envelope of discourse. We need once more to be something that people won't associate with, we need to bring in ideas, even if they're scandalous, so they'll be exploited and reworked by other people." Beyond these critical aspects, Mangeot says he has a certain sense of well-being in ACT UP, an organization where he can deal with being HIV-positive and homosexual:

ACT UP is a place of circulating desires. I have two fiancés right now: I found both of
them at ACT UP. I've sometimes thought the Aides guys were better-looking, though. But
the goal of ACT UP is to have the best-looking guys in Paris! ACT UP is a cruising group,
but it's also a group where people whose sexuality is not yet defined can come, and where
they often have their first homosexual experiences. For example, even the straights in
ACT UP are queer! That's a joy to me. There's a process of becoming queer in ACT UP.

Joy? Love? Cruising? Surprising words. Nevertheless, they may be a better
characterization of ACT UP's implicit calling, and especially of its power, than
such words as "activism" or "action." The key virtue of a movement like ACT UP is
how it operates in terms of mutual support. The need for support was the reason
Aides was created and is perfectly symbolized by the "buddy system." Aides is almost a family: people volunteer to help others as well as themselves, in a sense
combining private life and the life of the group. But ACT UP goes beyond this initial self-therapy and has sick people march in the streets. Activism offers militants a
sort of collective outlet, which—as interviews confirm—allows people to "better
bear the string of losses," to belong to a highly unified network and let off steam
through actions. "action=life" may be the most significant and best-known slogan
of ACT UP: it perfectly sums up this objective. Echoing this sentiment, Lestrade
comments on the death of his friend Luc Coulavin, cofounder of ACT UP: "Today,
after years of the epidemic, we are being inundated with more and more deaths,
and the 1990s are already the worst years of our lives."[41] What is even more significant, Lestrade said in an interview with *Gai Pied*, "We are overwhelmed by hatred."

Thus gay couples in ACT UP (Cleews Vellay and Philippe Labbey are the most
legendary) are part of the organization's history. A list of the "five hottest guys in
ACT UP" has been established, and the organization, like all homosexual groups,
is a big cruising spot, the best form of mutual support.

Through this support, ACT UP unites all the "communities" affected by AIDS,
with the aim of openly supporting the birth of a communitarian model in France.
To achieve it, ACT UP has set the goal of creating a coalition of minorities, which
might lead to an American-style communitarianism. "I'm very proud," Lestrade
explains,

because I managed to sell this idea to ACT UP–Paris. I backed the idea of a homosexual
community because we had to be collectively responsible for our peers. That was what
ACT UP was. Little by little, ACT UP became the driving force behind a greater awareness
within homosexual milieux of the existence of this community. We finally created a little
enclave in French society—a society that is so hostile to groups—by giving birth to a gay
community. The greatest and most significant success of ACT UP may turn out to be its
planting the roots of this communitarianism in France. Republican values are getting off
track, becoming more cynical every day. I expect society to go up in flames.

In terms of AIDS, however, this communitarianism could lead ACT UP to lay
claim to the title of exclusive spokesperson for people with AIDS. This tendency,

already criticized by Pollak, raises even more questions inasmuch as fewer and fewer members of the organization are HIV-positive. "Statistically, we are more an organization of queers than an organization of people with HIV," Mangeot confirms. "You cannot be in ACT UP without realizing that this is not an organization of sick people. However, we know that's the only language we can embrace, since no other organization is doing it."[42] In light of these words, we can more easily understand why it is no longer tenable for ACT UP to say it has a mandate to express itself on behalf of all people with AIDS. This is what an activist from ACT UP–New York has also recognized: "We no longer have the right to speak in the name of all those who are infected."[43]

The minority coalition plan, which is firmly anchored in ACT UP's approach, is obvious in the satellite organizations to which the organization has given rise. The workings and success of this coalition are instructive. Several collectives were spearheaded by ACT UP militants: ADMEF (to defend the rights of foreign patients whose immigration status is irregular) and, to a lesser degree, the organization "Limiter la casse" [Limit the damage] (in support of drug addicts).[44] In addition, pressure groups have been created or inspired by members of ACT UP–Paris: Communistes contre le Sida [Communists against AIDS], Marie-pas-Claire, Lesbiennes Se Déchainent [Lesbians lash out], and Sourds en Colère [Deaf and angry].[45] The Sisters of Perpetual Indulgence [Soeurs de la Perpétuelle Indulgence, as they are known in France], for their part, have affinities with the self-deprecation of the Gazolines of the FHAR and appeared in France in 1990 as an extension of ACT UP–Paris (although they originated in San Francisco in 1979, with no links to AIDS). A group of gay men dressed as nuns, the Sisters propose to battle Christian fanaticism through caricature, an intentionally blasphemous militancy, and fundraising.

Despite the sympathies that ACT UP has awakened in France, and despite the organizations it has more or less directly inspired, the organization's methods have been the target of various criticisms. Most of the tension that has surfaced between ACT UP and other groups has had to do with the recurrent themes of homosexual visibility and the question of private life. Although ACT UP militants are themselves divided on these issues, there has been a perceptible inclination toward attacks on private life, ad hominem attacks, or physical humiliation.[46]

On March 19, 1991, ACT UP–Paris also adopted the principle of outing. "We have not yet practiced outing," Lestrade explains:

We are probably wrong. The moral question of outing does not frighten ACT UP: it is a matter of telling the truth, and ACT UP is against lying. The only thing that frightens us is the legal aspect. There are laws in France that protect people's private lives. How can you advance the fight against AIDS in our country if the people most involved in it hide behind the eternal concept of private life? If there were no laws against outing, ACT UP would have used it a long time ago. It may be time to do it, and there are probably ways for ACT UP to be the instigator of outing without really acknowledging it—which would keep us from acting illegally. We're going to think about it.

Michael Pollak, again critical, prefers to contrast this argument with a different way of thinking:

In almost every AIDS organization, the question of whether to reveal one's homosexuality and one's HIV status is left to the person concerned. If he or she does not deliberately make that choice, discretion is required. ACT UP, by contrast, has voted for the principle of outing. . . . Respect for private life has been replaced by an obligation to be an activist, and the rule of discretion has been replaced by denunciation.[47]

ACT UP has also been harshly criticized for composing a list, "Know Your Enemies," on which recognized figures in the fight against AIDS appear (for example, Arnaud Marty-Lavauzelle, president of Aides; Frédéric Edelmann, director of Arcat; and Pierre Kneip, director of Sida Infos Service). "I was very hurt that my name appeared on a list like that," Kneip confided shortly before his death:

All of a sudden, I felt like I was in a movement that no longer had anything to do with the fight against AIDS, a movement that determined what was good and what was bad in a totalitarian way. For ACT UP to make doctors like Willy Rozenbaum and Michel Kazatchkine their enemies is a confusion reminiscent of fundamentalist or fascist groups. This kind of ACT UP list is totally incompatible with the fight against the disease.

ACT UP's Philippe Mangeot understands these criticisms:

There is bad faith in ACT UP, and it makes me laugh because it's strategic. I love it when ACT UP makes political use of stupidity, of the power of simplification, as when it moved from "Know Our Enemies" to "Know Your Enemies." But when ACT UP believes in its stupidity, that's idiotic. It happens, and this we're-the-ones-dying side of ACT UP pisses me off.

In Aides, the leaders have a tendency not to reply to ACT UP's criticisms, even though they sometimes have trouble concealing their exasperation at ACT UP's new media imperialism and monopoly on discourse. They often wisely confine themselves to recalling that Aides has more than 3,600 volunteers in ninety-nine cities in France, whereas ACT UP has only 300 members and is completely or nearly absent from the provinces.[48] All the same, Arnaud Marty-Lavauzelle, president of the Aides federation, understands the motivations of ACT UP: "If I had learned that I was infected at a younger age, at twenty, for example, things probably would have taken a relatively tempestuous course. However, direct physical threat to the person bothers me. Any action that entails physical humiliation is problematic."

On "Saint AIDS Day" (December 1, 1993), as ACT UP called it, the spectacular action of putting a giant fluorescent pink condom on the obelisk at the Place de la

Concorde[49] made all of France smile, allowing ACT UP to rally unanimous support. Yet the financing of this media coup by United Colors of Benetton was deeply resented by some people with AIDS, who remembered Oliviero Toscani's last advertising campaign, with its images of bodies, like sides of beef, stamped HIV-POSITIVE.[50]

Some people are less reserved in their reactions to ACT UP, even some from whom one would least expect such reactions. For Jacques Leibowitch, "ACT UP represents life: it is modernity. It moved AIDS from silence to politics, even to medicine, while the other organizations were pulling down a nice salary, finding fulfillment in AIDS. We're not here to benefit from the virus or have usufruct of it: we have to get rid of it. That's what ACT UP is doing." Even though he was himself the object of a zap, Jack Lang approves of ACT UP: "I imagine that someone like Guy Hocquenghem would be in ACT UP today. When I met with them, the people in ACT UP helped me a great deal in understanding what AIDS is all about." And the former state minister concludes, "You know, when there are no other solutions, it's sometimes good to kick some ass." The historian Paul Veyne has the same opinion: "It gives me pleasure when they attack the laboratories."

Beyond these positive and negative assessments, there is the power of the words of militants themselves. Although having AIDS or HIV does not justify everything, these often eloquent words allow us to understand the motivation of the militants, beyond any judgment we might form of ACT UP. "I came to ACT UP because I am queer" (Philippe M.). "I'm in ACT UP because my anger is inversely proportionate to the number of T cells I have. I'm in ACT UP because I'm going to die soon" (Cleews). "I'm in ACT UP because I'm haunted by twenty-year-old ghosts" (Jean-Christian). "I'm in ACT UP because, having become resigned to my fate, I wanted to die, and now I want to live so I can fight. . . . Because ACT UP gave me new hope" (Bernard). "In ACT UP, I acknowledged what I was. I found in it a political discourse and the seed of a community. What I loved was the collective elaboration of a political discourse" (Gwen). "ACT UP is group therapy. My anger is the final lie, created by ACT UP for its own purposes. What motivates people is not anger but love" (Didier). "I'm in ACT UP because they're never ashamed here of being queers, lesbians, druggies, prostitutes, prisoners, foreigners, or sadomasochists" (Benoît). "I stayed because in ACT UP I heard a real analysis of the AIDS crisis" (Anne). "I came here because I was at war, and you don't fight a war all alone" (Philippe). "I joined ACT UP with memories of the FHAR. We are the babies of the FHAR" (Philippe L.). "I came to ACT UP because I laugh a lot here—in an AIDS organization, I break out laughing like you wouldn't believe" (Christophe). "Because I dream of a homosexual community, and I don't see it happening elsewhere" (Philippe). "I found all my friends, lovers, and even my nanny there. What would become of me without them?" (Jean-Christian). "What does it give me? An intense feeling of solidarity. A strong queer community that reacts.

Friends. Moments of great joy, great exuberance. Pride as well. And I am stronger when friends die. It's not ideal, but it's good all the same. ACT UP is my home. My family" (Philippe).[51]

᠆ᢌ

The symbolic and militant power of ACT UP, and its power in the media, ought not to hide the fact that the organization is in crisis. Marked through and through by contradictory tendencies, the movement has almost imploded on many occasions, even though reconciliation has always taken place around homosexual solidarity. By becoming part of the state apparatus, ACT UP gradually placed itself inside a logic of institutionalization. Today, the organization has a growing budget and six half-time salaried employees. A slogan shouted as late as 1994 by Cleews Vellay, during a debate on salaried employees—"There are those who live off it and those who die from it"—is completely forgotten today.[52]

"What message can you put out when everyone else is putting out your message?" This seems to be the question that most preoccupies ACT UP today. Since the condom on the obelisk at the Place de la Concorde, and since Sidaction, on April 7, 1994, the organization has gained recognition. It attracts numerous militants, and Edouard Balladur borrowed one of its slogans, declaring "universal mobilization"; Robert Hue asserted that it was necessary to "declare a state of emergency." Moreover, "action=life" T-shirts are now marketed in women's magazines, Jean-Baptiste Mondino is making photographs for the organization, Christian Lacroix is creating T-shirts, and ACT UP's prevention video was presented at Beaubourg as part of the "Féminimasculin" retrospective.

Given this new consensus, the future of the group is hard to predict. One hypothesis is that, with greater use of technology in treatment, research, and a desire for training, this institutionalization will continue.[53] But Aides and Arcat-sida are already performing this role, to a great extent. Another hypothesis is that, conversely, ACT UP's radicalization will move it beyond the new consensual discourse on AIDS and to attacks on people like Minister of Health Philippe Douste-Blazy, who has made a habit of regularly consulting ACT UP. The organization would then become something with which no one would want to be associated, and the increased tension might be expressed in a kind of HIV-positive humor that is already very much a presence in ACT UP, probably as a symptom of militants' despair.[54] Thematically, this radicalism might focus on sensitive subjects, such as homosexual visibility, decriminalization of hard drugs, the distribution of heroin for medical purposes, sex in prisons, or immigrant patients of irregular status. ACT UP remains homosexual for the most part, however: there are few drug addicts, no foreigners with HIV, and no ex-prisoners. Here, perhaps, we see the limits of ACT UP's involvement in social arenas beyond the homosexual cause. And so the question is raised, cruelly, once again: Is ACT UP a fashion trend or a social movement?

Three other evolutions are possible for ACT UP. First, its discourse could become less prevalent and its influence on society less significant (like SOS Racisme, with its "beurs-geois" [middle-class, French-born North Africans], or like the feminist movement). Second, a split could occur—around the question of treatment, for example. Or, third, ACT UP could choose to dissolve (as did Daniel Defert's and Michel Foucault's Groupe d'Information sur les Prisons)—a noble act, which may be hoped for by some of the militants historically associated with ACT UP.

Apart from these scenarios for the future, it is still true that ACT UP has taken root as one of the most significant movements of the 1990s. ACT UP—a gold mine for any sociologist studying organizations, protest groups, or public policies; the hope of far-left militants who have finally found their heirs; the terror of administrations and ministerial cabinets—has been able to move considerably beyond the AIDS–homosexuality problematic (its initial reason for existence) by raising, to its credit, penetrating questions (such as the question of HIV's politicization). The answers to these questions will probably be of interest in the treatment of all serious pathologies. From the beginning, by embracing the idea of Americanizing French society, ACT UP set itself the goal of giving birth to a "gay community." As a result, the organization has triggered a new, quantitatively significant process of affirming identity. In this sense, it may be a harbinger of new forms of political action that are yet to come.

⮑

Twenty years after the FHAR, and ten years after the appearance of AIDS, ACT UP marked the entry of homosexual militancy into the fight against AIDS. With these beginnings, which obliterated the denial of the years between 1981 and 1985, ACT UP brought homosexuals to take a step that Guy Hocquenghem had not wanted to take. From the politicization of homosexuality, in 1971, to the politicization of AIDS, in 1991, the circle was complete. Lipstick became political again on Cleews Vellay's face. Homosexual liberation, momentarily interrupted by "gay cancer," has resumed its course. The FHAR has returned to bid the world farewell, the offices of *Gai Pied* are occupied once again, and the general meetings at Beaux-Arts are throwing a big wake: ACT UP has set up shop there.

The new procession of AIDS militants, now indissociable from the gay militants, is a long one, and the pom-pom girls are in the party. ACT UP anticipates the homosexual movement now under way, and it sets the tone. The new parade, with its familiar faces, has bright colors, and all its sails are set. In many ways, the "homosexual revolution" is returning to port.

15

The Second Homosexual Revolution

The AIDS patient is a social reformer.
—Daniel Defert

"Even in the least moralistic commentaries, AIDS seems to mark the end of the age of freedom, the end of a certain way of living homosexuality." This observation by the sociologist Michael Pollak offers confirmation, if any is needed, that "homosexuals have changed."[1]

In their sexual practices, cruising codes, and lifestyles, in their embracing of an identity, 1990s gays hardly resemble their elders. In ten years, AIDS moved homosexual life from the toilets to Queen "fog machine" parties, from Renaud Camus's *Tricks* to Hervé Guibert's *The Compassion Protocol*, from Patrice Chéreau's *L'homme blessé* to Jonathan Demme's *Philadelphia*. How distant Jean-Louis Bory's short sketches in *Le Nouvel Observateur* or the "Chéri(e)" personals in *Libération* now seem! The children of the FHAR have become experts in safer sex and have begun to sing the virtues of the "civil union contract," things that would have bewildered their predecessors. The use of condoms has become the rule; *dura lex, sed lex*: the law is harsh, but it is the law.

Daniel Defert sums up these changes: "AIDS, it must be said, changed our sexuality. But I don't like the word 'changed'; I prefer 'adapted.' For all of us, there's much less sex, many fewer penetrations, many fewer partners. There's also much less anonymous sex. ... For us, there are also many more couples in existence, many more who are alive."[2]

Although homosexuals have moved from one tragic world to another, from marginality to AIDS, they have also learned how to manage a new illness, invent new codes of love, new forms of emotional association. They have created disparate, "Deleuzian" couples. Paradoxically, they may have achieved a certain kind of banalization, if not recognition. This is no mere evolution: a whole world has been turned upside down.

Homosexuality used to be an individual adventure. For the first time, AIDS has given homosexuals a collective history. The central fact of the epidemic is probably that it was identified with the homosexual environment; and, conversely, we might hypothesize that the central fact of the history of homosexuality is now the emergence of AIDS. Homosexuality will never be what it once was, a fact that may have many ramifications.

↩

Given the public health imperatives, homosexuals received a great deal of attention in the second half of the 1980s. In the end, the government admitted it was obliged to take account of homosexuals in order to combat the illness. It thus created work groups and groups of experts, awarded grants to openly gay organizations, and became more tolerant of homosexual bathhouses, which were turned into relay points for prevention efforts.

In parallel to the new interest shown by public leaders, the scientific world apprehended homosexuality as an object of study, an amazing social laboratory, heretofore completely—and mysteriously—unexplored. Demographers had been silent on the issue, political scientists mute, sociologists nowhere to be found. From that point on, researchers began to speak out. To their credit, they stuck to ordinary facts; that is, they did not embrace the theories of their predecessors, the psychoanalysts and psychiatrists. They tried to understand homosexual behavior, to follow gay strategies with respect to AIDS, and even, for the first time since Kinsey, to count the number of homosexuals. Until recently, in fact, there had been only a very small number of studies,[3] most of them eliciting serious scientific reservations.

There are now two authoritative studies in France, as different as they are complementary: the early and original work undertaken in 1985 by Michael Pollak on a voluntary sample of *Gai Pied Hebdo* readers (work continued after his death by Marie-Ange Schiltz), and the study carried out by a team of twenty researchers under the direction of Alfred Spira and Nathalie Bajos, the largest survey to date on French sexuality.[4]

Because of the Spira and Bajos study, we now have recent data on homosexuals, though there may be a certain amount of underreporting in the data.[5] One of this study's principal outcomes is that it allows us to estimate, as far as possible, the number of people who are having (or have had) homosexual relations in France. According to the Spira and Bajos survey, 4.1 percent of men and 2.6 percent of women report having had at least one partner of the same sex during their lifetimes.[6] When the survey focuses on the past five years only, or on the current year ("the past twelve months"), the rate of homosexual practices stands at 1.4 percent for men and 0.4 percent for women in the past five years, and at 1.1 percent for men and 0.3 percent for women in the past year.

Given the probability of underreporting, these figures cannot be taken as definitive, but they do at least allow us to hypothesize that the prevalence of homosexuality has often been overestimated: in 1948, for example, in the infamous Kinsey report, and in the 1970s and 1980s by homosexual militants eager to create an illusion about their many "sympathizers," if not their troops. But this tendency to overestimate is not solely the result of a deliberate, ideologically motivated choice. It can also be explained by the high visibility of homosexuals in Paris, the battlefield of choice for militancy, and by their overrepresentation in certain socioprofessional groups that have contact with the public (the service sector, public relations, and so on).[7]

The number of homosexuals/bisexuals, both men and women, between the ages of eighteen and sixty-nine is by no means negligible in France. It can be roughly measured as being between 270,000 and 1.3 million at a minimum. This is not so much an exact figure as an indication of a tendency.[8] When underreporting and the French population as a whole are taken into account, we can assume, in the absence of reliable figures, that an estimate of between 500,000 and 2 million is acceptable. Making such estimates is a tricky business, because a great deal of ambiguity surrounds the notion of homosexual relations and because there are many gradations between bisexuality and exclusive homosexuality, but these figures are nevertheless impressive as well as significant.

⤿

The detailed data now available on homosexuals provide even more valuable information on contemporary homosexual lifestyles, despite the small size of the samples obtained.[9] We find the confirmation of a generally accepted idea: namely, that homosexual/bisexual males have, on average, a significantly higher number of partners than do heterosexuals. By contrast, female homosexuals/bisexuals seem to have a lower number of partners than do heterosexual women generally. Frequently, however, homosexuals of both sexes have also had heterosexual encounters, a finding that confirms the existence of a high rate of bisexuality, though such activity may be only occasional or limited to adolescence.[10] In short, heterosexual experiences among homosexuals may be more common than homosexual experiences among heterosexuals. The myth of lesbian or gay purity appears to be contradicted by a picture in which the ambivalence of desires is predominant.

If we limit ourselves to the male subsample of the survey—unfortunately, given the small size of the samples obtained, lesbians could not be the object of detailed study—we find some interesting information. Among 82 percent of the gay men surveyed, the first sexual experience was reported as having occurred before the age of twenty (the average was nineteen years), whereas heterosexuals were a bit more precocious (eighteen years on average, and just over seventeen years among those who are currently young). The age gap between the individual and his first partner shows an even more significant difference: on average, the age difference is six years for the first homosexual encounter, but only one and one-half years for the first heterosexual encounter. Thus gay initiation may be a difficult step that requires the experience of an older partner, particularly one who can make the first move. For the first sexual encounter, by contrast, homosexuals did not turn to prostitutes any more often than heterosexuals did, nor do they seem to have felt any difference in amorous intensity on that occasion.

Where the nature of sexual relations is concerned (in this case, the last male homosexual encounter of the individual being surveyed), it seems that, in addition to more or less systematic sexual practices (fondling, mutual masturbation), passive or active fellatio is very common (practiced by 72 to 82 percent of those surveyed), and the frequency of anal sex remains high (active for 36 percent, passive for 28 percent). Nevertheless, for homosexuals the expression "make love" does not necessarily imply penetration, whereas it does for heterosexuals, and although anal sex is neither uncommon nor programmatic in male homosexual relations, fisting is a fairly rare practice (reported by 6 percent). In addition, there is a higher number of homosexuals/bisexuals who are having no sexual relations at all (abstinence): 9.5 percent had stopped—temporarily at least—having sex five or more years before, as compared to 2.7 percent of heterosexuals.

With respect to life as a couple, the data provided by the male subsample partially contradict a commonplace belief. Nearly one homosexual/bisexual in three (about 30 percent) is coupled, and among this 30 percent the rate of cohabitation is close to 80 percent.[11] These male couples share a fairly long life together: on average, seven years for exclusively homosexual couples. Despite the new trend toward a form of homosexual "cocooning," gay couples are still proportionately less common than heterosexual couples, their rate of cohabitation is slightly lower, and the duration of these couples is notably shorter. Finally, although homosexuals living as couples reported frequent affairs outside their relationships, nearly 49 percent reported living as closed couples, with no "extramarital" relations.

Well beyond private life, homosexual orientation affects an individual's social life as a whole, particularly his professional life. The Spira and Bajos pollsters observed this phenomenon on a national scale: the vast majority (85 percent) of homosexuals who were surveyed lived in the Paris region or in cities with populations greater than 100,000. This finding confirms the link between homosexuality and geographic migration to the cities. The urban concentration of homosexuals is beyond dispute; it is statistically significant and represents a serious departure from the geographic distribution of the French population overall.[12]

Analysis of the differences in age, socioprofessional group, and educational level within homosexual couples also offers interesting results. In this respect, homosexuality makes possible within the couple a greater exogamy, not to mention heterogamy. To a significant but not excessive degree, differences in age, educational level, and socioprofessional group are greater within homosexual couples than within heterosexual couples. Even today, like the castrated young page married by the Roman emperor Nero, a humble hairstylist who wishes to see himself on the arm of his own little Prince of Wales can hit the jackpot with a rich industrialist.

There is a cultural logic that corresponds to this social logic: the survey brings to light an overrepresentation of college graduates. Thus the inequality of heterosexuals in the matter of education is not simply a tired cliché: the professional choices and geographical migration impelled by homosexuality may oblige gays to invest more than the average amount of time in education. Membership in a minority group may lead to social climbing and to a search for greater cultural capital. Still, such interpretations should be met with reservations; at the very least, they should not be taken too seriously.

Finally, on the so-called normative issues, homosexuality remains difficult to talk about within the family. Sexuality in general is a delicate area, of course, regardless of the adolescent's orientation: children become emancipated as a result of sexuality, and their silence on the issue within the family is a decisive part of their autonomy. Generally, talking about sex seems a bit easier between a heterosexual son and his mother than between a heterosexual son and his father. For the young homosexual, there is both a difficulty in acknowledging his homosexuality within the family circle and greater difficulty talking about personal problems with his parents, and this difficulty is independent of the declaration of homosexuality. The Spira and Bajos subsample confirms that adolescent male homosexuals have much better relationships with their mothers than with their fathers; the percentages on this question are extremely high, especially by comparison with those for heterosexuals. Talking to their fathers about sex was difficult or impossible for almost all the homosexual adolescents (98 percent). Nevertheless, despite the common belief that adolescent male homosexuals are their mothers' special confidants, gay teenagers seem to have a harder time talking to their mothers than do heterosexual adolescents.

↩

Homosexuals, now better known, are still atypical of French people in general, although their lifestyles now seem less unusual. In this respect, the changes that have come about in France in the past twenty-five years have led to two concurrent phenomena. On the one hand, as homosexuality became more commonplace it also became more visible, and homosexual identity was also "desexualized" during the AIDS years. Overlap among the social, political, and cultural aspects of homosexuals' lives has made the importance of their sexuality relative. Along with the illness, a certain gravity has appeared within homosexuality, replacing the frivolity or supposedly festive aspects that were characteristic in the past. Living in couples is also probably more widespread. On the other hand, as the image of gays was changing, heterosexual lifestyles were undergoing transformation in the opposite direction. Whereas homosexuals were once the only demographic outlaws and society called them "queers," an increasingly broad spectrum of the population at large has now become "deviant" and "wild," rejecting the confines of marriage as an institution.

In 1971, in the joint general meetings of the MLF and the FHAR—meetings with a certain edge—homosexuals of both sexes claimed to be waging the final battle against the capitalist order (phallocracy), marriage (heterosexuality), and the patriarchal order, which restricted the full expression of their sexuality. Twenty years later, who could deny that heterosexuality, marriage, and the family have been profoundly changed?

Most demographers acknowledge that feminist discourse and homosexual lifestyles have played a role in weakening the traditional family, but this weakening began before sexual liberation movements first appeared in France, and its causes, like its consequences, are both broader and more complex than the simple demand for more liberal mores. Nevertheless, these social movements did accompany changes in society, and the history of everyday life (homosexual liberation) occupies a place within a more comprehensive history (the sexual revolution). The efforts of the women's movement, combined with homosexuals' "destiny as troublemakers," in the words of Guy Hocquenghem, have tended to establish a distinction between sex and procreation. Sex has become a convenience. For heterosexuals, then, there was something to be appropriated from the lifestyles and eroticism of gays. The homosexual, a social outsider, a "source of disorder" (Bory), an internal exile, has proved to be a "homing device," a "pilot fish for new possibilities in sexuality."[13]

With the wisdom of scientists who weigh their words while commenting on phenomena as powerful as a tidal wave, the demographers have been astounded: Hervé Le Bras now speaks of "build-it-yourself families," and Louis Roussel explains that all families are "abnormal." Henri Mendras, even more radically, succinctly defines the changes that transformed France's moral life between 1965 and 1984 as "the second French revolution."[14]

The demographic elements of these upheavals among heterosexuals are well known: "People now marry less and later; they divorce more and earlier; they have fewer children, and these children are born to older couples; people remarry less often after divorce" (Roussel). The demographers' amazement is not out of proportion with the changes observed.

Amid the mountains of statistics, a few bits of data have caught the attention of observers: fertility and marriage rates have taken a nosedive; the percentage of divorces requested by wives reached 73.5 in 1985; the rate of children born out of wedlock has risen to nearly one birth in three. As for single-parent families, they now constitute nearly 13 percent of all families (23 percent in Paris, or nearly one family in four).[15] Finally, there has been an increase in the number of adults living alone, with single-person households now approaching one-quarter of all households. Paris, which has become the "capital of loneliness," holds the record.[16]

With all these single-parent families, blended families, and single-person households, the idea of a "natural" family—simple and universal—has been discredited. Marriage, where it survives, is often redefined as a contractual bond, with all the precariousness and fragility characteristic of such a bond. As the classic family model has weakened, it has been replaced by a recognition of sexual pleasure at the expense of fertility alone. The heterosexual with multiple partners has become more visible. The image of masculinity has also changed. There is a more pronounced lack of differentiation between the sexes, and "homosexuality has promoted a virile image of man unrelated to the authoritarian male domination of women."[17] In addition, sexual behaviors considered to be on the fringe have been revealed among heterosexuals: anal sex, for example, seems to be practiced by a considerable number of French heterosexual couples (30 percent of men and 24 percent of women have tried it at least once; 15 percent of men and 13 percent of women engage in it regularly; it was practiced in 3 to 8 percent of respondents' most recent sexual encounters).[18]

In this new sexual landscape, where the most diverse sexual practices are given free rein, homosexual lifestyles have come to seem more commonplace, and their specificity has become simply a lifestyle difference. The general threshold of tolerance has risen. Homosexual behavior is no longer reduced to the arena of sex alone; and, conversely, everything suggests that heterosexuals, now hungry for "bad company," are no longer above suspicion.[19] For them, the homosexual even has a certain prestige, that of a Don Juan. Bisexuality has become a label easy to embrace, as demonstrated by Collard's *Les nuits fauves* and by the gay bars and discos—Le Boy, Le Queen, Le Banana Café— that, in Paris and the provinces, attract large numbers of heterosexuals. The success of a film like Josiane Balasko's *French Twist*, despite its sitcom character and the cliché of the mannish lesbian, is probably a good indication of this movement, since it shows that homosexuality has become rather banal (in France, nearly four million people went to see the film in 1995). Finally, the fact that everyone has to use condoms has established a certain equality, at least at the unconscious level, between heterosexuals and homosexuals in the area of risk management.

Hence, through these two contradictory trends, homosexuals are becoming better integrated into society. Homosexuals, their feelings, and their particular behavior are more likely to be considered in all their diversity; gradually, they may escape the hypothetical label "homosexuality." In this shift, the very question of marginality has been challenged, and the notion of a sexual norm has eroded. As a result, we may have moved from *homosexuality* [as a noun] to *homosexual* [as an adjective], in a way that will benefit everyone concerned.

~

The results of recent surveys seem to confirm a greater public tolerance for homosexuality and a drop in "homophobia." This growing acceptance seems to have appeared in France in the mid-1980s (about 1985–87) and marks a departure from earlier surveys.[20] For 59 percent of individuals queried by CSA/*Le Monde* in January 1994, homosexuality is a personal matter, whereas 8 percent thought it is the effect of life experiences (by contrast, 11 percent said it is a mistake, 9 percent claimed it is a moral failing, and 8 percent saw it as a sin, with 5 percent giving no opinion).[21] This change seems even more noticeable when the respondents are younger than twenty-four: a Sofres/Ministère de la Jeunesse et des Sports survey in January 1993 shows that for 76 percent of the adolescents queried, homosexuality was "not really or not at all reprehensible."[22]

Paradoxical as it may seem, we can hypothesize that AIDS has accompanied this new tolerance—also perceptible at the international level[23]—even though the new attitudes began to form earlier, probably inspired by "sexual liberation."

Throughout the ordeal of AIDS, although the values of individual tolerance and freedom have been threatened, homosexuals have taken responsibility, reacting to the unexpected virus with new forms of solidarity. They have even made up for the government's delays. The history of Aides is a perfect illustration of this development.

The effectiveness of AIDS activists, in combination with the new practices adopted by individuals, has slowed the rate of infection. Homosexuals invented safer sex, and its practice in the gay population, even before heterosexuals rallied behind safer sex, has increased spectacularly since 1989. To judge by the surveys of *Gai Pied Hebdo*'s readers that Michael Pollak and Marie-Ange Schiltz have conducted, this evolution was notable between 1985 and 1987 and then slowed between 1987 and 1989, remaining steady after that. Thus 6 percent of the homosexuals queried in 1985 used condoms regularly or sometimes, 25 percent did so in 1986, 47 percent in 1987, 56 percent in 1988, and 64 percent in 1989. More recent studies (for example, the one conducted by Schiltz in 1991–1992; see the bibliography) allow us to refine these data: in active or passive penetration with an *occasional* partner, 74 percent of the people who were queried always used a condom, 9.9 percent sometimes used one, and 16.9 percent never used one. With a *stable* partner, the numbers were reversed: 43 percent always used a condom, 11 percent sometimes used one, and 46 percent never used one. Similarly, a significant drop in the number of partners is apparently observable between 1985 and 1992, and more of the people who were queried reported that they were looking for a stable relationship. In addition, some stable homosexual couples had abandoned safer sex within the relationship if they were HIV-negative but resumed it for any outside encounters (tolerated or secret). This large minority fluctuated between 10 and 13 percent of the homosexuals queried in 1992. At the same time, for all people surveyed, the sexual repertoire with occasional partners had been considerably impoverished; in particular, anal sex had frequently been abandoned in such encounters and was reserved for the stable partner.[24]

For a long time, this risk-avoidance strategy, primarily a vital reaction aimed at saving one's skin, resulted in a reduction in the rate of HIV infection in the homosexual milieu. It also meant that people who were infected could pursue a homosexual lifestyle, even in sex spots. Daniel Defert notes, this was probably "the first

time" there had been concern "not only with protecting those who [were] not infected but also with making pleasure accessible to those who [were]."[25]

↩

Wasn't the acquisition of the label "good managers of the epidemic" itself a
form of acknowledgment? We must be extremely careful in making this claim,
since it is very difficult to find anything positive about an epidemic that is affecting
more people every day.

The historian Paul Veyne, a professor at the Collège de France, likes to call
himself an "apologetic heterosexual." He was a fellow traveler of Michel Foucault,
and his son died of AIDS. According to Veyne, the issue of a certain acknowledgment of homosexuality by way of AIDS is unavoidable:

It may be difficult to admit, but AIDS has reduced antihomosexual prejudice. In my little
town, when people spoke of my son, they didn't say, "He's a queer," but rather "The poor
guy." His death was met with immense respect, even though we're in a rural area isolated
from the big cities. The horrible fact of the illness seems to have played a considerable
role in reducing homophobia. The irrational taboo on homosexuality has given way to a
need for rational and material precautions: condom use. I think that by the time the epidemic has been arrested, the taboo will have disappeared.

Aware of the delicate nature of his words, Veyne adds:

We must be very careful in this analysis so as not to be misunderstood, since it would be
easy to slip into an intolerable claim, as if you were saying that the gas chambers had the
advantage of reducing anti-Semitic prejudice. And yet the 5 percent of pity that every
human heart contains means people can no longer say bad things about homosexuals
who have suffered or who continue to suffer. I believe homophobia will no longer be
what it once was.

In the same vein, for the sociologist Alain Touraine, "the compensation for
AIDS will be an acknowledgment of homosexuals' moral citizenship." And for
Deputy Jean-Pierre Michel, "the French people no longer dare to be homophobic:
it's tragic, but the fact that there's been some progress is partly due to AIDS." Willy
Rozenbaum agrees with these analyses: "In spite of the tragedy, we might see a
positive side to the epidemic. The disease put male homosexuality on the map. It
made a previously clandestine reality visible. Homosexuals have found an identity,
and they are going through their enormous suffering together. Time will tell
whether some kind of revolution has taken place."

We should not push this matter too far. It is impossible to ignore the new
forms of "homophobia" and rampant hostility. In 1993, one homosexual in five
who was queried said he had been the object of insults, and one in twenty-five said
he had been assaulted because of his homosexuality. One homosexual in two says
he cannot tell his parents he is gay, and one in three never speaks to them about
having AIDS, not even in the end stage.[26] The image of homosexuality produced by
the illness links it to sympathy and compassion, but also to fear; none of these asso-

ciations appears beneficial at first glance. "Something is changing in the way people think," explains Françoise Héritier-Augé, a professor at the Collège de France
and former president of the Conseil National du Sida [National council on AIDS].
"Here's one hypothesis: there may have been a shift in the collective imagination
from homosexual as *scapegoat* to homosexual as *sacrificial victim*, someone who
has taken the illness upon himself to keep others from getting it."

Alain Molla, president of Aides–Provence and a man of practical experience,
also notes, "AIDS has triggered enormous changes in the way the public at large
views homosexuality. In Marseilles, I find people now raise the issue of homosexuality nonjudgmentally and understand the idea of the couple. Gay militants reject
the analysis that AIDS may have served the cause of gay identity, because this re-
duces their efforts to nothing. But the fundamental question is still raised: Does
AIDS destroy or reinforce homosexual identity? Personally, I think it must complement it."

THE NEW PITFALLS OF PREVENTION

Since the second half of the 1980s, the label "good managers of the epidemic"
has been applied to homosexuals as a result of their collective efforts to combat
AIDS, and this description is still generally accepted.

"Calculations based on simple probability allow us to posit that the epidemic
will tend to start up again in places where its prevalence is already highest, that is,
among male homosexuals."[27] In 1991, only a few months before his death, Michael
Pollak warned against a possible resurgence of infections in the homosexual milieu. Daniel Defert offered a similar analysis at the same time:

Although I am now convinced that organizing a response to the epidemic and establishing solidarity were important instruments in the individual and collective acknowledgment of homosexuality, I believe that homosexuals cannot stop at presenting a positive
image of themselves as controllers of the epidemic. If this image turned out to be a delusion, the cost in lives and social reaction would be high.[28]

Shortly before his death, Pierre Kneip, director of Sida Infos Service, declared,
more categorically, "There is nothing to be done. The myth of homosexuals as
good managers of the epidemic is false."

Since the early 1990s, prevention in the gay milieu has once again become
problematic. Pollak's and Schiltz's surveys have revealed a "pocket of resistance"
amounting to about 20 percent of homosexuals with occasional partners, who
continue to resist safer-sex practices (especially condom use). In addition, epidemiologists have hypothesized that the infection rate has begun to rise again in the
homosexual milieu. In this context, there has been mention of the phenomenon of
"relapse" [*relaps*], a kind of "fall" and a double reversal: safer sex is first adopted
and later abandoned, at least from time to time.[29] Indications of a new round of
HIV infections within the population most affected can be seen in the increase in

certain sexually transmitted diseases whose modes of transmission are similar to those for HIV; these indications have also been confirmed by the Schiltz surveys.[30] Observers who fear a second wave of infections in the homosexual population are particularly concerned by at least four problems: the phenomenon of relapse, the risks that continue to be taken in baths and back rooms, prevention among homosexual adolescents, and prevention among homosexuals who have been excluded from the larger society (those involved in "dark homosexuality," to use Guy Hocquenghem's expression).

Several hypotheses have been advanced to explain relapse and the abandoning of preventive measures. Homosexuals may be unable to assert themselves in negotiating matters of sexuality. Some may have burned out and grown weary after ten years of the epidemic ("they didn't tell us it would be forever"). Condoms may suddenly appear to be an obstacle to eroticism. New generations have appeared on the scene who are less sensitive to matters of prevention. Some homosexuals may have adopted irrational risk-avoidance strategies (selecting partners or cruising spots on the basis of illogical criteria). Some may lose control as a result of alcohol or drugs. Finally, some may have gradually developed "survivor's guilt," also observed after plane crashes.

In many ways, all these risky behaviors have appeared in the space left open by unresolved questions. What collective memory of AIDS do HIV-negative homosexuals have today?[31] How are we to conceptualize prevention over the long term, when one member of a couple is HIV-positive and the other is not? How are we to get information to individuals who are HIV-negative, who may not feel connected to the gay milieu, or who may not identify with this new homosexual destiny, which is sometimes too closely associated with the disease? How, conversely, can we put an end to this morbid fascination with HIV and sever the link between AIDS and homosexuality, with the implicit acknowledgment and claim of a symbolic gay identity that it entails? Finally, as the virus becomes familiar and vigilance wavers, how are we to avoid becoming complacent about the risk of AIDS?

Places of "high sexual yield" are still places where infection rates are high.[32] Although the number of people who visit such places dropped considerably in the second half of the 1980s, back rooms have reopened in significant numbers since 1992, both in Paris and in the provinces. Marie-Ange Schiltz, a statistician, can be credited with boldly asking a disturbing question: "The risk incurred is always higher in cruising spots of high sexual yield than it is elsewhere, whatever the degree of protection practiced in the places concerned. ... Might it not be useful to inform homosexuals that, according to our observations, as the number of partners and penetrations increases, the exposure to risk also increases proportionately?" In addition to psychological causes, there are mechanical factors, such as relatively frequent condom ruptures, which unquestionably increase in conjunction with the number of sex acts and, usually, with the number of partners.[33] For homosexuals who visit commercial establishments, lack of information about AIDS can no longer wholly explain the risks being taken.

Gay adolescents, by contrast, may not be adequately informed. "How can we reach a sixteen-year-old homosexual who has received information aimed at the general public but finds he is in a high-risk environment?" asks Alain Molla. Is it possible that there is a kind of self-discrimination syndrome, an unconscious valorization of the disease via its martyred heroes, as some studies suggest? What does "becoming a homosexual" mean in the AIDS years? How can the younger generations be persuaded to practice prevention the very first time (the "lapse" problematic)? Young homosexuals seem to be especially vulnerable because of the difficulty in negotiating the terms of the first sexual experience. For them, sexual initiation seems to occur almost invariably with older partners. It is undoubtedly up to these partners to be responsible, especially since the first encounter may be decisive in determining whether the adolescent practices prevention in the future.[34] Nevertheless, communication has to be handled very carefully, since, as Daniel Defert has explained, "If we try to conceive of prevention targeting young homosexuals, we run the risk from the outset of having nobody listen."

There is one more area where prevention among homosexuals remains tricky—namely, the area of "dark" homosexuality. When homosexuality is combined with drug use, prostitution, or simply life on the edge, the prevention measures of the traditional organizations no longer seem effective, and behaviors like these appear rarely or not at all in sociological studies. This is naturally true in the case of "survival sex," cases in which individuals agree to perform sexual acts for pay in order to procure drugs, and who are thus "condemned to homosexuality." These venal homosexual encounters are often indispensable if an individual is to be able to buy crack; and yet, to remain in control of his sex drive (which, all things considered, is necessary in male prostitution), he may have to use heroin as well.[35] But this is true as well for all "men among themselves" who do not define themselves as homosexuals, and who go out to "get some fresh air" in public parks, where from time to time they have "casual sex." "Dark" homosexuality is defined by a subtle geography (Frédéric-Mistral Park, in Grenoble; alongside the Quai de Jemmapes, in Paris; in the woods of Verrières-le-Buisson, in Essonne; near the Esplanade des Jacobins, in Le Mans, or Gerland Stadium, in Lyons; in the woods of Phalempin, in Lille, or Vaugrenier Park, in Nice; on some freeway interchange in Bordeaux, where hustlers rub shoulders with married men, transvestites, immigrants, exiles from eastern Europe, and swinging heterosexual couples) and by fleeting, short-lived codes.

This "dark" homosexuality is probably more common than we may think and more complex than we may want to admit. It sheds light on often confused individual histories, where uneasiness, exclusion, secrecy, and incomprehensible sexuality all intersect; in the end, such things are far removed from the carefree, festive gay life that has once more become an object of discussion.

Prevention campaigns targeting gays remain largely ineffective for populations in which sexual discrimination is often combined with ethnic or social discrimination. Any prevention measure based on a gay identity is rejected, obviously; Aides, despite its efforts, has had trouble establishing prevention efforts that can reach these individuals, a fact that has led its detractors to criticize it as elitist and out of touch. Nevertheless, the government has been just as ineffective in proposing solutions, and Aides finally chose to organize prevention efforts aimed specifically at sex workers—in September 1991, for example, near the Gare Saint-Charles, in Marseilles.

To get an idea of these situations, it is enough to listen to the calls made to Sida Infos Service, a free AIDS information line established by Pierre Kneip, and hear the bits and pieces of life stories. These calls constitute a formidable observatory for a homosexuality that is sometimes lived out among lies and doubts and that is not acknowledged—not even to oneself. All kinds of messages are found here, from general admissions of discomfort ("I'm calling because things aren't going well") to the pretense of a third party used to mask the fact that one wishes to get information for oneself ("I'm calling for my brother Alain"). "It's not a life, it's just fucking like rabbits," one HIV-positive man says regretfully, looking back on his past. "I need a shoulder to cry on," some of love's outcasts seem to say, seeking, in vain, a brief encounter or a lifelong relationship.[36]

↜

The universe of the playwright Bernard-Marie Koltès, who died of AIDS in April 1989, may serve to illustrate these encounters in which "illicit" destinies overlap in unauthorized places, and these people who worry about being fondled but expect to be slapped. Thus, toward the end of *Dans la solitude des champs de coton* [In the loneliness of the cotton fields], the customer looking for nothing can say to the dealer with nothing to sell, "There is no love, there is no love." Koltès's characters are convicts, outlaws, losers in the sex trade, but they also speak of their heartrending need for love. For Koltès, the needy homosexual resembles a drug addict looking for a dealer; there is a homo high just as there is a drug trip. As Koltès explained in 1983, "There is a form of rootlessness specific to homosexuals. It's something I sense but have not yet managed to figure out."[37] Since that time, the "rootlessness" of homosexuals has changed, and Koltès was probably alluding to his own illness in this line from the same play: "Do you talk to a roof tile that falls off and fractures your skull? You're a bee that has landed on the muzzle of a cow trying to graze on the other side of an electric fence; you shut up or you run away, you're sorry, you wait, you do what you can, nothing but senseless motivations, illegal acts, darkness."

↜

A snapshot of the epidemic's ravages in the French homosexual population is overpowering in its effect.[38] The hour is late and the toll is critical, but it is no less true that safer sex was initiated by homosexuals in 1985, that prevention in the gay milieu has been undertaken in exemplary fashion, and that risk reduction has been significant in the population most affected by the epidemic.

The future success of prevention among gays, and the number of lives saved, will probably depend on the responses that public leaders and organizations can bring to the new challenges of prevention: first homosexual encounters, establishments with a "high sexual yield," relapses, "dark" homosexuality. In the years to come, despite some demonstrated successes, prevention measures targeting homosexual populations will have to set a minimum goal of (to borrow, again, an expression popular among those working to curb drug addiction) limiting the damage.[39]

16

The Identity Movement

Homosexuals today form what Otto Bauer called, in reference to nations, a destiny group (*Schicksalsgemeinschaft*).
    —Alain Finkielkraut, interview with the author, *Journal du Sida*, April 1995

O n June 16, 1988, barely a thousand people marched in the streets of Paris for the annual demonstration called the Gay Pride parade—an incongruous, ridiculous parade, which persisted in denying the reality of AIDS. Aides was not there; ACT UP did not yet exist. French homosexual militancy was in jeopardy as the fight against AIDS intensified. The homosexual revolution was ending in jokes and irresponsibility.

On June 24, 1995, nearly 60,000 people marched in the streets of Paris for Lesbian/Gay Pride Day. Aides and ACT UP were a major presence in the demonstration. The lesbians were back, and everyone had rediscovered the history of the homosexual deportation during World War II. Everyone hoped to give birth to a "homosexual community." It was the greatest success of the French homosexual movement.

What had taken place between these two dates?

  ↩

Since the early 1990s, AIDS organizations have formed a complex of groups that play a role in a stormy, sometimes brutal history mirroring an epidemic whose victims have reacted with desperate energy. As the illness affected more heterosexuals, young people, women, children, and poor people, every aspect of the epidemic was taken in hand by new groups: organizations for people with HIV, associations for hemophiliacs and transfusion recipients, associations of young people, women, and artists.[1] As a result of this multitude of organizations—specialized groups representing real or potential "victims," who responded helpfully to the new challenges raised by the epidemic—an unexpected turnabout has occurred. The idea of "risk groups," vigorously challenged between 1981 and 1987, has become the focus of prevention, articulated as such and appearing as the social goal of the organizations. A comprehensive view of the illness did not disappear, but alongside it there emerged the idea that certain targeted populations had a specific, collective relationship to the threat. In the late 1980s, through a curious reversal in the situation, homosexual militants appropriated the concept of a "gay cancer," which they had initially rejected or dismissed ("The cancer is not gay," in 1983) and then gradually acknowledged ("The cancer is gay," in 1985). They did so at a time when epidemiologists, public opinion, and especially the press were keeping their distance from this idea, having once embraced it. Ten years after the beginning of the epidemic, in militants' eyes, the cancer was again becoming gay.[2]

THE REALITY OF GAY CANCER

To be sure, this tone marks a departure from the past. It is more radical, more militant. "If you disagree with our morals ... if you think homosexuality is good if you happen to be manly and hairy, but that anyone who's a bit thin and has a sing-song voice shouldn't attend official meetings, if you're one of those people, then I beg you, drop out!"[3] These were the words of the psychiatrist Arnaud Marty-Lavauzelle, the new president of the Aides federation, who replaced Daniel Defert at the conference in Nancy in October 1991.

Aides is the "premier gay organization, the premier organization of people with HIV, the premier organization of women," Marty-Lavauzelle warned from the outset. After announcing to Aides volunteers, "You have a president with AIDS," he chose as his slogan the words of the Japanese poet Yukata Hirati: "I would like to live a little bit longer." His evolution within the federation was classic. The doctor joined the Aides "psychiatrist" group in February 1987, shortly after the split with Arcat-sida. He specialized in training new volunteers and was elected vice president and then president of the Aides–Paris–Ile de France committee. He then became the only candidate to run for Defert's office as head of the federation. "I am not a hero, I have no ambition to be one, nor to be a man of duty," Defert explained, to justify his resignation. "I have reached my limit. I cannot go on. Like all of you, I cannot continue going to the cemetery, to the crematorium, every week."[4]

Marty-Lavauzelle brought a more institutional, more federative (less Parisian) philosophy to Aides, increasing the number of salaried employees and the number of grassroots activities. One might say he now presided over the destiny of a true "humanitarian enterprise," with 3,600 volunteers and 150 representatives distributed among thirty-two departmental branches within thirty-one regional committees, and with a consolidated annual budget of 110 million francs.[5] The Paris Aides committee itself became a structured and efficient organization; it alone had over a thousand volunteers, whom its new president, Pierre Lascoumes, an academic specializing in "public policy" and an enlightened fan of contemporary dance, mustered into battle order in the European city most affected by AIDS.

This professionalism did not rule out a more combative tone. "It's the pressure of the epidemic that pushed us to protest more," Marty-Lavauzelle comments. The influence of ACT UP was also a determining factor: when Aides was criticized for its passivity, and when its leadership was challenged, it had to adopt a more force-ful tone. It began to organize public demonstrations, became actively involved in preventing AIDS among drug addicts (in the "Limiter la casse" collective), and so-licited help from political parties. Marty-Lavauzelle, explaining this new involve-ment, said he had lived through "wasted political years—it was impossible to talk about AIDS during the last two years of the Socialist government."[6] As Aides be-came more oriented to protest, it also acquired greater homosexual visibility, which initially had been fairly foreign to the organization. The image of an Aides that transcended and embraced various groups became less desirable, as if this strategic choice had gradually become less tenable in an organization with few drug users, hemophiliacs, and foreigners.[7] This "homosexualization" of Aides's message reached significant proportions, beginning in 1989.[8]

"We all did extraordinary things for homosexuality," explains Thierry Gamby, founder of Aides–Provence in 1985. "We would never have dared do all that if it hadn't been for AIDS." This admission shows that homosexuality lay at the heart of the Aides dynamic from its beginnings. Like Gamby, other volunteers fre-quently declared that they had "surprised themselves."

Many volunteers came to Aides out of gay solidarity, to get information, to deal with being HIV-positive, to grieve, or to declare their homosexuality, al-though this declaration was not, as the sociologist Marie-Ange Schiltz has said, "within everyone's reach." The available data confirm that in 1993 the majority of Aides members were homosexual, though their proportion was lower than it had been in 1985.[9]

In the provinces, Aides committees and radio stations appeared in the late 1980s as places for homosexuals to socialize and find affirmation. "Going to Aides gave me a sense of my homosexuality," explains a volunteer from Bordeaux. "Aides is a place to talk about homosexuality. In the provinces, there are few places to talk," confirms Christophe Coussin of Aides–Nantes. One of his colleagues at another branch explains, "What's a good queer? For me, it's a homosexual who has become involved in the fight against AIDS to help his brothers." The words of the vice president of a regional Aides committee are less typical but also revealing:

My involvement in Aides is not innocent. It seems to me it was also an unconscious pact with my mother: going to Aides was a way of telling her I was homosexual and at the same time sending the message that, though I was different, I could be part of an organi-zation with high social value. Without putting it into words, I wanted my admission to be offset by a notion of seriousness and responsibility, to be accompanied by a certain rec-ognition.

Involvement in Aides was sometimes an implicit way of satisfying the desire for "more cordial" cruising than occurred in specialized establishments. "Before, I couldn't cruise and pick up men. I'm better at it with the Aides label," confirms a volunteer in Aides–Nice.[10] In Dax, Mâcon, and Bourg-en-Bresse, as in all isolated cities, the Aides radio station was friendlier than the parks or the beaches. "In part,

Aides is an excuse to meet people who are like you and whom you want to spend time with," explains Michel Bourrelly, director of Aides–Provence. Nevertheless, Aides militants seemed to reject identity politics, at least until the 1990s. Marty-Lavauzelle gives partial confirmation of this hypothesis: "The people involved in the organization from the beginning were homosexual militants, but on a much broader scale than those embracing traditional homosexual identity. The traditional homosexuals were relatively loud and provocative and very strongly based in an acknowledgment of their sexuality. Aides is not the Gazolines."

Homosexuality in Aides, somewhat as in the women's movement, may have been kept quiet or not talked about in dealings with the outside world, but it remained a determining factor within the organization. High visibility and strong legitimacy on the inside, absence of visibility on the outside: the same old song.

Beginning in the 1990s, however, homosexual identity, implicitly the force behind many volunteers' commitment, began to appear openly. "On many Aides committees, homosexual visibility was already an occasion for tension and sometimes played a role in causing splits," confirms Bruno Gachard of Aides–Poitiers. From that date on, the "buddies" saw that they were also gay militants. Aides was no longer just a place to meet peers or form a "family"; it had become a framework for activism. "I felt very strong pressure and the demand for a new homosexual visibility," Marty-Lavauzelle comments today.

About 1989, Aides created a specific group for activism in the gay milieu. In Paris, the name Dominik Le Fers is still associated with this group. The activism of this Bordeaux native was a determining factor; his death in February 1992 was the occasion for "national mourning" within the Aides federation. In April 1992, the group adopted a telling name: Pin'Aides [a homophone of *pinèdes,* "pine forests"]. At the same time, groups for "prévention en milieu gai" [prevention in the gay milieu], or PMGs, proliferated in the organization's regional committees.[11]

In the provinces in the early 1990s, the PMGs were once again running into owners of gay establishments who rejected the prevention materials offered by Aides, and some local homosexual organizations refused to pass them along, maintaining that this was not their job. These incidents were not isolated; their persistence into the 1990s is disconcerting. Cases were reported by all the PMGs: one owner who accepted Aides prevention materials during the week but rejected them on the weekend; another who made the Aides volunteers pay a cover charge to enter his disco; a bathhouse owner who denied, against all the evidence, that his business was a homosexual one. "Heterosexual discos are much more likely than gay establishments to accept prevention measures," notes a disabused Bruno Gachard. Pierre Kneip, director of Sida Infos Service, declared shortly before his death, "Gay establishments are even now overwhelmingly responsible for the hecatomb. That fact is irrefutable." Bruno Hup of Aides explains the proliferation of the PMGs: "If the network of organizations and commercial spots had truly mobilized before 1990, the PMGs probably never would have come into being."

The lack of involvement in prevention among some bathhouse and disco owners and gay organizations in the early 1990s is indisputably peculiar to France, and no one, not even ACT UP, was really troubled by it until a few years ago.[12]

"PMG leaders were often criticized by homosexual organizations," Alain Molla, president of Aides–Provence, confirms bitterly. "But there are far more homosexual militants in these gay Aides groups than in all the other Parisian homosexual organizations put together." This observation, if harsh, is at least clear and perhaps suggests that the Aides volunteers replaced the traditional homosexual militants.

It is possible, then, that the return of homosexual militancy in France came about in part as a result of the new desire on the part of Aides volunteers, incited by members of ACT UP, to publicly declare their homosexuality and engage in identity politics.[13] The sociologist Michael Pollak has made a similar observation: "In my opinion, the integration of homosexuality into organizational activism signals a self-assurance and a pride acquired through action."[14] The sense of belonging to a community may have begun here, between suffering and responsibility, between a spirit of resistance and the pride of a universalist struggle that has become a model for the rest of society.

    ↜

    The second sign indicating the return of militant identity politics in the late 1980s could be seen in lesbian settings. Given the predominance of male homosexuality in the issue of AIDS, we have to some extent lost track of homosexual women. What had become of them since the beginning of the epidemic?

In keeping with the American tradition, where the massive involvement of lesbians has been characteristic of the history of the AIDS movement, homosexual women made an early appearance in French AIDS organizations. Some French homosexual women became involved in Aides groups after a gay friend had died; others, having "joyfully" fought alongside homosexual men in the 1970s, "naturally" found themselves at their side once more in the "dark times of homosexuality" (as a woman Aides volunteer explained): "We had to stand behind the product we had sold in the battles of the 1970s." The individual or collective involvement of lesbians bears witness to a certain sense of solidarity among homosexuals, beyond gender.

Marie-Ange Schiltz, who had distanced herself from the feminists "because there were more serious problems," chose to fight against AIDS side by side with Pollak. "Our joint work on AIDS allowed me to acknowledge my own homosexuality," she confides. "I had never given any importance to this issue before."

The presence of homosexual women in the fight against AIDS and on the Aides committees should not mask the initial difficulties that heterosexual women encountered in these organizations. Although they represented nearly 35 percent of new Aides volunteers in 1987, their remarks are sometimes tinged with a certain disappointment. "I got in touch with Aides in 1986 but only became a volunteer two years later," says France Uebersfeld, former president of the Paris Aides committee. "For a long time I thought you couldn't volunteer if you were a woman. In the beginning, I felt invisible as a woman in the organization. I didn't exist. There were aspects of it that could be threatening for a heterosexual woman: a way of talking about sex, the way the men touched each other, the chumminess among the guys. Over time, these elements became secondary."

Women's presence in Aides continued to grow: they were 43 percent of the volunteers in 1993. Not all these women were homosexual; far from it.[15] Those who were not were called "fag hags" by the detractors of Aides. In reality, these women had more diverse backgrounds than might be expected. A number were the mothers of homosexual or drug-addicted sons who had died of AIDS: "Helping others fight the illness helps you bear the grief." Others fit a profile more typical in humanitarian organizations. Some belonged to paramedical, nursing, or nursing auxiliary organizations. Many had people close to them who had been affected by AIDS.

The presence of heterosexual women in Aides should not be underestimated. It demonstrates a more inclusive aspect of the fight against the epidemic, illustrates the dialogue between homosexuals and people who are not homosexual, and thus serves to qualify the new image of Aides as grounded in a gay identity.

In the history of Aides, lesbians have felt stigmatized by homosexuality, as if they too were being regarded as a risk group, in keeping with an irrational process of identification, more social than medical.[16] The risk of infection among women was the subject of intense debate, especially since, for some lesbian militants, the fight against AIDS represented an issue of identity politics specific to them.[17] The most radical homosexual women in this "lowest-risk" group wanted to raise the stakes—urging the use of dental dams, for example.[18] But this movement did not have any significant influence.[19]

"AIDS doesn't affect lesbians as a group the way it does queer men," says the novelist Anne Garreta. Professor Christine Rouzioux, codiscoverer of the AIDS virus, declares frankly, "I want to tell lesbians, Knock it off with your fear of AIDS; gay men are tallying up their dead." Nevertheless, ACT UP and Aides created prevention groups[20] targeting lesbians, using irrefutable arguments: lesbians could be drug addicts or have bisexual relationships.

The more militant presence of lesbians in ACT UP may have been driven by other factors. Homosexual women in this organization embraced radicalism with a new intensity; and in the early 1990s, this radicalism was scarcely able to find expression elsewhere. In their own way, lesbians were committed to the fight against a disease from which some people wanted to exclude them (as one militant woman in ACT UP explained). In fact, one slogan of the organization declared, "Women don't get AIDS, but it's killing them."

In this vein, the "women's committee" of ACT UP–Paris took an interest in the specifically female aspects of AIDS (the risk of HIV infection via menstrual blood, vaginal fisting, the use of dildos, the specifics of needle sharing within women's communities, mother-child relationships, the risk of infection during artificial insemination) and of illnesses associated with HIV (recurrent pelvic infections, dysplasia, invasive cervical cancer).[21]

⤙

A revival of lesbian militancy came about through these new debates, which led homosexual women to raise issues about all the health problems specific to women, if not to lesbians. And, once again, this remobilization should not conceal a generation gap. Catherine Gonnard, editor-in-chief of *Lesbia*, says:

I see an entirely new generation of lesbians in ACT UP, who are immersed in feminism but moving away from it. They want a coed radicalism. They're interested in sadomasochism, fascinated by the power of gay militancy against AIDS, attracted to the male ghetto, its clothes, its commercial spots. We sometimes play the mother role, even though they call us old fogies: in fact, they have little understanding of us.

In the tradition of ACT UP, the organization Lesbiennes Se Déchaînent [Lesbians lash out], or LSD, which developed in late 1994, fits this new model of militancy fairly well. It is radical and provocative, critical of feminism but close to the gay men's movement.

⤙

Anne Garreta alludes to the strange postfeminism she discovered, and from which she feels very removed: "When I got into feminism, all I found was the hysteria of microscopic dinosaurs caught up in a psychoanalytic frenzy. The word 'feminist' had become an insult. The feminist movements were paranoid and self-perpetuating. They had become cults." This harsh view is not unanimously shared, and the "historic" feminists have not disappeared. Some, such as Luce Irigaray, Hélène Cixous, and Monique Wittig, even seem to have quite a following in North America—more, anyway, than in France, as if "America were no longer the future of feminism, but its past."[22]

For most feminists in France, the debate now seems to focus on politics, and primarily on salary inequity and political parity (equal access to political office). "The majority of the parity lobby is lesbian," says Thérèse Clerc of Réseau Femmes pour la Parité [Women for parity network]. If feminists are to be believed, these political themes illustrate a "discontent within citizenship" or a "democracy deficit." More broadly, they are part of a crisis of conscience on the left and a disillusionment with, if not bitterness toward, the Socialists.

When Colette Codaccioni was appointed "minister of intergenerational harmony," in June 1995 (her duties include women's issues), feminism took on new life in its battle against her. Organizations denounced her cult of the family and her ties to fundamentalist Catholic and antiabortion forces. They were unimpressed with the appointment of Clara Lejeune-Gaymard, daughter of the famous professor Jérôme Lejeune (so fiercely fought against in the early 1970s) and wife of Secretary of Health Hervé Gaymard, as Codaccioni's cabinet director. But would Codaccioni's sudden departure from the government, on November 7, 1995, jeopardize the rebirth of feminism (constantly being announced) by depriving feminists of an enemy?[23]

Who has taken the feminists' place? The group and journal Marie-Pas-Claire, created in 1991 and appearing to be the daughters of the MLF militants, backs a modern form of feminism greatly influenced by ACT UP. Although several of these young women are openly homosexual—they fight against "lesbophobia" and attend the Gay Pride parade—they see themselves as feminists first. Their predecessors, some of whom actually are their mothers, regard them with "tenderness and weariness," in the words of one feminist from the old days. Marie-Pas-Claire, forgetting the MLF's teachings, achievements, and limitations, proposes to raise the issues of rape and sexual harassment once again. In this vein, a "sexual feminism," already under way in the United States, may come along to replace "egalitarian feminism."[24]

For the moment, feminism's battlefield of choice is international. Women's condition in Algeria and, more generally, within the Islamic world; the fate of the Bangladeshi writer Taslima Nasreen, or of Sarah Balabagan, the young Filipina raped by her Kuwaiti employer—these have inspired large-scale demonstrations of solidarity.

The most significant example of this approach involves the rape of women in Bosnia. The Collectif Féministe de la Solidarité avec les Femmes en ex-Yougoslavie [Feminist collective of solidarity with women in the former Yugoslavia] was created in France in October 1992. Many groups began to form in the provinces, until the Paris collective split apart in February 1993—over the issue of lesbianism: Should the name of the collective include the word "lesbian" or not?[25] It is telling that, as during the heyday of the women's movement (recall the split at *Questions Féministes*, in 1980), the issue of lesbianism has once more brought about divisions in the feminist organizations of the 1990s.[26] For French feminism, lesbianism has continued to be a point of both gathering together and splitting apart.

≈

Like lesbians' protests over Bosnia, militancy in connection with the commemoration of the homosexual deportation—the third sign indicating the return of identity politics in France—is also not free of ambiguity.

The boy has an angelic, androgynous beauty, a grave look about him. There is a bit of makeup around his eyes. He is erotic, wearing lipstick, but his head is shaved.

He is wearing a nice pinstriped shirt, more reminiscent of Jean-Paul Gaultier fashions than of the deportee's uniform. On this shirt, however, there is an inverted pink triangle with a number on it. The boy seems to be posing behind shiny new barbed wire, and his attraction to uniforms, maybe even his inclination for sadomasochism, can be discerned. This photo by the homosexual artists Pierre and Gilles sums up all the issues—and all the ambiguities—surrounding the homosexual deportation that it is supposed to illustrate.[27]

Since the early 1990s, the rebirth of the homosexual movement has included a new interpretation of its history, and especially of the homosexual deportation: memory is all the rage. We might hypothesize that the AIDS epidemic, by making people aware of collective grief, served as the trigger. ACT UP took the pink triangle as its symbol and established a comparison between the Holocaust and AIDS.[28]

On April 24, 1994, during official ceremonies for the national day of remembrance of the deportation, about a hundred gay militants tried to place a spray of flowers in memory of deported homosexuals. On that day, not far from Prime Minister Edouard Balladur and Simone Veil, the militants were blocked by police officers and denied access to the martyrs' memorial on the Ile de la Cité, in Paris. A few days earlier, the Union Nationale des Associations de Déportés [National union of deportee organizations], or UNADIF, had sent a letter to gay organizations claiming, in particularly vicious terms:

[The problem of homosexual deportation] never existed for French deportees. In fact, if there were any prisoners wearing the pink triangle in Nazi concentration camps . . . they were all of German nationality, and no French person was given that label. A few Alsatians also wore the pink triangle, but they were considered German at the time. The acknowledgment you are seeking will not come about through misrepresentation of historical events in which homosexuals did not participate as a group. . . . As a result, there is no reason to make a place of any kind for homosexuals in [commemorative observances of] the deportation. That is why we cannot tolerate any demonstration on your part, or on the part of your allies, at our patriotic demonstrations. Our security forces will oppose your intrusion with all their authority.[29]

In reply, homosexual militants naturally gave their own interpretation of the deportation, denounced the sectarianism or even revisionism that tended to obliterate the "other" victims, and buttressed their argument by pointing to monuments on behalf of homosexual deportees in Berlin, Amsterdam, and Mauthausen. They also distributed a poster with the slogan STOP THE MASSACRE OF MEMORY!

This misunderstanding shows that the homosexual deportation remains a difficult subject. The arguments on both sides do not bode well. In order to understand, we must consider some historical details, and at some length; only then will one of the most disconcerting aspects of the history of homosexuals appear. To a surprising degree, their fate in the concentration camps is still unknown.[30] No official survey has been done, no serious historical study has been devoted to the deportation, and what statistics there are not really reliable.

With respect to the deportation, three elements need to be considered: the geographical area studied, the "motives" for deportation,[31] and the conditions surrounding detention and death in the camps. Most historians are agreed in distinguishing the so-called concentration camps from the "extermination" camps. The former housed several categories of prisoners, recognizable by the color of the triangles sewn onto their clothing: red for the "politicals" (opponents of the Nazi regime, Communists, resistance fighters), green for "common criminals," violet for Jehohah's Witnesses, black for "antisocials," blue for stateless people, and pink for homosexuals. A total of 1.65 million people throughout the world are believed to have been deported to the concentration camps, and at least 550,000 died there. Of that total, homosexuals seem to have been decimated at a higher rate than the other populations. The historians Richard Plant and François Bédarida posit a mortality rate of 60 percent among deported homosexuals, who faced a particularly agonizing fate in these camps. They were considered "sexual delinquents," and macabre medical experiments (castration in particular) were sometimes performed on them. This was not systematic execution, however, nor was it "genocide" in the strict sense of the term.[32]

By contrast, the function of the extermination camps was to physically eliminate the greatest possible number of human beings, and as quickly as possible, with the maximum "yield." The six death camps, all in formerly Polish territory, were used to exterminate Jews (who wore the yellow star) and, to an extent, Gypsies. Soviet political prisoners and mentally ill people were also subject to the extermination policy.

Whatever their countries of origin, individuals deported for being homosexual were not taken to the extermination camps, even though the Nazis considered homosexuality to be not a moral or medical problem but a "racial" one.[33] Richard Plant estimates that, for all countries combined, between 5,000 and 30,000 homosexuals—but probably fewer than 20,000—died in concentration camps.[34] Most were German, Austrian, or Polish. On what pretext were they arrested, and how? What was their fate? How many survived? We do not know.

The few historians who have taken an interest in the question of homosexual deportees do not always agree on the figures, but most French historians do agree that there was no deportation of homosexuals as such from France.[35] The debate focuses on deportees from Alsace, a territory considered German at the time because it had been annexed by the Reich. How many deportees were there? We do not know that, either. It has been established, however, that government employees in the eastern departments made the police files of homosexuals available to the Germans at the Germans' request.

To avoid simply including French homosexuals under the Occupation rubric "victims," we need to recall that a part of the Paris homosexual intelligentsia collaborated with the Germans. The names most often cited are those of Maurice Sachs, Abel Bonnard (nicknamed "our little gestapo gal" [gestapette] by Pétain), and Robert Brasillach, who was probably bisexual. Another portion of this intelligentsia (Marcel Jouhandeau, Henri de Montherlant, and even, in an altogether personal manner, Jean Cocteau and Jean Genet) may have "accommodated itself" to the occupiers or indulged them. As a reflection of this situation, Daniel, the homosexual character in Sartre's *Chemins de la liberté* [The road to freedom], applauds the Germans' arrival in Paris. Finally, how can we fail to mention the deported homosexuals who, having become the "little buddies" of Nazis, managed to obtain the rank of Kapo?[36] Recognition of the homosexual deportation in Europe would be useful in offsetting these images and would demonstrate that homosexuality, notwithstanding some notorious collaborators, is politically "neutral."

ᗡ

In 1981 there appeared a controversial eyewitness account by Heinz Heger, a homosexual deportee who himself became a Kapo.[37] Guy Hocquenghem chose to write the preface to this book: "This may be what being homosexual means today: knowing you are linked to a genocide for which there will be no reparation." This legitimate concern with commemorating the homosexual deportation might have been acceptable if Hocquenghem, who ought to have known better, had not left disturbing doubts about his true intentions. In this preface and plea on behalf of homosexuals, Hocquenghem blamed "the power of the American Jewish community," and he denounced what he viewed as the "trickery" of Jewish martyrs who were concealing "authentic" homosexual "martyrs." He even went so far as to write these odiously defamatory words: "I would not have wanted to live in a barracks where Simone Veil was Kapo."[38] The philosopher Alain Finkielkraut, denouncing Hocquenghem's "rivalrous anti-Semitism," replied in a scathing article:

It is the same phobia in the revisionists and in Hocquenghem. What is different is the perspective: the issue is no longer to make Nazism banal but to resurrect unknown martyrs. ... [Hocquenghem's goal is to] dethrone the Jews—those pseudovictims, those ⧫usurpers, those fake pariahs—and reveal, in all their immaculate splendor, the ones who hold the true title of Most Abused.

Finkielkraut adds, "The equivalent of a Final Solution was not inflicted on this minority [homosexuals]. In Europe under the Nazi occupation, there was no queer hunt that had the methodical frenzy, the totalitarian efficiency, that was everywhere brought to bear against the Jews."[39] In 1981, Hocquenghem's "instrumentalism" with respect to the homosexual deportation, and his outlandish vehemence, brought to light the ambiguities of the "right to difference."

What more is there to say? The homosexual deportation was a historical event and cannot be denied. Even if there were only one documented case of a French [homosexual] deportee from Alsace, European organizations for homosexual former deportees unquestionably should be allowed to place a spray of flowers at ceremonies commemorating the deportation.[40] In what is a healthy development, young Jewish militants have moved in this direction, questioning the reservations of their elders: "How could young French people belonging to the Jewish faith stand by certain leaders in the Jewish community, who have been reluctant to grant Gypsies and homosexuals their request to join them at memorial ceremonies?"[41]

For his part, the only Alsatian homosexual deportee to be recognized as such was surprised by how he was being "exploited." He criticized gay militants who "strutted about" with their pink triangles in front of the monument to the dead: "I want to tell them, You've got no goddamn right to be in front of this monument! Leave the deportees alone! What a circus! As long as homosexual militants are there, I won't go to the ceremonies. What right do they have to wear the pink triangle?"[42]

Can you quell the debate by wearing an ACT UP T-shirt on Deportation Day, organizing a "mini–Gay Pride Day," being deliberately provocative, and thinly veiling the goals of identity politics? Is the purpose of recovering the history of homosexuals under the Nazi Occupation to reinforce the developing homosexual community? Is it possible to believe that an acknowledgment of the deportation would have an immediate effect on AIDS prevention?[43] Isn't this kind of historical instrumentalism implicitly designed to serve the contemporary gay cause, which claims that the Holocaust and AIDS are equivalent? In other words, must today's French homosexual militants raise suspicions about their intentions? To defend their own cause, must they take up the mantle of revisionists and Holocaust negators? Following Hocquenghem, must they set themselves up as rivals of the Jews (even misrepresenting their own memories, as Pierre and Gilles did when they put makeup on their deportee model)? Or should the contemporary French homosexual movement embrace its legitimate obligation to the past? This would entail, not making history speak, but inviting historians to break their bewildering silence about the Nazi persecution of homosexuals, encouraging them to understand why Jews, Gypsies, mentally ill people, and homosexuals had the misfortune of setting off the infernal machine—a question that remains "irksome" (Hannah Arendt).[44]

BIRTH OF A COMMUNITY?

These three signs of an identity movement under way—the radicalization and "homosexualization" of Aides, the rebirth of lesbian militancy, and the rediscovery of the history of homosexual deportation—are part of the militant revival inaugurated by ACT UP–Paris. As the toll of the homosexual dead mounted and the fight against AIDS became urgent, the social ties necessary for mobilization were forged. More conscious than ever of the exclusion from which they suffer, homosexual militants wanted to overvalue their marginality and chose a new communitarian path. For this "community" to come into being, however, the rights denied to homosexuals still had to be identified and demanded.[45] This last step was taken in France in 1992, and it centered on the project of a "civil union contract."

⌐⌐

During the 1980s, AIDS starkly revealed the vulnerable and problematic situations existing among homosexuals. Examples abound of homosexuals stripped of their legitimate role of mourner by the families of their deceased partners, as if the history of these love affairs could be denied and effaced. Some "longtime companions" have not even been invited to their partners' funerals, and "blood relatives" have sometimes taken the vicious step of giving a lover the wrong date or location, to keep him away. Daniel Defert concludes, "There is no greater taboo than the tears shed for a homosexual lover."[46] These difficulties sometimes become even more harrowing when the time comes to divide up the inheritance of a deceased homosexual or to renegotiate the lease for an apartment that a couple has occupied.

These situations, made even more intolerable by AIDS, reveal the daily difficulties faced by homosexual couples. What does civil law have to say about the "bizarre unions" composed of a gay and a lesbian couple, or to homosexual women raising a child together? How does inheritance work within a gay couple? How are job transfers handled for government employees who have homosexual partners? What about joint requests for government housing? How are case files handled for the various forms of social welfare? How can a couple of elderly homosexual women earn the right not to be separated in a retirement home? Why are women refused custody of their own children because they are homosexual? These particular questions, the answers to which remain unresolved, show—and this is an understatement—that legislation has not kept up with reality.

Jurisprudence has proved no more flexible than the law. In 1989, the Cour de Cassation issued two decrees banning homosexual couples from enjoying the same rights as heterosexual domestic partners. The first case had to do with a male flight attendant for Air France, Yves S., who wanted his partner, Serge, to get the reduced fares that are granted to employees' legal spouses and heterosexual domestic partners. The second case involved Nadia L., a stay-at-home mother of three children, who lived with her partner, Annie, and who had obtained a certificate of domestic partnership from the deputy mayor of the town where the couple lived. Nadia simply wanted to be covered by Annie's medical insurance, but Sécurité Sociale opposed the measure, citing the absence of a legal precedent.

After each case was appealed to the Cour de Cassation, the highest judicial authority in France rejected the arguments made by homosexuals, on the basis of existing precedents related to "marital law." A domestic partnership exists only if marriage is a possibility, the court held, and this is not the case for homosexuals.

In addition to these two symbolic cases, there are a large number of divorce cases in which child custody has been refused to a parent, or in which visitation rights have been curtailed or left to the discretion of the mother, on the sole ground of the ex-husband's homosexual orientation. By contrast, administrative precedents are very weak—"which is rather a good sign," says René Chapus, a senior official—and the Commission National Informatique et Libertés [National computer and freedom commission] has considered only one case since its creation.[47]

In this general context, made more urgent and more tragic by AIDS, it is possible that a future request for regulations regarding "homosexual bonds" may appear. This new demand illustrates that "emotional needs" seem to be replacing the "pleasure needs" of homosexual liberation's heyday. It also lends support to the intuition of Louise de Vilmorin, who is said to have replied to André Malraux, when he proposed marriage to her, "Don't you realize that priests and homosexuals are the only people who still want to get married?"

╰┐

Legislation on homosexual domestic partnerships was drafted several times in the 1980s by various organizations close to the Socialist Party, or even directly, by one of its elected officials, Senator Jean-Luc Mélenchon. Nevertheless, only in October 1991, under the rubric of the civil union contract, or CUC, did homosexual domestic partnerships became part of France's social history and meet with general approval.

The original idea of this legislation came from two former leaders in the Comité d'Urgence Anti-Répression Homosexuelle (CUARH), which had gradually dissolved around 1985. In the early 1990s, Jean-Paul Pouliquen and Gérard Bach-Ignasse noted that lifestyle changes and the tragic consequences of AIDS required changes in domestic-partnership legislation. Little by little, with dogged persistence, they managed to convince many leading figures and got three Socialist deputies—Jean-Pierre Michel and Jean-Yves Autexier (who at the time had close ties to the party's Chevènement camp), along with Jean-Michel Bélorgey—to agree to sponsor legislation.[48]

Initially, an omnibus bill was drafted to cover all the legal problems raised by the situation of individuals living together, regardless of their gender. It proposed something between a stripped-down marriage and an augmented domestic partnership. The most significant innovations of the bill, intended to provide a legal framework for a de facto arrangement, were its review of inheritance provisions and its awarding of the right to Sécurité Sociale benefits and "continued occupancy of a residence" if one of the partners died. On essential points, then, the legislation proposed to grant unmarried couples rights similar to those of married couples.

The proposed legislation received wide support. Among the many figures who supported it were those who had wanted to decriminalize homosexuality in 1981 (from Huguette Bouchardeau to Henri Caillavet, a group including Gisèle Halimi, Jean-Pierre Mignard, and Cécile Goldet), feminists (from Yvette Roudy to Françoise Gaspard), cultural figures prominent in homosexual debates in France (from Dominique Fernandez to Jocelyne François, and from Renaud Camus to

Yves Navarre), but also groups whose involvement in sexual matters was unremarkable: Planning Familial [a French counterpart of Planned Parenthood], the Verts [the Green Party], the National Union of French Students, and Génération Ecologie [Generation ecology]. By contrast, several leaders of homosexual organizations refused to be associated with the plan.

Elisabeth Badinter publicly supported the civil union contract, gradually emerging as one of its principal spokespersons. From the outset, this wife of a former president of the Conseil Constitutionnel presented the bill as a "universal idea for justice." According to her, "great reforms, which require true courage to fight prejudices of every stripe, are usually made at the beginning of a legislative term. I cannot help thinking that, if it had to be done today, we could never abolish capital punishment." For her, the CUC completed the shift from homosexuals' "right to difference" to their "right to indifference": "Leave us alone, we're just like everybody else. It's the right to difference that ghettoizes minority communities and makes the majority reject and oppress them."[49]

↩

Beyond the legal aspects, the ideas of the CUC were largely championed by activists in the fight against AIDS, who saw the plan as a means of promoting prevention. Willy Rozenbaum declared, "For a population as broadly affected as homosexuals have been, establishing a civil union contract will have an impact in the area of AIDS prevention that will be at least as significant as the impact of technological measures." In the same vein, the epidemiologist Jean-Baptiste Brunet explained, "You cannot ask an entire community to join in the fight against AIDS . . . and at the same time not acknowledge that community!"[50]

Even though the press spread the idea of the CUC and more than 3,000 people agreed to support the legislation, and even though a May 1992 survey revealed that 72 percent of those questioned were "very much" or "somewhat" in favor of the bill, the response of politicians was not unanimous; far from it.

Of course, the legislation's proponents may have made tactical mistakes. By drafting their bill more on the model of marriage than on that of cohabitation, they gave their detractors a valuable argument: they created the impression that they wanted to establish "gay marriage." Conversely, by disconnecting the CUC from the couple relationship, particularly its sexual dimension, they suggested that they stood for a trivial, fickle, merely utilitarian conception of the couple.[51] But this is not enough to explain the reluctance of political leaders. The first criticisms of the CUC came from right-wing figures (Jacques Toubon, for example), who rejected it on principle, and even from some (such as Elisabeth Hubert) who knew nothing about the legislation. It is not insignificant that the same deputies who denounced the "excesses" of promiscuous homosexuals were even more vehement in rejecting the civil union contract. This attitude, expressed by Philippe de Villers in particular, seems especially inconsistent.

On the left, the Socialist Party proved extremely chilly on the subject. In December 1992, after incomprehensible hesitations and refusals by a number of Socialist leaders, the bill was revised at the last minute, before the end of the parliamentary session. Thanks to the tenacity of Jean-Marie Le Guen (first secretary of the Socialist Party federation in Paris) and Marie Noëlle Lienemann, then minister of housing, Socialist deputies adopted two amendments to the CUC on the sly: one guaranteed the right of continued occupancy (it was later declared unconstitutional on technical grounds), and the other extended Sécurité Sociale benefits to the partner (the enforcement of this amendment was later ordered).[52] The responsibility for this near-failure, as absurd as it was unexpected by the left, lies with the Socialist group in the National Assembly and with the Bérégovoy government: both demonstrated an undeniable indifference and disingenuousness, which resulted in the reduction of several original ideas to their most minimalist expressions. Yet the implementation of these ideas was and still is an urgent matter. In this sense, the act of adopting two amendments to the CUC and scrapping the rest can be read as a reversal of the precedent set in 1982, when the decriminalization of homosexuality was supported publicly at every level of the state. In its proposal to strengthen the laws regarding cohabitation and to establish real protection for the domestic partner—male or female—without benefit of clergy, wasn't the CUC an eminently leftist bill? The Socialists in power in 1993 did not think so. "The Socialist group," Deputy Jean-Pierre Michel explains today, "behaved in a frightened and hypocritical manner. It was completely ridiculous. The civil union contract was secular legislation, in the purest tradition of Léon Blum."

The political right, having returned to power in 1993, was no more eager to include such a plan in its political agenda. In late November 1995, through Minister of Justice Jacques Toubon, Alain Juppé's government even confirmed its categorical rejection of the CUC. Speaking at the oral arguments session, the minister of justice replied to Deputy Jean-Pierre Michel in particularly emphatic terms, which would not have displeased the old deputy Jean Foyer:

On the contrary, I want to say very clearly that the government is not in favor of discussing or adopting [the civil union contract] because this bill is opposed to the public good and would create fundamental insecurities for the couples you wish to legalize in this way. . . . It is therefore out of the question to create a civil union contract; on the contrary, marriages and births ought to be favored in this country, so that France will become stronger![53]

For the moment, then, the bill seems to be compromised. It is likely, however, that the fight for similar legislation will intensify in the months and years to come.[54]

☞

"I am someone who believes that being homosexual also means not living as a couple, even if you happen to live with one other person." The film director Patrice Chéreau, responding to the idea of a civil union contract, explains why he did not support the legislation. Like others, he remembers the subversive years, when homosexuals and feminists denounced the norms of patriarchy, monogamy, and marriage. He is therefore surprised that their current successors are setting in- stitutionalization of the gay couple as the goal of their activism. Chéreau, atypical but not alone, admits that he cannot identify with what he sees as normalization, or as a sort of degraded utopia, at a time of spectacular consensus regarding the fight against AIDS. Chéreau prefers to see homosexuality as one of the last bastions of a necessary marginality:

Organized vacations, joint membership fees ... I'm shocked by people who cannot imagine a different model for relationships, who want to imitate the heterosexual couple, minus children, but with Sécurité Sociale. For me, being queer doesn't make ends meet, it doesn't settle everyday matters. Rightly or wrongly, I think that a totally integrated homo- sexuality is less attractive. I prefer to think there is still a tiny bit of marginality involved.

"Minus children, but with Sécurité Sociale," Chéreau notes with humor. And yet it is likely that organizations, having championed the right to a civil union contract, will turn to homosexuals' right to adopt children and lesbians' right to artificial insemination. These forthcoming social debates are already being dis- cussed in gay organizations. Such demands will no doubt elicit even stronger reac- tions of hostility than the CUC did. The right to adopt, in fact, goes against one of the most deep-seated assumptions about homosexuality: that bad examples or bad parenting can transform a "healthy" individual into a homosexual. This prepos- terous idea of "contagion" or "infectious" homosexuality, which is probably one of the main sources of homophobia, may persist for some time to come because it is so unconscious and irrational. As for artificial insemination, forcefully demanded by Lesbiennes Se Déchaînent, it speaks to homosexual women's desire to bear children without the usual complications. Some lesbians have in fact used personal ads to "recruit" male homosexuals—brilliant, physically attractive college gradu- ates, if at all possible (for example, an Australian student planning to return to his home country before the baby is due). One of the members of the lesbian couple then "devotes" herself to him for a few evenings. This decision can involve long bargaining sessions to decide which woman will bear the child, a decision that has sometimes been made by drawing lots. Artificial insemination, which belongs to the field of bioethics and the new technologies of reproduction, appears to be a solution, and supporters of medically assisted procreation have become dream merchants for homosexuals. Although these methods, whose aim is to treat infer- tility, are primarily designed for sterile couples as a means of supplementing sexual intercourse, lesbian groups have realized their own interest in supporting such practices, even though, for the moment, neither legislation nor legal precedent has decided in lesbians' favor.

In France, the decade of the 1980s was a tragic demonstration that the homosexual movement and the fight against AIDS do not completely overlap.[55] As a result, the scale of the fight against AIDS had a tendency to overshadow the homosexual movement during that period. Since 1990, new debates have emerged: militancy has begun to find its bearings again after the initial shock of the epidemic. Now the gay movement and the AIDS movement are exerting a mutual influence and are about to rediscover their shared foundations. In a particularly visible way, the revival of identity politics has surfaced at the spot where these two camps meet.

This rebirth, which can be perceived among various minorities in France, and even within feminism, began among gays about 1990. The AIDS epidemic, by designating at-risk populations and creating a high toll of the homosexual dead, created community ties, thus becoming a source of identity.

The signs of this phenomenon are varied, but the most remarkable one has to do with the increase in homosexual visibility within organizations previously favoring the "right to indifference," or even discretion. Foremost among these are Aides and feminist groups. In each case, homosexual difference has become more important—a departure from the 1980s, when the terms "feminist" and "homosexual militant" seemed so pejorative to most people that they became difficult to embrace.

~

Enthusiastically choosing the communitarian path, a whole movement is taking shape today whose aspiration is to form a "community." The Syndicat National des Entreprises Gaies, or SNEG [National union of gay enterprises], based on a unionist model, was created in 1990, bringing together several hundred of the 600 or so commercial gay establishments listed in France. Even more characteristically, the Salon de l'Homosocialité [Salon of homosociality] was created in 1992; two years later, it had nearly a hundred branches. This collection of groups constitutes a real communitarian breeding ground. Each organization meets a particular social demand. The Gai Moto Club, the Caramels Fous [Mad toffee] choir, and Quand les Lesbiennes Se Font du Cinéma [When lesbians make movies] are hobby groups. SOS Ecoute Gaie [SOS gay sounding board], Réseau Femmes d'Ile-de-France [Ile-de-France women's network], and Femmes entre Elles [Women among themselves] in Rennes are mutual-aid societies. Beit Haverin and the Centre du Christ Libérateur [Center of Christ the liberator] are religious groups. Gage–Association des Etudiants Gais [Gage–Gay students' association], the Mouvement d'Affirmation des Jeunes Gais [Young gays' affirmation movement], and Gais Retraités [Gay retirees] are age cohorts. Fraction Armée Rose [Lavender army faction], SOS Homophobie, and the Maquis are radical groups. Homosexualités et

Socialisme [Homosexualities and socialism], the Mouvement des Gais Libéraux [Liberal gay movement], and Ornicar are political organizations. In their diversity, all these interest groups attempt to construct an expression of difference and to respond to unexpected social situations that homosexuals seem unable or unwilling to resolve.[56]

Even though none of these organizations is truly national in scope, and though they are sometimes more like homosexual clubs than a real social movement, these organizations as a whole are by no means insignificant.

Arnaud Marty-Lavauzelle, president of the Aides federation, is well aware of the strength of this movement: "I am someone who thinks that if there was, at one time, no homosexual community, now there is one." Conversely, though he remains convinced that this phase of forming a "community" is necessary, Marty-Lavauzelle notes the possible missteps an exclusively homosexual militancy:

We at Aides live on Planet HIV, which means we have a lot of problems with the people who do not live here. So I would be very interested in knowing what homosexual organizations are doing if they are not involved in the fight against AIDS. The answer will be fairly short, I think. The situation is apparently dominated by the old fogeys from 1968; one of their Herculean labors is to go looking for things that might be homophobic. That's what I call backpedaling. Those of us fighting against AIDS know what people are up to.

As the logical outcome of the concern to form a community, the Centre Gai et Lesbien [Gay and lesbian center], or CGL, was created in Paris in March 1994.[57] A former project of the Maison des Homosexualités, it had encountered a substantial number of setbacks and disappointments until it managed to get itself organized, under the dual pressure of circumstances (the militant revival of the early 1990s) and the determined will of ACT UP.[58]

Philippe Labbey, the "brains" of ACT UP–Paris, became president of the CGL. "ACT UP was the catalyst that made the center possible," Labbey explains. "I came to homosexual militancy through ACT UP. I got involved with the center to make my husband, Cleews Vellay, happy; he was in despair about the state of gay militancy. Shortly before his death, he told me he was very proud of the work that had been accomplished." From that point on, the CGL's mission was to create, in a manner reminiscent of the Maison des Femmes in Paris, a community space for information and services. "I think this center fosters a gay identity," Labbey adds, "but I also want it to foster community. We created a reception hall and a service center designed primarily for its users, not for organizations. It is not simply a homosexual house." To date, the center houses about sixty organizations that it intends to make more widely known, if not to represent or even bring into a federation.[59] It is a coed group and has established a lesbian hotline, which now attracts many homosexual women, who are sometimes disappointed by the Maison des Femmes. "The coed nature of the place gives people a new sense of belonging to a community," explains Labbey. "For many people, ACT UP is the source of this philosophy."

In the provinces, gay and lesbian centers were created on the same model (in Montpellier, Lyons, Marseilles, Bordeaux, and Poitiers), and others are slated to open soon. Beyond the question of how representative they are, all these federative structures—all these gay centers, unions, and salons—reflect, in part, the new homosexual "configuration" of France.

From the "homosexualization" of Aides to the new lesbian debates, from the rediscovery of the homosexual deportation to the new symbolics of the pink triangle in ACT UP, the French homosexual movement has thus completed its transformation.

↩

As we reach the end of a rich and chaotic journey, beginning in 1968 and ending in the present, there is probably no better way to sum up the historical developments in the homosexual "minority" than the history of Gay Pride Day. A familiar symbol of militancy, it stands both as the thread running through the history of homosexuality in France and as the point where the current movements converge. It is also the best instrument by which to evaluate the impact of the identity movement.

Gay Pride Day is an annual demonstration whose beginnings can be traced directly to the American gay movement, the Stonewall uprising in New York on June 27, 1969. In France, the first autonomous demonstration of homosexuals occurred on June 25, 1977, after a call from lesbians in the MLF. It combined a commemoration of Stonewall with demands specific to French homosexuals. That march replaced the traditional May Day march of the trade unions, in which homosexual militants had participated since 1971. National gay marches became an annual event; they had limited success until the march of April 4, 1981. This time, nearly 10,000 demonstrators poured into the streets of Paris. Although they didn't know it, the militants, by sweeping Mitterrand into office, also sealed the fate of homosexual liberation. That date stands as the apogee of the French movement.

By 1983, Gay Pride Day was losing its importance. The homosexual movement was falling apart, and gay organizations were ending their run: the idea that had served as their standard was dying, along with several thousand gays. "The Sad Procession of Gays" was *Libération*'s headline in 1983. It was a peculiar time of ridiculous parades, which survived through the self-interested aid of the gay businesses that had come to promote themselves. On Gay Pride Day in June 1985, a disabused Daniel Defert published an Aides poster depicting homosexuals as ostriches, their heads buried in the sand and their rear ends in the air. Only about a thousand people turned out for the 1988 parade. That year, the indecency reached new heights: it was the businessman David Girard himself, owner of the unsafe baths, who organized Gay Pride Day. It appears to be a poisoned gift of historical circumstance that the voice of this carefree mountebank, because of a huge misunderstanding, should have found a temporary forum in the bankruptcy of militancy. And this smooth talker demonstrated precisely the talent that is most improbable in a business owner: unawareness. Moving against the current of AIDS organizations, which were thriving everywhere in France, he proclaimed publicly from the float representing his back-room disco, Le Haute Tension, "To hell with AIDS!"[60] AIDS was being masked behind "bearded majorettes" and the release of pink balloons. This instance of "gay pride," which had become "denial pride," can be interpreted in two ways: it was a sign either that some gay business owners were indifferent to homosexual misfortune or that they had been struck dumb by a disease that, in the end, also did not spare them (David Girard died of AIDS in 1990). In a sense, 1988 marked the twilight of Gay Pride Day and brought an end to the symbolic repertoire of the homosexual revolution.[61]

The year 1989 was a turning point and the beginning of a revival. For the first time, Aides officially—though still timidly—participated in the parade, and the first ACT UP militants appeared. They would soon proclaim, "AIDS: Queers, dykes, wake up!" As a result, the fight against AIDS became a subject of protests on Gay Pride Day, which came back to life to pay homage to victims of the disease. In many ways, it was no longer a parade but a funeral procession.

I WANT YOU TO LIVE was ACT UP's poignant slogan at the 1992 Gay Pride parade. That year, the organization's pompom girls marched en masse. The group Pin'Aides broadcast *Just a Gigolo* from a giant P.A. system, and *Gai Pied* backed the CUC: "Let's get CUCked!" That year, and even more so in 1993, the crowd grew: nearly 10,000 marched through the streets of Paris. ACT UP introduced two slogans. The first was rather sad ("This may be my last Gay Pride Day"); the second, more combative ("To dance is to live").

In 1994, the twenty-fifth anniversary of the Stonewall uprising, Paris's Gay Pride Day was again a success. Now organized by a specific organization (Lesbian & Gay Pride), the demonstration was subsidized by the Ministry of Health. For the first time, the regional Aides committees mobilized in force, guaranteeing a large share of the troops for Gay Pride Day. IF I'M HIV-POSITIVE, WILL YOU DANCE WITH ME? an ACT UP poster asked ironically. On June 18, 1994, nearly 20,000 marched in the streets of Paris.

The forces behind Gay Pride Day managed to effect a revival by cutting their losses: they reconciled with the past and fraternized with AIDS militants. From that point on, they brought together people who remembered the heroic militancy of the 1970s (survivors of the FHAR, the GLH, and the CUARH marched once again), and they welcomed soldiers in the fight against AIDS. Now they all shared the same desire: to fight "homophobia" and denounce the government, which, according to them, had failed in efforts to prevent the disease. These forces even outdid Aides in forgetting their most recent past. With this patch-up job, they were soon attracting enormous crowds.

Shoring up this tendency, and bringing the movement to completion, on June

24, 1995, French homosexual militants had the greatest success in their history: nearly 60,000 people marched from Montparnasse to the Bastille for what had become Lesbian/Gay Pride Day.[62] This success was spectacular and partly reminiscent of the great Beurs march of 1983.[63] The red ribbon replaced the badge proclaiming NE TOUCHE PAS À MON POTE, and a rather too inclusive banner with the slogan AGAINST EVERY FORM OF EXCLUSION! invited heterosexuals to march with gays. The atmosphere that day was festive: there were floats from gay businesses, and there was the Rainbow Flag, a gay emblem new to France.[64] Drag queens put out the call to arms with a self-assured batting of false eyelashes. Boulevard Saint-Germain was turned into a huge dance floor (with house music and techno-pop on the float for Le Queen disco). Young feminists (Marie-pas-Claire) marched beside Lesbiennes Se Déchaînent, and the return of mixed-sex activism reached an unprecedented scale. ACT UP slogans reminded people of the epidemic's presence: HELL HATH NO FURY LIKE A QUEEN DOOMED, LOOKING FOR A HUSBAND— MINE IS DEAD, THERE COULD HAVE BEEN 14,000 MORE OF US (14,000 homosexuals had died of AIDS in France since 1981).

The evening before, Canal Plus had broadcast an exceptional program, nearly nine hours in length, called *La nuit gay* [Gay nightlife]. The same week, two French weeklies devoted their front pages to homosexuals. Simultaneously, Pierre Bergé, head of Yves Saint-Laurent, and two of the founders of ACT UP, Didier Lestrade and Pascal Loubet, were launching a new glossy, light homosexual journal, *Têtu* [Obstinate].[65] Finally, a few influential elected officials from the Socialist Party and the Green Party saw, with a certain cynicism, that promoting communitarianism was a way of catering to the electorate, and they gave their support to Gay Pride 1995, implicitly backing the "right to difference." Their goal may simply have been to pay lip service to an idealized multiculturalism in which minorities would talk among themselves.[66]

This movement contains astonishing ambiguities. It also faces limitations when it undertakes the fight against AIDS.[67] Some militants, fearing that the disease is coming to define gayness, refuse to combine homosexuality and the fight against AIDS, which exasperates ACT UP. Some owners of gay businesses participate in Gay Pride Day while still refusing to practice prevention in their establishments, which alarms Aides. Still others march under the purity of a militant banner, poorly disguising their essentially commercial goals, which upsets other gay organizations.[68] AIDS remains both the driving (centrifugal) force and the disruptive (centripetal) element of this return to a gay identity.

Twenty-five years after some two dozen homosexuals stormed Ménie Grégoire's live broadcast, homosexuals had come full circle. In 1995, they invaded Paris to say publicly that they were "proud to be gay." It is possible that the first phase of the French homosexual movement (whatever this movement's future may be) ran its course between 1971 and 1995. A cycle has ended; a social agent has been born.

⌒

A determining factor will be the future positioning of individuals with respect to their membership or nonmembership in the nascent community. Most of
the tensions that have cropped up in the homosexual population can be attributed
to two conflicting aims: first, support for the communitarian lifestyle; and, second,
the search for a life outside the ghetto. How will homosexuals outside the ghetto
react?

Beyond these two aims, the dynamic of emancipation probably requires a few
periods of retreat, some phases of seeking an identity but also periods of openness
to the social environment. Most homosexuals seem to be more like "free electrons," having taken various paths to arrive at homosexuality. Membership in a
community may entail sometimes blurry gradations rather than sharp distinc-
tions. Homosexuals, especially younger ones, in leaving their isolation behind,
have had extremely varied life histories characterized by complex, ever-changing
relationships of attraction to and rejection of the gay community. The responses
that individual homosexuals give to these new "proposals" will determine how we
assess the importance of the movement.

This is why it is still too early to tell whether the new demand for a community,
the scope of which was indisputable at Gay Pride Day 1995, marks the apogee of a
movement now condemned to repeat itself and try to outdo itself, or whether,
conversely, it prefigures the French homosexual movement yet to come. If the first
possibility is the case, then "gay pride" may be merely a fashion trend, as empty as
it is short-lived. If the second possibility is the case, then "gay pride" may be the reflection of a social movement and may require us to reconsider the French model
of integrating minorities. For the moment, no one can see into the future. In any
case, homosexuals—perhaps to console themselves for being condemned to the
world in which we live—will begin to compose the score of the post-AIDS era.

Epilogue: A Dubious Communitarianism

I will begin with what you call "love of the Jewish people." . . . You are altogether right: I am not moved by any "love" of this kind, for two reasons. In the first place, I have never in my life "loved" any people, any community. . . . I love my friends exclusively, and the only kind of love I know and believe in is the love of individuals. In the second place, since I am myself Jewish, this "love of Jews" seems rather suspect to me. I cannot love myself, love something I know I am a part of, love a fragment of my own person. . . . So it is in that sense that I do not "love" the Jews and do not "believe" in them: I am simply one of them; that goes without saying, beyond discussion or controversy.

—Hannah Arendt

Modern democracies, to achieve better integration of minorities and vulnerable populations, and to fight more effectively against exclusion, have given in to the communitarian temptation. French homosexuals have not avoided this way of thinking. They have taken a path—on behalf of a "righteous cause," the fight against AIDS—whose aim is to give birth to a community. This may be the wave of the future, but it has adopted the ways of the past.

In this epilogue, I wish to situate this movement within the history of French homosexuals and to show its present ambiguities and limitations. In doing so, I can no longer maintain the reserve that has prevailed in the preceding pages—or that, at the very least, I attempted to privilege by reporting the facts objectively and respecting the unique perspectives of the people interviewed. This epilogue should therefore be read as a subjective account.

The genesis of French homosexual communitarianism is complex. It began diffusely and ended problematically. Sexual liberation movements, which in France began in the wake of May '68, produced a form of activism based on revolutionary themes. Homosexuality was linked to subversion and heterosexuality to conformity, if not to capitalism. For tactical reasons, everything related to private life necessarily had to become political. The Front Homosexuel d'Action Révolutionnaire (FHAR) became a kind of "political striptease" (to borrow Guy Hocquenghem's expression); the slogan "The personal is political" perfectly sums up the Mouvement de la Libération des Femmes (MLF). By sacrificing privacy, militants aimed to champion indeterminate sexuality and the fluidity of sexual orientation (bisexuality, "desiring machines") but also, and somewhat paradoxically, to

denounce the unforgiving way in which society looked on the person who was different. This composite view inextricably combined a critique of fixed identities
("Everyone is more or less homosexual inside," "One man in two is a woman")
and a defense of the very same identities ("Down with the heterocops," "Legalize
homosexuality," "Make war on normal people, make love among ourselves," "Every man is a potential rapist"). Despite the lessons of *Anti-Oedipus*, and probably
in opposition to the original intentions of the leading figures of the FHAR and the
MLF, these movements could not keep their universalist promise: many women
became imprisoned in the closed universe of "féminitude" (the Psychépo camp),
many "egalitarian" feminists joined the exclusively female Maison des Femmes
and were soon defending quotas, many lesbians chose the ghetto (lesbian separatism), and male homosexuals even began to nominate gay candidates for the legislative elections. Everyone pursued his or her particularism, forgetting that every
individual is the result of a process, of a history, and balks at being closed inside a
well-defined schema.

Homosexual visibility—"coming out of the closet"—imported from American movements, appeared in the 1970s as the be-all and end-all of French gay militancy. The context probably explains the forms this activism took. But the obligation to come out, the worry that exhibitionism would become a political obligation, and the temptation to "out" others emerged as paradoxical consequences of
sexual liberation, which in turn had become normative. Foucault can be credited
with showing that the issue of "confession"—which he never privileged—
functions as a mechanism of the very repression and shame that it claims to fight.

In reality, the claim to "homosexual liberation" is a great myth. However attractive it may be, the process calls for critical analysis so that we can evaluate its
benefits and its limitations. The limitations are especially obvious in the matters of
feminism and gay culture and in the issue of pedophilia.

It was certainly necessary to strip marriage of its normative role and to make a
distinction between sexuality and reproduction. It was just as essential to defend
women's freedom and, in the first place, allow women to make choices about their
own sexuality and methods of birth control; it was also essential to recognize their
right to abortion. These battles were part of an overall plan to emancipate individuals, or to "get along better in society." Not without a certain bad faith, however, female homosexuals emphasized hatred of men as a way of defending
women. Marriage, which lesbians did not want for themselves, was denounced as
one of the ways in which men exploited women. Soon heterosexual relationships
became suspect, even synonymous with rape, and feminist movements embraced
the notion of women's "victimization." Since then, women's gains have nuanced
the disastrous portrait still being drawn by a number of militants. They have forgotten that certain rhetorical excesses play a role in isolating men from women,
instead of facilitating dialogue between men and women. They have forgotten that
in presenting heterosexuality merely as a power relation, they eliminate seduction

and pleasure and so look like killjoys. All these factors may partially explain feminists' current lack of influence in French society.

The same is true of gay art and culture. Male and female homosexuals have
sometimes encouraged these forms of expression by privileging a specific body of
literature or art. The intention was laudable: to supply widely scattered individuals
with peers, to link them to a history, and bring them together in a "destiny group."
This is not insignificant. At the same time, however, the desire to pile ghetto upon
ghetto seems to be a hypermodern folly. Such a plan serves to negate the very purpose of art, which is to promote dialogue, openness, and freedom from isolation
and confinement. In addition, such a defense of gays may amount to "bending the
truth," to use Marguerite Yourcenar's expression. In fact, Yourcenar hates it when
one group "hogs all the blankets." It is certainly imperative that isolated minorities
learn not to give in to such easy solutions.

Homosexual men called for universal sexual liberation, even for adolescents.
Who could blame them, as long as the legal age of consent was still twenty-one
and, in the matter of consent, an unfair distinction was still being made between
heterosexual and homosexual relations? It is understandable that the defenders of
pedophilia could stand shoulder to shoulder with gay militants in public. In the
late 1970s, this solidarity was reinforced by the use of the word "pederast," the ambiguity of which made it possible to combine the two causes into a single movement. Where homosexuals defended freedom of desire, however, pedophiles
wanted to push back the age of consent and reject all norms. An impasse was unavoidable: soon pedophiles tried to lend legitimacy to rape, in total opposition to
the feminist movement, which was intent on criminalizing rape. From that point
on, legitimate fears about pedophilia fostered irrational criticisms of homosexuality. In order to end homosexual repression, supposedly intended to protect minors, it became necessary, once the legal age of homosexual consent had been lowered, to distinguish between pedophilia, which is morally reprehensible, and homosexuality, which is morally neutral. In the mid–1980s, pedophiles and homosexuals stopped putting out "joint petitions." In spite of everything, the extremely
complex issue of pedophilia caused lasting confusion for "homosexual liberation."

In these three cases—the ambiguities of feminism, "gay culture," and the pedophile cause—homosexual militants, instead of privileging their common
ground, defended separatism and situations proper to themselves alone, often forgetting such essential concrete issues as equal rights. It was not until the early 1980s
that homosexuals mobilized in defense of rights. After Mitterrand's victory, this
activism was translated into a liberalization of the repressive state.

And yet, beyond the tensions and the excesses, who could argue that no
"homosexual liberation" has taken place? At least for men, liberation did occur in
the late 1970s, as evidenced in the development of a commercial market, a diverse
collection of bars, baths, and discos. This "homosexual liberation"—which I prefer
to call "emancipation" or even, with Michael Pollak, "modernization"—took

shape as soon as homosexuality entered the marketplace. Even today, many homosexuals experience this commercialization as liberation, and we probably
should view it as the handiwork of gay business owners more than of militants. It
was these business owners who saw that the times were changing. It may be that
homosexuality "came out" by way of kitsch, the manufacture of sex toys and aids,
specialized newspapers, ritual sex, and an institutionalized urban nightlife. This is
not to say that the homosexual population became a "minority" in itself but simply that it came to assume the appearance of a community united only by its sexual
practices (which, after all, is something). This form of emancipation may have allowed homosexuals to come out of the closet, but it often meant their going back
into the ghetto.

↬

The homosexual debates of the 1970s certainly might have been forgotten,
and the few errors committed might not have had much importance, if homosexuals had not, unfortunately, encountered the AIDS virus on their way to liberation. In the early 1980s, a number of gays came out of the closet, entered the homogeneous homosexual milieu, but did not organize into a political and social community. Did they need to? This question naturally assumes key importance.

I have emphasized homosexuals' denial of AIDS during the first half of the
1980s, not in order to track down guilty parties but rather to show that all the errors committed during this period (political errors at first, then administrative and
medical errors, and, finally, errors on the part of the affected populations) resulted
from a combination of uncertainty, hesitation, and explicit self-censorship and
resistance. These errors, taken together, constitute a model of irresponsibility,
which needs to be analyzed. It is significant, however, that all the entities that were
based on a gay identity (organizations, newspapers, business establishments, the
Gay Pride Day committee), and that claimed to be protecting homosexuals from
society, paradoxically—or, perhaps we should say, tragically—deceived homosexuals about the reality of the epidemic that was menacing them. We may advance the hypothesis that this blindness played a significant role in the near-
dissolution of these entities in the mid–1980s, but we must never forget that fear of
homophobia, a recurrent obsession among homosexual militants, cruelly masked
the disease and considerably delayed the moment when people took stock of it. In
any case, the fear of a new stigma cannot fully justify the irresponsibility of homosexual militants.

Would a strong community structure have made it possible to avoid this denial? This argument is a tempting one, and it has sometimes been put forward. I
believe it is untenable, however, and for several reasons, the most important of
which is that the communitarian model par excellence—that is, the American
model—itself passed through a phase of denial. If this phase of denial did not last
as long, it was not because of the way in which American homosexuals were or-

ganized but rather because of the epidemiological situation, which by 1982 was more obvious in the United States. Conversely, although some believe that in France the fight against AIDS was organized around gay groups and gay militants, I have shown that this was not at all the case during the first decade of the epidemic. The fight against AIDS came about because of individuals who were in fact homosexual, but who for the most part were not involved in identity politics.

↬

But the story does not end there. Although AIDS was initially a factor in the demobilization of the homosexual movement, and although the ruins of the 1970s homosexual revolution were left in its wake, homosexuals' realization of the tragedy had three consequences.

First, in 1985 a change in lifestyles began to occur. The carefree life, abandon, and a form of sexuality demanding to be joyful, excessive, and irresponsible were called into question. Even in places where group sex was practiced, places that are resurfacing today, the rules of the sex game changed; AIDS precludes experimental frenzy and dispossession of one's own body. All the same, the benefits of the 1970s have not disappeared, and a return to the pre-'68 past is improbable. To put it simply, sexuality has acquired a new status, one that includes an obligation to be responsible, and this seems to mark a return to individualization as well as a new way of relating to other people. The adoption of safer-sex practices is the most salutary illustration of this shift. Make no mistake: such individual responses are also a communitarian reflex.

Second, and just as paradoxically, AIDS has condemned gays to the homosexual fate. Each one from now on is linked to all the others by an invisible thread: fear of the virus. Although homosexuals may appear separated, they form a "destiny group." In addition, although the identity politics of the early 1980s was unable to face up to AIDS, the disease, by designating an at-risk population, and especially by producing a homosexual hecatomb, created community ties. It is now the source of a sense of identity.

The third consequence flows from the second: a spectacular and collective form of activism has come into being, and it is summed up in the history of Aides. The government, because it ignored the importance of the disease and was slow to allocate the funds necessary to fight it, encouraged a community response to the epidemic. To survive, homosexuals had to take the path of a defensive communitarianism. In the end, when the people affected took charge of "their" problem, they largely satisfied the government of the time. A certain neoliberalism proved to be altogether compatible with communitarianism: it was, amazingly, shared by the government of Laurent Fabius (which hardly favored state involvement in this area) and by Minister of Health Michèle Barzach (who agreed to maintain a political discourse without translating her words into programs or funding).

Ten years after the epidemic began, the conjunction of these three factors (individuals taking responsibility, the sense of a gay identity, and a community-based fight against AIDS) gave birth, in due course, to an offensive communitarianism. Taking as their example the new ACT UP militants, who aimed to mobilize the ghetto, the "buddies" in Aides realized that they, too, were homosexual activists. When the organization was only modestly successful in its plan to unite its natural base of homosexual volunteers with other populations vulnerable to the virus (such as drug users and hemophiliacs), Aides's philosophy of a diverse community gradually gave way to an exclusive focus on the homosexual community. Despite a significant presence of heterosexual women in its ranks, Aides illustrates to perfection—and probably against its founders' intention—that communitarian logic almost necessarily leads to identity politics.

This shift, perceptible since 1993, unquestionably marked the end of a cycle. Over the course of twenty-five years, an "agent" was born, as the sociologists say. Whatever the future of these new forms of activism, we can posit that today the first phase of the French homosexual movement has been completed.

ᔥ

Will the future be communitarian? It is one thing to note the birth of a community and of the identity movement; it is something else altogether to approve of them. I remain persuaded that those who feel the need for an identity movement must fight for it, but how could I fail to emphasize the limitations and ambiguities of that fight?

Let us not exaggerate: the rift between the "identity" camp and a more "universalist" camp, however attractive the idea of such a rift may be, should not be overestimated. First, the identity movement is new only in appearance: it is linked to recurring debates among the homosexual militants of the late 1970s and is reminiscent of the well-known disputes within a number of ethnic and religious minorities. Universalist leanings often coexist with culturalist, "identitarian" leanings, and the call for difference and particularism often stands side by side with the call for indifferentiation and indifference. Therefore, we should not be too simplistic in opposing universalism and identity. Even if we suppose that all homosexual practices are alike and, in themselves, constitute an identity (already very debatable), most individuals still take positions, combining the particular with the universal. They defend the community to which they belong, as well as an all-encompassing humanity, and they combine them in a subtle, complex dialectic. Moreover, it is certainly possible to imagine an intermediate position, not yet defined—or invented—that would combine multiculturalism and defense of the republican state, and that would relentlessly seek the ideal combination between gesellschaft (a competitive, rationalized, universal society) and gemeinschaft (a particularist, affective community).

Second, we should not overestimate the strength of the current communitarian movement. It may have no lasting hold on French society, and it probably is only an imperfect reflection of the national situation (especially gay life in the provinces). Beyond the question of its representativeness, which ought to be considered, this movement is still trying to find its bearings and probably has not reached maturity. Therefore, it would be prudent not to predict its future, and hence not to judge it too harshly in advance. This identity movement is still, in large part, anachronistic. The aggressiveness of the virus alone allows us to understand this movement: without AIDS, the French model of assimilation (whereby society integrates individuals but does not recognize groups) probably would have prevailed over the American communitarian model.

Once these precautions have been taken, we cannot deny that communitarianism is very tempting. Some homosexual militants, who once observed a "denial of citizenship," now want to create a community; and, perhaps to console themselves over their many losses, they champion the right to difference—which, as we know, can quickly lead to inequality of rights. Some make use of history and "instrumentalize" the homosexual deportation, with the aims of identity politics in view; others make an irrational comparison between AIDS and the Holocaust. All brandish the pink triangle, and yet Jews would have found it indecent to intentionally brandish the yellow star, the symbol of their extermination. Let me add that both these examples of simplistically using history for one's own ends are open to criticism. In the fight against AIDS, the stakes are too high for anyone to dodge the debate by using misleading terms as loaded as "collaborator" and "revisionism."

↫

Should communitarianism be encouraged? By way of conclusion, three issues allow us to see the ambiguities of this movement and to explain why it should go no farther: first, the social union contract; second, Gay Pride Day; and, third, AIDS prevention in the gay milieu.

A demand may be judged justifiable when it can be erected into a law valid for all of humanity (the principle of universalism). Therefore, homosexuals' freedom to make life choices ought to be protected from a society that would deny them their rights: the "right to indifference" is not the right to nonexistence. In this respect, increased recognition of the rights of unmarried couples is an advance that interests domestic partners as a whole, both homosexual and heterosexual. Strengthening the rights of people living together is an important goal, which entails gradually extending real protections to the domestic partner—man or woman—unceremoniously, but with real effects. This is why homosexual couples ought to be issued certificates of life partnership. The ideas behind the social union contract (an improved version of the civil union contract) ought to be part of this framework, and laws opposing it ought to be revised. Such demands, applying to everyone and not to a specific category of individuals, are part of an expansion of individual freedoms and human rights. They are an adaptation of a universal framework, perhaps the illustration of a new state of personal relationships and a new solidarity within future couples. They also make it possible to avoid the privileging that is characteristic of identity politics. Homosexuals should not be alone in backing these demands, since they will be useful to everyone. The Socialist Party (but not it alone), instead of supporting a vague homosexual communitarianism in the hope of garnering votes, would be better advised to focus the debate on these issues.

By contrast, giving homosexuals special status, whatever its form, seems unacceptable, whatever the aim of doing so may be. In the first place, homosexuality in itself should not be considered a cause, a categorical imperative, or a model. A noncommunitarian view makes a precise distinction between the demand for rights and the defense of special interests, between championing respect for others and encouraging "propagandizing," to use Jean-Louis Bory's term.

Similarly, an antidiscrimination law on the model of Yvette Roudy's "antisexist" law does not seem an appropriate solution for homosexuals. Such measures, still demanded by some gay militants, would probably be ineffective and would be an obstacle to freedom of expression and the postulate it implies: that the individual alone should have the ability to accept or reject pernicious statements.

↪

Gay Pride Day should be mentioned at this point because it is a striking concentration of all the aspirations and criticisms of communitarianism. What do the supporters and organizers of this demonstration tell us? That Gay Pride Day is only a phase in the process of integration, a transitional phase that requires a demonstration of strength so that rights can be won. That it is a moment of visibility, a place of celebration, a carnival. I am aware of the burdensome nature of a society that seems to tell individuals, "Be yourself, but only in private." Perhaps the republican position needs to change, to become less "inhospitable" to difference. The current identity movement reflects a legitimate concern about the place of homosexuals in tomorrow's society. These communitarian demands also reveal modes of disarticulation, the dissolution of the bonds of society in contemporary France. And every society must be able to rely on all its members, who must be able to communicate among themselves. If some people, rightly or wrongly, are convinced that they are being excluded, if they feel that they are being urged to undervalue themselves, if they observe or feel that they are being denied citizenship, then society as a whole must come to understand this discomfort. Otherwise, the future of the whole group will be jeopardized. Today, it seems as if homosexuals are demanding not just equal rights but also, perhaps, collective recognition. This is a real phenomenon. The current identity movement can even be seen more as a demand for recognition than as a demand for rights—the telling absence, until now, of demands on Gay Pride Day [in France] may confirm this view. To a certain extent, and for a given length of time, this "right to recognition" probably entails the production of symbolic speeches—such as the one given by Robert Badinter to the

National Assembly in December 1981—and, no doubt, the defense of the social union contract. I would like to assert that there is something to be said for these demands.

But is Gay Pride Day simply that? It is possible that its organizers have no intention of acting as intermediaries between citizens and the state, and no expectation that individual homosexuals will let them negotiate collectively for recognition from the government, as well as no desire to achieve an American-style model of integrating minorities (in fact, the United States is increasingly fomenting its own fragmentation, in favor of a proliferation of separate communities). But how can we fail to see Gay Pride Day as a gradual move toward the "Americanization" of French society? People who attempt to imitate the American model, unless they are prepared to completely dismantle the French model of integrating individuals, need to realize that such surgical operations could prove perilous in a country where no tradition of communitarianism exists, at least not yet. The contributions and limits of Gay Pride Day must also be considered if we are to determine the role it plays in supporting—or undermining—the emancipation of homosexual individuals.

Gay militants tell us that homosexuals in France today are specifically being denied citizenship. Anyone who tries to block legislation like the social union contract simultaneously encourages homosexual communitarianism because there are rights that have not yet been won, as well as freedoms that are still limited. Let us give serious thought to the matter, however: if we concede that these delays will be eliminated over time as society evolves, can we really say that there is a social and economic exclusion specific to homosexuals in France today? Are living conditions poor in "gay neighborhoods?" Are homosexuals expelled from high school because they listen to house music or wear red ribbons? Nothing could be less obvious, and those who suggest that this kind of exclusion exists are encouraging an unjustified anxiety. In our own time, exclusion is practiced less against fringe elements who reject the dominant norm than against individuals who wish to embrace precisely that norm but fail to do so. This is why the assimilation of homosexuals as a minority comparable to other minorities—ethnic or religious—seems a questionable venture. Nor should we believe—and this is essential—in an eternal and, so to speak, natural homophobia. To put forth such a view is probably self-indulgent and self-interested. Those who suggest that homosexuals of necessity face a hostile world are not quite in touch with reality, and they show an immoderate interest in being cast as victims. Or perhaps the repeated denunciation of homophobia is a strategy aimed at maintaining a semblance of unity in the "homosexual community." If so, then it is a very risky business, since gays' salvation will not come from a logic of victimization or from the conviction that, as a people, they are pariahs.

For good measure, Gay Pride Day has also introduced ambiguity about the status of "gay pride." Despite the intentions of militants, the reasons motivating homosexuals who participate in the Gay Pride parade are difficult to analyze. Do individuals come out to say, "I'm proud to be gay" or "I'm here to demand my rights" or "I'm here to fight against AIDS" or even "I'm here to party"? Lacking a response, let us not speak for others. If they support "gay pride," as the organizers of Gay Pride Day seem to think, then I feel obliged to express reservations about this self-pride, an exacerbation of otherness and an ostentatious form of the right to difference. In the same way, it is a short step from self-affirmation to exhibitionism. Can you legislate gay pride? It seems instead to be a kind of inverted pink triangle, which may, temporarily at least, produce perverse effects. In the end, pride may work in the same way self-loathing does. In fact, the risk of reinforcing stereotypes, a criticism often made of Gay Pride Day's exuberance (drag queens and go-go dancers), is less to be feared than the risk of retreating into a gay identity, of valuing the minority at the expense of the national culture. This tendency denies the world we all share and its collective projects, and it privileges the community and membership in a particular group, with all this implies in terms of allegiance. It is not the carnival that we should criticize, but rather the long-range danger of a differentialist project negotiated not as a dialogue but as a rift. Must homosexuals choose this path, when the example of differentialist antiracism in France (SOS Racisme) has been showing, for the last fifteen years, that it is a dead end (something this movement has only recently acknowledged)? That ought to persuade homosexuals to be more careful.

The developing French gay community seems to have forgotten its origins and is overlooking the burdensome, alienating form that identity movements can take. It seems to lack role models and may be unaware of the perverse effects that such movements can have. Is it clear on these issues? Has it avoided these sorts of criticisms? It is up to its defenders to state and, probably, clarify their intentions, and it is up to their detractors to propose alternative solutions.

To respond to these issues and escape the dead ends, we need to revive democratic debate. From this standpoint, we first need to pick up the thread of history, which the AIDS epidemic seems to have broken. In many respects, we will need to summon the dead, a few of them at least. By invoking four guiding figures, four "statues of the Commendatore" for the French homosexual movement, we can hope to achieve four aims. With the Guy Hocquenghem of the early 1970s, we will defend the right to indetermination and polysexuality; with Simone de Beauvoir, we will seek a tolerant feminism that champions neither hatred of men nor lesbian separatism; with Jean-Louis Bory, we will aspire to banalize homosexuality and recognize the right to indifference; and, finally, with Michel Foucault, we will reject the logic of confession, criticize a fixed homosexual identity, and challenge the effectiveness of a "liberationist" way of thinking. Rather than see these individuals as anachronistic escapees from a vanished world, let us recognize that their views lie at the heart of contemporary thought.

〜

Apart from homosexual militancy in the narrow sense, AIDS prevention in the gay milieu provides the framework for asking new questions. In the 1990s, opposition that had existed earlier in homosexual debates emerged in the fight against AIDS. This "displacement" can be seen in the curious reversal that led homosexual militants to appropriate the concept of a "gay cancer" (which they had initially rejected) at a time when epidemiologists and the press were abandoning the notion, which they themselves had put forward. In a sense, the fight against AIDS lent itself both to universalist integration ("The disease is everyone's concern," "If one homosexual is suffering, all of society suffers") and to identity-based differentialism. This displacement can also be seen in the osmosis that sometimes exists between AIDS prevention in the gay milieu and the fight for gay causes. The central question remains, however: In order to fight AIDS more effectively, is it necessary to organize as a community?

It is clumsy to theorize, for example, that commemoration of the homosexual deportation would encourage prevention, but prevention is promoted by support for the ideas behind the social union contract, and prevention requires campaigns that target gays—not because they are a specific population but because they engage in specific kinds of sexual behavior. This fundamental distinction explains why supporters of the right to indifference are likely to accept specific measures of prevention aimed at targeted populations, whereas, paradoxically, some militants in the identity movement reject these measures because they fear that the AIDS problematic will come to blur gay identity. The fight against AIDS will not be more effective once a gay community has been established; rather, it will be more effective when we have analyzed and understood the risky behavior of individuals so that we may combat it more effectively.

At the same time, the fight against AIDS has been an opportunity to ask, with new urgency, how it is that privacy has lost ground to politicization of the private sphere. The fight against the virus was initially based—especially by way of the Aides ethic—on respect for medical confidentiality, the principle of voluntary testing, the defense of private life, and the principle of not passing judgment. That some militants have been tempted to abolish the boundary between private and public, claiming that the fight against AIDS is an urgent matter, is understandable, but it is not justifiable.

Outing, used as an instrument in the fight against AIDS, is the most symbolic form of this desire to politicize private life. On this new battlefield, as on the abandoned field of homosexual liberation, can attacks on individuals or on privacy be defended, whatever form these attacks may take? That is, can we support the adoption of the very forms of aggression to which homosexuals have always been subjected? This question implies another, which appears repeatedly in protest movements: Must we use the enemy's own weapons? It seems to me that the answer to these questions must be a resounding no.

〜

The government's guilty conscience has led it to help homosexual organizations in the fight against AIDS. In exchange for subsidies, the state delegates responsibility for prevention to organizations, reinforcing the belief that "everything is political," and neglecting its own responsibilities. As a direct result, these subsidies favor the formation of a gay community, and the political cost of encouraging a homosexual and HIV-positive identity is high. These organizations, citing the state's weaknesses, further vilify the government by showing the results of its actions. The issue is not whether these subsidies are useful—they are. The issue is whether the state ought to remain uninvolved, and what sort of plan it should have: a plan to fight against AIDS, or a plan to fight for the homosexual cause?

Therefore, we need to rethink AIDS prevention in terms of ethics. It is even necessary to declare that gay business establishments, homosexual organizations, and specialized newspapers have a duty to practice and promote prevention. This kind of solidarity and willingness to help do exist, and to a significant degree. All the same, prevention measures must continue to be understood as public service, with due regard for certain weaknesses in the sacrosanct notion of individual responsibility. They must be conceived as real acts of solidarity and altruism; those responsible for prevention must not confine themselves to systematically demanding remuneration from the state. It is even more urgent to distinguish clearly between the fight against AIDS and homosexual militancy, by constantly questioning our own implicit motives and real goals.

Every reader is free to accept or reject the preceding analyses. Tension will undoubtedly remain between universalism and particularism, and it will be difficult to pursue these goals in tandem, to define common ground. But a solution is not impossible: the disagreements are no greater than those that were confronted when AIDS first appeared. In any case, homosexual solidarity cannot and should not be unconditional.

〜

"Homosexuality taught me everything." A number of the men and women interviewed for this book have made this claim, and many homosexuals probably would agree. "The school of life," "My homosexuality is the best part of me," "I would not be the same if I had not been homosexual": these individual words and phrases are understandable, even rather touching. And yet, as this book ends, is it still possible to hear the joyful sounds of homosexuality?

For many, homosexuality has become just one more sexual choice. It is experienced more as a journey than as a destination. Homosexuals have begun to distance themselves from the "cruising, wandering Jew" (Serge Daney) and "the rootless homosexual" (Bernard-Marie Koltès). They have lost some of their "destiny as troublemakers," (Guy Hocquenghem). They are no longer really "a source of disorder" (Jean-Louis Bory). The homosexual world has left behind the

Pasolini of Ostia and Marguerite Yourcenar's Zeno of Bruges, the "nomad" who loved boys and who, unable to live in peace, "drifted."

The normalization of homosexuals—the prelude, perhaps, to a sanitized society—should not necessarily be encouraged, but the banalization of homosexuality should be. It may be time to abandon the histrionics, to leave the militant strait-jackets and media events behind, to be neither pariahs nor parvenus. Homosexuals must be reconciled with society, and society with them.

In order for this reconciliation to occur, homosexuals must become individuals without labels. Their specificity no longer functions as a disintegrative agent against society—on the contrary—and it is less and less a factor in the destructuring of the family. And yet homosexuality continues to divide French political life and, at an even deeper level, contemporary society. Obviously, this is unfortunate. But homosexuals are part of the social puzzle; they are one voice in the choir of our society. Should that voice be missing, the choir would lose some of its resonance. Often, homosexuals contribute an understanding of the world around us and exemplify the tensions of democratic modernity.

With the onset of the AIDS epidemic, homosexuals began to liberate themselves from the sexual label that has been attached to them; they began to show their uniqueness and diversity. Of course, they are still cast as sacrificial victims, eliciting compassion ("A good queer is a dead queer"), or as heroes, the new missionaries ("A good gay man is an AIDS activist"). Beyond these stereotypes, however, homosexuals appear to be gradually escaping the hypothetical label "homosexuality."

In the interest of dialogue and relief of tensions—which ought to be encouraged—homosexuals, understood as individuals capable of mastering their own relation to the world, need to distance themselves from "homosexuality." What distinguishes homosexuals from one another is now more important than what unites them. It may even be that, over the past twenty-five years, we have shifted away from "homosexuality" and toward "homosexuals." Individuals have increased their independence and autonomy and have become the agents of their own life stories. The "homo" is no longer simply "sexual."

If we are now to leave behind communitarianism and a reductive, "homogenizing" identity, if we are to abandon a form of sexual kinship that cannot keep its promise of community, we must do our best to make "homosexuality" a meaningless term, a word with no relation to reality. Only ever-changing individuals must remain. To recover the possibility of happiness, it is up to us to defend individual autonomy, to propose that the issue of homosexuality no longer has any meaning or reason for being. In spite of AIDS, "homosexuals" can begin to live. "Homosexuality" no longer exists.

Avignon, December 1995

REFERENCE MATTER

Chronology (1968–99)

1968

May. A mysterious Comité d'Action Pédérastique Révolutionnaire (Revolutionary pederastic action committee) hangs eight posters in the occupied Sorbonne. They are quickly torn down.

December 18. Fabrice Emaer opens Le Sept, a homosexual club on rue Saint-Anne; homosexual chic.

Songs: "Ob-la-di, ob-la-da" (The Beatles), "Sister May" (The Velvet Underground).

1969

June 27–28. In New York, in a Greenwich Village homosexual bar (the Stonewall Inn), police are greeted with bricks; ever since then, this event has been commemorated annually around the world on Gay Pride Day.

September. The Arcadie club is established on rue du Château-d'Eau, at the site of a former movie theater.

Films: Pier Paolo Pasolini's *Teorema* and *Pigsty*; Stanley Donen's *Staircase*; Federico Fellini's *Satyricon*; Radley Metger's *Thérèse and Isabelle*; Paul Morrissey and Andy Warhol's *Flesh.*

Songs: "Get Back" (The Beatles), "Fiddle About" (The Who).

1970

March 18. Broadcast of *Campus* by Michel Lancelot, on Europe I, is devoted to homosexuality; André Baudry, Jean-Louis Bory, Roger Peyrefitte, and Daniel Guérin participate.

May 21. First meeting of feminists at the Université de Vincennes. The same month, an issue of *L'Idiot International* is devoted to the "fight for women's liberation" (with an article, notably, by Monique Wittig).

August 26. Nine women place banners and a spray of flowers on the Tomb of the Unknown Soldier; this is the first action of the MLF.

September. Partisans issue "Women's Liberation: Year Zero."

September 23. First issue of *Tout!* (edited by Jean-Paul Sartre); an allusion to the struggle of women and homosexuals.

September 26. First general meeting of the MLF at the Paris Beaux-Arts. A group of Arcadie lesbians associated with the MLF begins to meet separately.

October. The vice squad lists 300 male prostitutes in Paris. In September 1970, the capital has thirty-four sex shops (there were only seven in March).

November 20–22. The Women's Conference, organized by *Elle* at the Palais des Congrès, is disrupted by the MLF.

November 25. The writer Yukio Mishima commits suicide on live TV.

Films: Visconti's *The Damned*, Ken Russell's *Love*, Paul Morrissey and Andy Warhol's *Trash*.

Songs: "Je suis un homme" (Michel Polnareff), "Keep the Customer Satisfied" (Simon and Garfunkel).

1971

February 10. The so-called Calf's-Lung Lecture by Professor Lejeune at the Université Catholique de Paris. Lesbian militants participate in the sabotage operation organized by the MLF. Repeated on March 5 at the Mutualité, at the Let Us Live meeting. The fight to legalize abortion is launched.

March 10. In Salle Pleyel, Ménie Grégoire's broadcast on is disrupted by MLF militants and homosexual women from Arcadie. The FHAR is born.

April 5. Manifesto signed by 343 women who have had abortions is published in *Le Nouvel Observateur*. Signers include Simone de Beauvoir, Catherine Deneuve, Jeanne Moreau, Ariane Mnouchkine, and Gisèle Halimi.

April 23. Issue 12 of *Tout!* devotes four pages to homosexuality. The issue is seized.

April 26. Debate on abortion organized by *Le Nouvel Observateur*. Signers of the "343" manifesto walk off the stage. Guy Hocquenghem calms things down.

May. First issue of *Le Torchon Brûle*, a new "menstrual."

May 1. The FHAR marches at the traditional May Day demonstration, taking up the rear between the MLF and high school students.

November 20. The FHAR joins the first public demonstration of the MLF, on Place de la République.

Films: Luchino Visconti's *Death in Venice*, John Schlesinger's *Sunday Bloody Sunday*, Ken Russell's *Music Lovers* (on Tchaikovsky), Harry Kümel's *Daughters of Darkness*, Kenneth Anger's *Pink Narcissus* (the film, uncredited, was not released in France until 1974).

Dance: Maurice Béjart's *Le chant du compagnon errant*, with Rudolf Nureyev.

Songs: "Le rire du sergent" (Michel Sardou), "Queen Bitch"(David Bowie).

1972

January 10. *Le Nouvel Observateur* publishes a long interview with Guy Hocquenghem ("The Revolution of Homosexuals").

March 7. Publication of Gilles Deleuze and Félix Guattari's *L'anti-Oedipe*. The book's aim is to found a politics of desire, combining a critique of orthodox Freudianism and libertarian Marxism. "Being anti-Oedipus" becomes a lifestyle choice.

May 13–14. Days of Denunciation of Crimes Committed Against Women, held at the Mutualité. The Gouines Rouges make their first public appearance.

September 21. Suicide of the writer Henri de Montherlant.

October. Michel Polnareff's *Polnarévolution* opens at the Olympia Theater. Polnareff appears bare-bottomed on thousands of posters and is fined several thousand francs.

October 11–November 22. Trial in Bobigny of a sixteen-year-old (Marie-Claire) who had an abortion, an abortionist (her mother, a metro ticket taker) and their accomplices. Gisèle Halimi defends them.

Films: Bob Fosse's *Cabaret*, Guy Casaril's *Le rempart des Béguines*, R. W. Fassbinder's *The Bitter Tears of Petra von Kant* and *Jail Bait*, Bertolucci's *Last Tango in Paris*.

Songs: "Pour ne pas vivre seule" (Dalida), "John, I'm Only Dancing (David Bowie), "Daniel" (Elton John), "Goodnight Ladies" and "Make Up" (Lou Reed).

1973

February. At the Palais-Royal Theater, the stage play *La Cage aux Folles* (with Jean Poiret and Michel Serrault) is a success.

March. The special issue of *Recherches* titled "Trois milliards de pervers" is published and then seized. (On May 25, 1975, Félix Guattari will be convicted of "public indecency.") A basic text.

June 17. In the vacant lot of the munitions factory at Vincennes, women's art is displayed at the Women's Fair.

December 18. First homosexual personal ads in the daily *Libération*, which was launched on January 4, 1973.

Films: Luchino Visconti's *Ludwig*, Michèle Rosier's *George qui?*

Songs: "Comme ils disent" (Charles Aznavour), "The Jean Genie" and "Cracked Actor" (David Bowie), "Helpless Danger" (The Who), "All the Girls Love Alice" (Elton John), "Walk on the Wild Side" (Lou Reed).

1974

February. End of the FHAR: at the request of the director of the Ecole des Beaux-Arts, the police raid the sixth floor. The FHAR, its general meetings deserted, had been moribund for eight months.

May 19. Valéry Giscard d'Estaing is elected president of the republic.

June. First leaflet of the Groupe de Libération Homosexuelle (GLH), made up of former FHAR militants and a group of young people expelled from Arcadie.

July 5. The age of legal consent is lowered to eighteen.

November 29. The Veil law, on voluntary interruption of pregnancy, is adopted by the National Assembly.

Films: R. W. Fassbinder's *Fox and His Friends*, Christopher Larkin's *A Very Natural Thing*, Chantal Ackerman's *Je, tu, il, elles*, Lothar Lambert's *Berlin Harlem*.

Songs: "Il venait d'avoir 18 ans" (Dalida), "Rebel Rebel" (David Bowie), "Killer Queen" (Queen), "L'amour et l'amitié" (Henri Tachan).

1975

January. The year is officially declared International Year of the Woman.

January 21. On Antenne 2, *Les dossiers de l'écran* is devoted to homosexuality. Jean-Louis Bory participates.

May 6. Sécurité Sociale reimburses costs for contraceptives, which minors are allowed to use.

November 1. Pier Paolo Pasolini is murdered on a beach in Ostia, probably by a male prostitute.

December 30. A law introduces the "X" rating, accompanied by a decree (January 6, 1976; three gay movie theaters will open in Paris in 1976).

Films: Pier Paolo Pasolini's *Salo, or the 120 Days of Sodom*, Visconti's *Conversation Piece*, Coline Serreau's *Mais qu'est-ce qu'elles veulent?*

Songs: "Bohemian Rhapsody" and "Death on Two Legs" (Queen).

1976

August. First "Chéri(e)" personal ads in *Libération*. (In March 1979, *Libération* will be taken to court for running them.)

October. Creation of the Centre du Christ Libérateur (Center of Christ the liberator) by Pastor Joseph Doucé.

Films: Derek Jarman's *Sebastiane*, Agnes Varda's *One Sings, the Other Doesn't.*

1977

April 20–26. Homosexual week organized by te GLH–Paris at Frédéric Mitterrand's Olympic Theater.

June 25. First autonomous demonstration by homosexuals, at the initiative of women in the MLF. The first French Gay Pride parade.

Films: Ettore Scola's *A Special Day*, Wolfgang Petersen's *The Consequence.*

Songs: "The Altar Boy and the Thief" (Joan Baez), "San Francisco" (Village People), "The Killing of Georgie" (Rod Stewart), "New York" (The Sex Pistols), *Starmania* (rock opera by Michel Berger, with theme song "Un garçon pas comme les autres—Ziggy," sung by Fabienne Thibeault).

1978

February. Most gay newspapers (*Gaie Presse, In, Andros, Dialogues Homophiles*) are banned by the minister of the interior.

March 5. Fabrice Emaer opens Le Palace disco in a former Paris theater. (Gay tea dances will begin in 1979.)

Films: Edouard Molinaro's *La Cage aux Folles* (I), R. W. Fassbinder's *The Year of Thirteen Moons* and *Germany in Autumn*, Coline Serreau's *Pourquoi pas?*

Songs: "Où sont les femmes?" (Patrick Juvet), "Les uns contre les autres" (Fabienne Thibeault), "We Are the Champions" (Queen), "Big Dipper" (Elton John), "Macho Man," "I Am What I Am," and "YMCA" (Village People).

1979

March. Renaud Camus's *Tricks* is published with a preface by Roland Barthes: casual sex and back rooms.

April. Birth of the monthly *Gai Pied.*

June 11. Jean-Louis Bory, the leading homosexual figure of the 1970s, commits suicide.

July 23–28. First "Université d'Eté Homosexuelle" in Marseilles, the founding act of the CUARH. (This "homosexual summer school" will take place every two years until 1987.)

October 30. The Psychépo camp registers the name "MLF." Lawsuit ensues. End of a dream.

December 15. For the first time in France, Pastor Joseph Doucé celebrates a "union of homosexual friendship" in a Protestant church in Paris. (The pastor will be kidnapped and murdered in July 1990.)

Films: Philippe Vallois's *Nous étions un seul homme*, Lionel Soukaz and Guy Hocquenghem's *Race d'Ep.*

Songs: "The Gay Paris" (Patrick Juvet), "In the Navy" (Village People), "Gimme! Gimme! Gimme!" and "A Man after Midnight" (Abba), "Boys Keep Swinging" (David Bowie), "On any Other Day" (The Police), "Depuis qu'il vient chez nous" (Dalida), "I Will Survive" (Gloria Gaynor).

1980

January. Schism at the journal *Questions Féministes* over the issue of lesbianism.

March 6. Marguerite Yourcenar is the first woman elected to the Académie Française.

November 19. Amendment to keep homosexuality a crime for people between fifteen and eighteen years old is passed on the third attempt by the National Assembly. During the same debate, a law against rape, demanded by feminists, is also adopted. It includes provisions on conjugal and homosexual rape.

Films. Pedro Almodóvar's *Pepi, Luci, Bom and Other Girls on the Heap,* Herbert Ross's *Nijinsky,* Paul Verhoeven's *Spetters.*

Songs: "La plus belle fois qu'on m'a dit 'Je t'aime'" (Francis Lalanne), "Si j'étais un homme" (Diane Tell), "Il jouait du piano debout" (France Gall), "Cherchez le garçon" (Taxi Girl), "Uptown" and "When You were Mine" (Prince), "I'm Coming Out" (Diana Ross).

1981

January. Paris city hall orders 400 Decaux public toilets. The end of the *tasses.*

April 4. Demonstration in Paris by 10,000 homosexuals, including many feminists. In support, Jack Lang leads the parade, flanked by Jean-Paul Aron and Yves Navarre.

April 28. During a meeting of the pro-choice association Choisir, presidential candidate François Mitterrand says yes to Josyane Savigneau's and Gisèle Halimi's question about whether homosexuality will cease to be a criminal offense.

June 5. The epidemiologist's report from the Centers for Disease Control in Atlanta, Georgia, announces the appearance of what could be a new illness. In Paris, Willy Rozenbaum establishes a link between this information and the clinical symptoms of one of his patients.

September. First article in *Gai Pied* on "at-risk love"; "gay cancer" appears.

September 10. Birth of Fréquence Gaie.

December 31. Eleven cases of AIDS are reported in France; seventeen total cases will be identified after the fact.[1]

Songs: "Cruisin' the Streets" (Boys Town Gang), "Controversy" (Prince).

1982

February. An AIDS-alert group is formed around Willy Rozenbaum and Jacques Leibowitch. The "homosexual community" is immediately informed.

April 24 and 25. "Training seminar" for the Association des Médecins Gais. One session of the colloquium is devoted to Kaposi's sarcoma.

May 13. André Baudry announces the dissolution of Arcadie.

July 27. Fulfilling a promise made by François Mitterrand as a presidential candidate, Gisèle Halimi and Robert Badinter win the decriminalization of homosexuality (repeal of article 331, paragraph 2 of the penal code; law of August 4, 1981).

October 13. The scandal over Le Coral erupts (pedophilia in group homes for problem children).

December. In the *Bulletin Epidémiologique Hebdomadaire,* the word *SIDA* [AIDS] first appears, and new at-risk groups (intravenous drug users, hemophiliacs, Haitians, immigrants) are identified.

December 31. Forty-eight cases of AIDS are reported in France (including twenty-eight among homo/bisexual males).

Films: R. W. Fassbinder's *Querelle* (based on Jean Genet's novel), Almodóvar's *Labyrinth of Passion*, Blake Edwards's *Victor Victoria*, Diane Kurys's *Coup de foudre*.

Songs: "Maman a tort" (Mylène Farmer), "Tainted Love" (Soft Cell), "De la main gauche" (Danielle Messia).

1983

January 3 –May 20. Luc Montagnier's team discovers the retrovirus named LAV, which may be responsible for AIDS (findings published in *Science* on May 20, 1983). The discovery will not be definitely confirmed until 1984.

March 9. The Conseil des Ministres adopts Yvette Roudy's "antisexist" bill, which will ultimately fail.

March 19. Libération runs the headline "Epidemic of Gay Cancer."

June 18. The Gay Pride parade is deserted.

June 20. A questionnaire is introduced to eliminate at-risk blood donors. The directive from the Direction Générale de la Santé will seldom be followed. Homosexual militants are critical of it.

September 5. Soap-opera homosexuality: *Dynasty* begins its run on FR3, competing with *Dallas*. Al Corley plays Steven Carrington, a liberated homosexual, but his "homophobic" father kills his lover.

December 31. A total of 140 cases of AIDS is reported in France (including 84 among homo/bisexuals).

Films: Patrice Chéreau's *L'homme blessé*, Marek Kanievska's *Another Country*, André Téchiné's *La Matiouette ou l'arrière-pays*, Paul Verhoeven's *The Fourth Man*.

Songs: "La rockeuse de diamants" (Catherine Lara), *Cargo*, video produced by Jean-Baptiste Mondino in the style of Querelle (Axel Bauer), "Modern Love" (David Bowie), "Miss Me Blind" and "Karma Chameleon"(Culture Club), "Jungle Jezebel" (Divine), "She Bop" (Cyndi Lauper).

1984

February 6. Exchange 3615 opens on Minitel.

April. The retrovirus LAV discovered by Luc Montagnier is definitively found to be the cause of AIDS. HTLV 3, discovered in the United States by Professor Robert Gallo, will turn out to be the same retrovirus.

June 25. Michel Foucault dies. Daniel Defert gets in touch with a few jurists and doctors during the summer. Birth of an enormous support group (Aides).

July 17. Laurent Fabius is named prime minister (Georgina Dufoix is minister of social affairs, and Edmond Hervé is minister of health).

September. The Association des Médecins Gais has a complete change of heart: after long denying the existence of AIDS, Dr. Claude Lejeune sounds the alarm. A turning point.

October 4. Daniel Defert invites several gay militants to his apartment to present them with a plan for the organization called Aides. They decline the invitation. Aides will not be a homosexual organization.

November 22, 1984–October 20, 1985. The state is judged to have committed "grave errors" in the contaminated-blood scandal between these two dates (contested ruling of the Conseil d'Etat, April 9, 1993).

December 4. The by-laws of Aides are officially registered. (The organization was created in October 1984, and *Libération* announced its existence on October 20.)

Late December. Frédéric Edelmann and Jean-Florian Mettetal join Aides. The Elisa [LAV antibody] test is introduced. It will gradually become available in France in 1985. Homosexual militants, worried that their names will be put on file, publicly oppose the test.

December 31. A total of 377 cases of AIDS is reported in France (including 232 among homo/bisexuals).

Films: Yannick Bellon's *La triche.*

Songs: "Dom Juane" (Catherine Lara), *Relax,* sadomasochistic video by Bernard Rose (Frankie Goes to Hollywood), "Small Town Boy," "Why," "I Feel Love," and "Johnny, Remember Me" (Bronski Beat), "Girls Just Want to Have Fun" and "She's So Unusual" (Cyndi Lauper), "People Are People" (Depeche Mode), "William, It Was Really Nothing" and "This Charming Man" (The Smiths), "I Want to Break Free" (Queen), "He's So Gay" (Frank Zappa).

1985

February 16. The first Aides brochure is published (55,000 copies) and inserted into *Gai Pied Hebdo.* Simultaneously, the Aides hotline opens, and the first debates in Paris homosexual bars take place.

April. Minister of Health Edmond Hervé, "unavoidably detained," does not meet with Aides, which has asked to see him.

July 23. Ministerial order requiring screening for LAV antibodies in every blood donation (applicable August 1; reimbursement for the cost of unheated antihemophiliac blood products is approved only on October 1, 1985).

July 25. The National Assembly adopts Jean-Pierre Michel's amendment extending antiracist laws to discrimination based on sexual behavior.

Summer. The first survey by the sociologist Michael Pollak appears in *Gai Pied Hebdo.*

October 2. Death of Rock Hudson, who has been hospitalized in Paris, gives AIDS a face.

November 16. An issue of *Gai Pied Hebdo* contains a condom.

December 31. A total of 959 cases of AIDS is reported in France (including 614 among homo/bisexuals).

Films: Stephen Frears's *My Beautiful Laundrette,* Jean-Charles Tacchella's *Escalier C.*
Songs: "Libertine" (Mylène Farmer).

1986

March 4. Television broadcast *Les dossiers de l'écran* is devoted to AIDS. Willy Rozenbaum, Luc Montagnier, and Aides volunteers participate.

March 20. Jacques Chirac is named prime minister; Michèle Barzach becomes deputy minister of health and family under Philippe Séguin.

November 13. Thierry Le Luron dies. He had "married" Coluche at the wax museum in Montmartre on September 25, 1985.

November 27. Michèle Barzach declares AIDS "a great national cause for 1987." Aides receives a small subsidy (490,000 francs) for 1986.

December 6. Louis Pauwels: "The young are infected with mental AIDS."

December 31. A total of 2,213 cases of AIDS is reported in France (including 1,363 among homo/bisexuals).

Films: Bertrand Blier's *Tenue de soirée*, Pedro Almodóvar's *Law of Desire*, Derek Jarman's *Caravaggio*, Pierre Granier-Deferre's *Cours privé*.

Songs: "Nuit magique" (Catherine Lara), "Rent" (Pet Shop Boys), "You Are My World" (The Communards).

1987

January 27. Condom advertising legalized.

March 7. Rift within Aides: Frédéric Edelmann and Jean-Florian Mettetal are defeated. They both resign (they will join Arcat-sida in 1988).

March 16. Charles Pasqua threatens to ban the sale of *Gai Pied Hebdo* to minors. (In April, he opens the Musée de l'Horrible.)

April 27. First government campaign: "AIDS Will Not Get by Me."

May 6. On *L'heure de la vérité*, Jean-Marie Le Pen exploits AIDS as a theme, proposing systematic screening and using the terms *sidaïques* and *sidatoriums*.

October 30. "Mon sida," influential interview in *Le Nouvel Observateur* with Jean-Paul Aron.

December 31. A total of 4,458 cases of AIDS is reported in France (including 2,614 among homo/bisexuals).

Films: Stephen Frears's *Prick Up Your Ears*, James Ivory's *Maurice*, André Téchiné's *Les innocents*, Giuliano Montaldo's *The Gold-Rimmed Glasses*, Paul Vecchiali's *Encore*, Geneviève Lefebvre's *Le jupon rouge*.

Songs: "Never Can Say Goodbye" (The Communards).

1988

May 12. Claude Evin becomes minister of social affairs and health in the Rocard government.

August 20. Jean-Paul Aron dies.

August 28. Guy Hocquenghem dies.

November. After Professor Claude Got's report on AIDS is published, Claude Evin decides to create the Agence Française de Lutte contre le Sida (AFLS), the Agence Nationale de Recherche sur le Sida (ANRS), and the Conseil National du Sida.

December 31. A total of 7,503 cases of AIDS is reported in France (including 4,191 among homo/bisexuals).

Songs: "Sans contrefaçon" (Mylène Farmer), "Une femme avec une femme" (Mecano), "No Clause 28" (Boy George), "Left to My Own Devices" (Pet Shop Boys), "The Halloween Parade" (Lou Reed).

1989

April–June. AFLS campaigns directed at the general public.

June 24. Aides and the brand-new organization ACT UP officially participate in the Gay Pride parade for the first time. "Silence = Death."

July 26. Didier Lestrade creates ACT UP–Paris.

November. First AFLS campaigns directed at gays.

December 31. A total of 11,287 cases of AIDS is reported in France (including 6,038 among homo/bisexuals).

Songs: "Read My Lips" (Jimmy Somerville).

1990

February–March. Hervé Guibert's *A l'ami qui ne m'a pas sauvé la vie* is published. Pierre Epkin-Kneip begins the "Les années sida" column in *Gai Pied.* HIV conference is organized in Paris at the Bataclan.

April. The prime minister's information office bans the condom-promotion campaign planned by the AFLS for the Paris, Lyons, and Marseilles metros. *Gai Pied:* "The Left as Censor."

· *November.* Sida Infos Service is created at the initiative of Pierre Kneip. (The former Aides volunteer will die of AIDS on December 2, 1995.)

December 31. A total of 15,573 cases of AIDS is reported in France (including 8,185 among homo/bisexuals).

Films: Norman René's *Longtime Companion,* Paul Bogart's *Torch Song Trilogy.*

Songs: "Being Boring" (Pet Shop Boys).

1991

April. AFLS director Dominique Charvet reports that his budget includes a "homosexuality expenditure" of 5 million francs.

May–July. Edith Cresson criticizes the latent homosexuality of the British people.

October 4, 5, and 6. At the Nancy conference, Arnaud Marty-Lavauzelle is elected president of the Aides federation.

December 27. Hervé Guibert dies from an overdose of his AIDS medication.

December 31. A total of 20,165 cases of AIDS is reported in France (including 10,322 among homo/bisexuals).

Films: André Téchiné's *J'embrasse pas,* P. J. Castellaneta's *Together Alone,* Nico Papatakis's *Les équilibristes.*

Songs: "Désenchantée" (Mylène Farmer).

1992

March. Continental Opéra baths close.

April 17. *Le Monde* announces on the last page that the creation of a civil union contract is being studied.

April 30. On Antenne 2, *Sida urgence* [AIDS emergency] is broadcast and raises 15 million francs.

June 7. Michael Pollak dies.

June 8. Dr. Jean-Florian Mettetal dies. (During the same period, the film critic Serge Daney and Aides director Jean-Michel Mandopoulos also die of AIDS.)

June 22–August 5. First trial in the matter of the contaminated-blood scandal.

September. Fréquence Gaie (now FH) switches to techno music. (In 1993, its audience will increase tenfold, to 80,000 listeners a day.)

October. *Gai Pied* folds.

December 21. Two amendments to the civil union contract are adopted by Parliament. One will be declared unconstitutional on technical grounds. Sécurité Sociale will now have to insure domestic partners, regardless of sex, for anyone who is covered and who makes such a request.

December 31. A total of 25,227 cases of AIDS is reported in France (including 12,600 among homo/bisexuals).

Films: Pedro Almodavar's *High Heels,* Chen Kaige's *Farewell, My Concubine,* Gus Van

Sant's *My Own Private Idaho*, Michel Béna's *Le ciel de Paris*, Paul Verhoeven's *Basic Instinct*, and four films on AIDS: Cyril Collard's *Les nuits fauves*, François Margolin's *Mensonge*, Kenneth Branagh's *Peter's Friends*, and Steve Levitt's *Deaf Heaven*.

Songs: "Do You Really Want to Know?" (George Michael).

1993

February. Survey on French sexuality by Alfred Spira is published: 4.1 percent of men questioned and 2.6 percent of women are homo/bisexuals. A gross estimate of between 500,000 and 2,000,000 homo/bisexuals in France can be advanced.

March. Simone Veil becomes minister of social, urban, and health affairs in Edouard Balladur's "cohabitation" government (Philippe Douste-Blazy is deputy minister of health).

March 5. Cyril Collard dies of AIDS.

March 8. Cyril Collard's *Les Nuits fauves* receives four César awards. (Between October 21, 1992, and the summer of 1993, it will be seen by 2.8 million moviegoers in France.)

September. The new edition of the *Petit Robert* dictionary changes with the times. *Amour*, previously defined as "a relationship between a man and a woman," becomes "a relationship between two individuals."

December 1. For International AIDS Awareness Day, ACT UP–Paris and Benetton bedeck the obelisk at the Place de la Concorde with a giant fluorescent-pink condom.

December 31. A total of 30,616 cases of AIDS is reported in France (including 14,718 among homo/bisexuals).

Films: Ang Lee's *The Wedding Banquet*, Derek Jarman's *Edward II*.

Songs: "Liberation" (Pet Shop Boys).

1994

April 7. "Tous contre sida," or "Sidaction," is broadcast on all five French television stations. A consensus has been reached in the fight against AIDS: the red ribbon is in fashion.

June 18. In Paris, nearly 20,000 participate in the Gay Pride parade, which marks the twenty-fifth anniversary of the Stonewall Riots.

June 24. The writer Yves Navarre commits suicide.

September 23–25. In Paris, the Aides conference marks the organization's tenth anniversary. Simone Veil attends. Aides now has nearly 3,600 volunteers, divided into thirty-one regional committees spread across ninety-nine cities.

September 25. Christophe Martet replaces Cleews Vellay as president of ACT UP–Paris.

October 18. Cleews Vellay dies. The Centre Gai et Lesbian, headed by Vellay's "husband," Philippe Labbey, organizes a political funeral.

December 31. A total of 35,717 cases of AIDS is reported in France (including 16,771 among homo/bisexuals).

Films: André Téchiné's *Les roseaux sauvages*, Jonathan Demme's *Philadelphia*, Rose Troche's *Go Fish*, Roger Spottiswoode's *And the Band Played On*, Thomas Gutierrez Alea's *Strawberry and Chocolate*, Stephen Elliott's *The Adventures of Priscilla, Queen of the Desert*.

Theater: Tony Kushner's *Angels in America*, directed by Brigitte Jacques, is staged at the festival in Avignon.

1995

April 2. "Let the Third Term Begin," joint demonstration by anti-AIDS groups, organized around Aides and ACT UP.

May 7. Jacques Chirac is elected president of the republic, backed by three figures close to François Mitterrand: Pierre Bergé, Frédéric Mitterrand, and Pascal Sevran.

June. The Aides federation mobilizes to grant unmarried couples legal status (the "social life contract," which in September will become the "social union contract").

June 23. A program devoted entirely to homosexuality, *La nuit gay*, debuts on Canal Plus.

June 24. Nearly 60,000 march in Paris for Gay Pride Day, the greatest success in the history of the French homosexual movement. Creation of a gay community?

July 6. At the request of Colette Codaccioni, the new minister of generational harmony, Minister of Health Elisabeth Hubert censors certain homosexual images in the ministerial campaign against AIDS.

August 29. Jean-Claude Poulet-Dachary, chief of staff for Toulon's new Front National mayor, is murdered.

September 4–15. Fourth International Women's Conference in Beijing: the return of 1970s radical feminism. (Some weeks later, on November 25, nearly 30,000 people, most of them women, will march in Paris to defend their rights: commemoration or revival?)

September 13. Joël Bateux, mayor of Saint-Nazaire, announces that his district will now issue certificates of life partnership to homosexual couples. The Socialist Party mayors of six Paris arrondissements and Mayor Catherine Trautman of Strasbourg follow suit. Anticipation of the social union contract?

November 29. Minister of Justice Jacques Toubon declares before the National Assembly: "It is . . . out of the question to create a civil union contract; on the contrary, marriages and births ought to be favored in this country."

December 31. A total of 39,800 cases of AIDS is reported in France (including 18,400 among homosexuals).

Films: Josiane Balasko's *French Twist*, John Greyson's *Zéro Patience*, Tom Kalin's *Swoon*, Antonia Bird's *Priest*, Xavier Beauvois's *N'oublie pas que tu vas mourir* (debut in Cannes; general release in January 1996).

1996

January 29. Hope raised by combined drug therapies (in particular, the prescription of three drugs combined with a protease inhibitor), presented during the third conference on retroviruses in Washington, D.C. It now appears that the "January 29 revolution" was a major and spectacular turning point in the fight against the AIDS epidemic. AIDS will gradually become a "chronic viral illness."

April 3. Publication in France of this book, which precipitates many lively debates; more than a hundred articles will be devoted to it in the weeks that follow.

May 10. The national railway company, the Société Nationale des Chemins de Fer, grants "joint passes" to homosexual couples.

June 6. The second "Sidaction," scheduled on all eight French television channels, is an abject failure. One line uttered by the president of ACT UP ("France, country of shit") will be particularly criticized. Donations for AIDS research and treatment drop precipitously (fewer than 40 million francs, compared to 300 million francs in 1994). This date is a turning point in the history of the fight against AIDS in France, and it marks the beginning of the decline in mobilization against the epidemic.

June 21. At the initiative of Martine Aubry, the leaders of various leftist parties (among them Michel Rocard, Pierre Mauroy, Charles Fiterman, and Jack Ralite) sign a petition, published in *Le Monde* on June 22, in favor of the Contrat d'Union Sociale (CUS). (Six of the signers—Martine Aubry, Elisabeth Guigou, Bernard Kouchner, Catherine Trautmann, Daniel Vaillant, and Dominique Voynet—will be named ministers in June 1997.) This text appears, retrospectively, to be the principal commitment on the part of the left in favor of the CUS (now the PACS).

June 22. Nearly 100,000 people march at the fifteenth French Lesbian and Gay Pride parade. The demand for the Contrat d'Union Civile et Sociale is put forward. François Hollande, Jack Lang, and Daniel Vaillant represent the French Socialist Party.

August. In France, six months after the "January 29 revolution," more than 13,300 people infected with HIV are receiving combined drug therapies that include a protease inhibitor. (These drugs will be available in pharmacies in 1997.)

Films: Hettie MacDonald's *Beautiful Thing*, Jean-Michel Carré's *Visiblement, je vous aime.*

1997

June 1. Victory of the *gauche plurielle* [the plural left] in the early legislative elections. Lionel Jospin becomes prime minister on June 2 (Elisabeth Guigou, minister of justice; Martine Aubry, minister of labor and social affairs; Bernard Kouchner, minister of health).

June 23. Minister of Justice Elisabeth Guigou declares that the new government will respect its commitments by creating the Contrat d'Union Sociale.

June 23–27. An international colloquium on gay and lesbian cultures is held at the Centre Georges Pompidou. The sociologist Pierre Bourdieu calls for homosexual militants to place themselves "in the service of the social movement as a whole" and "in the forefront" of subversive social movements.

June 28. "Europride" brings together nearly 250,000 people in Paris. It is the greatest success in the history of Gay Pride Day in France. Dominique Voynet, a new minister in the Jospin government, participates in the march.

July 15. Murder of fashion designer Gianni Versace in Florida.

December 1. The traditional day marking the fight against AIDS is a relative failure (lower participation by organizations, fewer programs).

1998

February. The term "Pacte Civil de Solidarité" (PACS) appears. It will gradually replace the earlier terms "Contrat d'Union Civile" and "Contrat d'Union Sociale."

April 28. In a report to the legislative committee, Deputies Patrick Bloche and Jean-Pierre Michel adopt the term "PACS." (The legislative bill will be made public by Catherine Tasca, chair of the legislative committee, on May 28.)

June. The anti-impotence drug Viagra, sold in the United States since March, is marketed in France.

June 17. During a decisive interministerial meeting at the Hôtel Matignon (involving the chiefs of staff of the prime minister, the minister of justice, and the minister of labor and social affairs), the government opts for the PACS and commits itself to having the Michel-Bloche bill considered at the fall session of the National Assembly. Shortly thereafter, Elisabeth Guigou confirms this decision in a letter to Catherine Tasca, chair of the legislative committee. The letter is made public the next day.

June 20. Nearly 100,000 people march in Paris for the traditional Gay Pride Day.

September 19. On the model of the Berlin "Love Parade," the first "techno-parade" in the streets of Paris. Nearly 130,000 people march.

September 24. The legislative committee passes the PACS legislation.

October 9. The National Assembly begins consideration of the PACS bill. After fewer than four hours of debate, the right passes a motion to table it, given the absence of many deputies on the left, who are in the minority at the time of the vote. The bill is killed: it is a brutal affront to the government and to the left. *Libération*'s headline (October 12): "The Socialist Party in Retreat." *Le Monde* (October 11): "Socialist Party Deputies Were Ashamed of the PACS."

November 3–December 9. After the October 9 defeat, a new bill in support of the PACS is introduced. It is discussed from November 3 to November 10, but its passage is postponed, given very strong opposition from the right (introduction of more than a thousand amendments, lively battles over procedures, a long-winded speech by Christine Boutin, a deputy from the Union de la Démocratie Française party).

December. Le Piano Zinc, one of the historic bars of Paris, closes its doors.

December 1. "Return to Silence" is the slogan adopted by ACT UP at the demonstration marking the global fight against AIDS. A revealing slogan.

December 9. After a new series of stormy debates, the PACS legislation is passed on the first vote by the National Assembly.

Films: Jacques Martineau and Olivier Ducastel's *Jeanne et le garçon formidable,* Patrice Chéreau's *Ceux qui m'aiment prendront le train,* Benoît Jacquot's *L'école de la chair.*

1999

January 28. Tennis: Amélie Mauresmo, women's singles finalist at the French Open, reveals her homosexuality.

January 27. Successful opening of David Hockney's painting exhibition at Beaubourg. (On the same day, a party is held in his honor at Le Queen; more than 100,000 visitors will see the exhibition in the month that follows.)

January 31. In Paris, more than 100,000 people mobilized by numerous religious organizations and about a hundred rightist deputies, march against the PACS. Banners proclaiming PACS = QUEERS are displayed in the capital. It is the largest demonstration since the Lionel Jospin government has come to power, and the largest implicitly "homophobic" demonstration ever held in France.

February–March. Trial of the ministers in the contaminated-blood scandal before the Cour de Justice de la République.

March 9. In the contaminated-blood scandal, former prime minister Laurent Fabius and the former minister of social affairs are exonerated by the Cour de Justice de la République. Former secretary of health Edmond Hervé is convicted, but no penalty is imposed.

March 12–13. A big flop: ACT UP, after threatening to reveal the homosexuality of a rightist deputy who had participated in the anti-PACS demonstration on January 31, is roundly criticized. French-style outing is a failure.

March 30–April 1. Second vote on the PACS legislation in the National Assembly. An amendment adopted by the Senate on domestic partnerships is revised and extended to homosexuals. (After some shuttling back and forth, as required by the constitution, the PACS legislation ought to be definitively adopted by the end of 1999; the first PACS could then be signed in France in early 2000.)

Interview Sources

This book is the result of a survey based on 280 original interviews conducted over three years, from 1993 to 1996, in Paris and eleven other cities in France (Avignon, Bordeaux, Dijon, Le Mans, Lyons, Mâcon, Marseilles, Montpellier, Nantes, Nice, and Strasbourg).

All unattributed quotations appearing in this book are taken from these interviews. The following observers and participants were interviewed.

GREAT OBSERVERS OF THE TIMES

Michèle André; Thierry de Beaucé; Jean-Michel Belorgey; Maurice Bénassayag; Daniel Bensaïd; Pirre Bergé; Hector Bianciotti; Huguette Bouchardeau; Christian Bourgois; Patrice Chéreau; William Christie; Hervé Claude; Lucien Clergue; André Comte-Sponville; Daniel Defert; Julien Dray; Frédéric Edelmann; Annie Ernaux; Laurent Fabius; Father Jean-Michel di Falco; Dominique Fernandez; Alain Finkielkraut; Jocelyne François; Anne Garreta; the late Jean Gattégno; Jean Guidoni; Gisèle Halimi; Françoise Héritier-Augé; Vaclav Jamek; Jean-Noël Jeanneney; Louis Joinet; Jack Lang; Didier Lapeyronnie; Daniel Larrieu; Jorge Lavelli; Annie Le Brun; Mathieu Lindon; Bruno Masure; Jean-Pierre Michel; Jean-Paul Montanari; the late Yves Navarre; Michelle Perrot; Roger Peyrefitte; Michel Pezet; Michel Polac; Madeleine Reberioux; Angelo Rinaldi; Monsigneur Albert Rouet; Henry Rousso; Willy Rozenbaum; Josyane Savigneau; Jacques Siclier; Pierre-André Taguieff; Alain Touraine; Michel Tournier; Paul Veyne; Edmund White; Michel Wieviorka.

PARTICIPANTS IN THE MOVEMENTS FOR
SEXUAL LIBERATION

Gérard Bach-Ignasse (CUARH); Mélanie Badaire (CUARH); André Baudry (Arcadie); Bernard Bousset (Syndicat National des Entreprises Gaies); Jean Boyer (CUARH); Patrick Cardon (GLH–Aix); René de Ceccatty (*Gai Pied, Masques*); Yves Charfe (*Gai Pied*); Jean-Marc Choub (CUARH); Jacques Cougnaud (David et Jonathan); the late Michel Cressole (FHAR, *Libération*); Laurent Dispot (FHAR); Laurent Doumerc (CUARH); Marc Epstein (*Fréquence Gaie*); Jacques Fortin (GLH–Marseilles); Jacky Fougerary (GLH–Orléans, *Gai Pied, Illico*); Philippe Fretté (CUARH); Philippe Guy (co-founder of FHAR); Didier Heller (*Gai Pied*); Jean-Luc Hennig (*Libération, Gai Pied*); Christian Hennion (FHAR, *Libération*); Alain Huet (FHAR, GLH); Georges Lapassade (FHAR); Claude Lejeune (Association de Médecins Gais); André Letowski (David et Jonathan); Christian de Leusse (GLH–Marseilles); Hervé Liffran (CUARH); Hugo Marsan (*Gai Pied*); Alain Neddam (GLH–Lyons, Sida Solidarité Spectacle); Blaise Noël (SOS Ecoute Gaie); Jan-Paul Pouliquen (CUARH, Contrat d'Union Civile collective); the late Jacques de Ricaumont (Arcadie); Albert Rosse (Parti Socialiste Unifié, *Gai Pied*); Pablo Rouy (FHAR, GLH, *Gai Pied*); Alain

Sanzio (*Masques*); René Schérer (FHAR); Jean Stern (*Gai Pied, Libération*, Aides); Gérard Vappereau (GLH, *Gai Pied*).

MILITANT FEMINISTS

Cathy Bernheim (Mouvement des Femmes); Sandrine Bodet (Marie-pas-Claire); Marie-Jo Bonnet (Gouines Rouges); Renée Broustal (Centre Simone-de-Beauvoir–Nantes); Jackie Buet (Festival de Femmes); Michèle Causse; Thérèse Clerc; Carole Crawford (Mouvement d'Information et d'Expression des Lesbiennes); Christine Delphy (Mouvement des Femmes, *Questions Féministes*); Catherine Deudon (Mouvement des Femmes); Renée Dufourt; Françoise d'Eaubonne, Anne-Marie Fauré (cofounders of FHAR); Catherine Gonnard (*Lesbia*); Maryse Guerlais (Centre Simone-de-Beauvoir–Nantes); Sonia Guessab (Lesbiennes Se Déchaînent); Luce Irigaray; Carole Keruzore (Lesbiennes Se Déchaînent); Michèle Larrouy (Archives Lesbiennes); Claudie Lesselier (Archives Lesbiennes); Nicole-Claude Mathieu (*Questions Féministes*); Hélène de Monferrand; Geneviève Pastre; Françoise Picq (Mouvement des Femmes); Claude Rejon; Evelyne Rochedereux (Mouvement des Femmes); Françoise Roncin; Annie Sugier (Mouvement des Femmes); Maya Surduts (Coordination Nationale des Associations pour le Droit à l'Avortement et à la Contraception); Suzette Triton (Ligue Communiste Révolutionnaire, *Masques, Vlasta*); Moruni Turlot (Marie-pas-Claire); Sandrine Vivelespérance (Lesbiennes Se Déchaînent); Anne (Tristan) Zelensky (Mouvement des Femmes).

PERSONALITIES AND PARTICIPANTS IN THE
FIGHT AGAINST AIDS

Michèle Arnaudiès (Agence Française de Lutte contre le Sida); Nadine Balcon; Françoise Baranne; Professor Françoise Barré-Sinoussi (Institut Pasteur; codiscoverer of HIV); Father Gérard Bénéteau (Sida-Solidarité–Saint-Eustache); Michel Bourrelly (Aides); Jean-Baptiste Brunet (Groupe d'Alerte sur le Sida); Michel Celse (ACT UP); Dominique Charvet (Agence Française de Lutte contre le Sida); Eric Conan (ex-reporter for *Libération*); Thierry Corde (Sida Infos Service); Christophe Coussin (Aides); Laurent Cribier (Aides); Jean-Pierre Derrien (Aides); Christophe Divernet (Aides); Jean-Michel Dorlet (Aides); Benoît Félix (Aides); Bruno Gachard (Aides); Thierry Gamby (Aides); Christophe Girard (Arcat); Mirko Grmek; Edmond-Luc Henry (Association Française des Hémophiles); Emmanuel Hirsch (Arcat); Professor Dider Jayle; Serge Hefez (*Gai Pied, Ruban Rouge*); Bruno Hup (Aides); Martine Jalta (Aides); Professor Christine Katlama; Professor Michel Kazatchkine; Professor David Klatzmann; the late Pierre Kneip (Aides, Sida Infos Service); Philippe Labbey (ACT UP, Centre Gai et Lesbien); Emeric Languérand (ACT UP); Pierre Lascoumes (Aides); Professor Jacques Leibowitch; Didier Lestrade (ACT UP); Antoine Lion (Chrétiens et Sida); Gilles Manas (Aides); Philippe Mangeot (ACT UP); Laurent Martin (Aides); Christophe Martet (ACT UP); Arnaud Marty-Lavauzelle (Aides); Marie-Yannick Merckx (Broussais Hospital); Antoine Messiah; Patrice Meyer (Vive la Révolution); Jean-Michel Misrai (Aides); Alain Molla (Aides); Jean-Yves Nau (*Le Monde*); Geneviève Paicheler (Centre d'Etudes et de Recherches Marxistes); Jacky Pedinielli (Aides); Samuel Planet (Aides); Roberto Polchi (Aides); Mathieu Potte-Bonneville (ACT UP); Anne Rousseau (ACT UP); Professor Christine Rouzioux (codiscoverer of HIV); Grégory Rowe (Aides); Marie-Ange Schiltz (Ecole des Hautes Etudes en Sciences Sociales); Michel Setbon; Alain Siboni (Aides); Professor Alfred Spira; Nathalie Truchet; France Uebersfeld (Aides); Laurent Vinauger (Aides).

OTHERS WHO WERE INTERVIEWED

Jean-Yves Autexier; Christian Belaygue; Denis Bernet-Rollande; Bernard Besret; Facundo Bo; Fédérico Botana; Jean-Daniel Cadinot; Michel Canesi; Bertrand Charneau; Jean-Martin Cohen-Solal (former director of the Comité Français d'Education pour la Santé); Muriel Courtot; Dominique Couvreur (former city editor for *Libération*); Thibaud Debray; Marion Doin; Patrick Drevet; Jean-Pierre Esperandieu; Bernard Faucon; Agathe Gaillard; Monique Golliet; Christine Guibert; Jacques Hauguel; Josy (owner of La Champmeslé); Sophie Koutouzov; Claude Laroche; Lindinalva Laurindo–Da Silva; Brother Jacques Laval; Jean-Claude Le Berre; Joël Leroux (Le Duplex); Claude L'Huillier; Maurice McGrath (Le Central); Michel Maffesoli; Françoise Marc; Jean-Charles Marsan (Le Vagabond); Jean-Pierre Meyer-Genton (Les Mots à la Bouche bookstore); Bernard Minoret; the late Jean-Baptiste Niel; Elula Perrin (Le Katmandou); Jean-Pierre Piticco; Jürgen Pletsch (Le Piano Zinc); Olivier Pouzet; Xavier Rosan; Carole Roussopoulos; Serge Tamagnot; Georges-Charles Veran; Thierry Voeltzel.

Notes

1. I was a journalist at the French homosexual weekly *Gay Pied Hebdo* from 1987 to 1990, president of the foremost gay student organization in France from 1988 to 1990, and adviser to former prime minister Michel Rocard on social problems and the fight against AIDS from 1993 to 1994. Since 1997 I have been an adviser to Martine Aubry, minister of labor and social affairs in the Lionel Jospin government.

2. The PACS, debated in the French National Assembly in 1998–99, would allow the legal recognition of unmarried couples, heterosexual or homosexual. The PACS legislation represents a synthesis of two earlier, similar bills: the Contrat d'Union Civile [Civil Union Contract], or CUC, in 1992–94, and the Contrat d'Union Sociale [Social Union Contract], or CUS, in 1995–98. I supported these various pieces of legislation from the beginning and was named a government representative for the PACS bill.

3. With the exception of the updated chronology and of this preface, published here for the first time.

4. Let me indicate, very briefly, that the fight against AIDS in France has undergone three major shifts since 1996: Aides has grown weaker and is struggling to recruit new members; ACT UP has become more radical and has been severely marginalized (the organization was unanimously criticized in March 1999 when it ventured into an act of "outing"); and fundraising through Sidaction has dropped considerably since 1996 (its joint programming on the various French television stations was a miserable failure). All these elements, obviously, are linked to the "revolution" of January 29, 1996: the introduction of combined-drug therapies, a major and spectacular turning point in the fight against the AIDS epidemic.

5. There are very few books on the history of the women's movement in France, and none deals with the role played within it by the issue of lesbianism. To my knowledge, there is also no history, not even a brief one, of lesbian groups in twentieth-century France.

6. Hannah Arendt, "Postscript," in *Eichmann in Jerusalem: A Report on the Banality of Evil*, revised and enlarged edition (New York: Penguin, 1977), p. 296.

7. [In September 1994, the French government issued guidelines, designed to crack down on Muslim fundamentalism, that restricted the wearing of religious symbols in schools. A number of Muslim schoolgirls were expelled for refusing to remove their traditional head scarves. Mass protests followed.—Trans.]

8. This is especially true of one journalist, Didier Eribon, who has vehemently attacked my book for personal reasons.

9. Support for homosexual marriage—clearly a universalist proposal (and not at all a communitarian one), and one that I do not criticize at the theoretical level—appears ex-

tremely marginal in France at this time, and, given the political power structure and public opinion, politically unrealistic for now.

PROLOGUE

1. [Later called *Gai Pied Hebdo*; see also chap. 6, n. 1. Throughout the text, the titles of French-language and other foreign-language works that exist in published English translations are followed by their English-language titles, italicized and in brackets, and the English title is used after the first mention. If there is no published English translation, an English translation of the title is given once in brackets but is not italicized. For a direct quotation from a work that does exist in a published English translation, but for which my own translation has been substituted, the corresponding note gives the original title of the work rather than the title of the published English translation, even though the text uses the work's English title.—Trans.]

2. [Where a woman can kiss the person of her choice on the dance floor.—Trans.]

3. [*Sept ans de bonheur:* literally, "Seven years of happiness." The phrase, which repeats the French title of the film *The Seven-Year Itch*, also alludes to the length of the presidential term in office.—Trans.]

4. The term "homosexual" will be used in this book in its most basic social sense. That is, it will refer to any woman or man who considers herself or himself "homosexual." The term "gay" will be used in an identical manner, but only in referring to the late 1970s and after (for a discussion of the figures cited, which may be a low estimate, see chap. 15).

5. [See chap. 2.—Trans.]

6. Guy Hocquenghem and Jean-Louis Bory, *Comment nous appelez-vous déjà?* (In these notes, the only works cited along with names of publishers and dates of publication are those that do not appear in the bibliography.)

7. Letter from Gilles Deleuze, Feb. 25, 1994. To encourage this debate, I invite readers to share their experiences with me, as well as their remarks on and reactions to this book.

CHAPTER 1: "MY NAME IS GUY HOCQUENGHEM"

1. Madeleine Hocquenghem, "Lettre à mon fils," *Le Nouvel Observateur*, Jan. 17, 1972.

2. In a posthumous text (*L'amphithéâtre des morts*), Guy Hocquenghem gives an account of his adolescent years.

3. Unless otherwise noted, words and phrases that appear in quotation marks, as well as numerous pieces of information cited in the body of the text, are taken from original interviews that I conducted with various informants between 1993 and 1996. [See the preceding section, "Interview Sources."—Trans.]

4. In a leftist meeting on rue d'Ulm, Hocquenghem, publicly accused of being homosexual, replied, "You're crazy. What an idea!" In *L'amphithéâtre des morts*, he confirms this anecdote and his response, of which he said he was "still ashamed, half a century later."

5. Since Guy Hocquenghem was a member of the occupation committee at the Sorbonne, some have said that he himself tore down the notices of the CAPR (a theory supported, unconvincingly, by Philippe Guy and Hélène Hazera).

6. *Répétition génerale* [Dress rehearsal] is the title of a book by Henri Weber and Daniel Bensaïd (Maspero, 1968).

7. *Le songe d'une nuit d'hiver* (1953), *Les sept tentations de Puck* (1953), *Symphonie pour un homme seul* (1955), and *Le sacre du printemps* (1959) had already anticipated this movement in Béjart's works.

8. Wilhelm Reich, *Die sexuelle Revolution* (published in France in Sept. 1968).

9. Jean-Paul Aron, *Les modernes*.

10. See also Guy Hocquenghem, "1970–1980, dix ans qui valent vingt siècles" *Libération*, July 29, 1980.

11. Ménie Grégoire, who published *Le métier d'être femme* in 1965, ended her broadcasts in 1981.

12. *France soir*, March 12, 1971; *Actuel*, Nov. 1972 (the words and slogans published here were directly retranscribed from one of the rare copies of the broadcast).

13. Françoise d'Eaubonne and Anne-Marie Fauré were not present the day of the broadcast, and Pierre Hahn, though present, was onstage as a guest.

14. Guy Hocquenghem, *Lettre ouverte à ceux qui sont passés du col mao au Rotary club*. In the same book, Hocquenghem explains that Roland Castro was opposed to his joining VLR.

15. Guy Hocquenghem, *Le Nouvel Observateur*, Jan. 10, 1972.

16. *Tout!*, issue 1. This issue caused quite a stir and elicited a great deal of mail. It also included an article about the events on Christopher Street and the birth of the Gay Liberation Front in the United States.

17. This text, published anonymously in issue 12 of *Tout!*, was reprinted by Guy Hocquenghem in the July 1972 issue of the bimonthly review *Partisans*—his way of signing it.

18. This manifesto was directly inspired by the manifesto on the issue of abortion, signed by 343 women and published on Apr. 5, 1971 (see chap. 2).

19. This quotation, interpreted in various ways, caused a great deal of controversy. Some said that this attraction to the physical beauty of Arabs, combined with anti-Zionism—if not anti-Semitism—drove Jean Genet to Yasser Arafat's fedayeen camps; see Angelo Rinaldi, "Notre-Dame-des-Salauds," *L'Express*, Sept. 5, 1991.

20. The charge was the result of a question addressed to the government by two members of the National Assembly, one of whom was Jean Royer (*Le Monde*, May 15, 1971).

21. In the historic decision of July 16, 1971, the Constitutional Council, exasperated by the zeal that Raymond Marcellin had shown in repressing leftist unrest, found in favor of Sartre, declaring that the attacks on freedom of expression and association were unconstitutional. To this day, it is the most important decision the constitutional judge has made.

22. Christian, "Notre dernier numéro est-il anti-ouvrier?" *Tout!*, issue 13.

23. *Tout!*, issue 12.

24. *Lutte Ouvrière*, May 4, 1971.

25. The saying "We don't get off within the system" was used in an FHAR pamphlet (archives of the Bibliothèque Nationale) distributed June 1, 1971, on the rue du Dragon, outside a screening of the film *Death in Venice*.

26. Slogan from Nanterre, 1968.

27. Marc Roy, "FHAR, le coup d'éclat," *Gai Pied*, Apr. 1981.

28. Interview with Pierre-André Boutang, 1985. Daniel Guérin was also the first to publish Malcolm X in France.

29. It is even possible that the anarchist camp, combined with the actions of the Gazolines, prevented the FHAR from taking reformist actions and from becoming better structured.

30. Pierre Juquin, interviewed in *Le Nouvel Observateur*, May 15, 1972.

31. A twenty-five-minute film on the beginnings of the FHAR (May–June 1971) was produced by Carole Roussopoulos. It provides information about the precise slogans and atmosphere of the time.

32. Leaflets in the archives of the Bibliothèque Nationale.

33. Daniel Mauroc, *Les étreintes foules* (Plasma, 1979).

34. Guy Hocquenghem, *Partisans*, July 1972.

35. [*Fard*, "makeup," is a homonym of "FHAR."—Trans.]

36. The Gazolines' desire for an indissociably aesthetic and political form of radical subversion linked them to the Situationiste Internationale. Some of the Gazolines made Guy Debord's *La société du spectacle* (Buchet-Chastel, 1967) their bedside reading, and a few FHAR manifestoes were published by Gérard Lebovici at Champ Libre. See also Jean-Pierre Voyer, *Lettre ouverte aux citoyens du FHAR*, Nov. 10, 1971. Nevertheless, their influence should not be overestimated.

37. Jean-François Bizot, *Les déclassés* (Le Sagittaire, 1976).

38. For the comments of Griselda and Daniel Guérin, see *Gai Pied*, Apr. 1981. See also Hélène Hazera, "Souvenirs gazogènes," *Gai Pied Hebdo*, March 7, 1991.

39. Also collaborating on this issue were Cathy Bernheim, Michel Cressole, Catherine Deudon, Daniel Guérin, Pierre Hahn, Christian Hennion, Guy Hocquenghem, Georges Lapassade, Marie-France, Christian Revon, and Anne Querrien.

40. About a dozen FHAR groups were created in the provinces, however—by Jean Le Bitoux and Pierre de Ségovia in Nice, by Pablo Rouy in Tours, and by Patrick Cardon in Aix-en-Provence.

41. Laurent Dispot, opinion piece published in *Gai Pied Hebdo*, March 7, 1991.

42. Even in *Tout!* an FHAR militant expressed regret that the movement had rejected reformism and the notion of gay rights as championed in the United States; see "Bilan," issue 15.

43. Between 1971 and 1973 there were reports of several suicides by young homosexuals in prison, in particular those of Guy Clergeot and Gérard Grandmontagne; Guy Hocquenghem dedicated one of his books to the latter.

44. For lifestyles, see chap. 4.

45. Guy Hocquenghem, *Le désir homosexuel*.

46. The article "Les pédés et la révolution" (issue 12 of *Tout!*) gives a detailed analysis of this litmus test.

47. The theme of bisexuality and polysexuality recurs in the theoretical documents of the FHAR, in the tradition of Deleuze and Guattari's "desiring machines."

48. See FHAR, *Rapport contre la normalité*; and *Partisans*, July 1972.

49. Hocquenghem speaks of the "language proper" to homosexuals, and his interview with *Le Nouvel Observateur* (Jan. 1972) already illustrates, though against his will, the path toward identity politics. Six years later, in 1978, Hocquenghem spoke of a [homosexual] "race" and ran in the legislative elections as a "homosexual" candidate.

50. *Gai Pied Hebdo*, March 7, 1991.

51. Guy Hocquenghem, in FHAR, *Rapport contre la normalité*.

CHAPTER 2: WOMEN'S LIBERATION

1. "Libération des femmes: Année zéro," *Partisans*, July–Oct. 1970.

2. The women's liberation movement in the United States also began with a spectacular act: on September 7, 1968, women disrupted the Miss America Pageant in Atlantic City and threw their underwear at the audience. [This is a variation on a popular misconception. The women threw some objects, including brassieres, into a "Freedom Trash Can" outside Convention Hall (a gesture that has been widely and persistently misrepresented for some thirty years now as a collective "bra burning"). No underwear was thrown

at the pageant's audience; the action proper consisted of the women's unfurling a banner reading WOMEN'S LIBERATION from the balcony of the hall as the new Miss America was crowned.—Ed.]

3. The disturbance occurred at what was in fact the first action of the MLF, organized on May 21, 1970, by several women, including Antoinette Fouque and Monique Wittig. "Not getting any?" [Mal baisées] was the response of leftist militants, and it led the feminists to choose to work in exclusively female groups. [See n. 20.—Trans.]

4. Cathy Bernheim, Perturbation, ma soeur and L'amour presque parfait. See also the article "Je suis moins désespérée qu'il y a quelques années," Libération, May 18, 1978.

5. In 1964 Andrée Michel published La condition de la Française d'aujourd'hui with Geneviève Texier (Gonthier). FMA was associated until 1970 with the Mouvement Démocratique Féminin [Women's democratic movement], led by Marie-Thérèse Eyquem, Colette Audry, and Yvette Roudy.

6. Tout!, issue 12 (unsigned text by Françoise Picq and Nadja Ringart).

7. William Masters and Virginia Johnson's Human Sexual Response (Little, Brown, 1966, translated into French in 1968), Kate Millett's Sexual Politics (Doubleday, 1970, translated into French in 1971), and Germaine Greer's The Female Eunuch (Bantam, 1971, translated into French in 1971) introduced or complemented these positions.

8. Betty Friedan continued Beauvoir's reflections on this issue in The Feminine Mystique (Norton, 1963, translated into French by Yvette Roudy in 1964).

9. In fact, this famous line of Mauriac's—which, moreover, is less obscene than some have said—is from a private letter sent to Roger Stéphane, but Sartre and Beauvoir took pleasure in making it public.

10. One part of that chapter, titled "The Lesbian," was based on the experiences of her friend Violette Leduc.

11. Moreover, in Lettres à Sartre, Beauvoir clearly alludes to her love affairs with women.

12. Simone de Beauvoir, "La lesbienne," in Le deuxième sexe.

13. On Simone de Beauvoir, see the biography by Deirdre Bair.

14. Simone de Beauvoir's preface to Anne Tristan and Annie de Pisan's Histoires du MLF.

15. Vicky, "Harmonie ou si l'homosexualité m'était contée," Les Temps Modernes, Apr.–May 1974.

16. "Debré nous n'te ferons plus d'enfants," from Mouvement de libération des femmes en chanson, histoire subjective, 1970–1980 (Tierce, 1981), a collection of MLF songs.

17. Monique Wittig, Actuel, Jan. 1974.

18. On the function of cruising in the movement, see "La femme de drague," a discussion among a dozen women, in the "Trois milliards de pervers" issue of Recherches.

19. In 1986, three-quarters of the same women declared themselves to be heterosexual, and the remaining quarter were still homo- or bisexual. Nadja Ringart, "Quand ce n'était qu'un début," Crises de la société, féminisme et changement (Tierce, 1991). Another survey of the women's movement in Lyons (Centre Lyonnais d'Etudes Féministes, Chronique d'une passion) reported slightly higher levels of homosexuality.

20. [The French expression "mal baisées" literally means "(you) poorly fucked (women)."—Trans.]

21. Anne Tristan (Zelensky), Histoires du MLF.

22. The apparent coherence and delimitation of these two camps should not lead us to forget that they were less rigid than they appeared, especially in the early 1970s. In addition,

at least one other camp, in sympathy with "the class struggle," was more directly linked to the far left. The MLF neighborhood groups came into being in 1971. The Pétroleuses (associated with the Ligue Communiste Révolutionnaire, or LCR), Femmes en Lutte [Women in struggle], and Femmes Travailleuses en Lutte [Working women in struggle] were their successors. Homosexuality seems to have played a lesser role in these neighborhood groups.

23. Egalitarian desire and universalism were not always well regarded among the Féministes Révolutionnaires, as the paradoxical life history of Monique Wittig seems to indicate. Nevertheless, their first slogan, "One man in two is a woman," is significant.

24. Editions des Femmes and the periodical *Des Femmes en Mouvement* for Psychépo; Tierce and *Questions Féministes, Histoires d'Elles* for the other feminists.

25. In the United States, this debate also occurred between cultural feminists and radical feminists. See Michel Feher, "Erotisme et féminisme aux Etats-Unis: Les exercices de la liberté," *Esprit*, Nov. 1993.

26. This notion of "visibility," in the sense of "politicization of the private sphere," took on particular importance in homosexual groups in France after 1968.

27. Antoinette Fouque developed her position on homosexuality at length in an essential interview (which I cite broadly here): "Notre terre de naissance," *Des Femmes en Mouvement: Midi-Pyrénées*, May 1982. See also the special issue "Homosexuelles, des femmes," *Des Femmes en Mouvement*, Aug. 22, 1980.

28. Guy Hocquenghem, *L'après-mai des faunes*.

29. Cathy Bernheim holds that this "circle of women" appeared in May–June 1970 and was responsible for placing the spray of flowers at the Tomb of the Unknown Soldier. By contrast, Christine Delphy assumes that "Petites Marguerites" was simply another name for the Féministes Révolutionnaires, and thus that the Petites Marguerites did not come first.

30. This legendary commando was formed by Françoise d'Eaubonne and Pierre Hahn (of the nascent FHAR). Supposedly it allowed militants to defend themselves with long sausages, used as blackjacks, which could be brought into the Mutualité without attracting the attention of the security forces.

31. Specifically, Monique Wittig, Christine Delphy, Cathy Bernheim, and Catherine Deudon were present at the Ménie Grégoire action.

32. Anne Tristan (Zelensky) and Annie de Pisan, *Histoires du MLF*.

33. The MLA, created in 1971, was a direct offshoot of the MLF. The Mouvement pour la Libération de l'Avortement et de la Contraception (MLAC) was created in April 1973, after a rift with Choisir; it had both men and women as members.

34. The woman who had had an abortion, Marie-Claire Chevallier, was defended by Gisèle Halimi. Simone de Beauvoir and Michel Rocard, among others, gave forceful depositions as witnesses for Chevallier.

35. *Le Torchon Brûle* was one of the movement's principal journals, with six issues between 1971 and 1973.

36. Guy Hocquenghem, "Les femmes sont un peu nos mamans," *Actuel*, Nov. 1972.

37. The FHAR also joined the first public demonstration of the MLF, on November 20, 1971.

38. Some feminists maintain that, given the concentric circles already described, "Gouines Rouges" was simply another name—internal, less visible from the outside, perhaps merely a bit less restrained—for the Féministes Révolutionnaires camp of the MLF.

39. Guy Hocquenghem, *Partisans*, July–Oct. 1972.

40. Anne Tristan (Zelensky), *Histoires d'amour, le cabinet de Barbe-Bleue*. ["*homosexualité mâle*": the play on words is double (*mâle*, "male" in the biological sense; and *mâle*, "male" in the sense of electrical equipment whose function is specifically to be inserted).—Trans.]

41. In this respect, the tumultuous relations of collaboration and separation among the Daughters of Bilitis (created in 1955), the National Organization for Women (NOW, created in 1966), and the Gay Liberation Front (GLF, dating from 1970) are telling.

42. Interview with Marie-Jo Bonnet in *Masques*, Summer 1980.

CHAPTER 3: "DOWN WITH DADDY'S HOMOSEXUALITY!"

In the article from which this chapter's epigraph is taken, Michel Foucault uses a pseudonym. See Didier Eribon, *Michel Foucault et ses contemporains* (Fayard, 1994).

1. As we have seen, Simone de Beauvoir was an exception, but she was a role model more for feminists than for homosexual militants. See the debate surrounding her chapter "La lesbienne."

2. André Gide, preface to *Corydon*.

3. Paul Claudel, letter to André Gide, March 2, 1914. In *Le livre d'or*, Jean Laurence d'Estoux claims Claudel said, "I hate Gide, Proust, and the cursed race of Sodom."

4. Dominique Fernandez, *Le rapt de Ganymède*.

5. In June 1936 André Gide went to Moscow with his companion, Pierre Herbart. But Gide, suspecting attacks on freedom, and having learned about the setbacks that homosexuals had experienced under the regime, predicted totalitarianism. See Gide's *Retour de l'URSS* (Gallimard, 1936), in which several observations have to do with homosexuals; and Pierre Herbart, *En URSS* (Gallimard, 1937).

6. André Gide, quoted by Roger Peyrefitte, *Le regard des autres* (Arcadie congress).

7. Angelo Rinaldi, *L'Express*, Sept. 30, 1983.

8. In spite of Aragon and, especially, Crevel, the Surrealists, with Breton in the lead, proved particularly hateful toward inverts. See especially "Recherches sur la sexualité," *La Révolution Surréaliste*, March 1928, reprinted in volume 4 of *Archives du surréalisme* (Gallimard).

9. Jean Cocteau, *Le livre blanc*.

10. Ibid.

11. Edmund White, *Genet: A Biography* (Knopf, 1993) (this volume will henceforth be an important reference text).

12. Ibid. Here, Genet definitively contradicts Sartre, who devoted an entire book to him, *Saint Genet, comédien et martyr*.

13. Jean Genet, interviewed by Robert Poulet, "Fouillez l'ordure," *Bulletin de Paris*, July 19, 1956.

14. Genet, Edmund White informs us, had planned to compile a long treatise on homosexuality titled *L'enfer* [Hell]. In addition, some American women militants consider his writings "feminist" because they show that "femininity" is a social role, not a biological reality. See Kate Millett, *Sexual Politics*.

15. See Jean Gattegno, "Du pécheur au militant," *Le Débat*, March 1981. Marie-Jo Bonnet's *Un choix sans équivoque*, which seeks out sapphic women throughout history, suggests that these claims need to be nuanced.

16. Radclyffe Hall was the author of *The Well of Loneliness*. In 1928, thirty years after Oscar Wilde, she was put on trial for the book and was supported by E. M. Forster, Virginia Woolf, and Aldous Huxley. On Gertrude Stein and Alice B. Toklas, see chap. 7.

17. Letter from Marguerite Yourcenar to Natalie Barney, July 29, 1963, in Marguerite Yourcenar, *Lettres à ses amis et à quelques autres* (Gallimard, 1995).

18. Colette's first novels were signed by her husband, Willy, who did not allow her to publish her books under her own name until 1904.

19. In 1948, notably, he published *Les amours buissonnières*, a realist novel about desire among boys. The book enjoyed a modest success.

20. Kinsey's figures were seriously challenged, especially because he recruited former prisoners for his survey. More recent studies (including one from the Kinsey Institute, published by *Science*, Jan. 1989) have confirmed that these estimates were too high.

21. Roger Peyrefitte, *Arts*, May 1964.

22. Peyrefitte also thought he could cite the homosexuality of King Baldwin I, the Duke of Edinburgh, and the Shah of Iran until he realized that he was the victim of a practical joke, since some journalists at *Globe* had deliberately provided him with false evidence (*Globe*, May 1989).

23. Angelo Rinaldi, *L'Express*, July 1977.

24. Angelo Rinaldi, "Ricaumont: Un chouan chez les curés," *L'Express*, March 14, 1981.

25. *Futur*, created in 1952, was a double monthly sheet that was sold in kiosks and that defined itself as a journal of information "for sexual equality and freedom." Charges were brought against *Futur*, and it folded in 1955. Its last issue displayed a young adolescent in a full-page photo: a last act of insolence, and an epitaph for the real battle of *Futur*.

26. A sign of the times: during the same period, American homosexual organizations, such as the Mattachine Society and the Daughters of Bilitis, were just as "respectable" as *Arcadie*.

27. Roger Stéphane, interview in *Lire*, Nov. 1992.

28. André Baudry, *Arcadie* 273.

29. Michel Foucault, *Libération*, July 12, 1983.

30. Angelo Rinaldi, *L'Express*, Aug. 12, 1974.

31. On May 29, 1955, for example, "Arcadians" performed excerpts from Oscar Wilde's trial. [*danses du tapis:* See Prologue, n. 2.—Trans.]

32. Feminists from the MLF were present at that meeting.

33. Angelo Rinaldi, *L'Express*, Apr. 16, 1973.

34. André Gide, quoted by Rinaldi, *L'Express*, Apr. 16, 1973, and Oct. 15, 1992.

35. Nearly 500 people attended the 1972 banquet. André Baudry defended his strategy, forging a path between reformism and revolution (the latter was the FHAR's choice). See Bruno Frappat, "Le droit d'être soi-même," *Le Monde*, Nov. 14, 1972. Shortly before his death, Pier Paolo Pasolini agreed to be guest of honor at an Arcadie banquet.

36. Genesis 19:1–29; Leviticus 18:22 and 20:13, King James Version. Nevertheless, it is possible to give a positive interpretation to this episode of the Bible, which tells the story of David and Jonathan (the son of King Saul).

37. Jacques Rivette's film *La religieuse*, twice banned (in 1965 and 1966), depicts a woman's homosexual relationship in a convent.

38. Jacques Laval has published his autobiography, titled *Un homme partagé* (Julliard, 1978), as well as *Mémoires parallèles* (Editions C. de Bartillat, 1994).

39. The sociological makeup of Arcadie is relatively well known (far better known than that of the FHAR), thanks to the 1974 survey by Michel Bon and Antoine d'Arc (*Rapport sur*

l'homosexualité de l'homme). Life in couples predominates, with the formation of quasi-familial structures, sexual practices similar in frequency to those of heterosexuals, and a wide age gap within couples. See the critical analysis by Michael Pollak, "Les vertus de la banalité."

40. Despite its clandestine nature (often criticized), this lobbying function ought not to be underestimated. The organization's principal merit may even be its having inaugurated a reformist, antidiscriminatory homosexual militancy in France, adopted in 1980 by the Comité d'Urgence Anti-Répression Homosexuelle (CUARH).

41. Letter from François Mitterrand to André Baudry, May 13, 1974 (unpublished document that André Baudry shared with me). On Mitterrand's position with respect to homosexuality, see chap. 7.

42. On the relationship between Michel Foucault and Arcadie, see chap. 6. In November 1980, the guest of honor at the Journées Nationales d'Arcadie was Robert Badinter, and his lecture received a great deal of media attention.

43. See *Le Monde*, July 2, 1982, and *Libération*, July 12, 1982. In this chapter, any of Baudry's remarks for which there are no corresponding notes come from two interviews that I conducted at his home in 1995.

44. Some former members of Arcadie attempted to create a new, short-lived organization, Présence.

CHAPTER 4: DRIFTING

1. *La dérive homosexuelle* [Homosexual drifting] is the title of an essential book by Guy Hocquenghem, dating from 1977. Dominique Fernandez confirms the use of this term in *Le rapt de Ganymède*, and in 1968 Marguerite Yourcenar used it to describe Zénon in *L'oeuvre au noir*.

2. Guy Hocquenghem, *Recherches*, March 1973.

3. Guy Hocquenghem, *La dérive homosexuelle*.

4. On the dichotomy, before 1968, between day and night, age and social background, I borrow certain elements proposed for reflection by Bernard Minoret and Daniel Defert.

5. Dognon describes the nightlife of Chez Graff at length in *Les amours buissonières*.

6. In slang, a *jésus* is a pretty, effeminate boy. In his novel *Jésus la Caille* (1914), Francis Carco uses the slang of homosexuals and male prostitutes from the early twentieth century (as Genet would later do in *Notre-Dame-des-Fleurs*). A linguistic dissymmetry went hand in hand with the social dissymmetry.

7. On prewar homosexual Paris, see Willy, *Le troisième sexe* (Paris Edition, 1927); and Gilles Barbedette and Michell Carassou, *Paris gay 1925* (Presses de la Renaissance, 1985).

8. The clientele at Le Boeuf is more conventional today.

9. L'Escale was later the name of a postwar lesbian cabaret that Suzy Solidor opened in Cagnes-sur-Mer.

10. On the Left Bank, Le Sélect, in Montparnasse, was an ambiguous spot before the war.

11. This affair of December 1968 involved rumors about the private life of Georges Pompidou and his wife.

12. According to Commissioner Ottavioli, who was head of the vice squad at that time (comments made during the "Campus" broadcast on Europe 1, March 18, 1970).

13. On Madame Madeleine, see Marcel Jouhandeau, *Journaliers* (vols. 23–28), and Angelo Rinaldi, *L'Express*, June 3, 1988.

14. The first "modern" public toilets, it seems, date from 1830, though they also existed in antiquity (the public latrines in Rome) and under the ancien régime (the public conveniences on the Feuillants terraces in the Tuileries, during the reign of Louis XVI). In 1843 there were 468 public toilets in Paris; in the 1950s, 1,300.

15. For a long time, Charlus visited the public toilet on Place de la Madeleine, which Proust could see from his window. Some commentators have drawn the conclusion, not without some exaggeration, that the public toilet played a key role in Proust's imagination. See, for example, Philippe Boyer, *Le petit pan de mur jaune* (Editions du Seuil, 1987).

16. Philippe Guy "Les Arabes et nous," in the "Trois milliards de pervers" issue of *Recherches*. On the complex problematic of latent homosexuality in the Maghreb, see Malek Chebel, *L'esprit du sérail* (Lieu Commun, 1988). It is possible to make the comparison with homosexuality in classical Greece, where individuals were not homosexuals in the strict sense. See Kenneth Dover, *Greek Homosexuality*.

17. Michael Pollak, "Les vertus de la banalité."

18. One text ("Paris est une fête") in the "Trois milliards de pervers" issue of *Recherches* is devoted to cruising in the Tuileries.

19. Paris had seven sex shops in March 1970 but thirty-four in September of the same year—a significant increase.

20. See Pierre Hahn, *Partisans*, 66–67.

21. See Michael Pollak, *Les homosexuels et le sida*.

22. TTT was the inspiration for Rocky, the perfect man in solid gold underpants in the *Rocky Horror Picture Show* (1975). Zaza Napoli was the battered transvestite (played by Michel Serrault) in *La Cage aux Folles*. Lady X held court at the Bois de Boulogne.

23. An ordinance of February 1, 1949, prohibited men from dancing with one another. In 1960, Arcadie suspended its dances for a time.

24. Michel Guy was minister of cultural affairs from June 1974 to September 1976.

25. In a historical irony, when rue Sainte-Anne stopped being homosexual, in the early 1980s, the hotel lost most of its clientele and went bankrupt.

26. Yves Navarre, "Une place entre l'ombre et le soleil," *Dossier de presse* (archival GLH document, 1977, courtesy of Albert Rosse).

27. On these criticisms of the "commercial ghetto," see issue 12 of *Tout!*; the various issues of *Fléau Social*, one of the FHAR journals created by Alain Fleig; and Fleig's *Lutte de con et piège de classe* (Stock, 1977).

28. On November 26, 1970, on live television, the Japanese homosexual writer Mishima Yukio disemboweled himself in accordance with the hara-kiri ritual; one of his lovers then cut off Mishima's head with a saber. On Pasolini, see the fictionalized autobiography by Dominique Fernandez, *Dans la main de l'ange*.

29. Even though he was fired for indecency when he was a teacher, Pasolini displayed reservations about sexual liberation, and he fought against abortion.

30. Guy Hocquenghem, "Tout le monde ne peut pas mourir dans son lit," *Libération*, March 29, 1976.

31. Guy Hocquenghem, *L'après-midi des faunes*. See also Jean-Paul Sartre's important article on Pasolini's murder, "Cette affaire italienne a une portée internationale," *Il Corriere della Sera*, March 6, 1982 (reprinted in *Gai Pied*, Apr. 1982).

32. Anne Tristan (Zelensky), *Histoires d'amour*.

33. Groupes de Libération Homosexualle, "Le sexe et l'ordre," *Libération*, Apr. 20, 1976.

CHAPTER 5: THE MILITANT EXPLOSION

1. Simone Veil, cited in Laure Adler, *Les femmes politiques* (Editions du Seuil, 1993).

2. In the United States, the debate was not decided at the political level, as it was in France, but rather by the courts: the famous Roe *v.* Wade decision handed down by the Supreme Court in 1973 recognized a woman's right to abortion as an aspect of her right to privacy.

3. Jean-Paul Aron, *Les modernes.*

4. Luce Irigaray, "Des marchandises entre elles," *La Quinzaine Littéraire*, Aug. 1975; and *Ce sexe qui n'en est pas un.*

5. Hélène Cixous, "Sorties," *La jeune née* (1975).

6. Anne Tristan (Zelensky), *Histoires d'amour.*

7. Anne Tristan and Annie de Pisan, *Histoires du MLF.*

8. *Les pétroleuses*, Sept. 1975; *Libération*, Oct. 16, 1975.

9. Rape was considered a crime, but the charge was usually reduced to "public indecency" or "assault and battery" and then judged by a court dealing with lesser offenses (the *tribunal correctionnel* rather than the *cour d'assises*).

10. In the interest of "the revolution," Louison had been reluctant to file a complaint. See Anne Tristan (Zelensky) and Annie de Pisan, *Histoires du MLF.*

11. For lesbians' radicalism on the question of rape, see Françoise Picq, *Libération des femmes, les années mouvement.*

12. Take Back the Night demonstration of March 4, 1978; demonstrations by prostitutes in Lyons, June 2, 1975.

13. The slogan "Every man is a potential rapist" did not find unanimous support and was finally withdrawn from the Manifesto Against Rape project on June 26, 1976. The idea, however, has remained.

14. Alice Braitberg, *Le Monde*, Nov. 30, 1978.

15. Susan Brownmiller, *Against Our Will* (Simon & Schuster, 1975); Ti-Grace Atkinson, *Amazon Odyssey* (Links, 1974).

16. This slogan, which appeared for the first time on May Day 1976, is said to have been invented by a heterosexual member of the Gouines Rouges.

17. For a detailed history of the center, see Centre Lyonnais d'Etudes Féministes, *CLEF: Chroniques d'une passion.*

18. This was the first specifically lesbian journal in France (six issues were published between April 1978 and June 1980, with approximately 1,500 copies printed).

19. A Groupe de Libération Homosexuelle had appeared in Lyons in 1975.

20. Françoise Picq, *Libération des femmes.*

21. On rape and sexual harassment, see Françoise Picq, *Liberation des femmes*; Janine Mossuz-Lavau, *Les lois de l'amour.*

22. Before that, on Nov. 29, 1973, an Antenne 1 "medical" broadcast (with Yves Navarre and André Baudry) had been devoted to homosexuality, but its audience had been less than one-quarter the size of the later broadcast's.

23. [The slang term *pédaler* refers to homosexual activity.—Trans.]

24. [The term *flûte* is slang for "penis."—Trans.]

25. During a planning meeting for the launch of *Libération*, Michel Foucault expressed the wish that this daily newspaper give homosexuals a forum; see Claude Mauriac, *Et comme l'espérance est violente* (Grasset, 1976).

26. Jean-Luc Hennig published several books, among them *Les garçons de passe*, en-

quête sur la prostitution masculine (Hallier, 1978); the book was dedicated to "Pasolini and his murderer."

27. On December 18, 1973, the newly created *Libération* published its first homosexual personal ad.

28. Serge Daney, *Persévérance* (POL, 1994).

29. One of his drawings was judged racist: "1960: Uncle Sam exhibits his breasts. In the year 2000, I'll get buggered by a black man" (front page of *Libération*, Aug. 8, 1979).

30. The dialogue (collaborative and uncollaborative) between the GLH–Lyons and the Centre des Femmes de Lyons is very revealing.

31. Until the early 1980s, many militants associated with the far left denounced the "commercial ghetto" (business establishments), preferring the "wild ghetto" (public toilets and the like).

32. On the lives of militants, see Michael Pollak, *Les homosexuels et le sida*.

33. In Paris, the GLH, which met at the Jussieu secondary school in 1975, was ousted after a split into three camps (GLH–PQ, GLH–GB, and GLH–14 Décembre). The main one, the GLH–PQ, associated with the far left, bore the label "Politique et Quotidien" [Political and personal] and existed until 1978.

34. In the late nineteenth century, the French writer Jean Lorrain was the model for the "queen" and for decadence, situating himself between dandyism and "campiness." See especially his *Histoire des masques* (Ollendorf, 1900).

35. This camp, accused of being "bourgeois" and sometimes nicknamed "Arcadie on the left," was represented in Paris by the GLH–Groupe de Base. In 1980, it was reincarnated as the Comité d'Urgence Anti-Répression Homosexuelle [CUARH]. Finally, the GLH–14 Décembre camp rejected far-left militancy, opposed feminism, and "was reminiscent of a libertarian teahouse."

36. See Jean Le Bitoux's own observation, "De la misère relationnelle en milieu militante," *Libération*, May 6, 1978.

37. To support these candidacies, the militants created the short-lived Comités Homosexuels d'Arrondissements [Homosexual arrondissement committees], or CHA, which, about 1979, replaced the GLH–PQ of Paris. The only candidacies to be validated, those of Jean Le Bitoux and Alain Secouet, received a total of seventy-five votes.

38. The debate on female homosexuality, organized by the militant women of the MLF's Psychépo camp, had protection from its own security officers.

39. In January 1978, the GLH was less successful with "La quinzaine du film homo" [A fortnight of homo film] at La Pagode. Some of the films were confiscated, and a few of the militants were assaulted by a far-right commando.

40. The Parisian film club, which became an all-woman festival in 1989, was created to combat "lesbian invisibility" at the Sceaux festival. In particular, lesbian pornographic films are shown. The festival has several thousand entries every year.

41. Serge Daney, *Persévérance*.

42. Films such as *Jeunes filles en uniforme*, by Léontine Sagan (1931), *La garçonne*, by Jean de Limur (1935), and *Mademoiselle de la Ferté*, by Roger Dallier (1949), played a role.

43. The play had 1,300 performances in the 1970s; the film version of *La Cage aux Folles* had 800,000 viewers between 1978 and 1980.

44. See "Gaycott aux USA" by Alain Finkielkraut, *Libération*, June 6, 1977.

45. Arrested in 1973 and sentenced to six years in prison for homosexuality, Sergei Paradjanov (*Fire Horses*, 1965; *Sayat Nova* [*Color of Grenades*], 1969) was freed in 1977 and then rearrested in 1982.

46. Reinaldo Arenas, *Avant la nuit*. On the initial illusions and subsequent disenchantment, see the fundamental book by François Furet, *Le passé d'une illusion* (Laffont/Lévy, 1995).

47. Simone de Beauvoir, *Journal de guerre* and *Lettres à Sartre*; Julia Kristeva, *Des Chinoises* (Editions des Femmes, 1974); Gisèle Halimi, *Choisir* (1975).

48. In the enigmatic words of Jean Le Bitoux, a GLH–PQ militant, in *Gai Pied*, Sept. 1982.

49. At the Centre du Christ Libérateur [Center of Christ the Liberator], founded by Pastor Joseph Doucé in October 1976, pedophiles were welcome, and "blessings on homosexual friendships" were celebrated every Saturday. The first such blessing took place on December 15, 1979.

50. According to *Douze ans de femmes au quotidien* (La Griffonne, 1981).

51. Guy Hocquenghem, "V.I.O.L.," *Libération*, March 29, 1977. He also mentions "delicious, insidious rape" (*Libération*, Aug. 11, 1979). On Hocquenghem and Pier Paolo Pasolini, see chap. 4.

52. Guy Hocquenghem, *La dérive homosexuelle*.

53. *Agence Tasse*, editorial, Apr. 20, 1977.

54. See, in particular, the surprising text "Enfermement, psychiatrie, prison," in *Change*, Oct. 1977 (*Dits et écrits*, p. 209), and "La loi de la pudeur," in *Dialogues*, coauthored with Guy Hocquenghem (*France Culture*, Apr. 4, 1978). (The original of this interview is different from the version published in *Dits et écrits*, p. 263.) On rape, Monique Plaza made an apt but scathing reply to Foucault, itself based on Foucauldian principles ("Nos dommages et leurs intérêts," *Questions Féministes*, May 1978).

55. Michel Foucault, interview with James O'Higgins, 1982; *Gai Pied Hebdo*, Jan. 5, 1985 (*Dits et écrits*, p. 317).

56. Cathy Bernheim, "Maman n'a plus de nom ... et d'ailleurs, elle n'est plus ici," *Libération*, Apr. 22, 1977.

57. The GLF, in existence between 1976 and 1977, met on rue Sauffroy. It claimed to be revolutionary and published a bulletin. The Groupe de Lesbiennes de Paris, associated with the LCR's neighborhood women's groups, was in existence from November 1977 to June 1980.

58. In *Usé par la mer*, Bory depicts the relationship between Félicien and Georgette, a tattooed military woman. In *Un Noël à la tyrolienne*, he reached a milestone, describing the love between Aloys and Pierre. In *La peau des zèbres*, we again meet Félicien, now a homosexual, and Aloys, who has become François-Charles.

59. Jean-Louis Bory, in *Comment nous appelez-vous déjà?*

60. Jean-Louis Bory, in *Masques*, Summer 1981.

61. This famous passage from *Ma moitié d'orange* is also quoted in Bory's *Comment nous appelez-vous déjà?*

62. Jean-Louis Bory, *Comment nous appelez-vous déjà?*

63. In 1973, Bory again participated in an Arcadie colloquium.

64. On *Le masque et la plume*, the critics Matthieu Galey and Jacques Siclier also made constant allusions to the issue of homosexuality.

65. "Jean-Louis est revenu," *L'Express*, Feb. 14, 1991.

66. Jean-Louis Bory, interview with Jérôme Hesse conducted in April 1978 and published posthumously (in three parts) in *Gai Pied*, Jan.–March 1982.

67. Angelo Rinaldi, *L'Express*, Feb. 14, 1991.

68. Jean-Louis Bory, interview with Jérôme Hesse, *Gai Pied*, Jan.–March 1982.

69. Oscar Wilde, *De Profundis.*

70. A 1974 German study on suicide among homosexuals indicates that 13 percent of homosexuals have attempted suicide (twice the presumed rate for the population at large). Nearly all these attempts take place when the individuals are between sixteen and eighteen years old; the phenomenon disappears almost entirely after the age of twenty-one. After that age, the suicide rate for homosexuals is lower than for the rest of the population. See M. Pollak, "Les vertus de la banalité." Michel Foucault ("Un plaisir si simple," *Gai Pied,* Apr. 1979) has expressed reservations about this sort of generalization: "Because they cannot marry the right sex, [homosexuals] marry death. ... In this ridiculous game, homosexuals and suicide give each other a bad name."

71. On Jean-Louis Bory, see the biography by Daniel Garcia (Flammarion, 1991) and perhaps the one by Marie-Claude Jardin (Belfond, 1991).

CHAPTER 6: "WE MUST BE RELENTLESSLY GAY"

1. [French for "for kicks" is *pour le pied,* and *guêpier,* "wasp's nest," is a homonym of *gai pied.*—Trans.]

2. Jean-Paul Sartre, "Cette profondeur que n'ont pas les hétérosexuels," *Gai Pied,* Apr. 1980. Thirty years after writing *Saint Genet, comédien et martyr,* Sartre again showed a certain analytical weakness on the issue of homosexuality.

3. Hugo Marsan published about a dozen novels and stories, including *Un homme, un homme* (Autrement, 1983) and *Le balcon d'Angelo* (Verdier, 1992). The head of GLH–Rennes, Gilles Barbedette was the author of several essays and novels, including two autobiographical works: *Une saison en enfance* (1991) and the posthumously published *Mémoires d'un jeune homme devenu vieux* (Gallimard, 1993). René de Ceccatty published nearly a dozen books, including *Violette Leduc, éloge de la Bâtarde* (Stock, 1994) and *L'accompagnement* (Gallimard, 1994). All three men contributed to the literary supplement to *Le Monde.*

4. David Macey, one of Foucault's biographers, takes credit for this legend; see *The Lives of Michel Foucault: A Biography* (New York: Pantheon Books, 1993). It also figures as a question in *Lovetrivia,* an erotic version of *Trivial Pursuit.*

5. Foucault used the English word "gay," which, especially after the creation of *Gai Pied,* became Gallicized into *gai.* The term, which became widespread in the United States between about 1965 and 1970, had an earlier, dual Franco–Anglo-Saxon paternity. On the one hand, it was borrowed from English prison slang; on the other, the word's origin is Latin (*vagus,* in the sense of "wandering," "mobile," and "of free morals") and French: in the Middle Ages, actors were "gay," and in the nineteenth century, women of ill repute, or who liked prohibited pleasures, were so designated.

6. Michel Foucault, interview with James O'Higgins (*Dits et écrits,* p. 317).

7. Michel Foucault, interview published in the review *Masques,* spring 1982 (*Dits et écrits,* p. 311).

8. See Didier Eribon, *Michel Foucault et ses contemporains.* This biography and David Macey's *The Lives of Michel Foucault* were used as sources in preparing this book.

9. Michel Foucault mentions the issue of homosexuality in about thirty interviews or articles. About a dozen of them, dating from 1980 or later, concern this issue exclusively, including two for *Gai Pied,* one for *Masques,* and one for *The Advocate* (see *Dits et écrits*). A meticulous analysis of these texts has been done by David Halperin in *Saint Foucault: Two Essays in Gay Hagiography* (Oxford University Press, 1995).

10. Nevertheless, Foucault took up the defense of issue 12 of *Tout!* and supported the "Trois milliards de pervers" issue of *Recherches*. Later, he arranged for the French translation of works by John Boswell, and especially by K. J. Dover, on the issue of homosexuality.

11. Originally, Jean Le Bitoux, who had conducted an interview with Foucault in July 1978 ("Le gai savoir"), wanted to publish it in the first issue of *Gai Pied*. When Foucault declined, one of Foucault's friends, Thierry Voeltzel, a contributor to the paper, was called on to approach him. Foucault gave in by offering not an interview but an ambiguous article ("Un plaisir si simple"). Jean Le Bitoux, furious with Foucault, whom he accused of being a "closet queen," published the interview in the Netherlands and then in France, in the short-lived *Mec Magazine*, but in a broadly modified version that was rewritten without Foucault's agreement, and this explains its absence from the collection *Dits et écrits*.

12. Michel Foucault, interview published in issue 25 of *Gai Pied*, Apr. 1981 (*Dits et écrits*, p. 293).

13. Michel Foucault, interview with James O'Higgins (*Dits et écrits*, p. 317).

14. Foucault was the only one in the history of Arcadie to turn down the 2,000-franc fee that André Baudry offered him for a speech. "A gay man does not need to be paid to express himself in front of other gays," he explained simply.

15. Foucault knew Baudry personally (they dined together several times) and sometimes referred friends in trouble (those who were looking for work, tormented by religion, or lonely) to Baudry.

16. "Le départ du prophète," *Libération*, July 12, 1984. The article was signed "D.E.," but one of his biographers has revealed that the author was Foucault. See Didier Eribon, *Michel Foucault et ses contemporains*.

17. On the contradictions in Foucault's conduct in France and North America and the debates they continue to inspire, see Didier Eribon, *Michel Foucault et ses contemporains*, and James Miller's very controversial *The Passion of Michel Foucault* (Simon & Schuster, 1993).

18. Josyane Savigneau, *Marguerite Yourcenar, l'invention d'une vie*.

19. Yourcenar did subscribe to *Arcadie*, however, and even wrote to Marcel Jouhandeau in 1964 to criticize his severity regarding the homophile platform. See her letters to Marc Daniel, in *Lettres à ses amis et à quelques-uns* (Gallimard, 1995); see also, in the same book, the letter to Simon Sautier expressing her ideas on homosexuality.

20. *Le Devoir*, Nov. 21, 1981; Françoise Routhier, "Les Chéri(e)s, la dépendance amoureuse," *Les Cahiers du Grif*, Fall 1985.

21. See Evelyne Le Garrec, *Un lit à soi* and *Des femmes qui s'aiment*. See also "Les communautés contre la famille," *Actuel*, Oct. 1970, and the issue "Femmes entre elles: Lesbianisme," *Les Cahiers du Grif*, Apr. 1978.

22. The Veil law (promulgated in January 1980) was finally ratified after a national demonstration that was attended by more than 40,000 on Oct. 6, 1979.

23. Françoise Picq, *Libération des femmes*.

24. François Mitterrand, quoted by Laure Adler, *Les femmes politiques* (Editions du Seuil, 1993).

25. Françoise Picq, *Libération des femmes*.

26. Barbara, the strike leader for prostitutes in Lyons and an employee at Editions des Femmes, had been fired in 1976. The Féministes Révolutionnaires supported her against the Psychépo group.

27. Simone de Beauvoir herself wrote the preface to a collective work titled *Chroniques*

d'une imposture: Du mouvement de libération des femmes à une marque commerciale (Archives of the MLF, 1981).

28. See Françoise Picq, *Liberation des femmes*. See also *Questions Féministes*, issues 7 and 8, Feb. 1980 and May 1980, as well as *Nouvelles Questions Féministes*, issue 1, March 1981.

29. The words being quoted are Catherine Deudon's in "Radicale-ment, nature-elle-ment," *La Revue d'en face*, issue 9–10.

30. Other, subjective elements, such as cases of emotional estrangement that became entangled with power plays, probably also came into play. As in the men's movements, several splits within the MLF began as breakups of romantic relationships.

31. Christiane Jouve, "Dis maman, c'est quoi une lesbienne?" *Le Matin de Paris*, Sept. 26, 1985.

32. Poster at the Rencontre Lesbienne of June 21–22, 1980, organized by the so-called Jussieu Group.

33. Monique Wittig, "On ne naît pas femme," *Questions Féministes*, issue 8, May 1980.

34. Testimony of Simone de Beauvoir, *Minutes du procès*, judgment of the *tribunal de grande instance* of Paris, Dec. 8, 1981.

35. The *tribunal de grande instance* of Paris ruled that the adjective *nouvelles* modified the title sufficiently to avoid confusion, especially since readers of the journals were well informed about the quarrel that had led to the dissolution of *Questions Féministes*.

36. The idea for the Front des Lesbiennes Radicales came during a tumultuous meeting of feminists on March 8, 1981, at the Salle Wagram, and the FLR was established in April. The first meetings took place in June 1981 at the Jussieu secondary school.

37. Pamphlets of June 21–22, 1980 (reproduced in *Nouvelles Questions Féministes*, issue 1).

38. The source of this phrase is the so-called mauve letter from "radical feminist lesbians of the ex-collective Questions Féministes," March 1981.

CHAPTER 7: "SEVEN YEARS OF HAPPINESS"?

1. Political scientists argue that in certain cases, when a population that has been discriminated against, or whose rights have been minimized, identifies itself in a conscious and positive manner, the result may be new political behavior, the "revenge of a community." This behavior neutralizes the effects of social class or of the usual voting habits. Therefore, it is not a positive vote but a negative one (a protest vote).

2. In addition to Josyane Savigneau and Gisèle Halimi, Christine Ockrent questioned Mitterrand on politics, as Hélène Mathieu did on daycare centers and Ménie Grégoire did on incest.

3. François Mitterrand was alluding not to the homosexual age of majority but to the old ordinance concerning public indecency, even though it had been abrogated by Parliament in December 1980.

4. Choisir, *Quel président pour les femmes?* Replies of François Mitterrand, with a preface by Gisèle Halimi (Gallimard, 1981).

5. Jean-Paul Aron, philosopher and writer, and the author, notably, of *Le pénis et la démoralisation de l'Occident* (with Roger Kempf) and *Les modernes*. He was a member of the Socialist Party committee in Neuilly in 1981 and became a technical adviser in Jack Lang's cabinet.

6. *Gai Pied*, June 1980, Jan. 1981.

7. Yves Navarre, interviewed by Albert Rosse, 1983.

8. Pierre Bérégovoy had already sent an official letter to the major homosexual organizations on March 19, 1981, and to Arcadie on April 2.

9. This interview, by Gilles Barbedette and Jacky Fougeray, was published in *Gai Pied* in May 1981. The interview had already appeared in *Le Matin de Paris* on April 4, 1981, the day of the homosexual march. Although Mitterrand declined to add his name to the interview's byline, he apparently did read it over, according to Maurice Bénassayag.

10. Letter from Valéry Giscard d'Estaing to the director of Arcadie, Apr. 13, 1981 (document shared with me by André Baudry).

11. It was also signed by Daniel Mayer, Constantin Costa-Gavras, Régine Deforges, and Marie-France Pisier. Louis Aragon signed it after the first round.

12. Gertrude Stein did not display her homosexuality openly, and although she had been seen at Natalie Barney's salon, she did not belong to lesbian circles. Her book of poems *Lifting Belly: A Sonatina Followed by Another* and her book *QED* are fairly explicit, however.

13. Recollection by François Mitterrand, quoted in *Le Monde*, Sept. 9, 1994.

14. This love affair is depicted in Virginia Woolf's *Orlando* (Violet is Sasha; Vita, Orlando) and in Trefusis's *Broderie anglaise* (Virginia is Alexa).

15. Cécile Wajsbrot, *Violet Trefusis* (Mercure de France, 1989); Violet Trefusis, *Instants de mémoire* (Bartillat, 1992).

16. *Journal Officiel*, National Assembly, second session of Dec. 3, 1954. It is significant that after this reply from François Mitterrand, Deputy Raymond Dronne sharply attacked him for "sporting by turns the fleur-de-lis and the *francisque d'honneur*." [The *francisque d'honneur* was an award conferred during the Vichy regime.—Trans.]

17. Other personalities also signed the petition: Louis Aragon, Huguette Bouchardeau, Edmonde Charles-Roux, Dalida, Marguerite Duras, Tony Duvert, Jocelyne François, Mathieu Galey, Benoîte Groult, Daniel Guérin, Amanda Lear, Gabriel Matzneff, Michel Piccoli, and François Truffaut.

18. In Marseilles, every other year between 1979 and 1985, the "homosexual summer school" attracted militants from homosexual organizations of every stripe.

19. The CUARH and the MLF-*déposé* jointly organized, with some difficulty, the 1981 "homosexual summer school"; see "Mixité ou mixture," *Gai Pied*, Sept. 1981. Luce Irigaray, notably, participated in a debate on July 27. [The acronym MIEL means "honey" (the foodstuff).—Trans.]

20. *Homophonies* was published between November 1980 and May/June 1985. (Gérard Maison and Vincent Legret were the editors, and Hervé Liffran served on the administrative staff.)

21. A key figure in the Syndicat National de la Magistrature [National union of the magistracy], Joinet played a critical role in eliminating discriminatory laws aimed at homosexuals. He served as adviser on human rights to all the Socialist prime ministers between 1981 and 1993 before serving the same function for the president of the republic (March 1993–May 1995).

22. When the Organisation Communiste des Travailleurs [Communist organization of workers], or OCT—Leninists, but usually not Trotskyists—merged with the LCR in 1980, some OCT members who were also in the CUARH (Hervé Liffran, for example) agreed to join the LCR, whereas others (Gérard Bach, for example) refused. Jean Nicolas left the leadership of the LCR for the Comités Communistes pour l'Autogestion [Communist committees for self-management], to which Gilles Casanova already belonged.

23. Using one "confidential" pseudonym in the political movement and, usually, an-

other in the homosexual movement, the militants mentioned here generally had three names each—a situation that does not facilitate clarity.

24. The LCR, especially its "class struggle" camp, exerted a strong influence on the MLF. Révolution, a splinter group of the LCR, was also sensitive to the problems of women; a "homosexuality committee" was created in 1974.

25. It was Albert Rosse, a staff administrator for the PSU, who led these actions. A salaried employee of *Gai Pied* in 1981, he became a technical adviser in the office of Huguette Bouchardeau, minister of the environment, and then, from 1985 to 1986, a technical adviser in Jack Lang's office. See Albert Rosse, "Vers un vote rose?" in *Tribune Socialiste*, March 1981.

26. Jean Ristat, *Le Matin de Paris*, Oct. 18, 1978. Michel Boué, formerly of the FHAR, organized, with Pierre Bergé, an Yves Saint-Laurent fashion show at the *L'Humanité* celebration. Emmanuel Guallino, an ex-militant from GLH–Marseilles, covered cultural events for *La Marseillaise*.

27. Suzette Triton, "Le PCF déclare," *Rouge*, Apr. 27, 1977; Jean-Luc Hennig, "Le PC, la morale et l'homosexualité," *Libération*, Apr. 1977; Pierre Joquin, *France Nouvelle*, July 4, 1977.

28. Philippe Boucher defended Croissant in "Le petit défaut," *Le Monde*, June 26, 1980.

29. *Liberté, libertés: Réflexions du comité pour une charte des libertés*, edited by Robert Badinter, with a preface by François Mitterrand (Gallimard, 1976).

30. For example, in a letter to André Baudry (Feb. 13, 1978), and in a lecture by Robert Badinter that received wide media coverage at Arcadie's national celebration, in November 1980.

31. Conversely, in Lille, before 1981, Pierre Mauroy attempted to oppose the activities of a homosexual organization.

32. Edmonde Charles-Roux, interview with the author published as "Le bon plaisir de Dominique Fernandez" in *France Culture*, March 11, 1995.

33. Memorandum of June 12, 1981 (*Le Monde*, June 14, 1981; *Gai Pied*, July 1981). The minister, having observed that the memorandum was still not being adequately implemented, sent another on December 21, 1981.

34. Michel Foucault, interview in *Gai Pied*, Oct. 1982 (*Dits et écrits*, p. 318).

35. Their offenses involved public indecency, indecent acts, or crimes against nature, under article 330–2. In December 1981 those charged under article 331–2 were pardoned.

36. Henri Caillavet—a former minister, a member of the National Assembly, and, later, a Radical senator—played an important role after the war, supporting women's right to vote and, later, issues related to sexual mores (abortion, homosexuality, bioethics, and the civil union contract).

37. Since paragraph 2 had been abrogated, paragraph 3 now became paragraph 2 of article 331. Notable among the deputies who voted to keep the paragraph were François d'Aubert, Jacques Chirac, Jean-Claude Gaudin, Gérard Longuet, Alain Madelin, Jacques Médecin, Charles Millon, Philippe Séguin, and Jean Tibéri.

38. *Journal Officiel* 49, National Assembly, June 25, 1980.

39. It was signed by Louis Aragon, Jean-Paul Aron, Robert Badinter, Simone de Beauvoir, Huguette Bouchardeau, Benoîte Groult, Jean-Denis Bredin, Patrick Chéreau, Gilles Deleuze, Dalida, Conrad Detrez, Fabrice Emaer, Alain Krivine, Françoise Gaspard, Gisèle Halimi, Yves Montand, Simone Signoret, and François Truffaut, as well as by the LCR and the PSU.

40. Decision no. 80–125 DC of Dec. 19, 1980.

41. Report 602, National Assembly. See also Gisèle Halimi, *Une embellie perdue* (Gallimard, 1995).

42. *Journal Officiel*, Assemblée Nationale, Dec. 21, 1981.

43. Jean Foyer also used a more pernicious argument: the punitive fine–based revenue (between 60,000 and 20,000 francs, according to the case) that would be lost to the state if it were to abrogate the article. Gisèle Halimi replied, "That's not law, that's comedy" (*Journal Officiel*, National Assembly, July 28, 1982).

44. *Libération*, Dec. 22, 1981. Taking his ideas to their logical extreme, Jean Foyer proposed, as a last resort, making the legal age of sexual relations the same for homosexuals and heterosexuals, but raising it to eighteen.

45. This abrogation was also part of a movement within Europe. On October 1, 1981, the parliamentary assembly of the European Council showed itself very liberal on issues related to homosexuality as a whole (recommendation 924; see also resolution 756). Inspired by these standards, the European Parliament, for its part, adopted a resolution on specific types of discrimination in the workplace (March 13, 1984).

46. The legislative bill became Law 83–683 on August 4, 1982 (*Journal Officiel*, Aug. 5, 1982). Since that time, a 1991 bill in the Senate that attempted, during debate on reform of the penal code, to reinstate the old paragraph 331–2 was rejected by the National Assembly, but it is still possible that a future majority will rescind the decriminalization.

CHAPTER 8: SWAN SONG

1. Françoise Renaud, cited by Evelyne Le Garrec, *Des femmes qui s'aiment*.

2. Annie Le Brun, well known for her work on the Marquis de Sade, published two pamphlets against the French feminists, *Lâchez tout* and *Vagit-prop*, both later published in book form (see the bibliography).

3. Yvette Roudy, *A cause d'elles* (Albin Michel, 1985; preface by Simone de Beauvoir).

4. A bill sponsored by Jean-Pierre Michel nevertheless became law on July 25, 1985; it extended the antiracist laws to women and to the issues of sexual mores. Finally, the law of January 17, 1986, protected homosexual employees by modifying workplace legislation.

5. On these issues, see Janine Mossuz-Lavau, *Les lois de l'amour*.

6. Michel Foucault, interviewed by James O'Higgins in *Gai Pied Hebdo*, Jan. 5, 1985 (*Dits et écrits*, p. 317).

7. This text was signed, notably, by Louis Aragon, Roland Barthes, Simone de Beauvoir, Jean-Louis Bory, Patrice Chéreau, Michel Cressole, Gilles Deleuze, Bernard Dort, Françoise d'Eaubonne, André Glucksmann, Félix Guattari, Daniel Guérin, Pierre Guyotat, Pierre Hahn, Jean-Luc Hennig, Christian Hennion, Guy Hocquenghem, Bernard Kouchner, Jack Lang, Georges Lapassade, Gabriel Matzneff, Gilles Sandier, Christiane Rochefort, Jean-Paul Sartre, and René Schérer. See *Le Monde*, Jan. 26, 1977.

8. Jean-Luc Pinard-Legry and Benoît Lapouge, *L'enfance et le pédéraste* (Editions du Seuil, 1980); Leila Sebbar, *Le pédophile et la maman* (Stock, 1980).

9. Tony Duvert, *L'enfant au masculin* (Minuit, 1980). See also *Le bon sexe illustré* (Minuit, 1974).

10. Jean-Marie Le Pen (quoted in *Masques*, Summer 1984) did not hesitate to publicly call Jack Lang an "enculturalisé." [*Enculturalisé* is a portmanteau word combining *enculé*, "buggered," and *culture*, "culture."—Trans.]

11. René Schérer, a known supporter of the pedophiliac cause and an emblematic FHAR figure, is the author, most notably, of *Emile perverti* (Robert Laffont, 1974).

12. The Groupe de Recherche pour une Enfance Différente [Research group for a different childhood], created at the 1979 "homosexual summer school" in Marseilles, was part of the CUARH.

13. Gabriel Matzneff was the author of, in particular, *Moins de 16 ans* (Julliard).

14. "Contre, tout contre la nouvelle droite" (*Libération*, July 5 and 6, 1979). Hocquenghem's apparent proximity to Alain de Benoist's group (the hard right if ever there was one) showed, at the very least, his complexity. Accompanying the article was a drawing by Copi of a dog sodomizing a cat while shouting, "I love the inferior races!"

15. Michel Foucault (who appears under the pseudonym "Professor Couffauld") reportedly came close to a complete break with Hocquenghem because of this affair; see David Macey, *The Lives of Michel Foucault: A Biography* (Pantheon, 1993).

16. Angelo Rinaldo, *L'Express*, May 30, 1986.

17. Jack Lang is alluding to an article by Guy Hocquenghem titled "La jeune censure" (*Libération*, Feb. 16, 1982).

18. Guy Hocquenghem, interviewed by Hugo Marsan in *Gai Pied Hebdo*, Aug. 4, 1984.

19. This fidelity to the values of May '68 allowed Hocquenghem to go head to head, masterfully, with Bernard Tapie on the set of the TV broadcast *Apostrophes* (May 23, 1986), when another former member of the FHAR, Laurent Dispot, sang Tapie's praises. [Bernard Tapie, erstwhile television salesman, '60s pop singer (under the stage name "Tapy"), high-flying businessman, and sometime movie actor, entered politics in 1989 with his election as deputy from Marseilles and in 1996 was convicted of embezzlement and match fixing in connection with his soccer team, Olympique Marseille.—Ed.]

20. Guy Hocquenghem, *Gai Pied Hebdo*, Aug. 4, 1984.

21. The review *Masques* was created in May 1979 by dissidents from the first national homosexual commission of the Ligue Communiste Révolutionnaire [Communist revolutionary league]. *Persona*, created in 1980, was an editorial spinoff of the journal. Finally, *Vlasta* was a journal created by radical lesbians who had left *Masques* in the spring of 1983 (notably because of Tony Duvert's pedophiliac articles).

22. Angelo Rinaldi, *L'Express*, Sept. 9, 1993.

23. Michel Foucault, interviewed by James O'Higgins (*Dits et écrits*, p. 317).

24. Michel Foucault, "De l'amitié comme mode de vie," interview with *Gai Pied*, Apr. 1981 (*Dits et écrits*, p. 293).

25. Michel Foucault, "Sex, Power, and the Politics of Identity," interview in *The Advocate*, Aug. 7, 1984 (*Dits et écrits*, p. 358).

26. Letter from Arthur Rimbaud to Paul Demey, May 15, 1871 (the so-called Letter from the Seer).

27. The minifestival of the MLF was the embryo of what would become a live performance by women.

28. This tendency is particularly visible in the United States, where feminists have wanted to impose words like *chairperson* or *mailperson* (instead of *chairman* and *mailman*), but also *womyn* instead of *woman* and *herstory* instead of *history*. Some feminists have taken to denouncing the culture of "dead white males" by the name of Shakespeare, Freud, and Goethe.

29. Simone de Beauvoir, *Tout compte fait* (Gallimard, 1972).

30. On this point, Mona Ozouf's criticism seems very convincing; see *Les mots des femmes, essai sur la singularité française* (Fayard, 1995).

31. In France, *Du côté des petites filles* (Editions des Femmes, 1974), written by an Italian

woman, Elena Giannini Belotti, and questioning the way girls are brought up, has been quite successful.

32. Jean-Luc Hennig, interview with *Gai Pied*, Sept. 1982.

33. Cathy Bernheim, *L'amour presque parfait*.

34. Organized in 1983, Homosexualité et Socialisme was headed first by Jan-Paul Pouliquen and then by Philippe Ducloux and Stéphane Martinet. Gais pour les Libertés, a splinter group of Homosexualité et Socialisme headed by Henri Maurel and associated with Laurent Fabius (the split occurred in 1984), figured prominently in several debates. Projet Ornicar, itself a splinter group of Gais pour les Libertés, was headed by Thierry Meyssan.

35. Olivier Mongin, *La peur du vide* (Editions du Seuil, 1991); Gilles Lipovetsky, *L'ère du vide* (1983). See also *Globe*, beginning in 1985, or the film *37,2 le matin* [*Betty Blue*].

36. In 1982, as a monthly, *Gai Pied* reached a circulation of 30,000; in 1983–85, as a weekly, its circulation was 22,000. After 1985 the paper lost 1,000 readers every year, ending up with 7,000 in 1992.

37. "Le fric ou le credo," *Globe*, Apr. 1989.

CHAPTER 9: HAPPINESS IN THE GHETTO

1. Michel Foucault, interviewed July 10, 1978, by Jean Le Bitoux (corrected version of the original typescript of "Le Gai savoir" preserved at the Centre Michel-Foucault; see chap. 6, n. 11).

2. Upon publication of *Fragments d'un discours amoureux*, *Libération* (Apr. 8, 1977) ran the rather provocative headline "Barthes, l'amoureuse" [Barthes, woman in love]. The photo by David Hockney that illustrates the article depicts two men.

3. For example, Georges Lapassade's despicable effort in *Le bordel andalou* (Editions de l'Herne, 1971), or, to a certain extent, Dominique de Roux in *Immédiatement* (Christian Bourgois, 1972).

4. Roland Barthes, *La chambre claire*.

5. According to Louis-Jean Calvet, *Roland Barthes* (Flammarion, 1990).

6. They find support especially in his meticulous exegesis (in *S/Z*, 1970) of a novella, *Sarrasine*, by Balzac. *S/Z* sheds light on the theme of sexual ambiguity and castration, as well as on certain passages in Barthes's *Sade, Fourier, Loyola*.

7. Roland Barthes, *Barthes by Barthes*, trans. Richard Howard (New York: Hill and Wang, 1977, pp. 63–64).

8. This is also attested in the map published in the 1970 edition of *L'empire des signes* (Skira), which includes a sketch of homosexual bars in Tokyo.

9. Philippe Sollers, *Femmes* (Gallimard, 1983). Roland Barthes appears under the pseudonym "Werth."

10. *Incidents*, published posthumously in 1984, is a compilation of texts and personal journals by Roland Barthes.

11. See Didier Eribon, *Michel Foucault et ses contemporains*.

12. *Façade*, published between 1979 and 1983, was a sort of underground newspaper for fringe elements and jaded nightowls. It had homosexual overtones and borrowed its style from Andy Warhol's *Interview*.

13. Interviews with Andy Warhol by Alain Pacadis, *Un jeune homme chic* (Le Sagittaire, 1978).

14. Didier Lestrade, music critic for *Gai Pied*, produced a history of disco in which he showed the key role of homosexuals (see "Planète disco, 1976–1991").

15. *Gay Pied* listed about fifty in January 1984, in practically every region.

16. This format was also duplicated in Michel Coquet's broadcast, and then in Pablo Rouy's *Pêche à la ligne* and *Ligne de fiel*. [The name of the broadcast, *Double Face*, was in English.—Trans.]

17. Geneviève Pastre, cited in Evelyne Le Garrec, *Des femmes qui s'aiment*.

18. *Le Monde*, Feb. 27, 1982.

19. Another demonstration was held on January 22, 1983, as was an operation that put "3,000 telegrams on Mitterrand's desk," after Michèle Cotta asked Fréquence Gaie to share its frequency with Radio Libertaire, Radio Verte, and Radio Ark-en-Ciel. Fréquence Gaie finally obtained a band, to be shared solely with Radio Ark-en-Ciel and Pink Radio, a more or less dummy or front station.

20. The Finnish illustrator Tom of Finland, author of the notorious Kakes, began his career in the 1950s in bodybuilding magazines, which were in fact gay magazines in disguise. His drawings, slightly S&M, were immensely popular throughout the world. In 1979, *Gai Pied* used them as iconography. [The phrase "comic-trip" is in English in the original.—Trans.]

21. According to Michael Pollak (*Culture Pub*, "special on gays" broadcast, M6, Apr. 21, 1991). See also Michael Pollak, "Les vertus de la banalité."

22. Michel Foucault, "De l'amitié comme mode de vie," *Gai Pied*, Apr. 1981 (*Dits et écrits*, p. 293).

23. The book Michael Pollak devoted to homosexuals is still a key reference work.

24. Guy Hocquenghem, *Libération*, March 29, 1976.

25. Guy Hocquenghem, *Comment nous appelez-vous déjà?*

26. It is noteworthy that certain films belonging to the genre of "concentration-camp porn," to use Godard's expression, were widespread in France during the same period. Although a marginal movement, this trite fantasy (sometimes combined with sadomasochism), which had to do with the interconnectedness of tormentors and their victims, deserves mention because of its persistence.

27. Michel Foucault, interviewed by James O'Higgins, 1982 (*Dits et écrits*, p. 317).

28. Hervé Guibert, *A l'ami qui ne m'a pas sauvé la vie*.

29. The Pentihièvre baths had existed since the nineteenth century. During the *années folles*, the baths on rue de Ticquetonne and rue des Ternes were visited regularly. In the 1950s, the Turkish baths on rue de Milan in Paris, the Miromesnil baths, the Rhône baths, the Poncelet baths, and the Poulbot and Louvre bathhouses were also famous for their "activity."

30. In the early 1980s, Le Villette became Le Dayton, near Le Pigalle.

31. See Michael Pollak, *Les homosexuels et le sida*.

32. Edmund White, "Paris gay," *Gay Pied Hebdo*, July 13, 1984.

33. Michel Foucault, interviewed by Jean Le Bitoux, July 10, 1978 ("Le Gai savoir"; see my earlier remarks on this interview, in n. 11 to chap. 6).

34. David Girard, *Cher David, les nuits de Citizen Gay* (Ramsay, 1986).

35. In parallel to these places, bisexual spots like Le Flore opened at Les Halles: Le Café Contes in 1984 and, in 1986, Le Café Beaubourg.

36. The architectural character of the Marais, which was designated a historic neighborhood in 1964, may have played a role; Georgetown (in Washington, D.C.), Chelsea (in London), and Greenwich Village (in New York) are also historic neighborhoods that have

become gay. The financial backing of a liquor dealer who underwrote bank loans may also have contributed to the proliferation of gay spots in the Marais.

37. A few young Jews on rue des Rosiers attacked Le Central in July 1983, protesting the disappearance of the Jewish tobacco shop and causing an altercation.

38. Because the Jewish restaurant Jo Goldenberg's, on rue des Rosiers, was attacked on August 9, 1982 (with six dead and twenty-two wounded), surveillance was increased in the neighborhood at the time of the 1986 attacks. On that occasion, young Jews, leaders in the neighborhood's defense committees, asked to meet with some of the owners of gay bars. See also Jeanne Brody, *Rue des Rosiers, une autre manière d'être juif* (Autrement, 1995).

39. A former GLH militant, he opened a first bookstore, which existed between 1980 and 1983, on rue Simart.

40. The phrase "happiness in the ghetto" is taken from the title of an article by Michael Pollak, "L'homosexualité masculine ou le bonheur dans le ghetto?"

41. Ibid.; emphasis added.

42. With *Flesh* (1969, released in France in 1973), *Trash* (1970, 1972), and *Heat* (1971, 1973), Paul Morrissey and Andy Warhol paved the way for a new realist underground cinema and set the tone for future erotic films. Joe Dallesandro was one of the young actors who symbolized this evolution.

43. See Alain-Emmanuel Dreuilhe's *La société invertie* (Flammarion, 1979), and Guy Hocquenghem's *Le gay voyage*.

44. "La femme de drague" [The woman cruiser] is the title of an essential article on lesbian sex in the "Trois milliards de pervers" issue of *Recherches*, March 1973.

45. Jean Cavailhes, Pierre Dutey, and Gérard Bach-Ignasse, *Rapport gai, enquête sur les modes de vie homosexuels*.

46. Elula Perrin published, notably, *Les femmes préfèrent les femmes* (Ramsay, 1977), *Tant qu'il y aura des femmes* (Ramsay, 1978), *Alice au pays des femmes* (1980), and *Pour l'amour des femmes* (1995).

47. Excerpted from "La femme de drague," *Recherches*, March 1973.

48. Michel Foucault, *The Advocate*, Aug. 7, 1984 (*Dits et écrits*, p. 358).

49. Thanks to an intelligent free-distribution policy, the number of Minitel accounts in France has grown exponentially: by the end of 1982, there were 11,000 such accounts; by the end of 1983, 110,000; by the end of 1984, 530,000; by the end of 1985, 1,017,000; by the end of 1986, 2,037,000; by the end of 1987, 3,000,000.

50. A recent study shows that people who use long-distance methods (Minitel, phone networks) for encounters are a relatively autonomous group of homosexuals who only rarely venture into commercial or public spots and are more likely to hide their homosexuality from those who know them (Marie-Ange Schiltz, "N'importe qui ne drague pas n'importe où," *Actes du Colloque Terrains d'Entente*, mimeographed document, June 1994).

51. It is possible that, even without the help of militant organizations, public opinion would have evolved in the direction of emancipation.

52. This exclusion of certain gay militants led in particular to a split within *Gai Pied* in 1983 (see chap. 8).

53. Alain Girard, *Le choix du conjoint* (Presses Universitaires de France, 1964). The main outlines of this study have been confirmed by more recent surveys: Claude Thélot, *Tel père, tel fils?* (Dunod, 1982); Louis Roussel, *La famille incertaine* (Odile Jacob, 1989); Michel Bozon and François Héran, "La découverte du conjoint," *Population* 6 (1987), and *Population* 7 (1988).

54. Vaclav Jamek, *Traité des courtes merveilles*.

55. Michael Pollak, citing an American study from 1978, has attempted to explain this inclination toward multiple partners in terms of the socialization that preceded homosexuals' coming out. See "Les vertus de la banalité."

56. Vaclav Jamek, *Traité des courtes merveilles*.

57. All the same, the social mixing involved in homosexual cruising should not be overestimated, as Marie-Ange Schiltz's has recently demonstrated once again; see "N'importe qui ne drague pas n'importe où."

58. Michael Pollak, "Les vertus de la banalité."

59. Michel Foucault, interviewed in 1982 by James O'Higgins ("Lorsque l'amant part en taxi," *Dits et écrits*, p. 317) and glossing the words of Casanova.

60. This stability is confirmed by several studies; see Jean Cavailhes, Pierre Dutey, and Gérard Bach-Ignasse, *Rapport gai* (1984), and Alfred Spira and Nathalie Bajos, *Les comportements sexuels en France* (1993).

61. The preceding pages were largely inspired by the work of Michael Pollak (for more recent developments, see chap. 15).

62. Beyond the context of French film, Fassbinder's *Querelle* (1982), based on Genet's novel, can be pointed to as an example of evolving homosexual relationships. It starred Brad Davis in the role of the homosexual sailor, Jeanne Moureau as the bordel madam, and Laurent Malet as the lover of Gil's murderer.

63. Interview in *Nouvelles Littéraires*, Feb. 17, 1975.

64. Patrice Chéreau and Hervé Guibert, *L'homme blessé, scénario et notes* (Minuit, 1983).

CHAPTER 10: THE CONFLAGRATION

1. Hervé Guibert, *A l'ami qui ne m'a pas sauvé la vie*. The doubtful authenticity of this fictional scene, in which Foucault appears as Muzil, requires some caution in its use.

2. In an almost prophetic novel, *Les Loukoums* (1973), Yves Navarre described the existence of a stubborn and very resistant sexually transmitted disease, a cause of death in homosexual circles. In *La maladie de la mort* (Minuit, 1983), Marguerite Duras did the same, in a more vivid way.

3. The first official announcement was published on June 5, 1981, by the Centers for Disease Control (CDC) in Atlanta, in its *Morbidity and Mortality Weekly Report* (*MMWR*). The first article for the general public was "Rare Cancer Seen in 41 Homosexuals," *New York Times*, July 3, 1981.

4. *Impact médecin*, Feb. 20, 1982.

5. [To better follow the chronology, the author used by turns "gay cancer" (a nonmedical term, used by the media for the most part), "opportunistic illness and Kaposi's sarcoma" (a medical term), the rarely used "GRID" (gay-related immunodeficiency), "AIDS" (summer 1982), the French equivalent "S.I.D.A." (gradually adopted in France between October 1981 and May 1983), "SIDA" (an acronym used beginning in mid-1983), "Sida" (mid-1984), and, finally, the noun "sida." In this edition, however, the terms "S.I.D.A.," "SIDA," "Sida," and "sida" are all translated as "AIDS."—Trans.]

6. Michael Pollak's studies on the readership of *Gai Pied* showed that in 1985 57 percent of the homosexuals who were questioned had had a sexually transmitted disease (gonorrhea, 46 percent; syphilis, 20 percent; herpes, 13.6 percent; hepatitis B, 10.5 percent; and genital warts, 9.5 percent). The categories are not mutually exclusive.

7. Gilles Deleuze, *L'autre journal*, Oct. 1985.

8. The profile of Don Francis, the famous American virologist, is fairly close to Rozenbaum's. After working in Africa on a number of fevers, the CDC brought him to Atlanta to seek the causal agent for AIDS.

9. On March 6, 1982, five doctors (among them David Klatzmann and Charles Mayaud) published an article in *The Lancet* based on Willy Rozenbaum's work. It had to do with "multiple opportunistic infections in a French male homosexual." These doctors were the kernel of the Groupe Français de Travail sur le Sida. At first they called their group Infections Opportunistes et Sarcome de Kaposi [Opportunistic infections and Kaposi's sarcoma]. Jacques Leibowitch, Jean-Claude Gluckmann, Odile Picard, Jean-Baptiste Brunet, and Claude Weisselberg later joined them.

10. It can be hypothesized that if the epidemic had appeared earlier, its association with homosexual practices might not have been detected so quickly. After the fact, it was noted that New York drug users had shown the same symptoms in 1981, but, more marginalized and less likely to receive medical treatment, they were not identified until somewhat later (after the summer of 1982).

11. The very precise reports of the AIDS-alert group allow us to follow the chronology of their interactions with gay militants (documents from unpublished archives shared with me by Willy Rozenbaum).

12. A second colloquium was arranged by the AMG for March 19 and 20, 1983 (Jean-Baptiste Brunet, Jacques Leibowitch, and Willy Rozenbaum were present), and another meeting took place on May 19, 1983, with the same participants in addition to Luc Montagnier and Jean-Claude Chermann of the Institut Pasteur.

13. An instructive account of this colloquium was published by Eric Conan in *Libération*, Apr. 27, 1982.

14. See the subsequent article in which he repeated this information (Gilles Barbedette, "French Notes on AIDS," *New York Native*, July 4, 1983).

15. In 1978, the American researcher Robert Gallo had discovered the first human retrovirus (HTLV-I).

16. In addition to Barbedette's information, an article in the review *Nature* (Sept. 1983) also played a determining role in the hypothesis of a retrovirus, as the report of the work group confirmed in October 1982.

17. Although he probably attended once or twice, Dr. Lejeune did not choose to participate in the group.

18. For example, Leibowitch was on Fréquence Gaie in February 1982; Rozenbaum, in October of that year.

19. Hervé Liffran was contacted, but the representative of the CUARH was Jean-Marc Choub. This physician, who headed the medical committee of the CUARH from 1981 to 1983 and followed "health" matters in the monthly journal *Homophonies*, gradually withdrew from the CUARH in 1983 because "it all depressed [him] terribly."

20. Daniel Defert, quoted in Emmanuel Hirsch, *Aides-Solidaires*.

21. This judgment ought to be qualified, since, in addition to their dealings with gay representatives, the group alerted homosexuals in numerous interviews and press releases published in the mainstream press. From this point of view, *Libération* was an essential relay point.

22. Dr. Patrice Meyer also played a role. A former member of the FHAR and the GLH, a member of the AMG, and the host of a medical broadcast on Fréquence Gaie, in August 1983 he founded the first French AIDS organization, Vaincre le Sida [Beat AIDS]. On March 8, 1983, along with Didier Seux, he joined the French work group on AIDS.

23. See Randy Shilts, *And the Band Played On*; Mirko Grmek, *Histoire du sida*.

24. The term *RUB* is an anagram of the first three letters (BRU) of the patient's last name. This anonymity, usual in research, was made necessary by the fact that Frédéric Brugière was at the time in relatively good health, displaying only enlarged glands. He died of AIDS in the fall of 1988.

25. Reverse transcriptase is an enzyme specific to retroviruses.

26. In 1984, Robert Gallo isolated HTLV-III, a retrovirus he believed to be different from the one discovered by Montagnier. Both names, BRU-LAV and HTLV-III, were used until 1985, when it was acknowledged that the two viruses were the same. The virus was named "HIV" in 1986 ("VIH" in French).

27. The name of Charles Dauget, an engineer specializing in electron microscopy, also appeared, along with those of five technicians: F. Rey, M.-T. Nugeyre, S. Chamaret, J. Gruest, and C. Axler-Blin.

28. Luc Montagnier, "Le sida dix ans après," *Le Monde*, Jan. 24, 1993.

29. Jean Le Bitoux served as editor in chief of *Gai Pied* from 1979 to July 1983; Franck Arnal and Hugo Marsan served together until August 1988; Yves Charfe served until October 1991; Jean-Yves Le Talec served until February 1992; and, finally, Eric Lamien served until the newspaper folded, in October 1992.

30. It is possible that this sentence by Le Bitoux, in the version published by *Gai Pied*, contained a typographical error: *agis* (acted upon) for *gais* (gay).

31. "The contaminated-blood scandal": a judgment on litigation by the Council of State (legal conclusions, Apr. 9, 1993) assigned "heavy blame" to the state for the period between November 22, 1984, and October 1985.

32. Michel Setbon, *Pouvoirs contre sida*.

33. Press release reprinted by Jean-Yves Nau in *Le Monde*, June 16, 1983.

34. Jean-Yves Nau, "Conflits et divergences de vues à propos du SIDA," *Le Monde*, June 30, 1983.

35. This response was not published by *Libération* (archival document provided by Eric Conan).

36. Antoine Perruchot spoke of the "dubious ethics" involved in prohibiting homosexuals from donating blood (*Gai Pied Hebdo*, June 4, 1983). Gay representatives in the AIDS-alert group were also quite opposed to screening. Claude Lejeune was more cautious, however, in "Sida et don du sang" (*Gai Pied Hebdo*, Oct. 8, 1983).

37. In fact, at the trials dealing with HIV contamination via blood products, some blood banks entered into evidence press releases and articles from homosexuals.

38. See, for example, Professor Didier Sicard's testimony (*Rapport au président de l'Assemblée nationale*) before the parliamentary investigative commission on homosexuals' reactions to the screening of donated blood.

39. The link between AIDS and homosexuality did not raise a problem for them, which amazed the French review *Homophonies* (Nov. 1983).

40. In late 1983, 29 patients were reported in England (compared to 107 in France); in late 1984, 106 (compared to 260 in France).

41. The reactions in the three countries between 1981 and 1985 can be schematized as follows:

Sweden   (1) homosexual alert, (2) administrative alert, (3) political alert
Great Britain (1) homosexual alert, (2) administrative alert, (3) political hesitation
France   (1) administrative alert, (2) political silence and homosexual denial

42. On these questions, see Michel Setbon, *Pouvoirs contre sida*; Aquilino Morelle, "Retour sur l'affaire du sang contaminé" (*Esprit*, Oct. 1993), and *La défaite de la santé publique* (Flammarion, 1996).

43. These interviews with *Gai Pied* were used by the parliamentary investigative commission in 1993.

44. The *Bulletin Epidémiologique Hebdomadaire* reported (Jan. 1, 1984) 107 total cases of AIDS in France (44 people had died): 63 were homosexuals, 33 were foreigners (particularly Zaireans and Haitians), 1 was a hemophiliac, and 10 were "undetermined." In the United States, the 3,000-patient threshold was crossed on December 1, 1983.

45. Letter circulated by the AMG, Oct. 26, 1983; response from Jean-Baptiste Brunet (undated document).

46. The antibody-detection test was developed by the Montagnier and Gallo teams from the viral strain of a young French homosexual patient (whose last name began with the letters LAI) treated by Willy Rozenbaum.

47. *Libération*, Oct. 20, 1984. Laurent Greilsalmer made the same observation in "Après un an de réserve, les militants gays prennent le sida au sérieux" (*Le Monde*, Sept. 9, 1984).

48. *Homophonies*, Oct. 1984. In the same issue, Dr. Patrice Meyer's criticism of Lejeune's new declarations was just as harsh.

49. The 280-page *Rapport Gai* (Jean Cavailhes, Pierre Dutey, and Gérard Bach-Ignasse), compiled within the CUARH in 1984, mentioned AIDS in only two absurd sentences.

50. Guibert, *A l'ami qui ne m'a pas sauvé la vie*.

51. In January 1986, the most famous gay bathhouse in the United States, Saint Mark's, was closed for good. See Randy Shilts, *And the Band Played On*.

52. Daniel Defert, interviewed in *New York Native*, July 1–14, 1985.

53. In the same issue, Franck Arnal published a second article, under the pseudonym Francis Lacombe; it was very much opposed to testing.

54. The decision was announced to the National Assembly on June 19, ministerial order of July 23, applicable on August 1, 1985. Among European countries, France was in the middle range in terms of the date when this decision was made: May 1985 for the Netherlands and Norway; June for Austria; July for Italy and Belgium; August for France; October for the United Kingdom and Germany; January 1986 for Denmark and Finland; May 1986 for Switzerland; and February 1987 for Spain.

55. In an ambiguous press release of June 19, 1985, Aides mentioned more urgent priorities than the systematic testing of donated blood, among them the unregulated sale of syringes.

56. Gay militants and newspapers emphasized the diagnostic errors that might lead to "false positives," totally dismissing the question of "false negatives."

57. The rate was 0.65 per thousand donors in 1985.

58. It is also troubling that the government refused until February 1986 to allow reimbursement by Sécurité Sociale for testing. It was only in May 1987 that the first two free testing centers were opened by the Department of Health in Corbeil and then by Médecins du Monde. Michèle Barzach finally decided, in late 1987, to create free centers for anonymous testing.

59. Laurent Fabius's decision did not completely eliminate infection by way of blood. In the first place, there was a delay in applying the order, and there was a "disposal" of the remaining stock on the part of some blood banks. Second, there was the problem of "false negatives" and of the "test window": during a period of dormancy, estimated at several

weeks, the blood of people infected by the virus does not yet contain antibodies to the virus, and testing therefore cannot detect their seropositivity. These residual infections affected hemophiliacs only between June and October of 1985 because blood products were systematically heated after that time. By contrast, this "window" remains a source of infection for people receiving transfusions, since such blood cannot be heated. For this reason, homosexuals with multiple partners are asked even today not to donate their blood.

60. The figure cited by Rozenbaum came from a 1985 study of 6,500 homosexual patients in San Francisco.

61. Calculated in terms of editorial space, the progression of information on AIDS in *Gai Pied* is even more significant: 62 column inches in 1981, 822 column inches in 1982, 3,349 column inches in 1983, 7,029 column inches in 1984, and 20,260 column inches in 1985. See E. Rusch, D. Bertrand, and J. Guénot, *Santé publique et MST* (INSERM / John Libbey Eurotext, 1990).

62. *Gai Pied* had a circulation of about 30,000 in 1982 and averaged about 22,000 when it became a weekly (1983–85). *Homophonies* and *Masques* distributed about 2,000 copies apiece. And let us not forget *Samouraï* and *GI*, or the more openly pornographic publications.

63. After challenging homosexual lifestyles, Michel Canesi was attacked by Claude Lejeune, a year before Lejeune himself finally adopted the same line (debate reported in *Le Monde*, Sept. 18, 1983).

64. *Samouraï*, which emerged in part from the rift within *Gai Pied*, seems to have followed the same evolution as *Homophonies*; see, for example, "Cancer gay, la vérité!" (issue 5, Feb. 1983), in which Claude Lejeune makes an appearance.

65. A new erotics was promoted in *Magazine*, however: safer sex was disparaged, and readers were advised to do exactly those things that were prohibited by preventive measures. In addition, beginning in 1985, Lestrade published several articles in *Gai Pied Hebdo*, but, before 1989, none concerned AIDS. For example, he published a complete survey of homosexuals in London (Sept. 21, 1985) and dismissed the issue of AIDS: "Londoners do not seem too upset," he observed simply.

66. "Dis, maman, c'est quoi une lesbienne?" *Le Matin de Paris*, Sept. 26, 1985.

67. Questioned today, the journalists Béatrice Vallaeys and Gilles Pialoux confirm these views.

68. See the AIDS denial in Renaud Camus's *Chroniques achriennes* and Laurent Dispot's *Le manifeste archaïque* (Grasset, 1986). For Guy Hocquenghem, see chap. 11.

69. These ties to gay business owners were denounced by Jean Le Bitoux at the time the split occurred (see *Homophonies*, Sept. 1983) and afterward by Albert Rosse, René de Ceccatty, and Marie-Jo Bonnet (interviews with the author). Beginning in 1983, *Gai Pied* increased the amount of its publicity-based reporting, often bowing to the will of advertisers.

70. This theory was supported by Pierre Kneip. According to him, if AIDS had first appeared in the USSR or in Cuba, militants would have paid greater attention to it (interview with the author).

71. Use of plasma concentrate rich in the antihemophiliac factor (factor VIII or factor IX) obtained through the so-called pooling method (which combines plasma lots from several thousand donors). Since every lot of these concentrates contained the clotting factor of between 2,500 and 10,000 donors, the risk of infection was enormous.

72. The dependence of organizations for hemophiliacs on blood transfusions is another important factor explaining this denial. On these problems as a whole, see the im-

portant article by Danièle Carricaburu, "L'AFH face au danger de contamination par le virus du sida," *Sciences Sociales et Santé* 11, 3–4 (Oct. 1993).

73. See Franck Arnal, *Histoire de la prévention du sida en milieu homosexuel en France de 1982 à 1992*, and the book and pamphlets of ACT UP.

CHAPTER 11: AIDES

1. On Foucault, see Didier Eribon, *Michel Foucault et ses contemporains*; David Macey, *The Lives of Michel Foucault*.

2. Gilles Deleuze had been a member of the administrative council of Aides since 1987.

3. Michel Foucault, conversation with Werner Schroeter (*Dits et écrits*, p. 308).

4. According to Hélène Hazera, in 1971 Daniel Defert even tore up one of Michel Cressole's posters depicting a fake marriage between Pierre Overney and the prisoner Gérard Grandmontagne. At the time, Cressole was a Gazoline in the FHAR (*Gai Pied*, March 7, 1991). Today, Defert replies he did not confuse "bitchiness with militancy."

5. Hervé Guibert, "Les secrets d'un homme," in *Mauve le vierge*.

6. Unless otherwise indicated, quotations from Daniel Defert are excerpted from an interview with the author ("Le malade du sida est un réformateur social," *Esprit*, July 1994) or with Emmanuel Hirsch, *Aides-Solidaires*.

7. Daniel Defert, interviewed in *Libération*, Sept. 24, 1994.

8. Paul Veyne, *Le quotidien et l'intéressant* (Belles Lettres, 1995).

9. Hervé Guibert, *A l'ami qui ne m'a pas sauvé la vie*.

10. Daniel Defert, "Plus on est honteux, plus on avoue," *Libération*, Oct. 31, 1987.

11. Article signed "D.E.," *Libération*, July 12, 1982; see Didier Eribon, *Michel Foucault et ses contemporains*.

12. In tribute to his dead friend, Defert initially considered calling the organization "Antinoüs," but that name was not retained.

13. Daniel Defert, interviewed in April 1985 (*New York Native*, July 1–14, 1985).

14. Defert's comments at the Actes des 7e assises d'Aides, Sept. 23–25, 1994.

15. In this important article ("Les homosexuels français et l'effet sida," *Libération*, Oct. 20–21, 1984), Eric Conan highlighted the contrast between, on the one hand, a strategy "lacking in judgment" on the part of the Association des Médecins Gais (AMG) and *Gai Pied* and, on the other, the strategy of Daniel Defert, who was implicitly hailed for his innovation and solidarity.

16. Also present were Terry Lomax, Antoine Lazarus, and the lawyer Christian Revon (who drafted the bylaws for Aides). The first officers of the organization were elected: Daniel Defert, president; Philippe Arnaud and Jean Blancart, vice presidents (a doctor and a patient); Alain Siboni, secretary; and Jean Stern, treasurer.

17. Frédéric Edelmann, *Agora* 18–19.

18. According to other observers, it was Edelmann who contacted Jean-Florian Mettetal, thus finding a way to see him again.

19. All the organization's directions were decided on at a meeting on January 24, 1985, a meeting essential to the birth of Aides but one that Defert was unable to attend. This is a good indication that Aides was a collective project.

20. The influence of Mettetal, who was backed on this point by Didier Seux, was apparent at a meeting of Aides on December 11, 1984.

21. Three other AIDS organizations were started by homosexuals. Vaincre le Sida was created by Dr. Patrice Meyer during the 1983 "homosexual summer school." An organiza-

tion for the general public, Vaincre le Sida languished in its first years before finding its calling in home care, in 1990. Arsida, founded in 1984 by Dominique Lachiver, Patrice Meyer, Claude Villalonga, and Didier Seux, replaced Willy Rozenbaum's Groupe Français de Travail sur le Sida [French work group on AIDS]. Finally, Solidarité Gaie Française, a mysterious organization created in 1984, simply vanished.

22. Jean-Baptiste Brunet was invited on February 27, 1985, Willy Rozenbaum on March 20, Françoise Barré-Sinoussi and Jean-Paul Escande on April 25, and Jacques Leibowitch on June 6.

23. Frédéric Edelmann, quoted in Emmanuel Hirsch, *Aides-Solidaires*. In fact, this judgment seems too harsh. Although *Gai Pied* did not always support Aides, Hugo Marsan warmly welcomed the creation of the organization (editorial, Feb. 16, 1985).

24. In his notebooks, Defert explains that on October 30, 1984, *Gai Pied*, through Gilles Barbedette, finally proposed to welcome Aides into its offices. "Caution and self-interest" are noted in the minutes of the October 30 meeting (personal archives of Daniel Defert).

25. David Girard, *Cher David, les nuits de Citizen Gay* (Ramsay, 1986).

26. Jean-Florian Mettetal, quoted by Emmanuel Hirsch in *Aides-Solidaires*.

27. Franck Arnal was in the room for these first meetings but did not think it useful to mention them in *Gai Pied*.

28. *Gai Pied*, through the AMG (June 1983), had already distributed the brochure "Gais à votre santé," which mentioned AIDS and Kaposi's sarcoma.   .

29. In his editorial of May 4, 1985, Franck Arnal approved of placing safer-sex messages in the personals. But since the advertisers themselves had to insert these messages in the body of paid ads, it was several years before such safer-sex messages appeared.

30. Daniel Defert, "La sodomie est la voie royale du sida" (*Gai Pied Hebdo*, July 13, 1985, with responses compiled by Roland Surzur). Daniel Defert was allowed to respond (Aug. 24, 1985).

31. In *Lettre ouverte* (March 1986), Hocquenghem devoted only one page to AIDS, again speaking of the "odious panic" about AIDS and suggesting that homosexuality (not AIDS) was the "real taboo."

32. Daniel Defert, "Aides, nous ne sommes pas Act Up," *Gai Pied Hebdo*, Nov. 24, 1988.

33. Daniel Defert, interview with the author.

34. For example, Franck Arnal, *Résister ou disparaître*, certain articles in *Gai Pied Hebdo*, and certain texts in *Action* (the newspaper of ACT UP).

35. See chap. 10.

36. Indeed, the other organizations of the period, such as Gay Health Action Dublin, the COC in Amsterdam, the RFSL in Sweden, and, of course, GMHC in New York, were openly homosexual.

37. In April 1983, along with Dr. Jacques Bacconnier, he followed the progress of the first homosexual with AIDS in Marseilles.

38. It was in Marseilles (July 1987) that the famous Aides brochure on condoms, with a butterfly on its cover, was produced.

39. Comments made at the local chapter of GLH–Marseilles (shared with the author by Jean-Yves Nau); archival files related to the contaminated-blood scandal.

40. This statement must be qualified. Identity politics was involved in the fight against AIDS in such groups such as Gais pour les Libertés [Gays for freedom], or GPL. But since such organizations fell into confusion, the exception seems to prove the rule (see below, n. 70).

41. Michael Pollak, *Agora*, Autumn 1991.

42. Gay organizations began to mobilize in the Netherlands, England, and Luxembourg in 1982; in Germany and Spain in 1983; in Denmark and Italy in 1984; in Belgium and France in 1985; and in Ireland in 1986 (see Michael Pollak, "Histoire d'une cause," *Politix*).

43. Jean-Florian Mettetal, quoted by Emmanuel Hirsch, *Aides-Solidaires*.

44. This seems equally true with respect to all the nongovernment (Doctors Without Borders, Médecins du Monde), social medicine, and charitable organizations that kept silent in the 1980s and today regret the preeminence of Aides.

45. Hervé Guibert, *A l'ami qui ne m'a pas sauvé la vie*.

46. Jean-Florian Mettetal, quoted by Emmanuel Hirsch, *Aides-Solidaires*.

47. On March 31, 1985, the sum of 70,000 francs was collected by Aides, thanks to the brochure inserted into *Gai Pied*.

48. Pierre Kneip, first an operator for the Aides hotline and then its head, organized the conference for people with HIV and, later, wrote a regular column called "Les années sida" [The AIDS years] for *Gai Pied* under the name Pierre Epkin. Having founded Sida Infos Service in November 1990, he died of AIDS on December 2, 1995.

49. During this time, HPA 23, a course of treatment many hoped would be effective, was available only in Paris.

50. *Gai Pied* again inserted an Aides brochure (Oct. 12, 1985) and published an important special issue on AIDS (Nov. 9, 1985). All the same, in late 1985 *Gai Pied* stopped publishing Aides inserts at no cost and began to charge the advertising fee. Daniel Defert criticized this move in a letter to Gérard Vappereau, who was the paper's managing editor (correspondence between Vappereau and Defert, March 25, 1986–April 14, 1986; shared with the author by Daniel Defert).

51. Aides covered as much as 50 percent of the costs for this operation. By contrast, the office of the Ministry of Health declined to provide *Gai Pied* with financial assistance. Nevertheless, Dr. Claude Weisselberg assured the paper's owners that they would not be prosecuted for illegal advertising. (Dr. Weisselberg began in February 1982 to participate in the AIDS-alert group formed around Willy Rozenbaum. He directed the epidemiology bureau at the Ministry of Health before joining the office of the undersecretary at the Department of Health in July 1983, to pursue the particular issue of AIDS. He occupied that post, under Edmond Hervé, until March 1986.)

52. Although the first Aides brochure, in February 1985, included the word "condom," condoms were not the centerpiece of preventive measures until the brochure of October 1985.

53. *Journal Officiel*, National Assembly, May 3, 1982.

54. National governmental campaigns to combat AIDS were mounted in the Netherlands in 1983; in Denmark in 1984; in Germany, Belgium, Spain, and Greece in 1985; in Ireland, Portugal, and England in 1986; in France in 1987; and in Italy in 1989 (see Michael Pollak, "Histoire d'une cause," *Politix*).

55. Edmond Hervé was minister of health in the first Mauroy government (May 21–June 23, 1981), minister delegate at the Department of Energy (June 1981–March 1983), and then undersecretary at the Department of Health in the third Mauroy government (March 1983–July 1984), where he worked under Pierre Bérégovoy, minister of social affairs. He remained a state secretary under Laurent Fabius until March 1986.

56. See n. 51.

57. In 1985, Aides spending on prevention rose to 301,500 francs (the grant thus accounted for more than 80 percent). In 1986, Edelmann renewed his request from the DGS, asking for 2 million francs (only 300,000 francs were granted in November 1986 under

Michèle Barzach, supplemented by another 190,000 francs at the end of the year). The contract signed with the DGS stipulated that Aides had to promote prevention "among the group most affected, male homosexuals" (letters from Edelmann to the DGS, July 20, 1985, and Feb. 21, 1986; DGS / Aides contracts, Oct. 14, 1985, and Nov. 18, 1986; information shared with the author by Jean-Baptiste Brunet, an agent working under contract for the DGS).

58. Cohen-Solal, national delegate to the Department of Health for the Socialist Party and a general practitioner before 1981, served as CFES director from June 1981 to September 1986. Between 1983 and 1986 he combined these duties with those of technical adviser to Edmond Hervé's office. He was later in charge of communications for Bruno Durieux's office. The CFES also had an adjunct delegate-at-large, Marc Danzon.

59. Even in 1986, the CFES limited itself to publishing a pamphlet for medical workers ("Le praticien et le sida," with a foreword by Edmond Hervé, was published on Dec. 30, 1985; 223,000 copies were printed and probably distributed in 1986), and a brochure for the general public ("A propos du sida," with 500,000 copies distributed in collaboration with Aides, beginning in July 1986).

60. In 1987, the new CFES delegate-at-large, under Michèle Barzach, failed to distribute a million AIDS pamphlets published and paid for by CFES. When the scandal broke, Barzach reacted promptly, asking for the delegate's resignation. Because of this scandal, however, the CFES, having demonstrated its ineffectiveness in fighting against AIDS, was in fact relieved of that responsibility in 1989, through the creation of the Agence Française de Lutte contre le Sida [French agency to combat AIDS], or AFLS.

61. Franck Arnal, *Résister ou disparaître.*

62. This idea has been supported by Edelmann in particular (*Le Monde,* June 12, 1991).

63. Laurent Fabius, interview with the author, Oct. 13, 1994.

64. The question also concerns those condom manufacturers who did no advertising even after the ban was lifted, in 1987.

65. Paradoxically, the ban on promoting methods of contraception was included within the framework of the law authorizing the sale of contraceptives (the so-called Neuwirth law of Dec. 28, 1967, complemented by the law of Dec. 4, 1974). Condom advertising was banned by article L. 282, which originated in the 1942 law on venereal disease, adopted in an ordinance of 1960. Therefore, in order to authorize advertising, it was necessary to revise documents that had the force of law, and this could not be done without a parliamentary debate.

66. On these issues, see Michel Setbon, *Pouvoirs contre sida.*

67. This note from the DGS to Edmond Hervé was drafted by Jean-Baptiste Brunet, whose initials appear on this undated document.

68. Weisselberg, questioned today, does not remember having spoken these words.

69. The legal sale of syringes was rejected at the interministerial level. As a result, it is probable that Hervé, burned by that refusal, did not see the point of going to bat for condom advertising.

70. In 1985–86, the homosexual and "Fabiusian" organization Gais pour les Libertés (GPL) received public funding earmarked for the fight against AIDS. Several publications—*Le Canard Enchaîné* (Nov. 10, 1993), *Le Monde, Libération* (Nov. 12, 1998), *Politix* (Fabrice Nicolino, "Sida: Les bonnes affaires de la gauche caviar," May 1993)—found the way the funds were being used, as well as the organization of a gala, "scandalous."

71. See especially "Les vertus de la banalité" and "L'homosexualité masculine ou le bonheur dans le ghetto?"

72. Michel Pollak, *Agora*, Autumn 1991.

73. The plan was accepted by MIRE, a joint project of the Ministry of Health and the Ministry of Research, headed by Lucien Brams and Yves Souteyrand.

74. According to Lindinalva Laurindo–Da Silva. In another misunderstanding between Pollak and *Gai Pied*, Pollak had to ask *Gai Pied* for the right to respond because the paper had changed the ending of one of his articles.

75. Michael Pollak, interviewed in 1986 by Emmanuel Hirsch; interview published in *Le sida, rumeurs et faits* (Le Cerf, 1987).

76. The voting process (slates of candidates, with no possibility of splitting one's vote) played a large role in pitting one bloc (the Defert slate) against the other (the Mettetal slate).

77. Hervé Guibert, *A l'ami qui ne m'a pas sauvé la vie*.

78. In 1986, the organization had 1,200 members and sympathizers and 200 volunteers, and its budget was 2.5 million francs. On March 12 and 13, 1987, Aides became a federation that united already existing regional committees (in Grenoble since June 1986, in Rennes since January 1987, and in Reims since February 1987). Most of the expansion in Aides took place after 1987 (see chap. 16).

79. Arcat-sida was created in November 1985 by Drs. Daniel Vittecoq and Marcel Arrouy. In early 1986, at the request of the founders of Arcat, Pierre Bergé and Christophe Girard of Yves Saint-Laurent became, respectively, its president and general secretary. Since January 1996, Edelmann has been president, having succeeded Pierre Bergé when the latter resigned.

80. Michael Pollak, "Histoire d'une cause," *Politix*.

CHAPTER 12: BACKLASH

1. "Le monôme des zombies," *Figaro* magazine, Dec. 6, 1986.

2. Daniel Defert, quoted by Emmanuel Hirsch, *Aides-Solidaires*.

3. So begins Michael Pollak's *Les homosexuels et le sida*.

4. The recent neologism "homophobia" is etymologically inaccurate, since it literally means "fear of the same" or "hatred of the same" (in 1971, militants in the FHAR also used "homosexual racism," "antihomosexual," and "heterocop"). The historian John Boswell proposes "homosexophobia" (literally, "fear of the homosexual"), while others have suggested "allophobia" (fear of the other) and even "heterophobia" (fear of the different). Nevertheless, the term "homophobia" has found a place in the lexicon, next to "xenophobia."

5. In 1986, the French poster for the Pedro Almodóvar film *Law of Desire* was banned because it showed two men in the same bed.

6. Mathieu Lindon, a literary journalist at *Libération*, also published *Le livre de Jim-Courage*, *Le coeur de To*, and *Je t'aime*.

7. In *Concordances des temps* (Editions du Seuil, 1987), Jean-Noël Jeanneney compares the ban on *Gai Pied* to the 1922 ban on *La Garçonne*.

8. Letter from Dominique Latournerie to *Gai Pied Hebdo*, March 23, 1987, reproduced in the special issue ("La menace") of March 28, 1987.

9. The real turning point for AIDS information in *Gai Pied* was an agreement between the newspaper and Arcat-sida whereby Arcat-sida participated in writing the medical columns, thanks especially to the efforts of Jean-Florian Mettetal and Franck Fontenay.

10. In fact, Le Pen's elaboration of his position, alluding to the scientific doubts of

1983–84, was two or three years out of date. In 1987, researchers had a better understanding of how the virus was transmitted and quickly contradicted his claims.

11. François Bachelot, *Libération*, Feb. 13, 1987. See also Bachelot's "On cache la vérité," *Minute*, Dec. 1986.

12. François Bachelot, *Une société au risque du sida, sidatorium* (Albatros, 1988, collective volume).

13. In making these decisions, Barzach relied on Professor Rapin's report (requested by Edmond Hervé in February 1986 and submitted only in May). Nevertheless, although Barzach lifted the ban on condom advertising, she did not encourage such advertising. Ad campaigns began to appear only in 1988.

14. In addition, her superior, Minister Philippe Séguin, largely insensitive to the fight against AIDS at that time, did not leave her a wide margin for maneuvering.

15. According to Daniel Defert, interviewed by the author for *Esprit*, July 1994.

16. *Minute*, Apr. 1987.

17. *Présent*, June 2, 1989.

18. Ernest Chénière, quoted in *Le Monde*, Dec. 14, 1993.

19. Pierre Gendron, quoted in "Le Front national, vingt ans après: La guerre culturelle," *Le Monde*, Feb. 6, 1992.

20. As quickly as it is banned, the review reappears under a different name.

21. Jean-Marie Le Pen, quoted in *Libération*, Sept. 4, 1995, and *Le Monde*, Sept. 8, 1995.

22. The schism with Monseigneur Lefebvre (July 1988) probably prevented the Catholic Church in France from asserting its own position on condoms, independent of Rome's, so that the fundamentalists could be kept from proclaiming that they were the only supporters of the pontifical line.

23. See "Le malade du sida, reformateur social," interview by the author with Daniel Defert in *Esprit*, July 1994; and "La chair, le corps et le latex," *Chrétiens et sida* 4. It was not until Monseigneur Albert Rouet's communication of Feb. 12, 1996, that the French bishops finally decided that condom use was "necessary" in the fight against AIDS.

24. Monseigneur Collini, quoted in *Le Monde*, June 5, 1993.

25. Jacques Gaillot, before being stripped of his duties as bishop of Evreux in January 1995, published an opinion column in *Gai Pied Hebdo* in which he declared that "homosexuals enter the kingdom of God ahead of us" ("Etre homosexuel et catholique aujourd'hui," Feb. 2, 1989).

26. See the fundamental text by John Boswell, *Christianity, Social Tolerance, and Homosexuality: Gay People in Western Europe from the Beginnings of the Christian Era to the Fourteenth Century*.

27. Several of John Paul II's biographers have uncovered the influence that a certain Jan Tyranowski had on the young Karol Wojtyla. The future pope was twenty years old when he met the forty-year-old fashion designer in Krakow in 1940. The future John Paul II's mentor, though not a priest, conducted a discussion group for adolescents, which Karol attended regularly. It was this contact that led him to give up his theatrical ambitions and choose the seminary.

28. See the evolution in the Congrégation pour la Doctrine de la Foi [Congregation for the doctrine of faith], from the "Déclaration sur quelques questions d'éthique sexuelle" to the "Lettres aux évêques de l'Eglise catholique sur la pastorale à l'égard des personnes homosexuelles" (Oct. 1986).

29. "Quelqes considérations concernant la réponse à des propositions de loi sur la non-discrimination des personnes homosexuelles," July 1992 (*Osservatore Romano*, Aug. 4,

1992). This text reportedly was published deliberately during the American presidential campaign, when Bill Clinton was expressing support for gays.

30. Pope John Paul II, quoted in *Le Monde*, Feb. 22, 1994.

31. Survey by Alfred Spira and Nathalie Bajos, Messiah-Mouret subsample (see chapter 16).

32. Text adopted by the ethics board during the council of the Fédération Protestante de France, June 4 and 5, 1994 (*Le Monde*, June 7, 1994).

33. On these issues, Eugen Drewermann's work remains important (see *Les fonctionnaires de Dieu*).

34. More than 500 scandals implicating members of the Catholic clergy in the United States were adjudicated by American courts between 1983 and 1993 (*Le Monde*, Aug. 12, 1993).

35. The Baptist pastor Joseph Doucé was murdered in July 1990 after the Renseignements Généraux [Central intelligence service] agents assigned to watch him had him arrested. His death has since become "the Doucé affair," which has uncovered serious abuses in the office of Renseignements Généraux, and which played a role in the resignation of its Paris director, Claude Bardon, in 1994. The cause of Joseph Doucé's death is still unclear, however. See Bernard Violet, *Mort d'un pasteur, l'affaire Doucé* (Fayard, 1993).

36. Interview by the author with Alain Finkielkraut, "Il faut résister au discours de dénonciation," *Journal du Sida*, Apr. 1995. On "homophobia," see also *La peur de l'autre en soi: Du sexisme à l'homophobie*, edited by Daniel Welzer-Lang, Pierre Dutey, and Michel Dorais (VLB Editeur, 1994).

37. Editorial in *Figaro* magazine, Nov. 12, 1993.

CHAPTER 13: THE HECATOMB

1. The rate of death from AIDS was 544.2 per 1,000 deaths. See Haton, Jougla, Bouvie-Colle, and Maguin, *Mortalité et causes de décès en France* (INSERM/Doin, 1988).

2. Daniel Defert, interview with the author, *Esprit*, July 1994.

3. In Berlin there was the creation of the *Denkraum*, a cobblestone street leading to a cemetery, with the name of someone who has died of AIDS on each of the street's stones.

4. Daniel Defert, preface to Jean Forest, *Le Patchwork des noms* (1993).

5. Fabrice Emaer, contrary to reports, did not die from complications of AIDS but rather of kidney cancer.

6. With respect to Foucault, Aron further explains in his book *Mon sida*, "I attacked him because of my allergy to philosophy, but also for another reason, which is partly illegitimate: I was jealous of his fame."

7. With the kind permission of the publisher, Christian Bourgois, I cite here lengthy excerpts from *Mon sida* (1988) as it appeared in book form. In brackets, as necessary, I note sentences (contained in sections that were suppressed by Aron for the publication of the book) from the original interview conducted by Elisabeth Schemla and published by *Le Nouvel Observateur*, Oct. 30, 1987.

8. *Les modernes* was a book Aron wrote in opposition to modernity.

9. In the United States, the preventive effects of Magic Johnson's November 1991 "confession" have been demonstrated ("Etude de l'effet de l'annonce de la séropositivité de Magic Johnson," *Transcriptase*, Nov. 1992).

10. Aron took part in the initial denial of AIDS, in interviews and articles that may be considered irresponsible today (for example, in *Masques*, Spring 1984).

11. "La mort d'Aron," *Gai Pied Hebdo*, Aug. 1988. Daniel Defert had the same reaction, but for different reasons; his reaction combined the lucid discourse proper to the president of Aides with the personal reaction proper to a friend of Foucault's ("Plus on est honteux, plus on avoue," *Libération*, Oct. 31, 1971); see chap. 11.

12. See chap. 10.

13. Hocquenghem had already expressed his admiration for the genetic theories of new-right thinkers, with Alain de Benoist in the lead; see chap. 8.

14. Georges Lapassade and Willy Rozenbaum have the same memory.

15. Laurent Joffrin, *Libération*, Aug. 30, 1988.

16. Roland Surzur, preface to Guy Hocquenghem, *L'amphithéâtre des morts*.

17. Ecstasy, which began to be sold in tablet form in 1987, and whose effects on the brain (for example, fits of delirium) are often dangerous, is, like crystal meth, a "sex drug," that is, an aphrodisiac. K [also known as PCP and Special K], which appeared in France in 1995, is a similar drug that comes from veterinary medicine.

18. The deejays Sonic and Didier Sinclair created "the house and techno identity" of Fréquence Gaie (which became FG), thanks especially to *Happy Hour*. When FG became the first techno station, its audience in Paris grew to 80,000 listeners a day, according to Médiamétrie. A special issue of the journal *Coda* ("La vision techno," Sept. 1995) traces the history of house music and its link to militant homosexuals and AIDS.

19. Didier Lestrade and Luc Coulavin, "Histoire de la mode gay," *Gai Pied Hebdo*, May 12, 1988.

20. These data come from the *Bulletin Epidémiologique Hebdomadaire* (*BEH–DGS*, June 1982–Aug. 1995). The relay-point hypothesis is taken from Michael Pollak, *Les homosexuels et le sida*, from which I borrow liberally.

21. On September 30, 1987, 47 percent of homosexual AIDS cases had been recorded for the age cohort of people between thirty and thirty-nine (*BEH* 42, 1987).

22. *BEH* 18 and 42, 1987.

23. *BEH*, Aug. 8, 1995. These figures include "male homosexuals/bisexuals." In addition, there are probably "homosexual/bisexual" cases recorded under "heterosexual transmission," "unknown transmission," and especially "homosexual drug addicts."

24. Monseigneur Collini, quoted by Daniel Defert in an interview with the author, *Esprit*, July 1994.

25. The remarks of Michel Pelegrin, quoted here, were published in *Télérama* (Nov. 24, 1993). The conference took place at Le Bataclan, in Paris; transcripts were published in *Vivre de sida, actes des Etats Généraux du sida* (Le Cerf, 1990).

26. The data that follow are taken from a March 1986 survey by Michael Pollak of about a hundred patients who were at La Pitié Hospital for medical appointments; see Pollak, *Les homosexuels et le sida*.

27. Study of San Francisco homosexuals (published in *Transcriptase*, June 1993) about revealing one's HIV-positive status to friends and family members.

28. Hervé Guibert, *A l'ami qui ne m'a pas sauvé la vie*.

29. For novels quoted in these pages, see the bibliography.

30. Hervé Guibert, interview in *Libération*, March 1, 1990.

31. Jean Cocteau, *La difficulté d'être*.

32. From Gilles Barbedette, *Mémoires d'un jeune homme devenu vieux* (Gallimard, 1993). Jean Blancart, the ex-militant from GLH–Rennes who became vice president of Aides, died in late 1986. Barbedette, with whom Blancart had been living since 1975, died on March 30, 1992.

33. The remarks of people with HIV or AIDS are excerpted from *Gai Pied Hebdo* columns ("Les années sida," published March 1990–Oct. 1992) by Franck Arnal and Pierre Epkin (Kneip), from Christian Martin's *Libération* columns, or from interviews conducted by the author.

34. Vaclav Jamek, *Traité des courtes merveilles.*

35. For these AIDS novels, see the bibliography.

36. Other films devoted to the same theme were P. J. Castellaneta's *Together Alone* (1991), Kenneth Branagh's *Peter's Friends* (1992), Steve Levitt's *Deaf Heaven* (1992), and Roger Spottiswoode's *And the Band Played On* (1994), based on the book by Randy Shilts.

37. See Frédéric Martel, "Guibert, Koltès, Copi: Littérature et sida," *Esprit*, Nov. 1994.

38. Hervé Guibert, *A l'ami qui ne m'a pas sauvé la vie.*

39. Hervé Guibert, interviewed in *Libération*, Oct. 20, 1988.

40. Jean-Luc Hennig, *Libération*, Apr. 30, 1977.

41. Angelo Rinaldi's description of Guibert, *L'Express*, Apr. 30, 1982.

42. Michel Foucault, quoted by Guibert himself in *Le protocole compassionnel.*

43. Hervé Guibert, *A l'ami qui ne m'a pas sauvé la vie.*

44. Guibert was in love with the bullfighter Juan Antonio Ruiz (Espartaco). Guibert's passion for bullfighting belongs to a tradition that includes Henri de Montherlant, Jean Cocteau, the cult film *Pink Narcissus*, and, more recently, Serge Daney and Pedro Almodóvar.

CHAPTER 14: ACT UP

1. The book was translated into French under the title *Fags* in 1981.

2. On the United States, see Randy Shilts, *And the Band Played On*; Larry Kramer, *Reports from the Holocaust*; and the survey by Guillaume Marche, *Identification et action face au sida dans le mouvement gai et lesbien aux Etats-Unis*, edited by Michel Wieviorka (Ecole des Hautes Etudes en Sciences Sociales, 1993).

3. Larry Kramer, "1,112 and Counting," in *Reports from the Holocaust* (St. Martin's, 1989), p. 46.

4. Larry Kramer, interview in *Tribus*, June 1995; see also *Reports from the Holocaust.*

5. Didier Lestrade, interview with Larry Kramer ("J'accuse") in *Gai Pied*, Apr. 6, 1989.

6. A famous line from "Ten Years of Plague," *Advocate* 580 (1991).

7. Still, there is nothing new about this reprehensible activity. Roger Peyrefitte made it his specialty in France, and the young writer Christophe Donner attempted to out the son of a famous philosopher. As a result, his book *L'esprit de vengeance* (Grasset, 1992) was censored by provisional order.

8. The adviser responsible for this issue in Matignon, having neglected to preview the broadcast, was forced to resign.

9. *Le Monde*, Jan. 18 and 19, 1991. On this affair, see Elisabeth Schemla, *Edith Cresson, la femme piégée* (Flammarion, 1993).

10. At the time, Françoise Gaspard was head of the Socialist Party's AIDS committee, in which Willy Rozenbaum and Michael Pollak, notably, participated. See also "Un appel pour Mitterrand," *Libération*, Jan. 1988.

11. Edouard Balladur (in 1993) and Jacques Chirac (in 1995) understood the political stakes of this subject. It is true that the contaminated-blood scandal had erupted in the meantime (1991).

12. Bruno Durieux was deputy minister at the Department of Health from October

1990 to April 1992 (first under Evin and then, beginning May 1991, under Jean-Louis Bianco, minister of social affairs). Bernard Kouchner was minister of health and humanitarian action from April 1992 to March 1993 (he belatedly decided to assume all responsibility for individuals with HIV).

13. The campaign, ordered by Véronique Neiertz, undersecretary for women's rights, linked contraception, condoms, and the fight against AIDS. It was finally mounted six months later.

14. Lestrade wrote an important article on American communitarianism ("Ce qu'il faut retenir des Etats-Unis et ce qu'il faut importer en France," *La Lettre de Gai Pied*, Apr. 1994).

15. Interview in *Illico*, May 1992; interview in *Globe*, Feb. 10, 1992.

16. On November 1, 1991, they also disrupted the All Saints' Day mass at Notre-Dame de Paris, interrupting the sermon.

17. According to Jean-Christian, a member of ACT UP (*Globe*, Feb. 10, 1992).

18. Mitterrand first said the word "AIDS" in a public speech during a televised greeting for the new year, Dec. 31, 1993.

19. This message was presented by Frédéric Mitterrand and read by Yves Navarre during a dance at Cirque d'Hiver (*Gai Pied Hebdo*, June 1, 1989, and *Le Monde*, May 31, 1989); emphasis added.

20. These data are from the poll taken under the direction of Olivier Fillieule in 1994. The complete results are available in his edited collection *Activisme et lutte contre le sida: Les mouvements Act Up en Europe et aux Etats-Unis* (L'Harmattan, 1996).

21. "Simone Veil did nothing to end these *deportations*," declared the editorial in *Action* (Oct. 27, 1994); emphasis added.

22. The FHAR was the antithesis of an organized movement. In a time of polymorphous desires, disorder was de rigueur. Nevertheless, the FHAR organized a commando operation against the Rocher drug labs around 1974, against "medication for sexuality." ACT UP's methods were more than a nod toward the FHAR.

23. The format for taking the floor was governed by precise codes: hand raised with index finger pointing down to interrupt a statement in progress; both hands raised and crossed to give up one's turn to speak; a special way of applauding (clapping the fingers) and of hissing ("kss, kss"); a "T" sign made with both hands by the facilitator before cutting someone off.

24. In a letter of Sept. 25, 1989, the writer Pascal de Duve distanced himself from "the reigning political bureaucracy" of ACT UP.

25. Lestrade was admitted as a member of the AC5 committee of the ANRS in December 1993. In the United States, ACT UP persuaded Wellcome Laboratories to lower the price of AZT.

26. Nevertheless, such influential members of ACT UP as Philippe Labbey embraced libertarianism and situationism. ACT UP maintained good relations with the Fédération Anarchiste and produced a regular broadcast on Radio Libertaire. In addition, its criticisms of the media, combined with its exploitation of them, are sometimes reminiscent of Guy Debord. In the film with Brigitte Cornant (*Guy Debord, son art et son temps*), Debord presents the burglars on the outskirts of Paris and the members of ACT UP as the only positive contemporary heroes.

27. See ACT UP–Paris, *Le sida, combien de divisions?*; *Action*, Nov. 1993; *Journée du désespoir*, Apr. 4, 1992.

28. "Hécatombe," *Action*, May 1995; "Prévention=visibilité," *Action*, Feb. 1995.

29. Michael Pollak, "Histoire d'une cause."

30. Ibid.

31. It was Joëlle Bouchet, mother of Ludovic, a young infected hemophiliac, who took this issue to ACT UP in 1991. She was later expelled from ACT UP—by certified letter—because of her extremism in pursuing justice in the contaminated-blood scandal. See also Joëlle Bouchet, *J'accuse médecins et malades* (De Magrie, 1992).

32. In this scandal, ACT UP forgot that what had played a decisive role in infecting hemophiliacs and people receiving transfusions was not so much the 1985 delay in implementing HIV antibody testing as the faulty selection of donors from 1983 on (in which gay militants had played their part).

33. *Globe*, Feb. 10, 1992.

34. *Gai Pied Hebdo*, Apr. 6, 1989.

35. Lestrade is referring to Aides's Arc-en-ciel [Rainbow] project of early 1996, whose aim was to create a gathering place and service center for people with HIV. Its initial budget and annual operating expenses were high.

36. Didier Lestrade, "L'ultime frontière," *Gai Pied Hebdo*, Apr. 4, 1991.

37. Michael Pollak, *Agora* 18–19.

38. Michael Pollak, "Histoire d'une cause."

39. Lestrade and Pascal Loubet have even gone so far as to claim that the dehomosexualization of Aides explains the failure of prevention in the gay environment (see *Lettre du CRIPS*, May 1990).

40. Several people influential in ACT UP came out of Couteau entre les Dents [Knife between the teeth], a group of Ecole Normale students (Philippe Mangeot, Michel Celse, Pierre Zaoui, Mathieu Potte-Bonneville, Laurence Duchêne, and Juliette Chemillier) who opposed the Gulf War and published the *Cahiers de résistance*.

41. Didier Lestrade, *Action* 23.

42. Philippe Mangeot, quoted by Emeric Languerrand, "Crise d'identité à ACT UP," *Journal du Sida*, June 1995.

43. Scott Sawyer, interviewed in *Journal du Sida*, Oct. 1994.

44. Aides, and especially its new president, Arnaud Marty-Lavauzelle, also had a strong presence in this collective.

45. Created in March 1993, Sourds en colère is very close to ACT UP. Its goal is to "fight against cochlear implants and for the visibility of the deaf community," to oppose the image of deaf people as handicapped, and to spread "deaf culture."

46. For example, the physical violence during the zap against Dominique Charvet (April 13, 1992) and against Dr. Bahman Habibi (March 13, 1992); the slogan "He killed my friend" accompanied by a photo of Jean de Savigny, head of the Agence Française de Lutte contre le Sida (June 1993); or the publication of the home phone number of the president of the government workers' mutual insurance company (*Action*, Nov. 1992).

47. Michael Pollak, "Histoire d'une cause."

48. ACT UP–Paris claimed about 300 members in 1994, but only 120 participated in the decisive election whereby Christophe Martet succeeded Cleews Vellay as president. A few groups have appeared recently in the provinces, notably in Strasbourg, Marseilles, Montpellier, Nice, Lille, Toulouse, and La Rochelle.

49. This action, which may have been the most important one ever carried out in the fight against AIDS (the images were picked up by every TV station in the world), had been prepared months in advance, with scale models of the Place de la Concorde and a complex set of logistics.

50. Unlike Aides, Arcat, and the Agence Française de Lutte contre le Sida, ACT UP did not denounce this campaign, against which four people with HIV filed suit—and won. The Concorde operation, conducted jointly with United Colors of Benetton, shows that the organization will sometimes join forces with a commercial brand name that uses AIDS for commercial ends, if such a venture allows it to gain media attention.

51. Succinct remarks from *Action* (Jan. 1993), *Globe* (Feb. 10, 1992), and *Journal du Sida* (June 1995), or words taken from weekly meetings or from interviews with the author.

52. Several members of ACT UP have obtained posts with the ANRS, the MNEF, or Doctors Without Borders. Hugues Charbonneau, former vice president of ACT UP, was named director of Ensemble contre le Sida [Group against AIDS].

53. The issue of training is central for an organization with high turnover. This is one of the principal weaknesses of ACT UP as compared to Aides, which began to hold weekend training sessions in 1985. ACT UP has recently instituted public information meetings.

54. This "HIV-positive humor" is particularly evident in the "Miction" [Urination] supplement to the ACT UP journal and in such slogans as "AIDS is disco." Another of the militants' favorite games is to spy out central intelligence agents who may have infiltrated the organization's weekly meetings.

CHAPTER 15: THE SECOND HOMOSEXUAL REVOLUTION

The epigraph, a line made famous by Daniel Defert, is taken from the title of a paper he presented at the Second World AIDS Conference in Montreal in 1989. Michael Pollak had earlier used the expression "AIDS, a social indicator" (David and Jonathan Society colloquium, Feb. 27, 1988).

1. Michael Pollak, *Les homosexuels et le sida*.

2. Speech at Aides conference (quoted in *Libération*, Sept. 24, 1994).

3. Kinsey (1948); Simon (1972); Bon and d'Arc (1974); Cavailhes, Dutey, and Bach-Ignasse (1984).

4. This was a telephone survey, conducted in 1992, of 20,055 people between the ages of eighteen and sixty-nine (a random and representative national sample). See Alfred Spira and Nathalie Bajos, *Les comportements sexuels en France*. For Pollak's studies, see chap. 11.

5. For a scientific discussion of underreporting, and for details on data about homosexuals in the Spira and Bajos poll, see the essential article by Antoine Messiah and Emmanuelle Mouret-Fourme, "Homosexualité, bisexualité: Eléments de socio-biographie sexuelle."

6. These estimates obtained from the Spira and Bajos team are in line with estimates in the French survey by Simon (1972) and with those in a Danish survey (1992) by Melbye. Nevertheless, this national average masks a high degree of sociogeographic variability: 1.6 percent of men in rural areas versus 5.9 percent of men in the Paris area (with the highest rates at 10.6 percent among Parisian men between the ages of thirty and thirty-four, 11.2 percent among Parisian men between fifty and fifty-four, 14.8 percent among Parisian women between thirty-five and thirty-nine, and 15.9 percent among Parisian women between sixty and sixty-four).

7. See especially Michael Pollak, "Les vertus de la banalité."

8. The calculation is based on a rate of 0.7 percent (average of 0.3 and 1.1) for a single year, and 3.35 percent (average of 2.6 and 4.1) for a lifetime. This figure refers to the population surveyed for the Spira and Bajos poll (that is, about 38 million people between the ages of eighteen and sixty-nine).

9. All data on homosexuals are taken from Messiah and Mouret-Fourme, "Homosexualité, bisexualité."

10. For the purposes of the survey, the term "bisexual" was defined as describing any person who reported having had at least one partner of the same sex and one partner of the opposite sex during the previous twelve months.

11. Nevertheless, detailed study shows that those who are exclusively homosexual are less often coupled (29 percent are, and 71 percent are not) by comparison to bisexuals (68 percent are coupled, with 28 percent of this group in homosexual couples and 40 percent in heterosexual couples).

12. Of the homosexuals surveyed, 46 percent lived in the Paris region, 40 percent in cities with populations greater than 100,000, 5 percent in cities having between 20,000 and 100,000 residents, and 9 percent in cities having fewer than 20,000 residents.

13. Expressions used by Guy Hocquenghem in *La dérive homosexuelle*.

14. Hervé Le Bras, *Marianne et les lapins* (Olivier Orban, 1991); Louis Roussel, *La famille incertaine* (Odile Jacob, 1989); Henri Mendras, *La seconde Révolution française* (Gallimard, 1988). See also Irène Théry, *Le démariage* (Odile Jacob, 1993).

15. Data from the 1990 census, published in *Economie et statistiques* (INSEE, Apr. 1992), *Insee première* (Jan. 1994), and *Population et sociétés* (Jan. 1994).

16. *Economie et statistiques*, March 1985 (1982 survey). Of course, these figures may also reflect single-person households of widows and widowers.

17. See Alain Ehrenberg (*Esprit*, Nov. 1992), and Elisabeth Badinter, *XY, de l'identité masculine* (Odile Jacob, 1992).

18. Data from the Spira and Bajos survey. By contrast, there are, to my knowledge, no studies of "swinging" couples, ménages à trois, or sadomasochism among heterosexuals.

19. This phenomenon is particularly noticeable on FM radio programs where adolescents freely express their views live, and where AIDS and homosexuality are often mentioned; in 1994, one such program had an audience of nearly 1.3 million adolescents every evening.

20. Homosexuality was "primarily just another kind of behavior" for 24 percent of people questioned in 1973 (Sondage Sofres/*L'Express*), for 29 percent in 1979 (IFOP/*Arcadie* survey), for 27 percent in 1980 (Sofres/*Le Nouvel Observateur*), for 29 percent in 1981 (Sofres/*Elle*), for 41 percent in 1984 (Sofres/*GI*), for 54 percent in 1985 (IFOP/*Le Nouvel Observateur*), and for 61 percent in 1988 (IFOP/*Le Nouvel Observateur*).

21. *Le Monde*, May 12, 1994. This trend was noted even earlier, by the IFOP/*Globe* survey of May 12, 1993.

22. *Le Nouvel Observateur*, Apr. 8, 1993. This trend was confirmed by the IFOP/*L'Express–Canal Plus* poll of May 24, 1995.

23. Decisive shifts occurred at the international level in the early 1990s: the World Health Organization decided to take homosexuality off its list of "mental disorders" (where it had been appearing since 1948) and to give it the neutral classification of a "sexual preference" (a revision passed in 1990 but implemented only on Jan. 1, 1993). During the same period, Amnesty International decided (Sept. 7, 1991) to keep homosexuality as a criterion for persecution, condemnation, or internment. Finally, homosexuality has recently been decriminalized in several countries (for example, in Russia and Ireland).

24. Marie-Ange Schiltz, data from the 1992 survey; see *Les homosexuels masculins face au sida, enquêtes 1991–1992* (1993). Given the survey's bias, these figures should be considered only as indications of general trends.

25. Daniel Defert, "L'homosexualisation du sida," opinion piece published in *Gai Pied Hebdo*, Nov. 29, 1990.

26. Marie-Ange Schiltz, *Les homosexuels masculins face au sida*.

27. Michael Pollak, "Histoire d'une cause."

28. Daniel Defert, "L'homosexualisation du sida."

29. The French term *relaps* is borrowed from religious vocabulary and means a falling back into heresy, after recanting.

30. Marie-Ange Schiltz, *Les homosexuels masculins face au sida*. On the phenomenon of relapse, see especially Hubert Lisandre, *Les homosexuels et le safer sex: Contributions psychanalytiques à la prévention du sida* (mimeographed document, 1994), and Michael Warner's article in the *Journal du Sida* (Apr. 1995), especially the section titled "Les ratés de la prévention."

31. In the Schiltz surveys, conducted from 1991 to 1992, between 20 and 37 percent of the homosexuals who were queried reported not knowing anyone infected with HIV; see Schiltz, *Les homosexuels masculins face au sida*.

32. Marie-Ange Schiltz, "N'importe qui ne drague pas n'importe où," *Actes du Colloque Terrains d'Entente* (mimeographed document, June 1994).

33. In 1993, 30 percent of the homosexuals surveyed who used condoms had experienced a rupture, and 16 percent had experienced the slippage of a condom. These accidents often appear to result from insufficient lubrication; in fact, nearly 38 percent of Schiltz's homosexual respondents who used condoms reported that they did not apply a lubricant.

34. See Franck Arnal, "L'adolescent homosexuel: L'oublié des politiques de prévention du sida," *Sociétés* 39 (1993).

35. Crack is cocaine, usually in the form of small rocks, that is smoked (burned and rapidly inhaled) or sometimes injected (hence there is an added risk of infection). The use of heroin as a tranquilizer is sometimes necessary to calm the overexcitement and psychological stimulation of crack. Naturally, this becomes a vicious circle.

36. Scraps of conversation collected by the author in monitored calls at Sida Infos Service in Paris and in the provinces. Reports by operators, published by Sida Infos Service, are equally revealing.

37. Bernard-Marie Koltès, interview with *Gai Pied Hebdo*, Feb. 19, 1983; for works by Koltès, see the bibliography.

38. The situation is all the more heartbreaking when France is compared to Great Britain: there are more cases of AIDS in the Paris region than in Great Britain as a whole. On June 30, 1995, France had 37,000 total cases, 17,200 of them among homosexuals/bisexuals and 17,369 of them reported in Ile-de-France. On the same date, the United Kingdom had 11,051 cases, a total that included 7,923 cases among homosexuals/bisexuals.

39. In addition to prevention, the future course of the epidemic will depend on the prospect of a cure. Since the third international conference on retroviruses, held in Washington, D.C., on January 29, 1996, it has been possible to view the future more optimistically, given the prospect that medical research may develop effective treatments. The effectiveness of a therapeutic approach consisting of several combined antiviral substances (the "cocktail" concept), including protease inhibitors in particular, is now being tested. Even though it is not yet possible to foresee the sequence of events—hope may be followed by disappointment—AIDS "increasingly appears to be a chronic viral disease whose progress can be effectively slowed in the short or medium term" (Jean-Yves Nau, "Les nouveaux traitements du sida prochainement commercialisés en France," *Le Monde*, Feb. 1, 1996). See also *Le Journal du Sida* 83 (March 1996) and *Transcriptase* 42 (Feb. 1996).

CHAPTER 16: THE IDENTITY MOVEMENT

1. AIDS organizations are not in themselves the subject of this book; therefore, I will not discuss the question of their funding. Nevertheless, these organizations—opportunely—enjoy large budgets today (from the state, local collectives, and the Ensemble contre le sida/Sidaction). Some public leaders occasionally raise doubts about the use of these funds. After the difficulties of Gais pour les Libertés [Gays for freedom], or in conjunction with the AIDS-related complex (ARC) scandal, the fight against AIDS as a whole could be damaged in the future should new "scandals" emerge in the months or years to come.

2. Another hypothesis about the appearance of the virus has been developed by Luc Montagnier, who links the origin of the illness to specifically homosexual cofactors and especially to families of mycoplasmas found in the rectum and intestinal tract; see Luc Montagnier, Des virus et des hommes (Odile Jacob, 1994).

3. Concluding speech, Aides conference in Lyons, 1993.

4. Libération, Oct. 5, 1991.

5. Since its creation, the ratio of Aides volunteers to AIDS cases has remained nearly constant, about 1:10 (37 volunteers for 347 cases in 1985; 3,600 volunteers for 37,000 cases in 1995).

6. On these political errors during the two Socialist terms, see chap. 10 for the Fabius–Dufoix–Hervé era and chap. 14 for the Durieux–Kouchner era.

7. The only hemophiliac in Aides whom Michael Pollak interviewed in 1989 was homosexual. In 1993, 1 percent of volunteers were drug users (3 percent were former users).

8. This shift was also noticeable in Arcat-sida, which produced its first pamphlet for homosexuals in April 1990 ("Ils en parlent, parlez-en," by Jean Le Bitoux). AIDS prevention among gays was promoted at the Agence Française de Lutte contre le Sida (Mark Anguenot-Franchequin) and even at Paris's city hall (Stéphane Mantion).

9. In 1993, more than half (52 percent) of Aides volunteers were homosexual, and men have always been in the majority (90 percent male until 1986, 65 percent in 1987, 57 percent in 1993). This overrepresentation of men distinguishes Aides from other humanitarian associations or organizations. In addition, 13 percent of volunteers were HIV-positive or had AIDS; see Marie-Ange Schiltz, Les homosexuels masculins face au sida.

10. The red ribbon [worn in solidarity with people who had AIDS] initially may have served the same purpose and been a sign of recognition.

11. For example, Alain Navaud's group, and then Martine Jalta-Riehm's, in Strasbourg (created in late 1990); Thierry Ruiz's, in Marseilles; Serge Mathurin and Claude Weber's, in Nice; For'hommes, in Bordeaux (created in September 1991); and Gilles Manas's group, Nuit Blanche, in Lyons.

12. Despite some largely inconsequential efforts by the Agence Française de Lutte contre le Sida ("Hommes entre eux," "Concours des damiers"), it was not until November 30, 1995, that a "responsibility charter" was established among homosexual establishments, the Syndicat National des Entreprises Gaies [National union of gay businesses], or SNEG, and Aides and ACT UP. Responsiblity for prevention in commercial spots is a contractual part of this charter.

13. It is equally revealing that some gay organizations were created from the Aides PMGs (for example, Homonyme, in Nancy, and For'hommes, in Bordeaux, which initially formed within Aides and gradually became autonomous).

14. Michael Pollak, "Histoire d'une cause."

15. Only 12 percent of female Aides volunteers in 1993 reported being lesbians.

16. Brigitte Lhomond, "Lesbiennes, un risque moins sexuel que social," *Journal du Sida*, Oct. 1992. Nevertheless, around 1985 some lesbians were not allowed to donate blood.

17. [By 1996, the date of this book's publication in France,] two cases of HIV transmission between women had been documented. This mode of transmission is thus "extremely rare." As for the reported 79 lesbians and 103 bisexual women infected with AIDS in the United States, 95 percent were infected through drug injection or through a bisexual relationship with a man who had HIV. On existing studies [at the time of this book's original publication], see *Transcriptase* (Oct. 1992).

18. A dental dam is a piece of latex used by dentists, which some lesbians recommended as an oral-genital prophylactic.

19. The "radical lesbians" who left the *Questions Féministes* collective in 1980 have resurfaced and published a brochure titled *Les lesbiennes et le sida* (ALS/CLEF/*Lesbia*, June 1989).

20. PILES is the lesbian group for prevention within Aides, which originated in Pin'Aides. Even though it is a mixed-sex group, it has in essence brought about the return of lesbian militancy.

21. On the scientific discussion of these questions, see the "Sida et femmes" section of the *Journal du Sida*, March 1993.

22. Eric Fassin, "Le féminisme au miroir transatlantique" (*Esprit*, Nov. 1993). Pascal Bruckner has given a good analysis of the changes that feminism is currently undergoing in *La tentation de l'innocence* (Grasset, 1995).

23. On November 25, 1995, a mixed-sex group of nearly 30,000 people (most of them women) and a delegation from Aides marched in the streets of Paris, at the initiative of the Coordination Nationale des Associations pour le Droit à l'Avortement et à la Contraception [National consortium of organizations for abortion and contraceptive rights], or CADAC. Was this the rebirth or feminism, or was it a memorial?

24. In the United States, the issue of rape has remained central to the feminist struggle. Thus, in recent years, the attorney Catharine MacKinnon has reconceptualized sexual harassment, assimilating heterosexual sex to rape.

25. Two groups housed at the Maison des Femmes have since formed: the Collectif Lesbien et Féministe de Solidarité aux Femmes de l'ex-Yougoslavie [Lesbian and feminist collective for solidarity with the women of the former Yugoslavia] and the Association de Solidarité Féministe avec les Femmes de l'ex-Yougoslavie [Organization for feminist solidarity with the women of the former Yugoslavia]. The Gemellières, an organization in Evreux, has also brought together about forty lesbians against rape in Bosnia.

26. This legitimate solidarity with Bosnian women has sometimes led to a misleading interpretation of the conflict in the former Yugoslavia: ethnic cleansing and the Serbian war of conquest disappear in favor of men's assault on women. See Frédéric Martel, "Pour servir à l'histoire de notre défaite: L'élite intellectuelle et morale française et la guerre en ex-Yougoslavie," in *Le messager européen* (Gallimard, 1994).

27. Pierre and Gilles, *Le triangle rose* (Laurent, 1993).

28. On this question, see chap. 14.

29. Letter from Pierre Eudes, general secretary of UNADIF, to the organization called Mémorial de la Déportation Homosexuelle, Apr. 15, 1994.

30. Despite the fact that the presence of homosexual deportees was documented in most of the concentration camps, eyewitness accounts are rare. Since homosexuality is particularly unspeakable, witnesses have not declared themselves, and calls for eyewitness accounts have yielded no results.

31. For example, we know little about homosexuals who were deported for political or racial reasons and who were identified as homosexuals only after they reached the camps. There is one account, however, by Aimé Spitz, an "NN"—*Nacht und Nebel*, night and fog—resistance fighter deported to Struthof. He was homosexual and describes the brutality that the French "pink triangles" endured in the camps. See *Gai Pied*, May 1980.

32. Richard Plant, *The Pink Triangle: The Nazi War Against Homosexuals* (Holt, 1986); see the review in *Holocaust and Genocide Studies* 2:2 (1987). See also François Bédarida, *Le nazisme et le génocide* (Nathan, 1989); François Bédarida, ed., *La politique nazie d'extermination* (Albin Michel, 1989), especially the article by Michael Pollak; Eric Conan and Henry Rousso, *Vichy, un passé qui ne passe pas* (Fayard, 1994); Franck Rector, *The Nazi Extermination of Homosexuals* (Stein & Day, 1980).

33. Certain speeches by Hitler (July 13, 1934, the speech justifying the Night of Long Knives on the basis of the "perversions" of Ernst Röhm and the SA), Himmler (Feb. 18, 1937), and Goebbels (Jan. 26, 1938, and Nov. 16, 1940) leave no doubt on this point. See Richard Plant, *The Pink Triangle*; Jean Boisson, *Le triangle rose: La déportation des homosexuels* (Robert Laffont, 1988).

34. This range is proposed by Richard Plant (*The Pink Triangle*), in agreement, he says, with three of the most distinguished U.S. gay scholars. Others make estimates—between 50,000 and 200,000—that are very open to debate. Simone Veil found the latter figures "too high" (interview in *Gai Pied*, March 8, 1986). Frank Rector estimates the figure at 220,000 deported homosexuals, and other gay militants give the unreasonable figure of one million (Jean Boisson, *Le triangle rose*). Thus the estimates fluctuate wildly.

35. Although homosexuals, unlike Jews, were not persecuted or rounded up under the Vichy government, Marshal Pétain did adopt an ordinance that limited the rights of homosexuals (Aug. 6, 1942); it became article 331–3 of the penal code (see chap. 7).

36. For example, a homosexual was the *Lagerälteste* (camp leader) of Birkenau for several months.

37. Heinz Heger, *Les hommes au triangle rose, journal d'un déporté homosexuel* (Persona, 1981).

38. Do we need to be reminded that Simone Veil was eighteen years old when she was deported to Ravensbrück? She was never a Kapo.

39. Alain Finkielkraut, *L'avenir d'une négation* (Seuil, 1982).

40. On April 30, 1995, for the first time, an official delegation sent by homosexual organizations (including, notably, the Socialist deputy Daniel Vaillant and Dominique Voynet) was allowed to place a spray of flowers.

41. Stéphane Trana, political editor of the weekly *Tribune Juive* (*Libération*, Sept. 29, 1994).

42. Pierre Seel, interned in the "security camp" of Schirmeck-Vorbrück, near Mulhouse, had just been granted the status of political deportee; see *Moi, Pierre Seel, déporté homosexuel* (Calmann-Lévy, 1994, with notes collated by Jean Le Bitoux). The remarks quoted here, however, are excerpted from a disturbing interview that Seel gave to the far-right newspaper *Minute* (Apr. 26, 1995).

43. An argument made during the Etats Généraux Homosexualité et Sida, Apr. 8–9, 1995.

44. My thanks to the historians Denis Peschanski and Henry Rousso of the Institut d'Histoire du Temps Présent for providing information and reviewing the section of this book that deals with the homosexual deportation. Thanks as well to Eric Conan for his attentive rereading and to François Furet and Jean-Noël Jeanneney for their advice.

45. Yves Roussel has given a good analysis of the phases of this movement in "Le mouvement homosexual français face aux stratégies identitaires," *Les Temps Modernes*, May–June 1995.

46. "Un nouveau réformateur social: Le malade," *Libération*, Aug. 15, 1989.

47. There has been only one judgment from the Council of State; it had to do with a homosexual deputy police sergeant who was cited for harboring a runaway minor (decree of June 13, 1990). The only deliberation of the Commission National Informatique et Libertés [National computer and freedom commission] (case no. 93-064), according to Jacques Fauvet, its president, involved a claim against the company UNI-Europe. But, in a judgment of July 25, 1995, the criminal court of Belfort became the first to recognize the existence of lesbian couples and awarded damages and interest from the insurance company Groupama Assurances to a surviving lesbian partner.

48. Jan-Paul Pouliquen has given a moving account of his battle to bring this project to completion: "Contrat d'union civile—le dossier," *Humœurs* special issue (Feb. 1994).

49. Elisabeth Badinter, "Union civile: Le courage est payant," interviewed in *Libération*, Apr. 23, 1992.

50. Willy Rozenbaum and Jean-Baptiste Brunet, *Rapport au président de l'Assemblé nationale*. Daniel Defert (Aides), Franck Arnal (*Gai Pied*), and Dominique Charvet (Agence Française de Lutte contre le Sida) expressed similar views.

51. The bill was also poorly worded, with superfluous provisions that covertly reintroduced elements of self-discrimination—for example, the provision regarding parental authority (article 10), already guaranteed by the law on domestic partnership; the application of the CUC to "brothers" or "elderly women"; and the possibility of unilateral voiding of the contract (article 8), which reintroduced repudiation, unacceptable under French law. More generally, homosexuals' need for a "contract" endorsed by the civil state is a notion that remains problematic.

52. For the most part, this amendment, the only one adopted, seems to have benefited heterosexual couples in marginal situations, proof that the bill does not apply solely to gays.

53. Second session of Nov. 29, 1995.

54. In the tradition of the CUC, in June 1995 the legal group of the Aides federation introduced a bill called "Contrat de vie sociale" [social life contract], or CVS, whose aim was to give legal standing to unmarried couples. Since then, both the CUC and the CVS have been combined under a new name, the "contrat d'union sociale" [social union contract], or CUS, which has earned the support of ACT UP–Paris. On September 13, 1995, the mayor of Saint-Nazaire—a member of the Mouvement des citoyens [citizens' movement], or MDC—decided to issue "certificates of life partnership" to homosexual couples. He was immediately seconded by other mayors in the MDC, and then by the six Socialist mayors of Paris arrondissements and by several Socialist mayors in other large cities (Catherine Trautman in Strasbourg, Bernard Poignant in Quimper, Georges Frêche in Montpellier, and Pierre Mauroy in Lille).

55. The head for this section is taken from the title of an article in the official newspaper for Gay Pride Day (*Pride*, June 1995).

56. Subsidies from the Ministry of Health or Sidaction (Ensemble contre le Sida [Group against AIDS]) may have played a role in breathing life into these groups.

57. The birth of the CGL was made possible by a grant of 570,000 francs from the Ministry of Health and by financial contributions from ACT UP and Gay Pride. Pierre Bergé also backed the center by signing the lease for the center's quarters on rue Keller.

58. Pressure from ACT UP was decisive in creating the CGL. Philippe Labbey, director Alix Meuner, and coordinator Anne Rousseau are all former ACT UP leaders. Moreover, the "political funeral" of Cleews Vellay, the late president of ACT UP, took place at the CGL in October 1994.

59. From time to time the CGL performs symbolic "marriages" (called "secular civil unions"), which appear on the center's registry and may be accompanied by a notice published in *Libération*. The first of these occurred on March 25, 1995.

60. This expression, which may serve to symbolize AIDS denial pushed to the extreme, is the charming title of a still-famous editorial by David Girard (*GI* 2, 1984).

61. AIDS was not an object of protest in Gay Pride parades between 1981 and 1986. The word *sidaïque* [afflicted with AIDS] did appear in 1987, less as part of the fight against AIDS than as a rejection of the homophobia championed by Jean-Marie Le Pen. The fight against AIDS was still not an object of protest on Gay Pride Day in 1988.

62. This shift from Gay Pride Day to Lesbian/Gay Pride Day is significant, indicating that the identity movement was trying to outdo itself. In the United States, this partitioning philosophy eventually led to Lesbian/Gay/Bisexual/Transgender Pride Day.

63. By the time the Beurs demonstration of December 3, 1983, was over, 60,000 people had marched through Paris. Two years later, on June 15, 1985, 300,000 would gather at the Place de la Concorde for the "buddies festival" with SOS-Racisme.

64. [The Rainbow Flag, designed in 1978 by Gilbert Baker, a San Francisco artist, was first used in the 1979 San Francisco Gay Pride Parade and is felt to offer a more colorful and optimistic alternative to the pink triangle, reappropriated by ACT UP in the 1980s.— Trans.] It has all but replaced the Greek letter *lambda*, a gay symbol since Stonewall. Its appearance in France dates from 1992–93.

65. The aim of *Têtu* was to accompany the birth of a homosexual community. Its collapse in 1995, less than five months after it was launched amid much so much brouhaha, may have been a demonstration of the fragility of French-style communitarianism.

66. The organization of people with AIDS who had been infected by blood transfusions protested *La nuit gay*, Gay Pride Day, and Aides. In a press release of June 21, 1995, the organization denounced "the legalization of homosexual practices, [a legalization that,] by spreading AIDS, is causing the death of so many hemophiliacs and transfusion recipients." It added that Arnaud Marty-Lavauzelle, president of the Aides federation, "is not the spokesperson for people with AIDS in France, even though he may be the spokesperson for homosexuals."

67. An important though controversial article (coauthored, notably, by Mathieu Verboud, Roland Landman, Pierre Kneip, Emeric Languérand, and Laurent de Villepin) has shed light on the current drifting within the movement; see "Sida: Où vont les associations?" *Le Monde*, Dec. 1, 1995.

68. This is naturally true of the gay businesses that come to advertise, but also of the group that organizes Gay Pride Day. It registered its name as a commercial trademark, a step that caused a spirited debate with ACT UP ("You're nothing but little bureaucrats of homosexuality," the president of ACT UP wrote to the organizers of Gay Pride Day in an open letter of June 6, 1995). The act of registering an umbrella term was clearly reminiscent of the appropriation, in October 1979, of the logo and name of the women's movement by the Psychépo camp of the MLF.

EPILOGUE

After the publication of Hannah Arendt's *Eichmann in Jerusalem* and the debates it inspired, Gershom Scholem, an Israeli professor, accused Arendt of being "without love for
the Jewish people." It is to this letter that the Jewish philosopher is responding here
(excerpts published in *Esprit*, June 1985).

CHRONOLOGY

1. To make these figures easier to interpret and compare, I will list the total number of
AIDS cases reported for each year as they are known today (figures from the Centre Européen pour la Surveillance Epidémiologique du Sida [European center for epidemiological information on AIDS]). Because of delays in reporting and changes in how the disease
was defined, these figures do not correspond exactly to those given at the time. At this
writing [1996], France had about 120,000 people living with HIV, among them 20,500 patients who had developed full-blown AIDS. During the first three months of 1998, 1,100 new
cases of AIDS were diagnosed.

Annotated Bibliography

This bibliography is organized thematically and consists of three sections: general nonfiction; journals and newspapers; and literary works.

I have given particular attention to works available and published in France. Literary works are listed only for the post–World War II period (except for a few rare classics); essays, only for the period after 1968.

This bibliography includes only general and specific works on the subject of homosexuality. Complete references for other works cited are given in the notes.

An asterisk next to a title indicates that a work is considered important because it is a fundamental text or a good introduction to the works of an author, or because it is easily available.

Specialized readers may wish to consult a more extensive annotated bibliography; see Frédéric Martel, *Matériaux pour servir à l'histoire des homosexuels en France, chronologies, bibliographies* (Lille: Cahiers GKC, 1996).

GENERAL NONFICTION

Essential Theoretical Works

Beauvoir, Simone de. *Le deuxième sexe.* Gallimard, 1949. 2 vols.*

Deleuze, Gilles. "Lettre à un critique sévère." In *Pourparlers.* Minuit, 1990.* Letter to Michel Cressole. An essential text on the relationship between Deleuze and the FHAR.

Deleuze, Gilles, and Guattari, Félix. *L'anti-Oedipe: Capitalisme et schizophrenie.* Minuit, 1972.

Foucault, Michel. *Histoire de la sexualité.* Vol. 1: *La volonté de savoir.* Gallimard, 1976.* Vol. 2: *L'usage des plaisirs.* Gallimard, 1984. Vol. 3: *Le souci de soi.* Gallimard, 1984.

———. *Dits et écrits, 1954–1988.* Gallimard, 1994. 4 vols. Collection of nearly three hundred articles by Foucault, about thirty mentioning homosexuality.* See also biographies of Foucault by Didier Eribon (*Michel Foucault,* Flammarion, 1989) and David Macey (*The Lives of Michel Foucault: A Biography,* Pantheon Books, 1993).

General History

Amour et sexualité en Occident. Special issue of the journal *La recherche.* Reprinted by Seuil, 1991. (Introduction by Georges Duby.)

Ariès, Philippe, and Duby, Georges. *Histoire de la vie privée.* Vol. 5 (1914 to the present). Antoine Prost and Gérard Vincent, eds. Seuil, 1987.

Boswell, John. *Christianity, Social Tolerance, and Homosexuality: Gay People in Western Europe from the Beginnings of the Christian Era to the Fourteenth Century.* University of Chicago Press, 1980.*

Dover, Kenneth. *Greek Homosexuality.* Harvard University Press, 1978.

Histoire des femmes en Occident. Georges Duby and Michelle Perrot, eds. Vol. 5 (twentieth century). Françoise Thébaud, ed. Plon, 1992.

Lever, Maurice. *Les Bûchers de Sodome.* Fayard, 1985. On homosexuality from early Christianity to the contemporary era.

Plant, Richard. *The Pink Triangle: The Nazi War Against Homosexuals.* Holt, 1986. A fundamental text on the deportation of homosexuals during World War II.

Sexualités occidentales. Philippe Ariès and André Bejin, eds. Special issue of *Communications.* Reprinted by Seuil, 1982.

Thompson, Mark, ed. *Long Road to Freedom: The Advocate History of the Gay and Lesbian Movement.* St. Martin's Press, 1994. Detailed history of the American gay movement.

History of Sexual Liberation in France

Finkielkraut, Alain, and Bruckner, Pascal. *Le nouveau désordre amoureux.* Seuil, 1977.

Hamon, Hervé, and Rotman, Patrick. *Génération, les années de poudre.* Vol. 2. Seuil, 1988.

Mossuz-Lavau, Janine. *Les lois de l'amour.* Payot, 1991. History of sexual politics in France: contraception, abortion, rape, homosexuality.*

Statistical Data on Homosexuality

Bon, Michel, and Arc, Antoine d'. *Rapport sur l'homosexualité de l'homme.* Editions Universitaires, 1974. Arcadie survey.

Cavailhes, Jean, Dutey, Pierre, and Bach-Ignasse, Gérard. *Rapport gai, enquête sur les modes de vie homosexuels.* Persona, 1984. Comité d'Urgence Anti-Répression Homosexuelle survey.

Kinsey, Alfred C. *Sexual Behavior in the Human Male.* W. B. Saunders, 1948.

Simon, Pierre, ed. *Rapport sur le comportement sexuel des Français.* Julliard, 1972.

Spira, Alfred, and Bajos, Nathalie. *Les comportements sexuels en France.* La Documentation Française, 1993. The "homo/bisexual" subsample of this survey is examined in a fundamental article: Antoine Messiah and Emmanuelle Mouret-Fourme, "Homosexualité, bisexualité: Eléments de socio-biographie sexuelle," *Population* 48 (Sept.–Oct. 1993).*

Works by Homosexual Activists

Baudry, André, and Daniel, Marc. *Les homosexuels.* Casterman, 1973.

Eaubonne, Françoise d'. *Eros minoritaire.* Balland, 1970.

Front Homosexuel d'Action Révolutionnaire FHAR. *Rapport contre la normalité.* Champ libre, 1972. Texts by Françoise d'Eaubonne, Pierre Hahn, and Guy Hocquenghem.*

Girard, Jacques. *Le mouvement homosexuel en France.* Syros, 1981.

Guérin, Daniel. *Autobiographie de jeunesse: D'une dissidence sexuelle au socialisme.* Belfond, 1971.

———. *Le feu du sang.* Grasset, 1977.

———. *Son testament.* Encre, 1978.

Hahn, Pierre. *Français, encore un effort: L'homosexualité et sa répression.* Martineau, 1970. Collection of texts.

———. *Nos ancêtres les pervers: La vie des homosexuels sous le Second Empire.* Olivier Orban, 1979.

Hocquenghem, Guy. *Le désir homosexuel.* Editions universitaires, 1972.

———. *L'après-mai des faunes.* Grasset, 1974. Collection of articles.

———. *Comment nous appelez-vous déja?* Calmann-Lévy, 1977. In collaboration with Jean-Louis Bory.*

————. *La dérive homosexuelle.* Delarge, 1977. Collection of articles.*

————. *La beauté du métis: Réflexions d'un francophobe.* Ramsay, 1979.

————. *Race d'Ep, un siècle d'images de l'homosexualité.* Hallier, 1979. In collaboration with Lionel Soucaz.

————. *Le gay voyage.* Albin Michel, 1980.

————. *Lettre ouverte à ceux qui sont passés du col Mao au Rotary.* Albin Michel, 1986.

————. *L'amphithéâtre des morts.* Gallimard, Digraphe, 1994. An early autobiography published posthumously. Preface by Roland Surzur. Afterword by René Schérer. See also "Présence de Guy Hocquenghem," special issue of *Cahiers de l'Imaginaire* (1992).

Pastre, Geneviève. *L'espace du souffle.* Christian Bourgois, 1977.

————. *De l'amour lesbien.* Horay, 1980.

————. *Athènes ou le péril saphique.* Les Octaviennes, 1987.

History of the Women's Movement in France

Bernheim, Cathy. *Perturbation ma soeur: Naissance d'un mouvement de femmes.* Seuil, 1983. Personal account.

Centre Lyonnais d'Etudes Féministes. *CLEF: Chronique d'une passion, le mouvement de libération des femmes à Lyon.* L'Harmattan, 1989.

Le Brun, Annie. *Lâchez tout.* Sagittaire, 1977. An essay critical of French feminists.

————. *Vagit-prop.* Ramsay, 1990.

Les femmes s'affichent. Syros, 1984. Collective work.

Picq, Françoise. *Libération des femmes, les années mouvement.* Seuil, 1993. The most serious history of the MLF.*

Rémy, Monique. *De l'utopie à l'intégration: Histoire des mouvements de femmes.* L'Harmattan, 1990.

Tristan (Zelensky), Anne, and Pisan, Annie de. *Histoires du MLF.* Calmann-Lévy, 1977. Preface by Simone de Beauvoir. Personal accounts.

Cultural Essays

Aron, Jean-Paul. *Le pénis et la démoralisation de l'Occident.* Grasset, 1978. With Roger Kempf.

————. *Les modernes.* Gallimard, 1984.

Benstock, Shari. *Women of the Left Bank: Paris, 1900–1940.* University of Texas Press, 1986. On the major sapphic figures.

Courouve, Claude. *Vocabulaire de l'homosexualité masculine.* Payot, 1985.

Fernandez, Dominique. *Le rapt de Ganymède.* Grasset, 1989.*

————. *L'arbre jusqu'aux racines.* Grasset, 1972.

————. *Eisenstein.* Grasset, 1975.

Galey, Matthieu. *Journal.* 2 vols. Grasset, 1987 and 1989.

Klaitch, Dolorès. *Femme et femme: Attitudes envers l'homosexualité.* Editions des Femmes, 1976.

Mayer, Hans. *Les marginaux: Femmes, Juifs et homosexuels dans la littérature européenne* (1975). Reprinted by Albin Michel, 1994.*

Philbert, Bertrand. *L'homosexualité au cinéma.* Veyrier, 1984.

Povert, Lionel. *Dictionnaire gay.* Grancher, 1994.

Women's Sexuality and Lesbian Love

Bonnet, Marie-Jo. *Un choix sans équivoque.* Denoël-Gonthier, 1981. Reprinted by Odile Jacob, 1995 (under the title *Les relations amoureuses entre femmes*).

Faludi, Susan. *Backlash: The Undeclared War Against American Women.* Crown, 1991. Critical overview of antifeminist myths of the 1980s in the United States.

Le Garrec, Evelyne. *Un lit à soi.* Seuil, 1979.

―――. *Des femmes qui s'aiment.* Seuil, 1984.

Hite, Shere. *The Hite Report: A Nationwide Study of Female Sexuality.* Dell, 1981.

―――. *The Hite Report on Male Sexuality.* Knopf, 1981.

―――. *The Hite Report. Women and Love: A Cultural Revolution in Progress.* Knopf, 1987.

Irigaray, Luce. *Speculum de l'autre femme.* Minuit, 1974.

―――. *Ce sexe qui n'en est pas un.* Minuit, 1977.

―――. *Amante marine.* Minuit, 1980.

―――. *Sexes et parentés.* Minuit, 1987.

―――. *Le temps de la différence.* Hachette, 1989.

Millett, Kate. *Sexual Politics.* Doubleday, 1970.

―――. *Flying.* Knopf, 1974. Autobiography.

Nobili, Nella, and Zha, Edith. *Les femmes et l'amour homosexuel.* Hachette, 1979.

Tristan (Zelensky), Anne. *Histoires d'amour, le cabinet de Barbe-Bleue.* Calmann-Lévy, 1979. Personal account.

Homosexuality and Religion

Drewermann, Eugen. *Fonctionnaires de Dieu.* Albin Michel, 1993.

McNeill, John J. *The Church and the Homosexual.* Beacon, 1993.

Oraison, Abbot Marc. *La question homosexuelle.* Seuil, 1975. A dated but valuable book.

Thevenot, Xavier. *Homosexualité masculine et morale chrétienne.* Le Cerf, 1985.

Homosexuality and AIDS

Michael Pollak's original analyses on these subjects are essential reading.

Pollak, Michael, et al., eds. "Homosexualités et sida," *Cahiers GKC* (1991).

Pollak, Michael. "Les vertus de la banalité," *Le Débat* (March 1981).*

―――. *Homosexualité masculine ou le bonheur dans le ghetto?, Communications* 35. Reprinted by Seuil, 1982 (in *Sexualités occidentales*).*

―――. *Les homosexuels et le sida: Sociologie d'une épidemie.* A. M. Métailié, 1988. A fundamental work.*

―――. *Une identité blessée.* A. M. Métailié, 1993. Collection of Pollak's principal articles.*

―――. "Histoire d'une cause." In *L'homme contaminé.* Autrement, 1991.* Another version was published in *Politix* (Autumn 1991).

―――. "Une identité inclassable," *Sociétés* 17.

―――. "Identité sociale et gestion d'un risque de santé: Les homosexuels face au sida," *Actes de la Recherche en Sciences Sociales* (June 1987).

AIDS Prevention

Assemblée Nationale. *Rapport de la Commission d'enquête sur l'état des connaissances scientifiques et les actions menées à l'égard de la transmission du sida.* Report to the president of the National Assembly, submitted Feb. 4, 1993.

Favre, Pierre. *Sida et politique, les premiers affrontements, 1981–1987.* L'Harmattan, 1992.

Garfield, Simon. *The End of Innocence: Britain in the Time of AIDS*. London, 1994.

Grmek, Mirko. *Histoire du sida*. Payot, 1989.

Schiltz, Marie-Ange. *Les homosexuels masculins face au sida, enquêtes 1991–1992*. Report of the Centre National de la Recherche Scientifique–Ecole des Hautes Etudes en Sciences Sociales, Dec. 1993.

Setbon, Michel. *Pouvoirs contre sida*. Seuil, 1993. Comparative study of France, Great Britain, and Sweden.*

Seytre, Bernard. *Les secrets d'une polémique*. PUF, 1993. History of the beginning of AIDS and the discovery of the virus.

History of AIDS Organizations

ACT UP–Paris. *Le sida, combien de divisions?* Dagorno, 1994.

Defert, Daniel. "Aides, nous ne sommes pas Act Up," *Gai Pied Hebdo*, Nov. 24, 1988.

———. "L'homosexualisation du sida," *Gai Pied Hebdo*, Nov. 20, 1990.

———. "Le malade du sida, réformateur social," *Esprit*, July 1994. Interview with Frédéric Martel.

———. "Plus on est honteux, plus on avoue," *Libération*, Oct. 31, 1987.

———. "Un nouveau réformateur social: Le malade." *Actes/Les Cahiers d'Action Juridique* 71–72 (1990).

Hirsch, Emmanuel. *Aides solidaires*. Le Cerf, 1991.*

Kramer, Larry. *Reports from the Holocaust: The Making of an AIDS Activist*. St. Martin's Press, 1989.

Martet, Christophe. *Les combattants du sida*. Flammarion, 1993. Study of ACT UP.

Shilts, Randy. *And the Band Played On: Politics, People and the AIDS Epidemic*. St. Martin's Press, 1987.*

Personal Accounts Concerning AIDS

Arnal, Franck. *Résister ou disparaître? Les homosexuels face au sida*. L'Harmattan, 1993. Militant essay.

Aron, Jean-Paul. *Mon sida*. Christian Bourgois, 1988.

Epkin, Pierre (Pierre Kneip). *Les années sida racontées par ceux qui vivent la maladie au quotidien*. Mimeographed installments of Pierre Epkin's (Pierre Kneip's) column in *Gai Pied Hebdo*.

Marsan, Hugo. *La vie blessée: Sida, l'ère du soupçon*. Maren-Sell, 1989. Personal account.

JOURNALS AND NEWSPAPERS
(ARRANGED CHRONOLOGICALLY)

Arcadie. Literary and scientific journal. 342 issues between 1954 and 1982. André Baudry.

Tout! Journal of Vive la Révolution. 16 issues between Sept. 23, 1970, and July 29, 1971. Jean-Paul Sartre.

Partisans. Bimonthly edited by François Maspero. 68 issues; folded in 1972. See "Libération des femmes: Année zéro," July-Oct. 1970.

Le Torchon Brûle. 6 issues between May 1971 and May 1973. "Menstruel" of the Mouvement de Libération des Femmes.

Recherches. "Comprehensive encyclopedia of the homosexualities." Félix Guattari. (See the historic issue "Trois milliards de pervers," March 1973.*)

Le Fléau Social. 4 issues in 1972. Mimeographed journal of Group 5 of the Front Homosexuel d'Action Révolutionnaire. Situationist in inspiration.

L'Antinorm. 1972–74. Mimeographed journal of Group 11 of the Front Homosexuel d'Action Révolutionnaire. First leftist, then Trotskyist in inspiration.

Les Cahiers du Grif. 24 issues between 1973 and 1978; resumed publication in 1982. Francophone feminist review created in Belgium and published three times a year. Françoise Collin. (See the special issue "Femmes entre elles, Lesbianisme," Apr. 1978.)

Agence Tasse. 35 issues between 1976 and 1979. Journal associated with the Groupes de Libération Homosexuelle–14 December. Alain Huet.

Questions Féministes. 8 issues between 1977 and 1980. Simone de Beauvoir, Christine Delphy.

Gaie Presse. 4 issues in 1978. Associated with the Groupes de Libération Homosexuelle–PQ.

Gai Pied. 541 issues between Apr. 1979 and Oct. 1992. A French monthly, then a weekly.

Masques, Revue des Homosexualités. May 1979 to 1986. Coed cultural journal published three times a year. Jean-Pierre Joecker.

Homophonies. 54 issues between Nov. 1980 and May–June 1985. Monthly of the Comité d'Urgence Anti-Répression Homosexuelle.

Magazine. 11 issues published at irregular intervals between 1980 and June 1986. Journal of interviews, erotic news, and photos. Didier Lestrade, Michel Bigot.

Nouvelles Questions Féministes. Published regularly since March 1981. Successor of *Questions Féministes.* Simone de Beauvoir, Christine Delphy.

Samouraï. 1982 to 1986. Monthly.

Vlasta. 4 issues between spring 1983 and 1985. Cultural review created out of split with *Masques.* Suzette Triton.

GI. Created in Nov. 1984. David Girard.

Lesbia. Monthly founded in Dec. 1982 by Christiane Jouve and Catherine Marjollet. Catherine Gonnard.

Gaie France. Created in Nov. 1986. Right-wing pedophiliac review.

Mec Magazine. 6 issues. Journal founded in 1988. Jean Le Bitoux, Audrey Coz.

Illico. Monthly founded by Jacky Fougeray in March 1988. Currently the principal homosexual journal in France. Jean-François Laforgerie.

Idol. Founded by Jacky Fougeray in July 1994. Monthly devoted to the homosexual lifestyle.

Cahiers Gai Kitsch Camp. Published in Lille since 1989. Historical review of the gay sensibility. Patrick Cardon.

Humoeurs. Review founded in May 1993 in conjunction with the legislative bill for the civil union contract. Gérard Bach, Jan-Paul Pouliquen.

3 Keller. Journal of the Centre Gai et Lesbien.

Têtu. 3 issues between June and Oct. 1995; resumed publication in May 1996. Homosexual monthly. Pierre Bergé, Didier Lestrade.

Journal du Sida. Monthly created in Dec. 1988 and published by Arcat-sida. Medical, social, ethical, and political aspects of the AIDS epidemic. Frédéric Edelmann, Laurent de Villepin.

Transcriptase. Review giving an international overview of AIDS. Didier Jayle, Gilles Pialoux.

Plus Infos, Remaides, Le Volontaire. Three publications of Aides.

Action. Monthly newsletter of ACT UP–Paris.

LITERARY WORKS

Arenas, Reinaldo. *Arturo, la estrella más brillante*. Montesinos, 1984.

———. *Before Night Falls*. Viking, 1993. Autobiography.

Audry, Colette. *La statue*. Gallimard, 1983.

Augieras, François. *Le vieillard et l'enfant* (1947). Reprinted by Minuit, 1963.

———. *L'apprenti sorcier*. Julliard, 1964. Reprinted by Grasset, 1996.

Baldwin, James. *Giovanni's Room*. Dial, 1956.

Barbarant, Olivier. *Douze lettres d'amour au soldat inconnu*. Champ Vallon, 1993.

Barnes, Djuna. *Ladies Almanack* (1928). New York University Press, 1992.

———. *Nightwood*. New Directions, 1937.

Barney, Natalie C. *Quelques portraits*. 1900.

———. *Cinq petits dialogues grecs*. 1901.

———. *Eparpillements* (1910). Persona, 1982.

———. *Pensées d'une amazone*. Mercure de France, 1939. Reprinted by Ivrea, 1996.

———. *Traits et portraits*. Mercure de France, 1963.

———. *Aventures de l'esprit* (1929). Persona, 1983.

———. *Souvenirs indiscrets*. Flammarion, 1960. See also Jean Chalon, *Portrait d'une séductrice* (Stock, 1976), republished by Flammarion, 1992 (under the title *Chère Natalie Barney*); Michèle Causse, *Berthe ou un demi-siècle auprès de l'amazone* (Tierce, 1980).

Barthes, Roland. *Fragments d'un discours amoureux*. Seuil, 1977.*

Bassani, Giorgio. *Gli occhiali d'oro*. Mondadori, 1970. Beauvoir, Simone de. *L'invitée*. Gallimard, 1943.

———. *Les mandarins*. Gallimard, 1954.

———. *Mémoires d'une jeune fille rangée*. Gallimard, 1958.

———. *La force de l'âge*. Gallimard, 1960.

———. *La force des choses*. Gallimard, 1963.

———. *Journal de guerre*. Gallimard, 1990.

———. *Lettres à Sartre*. 2 vols. Gallimard, 1990. Published posthumously. See also the biography by Deirdre Bair (Fayard, 1991).

Beck, Béatrix. *Léon Morin prêtre*. Gallimard, 1952.

———. *Noli*. Sagittaire, 1978.

Bernheim, Cathy. *Côte d'Azur*. Gallimard, 1989.

———. *L'amour presque parfait*. Felin, 1991.

Best, Mireille. *Les mots de hasard*. Gallimard, 1980.

———. *Hymne aux murènes*. Gallimard, 1986.

———. *Une extrême attention* (1985).

———. *Camille en octobre*. Gallimard, 1988.

———. *Le méchant petit jeune homme*. Gallimard, 1983.

———. *Orphéa trois*. Gallimard, 1991.

———. *Il n'y a pas d'hommes au paradis*. Gallimard, 1995.

Bianciotti, Hector. *Seules les larmes seront comptées*. Grasset, 1989.

———. *Le pas si lent de l'amour*. Grasset, 1995.

Borel, Vincent. *Un ruban noir*. Actes Sud, 1995.

Bory, Jean-Louis. *La peau des zèbres*. Gallimard, 1969.

———. *La moitié d'orange*. Julliard, 1973.

———. *Tous nés d'une femme*. Gallimard, 1976.

———. *Un prix d'excellence*. Gallimard, 1986. Published posthumously.

Bourdin, Christophe. *Le fil*. La Différence, 1994. Novel about AIDS.

Braudeau, Michel. *Le livre de John*. Editions du Seuil, 1992.

Brossard, Nicole. *Amantes*. Quinze, 1980.

———. *Le sens apparent*. Flammarion, 1980.

———. *La lettre aérienne*. Remue–Ménage, 1985.

Burroughs, William. *Naked Lunch* (1959). Grove Press, 1975.

———. *The Soft Machine*. Grove Press, 1968.

———. *Cities of the Red Night* (1971). Holt, Rinehart & Winston, 1981.

———. *The Wild Boys* (1971). Grove Press, 1992.

———. *Queer*. Penguin, 1987.

Busi, Aldo. *Standard Life of a Temporary Pantyhose Salesman*. Faber & Faber, 1990.

Camus, Renaud. *Tricks*. Persona, 1979. Reprinted by POL, 1988. Preface by Roland Barthes.

———. *Notes achriennes*. POL, 1982.

———. *Chroniques achriennes*. POL, 1984. Collection of articles published in *Gai Pied*.

———. *Elegies pour quelques-uns*. POL, 1988.

Causse, Michèle. *L'encontre*. Editions des Femmes, 1975.

———. *Voyages de la grande naine en Androssie*. Trois, 1993.

Cavafy, Constantin. *The Complete Poems of Constantin Cavafy*. Hogarth, 1961.

Ceccatty, René de. *L'accompagnement*. Gallimard, 1994.

Chéreau, Patrice, and Guibert, Hervé. *L'homme blessé, scénario et notes*. Minuit, 1983.

Cixous, Hélène. *Dedans*. Editions des Femmes, 1969. Winner of the Prix Médicis.

———. *Souffles*. Editions des Femmes, 1975.

———. *La ville parjure ou le réveil des Erinyes* (1994). Theatrical piece on the contaminated-blood scandal.

Cocteau, Jean. *Le livre blanc*. Published anonymously in 1927, republished with drawings in 1930.

———. *La difficulté d'être*. Morihien, 1947. Reprinted by Du Rocher, 1983.

Colette. *Ces plaisirs*. Ferenczi, 1932. Republished by Armes de France, 1941 (under the title *Le pur et l'impur*).

———. *Claudine à l'école* (1900).

———. *Claudine à Paris* (1901).

———. *Aventures quotidiennes* (1924).

———. *La femme cachée* (1924). Short stories. See especially "L'habitude."

———. *Mes apprentissages* (1936).

Collard, Cyril. *Les nuits fauves*. Flammarion, 1989.

Copi. *Théâtre*. 2 vols. Christian Bourgois, 1986. This edition includes most of the plays, such as *L'homosexuel ou la difficulté de s'exprimer*, *Le frigo*, and *Les escaliers du sacré-coeur*.*

———. *Le bal des folles*. Christian Bourgois, 1977. Novel.

———. *La guerre des pédés*. Albin Michel, 1982. Novel.

———. *Virginia Woolf a encore frappé*. Persona, 1983. Short stories.

———. *Une visite inopportune*. Christian Bourgois, 1988. Play about AIDS.*

Crevel, René. *Mon corps et moi* (1926).

———. *La mort difficile* (1927).

Deforges, Régine. *O. m'a dit*. Pauvert, 1975. Interviews with Pauline Réage (Dominique Aury).

———. *Le cahier volé*. Fayard, 1978.

———. *Pour l'amour de Marie Salat*. Albin Michel, 1986.

Detrez, Conrad. *L'herbe à brûler*. Calmann-Lévy, 1978.

———. *Ludo.* Calmann-Lévy (1947). Reprinted by Babel, 1995.

———. *Les plumes du coq.* Calmann-Lévy, 1975. Reprinted by Babel, 1996.

———. *Le dragueur de Dieu.* Calmann-Lévy, 1981.

———. *Les noms de la tribu.* Seuil, 1981.

———. *La mélancholie du voyeur.* Denoël, 1986. Novel about AIDS.

Dognon, André du. *Les amours buissonières.* Scorpion, 1948.

Donner, Christophe. *Les sentiments.* Seuil, 1990.

———. *Giton.* Seuil, 1990.

———. *Lettres de mon petit frère.* Ecole des loisirs, 1991.

Dreuilhe, Emmanuel. *Corps à corps.* Gallimard, 1987. About AIDS.

Duteurtre, Benoît. *Gaieté parisienne.* Gallimard, 1996.

Duve, Pascal de. *Cargo vie.* Lattès, 1992. About AIDS.

Duvert, Tony. *Récidive.* Minuit, 1967.

———. *Paysage de fantaisie.* Minuit, 1972.

———. *Journal d'un innocent.* Minuit, 1976.

———. *Quand mourut Jonathan.* Minuit, 1978.

———. *L'île Atlantique.* Minuit, 1979.

Fernandez, Dominique. *Porporino ou les mystères de Naples.* Grasset, 1974. Winner of the Prix Médicis.

———. *L'étoile rose.* Grasset, 1978.*

———. *Dans la main de l'ange.* Grasset, 1982. Winner of the Prix Goncourt. Fictional autobiography of Pier Paolo Pasolini.

———. *L'amour.* Grasset, 1986.

———. *La gloire du paria.* Grasset, 1987. About AIDS.

———. *Tribunal d'honneur.* Grasset, 1997. About Tchaikovsky.

Forster, E. M. *Maurice.* Norton, 1971.

François, Jocelyne. *Les bonheurs.* Robert Laffont, 1970.

———. *Les amantes.* Mercure de France, 1978.

———. *Joue-nous España.* Mercure de France, 1980. Winner of the Prix Fémina.*

———. *Le sel.* Mercure de France, 1992.

———. *Histoire de Volubilis.* Mercure de France, 1985.

———. *Le cahier vert.* Mercure de France, 1990. Diary.

———. *La femme sans tombe.* Mercure de France, 1995.

Galzy, Jeanne. *La surprise de vivre.* Gallimard, 1969.

Garreta, Anne. *Sphinx.* Grasset, 1986.*

———. *Ciels liquides.* Grasset, 1990.

Genet, Jean. *Notre-Dame-des-Fleurs.* 1946.

———. *Miracle de la rose.* 1947.

———. *Le journal du voleur.* Skira, 1948 (published anonymously). Republished by Gallimard, 1949 (under Genet's name).*

———. *Querelle de Brest.* Gallimard, 1981. See also Jean-Paul Sartre, *Saint Genet, comédien et martyr* (Gallimard, 1952), and the biography by Edmund White.

Gide, André. *Corydon* (1911).

———. *Saül* (1903). Theatrical piece.

———. *L'immoraliste* (1902).

———. *Les caves du Vatican* (1914).

———. *Si le grain ne meurt* (1920).

———. *L'ecole des femmes* (1929).

————. *Amyntas* (1906).

Gomez-Arcos, Agustin. *L'agneau carnivore*. Stock, 1975. Reprinted by Points Seuil, 1985.

Green, Julien. *L'autre sommeil* (1931).

————. *Sud* (1953). Theatrical piece.*

————. *Moïra* (1950).

————. *Le malfaiteur* (1956).

————. *Chaque homme dans sa nuit*. Plon, 1960.* See also Green's *Journal*, 14 vols., and especially his "autobiography," printed under the joint title *Jeunes années, I et II* (Seuil,
1984). Includes *Partir avant le jour* (Grasset, 1963); *Mille chemins ouverts* (Grasset, 1964);
Terre lointaine (Grasset, 1966); and *Jeunesse* (Plon, 1974).

Guersant, Marcel. *Jean Paul*. Minuit, 1953.

Guibert, Hervé. *La mort propagande*. Régine Deforges, 1977.

————. *L'image fantôme*. Minuit, 1981.

————. *Les aventures singulières*. Minuit, 1982.

————. *Les chiens*. Minuit, 1982.

————. *Voyage avec deux enfants*. Minuit, 1982.

————. *Les lubies d'Arthur*. Minuit, 1983.

————. *Des aveugles*. Gallimard, 1985.

————. *Mes parents*. Gallimard, 1986.

————. *Vous m'avez fait former des fantômes*. Gallimard, 1987.

————. *Les gangsters*. Minuit, 1988.

————. *Mauve le vierge*. Gallimard, 1988.

————. *Fou de Vincent*. Minuit, 1989.*

————. *L'incognito*. Gallimard, 1989.

————. *A l'ami qui ne m'a pas sauvé la vie*. Gallimard, 1990.*

————. *Le protocole compassionnel*. Gallimard, 1991.

————. *Mon valet et moi*. Seuil, 1991.

————. *Vice*. Bertoin, 1991.

————. *Cytomégalovirus*. Seuil, 1992. Diary of a hospital stay.

————. *L'homme au chapeau rouge*. Gallimard, 1992.

————. *Le paradis*. Gallimard, 1992.

————. *Vole mon dragon*. Gallimard, 1994.

————. *La piqûre d'amour*. Gallimard, 1994.

Guyotat, Pierre. *Tombeau pour 500,000 soldats*. Gallimard, 1967. Censored.

————. *Eden, eden, eden*. Gallimard, 1970. Censored.

Hall, Radclyffe. *The Well of Loneliness*. Doubleday, 1928, 1990.

Herbart, Pierre. *Alcyon*. Gallimard, 1945. Reprinted by L'Imaginaire, 1980.

————. *A la recherche d'André Gide*. Gallimard, 1952.

————. *L'âge d'or*. Gallimard, 1953. Reprinted by Le Dilettante, 1992.*

Highsmith, Patricia. *The Price of Salt* (1952). Republished by Random House, 1993. (Initially
published under the pseudonym Claire Morgan.)

Hocquenghem, Guy. *L'amour en relief*. Albin Michel, 1981.

————. *Les petits garçons*. Albin Michel, 1983.

————. *La colère de l'agneau*. Albin Michel, 1985.

————. *Eve*. Albin Michel, 1987.

————. *Voyages et aventures extraordinaires de frère Angelo*. Albin Michel, 1988. Published
posthumously.

Hollinghurst, Alan. *Swimming Pool Library*. Random House, 1989.

————. *The Folding Star*. Vintage, 1994.

Isherwood, Christopher. *Christopher and His Kind*. Farrar, Straus & Giroux, 1976.

————. *A Single Man*. Farrar, Straus & Giroux, 1987.

Jamek, Vaclav. *Traité des courtes merveilles*. Grasset, 1989.*

Jarman, Derek. *At Your Own Risk*. Hutchinson, 1992.

Jouhandeau, Marcel. *De l'abjection*. Gallimard, 1939. Initially published anonymously.

————. *Chroniques maritales* (1935).

————. *Ces messieurs*. Lilac, 1951.

————. *Du pur amour*. Gallimard, 1955.

————. *Chronique d'une passion* (1949). Reprinted by Gallimard, 1964.

————. *La vie comme une fête*. Pauvert, 1977.

————. *Pages égarées*. Pauvert, 1980. Erotic short stories, published posthumously.

————. *Ecrits secrets*. Three volumes published anonymously: vol. 1, *Tirésias* (1954); vol. 2, *Carnets de Don Juan*; vol. 3, *Le voyage secret*. Reprinted by Arléa, 1988. See also *Journaliers* (Gallimard), notebooks beginning in 1961.

Koltès, Bernard-Marie. *Combat de nègre et de chiens* (1979). Reprinted by Stock, 1980; Minuit, 1989.

————. *La fuite à cheval très loin dans la ville*. Minuit, 1984.

————. *Quai Ouest*. Minuit, 1985.

————. *Dans la solitude des champs de coton*. Minuit, 1986.*

————. *La nuit juste avant les forêts*. Minuit, 1988.

————. *Le retour au désert*. Minuit, 1988.

————. *Roberto Zucco, suivi de Tabataba*. Minuit, 1990.

————. *Prologue et autres textes*. Minuit, 1991.

————. *Sallinger*. Minuit, 1995.

Kramer, Larry, *Faggots*. Random House, 1978.

————. *The Normal Heart*. New American Library, 1985.

Leavitt, David. *The Lost Language of Cranes*. Knopf, 1986.

————. *Equal Affections*. Weidenfeld and Nicolson, 1989.

————. *Family Dancing*. Knopf, 1984. Short stories.

Leduc, Violette. *Thérèse et Isabelle*. Gallimard, 1966. Censored pages from *Ravages*.*

————. *La bâtarde*. Gallimard, 1964. Preface by Simone de Beauvoir.

————. *L'asphyxie*. Gallimard, 1946.

————. *L'affamée*. Jean-Jacques Pauvert, 1948.

————. *La chasse à l'amour*. Gallimard, 1973.

Le Touze, Guillaume. *Comme ton père*. L'Olivier, 1994.

Mallet-Joris, Françoise. *Le rempart des béguines*. Julliard, 1951.

————. *Chambre rouge* (1955).

Mann, Thomas. *Death in Venice* (1910). Vintage, 1954.

Martin du Gard, Roger. *Les mémoires du lieutenant-colonel de Maumort*. Gallimard, 1983. Published posthumously.

Maupin, Armistead. *Tales of the City*. Harper Perennial, 1979–89.*

Mauriac, François. *Un adolescent d'autrefois*. Flammarion, 1969.

Millett, Kate. *Sita*. Farrar, Straus & Giroux, 1977.

Mishima, Yukio. *Thirst for Love*. Knopf, 1969.

————. *Confessions of a Mask*. New Directions, 1958.

Monette, Paul. *Borrowed Time: An AIDS Memoir*. Harcourt Brace Jovanovich, 1988.

————. *Becoming a Man*. Abacus, 1992.

Monferrand, Hélène de. *Les amies d'Héloïse*. De Fallois, 1990.

———. *Le journal du Suzanne*. De Fallois, 1991.

Montherlant, Henri de. *La ville dont le prince est un enfant* (1951). Reprinted by Gallimard, 1952. Theatrical piece.

———. *Les garçons* (1969).

———. *Moustique*. La Table Ronde, 1986. Published posthumously.

———. *Mais aimons-nous ce que nous aimons?* Gallimard, 1973. Published posthumously.

Musil, Robert. *Les désarrois de l'élève Törless* (1906). Reprinted by Seuil, 1960.

Navarre, Yves. *Lady Black*. Flammarion, 1971.

———. *Les Loukoums*. Flammarion, 1973.*

———. *Killer*. Flammarion, 1975.

———. *Le petit galopin de nos corps*. Robert Laffont, 1977.

———. *Le temps voulu*. Flammarion, 1979.

———. *Le jardin d'acclimatation*. Flammarion, 1980. Winner of the Prix Goncourt.

———. *Biographie*. Flammarion, 1981.

———. *Ce sont amis que vent emporte*. Flammarion, 1991. About AIDS.

———. *Hôtel Styx*. Albin Michel, 1989.

Olivia (pseud. Dorothy Strachey Bussy). *Olivia* (1950). Hogarth, 1966.*

Pancrazi, Jean-Noël. *Les quartiers d'hiver*. Gallimard, 1990. About AIDS.

Pasolini, Pier Paolo. *Ragazzi di vita*. Garzanti, 1955.

———. *Actes impurs*, followed by *Amado mio* (1981). Gallimard, 1984.

———. *Selected Poems*. Calder, 1984. English and Italian.

Penna, Sandro. *This Strange Joy*. Ohio State University Press, 1982.

Peyrefitte, Roger. *Les amitiés particulières* (1943). Reprinted by Flammarion, 1951.

———. *L'exilé de Capri*. Flammarion, 1959.

———. *Notre amour* (1972).

Pougy, Liane de. *Idylle saphique* (1901). Reprinted by Editions des Femmes, 1987.

———. *Mes cahiers bleus*. Plon, 1977.

Prou, Suzanne. *L'été jaune*. Calmann-Lévy, 1968.

———. *La terrasse des Bernardini*. Calmann-Lévy, 1973.

Proust, Marcel. *A la recherche du temps perdu* (1913–27).

———. *Les plaisirs et les jours* (1896).

———. *Avant la nuit* (1893). Short story.

———. *Contre Sainte-Beuve*. Gallimard, 1954. See chap. 13, "La race maudite." See also biographies by G. D. Painter (Mercure de France, 1966) and Jean-Yves Tadié (Gallimard, 1996).

Purdy, James. *Narrow Rooms*. Arbor House, 1978. Reprinted by Gay Men's Press, 1995.

Rechy, John. *City of Night*. Grove Press, 1963.*

Rinaldi, Angelo. *La dernière fête de l'Empire*. Gallimard, 1980.

———. *Les jours ne s'en vont pas longtemps*. Grasset, 1993.

Rochefort, Christiane. *Les petits enfants du siècle*. Grasset, 1961.

———. *Les stances à Sophie*. Grasset, 1963.

———. *Une rose pour Morrison*. Grasset, 1966.

———. *Printemps au parking*. Grasset, 1969.

Saba, Umberto. *Ernesto*. Editions du Seuil, 1978.

Sachs, Maurice. *Alias* (1935).

———. *Au temps du boeuf sur le toit* (1939).

———. *Le sabbat* (1946).

———. *La chasse à courre*. Gallimard, 1948.

Sackville-West, Vita. *The Letters of Vita Sackville-West to Virginia Woolf*. Morrow, 1985.

Sagan, Françoise. *Des yeux de soie*. Flammarion, 1975. Short stories. See "L'inconnue."

———. *Bonjour tristesse*. Julliard, 1954.

Schneider, Marcel. *L'éternité fragile, mémoires intimes*. 4 vols. Grasset, 1989–92.

Spender, Stephen. *Journals, 1939–1983*. Random House, 1986.

———. *The Temple*. Grove Press, 1988.

Stein, Gertrude. *The Autobiography of Alice B. Toklas* (1933). Vintage, 1960.

———. *Three Lives*. New Directions, 1941. Short stories.

———. *QED*. P. Owen, 1972.

Stéphane, Roger. *Parce que c'était lui*. La Table Ronde, 1953.

———. *Toutes choses ont leur saison*. Fayard, 1979.

———. *Tout est bien*. Quai Voltaire, 1989.

Toklas, Alice B. *The Alice B. Toklas Cookbook* (1954). HarperCollins, 1986.

Tondelli, Pier Vittorio. *Separate Rooms*, trans. Simon Pleasance. Serpent's Tail, 1992.

Tournier, Michel. *Le roi des Aulnes*. Gallimard, 1970. Winner of the Prix Goncourt.

———. *Les météores*. Gallimard, 1975.

Trefusis, Violet. *Broderie anglaise*. Plon, 1935.

———. *Il court, il court*. Gallimard, 1938. Reprinted by Stock, 1992.

———. *Causes perdues*. Gallimard, 1941.

———. *Don't Look Round* (1952). H. Hamilton, 1989. Autobiography.

———. *Echo*. Christian Bourgois, 1989.

———. *Violet to Vita: The Letters of Violet Trefusis to Vita Sackville-West, 1910–1921*. Penguin, 1991.

———. *Instants de mémoire*. Bartillat, 1992. See also Nigel Nicolson, *Portrait of a Marriage* (Weidenfeld and Nicolson, 1990).

Tremblay, Michel. *Le coeur découvert*. Leméac, 1986.

———. *Le coeur éclaté*. Leméac, 1993.

———. *La nuit du prince charmant*. Leméac, 1995.

Vidal, Gore. *Palimpsest: A Memoir*. Random House, 1995.

Vivien, Renée. *Poèmes*. 2 vols. Lemerre, 1923–24. Reprinted by Régine Deforges, 1977. Complete poetic works.

———. *Une femme m'apparut* (1904). Novel. See also biographies by Paul Lorrentz (Julliard, 1977) and J.-P. Goujon (Régine Deforges, 1986).

White, Edmund. *A Boy's Own Story*. Dutton, 1982.*

———. *Nocturnes for the King of Naples*. St. Martin's Press, 1988.

———. , with Adam Mars-Jones. *The Darker Proof: Stories from a Crisis*. St. Martin's Press, 1988. Short stories about AIDS.

———. *The Beautiful Room Is Empty*. Random House, 1994.

———. *Forgetting Elena*. Knopf, 1994.

———. *Skinned Alive*. Random House, 1996.

Wilde, Oscar. *The Picture of Dorian Gray* (1891). Penguin, 1985.

———. *De Profundis* (1897). Dover, 1996.*

———. *The Ballad of Reading Gaol* (1898). Heritage, 1937. Published first under the pseudonym C.33, then under Wilde's name in 1899. See also Robert Badinter, *C.33* (Actes Sud, 1995).

Williams, Tennessee. *Collected Stories*. New Directions, 1985. See especially "The Black Masseur."

Winterson, Jeanette. *Oranges Are Not the Only Fruit.* Pandora Press, 1985.

———. *Written on the Body.* Random House, 1994.

Wittig, Monique. *L'opoponax.* Minuit, 1964. Winner of the Prix Médicis.*

———. *Les guérillères.* Minuit, 1969.

———. *Le corps lesbien.* Minuit, 1973.

———. *Brouillon pour un dictionnaire des amantes.* Grasset, 1976. Collective work.

———. *Virgile, non.* Minuit, 1985.

Woolf, Virginia. *Orlando* (1928). Harcourt Brace Jovanovich, 1973.*

———. *A Room of One's Own* (1929). Harcourt Brace Jovanovich, 1976.*

———. *Three Guineas* (1938). Harcourt Brace Jovanovich, 1966. See also *The Diary of Virginia Woolf* (Harcourt Brace Jovanovich, 1980–85); *The Letters of Virginia Woolf,* ed. Nigel Nicolson (Harcourt Brace Jovanovich, 1975–80).

Yourcenar, Marguerite. *Alexis ou le traité du vain combat* (1929). Reprinted by Plon, 1952; Gallimard, 1971.*

———. *Feux.* Grasset, 1936. Prose poems.

———. *Le coup de grâce.* Gallimard, 1939.

———. *Mémoires d'Hadrien.* Plon, 1951.*

———. *L'oeuvre au noir.* Gallimard, 1968.*

———. *Souvenirs pieux.* Gallimard, 1974. Vol. 1 of *Labyrinthe du monde;* vol 2, *Archives du Nord* (Gallimard, 1977); vol 3, *Quoi? L'éternité* (Gallimard, 1988).

———. *Anna, soror.* Gallimard, 1981.

———. *En pèlerin et en étranger.* Gallimard, 1989. See also Josyane Savigneau, *Marguerite Yourcenar, l'invention d'une vie* (Gallimard, 1990).

Zweig, Stefan. *Verwirrung der Gerfühle.* S. Fischer, 1960.